Readings from

Programming with

Python™

Kyla McMullen

Elizabeth Matthews

June Jamrich Parsons

✸ Cengage

Australia • Brazil • Canada • Mexico • Singapore • United Kingdom • United States

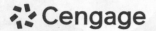

Readings from Programming with Python
Kyla McMullen, Elizabeth Matthews, June Jamrich Parsons

SVP, Higher Education Product Management: Erin Joyner

VP, Product Management, Learning Experiences: Thais Alencar

Product Director: Mark Santee

Associate Product Manager: Tran Pham

Product Assistant: Ethan Wheel

Learning Designer: Mary Convertino

Senior Content Manager: Maria Garguilo

Associate Digital Delivery Quality Partner: David O'Connor

Technical Editor: Danielle Shaw

Developmental Editor: Lisa Ruffolo

VP, Product Marketing: Jason Sakos

Director, Product Marketing: April Danaë

Portfolio Marketing Manager: Mackenzie Paine

IP Analyst: Ann Hoffman

IP Project Manager: Lumina Datamatics

Production Service: Straive

Senior Designer: Erin Griffin

Cover Image Source: echo3005/ShutterStock.com

For product information and technology assistance, contact us at
**Cengage Customer & Sales Support, 1-800-354-9706
or support.cengage.com.**

For permission to use material from this text or product, submit all requests online at **www.copyright.com.**

Library of Congress Control Number: 2021924889

ISBN: 978-0-357-63745-6

Cengage Learning
200 Pier 4 Boulevard
Boston, MA 02210
USA

Cengage is a leading provider of customized learning solutions with employees residing in nearly 40 different countries and sales in more than 125 countries around the world. Find your local representative at **www.cengage.com**.

To learn more about Cengage platforms and services, register or access your online learning solution, or purchase materials for your course, visit **www.cengage.com**.

Notice to the Reader

Printed at CLDPC, USA, 03-22

Brief Contents

Table of Contents

Preface

Welcome to *Readings from Programming with Python*. This text includes the stand-alone lessons and readings from MindTap for *Programming with Python* and is intended to be used in conjunction with MindTap for a complete learning experience.

This first edition title is a programming text that teaches the constructs of programming through the lens of Python. This text provides a comprehensive overview of concepts that can also be applied across other programming languages.

Programming with Python is designed for instructors who want the autonomy to create their own robust learning experiences and who prefer to utilize their own selected lab assignments and integrated development editor. The content is introductory and will fit with a wide range of students entering the course. This text does not assume that students have prior programming experience. Modules are designed to give students a real-world introduction to programming using common concepts and terminology.

MindTap Overview

Programming with Python presents a conceptual narrative overview of the Python programming language. Included in the MindTap product are ungraded Python coding Snippets for practice, test banks for assessment creation, and additional instructor resources.

The goal of this digital product is to present content around the concepts that are essential for understanding computer science from a Python programming perspective. Learners will gain a foundational understanding of computer science concepts, procedural programming, and object-oriented programming. Instructors have identified the need for comprehensive, conceptual content that can be paired with hands-on practice in a specific language. This 31-module course

is designed to provide rich examples and hands-on learning activities that convey the particular components and structure of the Python programming language.

Course Objectives

- Develop foundational knowledge of coding principles, terminology, and core concepts.
- Apply new foundational knowledge to Python programming skills.
- Practice emerging coding skills in a low-risk environment.
- Apply learned concepts and skills to assignments and activities that mimic real-world experiences and environments.

Organization of Content

Programming with Python is comprised of 31 modules that cover a wide range of foundational material, from programming language concepts and data structures to advanced programming applications.

Modules 1 and 2 provide a solid foundation for programming by introducing computational thinking and presenting various programming tools. Modules 3–9 and 12 introduce the common control flow statements in programming: sequential, decision, repetition, functions, and recursion. Module 10 helps students to anticipate unexpected events through exception handling. Module 11 covers file operations and helpful tools for file manipulation in Python. Using Python modules to organize code is introduced in Module 13. Modules 14–18 provide a thorough framework for object-oriented programming by defining classes and objects, using methods to modify objects, enhancing coding through encapsulation, and demonstrating code flexibility through inheritance and polymorphism. To enable students to create code that can be used by anyone, interfaces are covered in Module 16. Students learn to create data structures for information storage and retrieval in Modules 19–21. Modules 22–24 teach students how to evaluate the complexity of their code and efficiently sort and search for data. Modules 25 and 26 provide support for understanding computing and data through processor architecture and data representation. Modules 27–31 support students' development as real-world programmers by teaching various programming paradigms, discussing types of user interfaces, examining common software development methodologies, expressing program flow graphically, and using Unified Modeling Language to communicate with teams. Some concepts, such as templates, are not applicable in Python and are therefore omitted.

MindTap Features

In addition to the readings included within this text, the MindTap includes the following:

Course Orientation: Custom videos and readings prepare students for the material and coding experiences they will encounter in their course.

Videos: Animated videos demonstrate new programming terms and concepts in an easy-to-understand format, increasing student confidence and learning.

Coding Snippets: These short, ungraded coding activities for practice are embedded within the MindTap Reader and provide students with an opportunity to practice new programming concepts as they learn about them.

Python Code Examples: Figures illustrate the application of general concepts in Python code. Students are able to study code segments within the larger context of the code, as well as copy, paste, and run complete programs. The full source code to all Python figures is available online and provides students with the opportunity to test and manipulate the code presented in the modules in their preferred IDEs.

Q & A: An interactive series of brief critical thinking questions review the main points introduced in the module and reinforce new concepts at the moment of learning.

Python Version

We recommend downloading the latest version of Python before beginning this text. Python 3.9.6 was used to test all Python code presented in the module figures.

Instructor and Student Resources

Additional instructor and student resources for this product are available online. Instructor assets include an Instructor's Manual, Teaching Online Guide, PowerPoint® slides, and a test bank powered by Cognero®. Student assets include source code files and coding Snippets ReadMe. Sign up or sign in at www.cengage.com to search for and access this product and its online resources.

About the Authors

Dr. Kyla McMullen is a tenure-track faculty member in the University of Florida's Computer & Information Sciences & Engineering Department, specializing in Human-Centered Computing. Her research interests are in the perception, applications, and development of 3D audio technologies. Dr. McMullen has authored over 30 manuscripts in this line of research and is the primary investigator for over 2 million dollars' worth of sponsored research projects.

Dr. Elizabeth A. Matthews is an Assistant Professor of Computer Science at Washington and Lee University. She has taught computer science since 2013 and has been an active researcher in human–computer interaction and human-centered computing. Dr. Matthews has published research in the areas of procedural generation, video game enjoyment factors, and freshwater algae identification with HCI.

June Jamrich Parsons is an educator, digital book pioneer, and co-author of Texty and McGuffey award-winning textbooks. She co-developed the first commercially successful multimedia, interactive digital textbook—one that set the bar for platforms now being developed by educational publishers. Her career includes extensive classroom teaching, product design for eCourseware, textbook authoring for Course Technology and Cengage, Creative Strategist for MediaTechnics Corporation, and Director of Content for Veative Virtual Reality Labs.

Acknowledgments

The unique approach for this book required a seasoned team. Our thanks to Maria Garguilo, who ushered the manuscripts through every iteration and kept tight rein on the schedule; to Mary E. Convertino, who supplied her expertise in learning design; to Lisa Ruffolo for her excellent developmental edit; to Tran Pham, who coordinated the project; to Rajiv Malkan (Lone Star College) for his instructional input; to Wade Schofield (Liberty University), Eric James Williamson (Liberty University Online Academy), and Dr. Christian Servin (El Paso Community College) for their reviewing expertise; and to Danielle Shaw for her meticulous code review. It was a pleasure to be part of this professional and talented team. We hope that instructors and students will appreciate our efforts to provide this unique approach to computer science and programming.

Kyla McMullen: Above all things, I would like to thank God for giving me the gifts and talents that were utilized to write this book. I would like to thank my amazing husband Ade Kumuyi for always being my rock, sounding board, and biggest cheerleader. I thank my parents, Rita and James McMullen, for all of their sacrifices to raise me. Last but not least, I thank my spirited friends who help me to remain sane, remind me of who I am, and never let me forget whose I am.

Elizabeth Matthews: I want to thank my parents, Drs. Geoff and Robin Matthews, for their support and understanding in my journey. I would also like to thank my advisor, Dr. Juan Gilbert, for seeing my dream to the end. Finally, I would like to thank my cats, Oreo and Laptop, who made sure that writing this book was interrupted as often as possible.

June Jamrich Parsons: Computer programming can be a truly satisfying experience. The reward when a program runs flawlessly has to bring a smile even to the most seasoned programmers. Working with three programming languages for this project at the same time was certainly challenging but provided insights that can help students understand computational thinking. I've thoroughly enjoyed working with the team to create these versatile learning resources and would like to dedicate my efforts to my mom, who has been a steadfast cheerleader for me throughout my career. To the instructors and students who use this book, my hope is that you enjoy programming as much as I do.

Module 1

Computational Thinking

Learning Objectives:

1.1 Algorithms

1.1.1 Define the term "algorithm" as a series of steps for solving a problem or carrying out a task.

1.1.2 State that algorithms are the underlying logic for computer programs.

1.1.3 Define the term "computer program."

1.1.4 Provide examples of algorithms used in everyday technology applications.

1.1.5 Confirm that there can be more than one algorithm for a task or problem and that some algorithms may be more efficient than others.

1.1.6 Explain why computer scientists are interested in algorithm efficiency.

1.1.7 List the characteristics of an effective algorithm.

1.1.8 Write an algorithm for accomplishing a simple, everyday technology task.

1.1.9 Write an alternate algorithm for an everyday technology task.

1.1.10 Select the more efficient of the two algorithms you have written.

1.2 Decomposition

1.2.1 Define the term "decomposition" as a technique for dividing a complex problem or solution into smaller parts.

1.2.2 Explain why decomposition is an important tool for computer scientists.

1.2.3 Differentiate the concepts of algorithms and decomposition.

1.2.4 Identify examples of structural decomposition.

1.2.5 Identify examples of functional decomposition.

1.2.6 Identify examples of object-oriented decomposition.

1.2.7 Provide examples of decomposition in technology applications.

1.2.8 Explain how dependencies and cohesion relate to decomposition.

1.3 Pattern Identification

1.3.1 Define the term "pattern identification" as a technique for recognizing similarities or characteristics among the elements of a task or problem.

1.3.2 Identify examples of fill-in-the-blank patterns.

1.3.3 Identify examples of repetitive patterns.

1.3.4 Identify examples of classification patterns.

1.3.5 Provide examples of pattern identification in the real world and in technology applications.

1.4 Abstraction

1.4.1 Define the term "abstraction" as a technique for generalization and for simplifying levels of complexity.

1.4.2 Explain why abstraction is an important computer science concept.

1.4.3 Provide an example illustrating how abstraction can help identify variables.

1.4.4   Provide examples of technology applications that have abstracted or hidden details.

1.4.5   Provide an example illustrating the use of a class as an abstraction of a set of objects.

1.4.6   Explain how the black box concept is an implementation of abstraction.

1.4.7   Identify appropriate levels of abstraction.

1.1 Algorithms

Algorithm Basics (1.1.1, 1.1.4)

A password might not be enough to protect your online accounts. Two-factor authentication adds an extra layer of protection. A common form of two-factor authentication sends a personal identification number (PIN) to your cell phone. To log in, you perform the series of steps shown in **Figure 1-1**.

Connect to the site's login page.
Enter your user ID.
Enter your password.
Wait for a text message containing a PIN
   to arrive on your smartphone.
On the site's login page, enter the PIN.

Figure 1-1   Steps for two-factor authentication

The procedure for two-factor authentication is an example of an algorithm. In a general sense, an **algorithm** is a series of steps for solving a problem or carrying out a task.

Algorithms exist for everyday tasks and tasks that involve technology. Here are some examples:

- A recipe for baking brownies
- The steps for changing a tire
- The instructions for pairing a smart watch with your phone
- The payment process at an online store
- The procedure for posting a tweet

Programming Algorithms (1.1.2, 1.1.3, 1.1.5)

Algorithms are also an important tool for programmers. A **programming algorithm** is a set of steps that specifies the underlying logic and structure for the statements in a computer program. You can think of programming algorithms as the recipes for computer programs. A recipe has a sequence of steps you follow to create something (such as a cake). Similarly, an algorithm is a sequence of steps for a computer to follow to create something (such as a program).

A **computer program** is a set of instructions, written in a programming language such as Python, that performs a specific task when executed by a digital device. A computer program is an implementation of an algorithm.

Q Programming algorithms tell the computer what to do. Can you tell which of these algorithms is a programming algorithm?

Algorithm 1:

Connect to the website's login page.

Enter your user ID.

Enter your password.

Wait for a text message containing a PIN to arrive on your smartphone.

On the website's login page, enter the PIN.

Algorithm 2:

Prompt the user to enter a user ID.

Prompt the user to enter a password.

Make sure that the user ID and password match.

If the user ID and password match:

Generate a random PIN.

Send the PIN to the user's phone.

Prompt the user to enter the PIN.

If the PIN is correct:

Allow access.

A Algorithm 1 is not a programming algorithm because it outlines instructions for the user. Algorithm 2 is a programming algorithm because it specifies what the computer is supposed to do. When you formulate a programming algorithm, the instructions should be for the computer, not the user.

There can be more than one programming algorithm for solving a problem or performing a task, but some algorithms are more efficient than others.

Q Here are two algorithms for summing the numbers from 1 to 10. Which algorithm is more efficient?

Algorithm 1:

Add 1 + 2 to get a total.

Repeat these steps nine times:

Get the next number.

Add this number to the total.

Algorithm 2:

Get the last number in the series (10).

Divide 10 by 2 to get a result.

Add 10 + 1 to get a sum.

Multiply the result by the sum.

A Both algorithms contain four instructions, but Algorithm 2 is more efficient. You can use it to amaze your friends by quickly calculating the total in only four steps. Algorithm 1 is also four lines long, but two of the instructions are repeated nine times. Counting the first step, that's 19 steps to complete this task!

"Good" Algorithms (1.1.6, 1.1.7)

Computer scientists are interested in designing what they call "good" algorithms. A good algorithm tends to produce a computer program that operates efficiently, quickly, and reliably. Good algorithms have these characteristics:

Input: The algorithm applies to a set of specified inputs.
Output: The algorithm produces one or more outputs.
Finite: The algorithm terminates after a finite number of steps.
Precise: Each step of the algorithm is clear and unambiguous.
Effective: The algorithm successfully produces the correct output.

When formulating an algorithm, you can easily check to make sure it satisfies all the criteria for a good algorithm. You can see how these criteria apply to an algorithm in **Figure 1-2**.

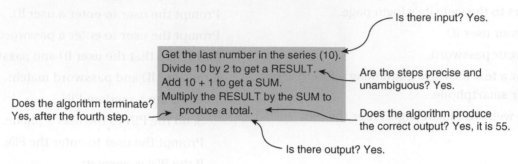

Figure 1-2   Is this a good algorithm?

Selecting and Creating Algorithms (1.1.8, 1.1.9, 1.1.10)

Before coding, programmers consider various algorithms that might apply to a problem. You can come up with an algorithm in three ways:

Use a standard algorithm. Programmers have created effective algorithms for many computing tasks, such as sorting, searching, manipulating text, encrypting data, and finding the shortest path. When you are familiar with these standard algorithms, you can easily incorporate them in programs.

Perform the task manually. When you can't find a standard algorithm, you can formulate an algorithm by stepping through a process manually, recording those steps, and then analyzing their effectiveness.

Apply computational thinking techniques. **Computational thinking** is a set of techniques designed to formulate problems and their solutions. You can use computational thinking techniques such as decomposition, pattern identification, and abstraction to devise efficient algorithms. Let's take a look at these techniques in more detail.

1.2 Decomposition

Decomposition Basics (1.2.1)

A mobile banking app contains many components. It has to provide a secure login procedure, allow users to manage preferences, display account balances, push out alerts, read checks for deposit, and perform other tasks, as shown in **Figure 1-3**.

The algorithm for such an extensive app would be difficult to formulate without dividing it into smaller parts, a process called **decomposition**. When devising an algorithm for a complex problem or task, decomposition can help you deal with smaller, more manageable pieces of the puzzle.

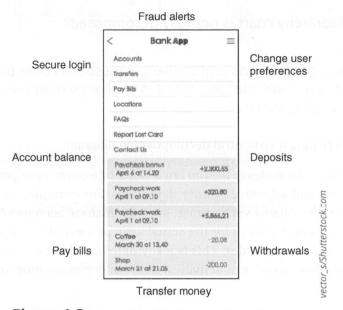

Figure 1-3   A mobile banking app handles many interacting tasks

Structural Decomposition (1.2.2, 1.2.3, 1.2.4, 1.2.7)

The first step in decomposition is to identify structural units that perform distinct tasks. **Figure 1-4** illustrates how you might divide a mobile banking app into structural units, called **modules**.

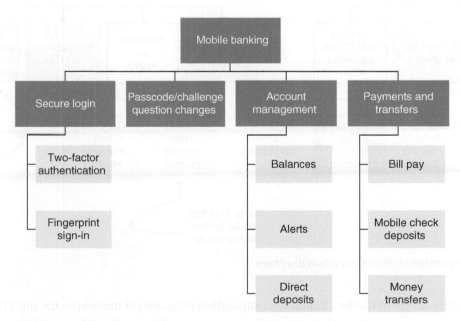

Figure 1-4   Structural decomposition diagram

Structural decomposition is a process that identifies a hierarchy of building-block units for a program concept. At the lowest levels of the hierarchy are modules, indicated in yellow in Figure 1-4, that have a manageable scope for creating algorithms. The higher-level blocks, indicated in blue, convey the bigger picture or goal the program will achieve.

Q Which block of the hierarchy chart is not fully decomposed?

A The block for modifying passwords and challenge questions could be further decomposed into two modules: one module that allows users to change their passwords and one for changing their challenge questions.

Here are some tips for creating a structural decomposition diagram:

- Use a top-down approach. The nodes at the top break down into component parts in the nodes below them.
- Label nodes with nouns and adjectives rather than verbs. For example, "Account management" is the correct noun phrase, rather than a verb phrase, such as "Manage accounts."
- Don't worry about sequencing. Except for the actual login process, the components in a mobile banking system could be accessed in any order. This is a key difference between an algorithm and decomposition. An algorithm specifies an order of activities, whereas decomposition specifies the parts of a task.

Functional Decomposition (1.2.5)

Functional decomposition breaks down modules into smaller actions, processes, or steps. **Figure 1-5** illustrates a functional decomposition of the two-factor authentication module.

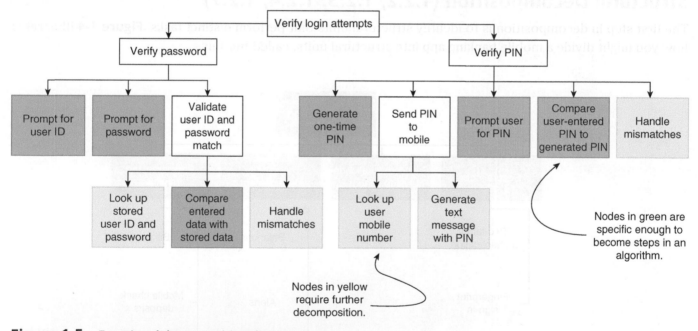

Figure 1-5   Functional decomposition diagram

Notice how the levels of the functional decomposition diagram get more specific until the nodes in the lowest levels begin to reveal instructions that should be incorporated in an algorithm.

Here are some tips for constructing functional decomposition diagrams and deriving algorithms from them:

- Label nodes with verb phrases. In contrast to the nodes of a structural decomposition diagram, the nodes of a functional decomposition diagram are labeled with verb phrases that indicate "what" is to be done.
- Sequence from left to right. Reading left to right on the diagram should correspond to the sequence in which steps in the algorithm are performed.

Object-Oriented Decomposition (1.2.6)

Another way to apply decomposition to a module is to look for logical and physical objects that a computer program will manipulate. **Figure 1-6** illustrates an **object-oriented decomposition** of the two-factor authentication module.

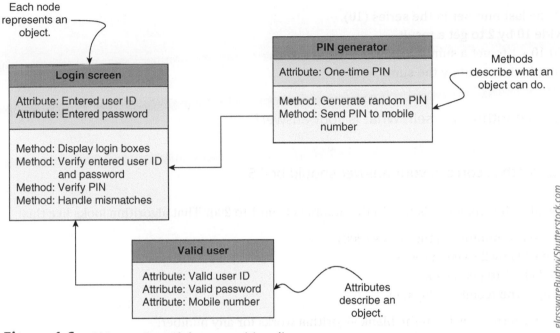

Figure 1-6   Object-oriented decomposition diagram

An object-oriented decomposition does not produce a hierarchy. Instead, it produces a collection of **objects** that can represent people, places, or things.

Tips for object-oriented decomposition:

- Node titles are nouns. Each node in the object-oriented decomposition diagram is labeled with a noun.
- Attributes are nouns. A node can contain a list of **attributes**, which relate to the characteristics of an object.
- Methods are verb phrases. An object can also contain **methods**, which are actions that an object can perform. You may need to devise an algorithm for each method.
- Sketch in connection arrows. Connection arrows help you visualize how objects share data.

Dependencies and Cohesion (1.2.8)

You might wonder if there is a correct way to decompose a problem or task. In practice, there may be several viable ways to apply decomposition, but an effective breakdown minimizes dependencies and maximizes cohesion among the various parts.

The principles of decomposition are as follows:

- *Minimize dependencies.* Although input and output may flow between nodes, changing the instructions in one module or object should not require changes to others.
- *Maximize cohesion.* Each object or module contains attributes, methods, or instructions that perform a single logical task or represent a single entity. If you find that your instruction is trying to do two things at once, break it into smaller pieces.

1.3 Pattern Identification

Pattern Identification Basics (1.3.1, 1.3.2)

The Amaze-Your-Friends math trick for quickly adding numbers from 1 to 10 is very simple:

1. Get the last number in the series (10).
2. Divide 10 by 2 to get a result.
3. Add 10 + 1 to get a sum.
4. Multiply the result by the sum.

Q Try the algorithm yourself. What is your answer?

A If your math is correct, your answer should be 55.

Now, what if the challenge is to add the numbers from 1 to 200? That algorithm looks like this:

1. Get the last number in the series (200).
2. Divide 200 by 2 to get a result.
3. Add 200 + 1 to get a sum.
4. Multiply the result by the sum.

Notice a pattern? This fill-in-the-blank algorithm works for any number:

1. Get the last number in the series (_____).
2. Divide _____ by 2 to get a result.
3. Add _____ + 1 to get a sum.
4. Multiply the result by the sum.

The process of finding similarities in procedures and tasks is called **pattern identification**. It is a useful computational thinking technique for creating algorithms that can be used and reused on different data sets. By recognizing the pattern in the Amaze-Your-Friends math trick, you can use the algorithm to find the total of any series of numbers.

Repetitive Patterns (1.3.3)

In addition to fill-in-the-blank patterns, you might also find repetitive patterns as you analyze tasks and problems. Think about this algorithm, which handles logins to a social media site:

1. Get a user ID.
2. Get a password.
3. If the password is correct, allow access.
4. If the password is not correct, get the password again.
5. If the password is correct, allow access.
6. If the password is not correct, get the password again.
7. If the password is correct, allow access.
8. If the password is not correct, get the password again.
9. If the password is correct, allow access.
10. If the password is not correct, lock the account.

Q How many repetition patterns do you recognize?

A Two lines are repeated three times:
If the password is not correct, get the password again.
If the password is correct, allow access.

Recognizing this repetition, you can streamline the algorithm like this:

1. Get a password.
2. Repeat three times:
   a. If the password is correct, allow access.
   b. If the password is not correct, get the password again.
3. If the password is correct, allow access.
4. If the password is not correct, lock the account.

Classification Patterns (1.3.4, 1.3.5)

Everyone who subscribes to a social media site has a set of login credentials. Here are Lee's and Priya's credentials:

Lee's login credentials:

Lee's user ID: LeezyBranson@gmail.com

Lee's password: MyCat411

Lee's mobile number: 415-999-1234

Priya's login credentials:

Priya's user ID: PriyaMontell@gmail.com

Priya's password: ouY52311v

Priya's mobile number: 906-222-0987

The series of attributes that defines each user's login credentials have a pattern of similarities. Each user has three attributes: a user ID, a password, and a mobile number. By recognizing this pattern, you can create a template for any user's login credentials like this:

User ID: _____
Password: _____
Mobile number: _____

You can often discover **classification patterns** in the attributes that describe any person or object. Identifying classification patterns can help you design programs that involve databases because the template identifies fields, such as User ID, that contain data.

Classification patterns also come in handy if you want to design programs based on the interactions among a variety of objects rather than a step-by-step algorithm. In some programming circles, templates are called **classes** because they specify the attributes for a classification of objects. For example, people classified as social media subscribers have attributes for login credentials. Vehicles classified as cars have attributes such as color, make, model, and VIN number. Businesses classified as restaurants have a name, hours of operation, and a menu.

1.4 Abstraction

Abstraction Basics (1.4.1, 1.4.2, 1.4.3)

Think back to the Amaze-Your-Friends math trick. By identifying a pattern, you formulated a general algorithm that works for a sequence of any length, whether it is a sequence of 1 to 10 or 1 to 200.

1. Get the last number in the series (_____).
2. Divide _____ by 2 to get a result.

3. Add _____ + 1 to get a sum.

4. Multiply the result by the sum.

In this algorithm, the blank line is an abstraction that represents the last number in the sequence. An **abstraction** hides details, simplifies complexity, substitutes a generalization for something specific, and allows an algorithm to work for multiple inputs.

Abstraction is a key element of computational thinking and helps programmers in a multitude of ways.

If you've programmed before, you'll recognize that in the Amaze-Your-Friends algorithm, the blanks could become a stand-in name such as `last_number`. Result and sum are also placeholder names because they represent values that change depending on the numbers in the sequence:

1. Get the `last_number`.

2. Divide `last_number` by 2 to get a `result`.

3. Add `last_number` + 1 to get a `sum`.

4. Multiply the `result` by the `sum`.

Substituting a descriptive name for a value is an abstraction because rather than representing a specific number, the name can be used to represent many different numbers.

Classes and Objects (1.4.4, 1.4.5)

Abstraction has uses other than identifying variables. It is important for understanding how to represent real-world and conceptual objects. Remember the pattern you discovered for social media login credentials? With a little modification, it becomes a template that can be applied to any subscriber:

Class: LoginCredentials
Attribute: user_ID
Attribute: user_password
Attribute: mobile_number

The LoginCredentials class is an abstraction that contains a set of attributes. The class was formed by abstracting away, or removing, details for any specific subscriber.

Abstractions are handy for any programs that deal with real-world objects in addition to technology objects, such as login credentials.

Q Can you envision a class that's an abstraction of the collection of objects shown in **Figure 1-7**?

12 oz water glass   5 oz martini glass   8 oz wine glass   10 oz water goblet

Savany/iStock/Getty Images   Jane Rix/Shutterstock.com   Kaczka/E+/Getty Images   Jaykayl/iStock/Getty Images

Figure 1-7   Abstract the details from this collection of glassware

A The glassware class could have these attributes:
Class: Glassware
Attribute: Color
Attribute: Capacity
Attribute: Style

Black Boxes (1.4.6)

To drive a car, you don't have to know exactly what goes on under the hood. The engine is essentially a "black box" that you control using a few simple inputs such as the gas pedal, brake, and steering wheel. The details of the engine are hidden. In computer science terminology, these details have been "abstracted away." See **Figure 1-8**.

You can drive a car without knowing the details of what's under the hood.

Figure 1-8   The controls for a car are an abstraction of its detailed mechanics

In concept, a black box is anything that accepts some type of input and performs a specific process to produce output without requiring an understanding of its internal workings. See **Figure 1-9**.

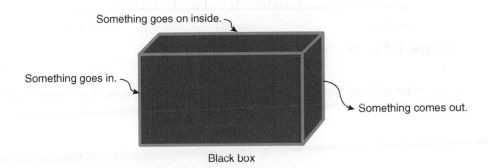

Something goes on inside.

Something goes in.

Something comes out.

Black box

Figure 1-9   Black box abstraction

The black box concept of abstraction is a fundamental aspect of computer science. Think about it. Computer programs are abstractions. For example, you can use a social media app without knowing anything about the programming that makes it work. The icons that you touch on the screen abstract away the details of the underlying programming.

Programmers make extensive use of abstraction within programs by creating a set of instructions that functions like a black box. For example, you could bundle the instructions that handle login attempts into a black box like the one in **Figure 1-10**.

Programming languages also have built-in abstractions that perform standard tasks. For example, the built-in random function generates a random number when given a range, such as 1–100. You can incorporate the random function in a program without knowing how it works internally.

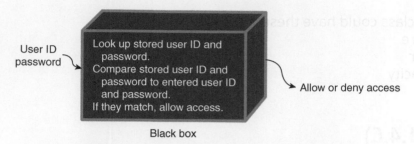

Black box

Figure 1-10   A login abstraction

Levels of Abstraction (1.4.7)

After you get the hang of abstraction, you'll see examples of this computational thinking concept everywhere. Applying the correct level of abstraction to your programs may take a little practice.

A **level of abstraction** relates to the amount of detail that is hidden. Abstracting out too much detail can make a program too generalized. Neglecting abstraction can produce programs that are too specific to work with a wide variety of data. See **Figure 1-11**.

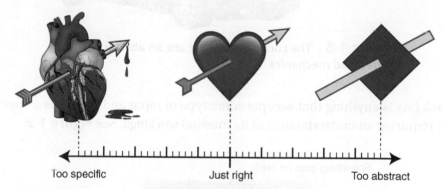

Too specific   Just right   Too abstract

Figure 1-11   Levels of abstraction

With experience, you'll be able to identify useful abstractions and gauge the correct level of abstraction to use.

Summary

- Computational thinking techniques help programmers define problems, find solutions, delineate tasks, and devise algorithms.
- An algorithm is a series of steps for solving a problem or carrying out a task. Programming algorithms are the blueprints for computer programs.
- Standard algorithms exist for many computing tasks. When an algorithm does not exist, you can step through a process manually and record the steps, or you can apply computational thinking techniques, such as decomposition, pattern identification, and abstraction.
- Decomposition divides a complex problem or task into manageable units.
- Pattern identification reveals sequences and repetitive tasks that can lead to algorithm efficiencies.
- Abstraction is a key computer science concept that suppresses details, substitutes a generalization for something specific, and allows an algorithm to work for multiple inputs.

Key Terms

abstraction	computer program	objects
algorithm	decomposition	object-oriented decomposition
attributes	functional decomposition	pattern identification
classes	level of abstraction	programming algorithm
classification patterns	methods	structural decomposition
computational thinking	modules	

Module 2

Programming Tools

Learning Objectives:

2.1 Programming Languages

2.1.1 Explain the significance of the Hello World! program.

2.1.2 Reiterate that programming languages are used to create software.

2.1.3 Name some popular programming languages.

2.1.4 Distinguish between syntax and semantics in the context of programming languages.

2.1.5 Identify the key characteristics common to programming languages.

2.1.6 Explain options for accessing programming language implementations.

2.1.7 Identify programming tools.

2.2 Coding Tools

2.2.1 Define a program editor as the tool used to enter program code.

2.2.2 List the types of editors that can be used for coding.

2.2.3 List some handy features of code editors, and explain how they help programmers create clean code.

2.2.4 Identify the basic structure and syntactical elements for a program written in the programming language you use.

2.3 Build Tools

2.3.1 Explain the purpose of build tools.

2.3.2 Explain the difference between source code and object code.

2.3.3 Describe how a compiler works.

2.3.4 Associate virtual machines with Java and bytecode.

2.3.5 Explain how an interpreter works.

2.3.6 Differentiate between source code, bytecode, object code, and executable code.

2.4 Debugging Tools

2.4.1 Explain the purpose of debugging.

2.4.2 List common syntax errors.

2.4.3 List common runtime errors.

2.4.4 List common logic errors.

2.4.5 Classify program errors as syntax errors, logic errors, or runtime errors.

2.4.6 Classify a debugger as utility software that allows programmers to walk through the code of a target program to find errors.

2.4.7 List handy features provided by a debugger.

2.5 IDEs and SDKs

2.5.1 List the purpose and typical features of an integrated development environment (IDE).

2.5.2 Explain how IDEs support visual programming.

2.5.3 Confirm that some IDEs are installed locally while other IDEs are accessed online.

2.5.4 Identify popular IDEs.

2.5.5 Identify IDLE as a built-in Python IDE.

2.5.6 Contrast IDLE's shell and script modes.

2.5.7 List the purpose and typical features of a software development kit (SDK).

2.5.8 Provide examples of SDK functionality.

2.5.9 Identify popular SDKs.

2.1 Programming Languages

Hello World! (2.1.1)

Hola! Bonjour! Hi! Ciao! Namaste! Salaam! Nihau! Greetings like these are the first thing you learn when studying a spoken language. Programmers have a similar starting point. It is the Hello World! program.

Hello World! is without doubt the most famous computer program of all time. It has been written in every one of the 700+ programming languages. It is typically the first program written by aspiring programmers.

Q Take a look at the Hello World! programs in **Figure 2-1**. They are written in three popular programming languages: C++, Java, and Python. What differences can you identify?

Hello World! in C++	Hello World! in Java	Hello World! in Python

```#include <iostream>```
```using namespace std;```
```int main()```
```{```
```   cout << "Hello World!" << endl;```
```   return 0;```
```}```
	```class HelloWorld {```
	``` public static void main(String[] args) {```
	``` System.out.println("Hello World!");```
	``` }```
	```}```
		```print("Hello World!")```

Figure 2-1   Hello World in C++, Java, and Python

A You probably noticed the following differences:
Length: Some Hello World! programs required more instructions than others.
Punctuation: Some programs used lots of curly brackets and semicolons.
Wording: To write the "Hello World!" statement, each programming language used a different command: `cout`, `System.out.println`, and `print`.
Complexity: Some programs seemed easier to interpret than others.

A lot of backstory is bundled into the Hello World! program that can be applied to learning a programming language. Let's unbundle this famous program to discover the basics about Python, as well as commonalities across languages.

Programming Language Basics (2.1.2, 2.1.3)

A **programming language** is a notation for specifying the steps in an algorithm that are supposed to be performed by a digital device. Programming languages such as C++, Java, and Python are classified as **high-level programming languages** because they provide a way for you as a programmer to compose human-readable instructions that direct the operations performed by a computing device.

How does your programming language stack up to other popular languages, and where does it shine? Check out the list in **Figure 2-2**.

Using a high-level programming language, you can specify a set of instructions that correspond to the steps in an algorithm. Each instruction is referred to as a **statement**. The set of statements you generate using a programming language is called **program code**, or simply code. Your code can become a **computer program**, which can be distributed as computer software, desktop applications, web apps, and mobile apps.

Logo	Programming Language	Where It Shines
JS	JavaScript	Consumer-facing web development, server-side web development
	Python	Server-side web development, scripting, machine learning, data science, desktop applications, robotics
Java	Java	Server-side web development, desktop applications, mobile development, Internet of Things
C	C	Systems programming, embedded applications, Internet of Things
C++	C++	Systems programming, game development, desktop applications embedded applications, robotics
php	PHP	Server-side web development
	Swift	Desktop and mobile applications for Apple devices
C#	C#	Desktop applications, game development, virtual reality, mobile development
	Ruby	Server-side web development
	Go	Server-side web development, systems programming, Internet of Things

Figure 2-2   Popular programming languages

Syntax and Semantics (2.1.4)

When learning a programming language, where do you start? Programming languages have two key elements: semantics and syntax.

Semantics refers to the meaning and validity of program statements. In a natural language, such as English, it is perfectly fine to say, "Let's start the game" or "Let's start the car," but "Let's start the pen" doesn't make any sense. It is not semantically valid.

Programming languages include **keywords**, such as `cout`. These words are a subset of a programming language's **reserved words**, which are reserved for special purposes. In this module, these words are colored orange, as in `include`. You can use reserved words only in the context defined by the programming language. Python also has something called built-in functions. These words are colored purple, as in `print`. In programs, you can use words to serve a purpose that you define except you cannot use any of the reserved words or built-in functions for Python.

One aspect of learning a programming language is to become familiar with its keywords/built-ins and their use. When learning C++, for example, you need to remember that `cout` sends output to a display device. But if you're learning Python, the code to use is `print`. **Figure 2-3** lists a few keywords you use while programming in Python. Built-in functions are covered more thoroughly in a later module.

Keyword	Purpose
class	Define the characteristics of a person, place, or thing.
def	Define a sequence of instructions.
for while	Begin a section of code that repeats one or more times.
if elif else	Execute program statements when a condition is true.
import	Incorporate a prewritten code module in a program.
return	Bring a value back from a function.
try	Catch errors and handle them gracefully.

Figure 2-3   Keywords for Python

Q Suppose you want to code a program to output "Hello World!" 10 times. What keyword could you use?

A Figure 2-3 lists the `for` and `while` keywords for specifying code that repeats one or more times.

You'll acquire a vocabulary of keywords for your programming language gradually. Language references provide a list of keywords and examples of their use. You can find language references online. In fact, it is often helpful to create or find a "cheat sheet" of keywords to keep beside your computer as you learn a new language.

The **syntax** of a programming language is equivalent to the grammar rules of a written language, such as English or Cyrillic. Syntax defines the order of words and the punctuation you are required to use when composing statements.

Various programming languages use different punctuation syntax. One of the early steps in learning a programming language is to get a handle on its syntax.

Remember the different use of punctuation in the C++, Java, and Python Hello World! programs? Take a closer look at **Figure 2-4**, and notice how punctuation helps to separate and structure the statements in a C++ program.

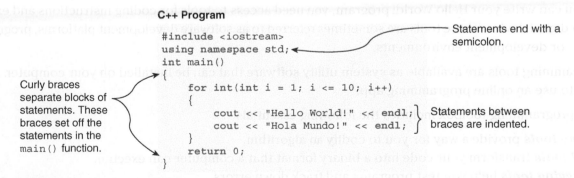

C++ Program

```
#include <iostream>
using namespace std;
int main()
{
    for int(int i = 1; i <= 10; i++)
    {
        cout << "Hello World!" << endl;
        cout << "Hola Mundo!" << endl;
    }
    return 0;
}
```

Statements end with a semicolon.

Curly braces separate blocks of statements. These braces set off the statements in the `main()` function.

Statements between braces are indented.

Figure 2-4   C++ syntax style

Python uses quite a different approach to punctuation. Examine the differences in **Figure 2-5**.

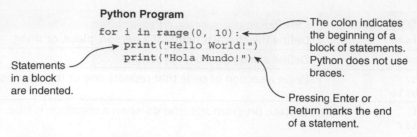

Figure 2-5   Python syntax style

In C++, statements are enclosed in a structure of curly braces, and each statement ends with a semicolon. In contrast, Python uses indents to structure statements, and the linefeed generated when you press the Enter key marks the end of a statement. This means that, unlike in other languages, white space has important meaning in Python. Pay careful attention to how much white space is on each line while programming. The standard for Python is to use exactly four spaces for each level of indent, as shown in all the code examples in this course.

Core Elements (2.1.5)

Although syntax and semantics in various programming languages differ, they have common elements. If you look for the ways that your programming language implements the elements in the following list, you will be well on your way through the initial learning curve.

Variables that can be assigned values and structures
Arithmetic operators that can be used to perform calculations
Keywords and Built-Ins that perform operations such as print or import
Data types that define values and text
Branching controls that change the sequence in which statements are executed
Repetition controls that repeat a series of statements
Syntax rules for constructing valid statements
Terminology for describing the components of a language and their functions

Your Toolbox (2.1.6, 2.1.7)

Before you can write your Hello World! program, you need access to tools for coding instructions and executing them on a digital device. These tools are sometimes referred to as software development platforms, programming platforms, or development environments.

Programming tools are available as system utility software that can be installed on your computer. Another option is to use an online programming app.

Your programming toolbox includes the following essentials:

Coding tools provide a way for you to codify an algorithm.
Build tools transform your code into a binary format that a computer can execute.
Debugging tools help you test programs and track down errors.

You can acquire these programming tools as individual components, or you can look for a comprehensive development environment. Let's explore these tools in more detail to find out how they can help you develop brilliant programs.

2.2 Coding Tools

Program Editors (2.2.1, 2.2.2, 2.2.3)

Coding tools provide you with a way to express an algorithm using the vocabulary of a programming language. Just how much of the code you have to manually type depends on your development platform. Here are the options:

Visual platform: You might have the option of arranging visual elements that represent various statements, as shown in **Figure 2-6**.

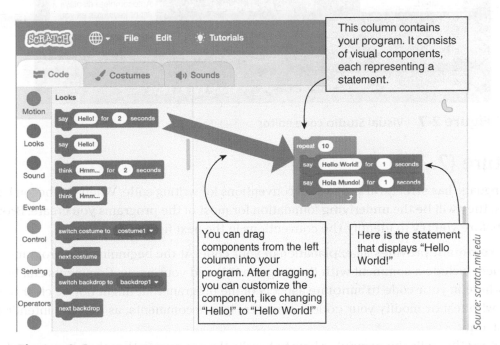

Figure 2-6   Visual programming

Text editor: A **text editor** such as Windows Notepad can produce plain ASCII text but offers no features designed to help programmers. Using a generic text editor is a bare-bones approach. There are much better coding tools.

Code editor: A **code editor** is a type of text editor specially designed for entering high-level programming code. It can help you correctly use punctuation and indents, as well as remember variable names and ensure that you use valid keywords. Some handy features of code editors are highlighted in **Figure 2-7**.

When using a code editor, you can simply type your commands. As you type, pay attention to color coding, autocomplete, and other helpful cues that the editor offers.

A traditional word processing program is not a good choice for a coding tool because its purpose is to create documents that are readable by humans, not computers. Word processors add hidden symbols that make text easy to read, such as for making a word bold or italic or for changing fonts. For a computer to read text, it needs to be formatted in a specific, plain way, with no hidden symbols.

Code editors are designed to manage the conflicting text types for humans and computers. While you edit code, a code editor makes the text easy to read by making certain words bold or different colors. When you save the code and send it to a programming language, however, none of that formatting is carried over, so the computer receives only the code it needs.

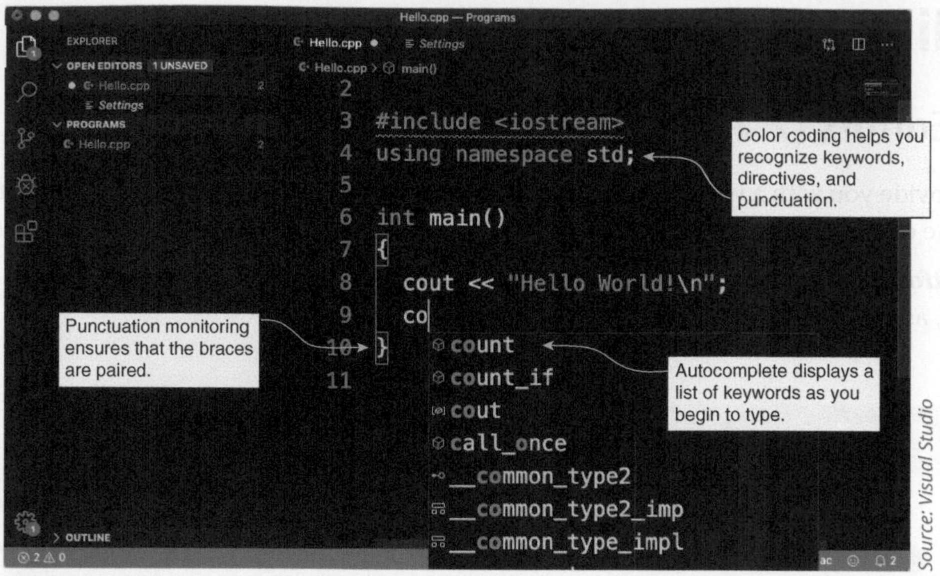

Figure 2-7   Visual Studio code editor

Basic Structure (2.2.4)

A programming language has structural and syntax conventions for writing code. When you become familiar with these conventions, they will be the underlying foundation for most of the programs you create. Browse through the following list before you try to identify the conventions in the next figure.

Comments: A **comment** provides an explanation of your code. At the beginning of a program, you can routinely include a comment with the program title and your name. Comments can be included anywhere in your code to annotate aspects of the program that might not be clear to other programmers who test or modify your code. Computers ignore comments, as they are intended for documentation only.

Directives: A **directive** tells the computer how to handle the program rather than how to perform an algorithm. For example, a directive might specify the name of an external file that is supposed to be incorporated with the rest of your program code. Directives may begin with keywords such as `#include`, `import`, or `using`.

Statements: Just as human-readable text is divided into sentences and paragraphs, your code should be divided into statements and blocks. A program statement is similar to a sentence; it contains one instruction. In Python, you end a statement by pressing the Enter or Return key.

Code blocks: A **code block** is like a paragraph; it contains multiple statements that have a specific purpose. In Python, code blocks are indented. This is how white space conveys meaning in Python.

Q Take a look at **Figure 2-8**, and see if you can identify any comments, directives, statements, and code blocks.

```
#Hello World! in English and Spanish

for i in range(10):

    print("Hello World!")

    print("Hola Mundo!")
```

Figure 2-8   Find the structural and syntax conventions in this code

A The comment is `#Hello World!` in English and Spanish.
There are no directives in this piece of code.
Every line of the program is a statement.
The statements after the `for` keyword are indented by the same amount, indicating they create one block. The two `print` statements form a block within the `for` block.

2.3 Build Tools

The Toolset (2.3.1)

The high-level code that you produce using an editor cannot be directly executed by a computer's microprocessor. Microprocessors have a machine language instruction set based on binary codes. There is no `print` instruction in the microprocessor's instruction set, for example.

Before a program can run, your code must be converted into **machine code** consisting of machine language instructions. This executable code is stored in an **executable file** that can be run, processed, and executed by the microprocessor. **Build tools** convert your code into a program that a computer can execute.

As a programmer, you'll eventually want to package your programs and distribute them so that they can be installed on a digital device and run with a click, just like the Hola Mundo! program in **Figure 2-9**.

A little background about build tools can help you understand some of the weird statements, such as `#include<iostream>`, that you have to include in programs. Also, a passing knowledge of build tools such as compilers, virtual machines, and interpreters will help you hold your own at late-night parties in Silicon Valley.

Figure 2-9 Hola Mundo! installed on a Windows computer

Compilers (2.3.2, 2.3.3)

A **compiler** translates code written in one programming language into another language. The original code is called **source code**, and the code a compiler produces is called **object code**. Object code is stored in a stand-alone file that is separate from the file that holds your source code. C++ programs use compilers. See **Figure 2-10**.

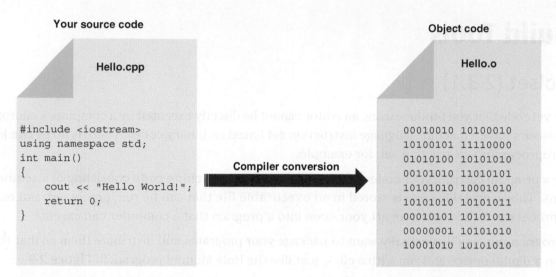

Figure 2-10   When the compiler creates machine code, the resulting file is executable

Q If a compiler is converting C++ code into machine code, what is the source code and what is the object code?

A The C++ code is the source code. The machine code is the object code.

Virtual Machines (2.3.4)

The product of a compiler is not necessarily machine code. Some compilers convert source code into semi-compiled code called **bytecode**. Software called a **virtual machine** converts the bytecode into machine code as the program executes.

What's the point of a virtual machine? The **Java Virtual Machine (JVM)** offers some insight. The backstory is that an executable file designed to run on a computer with the Microsoft Windows operating system won't work on a computer running macOS. You could develop one version of a program for Microsoft Windows and one for macOS, or you can use the Java programming language to create one version of the program and compile it to bytecode.

You can distribute the same bytecode to Windows and Mac users. Windows users have the Windows version of the JVM; Mac users have another version. The virtual machine software converts the bytecode into code that works on the host platform. **Figure 2-11** can help you understand how the JVM works and the value of bytecode.

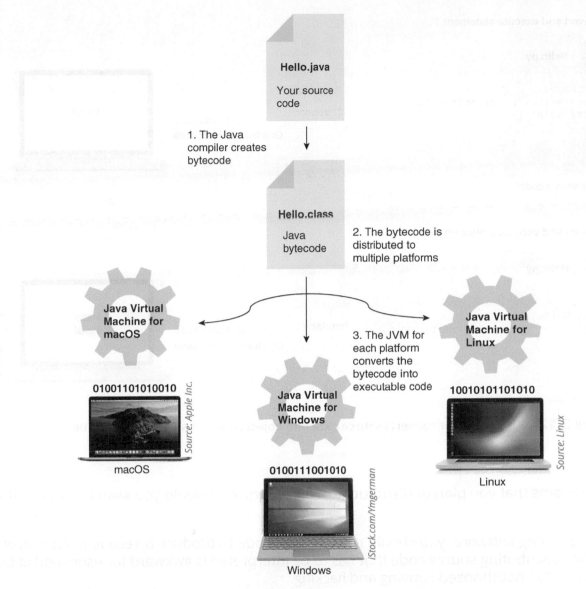

Figure 2-11 The Java Virtual Machine

Interpreters (2.3.5, 2.3.6)

Python uses a different tool for executing software. An **interpreter** is a software utility that begins with the first statement in your program, preprocesses it into a binary instruction, and then executes it. One by one, each statement in your program is interpreted and run, as illustrated in **Figure 2-12**.

The way an interpreter works is a huge contrast to the activity of a compiler, which preprocesses and converts all the statements in a program into a binary file before handing it over for execution.

Using an interpreter is convenient for coding and testing your programs because the code executes one line at a time. Execution stops if there is an error, and you can easily see where that error occurred. Modern programming development environments may come bundled with tools for interpreting code, compiling it, or doing both.

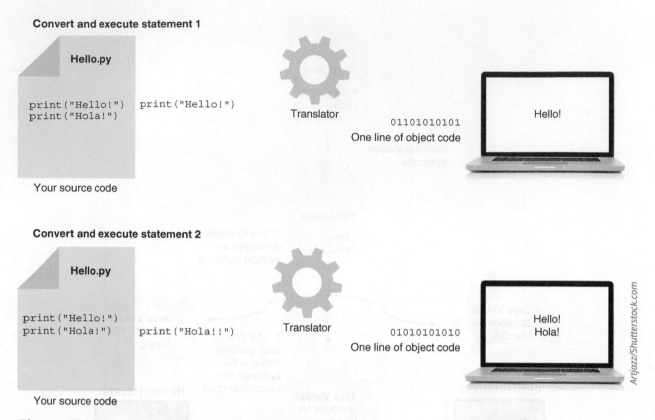

Figure 2-12 An interpreter converts source code into object code one statement at a time

Q For programs that you plan to distribute to other users, why would you want to compile them?

A For distributing software, you should compile your code to produce bytecode or an executable file. Distributing source code that has to be interpreted is awkward for users and exposes your code to unauthorized copying and hacking.

2.4 Debugging Tools

Programming Errors (2.4.1)

Yikes! You've written a Spanish version of the Hello World! program, but when you try to run it, all you see is an error message like the one in **Figure 2-13**.

Every programmer makes programming errors, but don't worry. You can quickly track down and fix errors using a variety of programming and debugging tools.

Debugging is programming jargon for finding and correcting errors, or "bugs," that prevent software from performing correctly. A popular meme dates the origin of the term "debug" to an event in 1947, when a programmer named Grace Hopper fixed a malfunctioning computer by removing a moth. That fact may come in handy when you play trivia. Think of debugging as a murder mystery game in which you are the detective, the culprit, and the victim all at the same time, trying to solve the mystery, "What did I do to my program?!"

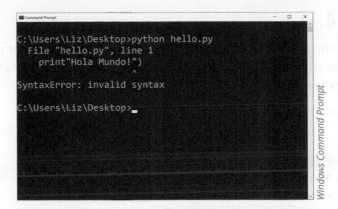

Figure 2-13   Error message from the command prompt reveals a glitch in program code

Programming errors can be classified into three categories: syntax errors, runtime errors, and semantic errors. Knowing the common errors in each of these categories can help you quickly spot bugs in your programs and fix them.

Syntax Errors (2.4.2)

A **syntax error** occurs when a source code statement does not conform to the punctuation and structural rules of the programming language. To track down the cause of a syntax error in your code, look for the following:

- A missing keyword
- A misspelled keyword
- A keyword in the wrong place
- A capitalized keyword
- Incorrect type of punctuation
- Unpaired quotes or brackets
- Incorrect indentation
- An empty block
- Embedded characters
- Incorrect method parameters

Q Syntax errors are typically caught by the compiler, which generates an error message. In Figure 2-13, can you use the error message to figure out what is wrong with the program?

A A parenthesis is missing at the start of `"Hola Mundo!"` The error message says, `"SyntaxError: invalid syntax."` The green ^ symbol indicates the general location of the error but points too far to the right. Python's syntax checker found the correct line on which the error occurred but only knows something went wrong on the line.

Runtime Errors (2.4.3)

Whoa! Your program just crashed. It cleared the syntax check, so what caused your program to come to an unexpected halt? A **runtime error** occurs when something in your program code goes wrong during runtime while it is executed by the microprocessor.

If you encounter a runtime error, look for these common problems:

- Division by zero
- Expressions that use incompatible data types
- Forgetting to declare a variable before using it
- Accessing a file that does not exist
- Running out of memory

In **Figure 2-14**, notice that the computer executed the first two lines of the program, but then it crashed when attempting to execute the last line containing a statement to divide by zero, which is not possible.

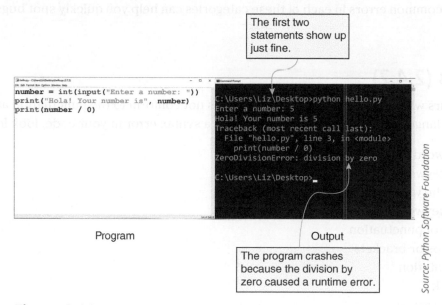

The first two statements show up just fine.

```
number = int(input("Enter a number: "))
print("Hola! Your number is", number)
print(number / 0)
```

Program

```
C:\Users\Liz\Desktop>python hello.py
Enter a number: 5
Hola! Your number is 5
Traceback (most recent call last):
  File "hello.py", line 3, in <module>
    print(number / 0)
ZeroDivisionError: division by zero

C:\Users\Liz\Desktop>
```

Output

The program crashes because the division by zero caused a runtime error.

Source: Python Software Foundation

Figure 2-14   What is wrong with this program?

When a program partially executes and then unexpectedly halts, you can be fairly certain of a runtime error. Some compilers can spot common runtime errors and will not allow your program to run until you've corrected them. Even though these common errors might be caught by the compiler, be aware that they are still classified as runtime errors, not syntax errors.

Semantic Errors (2.4.4, 2.4.5)

Recall that the semantics of a program statement relate to its meaning. A **semantic error** occurs when your program runs without crashing but produces an incorrect result. Semantic errors are also called **logic errors** because the algorithm might be based on flawed logic.

More commonly, semantic errors are caused by careless mistakes such as these:

- Using the wrong expression for a decision
- Using the wrong name for a variable
- Forgetting the order of operations
- Setting the wrong loop counter
- Indenting a block to the wrong level or incorrect placement of braces

Q In **Figure 2-15**, can you spot the logical error?

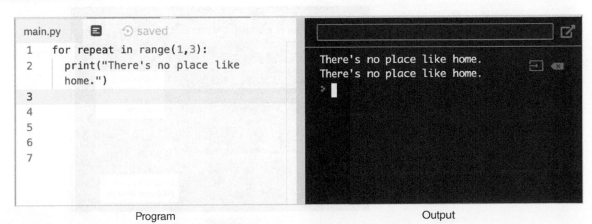

Figure 2-15   Logic errors produce the wrong result

A The `if` statement is incorrect. The `<` symbol should be `>=` so that the program says you can vote when your age is greater than or equal to 18.

Debugging Utilities (2.4.6, 2.4.7)

Compilers and interpreters can catch some programming errors. Special-purpose **debugging utilities** are also available for your use. These tools offer two nifty features: breakpoints and program animation.

A **breakpoint** specifies a line of code where execution should pause to let you look at the contents of variables, registers, and other execution elements. If you find unexpected data, a breakpoint can often help you identify the source of an error.

Suppose you write a program that is supposed to output **"There's no place like home."** three times. In **Figure 2-16**, you can see the program and its output, which is not what you expected. There are only two lines of output, not three.

```
main.py
1    for repeat in range(1,3):
2        print("There's no place like
         home.")
3
4
5
6
7
```

There's no place like home.
There's no place like home.

Program   Output

Figure 2-16   Something isn't working

By setting a breakpoint after the line containing `"There's no place like home."` you could examine the content of the variable called `repeat`. The variable `repeat` controls the number of times `"There's no place like home."` is output. In **Figure 2-17**, notice how the breakpoint pauses execution so that you can see the value of `repeat` as the program progresses.

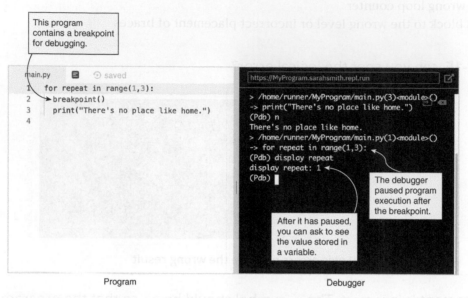

Figure 2-17 Using a debugger to check stored values

In Figure 2-17, `repeat` currently stores a value of 1. Everything seems normal, so you let the program continue and check the values later. By looking at the value of `repeat` when the program is complete, you'd find that it contains 2, which means `"There's no place like home."` was only output twice, not three times. That discrepancy would direct your attention to the `range(1,3)` statement that controls the number of times the `print` statement is repeated. It should be `range(0,3)` or `range(1,4)` because the first number in the range is where it starts, but the repetition stops *before* getting to the other number.

Debugging utilities also have a **program animation** feature that lets you watch the status of variables and other program elements as each line of your program is executed. This feature is useful when you run into an error that has you confounded. The program in **Figure 2-18** produced an error. The debugger helps you discover the source of that error.

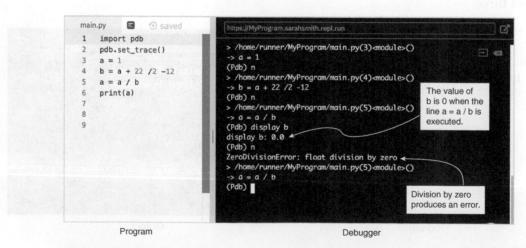

Figure 2-18 A step-by-step search for errors using a debugger's program animation

2.5 IDEs and SDKs

Integrated Development Environments (2.5.1, 2.5.2, 2.5.3, 2.5.4)

Some experienced programmers like to create a customized development environment containing their favorite editing, compiling, and debugging tools. For your initial foray into programming, it is easier to use an **integrated development environment (IDE)** that includes all the tools you need to code, compile, link, and debug your work.

Many IDEs support some level of visual programming so that you can define program elements using menus while dragging and dropping variables into program statements. Popular IDEs include Visual Studio, Xcode, Eclipse, Netbeans, and PyCharm. To use these IDEs, you download and install them on a computer. If you prefer to work with an **online IDE** (or web IDE) that requires no installation, check out services such as repl.it, codeanywhere, Ideone, and AWS Cloud9. With Python, you will likely want to use IDLE.

Using IDLE (2.5.5, 2.5.6)

The installation of Python comes with a built-in, easy-to-use IDE called IDLE, an ideal IDE for starting out in Python. You can use IDLE in one of two modes: shell mode or script mode.

The **shell mode** is useful for quick tests of code. **Figure 2-19** shows a simple Python command in shell mode. To run commands in the IDLE shell, type the code on one line and press Enter. Python will run the code immediately after you press Enter and then show the result. No work is saved, so once you close the shell window, the code you created will vanish.

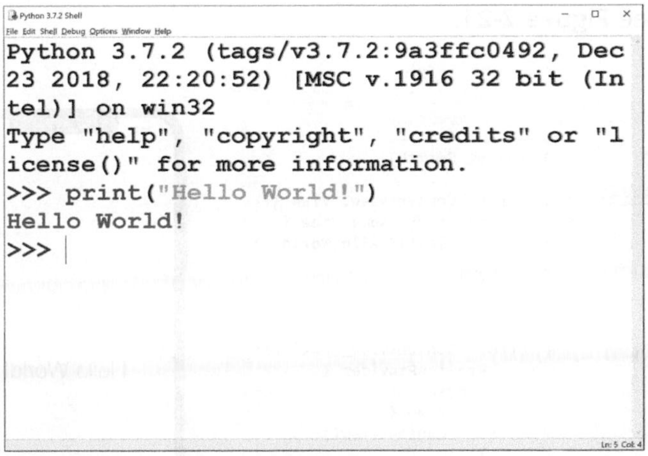

```
Python 3.7.2 Shell                                    —  □  ×
File Edit Shell Debug Options Window Help
Python 3.7.2 (tags/v3.7.2:9a3ffc0492, Dec
23 2018, 22:20:52) [MSC v.1916 32 bit (In
tel)] on win32
Type "help", "copyright", "credits" or "l
icense()" for more information.
>>> print("Hello World!")
Hello World!
>>> |
                                            Ln: 5 Col: 4
```

Source: Python Software Foundation

Figure 2-19   Shell mode in IDLE

You use **script mode** for larger projects that need to be saved to your computer, like a report created in a word processor. To run code in script mode, you save the file and then press F5. The output of your script file is shown in an IDLE shell, though it is run from the script mode. **Figure 2-20** shows the same code created and run as in Figure 2-19 but in script mode.

Source: Python Software Foundation

Code in script mode   Output in shell window

Figure 2-20   Script mode in IDLE with output in the shell window

Software Development Kits (2.5.7, 2.5.8, 2.5.9)

How would you create a program for iPhones that displays "Hola!" anytime the phone is picked up? Your program will have to access the phone's accelerometer to sense when the phone is lifted. To get this project off the ground, you need the iOS SDK.

A **software development kit (SDK)** is a set of tools for developing platform-specific software. SDKs include preprogrammed code libraries, code samples, documentation, and other utilities. Often these tools are wrapped in an integrated development environment that provides coding, compiling, and debugging tools.

The iOS SDK even provides an iPhone simulator so that you can test your app on the computer you are using as a development platform. See **Figure 2-21**.

Source: Apple Inc.

Figure 2-21   iOS SDK with iPhone simulator

SDKs are a required tool for programmers developing software for Windows, macOS, iOS, Android, and other platforms. Popular SDKs include the Java Development Kit for Android apps, iOS SDK, Windows SDK, and Facebook SDK.

Summary

- Programming languages such as C++, Java, and Python are classified as high-level programming languages because they provide a way for you as a programmer to compose human-readable instructions that direct the operations performed by a computing device.
- Semantics refers to the meaning and validity of program statements. Keywords have specific semantic purposes, and programmers must learn how to use them correctly.
- Syntax defines the order of words and the punctuation you are required to use when composing statements. Each programming language has a unique syntax.
- Programming requires code editors, compilers, and debugging utilities.
- Code editors help you enter statements correctly, using standard conventions for comments, directives, functions, statements, and code blocks.
- Before a program can run, your code must be converted into machine code, which is stored in an executable file. Compilers and interpreters convert your code into a program that a computer can execute.
- A compiler translates source code written in one programming language into a file containing object code in another language.
- Some compilers convert source code into semi-compiled code called bytecode. Software called a virtual machine translates bytecode into machine code just prior to its execution.
- An interpreter is a software utility that begins with the first statement in your program, preprocesses it into a binary instruction, and then executes it.
- Debugging is programming jargon for finding and correcting errors—or "bugs"—that prevent software from performing correctly. Debugging can reveal syntax, runtime, and semantic errors in a program.
- An IDE is an integrated development environment that typically includes a code editor, debugger, compiler, and linker. It might offer a visual environment to simplify coding.
- IDLE is an IDE that comes with Python. It has both a shell and script mode, with shell mode used for short code tests and script mode used for larger programs.
- In addition to an IDE, a software development kit (SDK) provides platform-specific development tools.

Key Terms

breakpoint
build tools
bytecode
code block
code editor
comment
compiler
computer program
debugging
debugging utilities
directive
executable file
high-level programming languages

integrated development
   environment (IDE)
interpreter
Java Virtual Machine (JVM)
keywords
logic errors
machine code
object code
online IDE
program animation
program code
programming language
reserved words

runtime error
script mode
semantic error
semantics
shell mode
software development kit (SDK)
source code
statement
syntax
syntax error
text editor
virtual machine

Module

3

Literals, Variables, and Constants

Learning Objectives:

3.1 Literals

3.1.1 Define the term "literal" in the context of programming.

3.1.2 Identify numeric literals.

3.1.3 Provide examples of integer literals and floating-point literals.

3.1.4 Identify character and string literals.

3.1.5 Provide use cases for string literals that look like numbers.

3.1.6 Identify Boolean literals.

3.2 Variables and Constants

3.2.1 List the characteristics of a program variable.

3.2.2 Create descriptive variable names using appropriate style conventions.

3.2.3 Describe the purpose of a constant.

3.2.4 Use standard naming conventions for constants.

3.2.5 Explain the difference between a variable, a constant, and a literal.

3.2.6 Explain the relationship between variables and memory.

3.3 Assignment Statements

3.3.1 Differentiate between undefined and defined variables.

3.3.2 Identify statements that declare variables.

3.3.3 Identify statements that initialize variables.

3.3.4 Explain how Python uses dynamic typing and determines data types.

3.3.5 Explain the meaning of type inference.

3.3.6 Explain the concept of a null variable.

3.3.7 Identify assignment statements that change the value of a variable.

3.3.8 Differentiate declaring, initializing, and assigning variables.

3.4 Input and Output

3.4.1 State the algorithm for collecting input from a user and placing it in a variable.

3.4.2 Transform the user input algorithm into pseudocode.

3.4.3 Trace the pseudocode that outputs the value of a variable that is input by a user.

3.1 Literals

Numeric Literals (3.1.1, 3.1.2, 3.1.3)

In J.R.R. Tolkien's classic fantasy series, *The Lord of the Rings*, 19 rings are endowed with magic powers and distributed to elves, dwarves, and humans in Middle Earth. The rings, which might look like those in **Figure 3-1**, can help explain the concept of literals, which are a basic element in programming.

Figure 3-1   Three rings for the elven kings under the sky...

When you get down to basics, programming is a simple activity. You put data into the memory of a computer; then you tell the computer how to manipulate the data according to an algorithm.

Any element of data that you specify for a program is referred to as a **literal**. In Middle Earth, the elven kings had three rings. You can express this idea as

```
elven_rings = 3
```

In this statement, 3 is a literal. It is a value that you specify as representing a quantity. The literal 3 always means three things, never four things. In that sense, 3 is a fixed value. But this is important: `elven_rings` is not fixed. If one ring is lost, then `elven_rings` can become 2.

Literals 3 and 2 are classified as numeric literals. A **numeric literal** is composed of one or more digits that can represent integers or floating-point numbers containing a decimal point.

Q What are the numeric literals in the following list?

```
dwarf_rings = 7

One
1

ring_thickness = 2.7

dark_lord = "Sauron"
```

A The numeric literals are 7, 1, and 2.7. Literals 7 and 1 are integers, while 2.7 is a floating-point number.

Okay, so numeric literals can be divided into integers and floating points. **Figure 3-2** illustrates the variety of numeric literals you can use in your programs.

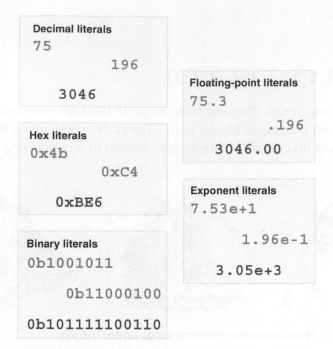

Figure 3-2   Common numeric literals

Q   What is the literal in the following statement?

```
elven_rings = 0b00000011
```

A   The literal is 0b00000011, which is the binary integer 3.

Character and String Literals (3.1.4)

In addition to numeric data, you'll want your programs to work with data such as letters, symbols, words, and sentences. These non-numeric literals come in two categories: character and string.

A **character literal** is a single letter or symbol. Programmers usually enclose character literals in single quotes, like these examples:

```
'a'
```

```
'@'
```

A **string literal** contains one or more characters and is typically denoted with double quotes, like these examples:

```
"Mordor"
```

```
"Three rings for the elven kings…"
```

```
"bilbo@theshire.com"
```

Q   How would you classify `"J.R.R. Tolkien"`?

A   It is a string literal because it contains more than one character.

In Python, a character literal is identical to a string literal containing only one character. You can actually use double quotes or single quotes for character and string literals, but you should be consistent, such as using single quotes for character literals and double quotes for string literals. Examples in this course use double quotes for characters and strings. **Figure 3-3** shows string and character literals.

```
Character literals
"a"
        'T'
   "#"
```

```
String literals
"cat"
        'A full sentence.'
   "1932"
```

Figure 3-3   Character literals and string literals

Tricky Literals (3.1.5, 3.1.6)

Literals that look like numbers could be strings. Surprisingly, 202 can be a numeric literal for the value two hundred and two, or it can be a string literal for the area code of Washington, D.C. When working with numerals in a context where they are not manipulated mathematically, you can designate them as string literals by enclosing them in double (or single) quotes.

Q Where is the string literal in the following statements?

```
distance_to_mordor = 156
unlock_code = "156"
```

A The unlock code **"156"** is a string literal. PINs, house numbers, Social Security numbers, area codes, and zip codes are examples of string literals that look like numbers.

Boolean literals are another surprise. The value of a **Boolean literal** is either **True** or **False**. Whether those words are capitalized depends on the programming language you are using. The point, however, is that the words **True** and **False** look like string literals, but because they are Boolean literals, they are not enclosed in single or double quotes.

Booleans have lots of uses in programming, such as setting a fact as true. At the start of *The Lord of the Rings* series, the character Bilbo is in possession of "The One Ring." This can be expressed in code:

```
bilbo_has_ring = True
```

This statement means that Bilbo has a ring. In contrast, the statement **bilbo_has_ring = "True"** might mean that the ring in Bilbo's possession is named "True" rather than "The One Ring."

3.2 Variables and Constants

Variables (3.2.1, 3.2.2)

To use literals, you must put them in a known location so that they can be accessed by the statements in your programs. At one point in The One Ring's history, it is lost during a swim through a river. No one can find it for a very long time, causing all kinds of trouble. To avoid trouble in your programs, you need to keep track of the location of literals. Variables and constants provide the locations for literals.

In the context of programming, a **variable** is a named memory location that temporarily holds text or a numeric value. See **Figure 3-4**.

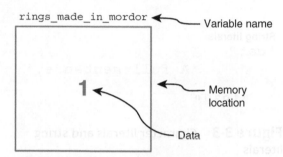

Figure 3-4   A variable is a named memory location that temporarily holds data

Variables have three important characteristics:

- A variable has a name.
- A variable corresponds to a memory location where data can be stored.
- The data in a variable can be changed.

You have lots of flexibility when naming variables, with the exception that you cannot use any of your programming language's built-in function names. A **built-in function**, such as `print`, is used by a programming language for a specific purpose. Your knowledge of what is or isn't a built-in function will grow as you learn about Python.

The names you use for variables should be descriptive. Can you guess what the programmer had in mind by calling a variable **er** and putting **3** into it?

```
er = 3
```

The variable name **er** might refer to an emergency room, explicit rate, or the small country of Eritrea. If **3** is the number of elven rings, however, a variable name such as **elven_rings** is much more descriptive.

```
elven_rings = 3
```

The style for variable names differs based on programming language syntax and project team standards. Some programming languages require variable names to begin with a lowercase letter, while other languages require an uppercase letter. Python variable names must start with a letter (uppercase or lowercase) or an underscore.

Variable names cannot contain any spaces, but a single word may not provide a very descriptive variable name. The two most prevalent conventions for combining words for variable names are camel case and snake case.

Camel case begins with a lowercase letter, but each subsequent word is capitalized. **Snake case** uses all lowercase and separates words with an underscore. **Figure 3-5** provides examples. Python typically uses **camelCase** for variable names.

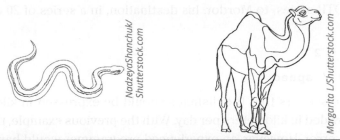

Snake case	Camel case
elven_rings	elvenRings
made_in_mordor	madeInMordor
hobbit	hobbit
multiples_of_2	multiplesOf2

Figure 3-5   Snake case and camel case for formatting variable names

Constants (3.2.3, 3.2.4, 3.2.5)

A **constant** is a named memory location that holds data, which is used but not changed by the statements in a program. See **Figure 3-6**.

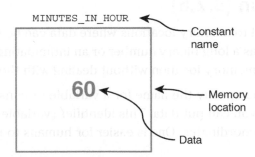

MINUTES_IN_HOUR ← Constant name

60 ← Memory location

← Data

Figure 3-6   A constant is a named memory location that holds data that does not change

These are the three important characteristics of constants:

- A constant has a name,
- A constant corresponds to a memory location where data can be stored.
- The data in a constant is not meant to be changed.

Constants are sometimes confused with literals because both may be described as "fixed." Your takeaway is that a literal is a data element, but a constant is a *place* in memory that holds a value that does not change.

As with variables, the name you use for a constant should be descriptive. The convention of differentiating constants from variables in Python is to name constants in all uppercase text with an underscore separating words. Here are some examples:

```
MINUTES_IN_HOUR = 60

MAXIMUM_USERS = 1024

OHIO_ABBREVIATION = "OH"
```

You might wonder why programmers use named constants instead of simply using the actual value in calculations or processes. Suppose a programmer uses 1,779 miles as the distance from the Shire, the starting location of Frodo's journey in the LOTR series, to Mordor, his destination, in a series of 20 or more formulas, beginning with these:

```
round_trip = 1779 * 2

travel_time = 1779 / speed
```

Later, the programmer discovers that the distance should be expressed in kilometers, not miles, because Frodo's walking speed is provided in kilometers per day. With the previous example, the programmer must change multiple formulas to fix this error. However, an experienced programmer would have set up the formulas with a constant such as **DISTANCE_SHIRE_MORDOR** like this:

```
DISTANCE_SHIRE_MORDOR = 1779

round_trip = DISTANCE_SHIRE_MORDOR * 2

travel_time = DISTANCE_SHIRE_MORDOR / speed
```

Changing the distance to kilometers then requires a change in only one line instead of all the formulas.

```
DISTANCE_SHIRE_MORDOR = 2863

round_trip = DISTANCE_SHIRE_MORDOR * 2

travel_time = DISTANCE_SHIRE_MORDOR / speed
```

The Memory Connection (3.2.6)

Variables and constants correspond to memory locations where data can be stored. Each memory location has a unique address that is expressed as a long binary number or an intimidating hex number such as 0xE2452440. Thankfully, you can put data into a memory location without dealing with those addresses.

Figure 3-7 shows that when you specify the name for a variable or constant, your programming language ties it to a memory location where you can put data. This identifier (variable name) is to computer memory as a street address is to geographical coordinates. One is easier for humans to remember and reference, but they both lead to the same location.

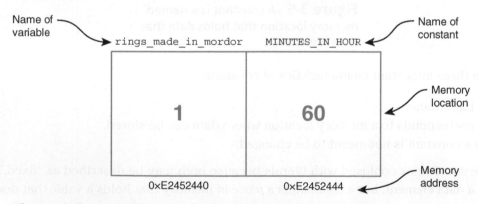

Figure 3-7   Variable names correspond to memory locations

3.3 Assignment Statements

Declaring Variables (3.3.1, 3.3.2)

The computer doesn't recognize a variable until it is named and set to a value. Otherwise, the variable is undefined. Using an **undefined variable** produces a runtime error, so it is essential to define the variables that you use in programs.

Variables can be declared, initialized, and assigned. Depending on your programming language and your algorithm, each of these operations might require a separate step, or all of them can be combined.

To **declare a variable** means specifying a name that is assigned, or bound, to a memory location. Python requires you to assign a value to all variables while declaring them. You do so with an initialization statement.

Initializing Variables (3.3.3, 3.3.4, 3.3.5, 3.3.6)

To **initialize a variable** means specifying a name and a value. In pseudocode, you can specify an initialization statement like this:

```
Store the value 20 in total_rings
```

Pseudocode expresses what the code will try to achieve without using the syntax and other rules of a programming language. When creating pseudocode, you write sentences that someone else could understand without knowing any Python syntax.

The pseudocode initialization statement `Store the value 20 in total_rings` suggests creating a variable called `total_rings` and setting its value to 20.

To translate pseudocode into actual code, you need to know how to translate one language (human/pseudocode) to another (computer/Python). **Figure 3-8** shows another way pseudocode could describe initializing a variable and the equivalent Python code.

Style	Initialization Statements
Pseudocode	There are 20 total rings
	The first letter is the character A
Python	total_rings = 20
	first_letter = "A"

Figure 3-8   Initializing a variable

Python is a **dynamically typed** programming language that allows a variable to take on any type of data during program execution. The language deduces the data type based on the presence or absence of a decimal point and quote marks. This process is referred to as **type inference**. The meaning is inferred from the context in which it is used. For example, in a dynamically typed language, the following code is perfectly acceptable:

```
total_rings = 19

total_rings = 20

total_rings = "unknown"
```

With dynamic typing, you can initialize `total_rings` as 19, which is a number. You can then change the value to 20 and then change it to the text string `"unknown"`.

Other languages may require you to store only one type of data in a variable. These languages are called **statically typed**.

What role does initialization play in your programming? Let's look at some examples.

Starting values. You can initialize a variable with a literal if you know its starting value when the program begins. You can specify that there are three elven rings as follows:

```
elven_rings = 3
```

Initial value of counter. The integer variables that you plan to use to count repetitions can be initialized with 0 or 1, depending on the control structure that operates the loop. Here is an example:

```
counter = 0
```

Sometimes the starting value is known, but other times you have to wait until someone enters a value. A temporary value to represent the unknown is used in these situations.

Q How could you initialize the ring location if you don't know where the ring can be found at the beginning of the program?

A You could use this initialization statement:

```
ring_location = "Unknown"
```

Null variables. A **null variable** is one that has no value. A null variable is not the same as a variable that has been initialized with 0. Zero is a value; null means no value. Programming languages handle null values in different ways. Python uses the keyword `None` to signal that a variable contains nothing.

```
ring_location = None
```

When you should use a null value or a temporary value, such as `"Unknown"`, is a nuance of programming you will learn with experience. You need to consider whether the variable is truly empty or contains an initial value, like a counter.

Assigning Variables (3.3.7, 3.3.8)

Assigning variables refers to any process that sets or changes the value of a variable. An **assignment statement** sets or changes the value that is stored in a variable. **Figure 3-9** explains the syntax of an assignment statement.

```
variable_name  =  expression

dwarf_rings    =  7 - 1
dwarf_rings    =  dwarf_rings - 1
total_rings    =  3 + 7 + 9 + 1
ring_location  =  "Anduin River"
ring_location  =  "Bilbo's pocket"
```

Figure 3-9   General syntax for assignment statements

Assignment statements and initialization statements are the same. An initialization is a type of assignment. Initialization is the term used for the first time you set the value of a variable. Later in your program, you can use an assignment statement to change the value of a variable.

In the following code, the variable `total_rings` is initialized as 0; then an assignment statement changes that value to the total number of rings.

```
total_rings = 0
total_rings = 3 + 7 + 9 + 1
```

As you can see, assignment statements are a handy way to perform calculations and place the result into a variable. You can then use that variable for further calculation or as the source of output you display to users.

You can also use assignment statements to change the value of a string literal that is stored in a variable. Here is an example:

```
who_has_the_ring = "Sauron"

who_has_the_ring = "Isildur"
```

Variables play several essential roles in your programs:

- Variables provide the perfect place to put the literals that your programs use as input, manipulations, and output.
- Variables can hold intermediate data while multistep calculations are performed.
- Variables can act as counters to control the number of repetitions a program performs.
- The value in a variable can be used as the basis for sections of an algorithm that hinge on decisions.

3.4 Input and Output

Input to a Variable (3.4.1, 3.4.2)

As a programmer, you can collect data from an outside source and place it into a variable. It is a handy way to obtain some or all the data your program is designed to process. The algorithm for collecting data from a user goes like this:

Initialize a variable to hold the user's input.
Prompt the user to enter data.
Collect the data in the initialized variable.

To get data from a user, you typically supply a **prompt** that explains what you want the user to enter. For example, if your program is collecting answers for a trivia game, one prompt might be, "In Middle Earth, how many rings were given to the dwarf lords?"

Using this prompt, here is the code to initialize a variable, display a prompt, and then collect an answer from the user:

```
dwarf_rings = 0

print("In Middle Earth, how many rings were given to the dwarf lords? ")

dwarf_rings = input()
```

When you code and run this program, the trivia player would see something like **Figure 3-10**.

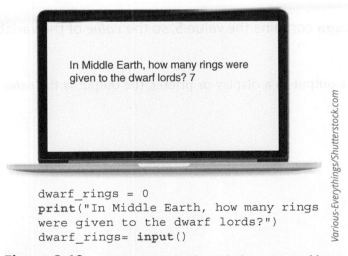

Figure 3-10   Loading a variable with data entered by a user

Q In Figure 3-10, which line of code initializes the variable **dwarf_rings**, and which line places the user's input in that variable?

A The line **dwarf_rings = 0** initializes the variable. The line **dwarf_rings = input()** places the user's input into the variable.

Python allows you to include an initialization, a display, and an input instruction on the same line. For example, you can write one line of code to load (initialize) the **dwarf_rings** variable with user input. To display text such as **In Middle Earth, how many rings were given to the dwarf lords?** as input instructions to the user, put the display string inside the parentheses that follow **input**. **Figure 3-11** compares the previous code to an abbreviated version that reduces three lines to one.

```
dwarf_rings = 0
print("In Middle Earth, how many rings were given to the dwarf lords?")
dwarf_rings = input()


dwarf_rings = 0
dwarf_rings = input("In Middle Earth, how many rings were given to the dwarf lords? ")
```

Figure 3-11   Loading a variable with data entered by a user

Output from a Variable (3.4.3)

Suppose the trivia player responds to the question about dwarf rings by entering 5. That is not the correct answer. You can then ask if 5 is the final answer. Here's the code:

```
dwarf_rings = 0

print("In Middle Earth, how many rings were given to the dwarf lords? ")

dwarf_rings = input()

print("Is", dwarf_rings, "your final answer?")
```

Q Look at the output of the program in **Figure 3-12**. Where does the 5 come from in the last line?

A The variable **dwarf_rings** contains the value 5, so the *value* of the variable appears in the displayed line.

When variables are sent as output to a display or printer, the output is the *value* of the variable, not the variable name.

In Middle Earth, how many rings were given to the dwarf lords? 5

Is 5 your final answer?

```
dwarf_rings = 0
print("In Middle Earth, how many rings were given to the dwarf lords? ")
dwarf_rings = input()
print("Is", dwarf_rings, "your final answer?")
```

Figure 3-12 Displaying the value of a variable

Various-Everything-/Shutterstock.com

Summary

- Any element of data that you specify for a program is referred to as a literal. There are several types of literals, such as integer, floating point, character, string, and Boolean.
- Literals that look like numbers are sometimes treated as strings when they are not intended to be used in calculations. Telephone numbers, PINs, house numbers, Social Security numbers, area codes, and zip codes are examples of string literals that look like numbers.
- A variable is a named memory location that temporarily holds text or a numeric value.
- Variable names should be descriptive but cannot be built-in function names used for special purposes by the programming language. Variable names are usually formatted in camel case or snake case.
- A constant is a named memory location holding data that is not changed by the statements in a program.
- Variables and constants correspond to memory locations where data can be stored. When you specify the name for a variable or constant, your programming language ties it to a memory location where you can place data.
- Using undefined variables can produce runtime or compile-time errors. To define a variable, you must initialize it. Dynamically typed languages do not require you to specify a data type. Type is inferred by the assignment and may be changed with a new assignment.
- Assignment statements can be used to initialize a variable or change its value.
- Programmers can assign values to variables, or they can collect values from external sources, such as user input. The values of variables can be sent as output to a printer, display, or other device.

Key Terms

assignment statement
Boolean literal
built-in function
camel case
character literal
constant
declare a variable

dynamically typed
initialize a variable
literal
null variable
numeric literal
prompt
snake case

statically typed
string literal
type inference
undefined variable
variable

Module 4

Numeric Data Types and Expressions

Learning Objectives:

4.1 Primitive Data Types

4.1.1 Define the term "data type."

4.1.2 List four common primitive data types.

4.1.3 Explain the purpose of primitive data types.

4.1.4 Distinguish between primitive data types and composite data types.

4.2 Numeric Data Types

4.2.1 List the characteristics of integer data.

4.2.2 Provide examples of integer data that might be incorporated in a computer program.

4.2.3 Explain the difference between a signed and an unsigned integer.

4.2.4 State the memory requirements for signed and unsigned integers.

4.2.5 List the characteristics of floating-point data.

4.2.6 Provide examples of floating-point data that might be incorporated in a computer program.

4.2.7 Recall that floating-point data is not stored in conventional binary format.

4.2.8 Compare and contrast the use of integer data with floating-point data.

4.3 Mathematical Expressions

4.3.1 List the symbols used for the following mathematical operations: addition, subtraction, multiplication, division, exponentiation, and modulo division.

4.3.2 Provide examples of program statements in which the result of a mathematical operation is stored in a variable.

4.3.3 Describe the mathematical order of operations.

4.3.4 Provide examples illustrating the use of parentheses to change the order of operations.

4.3.5 Explain the use of compound operators such as += -= *= /= and %=.

4.4 Numeric Data Type Conversion

4.4.1 Provide examples of when a programmer might convert integer or floating-point data to a different data type.

4.4.2 Explain the disadvantage of converting floating-point data to integer data.

4.4.3 Explain the significance of rounding for floating-point calculations.

4.5 Formatting Output

4.5.1 Explain the advantage of formatting output.

4.5.2 List the elements that can be specified when formatting numeric output.

4.5.3 Use formatting parameters to specify the output format of numeric data.

4.1 Primitive Data Types

Data Types (4.1.1)

iTunes provides detailed information about each of the albums in its collection. In **Figure 4-1**, you can easily identify the album price, release date, the number of reviewers, song list, song times, popularity, and song prices.

Figure 4-1   Data displayed for a music album is stored in variables

Source: Apple.com/itunes

This data can be stored in variables, but there's a small problem. If you are writing a program and want to assign the value of 3:56 to a variable called **song_time**, your programming language will generate an error. The problem with values such as 3:56 is related to data types, so let's dive into the topic.

The term **data type** refers to a way of categorizing data. For example, the number 21 could be categorized as an integer data type because it is a whole number without decimal places. As a programmer, you need a good understanding of data types because they are a key element of the variables that are the foundation for your programs.

Programmers work with two main classifications of data types: primitive data types and composite data types.

Primitive Data Types (4.1.2, 4.1.3)

Primitive data types are built into your programming language. **Figure 4-2** provides a list of them.

Primitive data types are important time savers because your programming language knows how to allocate memory for storing these data types. For example, suppose you want to store the number of songs (23) for the first act of the *Hamilton* soundtrack in a variable called **act1_song_count**. Because the integer 23 is classified as a primitive data type, your programming language knows how much memory space to allocate for it.

Primitive Data Type	Python Code	Description	Examples
Integer	`var = 5`	Whole number without any decimal places	1 128 3,056 –2
Floating-point	`var = 5.0`	Number that includes decimal places	12.99 0.26 –3.56

Boolean	`var = False`	Logical value of `True` or `False`	`True`
			
			`False`

Valueless	`var = None`	No value	No real-world equivalent examples

Figure 4-2   Primitive data types

Your programming language also knows how to manipulate primitive data types. For numbers such as 23, your language can perform addition, subtraction, and other mathematical operations.

Programming languages provide functions to manipulate data. A **function** is a named procedure that performs a specific task. The **abs()** function, for example, returns the absolute, unsigned value of an integer.

Q What are the two key characteristics of primitive data types?

A The key characteristics are as follows:

1. The programming language knows how much memory to allocate.
2. The programming language knows how to manipulate that type of data.

The takeaway for primitive data types is that you can tell the programming language what to do with them, but you don't have to explain how to do it. You don't have to specify the mechanics of storing or adding two numbers; you just specify the variables or values that you want to add.

Composite Data Types (4.1.4)

Composite data types are not built into your programming language but can be constructed from primitive data types. Composite data types are programmer defined or available in add-on libraries of program code. In most programming languages, data that represents time would be handled as a composite data type.

The first song on the *Hamilton* soundtrack is 3:56 minutes long. This value is not an integer, floating-point number, or other primitive data type. To use this value in a program, you would need to create a composite data type and code routines for manipulating it.

You will discover more about composite data types as you continue to learn about functions and data structures. For now, let's focus on primitive data types that involve integers and floating-point numbers.

4.2 Numeric Data Types

Integer Data Types (4.2.1, 4.2.2, 4.2.3, 4.2.4)

Whole numbers are classified as **integer data types**. Integer data types have the following characteristics:

- Must be whole numbers without decimal places or fractions.
- Can be positive or negative. An integer without a plus or minus symbol is called an **unsigned integer** and is assumed to be a positive number. An integer that begins with a plus or minus symbol is a **signed integer**.
- Can be a decimal, binary, or hexadecimal number.

Figure 4-3 contains examples of signed and unsigned integer data that you might incorporate into computer programs.

Integer Data	Is it Signed?	Description
23	Unsigned	Number of songs
+363	Signed	Number of reviewers
1460000	Unsigned	Number of *Hamilton* albums sold
7722333444	Unsigned	World population
−40	Signed	Coldest temperature recorded in Kansas
0b00000101	Unsigned	Binary 5
0x6C	Unsigned	Hexadecimal 108

Figure 4-3   Integer data types

Python infers the data type for a variable by the way the assignment statement is written. When you write the statement **var = 23**, Python assumes you intend **var** to contain an integer with a value of 23.

Integers, such as 23, are stored as binary numbers in memory locations. Each memory location holds one byte of data composed of eight digits. The binary number 11111111, which is 255, is the largest number that fits in one byte. One byte can hold unsigned integers ranging from 0 to 255.

A signed integer requires one digit as the sign, so only seven digits remain for the number. One byte provides enough storage space for signed integers ranging from −127 to +127. **Figure 4-4** further explains this important idea.

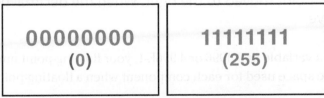

One byte of memory holds eight binary digits. Unsigned integers range from 00000000 to 11111111, which is 0 to 255.

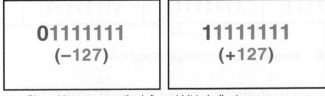

Signed integers use the leftmost bit to indicate a + or − sign. The range for signed integers is −1111111 to +1111111, which is −127 to +127.

Figure 4-4   Integer storage allocation

Because integers are a primitive data type, your programming language sets aside an appropriate amount of memory to store them. Your programs generally deal with integers that are larger than 255, so Python sets aside more than four bytes of memory for each integer. Four bytes can hold integers ranging from –2,147,483,648 to +2,147,483,647. More bytes can hold even larger numbers. As long as you are working with numbers in these ranges, the basic integer data type is all you'll need.

Floating-Point Data Types (4.2.5, 4.2.6, 4.2.7, 4.2.8)

Numbers with decimal places are classified as **floating-point data types**. These numbers include a decimal point and values to the right of the decimal point. **Figure 4-5** contains examples of signed and unsigned floating-point data that you might incorporate into computer programs.

Floating-Point Number	Is it Signed?	Description
19.99	Unsigned	Price of the *Hamilton* album
4.8	Unsigned	Customer rating
0.08	Unsigned	Tax rate
2.998E8	Unsigned	Speed of light (meters/second)
–4.5967E2	Signed	Absolute zero

Figure 4-5   Floating-point data types

Floating-point numbers can be positive or negative, and they can be expressed in decimal notation or E notation. **E notation** is similar to scientific notation, which formats numbers as powers of 10. For example, 459.67 in E notation is 4.5967E2. Notice the 2 to the right of E. It means the decimal point was moved two places to the left, with each place representing a power of 10.

Q What is the E notation for 0.4996?

A It is 4.996E-1. E notation always displays one number (that is not zero) to the left of the decimal, so the decimal point moved to the right. When the decimal point moves to the right, the exponent is negative.

Whether you initialize a variable as 0.4996 or 4.996E-1, your floating-point numbers are stored in E notation. In **Figure 4-6**, you can see the space used for each component when a floating-point number is stored in four bytes.

Byte 1	Byte 2	Byte 3	Byte 4
11111111	11111111	11111111	11111111

1 Sign bit   8 Exponent bits   23 Data bits

Figure 4-6   Floating-point storage allocation

Because of the space used to store the sign and exponent, four bytes can store floating-point numbers in the range of ±3.4E-38 to ±3.4E38. These four-byte numbers are referred to as **single precision** numbers. When floating-point data is stored in eight bytes, it is referred to as **double precision** data. Double precision numbers can range from ±1.7E–308 to ±1.7E308.

Statically typed languages use a keyword to designate single and double precision floating-point numbers. All floating-point numbers in Python are double precision (eight bytes), called "floats," inferred from the decimal point in the assignment statement, as in the following:

```
price = 5.99
```

4.3 Mathematical Expressions

Arithmetic Operators (4.3.1, 4.3.2)

Integers and floating-point numbers are used for calculations. The result of a calculation is generally stored in a variable. Here is an example:

```
discount_price = album_price - 2.99
```

The variable `discount_price` will hold the result of the calculation. On the right side of the = symbol, `album_price - 2.99` is an expression. An **expression** is a programming statement that has a value and usually includes one or more **arithmetic operators**, such as - or +, and one or more operands, such as `album_price` or `2.99`.

To construct expressions, you can use the arithmetic operators listed in **Figure 4-7**.

Operator	Operation	Example
+	Addition	`song_count = 23 + 22`
-	Subtraction	`discount_price = album_price - 2.99`
*	Multiplication	`tax = discount_price * tax_rate`
/	Division	`average_rating = total / number_of_reviewers`
//	Integer division	`truncated_average = total // number_of_reviewers`
%	Modulo division	`remainder = 23 % 6`

Figure 4-7   Arithmetic operators

Q From the examples in Figure 4-7, can you conclude that arithmetic operators work only for literals?

A No. You can see that arithmetic operations can manipulate variables, such as `tax_rate`, as well as literals, such as `2.99`.

Arithmetic operators generally work as you'd expect, but note these important takeaways:

Integer division. When integer division produces a fractional part, it may not be included in the result. For example, `7 / 2 = 3.5`, but the result might be `3` if you use the integer division operator `//`.

Modulo division. The % operator produces the remainder of a division operation. The result of dividing 11 by 3 is 3, with 2 as the remainder. So, `11 % 3` produces `2` as the result.

Q What is the result of 6 % 2?

A The result is 0 because 6 divided by 2 is 3 with no remainder. The remainder is 0. So, 6 % 2 is 0.

You can use the modulo operator in an algorithm to determine if a number is odd or even. Here is the pseudocode:

```
store 6 in a variable called my_number

if my_number is even then

    display the words "The number is even."

otherwise

    display the words "The number is odd."
```

How can you program the pseudocode line if my_number is even then? You can detect if a number is even by the remainder. If a number can be divided by 2 and have no remainder, then it is even. When my_number % 2 == 0, my_number is even.

In **Figure 4-8**, you can see how this algorithm translates into actual code. The operators = and == are different. You use = to assign values to variables, and you use == to compare values.

```
my_number = 6

if my_number % 2 == 0:

    print("The number is even.")

else:

    print("The number is odd.")

OUTPUT:

The number is even.
```

Figure 4-8   Checking whether a number is even or odd

Order of Operations (4.3.3, 4.3.4)

What is the solution to the expression 2 + 3 * (5 + 1)? If you answered 20, you're on point with the **order of operations**, which specifies the sequence in which to perform arithmetic operations. Here's the sequence:

1. Do the math in parentheses first.

2. Carry out exponentiation and roots.

3. Perform multiplication, floating-point division, integer division, and modulo as they appear from left to right.

4. Execute addition and subtraction as they appear from left to right.

To solve 2 + 3 * (5 + 1), first add 5 + 1 because it is in parentheses. Now you have 2 + 3 * 6. Next, do the multiplication, so the expression becomes 2 + 18. Finally, add those numbers and the result is 20. Try another one:

Q What is the result of `2 + 3 % 2 * (4 + 1)`?

A The result is 7. First add `4 + 1` because it is in parentheses. The modulo division `3 % 2` is next to yield a remainder of 1. Then multiply `1 * 5` and add the result to `2`.

Parentheses are the key for changing the order of operations. Here is a simple example. `3 + 2 * 5 == 13` because the order of operations specifies that the multiplication comes before the addition. But suppose you want to add `3 + 2` before multiplying it by `5`. Simply add parentheses around the operation you want to go first: `(3 + 2) * 5`. Now the result is `25`. **Figure 4-9** shows both expressions in code and the results.

```
without_parenths = 3 + 2 * 5
with_parenths = (3 + 2) * 5
print("Without parentheses:", without_parenths)
print("With parentheses:", with_parenths)
OUTPUT:
Without parentheses: 13
With parentheses: 25
```

Figure 4-9   Changing the order of operations

Compound Operators (4.3.5)

Most programming languages offer a set of **compound operators** that provide handy shortcuts for some common arithmetic operations. Programmers frequently want to keep track of repetitions by incrementing a counter by 1. One way of incrementing a counter is shown in **Figure 4-10**.

```
counter = 1
counter = counter + 1
print(counter)
OUTPUT:
2
```

Figure 4-10   Incrementing a counter

The variable `counter` begins with the value 1. The computation adds `1` to the `counter`, so its value becomes `2`. The compound `+=` operator does the same thing with the code shown in **Figure 4-11**.

```
counter = 1
counter += 1
print(counter)
OUTPUT:
2
```

Figure 4-11   Using a compound operator

Figure 4-12 provides examples of the most commonly used compound operators.

Compound Operator	Example	Result
+=	counter = 1 counter += 1	2
-=	counter = 1 counter -= 1	0
*=	counter = 10 counter *= 2	20
/=	counter = 12 counter /= 2	6
%=	counter = 7 counter %= 2	1

Figure 4-12 Compound operators

4.4 Numeric Data Type Conversion

Convert Integers and Floating-Point Numbers (4.4.1, 4.4.2)

Sometimes mathematical expressions contain different data types, such as an integer and a floating-point number. Here is a simple example designed to calculate the price of purchasing two albums:

```
number_of_albums = 2

individual_price = 19.99

total = number_of_albums * individual_price
```

The 19.99 price of one album is a floating-point number. The number of albums (2) is an integer. Python handles this expression gracefully using a process called coercion. **Coercion** automatically determines which data type to use for a calculation. For the expression 2 * 19.99, written as **number_of_albums * individual_price** in the example using variables, Python uses coercion to handle the integer 2 as a floating-point 2.0 when carrying out the calculation.

Coercion doesn't change the data type of the variable. The variable **number_of_albums** continues to hold the integer 2. Its value is coerced into a floating-point number only for the calculation. You can think of the calculation as happening on a scratch pad. This is the only place that the integer 2 becomes 2.0. Python always uses coercion during normal division with the / symbol.

Depending on coercion is not necessarily a best practice, especially if you don't carefully track its effects through a series of calculations. You can manually convert a value to a different data type through a process that is sometimes called **type casting**, or simply "casting."

Suppose that you have collected ratings for the *Hamilton* soundtrack from thousands of music fans. The combined rating for 2,361 customers is 10,456. To find the average rating, you can use a statement like this:

```
average_rating = 10456.2 / 2361
```

The result stored in **average_rating** is 4.42872, but if you want to convert that number to an integer, you can use the int() function. Look for the int() function in **Figure 4-13** to see how it converts the floating point **average_rating** into an integer stored in **integer_average**.

```
customers = 2361

sum_of_ratings = 10456

average_rating = sum_of_ratings / customers

integer_average = int(average_rating)

print("Average:", average_rating)

print("Truncated average:", integer_average)
OUTPUT:
Average: 4.4286319356204995

Truncated average: 4
```

Figure 4-13   Converting a floating-point number to an integer

Using the int() function converts the value in **average_rating** to an integer and stores 4 in **integer_aver-age**. Be aware, however, that the conversion has lost information. The fractional part to the right of the decimal is not stored in **integer_average**. Integer conversion isn't the same as rounding. It simply removes anything to the right of the decimal point, so int(5.9) is 5. You can explicitly convert numbers to floating point by using the function **float()** without relying on coercion.

Rounding Quirks (4.4.3)

Programming languages have some quirks when it comes to numeric data. Here's a puzzler:

What is the integer value of dividing 1 by 2 then multiplying by 2 again? You would be astonished if the computer produced 0 as the result. However, if you want the result to be an integer instead of a float, you would use integer division in Python with the // operator. The result of 1 // 2 is 0. **Figure 4-14** shows this in further detail.

```
Using // creates an integer value.
solution = 1 // 2 * 2

print(solution)
OUTPUT:

0
To get the expected result, use normal division and then cast to an integer.
solution = int(1 / 2 * 2)

print(solution)
OUTPUT:

1
```

Figure 4-14   Floating-point quirks

Here is another oddity. What do you expect as the result of the expression .1 + .2? Would it surprise you if the computer produced 0.3000000119 or 0.30000000000000004? **Figure 4-15** reveals this strange result.

The result of .1 + .2 should be .3, so where do the other numbers come from?

```
solution = .1 + .2
print("What's in the variable:", solution)
print("Hiding the value: {:.1}".format(solution))
OUTPUT:
What's in the variable: 0.30000000000000004
Hiding the value: 0.3
```

Figure 4-15 Floating-point decimal quirks

These odd results stem from a rounding quirk related to the computer's reliance on binary numbers. The binary representation of a floating-point number is an approximation because binary numbers don't yield the same fractions as decimal numbers.

When working with numbers that have many significant decimal places, you may have to use math functions to truncate or round the numbers. Python can round and format numbers in many ways.

4.5 Formatting Output

Formatted Output (4.5.1)

The danger of converting floating-point data to integers is that significant data can be lost. When you want to eliminate trailing zeros or decimal places from displayed data, you can specify an output format without changing the actual data in a variable.

When you format output, variables retain their values, but you specify how much or how little of that information is displayed. Suppose the variable **average** contains 4.43050. You can use formatting to output any of the following:

4.43050

4

4.4

4.4305000

  4.431

Formatting Parameters (4.5.2, 4.5.3)

Python has a unique syntax for formatting output where you can control the following elements, called **formatting parameters**:

Type. Integer, floating point, decimal, binary, hexadecimal, character, or E notation.

Precision. The number of places displayed after the decimal point.

Width. The number of spaces allocated to the output. This element is especially useful when outputting columns of numbers.

Alignment. Align left or right within the specified width.

To format a number in Python, you use the `format()` method. The `format()` method is applied to a series of letters inside double quotes with empty spots represented by two curly braces:

`"Your lucky numbers are {} and {}."`

You can apply the `format()` method to this series by adding `.format()` after the last double quote. Python fills in these empty spots by applying each piece of data in the parentheses that follow the word format:

`"Your lucky numbers are {} and {}.".format(42, 7.3)`

You specify the format of the numbers by providing formatting parameters. The parameters appear inside the curly braces, preceded by a colon. **Figure 4-16** shows how to provide formatting parameters in Python. The underscores indicate a space when printing.

Parameter	Letter or Symbol	Example code	Output
Type	d for decimal integers f for floating-point	`"{:d}".format(100)` `"{:f}".format(15.3)`	100 15.300000
Precision	Decimal point followed by the precision; only works for float numbers	`"{:.3}".format(15.3)`	15.3
Width	A number representing the number of characters for the total width	`"{:10}".format(2)`	_____2
Left-aligned	<	`"{:<10}".format(2)`	2_____
Centered	^	`"{:^10}".format(2)`	____2_____
Right-aligned	>	`"{:>10}".format(2)`	_____2

Figure 4-16   Formatting parameters

These formatting parameters can be used in combination. If you want to center a number and pad it to a width of 20 with a precision of 3 digits, use `"{:^20.2}".format(5.3)`. This formatting parameter uses the ^ symbol to center, the number **20** to indicate a width, and the **.2** to indicate 2 decimal points.

The program in **Figure 4-17** illustrates how you can use formatting parameters to change the appearance of numeric output.

One note of practical caution here: If your program outputs a formatted value but continues to use the more precise value in subsequent calculations, the user may see apparent discrepancies in the data.

Underscores are provided in the output to show where the spaces are in the output; these do not normally appear in IDLE.

```
average = 4.43050
print("Original: {:f}".format(average))
print("Three decimal places: {:.3f}".format(average))
print("Width of 9:")
print("{:9.3f}".format(average))
print("Centered with a width of 9:")
print("{:^9.3f}".format(average))
OUTPUT:
Original: 4.430500
Three decimal places: 4.431
Width of 9:
_____4.431
Centered with a width of 9:
__4.431__
```

Figure 4-17   Formatting numeric output

Summary

- The term data type refers to a way of categorizing data. Primitive data types are built into your programming language. Composite data types are programmer defined, available in functions, or provided by methods.
- Whole numbers are classified as integer data types. They can be signed or unsigned, decimal, binary, or hexadecimal.
- Integers are typically stored in four bytes of data, but long integers are stored in eight bytes and can take on larger values.
- Numbers with decimal places are classified as floating-point data types. Floating-point numbers can be positive or negative and expressed in decimal notation or E notation, which is similar to scientific notation.
- Single precision floating-point numbers can be stored in four bytes of memory. Double precision numbers are typically stored in eight bytes of memory.
- Integer and floating-point numbers can be used in expressions, along with arithmetic operators, such as + − * / and %. These operators are processed in a sequence called the order of operations.
- Programmers need to be aware of data types because mixing them in a single expression sometimes produces unexpected results. Also, rounding errors may produce quirks that can affect the results of calculations.
- Python uses coercion to automatically change the data type of a value as a calculation proceeds. Programmers can manually change the data type of a value by type casting. The int() and float() functions allow programmers to specify or change a numeric data type.
- Python provides extensive formatting parameters that can be used to change the appearance of a number without changing the data stored in the corresponding variable.

Key Terms

arithmetic operators	E notation	order of operations
coercion	expression	primitive data types
composite data types	floating-point data types	signed integer
compound operators	formatting parameters	single precision
data type	function	type casting
double precision	integer data types	unsigned integer

Module
5

Character and String Data Types

Learning Objectives:

5.1 Characters

5.1.1 List the variety of data that is classified as a character.

5.1.2 Initialize data as a character.

5.1.3 Describe the punctuation conventions used for character data.

5.1.4 State the storage required for ASCII character data.

5.1.5 Explain the difference between numbers and digits.

5.1.6 Format character output separated by spaces or on separate lines.

5.1.7 List some common functions or methods available for manipulating character data.

5.2 String Data Type

5.2.1 Explain that characters combine to form strings.

5.2.2 State that Python strings are sequences of characters.

5.2.3 Describe the punctuation conventions used for string literals.

5.2.4 Specify when an escape sequence is necessary.

5.2.5 Describe the memory allocation for strings.

5.2.6 Identify the index values for characters in a string.

5.3 String Functions

5.3.1 List commonly used functions and methods that programming languages provide to manipulate strings.

5.3.2 Identify code that produces the length of a string.

5.3.3 Identify code that changes the case of a string.

5.3.4 Explain the significance of case sensitivity.

5.3.5 Provide use cases for finding a character in a string.

5.3.6 Explain the general approach to retrieving substrings.

5.4 Concatenation and Typecasting

5.4.1 Explain the meaning of concatenation, and identify the concatenation operator.

5.4.2 Provide an example of when a programmer would concatenate a string.

5.4.3 Concatenate a string during output.

5.4.4 Concatenate the contents of multiple variables.

5.4.5 State which data types can be successfully concatenated.

5.4.6 Explain the meanings of coercion and typecasting in the context of data types.

5.1 Characters

Working with Character Data (5.1.1, 5.1.2, 5.1.3)

"Alphabet soup." The term can refer to letter-shaped pasta floating in a salty broth (**Figure 5-1**) or to the slew of acronyms—such as the WPA, CCC, CWA, SEC, FHA, and PWA—that stand for government agencies created by President Franklin Roosevelt in the 1930s. Let's see how programmers work with an alphabet soup of data: letters, words, sentences, and documents.

CorinnaL/Shutterstock.com

Figure 5-1   Character data is like the letters in alphabet soup

A **character** is the classification that programmers use for variables that hold a single letter of the alphabet, a numeral from 0 to 9, or a symbol. You might use character data in a program that asks for a person's middle initial or when designing an alphabet program for a preschooler.

When you initialize or assign a character literal to a variable, the convention is to surround the literal with double quotes. You are allowed to use single quotes around the literal as well, but this text uses double quotes.

```
first_letter = "a"
```

The quotes are stripped off when the literal is stored and are not included when the character is output. In **Figure 5-2**, the program outputs the contents of `first_letter` without quotes.

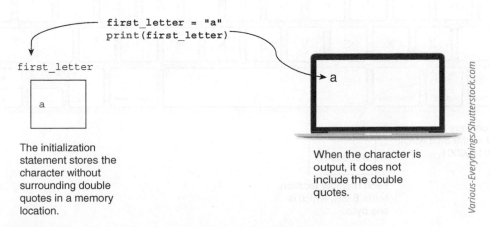

```
first_letter = "a"
print(first_letter)
```

first_letter

```
a
```

a

The initialization statement stores the character without surrounding double quotes in a memory location.

When the character is output, it does not include the double quotes.

Various-Everythings/Shutterstock.com

Figure 5-2   Character data initialization and storage

A standard initialization statement creates a variable containing character data, as shown in **Figure 5-3**.

Syntax:

`variable_name = "x"` where x is a single character.

Example:

`first_letter = "a"`

Character data can be output using `print()`. Because the variable does not store the double quotes, they are not displayed in the output stream.

`first_letter = "a"`

`print(first_letter)`

OUTPUT:

`a`

Figure 5-3   Character initialization and sample code

Character Memory Allocation (5.1.4)

Character data is stored in ASCII format. **ASCII (American Standard Code for Information Interchange)** is an encoding method that assigns a unique sequence of eight bits to each character. For example, the letter "a" is represented by the eight-bit ASCII code 01100001, which happens to be decimal 97.

All of the uppercase letters, lowercase letters, numerals, and symbols on your computer keyboard have a unique ASCII value. These commonly used characters can be stored in one byte of memory. See **Figure 5-4**.

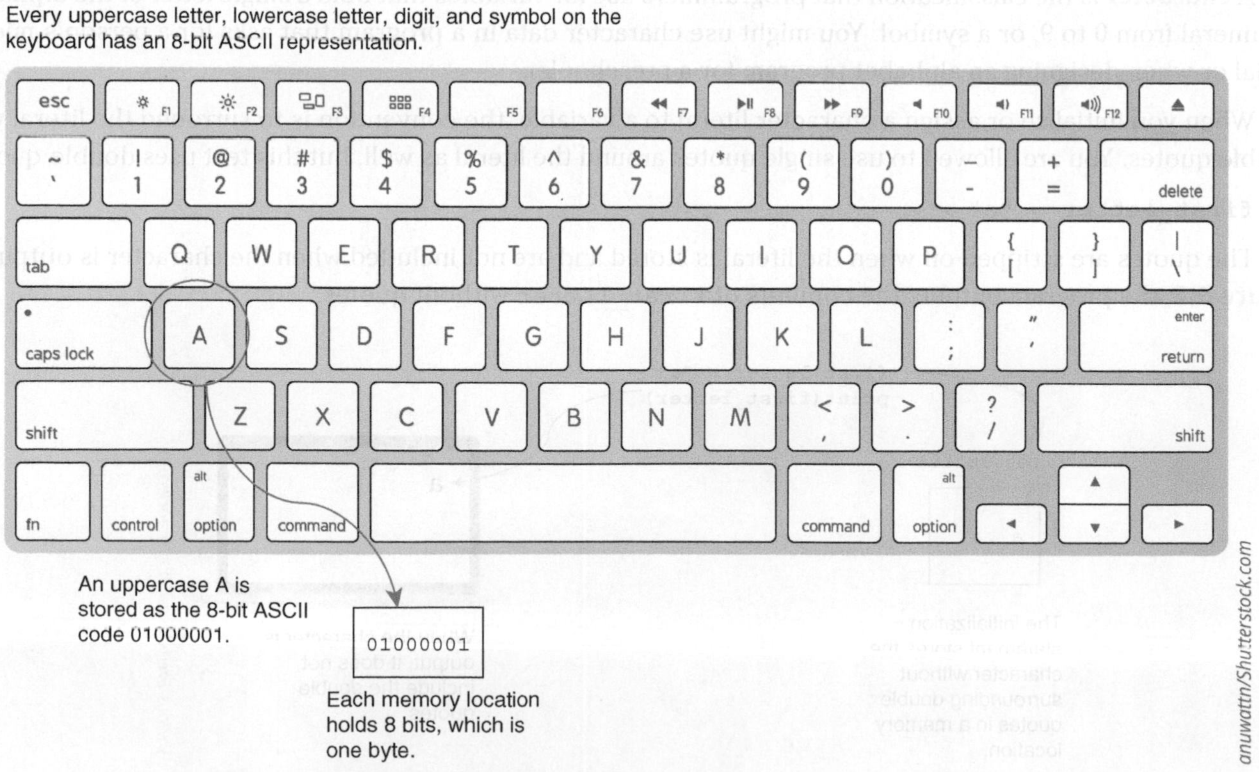

Every uppercase letter, lowercase letter, digit, and symbol on the keyboard has an 8-bit ASCII representation.

An uppercase A is stored as the 8-bit ASCII code 01000001.

`01000001`

Each memory location holds 8 bits, which is one byte.

anuwattn/Shutterstock.com

Figure 5-4   Basic character data requires one byte of storage

Digits (5.1.5)

The double quotes surrounding character literals are important, especially when you are working with digits 0 to 9. Without surrounding punctuation, 2 is an integer that you can use in calculations. With surrounding punctuation, "2" is simply a squiggly shape that does not have the actual value of two.

Q What would you expect as output from the code for the following digits program?

```
first_digit = "2"
second_digit = "5"
print(first_digit + second_digit)
```

A Did you answer **7** or **"25"**? The correct answer is **"25"**!

If the values assigned to the variables were **2** and **5** instead of **"2"** and **"5"**, then the answer would indeed be **7**, using mathematical addition. Characters are a different data type, and the **+** operator glues them together. **Figure 5-5** illustrates the difference between digits used as characters and numbers used as integers.

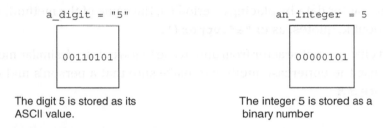

a_digit = "5"

00110101

The digit 5 is stored as its ASCII value.

an_integer = 5

00000101

The integer 5 is stored as a binary number

Figure 5-5   Digits are stored as ASCII codes, but integer numbers are stored as binary numbers

Attempting to add digits that are character data types can produce surprising results, depending on your programming language. Just remember that the data for calculations should be assigned numeric data types, not character data types.

Character Output Format (5.1.6)

In the digits program, the output looked like the value 25, but the output was actually the digit 2 and the digit 5. To make that clear, you can insert a space between the digits by including a blank space in the print statement or separating the output by commas, as shown in the program in **Figure 5-6**.

```
first_digit = "2"
second_digit = "5"
print(first_digit + " " + second_digit)
print(first_digit, second_digit)
OUTPUT:
2 5
2 5
```

Figure 5-6   Inserting a space in the output stream

Another option would be to output each digit on a separate line, as shown in **Figure 5-7**.

> Using one print statement per variable will place each digit on its own line.
>
> ```
> first_digit = "2"
>
> second_digit = "5"
>
> print(first_digit)
>
> print(second_digit)
> ```
> OUTPUT:
>
> 2
>
> 5

Figure 5-7   Output to separate lines

Character Manipulation (5.1.7)

Programming languages provide built-in tools for manipulating character data. These tools are called methods. Methods are applied to character data by placing a period (.), the name of the method, and a set of parentheses directly after the ending double quotes, as in **"a".upper()**.

One common method changes a character from uppercase to lowercase. A similar method changes lowercase to uppercase. You might use the uppercase method to make sure that a person's middle initial is stored as an uppercase letter. See **Figure 5-8**.

> The **upper()** method produces the uppercase version of a character. If there is no uppercase version, such as for the # sign, then the character remains unchanged. The syntax for this method is:
>
> ```
> variable_name = variable_name.upper()
> ```
>
> In the following program, **input()** is used to collect input from the keyboard and place it in the variable called **initial**. Notice that the uppercase character replaces the lowercase character in the variable called **initial**.
>
> ```
> initial = input("Enter initial: ")
>
> initial = initial.upper()
>
> print(initial)
> ```
> OUTPUT:
>
> **Enter initial:** b [Enter]
>
> **B**

Figure 5-8   Changing the case of a character

The syntax for **upper()** and other handy methods is shown in **Figure 5-9**.

Character Function/Method	Example	Data	Result
Check if the character is a letter of the alphabet	`initial.isalpha()` `choice.isalpha()`	`initial = "a"` `choice = "2"`	`True` `False`
Check if the character is a digit	`initial.isdigit()` `choice.isdigit()`	`initial = "a"` `choice = "2"`	`False` `True`
Change to uppercase	`initial.upper()`	`initial = "a"`	`A`
Change to lowercase	`initial.lower()`	`initial = "A"`	`a`

Figure 5-9 Character methods and functions

5.2 String Data Type

Working with String Data (5.2.1, 5.2.2, 5.2.3)

A sequence of characters is classified as a **string**. You can use the **string data type** for working with variables that contain words, phrases, sentences, and other text.

String literals are also enclosed in double quotes for initialization statements, assignment statements, and prompts. The code in **Figure 5-10** uses strings in several ways.

`your_name = ""`	Initializes `your_name` as an empty string.
`message = "likes alphabet soup."`	Initializes a variable containing a string. Quotes are required in the program statement.
`print("What is your name? ")`	Displays a prompt containing a string.
`your_name = input()`	Collects a user-input string such as Skylar Jones. No quotes are needed when the user enters the string.
`print(your_name, message)`	Outputs the string contents of `your_name` followed by the string stored in the variable called message separated by a space.

Figure 5-10 Strings can be initialized, input, and displayed

When initializing string variables, be sure to enclose the string in quotation marks. The quotation marks are not stored in the variable and will not appear in the output. Let's use the code from Figure 5-10 in a program. See **Figure 5-11**.

```
your_name = input("What is your name? ")
message = "likes alphabet soup."
print(your_name, message)
OUTPUT:
What's your name?
Skylar Jones [Enter]
Skylar Jones likes alphabet soup.
```

Figure 5-11 Code for the Alphabet Soup program

Escape Characters (5.2.4)

The trouble with enclosing a string in quotation marks is that they are also used as punctuation in real world data, such as poem titles, quotes, and words used in unusual ways. Here are some examples:

- Philip Parker wrote the song "Alphabet Soup."
- The song begins, "Oh, we're all right here, making alphabet soup."
- This song's kind of "soupy."

Storing quoted text results in more than one set of quotation marks:

```
fun_fact = "Philip Parker wrote the song "Alphabet Soup.""
```

Your programming language will look for the first set of quotes and process `"Philip Parker wrote the song "` as the complete string. The remaining text, `Alphabet Soup.""`, produces an error.

You can use an escape sequence to remedy this problem. An **escape sequence** embeds a command within a string. It begins with a backslash \. The `\"` escape sequence embeds a quotation mark that is not regarded as the start or end quotation mark for the string.

```
fun_fact = "Philip Parker wrote the song \"Alphabet Soup.\""
```

When using escape sequences, do not include a space after the backslash. **Figure 5-12** lists common escape sequences.

Escape Sequence	Name	Use
\"	Quotation mark	For strings that include quotation marks
\\	Backslash	For strings that include a backslash
\n	Newline	To insert a line break in a string
\t	Tab	To insert a tab in a string

Figure 5-12   Escape sequences

Q Based on the escape sequences in Figure 5-12, what do you expect as the output from this code?

```
review = "This song's kind of \n \"SOUPY!\""
print(review)
```

A Did you catch that SOUPY! is output on a separate line?

```
This song's kind of
"SOUPY!"
```

String Indexes (5.2.5, 5.2.6)

Strings are stored in a succession of memory locations. Each character in the string has an **index**, which is a number that indicates its position in the string. The first character in the string is referenced by index 0; the next character is index 1. Index numbers are enclosed in square brackets, as in **Figure 5-13**.

Memory Location	0x0075	0x0076	0x0077	0x0078	0x0079	0x007A	0x007B	0x007C	0x007D	0x007E
Data	C	a	m	p	b	e	l	l	'	s
Index	[0]	[1]	[2]	[3]	[4]	[5]	[6]	[7]	[8]	[9]

Figure 5-13 Each character in a string is stored in a memory location referenced by an index

You can find the character at any position in a string based on its index number. For example, suppose you want to make sure that the first letter of a person's name is an uppercase letter. Trace through the following code to see how indexing works to produce the first letter of a word.

```
company_name = "Campbell's"
letter = company_name[0]
print(letter)
OUTPUT:
C
```

Q What would you change in the following line of code to find the third letter of the company name?

```
letter = company_name[0]
```

A You would change the index for **company_name** to 2. Remember that the index begins with 0, so the third letter's index is 2. **Figure 5-14** shows the code and output.

```
company_name = "Campbell's"
letter = company_name[2]
print(letter)
OUTPUT:
m
```

Figure 5-14 Using the index to retrieve a specific element in a string

5.3 String Functions

String Manipulation (5.3.1)

In addition to using indexes, you may want to manipulate strings in other ways. Here are some examples:

- Find the length of a string.
- Change the case of a string.
- Check if a string contains a specific character.
- Retrieve a substring from a longer string.

Let's take a look at some examples to assess their usefulness.

String Length (5.3.2)

Knowing the length of a string can come in handy to ensure that the string is complete. It might also be a step in an algorithm for reversing a string or checking that a string is not too long for a data entry box. **Figure 5-15** details the syntax for the `len()` function and illustrates its use to determine if a string containing the alphabet contains all 26 letters. Note the difference in format between the function and methods used earlier on character data.

The output of the `len()` function is stored in an integer variable. The syntax for the `len()` function is:

```
the_length = len(variable_name)
```

Here's the code that checks the length of a string containing the alphabet.

```
alphabet = "ABCDEFGHIJKLMOPQRSTUVWXYZ"

the_length = len(alphabet)

print(the_length)
```

OUTPUT:

```
25
```

Figure 5-15   Finding the length of a string

Q The alphabet has 26 letters, but the length of the string in the `alphabet` variable is only 25. Assuming no duplicates, that means one letter must be missing from the string in the initialization statement. Can you see which letter is missing?

A The missing letter is N.

Change Case (5.3.3, 5.3.4)

As with character data, you can change a string to uppercase or lowercase. In Python, all the methods and functions that work with character data also work with string data. That is because, to Python, a character is simply a string of length 1. **Figure 5-16** shows some additional string methods.

A letter's case (UPPER or lower) can be significant when searching and sorting data. The string `"Soup"` is not the same as `"SOUP"` or `"soup"`. Why? Because uppercase characters have different ASCII codes than lowercase characters. An uppercase S has an ASCII code of 01010011, whereas a lowercase s has an ASCII code of 01110011.

The ASCII codes for S and s are not the same, so Soup does not match soup. The concept that uppercase letters are different from lowercase letters is called **case sensitivity**. Passwords and variable names are common examples of case-sensitive data.

String comparisons used for searching and sorting are case sensitive. When creating a program to search through an inventory of groceries, be aware that a search for "alphabet soup" will not match "Alphabet Soup" unless you include code to handle variations of upper and lowercase.

Note that none of these methods change the string but create a new value that you can then store in a new variable.

Method	Description	Code	Output
count()	Returns the number of times a specified value occurs in a string.	"banana".count("a")	3
endswith()	Returns True if the string ends with the specified value.	"alphabet".endswith("bet")	True
find()	Returns the first index of the specified value or −1 if it can't be found.	"apple".find("p")	1
startswith()	Returns True if the string starts with the specified value.	"caterpillar".startswith("cat")	True
title()	Capitalizes the first letter of each word in the string.	"hello world!".title()	Hello World!

Figure 5-16   Some string methods

One solution to case variations is to use the lowercase method. Here is a program that checks if two strings are the same regardless of case.

```
first_item = "Soup"

second_item = "soup"

if first_item.lower() == second_item.lower():

    print("The words are the same.")
```

The double equal sign == compares the values on either side for equality. The **lower()** method applies the logic to every character in a string, forcing every letter into lowercase.

Find the Location of a Character (5.3.5)

You can determine if a string contains a specific character. When a string contains a space, you can assume that the string holds more than one word. A comma might indicate that a string holds a list of words. You might then write code to break the string into separate words.

The method for finding the position of a character produces the index position of the first occurrence of the specified character. Remember that the first character in the string is index position 0.

Q In the following code, what does the **find()** method produce?

```
product_name = "Campbell's Alphabet Soup"

where = product_name.find(" ")
```

A It produces 10. Make sure you understand why.

Retrieve a Substring (5.3.6)

Sometimes you might want to deal with a substring rather than the entire string. Working with substrings is a component of search engines and several text-processing algorithms. **Figure 5-17** explains how to find a substring and store it in a variable.

You can retrieve a substring by indicating where it should begin and where it should end. The ending index will not be included in the substring. Remember that the elements of a string are indexed beginning with 0.

The syntax for retrieving a substring is:

```
new_string = variable_name[start:end]
```

Trace through the code and see if you can determine what the variable **sub_string** will contain.

```
alphabet = "ABCDEFGHIJKLMNOPQRSTUVWXYZ"

sub_string = alphabet[3:8]

print(sub_string)
```

OUTPUT:

```
DEFGH
```

The variable **sub_string** contains DEFGH as specified by the parameter [3:8]. The substring begins at D because A is index 0, B is index 1, and C is index 2, so D is index 3, up to H at index 7. Index 8 is not included, so I is not part of the substring.

Figure 5-17   Collecting a substring

5.4 Concatenation and Typecasting

Concatenated Output (5.4.1, 5.4.2, 5.4.3)

Asking for a person's first and last name in one statement might not be the best practice. Sometimes, you might want to output Philip Parker as Parker, Philip. It would be best to store the first name in one variable and the last name in another variable.

To output the strings in two or more variables, you can use a process called **concatenation**. Concatenation means chaining two or more values in sequence. The + sign is the concatenation operator. Trace through the following pseudocode to see how the **first_name** and **last_name** variables can be concatenated in output statements.

```
prompt the user for their first and last names

read the first and last names

display a message to the last name, first name format
```

EXPECTED OUTPUT:

```
What is your first name? Philip [Enter]

What is your last name? Parker [Enter]

Hello, Philip

You are filed as Parker, Philip
```

Let's see how this algorithm works in Python. Check out the last line of code in **Figure 5-18** to see how to concatenate output.

```
first_name = input("What is your first name? ")

last_name = input("What is your last name? ")

print("Hello,", first_name)

print("You are filed as", last_name + ", " + first_name)
OUTPUT:
Hello, Philip

You are filed as Parker, Philip
```

Figure 5-18   Concatenated output

Concatenated Variables (5.4.4)

Concatenation is not just for output. You can also concatenate one or more variables and store the combined string in a new variable.

```
company_name = "Campbell's"

soup_name = "Alphabet Soup"

product_name = company_name + " " + soup_name

print(product_name)
```

Q What ends up in the variable `product_name`?

A The variable `product_name` contains the string `Campbell's Alphabet Soup`.

The key takeaway here is that the variable `product_name` contains `Campbell's Alphabet Soup`, which is a result of concatenating the contents of the `company_name` and `soup_name` variables with the addition of a space in between.

The best practice for concatenating variables is to use a new variable for the concatenated string. It would be possible, but confusing, to put `company_name + soup_name` into the `company_name` variable. So using a third variable called `product_name` is a better option.

Coercion and Typecasting (5.4.5, 5.4.6)

With most programming languages, strings can be concatenated with other strings and character data, but not with integer or floating-point data. Concatenating or appending mixed data types often leads to trouble. Here's an example of an attempt to concatenate a house number stored as an integer with a street name stored as a string.

```
house_number = 101

street_name = "Main Street"

print(house_number)

print(street_name)

full_address = house_number + " " + street_name

print(full_address)
```

OUTPUT:

```
101

Main Street

TypeError: unsupported operand type(s) for +: 'int' and 'str'
```

An attempt to concatenate an integer with a string can produce an error. What does the error message say? Python cannot use + for an integer 'int' and a string 'str'. To fix an integer–string type mismatch, you can use typecasting to convert the integer to a string. **Figure 5-19** explains how to do it.

The `str()` function converts an integer or floating-point number into a string. The syntax is:

```
converted_string = str(variable_name)
```

This code converts the integer 101 to a string so it can be concatenated with the string "Main Street".

```
house_number = 101

street_name = "Main Street"

full_address = str(house_number) + " " + street_name

print(full_address)
```

OUTPUT:

```
101 Main Street
```

Figure 5-19   Typecasting: Integer to string

How about converting a string to an integer? You might want to do that when you have a string that contains digits you'd like to use for a calculation. The program in **Figure 5-20** gets the first two elements of a string, converts them to an integer, and then adds 1.

The `int()` function converts a string to an integer. Make sure the string value in parentheses has an integer value. Here is the syntax:

```
integer_variable = int(string_variable)
```

In this program, the first two characters of the date are collected using the substring syntax, then converted into an integer. Adding 1 to the day number produces the next day's date.

```
today = "15 February"

today_substring = today[0:3]

day_number = int(today_substring)

tomorrow = day_number + 1

print(tomorrow)
```

OUTPUT:

```
16
```

Figure 5-20   Typecasting: String to integer

Summary

- A character is a classification that programmers use for variables that hold a single letter of the alphabet, a numeral from 0 to 9, or a symbol.
- When you initialize or assign a character literal to a variable, the convention is to surround the literal with double quotes.
- Commonly used character data is stored in ASCII format, encoded as eight binary digits.
- Programming languages supply built-in methods for manipulating character data.
- Variables that hold a sequence of characters are assigned the string data type.
- Strings are stored in a succession of memory locations, each referenced by an index value. The first character in a string has an index value of [0].
- When you initialize or assign a string to a variable, the convention is to surround the string with double quotes.
- An escape sequence beginning with a backslash \ embeds a command within a string. Use the \" escape sequence for strings that already include quotation marks.
- Programming languages provide built-in string methods for tasks such as finding the location of a character in a string or converting a string to a title.
- Strings can be combined in a process called concatenation. It is also possible to change the data type using typecasting functions `int()` or `str()`.

Key Terms

ASCII (American Standard Code for Information Interchange)

case sensitivity

character

concatenation

escape sequence

index

string

string data type

Module 6

Decision Control Structures

Learning Objectives:

6.1 If-Then Control Structures

6.1.1 Describe the purpose of control structures.

6.1.2 Identify parts of algorithms that require decision control structures.

6.1.3 Provide examples of algorithms that incorporate conditions or decisions.

6.1.4 Illustrate an if-then structure using a flowchart.

6.1.5 Write an if-then structure in pseudocode.

6.1.6 Identify the conditional statement in an if-then structure.

6.1.7 Use programming language syntax to code an if-then structure.

6.2 Relational Operators

6.2.1 Differentiate between the = operator and the == operator.

6.2.2 List and define relational operators.

6.2.3 Identify the relational operators in example expressions.

6.2.4 Provide examples of Boolean expressions.

6.2.5 Initialize a Boolean variable using an assignment statement.

6.2.6 Differentiate a Boolean expression from a Boolean data type.

6.3 Multiple Conditions

6.3.1 Write an if-then-else structure in pseudocode.

6.3.2 Illustrate an if-then-else structure using a flowchart.

6.3.3 Code an if-then-else structure.

6.3.4 Trace the flow of an algorithm that contains a nested-if structure.

6.3.5 Trace the flow of an algorithm that contains an else-if structure.

6.3.6 Explain the concept of fall through in the context of decision control structures.

6.4 Conditional Logical Operators

6.4.1 Identify logical operators in expressions.

6.4.2 Identify the outcomes for **and** operations, as illustrated in a truth table.

6.4.3 Identify the outcomes for **or** operations, as illustrated in a truth table.

6.4.4 Create expressions using logical operators.

6.4.5 Identify the purpose and use for **not** operators.

6.1 If-Then Control Structures

Control Structures (6.1.1, 6.1.2)

Got a problem with your cable or Internet service? Customers who call their service providers typically interact with an automated voice response system. You know how it goes: "Press 1 if you need account information; press 2 if you need to troubleshoot your cable service …" See **Figure 6-1**.

Figure 6-1   Voice response systems require programming logic

Computer programs for these automated systems contain control structures that branch off to different paths based on options selected by the user. A **control structure** alters the sequential execution of statements in a computer program. A **decision control structure** alters the sequential flow by branching to specific statements based on a condition or decision.

Here is an algorithm for a sequential program that begins with a menu of choices. The program proceeds in sequence by asking for the customer's details; connecting to an agent, the cable troubleshooter, and then to the Internet troubleshooter; and finally ending the call.

Output "Press or say 1 to connect to an account agent."
Output "Press or say 2 to troubleshoot your cable service."
Output "Press or say 3 to troubleshoot your Internet service."
Output "Press or say 0 to quit."
Ask for customer's name.
Ask for customer's account number.
Provide current account status.
Connect to next available agent.
Connect user to automated cable troubleshooter.
Connect user to automated Internet troubleshooter.
Make sure the user really wants to quit.
Output goodbye message.

Clearly, this algorithm should not be sequential. It needs to branch to a specific action depending on the customer's menu selection. If the customer has an intermittent Internet connection, for example, selecting 3 should branch directly to the Internet troubleshooter.

Q How many distinct branches should this algorithm have?

A The algorithm should have four branches, one for each of the menu options to select 1, 2, 3, or 0.

Decision Logic (6.1.3)

Decision control structures play a key role in just about every computer program. These structures help programs seem intelligent because they can make responses that correspond to user input.

Decision control structures also allow programs to handle data based on differing values. Here are just a few examples.

- Deciding who is eligible to vote based on age and citizenship
- Determining if a polynomial has zero, one, or two real roots
- Assigning a letter grade based on a quiz score
- Figuring out whether to apply a bank service charge based on the account balance
- Operating a furnace or air conditioner based on room temperature
- Checking if a number is odd or even based on modulo division
- Offering free shipping based on the amount purchased or VIP status

Let's break down decision control structures to see how they work and how to incorporate them in your programs.

If-Then Structure (6.1.4, 6.1.5, 6.1.6, 6.1.7)

A basic voice response system might simply tell customers to find their account number and then press 1 when they are ready to connect to an agent. You can diagram this logic as a flowchart using a diamond shape for the decision. See **Figure 6-2**.

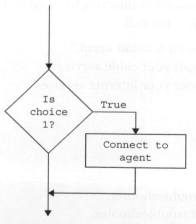

Figure 6-2 Flowchart for an if-then structure

The diamond symbol in a flowchart indicates a decision point and contains a question that specifies a condition. When the answer to the question is `True`, an arrow directs the flow to one or more statements in the conditional block. When the answer is `False`, the flow bypasses the conditional block. This logic is referred to as an **if-then structure** and can be presented in pseudocode by making a conditional statement such as "If it is raining, I will need an umbrella."

In pseudocode, any statements that are executed on the True branch should be indented.

```
if the choice is 1 then

    connect user to an agent

show the message "Bye"
```

The if-then structure is based on a **conditional statement** that directs the program flow to the correct set of statements when the condition is `True`. So, when the input is 1, the program directs the customer to an agent. When the conditional statement is not `True` (if the customer presses 9, for example), the program continues on a sequential path to the next statement, which in this case terminates the program with a message that says "Bye."

Figure 6-3 illustrates the general syntax and usage rules for an if-then structure in Python.

Syntax:

```
if condition:
    statement

if condition:
    statement1
    statement2
```

Rules and best practices:

- Place a colon after the condition.
- Indent any statements included in the if-then structure.
- Make sure to keep all statements to be contained within the if-then indented the same amount.

Figure 6-3   Syntax for an if-then structure

Figure 6-4 shows a simple Python program that uses an if-then structure. Note the quotations around the `"1"` in the condition. In Python, `input()` always returns a string. You can typecast it to an integer with `int()` later.

```
print("Press 1 when you are ready to")

choice = input("connect to an account agent: ")

if choice == "1";

    print("You chose option " + choice)

    print("Connecting you now")

print("Bye")

OUTPUT:

Press 1 when you are ready to

connect to an account agent: 1 [Enter]

You chose option 1

Connecting you now

Bye
```

Figure 6-4   Program with a simple if-then structure

Q Trace through the program code in Figure 6-4. What happens if the user presses a number other than 1?

A The program outputs **Bye** and the program ends. Statements not indented after an if-then structure are always run.

6.2 Relational Operators

The Equal Operator (6.2.1)

The conditional statement in the simple voice response system is peculiar. It contains double equal symbols:

```
if choice == 1:
```

The == is the **equal operator**, which checks to see if two operands, such as **choice** and **1**, are equal to each other. The == equal operator is quite different from the = assignment operator that you use to initialize variables. Using the assignment operator in a conditional statement is likely to produce an error. If you are using IDLE, it will catch this mix-up as a syntax error. **Figure 6-5** points out the difference between the assignment operator and the equal operator.

```
choice = 1

if choice = 0:  ◄————— Incorrect syntax

    print("choice is zero")

if choice == 1:  ◄

    print("choice is one")        Correct syntax
```

Figure 6-5 Using the assignment operator in a conditional statement is likely to produce an error

Using Relational Operators (6.2.2, 6.2.3)

The equal operator is one of several relational operators that you can use when constructing conditional expressions. A **relational operator** specifies a comparison between two operands. The operands could be

- Two literals, such as **7** and **9**
- Two variables, such as **airtime** and **limit**
- One variable and one literal such as **airtime** and **1000**

Figure 6-6 provides a list of relational operators and examples of their use.

Relational operators provide lots of flexibility for crafting conditional expressions. For example, you can use the ! = operator to validate input for the voice response system in the following pseudocode:

```
Prompt the user to press 1 to connect to an agent

Obtain the user's choice

if the value in choice is not 1

. . . . display an error message
```

Figure 6-7 illustrates this algorithm in code.

Operator	Description	Examples where airtime = 1056	Result
==	Equal to	`(airtime == 1056)` `(airtime == 566)`	`True` `False`
!=	Not equal to	`(airtime != 1056)` `(airtime != 566)`	`False` `True`
<	Less than	`(airtime < 2000)` `(2000 < airtime)`	`True` `False`
>	Greater than	`(airtime > 56)` `(56 > airtime)`	`True` `False`
<=	Less than or equal to	`(airtime <= 1056)` `(airtime <= 29)`	`True` `False`
>=	Greater than or equal to	`(airtime >= airtime)` `(airtime >= 2000)`	`True` `False`

Figure 6-6   Relational operators

```
print("Press 1 when you are ready to")
choice = input("connect to an account agent: ")
if choice != "1":
    print("You chose option " + choice + "\n")
    print("Invalid input" + "\n")
OUTPUT:
Press 1 when you are ready to
connect to an account agent: 9 [Enter]
You chose option 9
Invalid input
```

Figure 6-7   Using a decision structure to validate input

Boolean Expressions and Data Types (6.2.4, 6.2.5, 6.2.6)

Relational operators and operands form **Boolean expressions** that evaluate to True or False. For example, `choice != "1"` is a Boolean expression that is True when the customer does not select 1. The Boolean expression is False when the customer selects 1.

Boolean expressions have similarities to Boolean data types. Both carry a value of `True` or `False`. In practice, however, you use a Boolean expression as part of a conditional statement, whereas you use a Boolean data type when making declaration or assignment statements.

For example, you might want a variable called `vip` to hold `True` or `False`, depending on whether the customer has VIP status. In Python, you can initialize a Boolean variable like this:

`vip = True`

In memory, Boolean variables hold 0 representing False, or 1 representing True. Theoretically, a Boolean requires only one bit of storage, but the actual storage requirements vary by language.

In Python, `True` and `False` must be capitalized. Now take a look at the following Python code:

```
vip = True

if vip:

    print("Transferring you to the VIP agent.")
```

Q What is the Boolean variable in the previous pseudocode? What is the conditional statement? What is the Boolean expression?

A The Boolean variable is `vip`, which appears in the declaration and assignment statements. The conditional statement is `if vip`. The Boolean expression is simply `vip` in the conditional statement.

You can also write `if vip == True`. However, when a Boolean variable is used in a conditional statement, it does not need a relational operator. The Boolean variable is already either `True` or `False`, so the `== True` is redundant. By itself, the variable is the Boolean expression.

6.3 Multiple Conditions

If-Then-Else Structure (6.3.1, 6.3.2, 6.3.3)

Suppose a voice response system gives customers two options:

Press or say 1 when you are ready to connect to an account agent.
Press or say 0 to quit.

Figure 6-8 illustrates a flowchart for this algorithm. Notice that both the True and False branches contain statements. The program follows one of these branches based on the outcome of the Boolean expression.

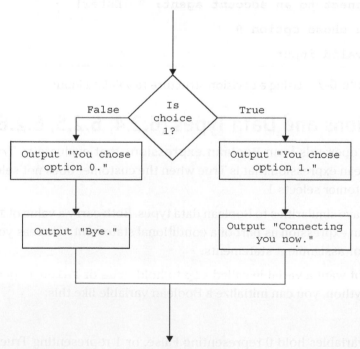

Figure 6-8 The if-then-else structure

While this two-way path could be coded as two separate if-then statements, there's an easier way. A decision coded as two possible paths is called an **if-then-else structure**. Python uses the keyword `else` to designate the alternative execution path. **Figure 6-9** illustrates the syntax, rules, and best practices for the if-then-else structure.

Syntax:
```
if condition:
        statement1
        statement2
else:
        statement3
        statement4
```

Rules and best practices:

- Place the `else` keyword on a separate line and at the same indent level as the `if` statement.
- Use a colon immediately after the `else` keyword with no condition statement.

Figure 6-9   If-then-else syntax

The Python code in **Figure 6-10** includes an if-block containing two statements. It also contains an else-block with two statements.

```
print("Press 1 when you are ready to")
print("connect to an account agent.")
print("Press anything else to quit.")
choice = input()
if choice == "1":
        print("You chose option 1.")
        print("Connecting you now.")
else:
        print("You chose to quit.")
        print("Bye.")
OUTPUT;
Press 1 when you are ready to
connect to an account agent.
Press anything else to quit.
0 [Enter]
You chose to quit.
Bye.
```

Figure 6-10   Sample code for the if-then-else structure

Nested-If Structures (6.3.4)

Sometimes programs need to make decisions within decisions. As an example, suppose that after a customer selects the Quit option, you want to check if the customer really wants to quit. The Quit option involves one decision, but within that decision is the second decision to quit or send the customer to the help desk.

Decisions within decisions are often referred to as **nested-if structures**. **Figure 6-11** illustrates the nested-if flowchart for customers who want to quit.

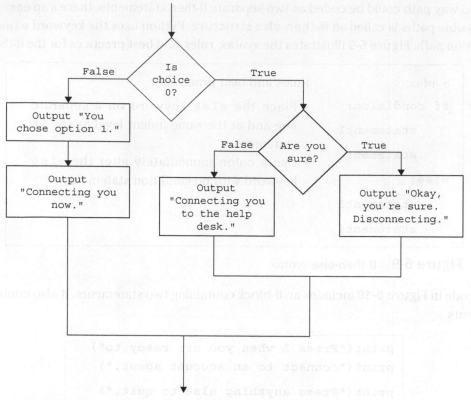

Figure 6-11 The nested-if structure

The Python code in **Figure 6-12** contains a nested-if structure that confirms if the customer wants to quit. Based on the input, the customer is either disconnected or connected to the help desk. When you implement a nested-if structure in code, be sure to use a second indent level for the inner decision structure. Trace through the code in Figure 6-12 to find the nested-if structure.

```
print("Press 1 when you are ready to")
print("connect to an account agent.")
print("Press 0 to quit.")
choice = input()
if choice == "0":
    print("Are you sure you want to quit?")
    sure_thing = input()
    if sure_thing == "y":
        print("Okay, you're sure. Disconnecting.")
    else:
        print("Connecting you to the help desk.")
else:
    print("You chose option 1.")
    print("Connecting you now.")
```

Figure 6-12 Sample code for the nested-if structure

Q Which lines of the Python code in Figure 6-12 are the inner level of the nested-if structure?

A
```
if sure_thing == "y":

    print("Okay, you're sure. Disconnecting.")
else:

    print("Connecting you to the help desk.")
```

Else-If Structure (6.3.5)

Python provides syntax for structures that involve multiple conditions. Suppose you want to offer customers a menu of the following options:

Press or say 1 to connect to an account agent.
Press or say 2 to troubleshoot your cable service.
Press or say 3 to troubleshoot your Internet connection.
Press or say 0 to quit.

To handle algorithms that require multiple conditions, you can use an **else-if structure**. Python combines the two keywords `if` and `else` into a new keyword to represent this concept: `elif`. **Figure 6-13** provides the syntax, rules, and best practices for the else-if structure.

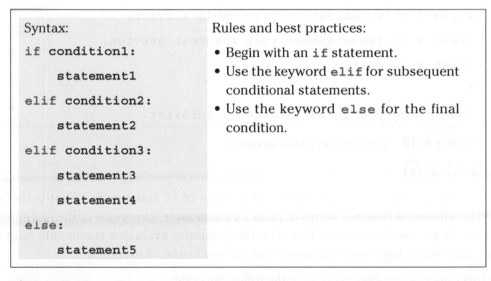

Syntax:
```
if condition1:
    statement1
elif condition2:
    statement2
elif condition3:
    statement3
    statement4
else:
    statement5
```

Rules and best practices:
- Begin with an `if` statement.
- Use the keyword `elif` for subsequent conditional statements.
- Use the keyword `else` for the final condition.

Figure 6-13   Syntax for an else-if structure

Figure 6-14 contains code for a program that uses an else-if structure to handle menu selections.

Q When you trace through the program, what is the output if a customer enters 2? What is the output if the customer enters 7?

A When the customer enters 2, the output is **Connecting you to a cable technician**. When the customer enters 7, the output is **Invalid input**.

```
print("Press 1 to connect to an account agent.")
print("Press 2 to troubleshoot your cable.")
print("Press 3 to troubleshoot your Internet.")
print("Press 0 to quit.")
choice = input()
if choice == "0":
    print("Bye.")
elif choice == "1":
    print("Transferring you to an account agent.")
elif choice == "2":
    print("Connecting you to a cable technician.")
elif choice == "3":
    print("Connecting you to an Internet specialist.")
else:
    print("Invalid input.")
OUTPUT:
Press 1 to connect to an account agent.
Press 2 to troubleshoot your cable service.
Press 3 to troubleshoot your Internet service.
Press 0 to quit.
3
Connecting you to an Internet specialist.
```

Figure 6-14   Code for an else-if structure

Fall Through (6.3.6)

You might ask, Why use an else-if structure instead of a series of `if` statements? What is the advantage of an else-if structure? The answer is that in a series of plain `if` statements, every one of the statements is evaluated and executed if true. In an else-if structure, however, the computer evaluates statements only until one of the conditions is true. The remaining else-if statements are not evaluated or executed.

To illustrate this concept, suppose you have the following code:

```
if choice == 1:
    print("One")
elif choice == 2:
    print("Two")
elif choice <= 2:
    print("Daisy")
else:
    print("Stop")
```

Q What is the output when a user enters 2?

A The output will be **Two**. The output will not include **Daisy** even though the condition **choice <= 2** is True because execution of the else-if structure terminated after the first True condition.

In programmer lingo, the else-if structure has no *fall through*. **Fall through** refers to program execution that continues to the next conditional statement within a structure. If the previous code used a fall-through structure, the output would be **Two Daisy**. Unfortunately, Python does not have a fall-through structure. Some other languages have the syntax to handle this situation, but in Python, you'll need to think carefully about your if-elif-else code.

6.4 Conditional Logical Operators

The and Operator (6.4.1, 6.4.2)

A simple conditional statement such as **choice == 1** contains a Boolean expression with one relational operator. You can specify more complex logic by adding conditional logical operators for **and** and **or** conditions. A **conditional logical operator** combines the outcomes of two or more Boolean expressions.

Suppose that you have a menu such as the following:

```
Press or say 1 to connect to an account agent.
Press or say 2 to troubleshoot your cable service.
Press or say 3 to troubleshoot your Internet service.
Press or say 9 to get help.
Press or say 0 to quit.
```

Valid input is 0, 1, 2, 3, and 9. You can filter out invalid input such as 4, 5, 6, 7, and 8 with the following:

```
choice = input()
if choice > 3 and choice != 9:
    print("Invalid input.")
```

In the conditional expression, when **choice** is greater than 3 and **choice** is not 9, then the input is not valid.

To determine if the program takes the True or the False path out of the **if** statement, each of the relational expressions is evaluated, and then the results are combined. Suppose the variable **choice** contains 7. Here's what the program does:

1. Evaluates **choice > 3**, which is True because 7 > 3.
2. Evaluates **choice != 9**, which is True because 7 != 9.
3. Evaluates **True and True** from steps 1 and 2, which is True.
4. The result is True, and the output is **"Invalid input."**.

Q What happens if `choice` contains 9?

A The `if` statement evaluates to `True and False`, which is `False`. The invalid output message is not produced.

The `and` operator requires that both conditions are true. A table summarizing the possible outcomes for logical operations is called a **truth table**. The truth table in **Figure 6-15** summarizes all the possible combinations for the `and` operator and provides a code snippet to show it in action.

The `and` Operator

`choice > 3`	`choice != 9`	`choice > 3 and choice != 9`
True	True	True
True	False	False
False	True	False
False	False	False

```
choice = 9
if choice > 3 and choice != 9:
    print("Invalid input.")
else:
    print("Valid input.")
```

OUTPUT:

```
Valid input.
```

Figure 6-15 Truth table for the `and` operator

The `or` Operator (6.4.3, 6.4.4)

The `or` operator requires that only one of the conditions is true. Suppose an online store offers free shipping to customers who purchase more than $100.00 of merchandise or are VIP club members. As you can see from the table and the code snippet in **Figure 6-16**, only one of the conditions has to be true for free shipping. Note that if both operands are `True`, the result is still `True`.

The `or` Operator

`purchase > 100.00`	`vip`	`Purchase > 100.00 or vip`
True	True	True
True	False	True
False	True	True
False	False	False

```
purchase = 80.00
vip = True
if purchase > 100.00 or vip:
    print("Free shipping!")
```

OUTPUT:
```
Free shipping!
```

Figure 6-16 Truth table for the `or` operator

You might find it necessary to use more than one logical operator in a conditional statement. When writing a Boolean expression, such as `if (vip == True and purchase >= 100) or free_shipping_coupon == True`, use parentheses to ensure that the logic is carried out in the correct sequence. Someone gets free shipping if the person is a VIP with a purchase of greater than $100.00 or if the person has a coupon.

The `not` Operator (6.4.5)

The `not` operator is the negation operator. It flips any Boolean value to the other; `False` becomes `True` or `True` becomes `False`. Sometimes it is easier to think of the condition for your if statement in terms of what you don't want to be true.

Q What's the Boolean expression to represent the pseudocode phrase "a coupon can be applied if the item isn't on clearance and it isn't jewelry"? Try to use the `not` operator.

A One solution is `can_apply_coupon = not (is_on_clearance or is_jewelry)`.

Summary

- A control structure alters the sequential execution of statements in a computer program. A decision control structure alters the sequential flow by branching to specific statements based on a condition or decision. Decision control structures help programs seem intelligent because they can make responses that correspond to user input.
- Decision control structures can be classified as if-then, if-then-else, nested-if, and else-if.
- Decision control structures begin with a conditional statement such as `if choice == 1`.
- Conditional statements include relational operators, such as `==`, `!=`, `>`, `<`, `>=`, and `<=`.
- The `==` equal operator, not the `=` assignment operator, is used in conditional statements.
- Relational operators and operands form Boolean expressions, such as `choice == 1`, that evaluate to True or False.
- Boolean expressions have similarities to Boolean data types. Both carry a value of `True` or `False`. In practice, however, you use a Boolean expression as part of a conditional statement, whereas you use a Boolean data type when making declaration or assignment statements. Sometimes a Boolean expression is a variable containing a Boolean value.
- Fall through refers to program execution that continues to the next conditional statement within a structure.
- The conditional logical operators `and` and `or` can be used to specify more complex logic for conditional statements. The results of `and` and `or` operations are summarized in truth tables.
- The conditional logical operator `not` is used to negate a Boolean value.

Key Terms

Boolean expressions	else-if structure	nested-if structures
conditional logical operator	equal operator	relational operator
conditional statement	fall through	truth table
control structure	if-then structure	
decision control structure	if-then-else structure	

Module

7

Repetition Control Structures

Learning Objectives:

7.1 Count-Controlled Loops

7.1.1 Identify parts of algorithms that require repetition controls.

7.1.2 Define an iterative sequence in the context of Python.

7.1.3 Show how to create an iterative sequence with the range function.

7.1.4 Specify how for-loops use the range function.

7.1.5 Specify the use case for count-controlled loops.

7.1.6 Specify the wording for count-controlled loops in pseudocode.

7.1.7 Identify loop control statements, loop counters, and test conditions.

7.1.8 Use language-specific syntax to code a count-controlled loop.

7.1.9 Provide an example of an algorithm that requires a user-controlled loop.

7.1.10 Collect user input to control a loop.

7.2 Counters and Accumulators

7.2.1 Provide an example of a loop that requires a counter.

7.2.2 Explain the advantages and disadvantages of using the loop counter variable as an output source.

7.2.3 Provide examples of loops that require an accumulator.

7.2.4 Describe the general syntax for expressions that serve as accumulators.

7.3 Nested Loops

7.3.1 Draw a flowchart that illustrates a nested loop.

7.3.2 Identify nested loops in Python code.

7.3.3 Describe common naming conventions for the variables used as counters in nested loops.

7.3.4 Use language-specific syntax to code a nested loop.

7.3.5 Analyze a nested loop to understand the results it produces.

7.4 Pre-Test Loops

7.4.1 Draw a flowchart that illustrates a pre-test loop.

7.4.2 Identify algorithms that require a pre-test loop.

7.4.3 Identify pre-test loops in Python code.

7.4.4 Use language-specific syntax to code a pre-test loop.

7.4.5 Identify infinite loops.

7.4.6 State how to terminate an infinite loop.

7.4.7 Explain the advantages and disadvantages of using the break statement to exit a loop.

7.1 Count-Controlled Loops

Loop Basics (7.1.1)

Pumping iron. Every lift requires repetitions using barbells, kettlebells, or free weights like those in **Figure 7-1**.

Figure 7-1   Barbells, kettlebells, and free weights

Like weight-lifting exercises, computer programs can perform reps using **repetition control structures**, or "loops," as they are called in the programming world. You can visualize a **loop** as a block of code with an entry point, a few statements that repeat, and an exit point. See **Figure 7-2**.

Loops are handy for many tasks within an algorithm, such as the following:

- Processing a series of records in a database or the items in a list
- Keeping a running count
- Accumulating totals
- Solving recursive math problems

There are two basic types of repetition control structures:

- Count-controlled loops
- Pre-test loops

In this module, you'll learn how to use both of these control structures. Are you ready to strengthen your programming skills by discovering loops? Let's get started.

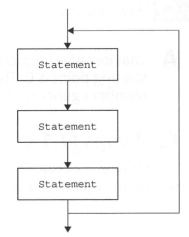

Figure 7-2   Repetition control structures repeat blocks of code

Control Statements (7.1.2, 7.1.3)

The simplest repetition control structure is the **count-controlled loop**, which repeats a specified number of times. This type of loop begins with a **control statement** that contains the following parameters for controlling the loop:

- A variable for the **loop counter** that tracks the number of times a loop has repeated
- An **iterative sequence** for the loop counter to use to control the loop

An iterative sequence is data in Python that can be linearly traced. For example, the numbers 1, 2, 3, 4 could be an iterative sequence. Additionally, "abc" is iterative. The most frequently used iterative sequence uses the **range function**. The `range()` function will create a numerical iterative sequence for you based on its own parameters:

- A starting number
- An ending number
- An incremental value, used to skip numbers in the sequence

Figure 7-3 shows examples of the iterative sequences created by the `range()` function. The starting number and increment values are optional to include. If the starting number is omitted, Python assumes it is 0. If the incremental value is omitted, Python assumes it is 1. Note how in Figure 7-3 the ending number is never included in the resulting sequence. Instead, `range()` will create the sequence up to but not including the ending number.

Range Function Parameters	Iterative Sequence
`range(10)`	0 1 2 3 4 5 6 7 8 9
`range(1, 10)`	1 2 3 4 5 6 7 8 9
`range(1, 10, 2)`	1 3 5 7 9
`range(0, 10, 2)`	0 2 4 6 8

Figure 7-3   Range sequences

Q How many numbers are in the iterative sequence created by `range(5)`?

A That iterative sequence contains five numbers. The starting number is not present, so the starting point is 0. The incremental value is also missing, so Python uses the default 1. The numbers generated are 0, 1, 2, 3, and 4.

For-Loops (7.1.4, 7.1.5, 7.1.6, 7.1.7, 7.1.8)

The **for-loop** is a count-controlled loop that is appropriate for when you know how many times you want a loop to repeat. The flowchart in **Figure 7-4** shows a for-loop.

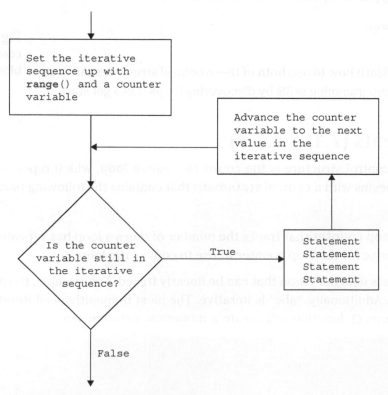

Figure 7-4   For-loop flowchart

You can write pseudocode for a for-loop using a statement like "repeat four times:". Here is the pseudocode for a program that displays verbal guidance for two repetitions of the bench press lift.

```
repeat twice:
    Display "Lift", "Pause", and "Lower"
```

EXPECTED OUTPUT:

```
Lift

Pause

Lower


Lift

Pause

Lower
```

Q Can you identify the equivalent `range()` function call for the preceding pseudocode?

A `range(2)` or `range(1, 3)` will work.

First, you need to name your loop counter variable. Programmers typically use the letter `i` for the loop counter's variable name. The `i` probably stands for **iteration**, which is a synonym for repetition. **Figure 7-5** provides the general syntax for a basic for-loop.

Syntax:

```
for i in range(iteration):
    statement1
    statement2
```

Rules and best practices:

- The loop variable should be a simple identifier, usually `i`.
- The `range` function provides a sequence for `i` to iterate over.
- The loop variable will visit each value in the sequence provided by the range function, even if you change the loop variable inside the loop.
- Avoid modifying the loop counter variable within the loop. For example, do not assign to `i` inside the loop.

Figure 7-5 For-loop syntax, rules, and best practices

By applying the for-loop syntax, you can code the following program that guides a bench press exercise by displaying "Lift Pause Lower" for three repetitions. Take a close look at in the solution in **Figure 7-6**.

User-Controlled Loops (7.1.9, 7.1.10)

You can allow users to determine the number of times a loop repeats. A **user-controlled loop** specifies the value for the `range()` function during runtime by obtaining user input for its value. Users can control for-loops as well as pre-test loops.

Suppose that a weightlifter wants to do five reps of the bench press exercise. The following pseudocode collects the input for reps and uses it to control the loop.

```
Ask weightlifter "How many reps? " and store in a
variable repeat based on input:

    Display "Lift, pause, lower"
```

EXPECTED OUTPUT:

```
How many reps?  5 [Enter]

Lift, pause, lower

Lift, pause, lower

Lift, pause, lower

Lift, pause, lower

Lift, pause, lower
```

Coding this algorithm produces the program in **Figure 7-7**. Look for the use of the variable **reps** in the input statement and in the **range()** function.

```
reps = int(input("How many reps? "))

for i in range(reps):

    print("Lift, pause, lower")
```
OUTPUT:
```
How many reps? 5 [Enter]

Lift, pause, lower

Lift, pause, lower

Lift, pause, lower

Lift, pause, lower

Lift, pause, lower
```

Figure 7-7   User-controlled for-loop

```
for i in range(1, 4):

    print("Lift")

    print("Pause")

    print("Lower")

    print()
```
OUTPUT:
```
Lift

Pause

Lower


Lift

Pause

Lower


Lift

Pause

Lower
```

Figure 7-6   Code for three repetitions of bench press guidance

7.2 Counters and Accumulators

Loops That Count (7.2.1, 7.2.2)

Count-controlled loops have a built-in counter that you can use for algorithms that need to count or accumulate totals. The values in the loop counter follow a sequence of numbers similar to counting 1 2 3 or 2 4 6.

You can set the **range** function to count by ones, by twos, by tens, or by other whole numbers using three parameters to **range()**. You must provide all three inputs to **range()** to skip numbers in the sequence. This feature is useful when you create programs that include some counting component, such as a math program to count by twos or to output multiplication tables.

After setting the loop counter parameters for a counting sequence, you can simply output the value for **i** during each iteration. **Figure 7-8** contains the code for a program that outputs even numbers from 2 to 10. Be sure to study the parameters for the **range()** function.

```
for i in range(2, 11, 2):

    print(i)
OUTPUT:
2
4
6
8
10
```

Figure 7-8   Loop that counts by twos

It is good programming practice to avoid using the loop counter variable in other statements within the loop. The previous program used **i** in the output statement. To avoid reuse, and the possibility that the counter variable might be inadvertently changed, you can set up a separate variable for the output and increment it within the loop, as shown in **Figure 7-9**.

```
count_out = 0
for i in range(2, 11, 2):

    count_out += 2

    print(count_out)
OUTPUT:
2
4
6
8
10
```

Figure 7-9   Loop that uses a variable called **count_out** as a separate counter

Q Instead of outputting **i** in the preceding program, which variable is used as a counter and for output?

A The variable **count_out** is used as a counter and for output.

Loops That Accumulate (7.2.3, 7.2.4)

Another application of loops is to accumulate a total by repeatedly adding values. Suppose you are bench pressing 15-pound weights in each hand and want to know the total weight that you've lifted after three repetitions.

You can set up a variable called `total_weight` that accumulates the sum of weight lifted during the bench press session. As a bonus, the cumulative totals can be output for each repetition. The pseudocode looks like this:

```
Ask how many reps and store response in a variable
Ask how much the weights weigh and store response in a variable
Initialize a total weight variable at 0
Repeat based on input:
     Increase the total weight by twice the weight
     Display the rep number and total weight so far
```

Notice the two statements that suggest the accumulator: `Initialize a total weight variable at 0` and `increase the total weight by twice the weight`. In general, the syntax for an accumulator spans two steps. One step sets the accumulator to a starting value (0 for addition) and the other increases the accumulator by some amount.

The code and output for the total-weight algorithm are in **Figure 7-10**.

```
total_weight = 0
reps = int(input("How many reps? "))
weight = int(input("What size weights are you using? "))
for i in range(reps):
    total_weight = total_weight + (weight * 2)
    print("Rep", i, total_weight, "lbs so far.")
print("Your total lift is:", total_weight, "lbs.")
OUTPUT:
How many reps? 3 [Enter]
What size weights are you using? 15 [Enter]
Rep 1 30 lbs so far.
Rep 2 60 lbs so far.
Rep 3 90 lbs so far.
Your total lift is: 90 lbs.
```

Figure 7-10 Loop that includes an accumulator for `total_weight`

Q Why is the weight multiplied by 2 before adding it to the accumulator?

A Because each hand is holding a weight. If each hand holds a 15-pound weight, then each lift is 30 pounds.

7.3 Nested Loops

Loops Within Loops (7.3.1, 7.3.2)

A **nested loop** is a loop within a loop. These loops contain multiple control statements and loop counters. Lifting weights provides an insight into how these nested loops work.

Weight-training exercises usually involve sets of repetitions. For example, set 1 for a bench press might involve four repetitions. Set 2 might involve another four repetitions, and a third set might involve four more repetitions. The sets repeat three times, and each set has four reps. The sets are the outer loop. The reps are the inner loop.

A flowchart for a nested loop is illustrated in **Figure 7-11**. Trace the True paths through the loop to reinforce the idea that the computer does one outer loop and then repeats the inner loops before doing the next outer loop.

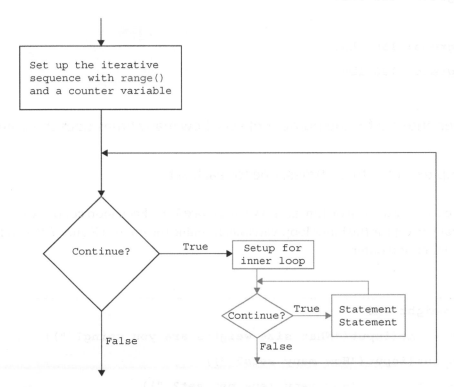

Figure 7-11   Nested-loop flowchart

Inner and Outer Loops (7.3.3, 7.3.4, 7.3.5)

When writing nested loops in pseudocode, the inner loop is indented from the outer loop.

```
Ask for the weight size and store response in a variable
Ask for how many sets and store response in a variable
Ask for how many reps per set and store response in a variable
Repeat based on the number of sets:
    Display the set number
    Repeat based on the number of reps:
        Increase the total weight by twice the weight size
        Display the rep number and total weight lifted so far
```

EXPECTED OUTPUT:

```
What size weights are you using? 15 [Enter]

How many sets? 3 [Enter]

How many reps per set? 2 [Enter]

Set: 1

    Rep: 1 Progress: 30 lbs.

    Rep: 2 Progress: 60 lbs.

Set: 2

    Rep: 1 Progress: 90 lbs.

    Rep: 2 Progress: 120 lbs.

Set: 3

    Rep: 1 Progress: 150 lbs.

    Rep: 2 Progress: 180 lbs.
```

Q When the user enters 3 for the number of sets, how many times does the outer loop iterate?

A The outer loop executes three times, one for each set.

The code for the training-sets algorithm is shown in **Figure 7-12**. Each loop control variable must be unique. Programmers typically use **j** for the inner loop variable. Examine the code in Figure 7-12 carefully to identify the two loop variables, inner and outer.

```
total_weight = 0

weight = int(input("What size weights are you using? "))

sets = int(input("How many sets? "))

reps = int(input("How many reps per set? "))

for s in range(sets):

    print("Set:", s)

    for r in range(reps):

        total_weight = total_weight + (weight * 2)

        print("    Rep:", r, "Progress:", total_weight, "lbs.")

print("Your total lift is:", total_weight, "lbs.")

OUTPUT:

What size weights are you using? 15 [Enter]

How many sets? 3 [Enter]

How many reps per set? 2 [Enter]
```

Figure 7-12   Code for a nested for-loop

```
Set: 1
    Rep: 1 Progress: 30 lbs.
    Rep: 2 Progress: 60 lbs.
 Set: 2
    Rep: 1 Progress: 90 lbs.
    Rep: 2 Progress: 120 lbs.
 Set: 3
    Rep: 1 Progress: 150 lbs.
    Rep: 2 Progress: 180 lbs.
Your total lift is: 180 lbs.
```

Figure 7-12   Code for a nested for-loop (Continued)

Q In the preceding program, why isn't "Set: 1" printed on the line for each repetition in the set, as follows?

```
Set: 1 Rep: 1 Progress: 30 lbs.
Set: 1 Rep: 2 Progress: 60 lbs.
```

A The statement that outputs the set number is before the beginning of the inner loop. If you want tasks performed only by the outer loop, do not place them within the code for the inner loop.

7.4 Pre-Test Loops

While-Loops (7.4.1, 7.4.2, 7.4.3, 7.4.4)

Loops are not always controlled by a counter. A **condition-controlled loop** is regulated by conditional statements containing Boolean expressions similar to those that control decision structures, such as if-then and else-if.

A **pre-test loop** begins with a condition. A condition-controlled pre-test loop executes only if the test condition is true and continues executing until the condition is no longer `True` or until the loop encounters a `break` statement.

A flowchart for a pre-test loop is illustrated in **Figure 7-13**.

Pre-test loops are handy for validating input. You can set up a loop that implements the following algorithm:

Ask user for input.

If the input is not valid, output a message that asks for a valid entry.

Check the entry again and repeat until the entry is valid.

The pseudocode for a pre-test loop typically uses the words **while** or **until**. Here is the pseudocode that validates input in the range 1 to 25. This pre-test loop repeats as many times as necessary until the user enters a value in the range 1 to 25.

Request the number of reps and store in a variable.

While the number of reps is less than 1 or greater than 25:

    Display an error message and request the number of reps again

Display a message which shows the number of valid reps

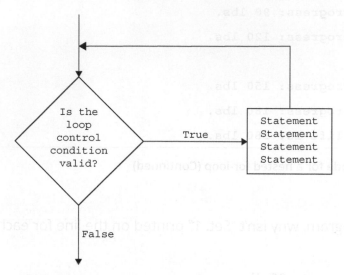

Figure 7-13   Pre-test loop flowchart

A **while-loop** provides the syntax for implementing a pre-test loop. In **Figure 7-14**, pay attention to the syntax, and then see how it is applied in the example code.

Syntax:

```
while condition:
    statement1
    statement2
```

Example:

```
reps = int(input("Enter the number of reps for this lifting exercise: "))
while reps < 1 or reps > 25:
    reps = int(input("Try again. Reps have to be in the range 1 to 25: "))
print("Okay, you want to do", reps, "reps.")
```

OUTPUT:

```
Enter the number of reps for this lifting exercise: 38 [Enter]
Try again. Reps have to be in the range 1 to 25: 20 [Enter]
Okay, you want to do 20 reps.
```

Figure 7-14   While-loop syntax and example

Infinite Loops (7.4.5)

When validating input, what happens if the weightlifter continues to enter 0? The validation loop could continue forever, a condition known as an **infinite loop**. Infinite loops can be caused by several factors, including the following:

- Invalid input that does not end an input loop
- Input that changes the value of the loop counter
- A programmer error in specifying the loop conditional statement
- Using the loop counter variable in a mathematical operation inside the loop
- Using the same loop counter variable for the inner and outer loops of a nested loop

Trace through the following Python code, and see if you can discover the error that creates an infinite loop.

```
reps = int(input("Enter the number of reps: "))

while reps < 1 or reps > 25:
    int(input("Try again. Enter a number in the range 1 to 25: "))

print("Okay, you want to do " + reps + " reps.")
```

OUTPUT:

```
Enter the number of reps: 0 [Enter]
Try again. Enter a number in the range 1 to 25:
Try again. Enter a number in the range 1 to 25:
Try again. Enter a number in the range 1 to 25:
Try again. Enter a number in the range 1 to 25:

. . .
```

Q Did you find the error?

A The error is that the input statement within the loop does not override the value in the `reps` variable. The user never has a chance to enter a value other than the 0 entered at the first prompt.

If your program inadvertently goes into an infinite loop, you may be able to terminate it by pressing Ctrl+C until the program exits the loop. Online compilers usually have a Stop button for use in such a situation.

Breaking Out of Loops (7.4.6, 7.4.7)

Using Ctrl+C to terminate a loop is not something you can expect users to do. Your program always should provide a clean exit path from a loop, preferably from within the logic of the loop control statement.

To prevent an endless loop when validating input, you can provide an exit strategy in the body of the loop. Look for the exit strategy in the following Python code.

```
reps = int(input("Enter the number of reps: "))

while (reps < 1 or reps > 25) and (reps != 999):
```

```
    reps = int(input ("Try again. Enter a number in the range 1 to
25, or enter 999 to exit: "))
if reps == 999:
    print("Bye.")
else:
    print("Okay, you want to do", reps, "reps.")
```

OUTPUT:

Enter the number of reps: 0 [Enter]

Try again. Enter a number in the range 1 to 25,

or enter 999 to exit: 999 [Enter]

Bye.

The user is given the option of entering 999 to exit the loop. This logic is handled by the parameters for the `while` statement (reps < 1 or reps > 25) and (reps != 999). The `if` and `else` statements later in the code provide additional logic necessary to either quit or output the number of reps.

It is also possible to use a `break` statement to exit a loop as in the following Python code, but the result might have unintended consequences.

```
reps = int(input("Enter the number of reps: "))
while (reps < 1 or reps > 25):
    reps = int(input ("Try again. Enter a number in the range 1 to
25, or enter 999 to exit: "))
    if reps == 999:
        print("Bye.")
        break
print("Okay, you want to do", reps, "reps.")
```

OUTPUT:

Enter the number of reps: 0 [Enter]

Try again. Enter a number in the range 1 to 25,

or enter 999 to exit: 999 [Enter]

Bye.

Okay, you want to do 999 reps.

Q What is wrong with the logic in the preceding Python?

A The loop exits with 999 in the variable **reps**, and the last statement outputs the "Okay ..." message, even though the loop terminated.

Because `break` statements can have unexpected effects, it is best to avoid their use within the body of a loop. The better practice is to design the control parameters to provide a graceful way to exit loops. Loops containing `break` statements are widely used by professional developers; however, as a programmer you should have the flexibility to use them or avoid them as required by the specifications for each project.

Summary

- A repetition control structure creates a loop that has an entry point, a number of statements that repeat, and an exit point.
- A count-controlled loop repeats a specified number of times. This type of loop begins with a control statement that establishes a loop counter. A loop counter sets up a variable that tracks the number of times the loop repeats.
- The for-loop is a count-controlled loop that is appropriate when you know how many times you want a loop to repeat.
- The `range()` function is used in for-loops to specify an iterative sequence to be used for the loop.
- Users can specify the value for a loop counter during runtime by providing input for the value of the loop counter. Users can control for-loops as well as pre-test loops.
- Loops can be used to output counting sequences and to sum values in an accumulator.
- Nested loops are loops within loops. The outer loop and inner loop are controlled by different variables.
- A pre-test loop begins with a condition. The loop executes only if that condition is true and continues executing until the condition is no longer true or until it encounters a `break` statement. Pre-test loops are handy for validating input.
- An infinite loop has no means of termination other than user intervention and is generally considered an error condition. To manually terminate an infinite loop, press Ctrl+C or the Run/Stop button provided by a development environment. Although it is possible to include `break` statements to exit a loop, a better practice is to provide a clean exit path from within the logic of the loop's control statement.

Key Terms

condition-controlled loop
control statement
count-controlled loop
for-loop
infinite loop

iteration
iterative sequence
loop
loop counter
nested loop

pre-test loop
range function
repetition control structures
user-controlled loop
while-loop

Module

8

Lists

Learning Objectives:

8.7.3   Understand the difference between the keys of a dictionary and the values.

8.7.4   Access a value from a dictionary using a key.

8.7.5   Output the keys of a dictionary.

8.7.6   Output the values of a dictionary.

8.7.7   Add a new key, value pair to a dictionary.

8.7.8   Update the value associated with a key in a dictionary.

8.7.9   Remove a key from a dictionary.

8.1 List Basics

Tic-Tac-Toe Board (8.1.1, 8.1.2)

In other modules, you've used variables to represent a single piece of data. Sometimes, data for a situation requires a lot of variables, but those variables need to be kept together. Consider a simple game board for tic-tac-toe, as in **Figure 8-1**. Six spaces could be represented by six unique variables. You can look at a location on the board to see what symbol it contains, or you can place an X or O in an empty spot to complete your turn. Suppose you are playing as O. Can you see a winning move?

dekzerphoto/Shutterstock.com

Figure 8-1   Incomplete game of tic-tac-toe

Individually creating the six variables needed for the entire board means you have to work harder to keep them all together; you can't do anything with just a `top_left` or `middle` variable because you need all six at once. A better (and easier) way to manage multiple pieces of data is with a list. In the context of programming, a **list** is a data structure that stores a collection of elements in a specific order or location. In this case, the tic-tac-toe board is a list that contains a collection of strings. Lists are classified as composite data types because they are constructed from primitive data types, such as integers.

Programmers typically work with one-dimensional and two-dimensional lists. Lists can have as many dimensions as you need, but for now, stick with one and two dimensions.

- A **one-dimensional list** is linear. The first row of the game board with its three elements is a one-dimensional list.
- A **two-dimensional list** has rows and columns that form a grid, or matrix. The entire board is a two-dimensional list.

List Characteristics (8.1.3, 8.1.4, 8.1.5, 8.1.6)

Lists are heterogeneous, ordered, and infinite.

Heterogeneous. A list can contain any type of data, but the elements of a list do not have to be the same data type, a characteristic referred to as **heterogeneous**. A list can contain any combination of data types, such as strings, integers, floats, and Booleans. A list typically contains the same type for each entry, but you are not limited in what you can store in a list.

Ordered. Lists store consecutive data where each element is identified by a sequential **list index** enclosed in square brackets. List indexes are sometimes referred to as subscripts. The first element in a list has an index of 0. The remaining list elements in a one-dimensional list are indexed in sequence, as shown in **Figure 8-2**.

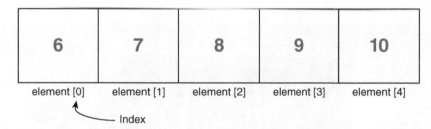

Figure 8-2   Indexing a one-dimensional list

Infinite. Lists need a size when they are created, even if the size is zero. After that, however, the list can grow as large as the memory on your computer allows, becoming basically "infinite."

A list is initially fixed to the size you specify. To expand a list, you append new items to the end, middle, or beginning of the list.

Here's a little gotcha. The first row of the tic-tac-toe board is a list of three elements, but the index for the final element is 2, not 3, as shown in **Figure 8-3**. Keep this in mind as you work with lists!

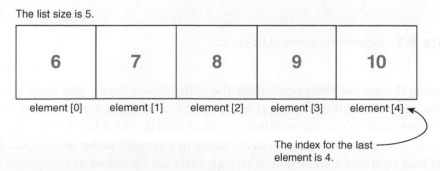

Figure 8-3   The index value for the last element in a list is one less than the number of elements in the list

List Use Cases (8.1.7)

Lists are an indispensable part of your programming toolbox. Suppose you want to find the average of 100 rainfall measurements. Initializing 100 variables would be tedious. Instead, you can create a single named list, such as **rainfall**, with a size of 100 to hold all the data.

Lists are useful when you need to do the following:

- Store lists of data
- Represent a collection of integer or floating-point data that you want to process using the same algorithm
- Sort a collection of numeric or string data
- Manipulate the characters in a word or phrase by reversing or encrypting them
- Process images that are stored as a matrix of pixels
- Implement data structures such as stacks, queues, and hash tables
- Store and manipulate mathematical matrices
- Search through lists and collections of data
- Process lists or tables of data

To discover more about this handy programming tool, let's begin by exploring one-dimensional lists.

8.2 One-Dimensional List Initialization

Initialize Lists (8.2.1, 8.2.2, 8.2.3)

A one-dimensional list has a name and uses a single index to identify list elements. When naming a list, use the same conventions as when naming a variable. The first row of the tic-tac-toe board can be coded as a list called **first_row**. The list contains three strings indexed 0 through 2 as shown in **Figure 8-4**.

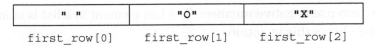

first_row[0]   first_row[1]   first_row[2]

Figure 8-4   List called **first_row** contains three elements

Q What is the value stored in index 2 of **first_row** in Figure 8-4?

A It is **"X"**.

To create a list, you can use the **list()** function or square brackets. Use the following Python code to create empty lists:

```
a_list = list()
b_list = []
```

The contents of the list can be specified at initialization. Surround the elements with square brackets, separating each element by a comma. **Figure 8-5** provides details on how to set up one-dimensional lists in Python with various data.

```
Syntax to declare an empty list:
empty_list = []
empty_list = list()

Syntax to declare and initialize a list:
numbers_list = [2, 6, 2, 3, 9, 12]
letters_list = ["A", "H", "C", "B"]
mixed_list = [2, 4, "B", 2, "Z"]
```

Figure 8-5 Declare and initialize one-dimensional lists

8.3 One-Dimensional List Input and Output

Output a List Element (8.3.1)

You can output a single element of a list using its index value. **Figure 8-6** showcases printing the value stored in index 3. Remember that indexes start at 0!

```
numbers = [6, 7, 8, 9, 10]
print(numbers[3])
OUTPUT:
9
```

Figure 8-6 Outputting a list element

Indexes in Python can also use negative numbers. The last element in a list is at index **-1**. Second to last is at **-2**, and so on. **Figure 8-7** shows this in action.

```
numbers = [6, 7, 8, 9, 10]
print(numbers[-3])
OUTPUT:
8
```

Figure 8-7 Outputting a list element with a negative index

Index Errors (8.3.2)

Using an index value that is too large for the list produces an **index error** or a runtime warning. For example, if you have the variable **numbers** holding five elements and you attempt to access or output **numbers[6]**, your programming environment might produce a message like the one in **Figure 8-8**. This also applies to negative numbers that are too big, such as **-6** for **numbers**.

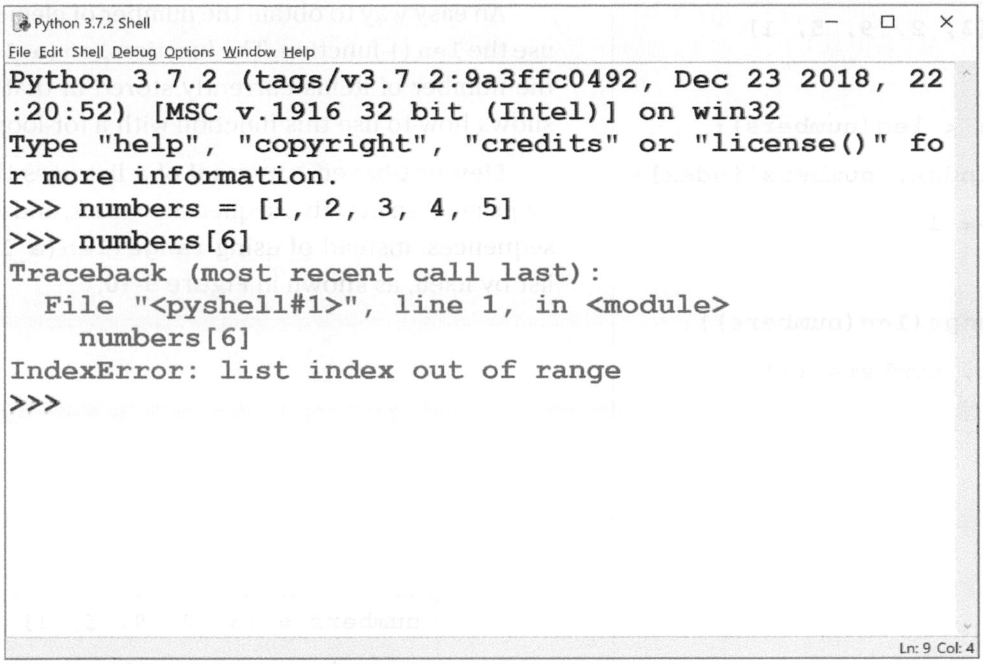

Source: Python Software Foundation

Figure 8-8 Index error message

Index errors are sometimes referred to as boundary errors, out-of-bounds exceptions, or subscript errors. These errors are easy to make, but they are also easy to correct by paying attention to the index values in loops, calculations, and output statements.

Traverse a List (8.3.3)

Lists have multiple elements. To output all the elements in **`numbers`**, you could use a brute-force algorithm like this:

```
print(numbers[0])
print(numbers[1])
print(numbers[2])
print(numbers[3])
print(numbers[4])
```

Obviously, that algorithm is not very efficient. In Python, you can call **`print(numbers)`** to display the list inside square brackets. Use a loop if you want more control over the display of elements. Accessing each list element in sequence is called **traversing a list**. You can traverse a list to output every element, count the total number of elements, search for an element, or sum the elements. There are two options for traversing a list: index-based traversal and element-based traversal.

Index-based traversal of a list requires a loop counter variable so the code visits each valid index of the list.

Q What is the range of valid indexes for a list?

A Between 0 and the number of elements in the list minus 1. If the list has five elements, the indexes range between `0` and `4`.

```
numbers = [3, 2, 9, 5, 1]
index = 0
while index < len(numbers):
    print(index, numbers[index])
    index += 1
print()
for i in range(len(numbers)):
    print(i, numbers[i])
print()
OUTPUT:
0 3
1 2
2 9
3 5
4 1

0 3
1 2
2 9
3 5
4 1
```

Figure 8-9   Index-based traversal

An easy way to obtain the number of elements in a list is to use the `len()` function. The function `len(a_list)` will return the number of items currently stored in that list. **Figure 8-9** shows how to use this function with a for-loop or while-loop.

Element-based traversal of a list uses the fact that for-loops need an iterative sequence to work, and lists are iterative sequences. Instead of using `range(len(a_list))`, use the list by itself, as shown in **Figure 8-10**.

```
numbers = [3, 2, 9, 5, 1]
for element in numbers:
    print(element)
OUTPUT:
3
2
9
5
1
```

Figure 8-10   Element-based traversal

Input List Elements (8.3.4)

Your programs can collect elements for a list at runtime. With Python, you can create an empty list and then append each new element as it is input. You use the append method to append to a list. The following syntax will append the number 5 to `a_list`:

```
a_list.append(5)
```

The only tricky part is knowing when to stop appending. You have two options: use a known amount or use sentinel values.

The known-amount approach specifies the number of elements to store ahead of time. This can be done within the program or as another input statement. **Figure 8-11** showcases the known-amount approach.

```
some_numbers = []
for i in range(5):
    number = int(input("Enter number " + str(i) + ": "))
    some_numbers.append(number)
print(some_numbers)


some_more_numbers = []
how_many = int(input("How many numbers do you want to enter? "))
for i in range(how_many):
    number = int(input("Enter number " + str(i) + ": "))
    some_more_numbers.append(number)
print(some_more_numbers)
OUTPUT:
Enter number 0: 3 [Enter]
Enter number 1: 2 [Enter]
Enter number 2: 6 [Enter]
Enter number 3: 4 [Enter]
Enter number 4: 9 [Enter]
[3, 2, 6, 4, 9]
How many numbers do you want to enter? 3 [Enter]
Enter number 0: 7 [Enter]
Enter number 1: 2 [Enter]
Enter number 2: 3 [Enter]
[7, 2, 3]
```

Figure 8-11   Runtime input to a list

Q In Figure 8-11, the variable `how_many` is used in two locations. Where does the value for `how_many` originate?

A The value for `how_many` is obtained by the `how_many = int(input("How many numbers do you want to enter? "))` statement when the user responds to the prompt.

A sentinel value is a value that signals that the user is done with input. The program will read input until it sees the sentinel value, appending each input until then. Take this approach when the user may not know how many items to enter at the start. See **Figure 8-12** for an example of using a sentinel value with a while-loop.

```
some_numbers = []
print("Enter numbers or -1 to quit:")
number = int(input())
while number != -1:
    some_numbers.append(number)
    number = int(input())
print(some_numbers)
OUTPUT:
Enter numbers or -1 to quit:
4 [Enter]
8 [Enter]
2 [Enter]
4 [Enter]
1 [Enter]
7 [Enter]
-1 [Enter]
[4, 8, 2, 4, 1, 7]
```

Figure 8-12   Sentinel-controlled input

8.4 One-Dimensional List Operations, Functions, and Methods

Change a List Element (8.4.1, 8.4.2)

You can change the value of any list element using an assignment statement. Just remember to include the index value for the element you want to change. Take a look at the code in **Figure 8-13**. Which element is changed?

```
numbers = [6, 7, 8, 9, 10]
numbers[3] = 22
print(numbers)
OUTPUT:
[6, 7, 8, 22, 10]
```

Figure 8-13   Changing a list element

A statement such as **numbers[3]** = **22** changes the value of the fourth element in the list because the first element's index is **0**. The program changed the list value **9** to **22**.

Earlier, you learned about two ways to traverse a list. The element-based traversal has a simple structure but can't modify values inside the list. Modifying every item in a list requires the index-based loop. **Figure 8-14** shows how to increase each element in a list by **1**.

```
numbers = [6, 7, 8, 9, 10]
for i in range(len(numbers)):
    numbers[i] += 1
print(numbers)
OUTPUT:
[7, 8, 9, 10, 11]
```

Figure 8-14 Changing all list elements

Find a List Element (8.4.3)

Suppose you have a long list and want to know if it contains the value **22**. Or suppose you want to know how many times **22** appears in the list. You can loop through the list and compare each list item to the target value. You can also include an accumulator that records the number of times the target element appears in the list. **Figure 8-15** shows one way to search a list.

```
count = 0
numbers = [6, 22, 8, 22, 12, 6, 99, 20, 2, 4]
for element in numbers:
    if element == 22:
        count += 1
print("The array contains", count, "instances of 22.")
OUTPUT:
The array contains 2 instances of 22.
```

Figure 8-15 Finding elements in a list

Q Why can the code in Figure 8-15 use an element-based loop instead of an index-based loop?

A Searching for a value within a list does not need to modify the list, so either loop style is valid.

Python has many functions and methods for use in list operations. The code in Figure 8-15 can be simplified by using one of these methods, the **count** method, as shown in **Figure 8-16**. The code in Figure 8-16 has the same results as Figure 8-15.

```
numbers = [6, 22, 8, 22, 12, 6, 99, 20, 2, 4]
total = numbers.count(22)
print("The array contains", total, "instances of 22.")
OUTPUT:
The array contains 2 instances of 22.
```

Figure 8-16 Finding elements in a list with count method

Sum List Elements (8.4.4)

The code in **Figure 8-17** uses an accumulator named `total` to find the sum of the elements in numbers.

```
total = 0
numbers = [6, 7, 8, 9, 10]
for element in numbers:
    total += element
print("The sum of the array:", total)
OUTPUT:
The sum of the array: 40
```

Figure 8-17   Finding the sum of list elements

The built-in function `sum()` can simplify the code shown in Figure 8-17. See **Figure 8-18**.

```
numbers = [6, 7, 8, 9, 10]
total = sum(numbers)
print("The sum of the array:", total)
OUTPUT:
The sum of the array: 40
```

Figure 8-18   Finding the sum of list elements using `sum()`

Some common built-in methods and functions are listed in **Figure 8-19**. You should understand the logic behind these methods and functions and know how Python handles one- and two-dimensional data.

Function or Method	Description	Syntax	Output
`min()`	Find the minimum value in a list.	`min([2,5,3,1])`	1
`max()`	Find the maximum value in a list.	`max([2,5,3,1])`	5
`sum()`	Add all elements in the list together.	`sum([2,5,3,1])`	11
`count()`	Count the elements that match the given parameter.	`[2,5,3,3,1].count(3)`	2
`index()`	Find the index of the first element which matches the given parameter.	`[2,5,3,2,1].index(2)`	0

`sort()`	Sort the contents of the list in place. Requires the list to be a variable and changes the variable.	`numbers = [4,2,3,5,1]`
		`numbers.sort()`
		`print(numbers)`
			`[1,2,3,4,5]`

Figure 8-19   Some useful list functions and methods

8.5 List Comprehension

Dimensional Manipulation (8.5.1, 8.5.2)

Suppose you want to list all the numbers between 0 and 99. You could create an empty list and then write a for-loop to append each number, as in **Figure 8-20**.

```
numbers = []
for i in range(100):
    numbers.append(i)
print(numbers)
OUTPUT:
[0, 1, 2, 3, 4, 5, 6, 7, 8, 9, 10, 11, 12, 13, 14, 15, 16,
17, 18, 19, 20, 21, 22, 23, 24, 25, 26, 27, 28, 29, 30, 31,
32, 33, 34, 35, 36, 37, 38, 39, 40, 41, 42, 43, 44, 45, 46,
47, 48, 49, 50, 51, 52, 53, 54, 55, 56, 57, 58, 59, 60, 61,
62, 63, 64, 65, 66, 67, 68, 69, 70, 71, 72, 73, 74, 75, 76,
77, 78, 79, 80, 81, 82, 83, 84, 85, 86, 87, 88, 89, 90, 91,
92, 93, 94, 95, 96, 97, 98, 99]
```

Figure 8-20   Manually creating a list with many numbers

Python lets you put the for-loop logic inside the square brackets to create lists, a technique called **list comprehension**. **Figure 8-21** produces the same output as Figure 8-20 but uses list comprehension to achieve it.

```
numbers = [i for i in range(100)]
print(numbers)
OUTPUT:
[0, 1, 2, 3, 4, 5, 6, 7, 8, 9, 10, 11, 12, 13, 14, 15, 16,
17, 18, 19, 20, 21, 22, 23, 24, 25, 26, 27, 28, 29, 30, 31,
32, 33, 34, 35, 36, 37, 38, 39, 40, 41, 42, 43, 44, 45, 46,
47, 48, 49, 50, 51, 52, 53, 54, 55, 56, 57, 58, 59, 60, 61,
62, 63, 64, 65, 66, 67, 68, 69, 70, 71, 72, 73, 74, 75, 76,
77, 78, 79, 80, 81, 82, 83, 84, 85, 86, 87, 88, 89, 90, 91,
92, 93, 94, 95, 96, 97, 98, 99]
```

Figure 8-21   Using list comprehension to create a list with many numbers

Filtering and Mapping (8.5.3, 8.5.4, 8.5.5, 8.5.6)

If you are working with large sets of data, sometimes you want to only look at certain elements. Two techniques you can use in Python are filtering and mapping. **Filtering** a list is a way of retaining only those elements that meet a specific condition. This can be accomplished by using a for-loop that contains an if-statement or by using a for-loop within square brackets. **Figure 8-22** shows both the manual and list comprehension approaches to selecting even numbers from a list.

```
evens = []
for i in range(100):
    if i % 2 == 0:
        evens.append(i)
print("Manual even numbers:")
print(evens)
print()


evens_LC = [i for i in range(100) if i % 2 == 0]
print("List comprehension even numbers:")
print(evens_LC)
print()
OUTPUT:
Manual even numbers:
[0, 2, 4, 6, 8, 10, 12, 14, 16, 18, 20, 22, 24, 26, 28, 30,
32, 34, 36, 38, 40, 42, 44, 46, 48, 50, 52, 54, 56, 58, 60,
62, 64, 66, 68, 70, 72, 74, 76, 78, 80, 82, 84, 86, 88, 90,
92, 94, 96, 98]


List comprehension even numbers:
[0, 2, 4, 6, 8, 10, 12, 14, 16, 18, 20, 22, 24, 26, 28, 30,
32, 34, 36, 38, 40, 42, 44, 46, 48, 50, 52, 54, 56, 58, 60,
62, 64, 66, 68, 70, 72, 74, 76, 78, 80, 82, 84, 86, 88, 90,
92, 94, 96, 98]
```

Figure 8-22   Two ways to create a list of even numbers

When working with data, you may want to apply the same behavior to each value. For example, you might want to find the absolute value of each number or the string equivalent of each number. You achieve this behavior by mapping a function or programming statement onto each element in a list. **Mapping** a list involves using a programming statement in addition to the for-loop within square brackets. **Figure 8-23** shows how to double each element in a list manually and with list comprehension.

```
doubled = []
for i in range(50):
    doubled.append(i * 2)
print("Manual doubled numbers:")
print(doubled)
print()
doubled_LC = [i * 2 for i in range(50)]
```

Figure 8-23   Two ways to create lists of doubled numbers

```
print("List comprehension doubled numbers:")

print(doubled_LC)

print()

OUTPUT:

Manual doubled numbers:

[0,  2,  4,  6,  8,  10,  12,  14,  16,  18,  20,  22,  24,  26,  28,  30,
32,  34,  36,  38,  40,  42,  44,  46,  48,  50,  52,  54,  56,  58,  60,
62,  64,  66,  68,  70,  72,  74,  76,  78,  80,  82,  84,  86,  88,  90,
92,  94,  96,  98]


List comprehension doubled numbers:

[0,  2,  4,  6,  8,  10,  12,  14,  16,  18,  20,  22,  24,  26,  28,  30,
32,  34,  36,  38,  40,  42,  44,  46,  48,  50,  52,  54,  56,  58,  60,
62,  64,  66,  68,  70,  72,  74,  76,  78,  80,  82,  84,  86,  88,  90,
92,  94,  96,  98]
```

Figure 8-23   Two ways to create lists of doubled numbers (Continued)

You can use mapping and filtering together. **Figure 8-24** shows how to triple each number while selecting only numbers divisible by 3.

```
result = []

for i in range(50):

    if i % 3 == 0:

        result.append(i * 3)

print("Manual tripling every third number:")

print(result)

print()


result_LC = [i * 3 for i in range(50) if i % 3 == 0]

print("List comprehension tripling every third number:")

print(result_LC)

print()

OUTPUT:

Manual tripling every third number:

[0, 9, 18, 27, 36, 45, 54, 63, 72, 81, 90, 99, 108, 117, 126, 135, 144]


List comprehension tripling every third number:

[0, 9, 18, 27, 36, 45, 54, 63, 72, 81, 90, 99, 108, 117, 126, 135, 144]
```

Figure 8-24   Two ways to create lists when tripling every third number

Q What should I do if I want to map complicated behavior to elements in a list?

A You can use any function in list comprehension, including ones you define yourself. For example, you could define a function called `my_mapping()` and then use it in list comprehension: `[my_mapping(x) for x in numbers]`.

8.6 Two-Dimensional Lists

Two-Dimensional List Basics (8.6.1, 8.6.2, 8.6.3)

A tic-tac-toe board is a two-dimensional list that has multiple rows and columns. Conceptually, two-dimensional lists appear to be tables, grids, or matrices. Each cell in a two-dimensional list is referenced by two index values: one to indicate the row and one to indicate the column, as shown in **Figure 8-25.**

	Column 0	Column 1	Column 2
Row 0	" " [0][0]	"O" [0][1]	"X" [0][2]
Row 1	"O" [1][0]	"O" [1][1]	" " [1][2]
Row 2	"X" [2][0]	" " [2][1]	"X" [2][2]

Figure 8-25   Two-dimensional list indexes

Q If the tic-tac-toe board in Figure 8-25 is represented by a two-dimensional list called `board`, how would you refer to the cell in the middle column and bottom row?

A The last row is row 2, and the middle column is 1. Using two indexes, the bottom-middle cell is `board[2][1]`.

Although a two-dimensional list appears to be a grid of rows and columns, you can think of it as a list that contains lists. Anything you can do with a one-dimensional list you can do to two-dimensional lists. Each element in a list is a variable, and each variable can be a list. **Figure 8-26** can help you visualize the layout.

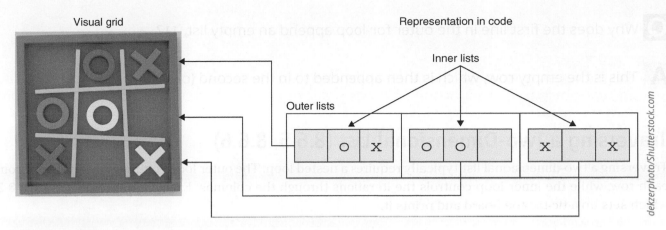

Figure 8-26 A two-dimensional list is a list that contains lists

Initialize a Two-Dimensional List (8.6.4)

In Python, you can declare a two-dimensional list using nested square brackets. It's the same as if each element in a one-dimensional list were also a list. The following code declares a two-dimensional list with three rows and three columns. The indentation and new lines are optional but help visualize the two-dimensional structure. Note the comma after each internal list.

```
grid_of_numbers = [[1, 2, 3],
                   [4, 5, 6],
                   [7, 8, 9]]
```

Figure 8-27 provides details for building a two-dimensional list from an empty list. All elements are set to 0. Note how `print()` will display the matrix for you.

```
matrix = []
rows = int(input("How many rows? "))
columns = int(input("How many columns? "))
for r in range(rows):
    matrix.append([])
    for c in range(columns):
        matrix[r].append(0)
print(matrix)
OUTPUT:
How many rows? 3
How many columns? 4
[[0, 0, 0, 0], [0, 0, 0, 0], [0, 0, 0, 0]]
```

Figure 8-27 Building a two-dimensional list

Q Why does the first line in the outer for-loop append an empty list, `[]`?

A This is the empty row, which is then appended to in the second (or inner) for-loop.

Traversing a Two-Dimensional List (8.6.5, 8.6.6)

Traversing a two-dimensional list typically requires a nested loop. The outer loop controls the iteration through each row, while the inner loop controls the iterations through the columns. Examine the code in **Figure 8-28**, which sets up a tic-tac-toe board and prints it.

```
board = [[" ", "O", "X"],

         ["O", "O", " "],

         ["X", " ", "X"]]


for i in range(len(board)):
    for j in range(len(board[i])):
        print(board[i][j], end="")
    print()
OUTPUT:
 OX
OO
X X
```

Figure 8-28   Printing a two-dimensional list

For **board**, the outer loop begins in row 0. As the inner loop iterates over each column in that row, cells with the following indexes are printed:

`[0] [0]   [0] [1]   [0] [2]`

Next, the loop outputs the values in row 1. These cells have the following indexes:

`[1] [0]   [1] [1]   [1] [2]`

Finally, the cells in the last row have the following indexes:

`[2] [0]   [2] [1]   [2] [2]`

When coding list output beyond what `print()` provides, you can add formatting parameters to align the output values. The `join()` method will "glue" together iterative sequences of strings. If your list contains strings already, you could use the following syntax to join each element in the list together with a space:

`" ".join(letters)`

Enter the joining string as the first part, followed by the method name (`.join`), and then the iterative sequence (your list) inside the parentheses to be passed as a parameter to `join()`. If your list contains numbers, you can use list comprehension and mapping to convert each element to a string before joining the elements:

`" ".join([str(x) for x in numbers])`

Using the mapping syntax creates a copy of each element in the list, but as a string. **Figure 8-29** shows how to use this pattern with a two-dimensional list. Vertical bars are added between the spaces for visibility.

```
board = [[" ", "O", "X"],
         ["O", "O", " "],
         ["X", " ", "X"]]
print("\n".join(["|".join(row) for row in board]))
OUTPUT:
 |O|X
O|O|
X| |X
```

Figure 8-29   Using join and list comprehension to print a two-dimensional list

The Tic-Tac-Toe Game (8.6.7, 8.6.8)

A game in tic-tac-toe is considered won when three spots in a row, column, or diagonal contain the same symbol. Figures 8-28 and 8-29 created a variable named **board** that contained spaces, Xs, and Os. To make a move in the game, the player needs to select a row and column in which to place their symbol. **Figure 8-30** shows a blank board and how you might begin to structure this game.

```
board = [[" ", " ", " "],
         [" ", " ", " "],
         [" ", " ", " "]]

print("\n".join(["|".join(row) for row in board]))

rowX = int(input("Player X row: "))
colX = int(input("Player X column: "))
board[rowX][colX] = "X"
print("\n".join(["|".join(row) for row in board]))

rowO = int(input("Player O row: "))
colO = int(input("Player O column: "))
board[rowO][colO] = "O"
print("\n".join(["|".join(row) for row in board]))
OUTPUT:
 | |
```

Figure 8-30   Part of a game of tic-tac-toe

```
   | |
   | |
Player X row: 0 [Enter]
Player X column: 2 [Enter]
   | |X

   | |

   | |
Player O row: 1 [Enter]
Player O column: 0 [Enter]
   | |X

O| |

   | |
```

Figure 8-30 Part of a game of tic-tac-toe (Continued)

Q Does the code in Figure 8-30 play a full game?

A No, it only reads two turns. To complete a full game, the game would need to use a looping structure to run until a winning move is detected somewhere on the board.

When you design programs that handle two-dimensional lists, use decomposition techniques to break down the algorithm into manageable chunks. For example, you can work out the algorithm for a one-dimensional list first, and then adapt it for a two-dimensional list.

A winning combination can occur in many places on a tic-tac-toe board, but the logic for each winning orientation is the same: Do the symbols in all three spots in a line match? If you had one variable, **row**, which represented a row of the board, detecting a winning combination in that row might look like **row[0] == row[1] and row[1] == row[2]**. Replacing the variable **row** with a two-dimensional variable, **board**, and accessing the first row will convert this one-dimensional logic to two-dimensional logic. **Figure 8-31** sets up a game board with some Xs and Os along with an attempt to detect a winning move horizontally on the first row.

```
board = [[" ", " ", " "],
         ["O", "O", "X"],
         ["X", "X", "O"]]


print("\n".join(["|".join(row) for row in board]))


if board[0][0] == board[0][1] and board[0][1] == board[0][2]:
```

Figure 8-31 An attempt to detect a winning move on the top row

```
        print("There is a winning combination on the top row!")
else:
        print("No winning combinations yet!")
OUTPUT:
 | |
O|O|X
X|X|O
There is a winning combination on the top row!
```

Figure 8-31 An attempt to detect a winning move on the top row (Continued)

Q Why does the game detect a winning move when the top row is empty?

A The logical expression inside the if-statement only checks to see if the three characters are the same, not if they are X or O. Three spaces are all equal to each other.

To account for empty spaces, you can check one of the locations on the board to see if it isn't empty first before comparing it to the remaining spaces. **Figure 8-32** has the corrected logic.

```
board = [[" ", " ", " "],
         ["O", "O", "X"],
         ["X", "X", "O"]]


print("\n".join(["|".join(row) for row in board]))


if board[0][0] != " " and board[0][0] == board[0][1] and
board[0][1] == board[0][2]:
        print("There is a winning combination on the top row!")
else:
        print("No winning combinations yet!")
OUTPUT:
 | |
O|O|X
X|X|O
No winning combinations yet!
```

Figure 8-32 Another attempt to detect a winning move on the top row

8.7 Dictionaries

Dictionary Basics (8.7.1, 8.7.2, 8.7.3, 8.7.4)

With lists, you use a number (an index) to reference the values stored, but sometimes the number is hard to remember. Suppose you're storing the tic-tac-toe scores for your friends. You could try to use a list to store the scores, as in **Figure 8-33**. You would create a list with the scores and variables representing an index for each friend's score.

```
mandy_index = 0
fernando_index = 1
jessica_index = 2
prateek_index = 3

scores = [2,4,1,1]

print("Mandy's score:", scores[mandy_index])
print("Fernando's score:", scores[fernando_index])
print("Jessica's score:", scores[jessica_index])
print("Prateek's score:", scores[prateek_index])
OUTPUT:
Mandy's score: 2
Fernando's score: 4
Jessica's score: 1
Prateek's score: 1
```

Figure 8-33   Keeping track of scores with a list

This approach technically works but is tiresome to maintain. Every time someone new joins your group of friends, you have to create a new variable to associate with the new friend. If someone leaves the group (for example, if Mandy moves across country and can no longer participate in the tic-tac-toe tournaments), you'd have to change the index for everyone listed after her. Fernando's index would change to 0, Jessica's index would change to 1, and Prateek's index would change to 2. To avoid this kind of programming overhead with a list, you could use a dictionary instead.

A **dictionary** is a data structure like a list, but instead of using numbers as references to the data, you can use strings. To create a dictionary in Python, you enclose the dictionary values in curly braces { } instead of the square brackets used for lists.

When creating a dictionary, you need to provide two values for each entry: the **value** to store and a **key** to reference the entry. The key is what you use to look up values stored in a dictionary and is usually a string, unlike the integer index for lists. Using a dictionary, the score set from Figure 8-33 becomes the code in **Figure 8-34**.

```
scores = {"mandy": 2,
          "fernando": 4,
          "jessica": 1,
          "prateek": 1}


print("Mandy's score:", scores["mandy"])
print("Fernando's score:", scores["fernando"])
print("Jessica's score:", scores["jessica"])
print("Prateek's score:", scores["prateek"])
OUTPUT:
Mandy's score: 2
Fernando's score: 4
Jessica's score: 1
Prateek's score: 1
```

Figure 8-34   Keeping track of scores with a dictionary

Instead of using index variables, the code in Figure 8-34 uses string keys in a dictionary. To initialize an empty dictionary, you can use empty curly braces, as in {}, or you can provide comma-separated key and value pairs. Each key and value pair includes a colon (:) symbol, where the left side of the colon is the key, and the right side is the value. Accessing values from a dictionary is just like using a list, except you specify the key instead of an index. To print Fernando's score, you write `print(scores["fernando"])`. Trying to use a string that is not in the dictionary causes an error. **Figure 8-35** shows code that attempts to print Jessica's and Mandy's score. However, because Mandy's name is misspelled, an error occurs.

```
scores = {"mandy": 2,
          "fernando": 4,
          "jessica": 1,
          "prateek": 1}


print("Jessica's score:", scores["jessica"])
print("Mandy's score:", scores["mamdy"])
OUTPUT:
Jessica's score: 1
Traceback (most recent call last):
  File "highScores.py", line 7, in <module>
    print("Mandy's score:", scores["mamdy"])
KeyError: 'mamdy'
```

Figure 8-35   Trying to access a key that isn't in the dictionary results in an
error

Dictionary Access (8.7.5, 8.7.6)

You can print a dictionary directly, just as you can with a list. The dictionary will appear in the same format as when initialized: curly braces around key and value pairs, with a comma separating each key and value pair, and a colon separating each key and value within the pair. Python dictionaries also let you access the keys as an iterative sequence. **Figure 8-36** uses the **keys()** method to produce all the keys stored in **scores**.

```
scores = {"mandy": 2,
            "fernando": 4,
            "jessica": 1,
            "prateek": 1}


keys = scores.keys()


print("Keys:", ", ".join(keys))
OUTPUT:
Keys: mandy, fernando, jessica, prateek
```

Figure 8-36   The keys() method returns the keys of the dictionary

You can iterate over the returned sequence from **keys()** with a for-loop. Doing so gives you greater control over visiting each key stored in the dictionary, and you can use it to print the value associated with that key. **Figure 8-37** uses the square brackets to access each value for each key in **keys()**.

```
scores = {"mandy": 2,
            "fernando": 4,
            "jessica": 1,
            "prateek": 1}


for key in scores.keys():
    print("Name, score:", key + ",", scores[key])
OUTPUT:
Name, score: mandy, 2
Name, score: fernando, 4
Name, score: jessica, 1
Name, score: prateek, 1
```

Figure 8-37   Using a for-loop to iterate over the keys and values in a dictionary

Dictionary Modification (8.7.7, 8.7.8, 8.7.9)

You can add a new friend to your scores dictionary without much coding. To create a new dictionary entry, use a unique key along with an assignment. When you assign a value to a new key, you create the entry. In contrast to trying to access the value for a key that does not exist and causing an error, assigning a value for a key that does not exist results in a new entry. Adding a new friend via input is shown in **Figure 8-38**. The input for the name is **"george"**, which is not a key in the **scores** dictionary. When the **scores[name]** = **score** statement is executed, a new key/value pair is added to the dictionary.

```
scores = {"mandy": 2,
          "fernando": 4,
          "jessica": 1,
          "prateek": 1}


name = input("Enter your name: ")
score = int(input("Enter your score: "))


scores[name] = score


for key in scores.keys():
    print("Name, score:", key + ",", scores[key])
OUTPUT:
Enter your name: George [Enter]
Enter your score: 0 [Enter]
Name, score: mandy, 2
Name, score: fernando, 4
Name, score: jessica, 1
Name, score: prateek, 1
Name, score: george, 0
```

Figure 8-38   Assignment with a nonexistent key adds the key and value pair to the dictionary

In dictionaries, only one value can be associated with each key. You can't have two or more identical keys. Using an assignment statement with a key that already exists in the dictionary will overwrite or update the value associated with that key. **Figure 8-39** has the same code as Figure 8-38, but the output shows what happens when you use a name that is already stored in **scores**. The input for the name is **"jessica"**, which is already in the **scores** dictionary. When the assignment statement is run, the value associated with the key **"jessica"** is updated to 3. If you have two friends named Jessica, you need to give them unique keys, such as **"jessicaA"** and **"jessicaJ"**.

```
scores = {"mandy": 2,
          "fernando": 4,
          "jessica": 1,
          "prateek": 1}
```

Figure 8-39   Assignment with an existing key updates the value in the dictionary for that key

```
name = input("Enter your name: ")
score = int(input("Enter your score: "))


scores[name] = score


for key in scores.keys():
    print("Name, score:", key + ",", scores[key])
```
OUTPUT:

Enter your name: Jessica [Enter]

Enter your score: 3 [Enter]

Name, score: mandy, 2

Name, score: fernando, 4

Name, score: jessica, 3

Name, score: prateek, 1

Figure 8-39 Assignment with an existing key updates the value in the dictionary for that key (Continued)

When Mandy moves away and no longer participates in the tic-tac-toe scoreboard, use the **pop()** method to remove a key from the dictionary. The method has one required argument—the key you want to remove—and modifies the dictionary. The **pop()** method does not return anything, so to see the changes, you need to print the dictionary. **Figure 8-40** shows how to remove Mandy from the dictionary (after a tearful goodbye in person).

```
scores = {"mandy": 2,
          "fernando": 4,
          "jessica": 1,
          "prateek": 1}


scores.pop("mandy")


for key in scores.keys():
    print("Name, score:", key + ",", scores[key])
```
OUTPUT:

Name, score: fernando, 4

Name, score: jessica, 1

Name, score: prateek, 1

Figure 8-40 The pop() method removes a key and value pair from a dictionary

Summary

- A list is a data structure that stores a collection of elements. Lists are also classified as composite data types because they are constructed from primitive data types, such as integers or characters.
- Lists are heterogeneous, ordered, and infinite. They have a variety of use cases for working with collections of data.
- Programmers typically work with one-dimensional and two-dimensional lists. A one-dimensional list is linear. A two-dimensional list has rows and columns that form a grid, or matrix.
- In program code, each element of a list is identified by an index value enclosed in brackets. The index can be positive or negative, counting from the front or back of the list, respectively.
- One-dimensional list elements have one index. Two-dimensional list elements have a row index and a column index. Index errors in program code are common but are easy to identify and correct.
- Accessing each list element in sequence is called traversing a list. Loops are typically used to traverse lists. Lists can be index-based or element-based.
- A single loop can traverse a one-dimensional list. A nested loop is required to traverse a two-dimensional list.
- Common list operations include outputting elements, changing elements, searching for elements, inputting elements at runtime, and summing elements.
- Dictionaries are like lists but use strings as keys instead of numbers as indexes. To specify a dictionary, store key and value pairs stored within curly braces.
- Traversing a dictionary uses the **keys()** method, which returns an iterative sequence of all keys in a dictionary.
- Using an assignment statement either adds a new key and value pair to the dictionary if the key is not already in the dictionary or updates the value associated with the key if the key is in the dictionary.

Key Terms

dictionary	index-based traversal	mapping
element-based traversal	key	one-dimensional list
filtering	list	traversing a list
heterogeneous	list comprehension	two-dimensional list
index error	list index	value

Module

9

Functions

Learning Objectives:

9.1 Function Basics

9.1.1 Differentiate between built-in functions, imported functions, and programmer-defined functions.

9.1.2 Associate functions with modular programming.

9.1.3 State the purpose of a function call.

9.1.4 Trace the flow of a program that includes programmer-defined functions.

9.1.5 State the advantages of programmer-defined functions.

9.1.6 Provide an example of a programmer-defined function.

9.2 Void Functions

9.2.1 Describe the key characteristics of a void function.

9.2.2 Compare the naming conventions for functions with those of variables.

9.2.3 Identify the components in the declaration and body of a void function.

9.2.4 Identify functions and function calls in source code.

9.2.5 Identify functions and function calls in pseudocode.

9.3 Functions with Parameters

9.3.1 Explain the purpose of function parameters in a function declaration.

9.3.2 Identify the arguments in a function call.

9.3.3 Differentiate arguments from parameters.

9.3.4 Identify the correspondence between the arguments in a function call and the parameters declared in a function declaration.

9.3.5 Trace data as it is handed off from a function call to a function.

9.4 Return Values

9.4.1 State the purpose of a function's return value.

9.4.2 Compose an assignment statement that collects a return value in a variable.

9.4.3 Trace the logic of a program that passes values to a function and returns a value to the main program.

9.4.4 Show how two different values can be returned at the same time.

9.4.5 Define the term "function signature" and identify examples.

9.4.6 Identify default parameters and their use.

9.5 Scope

9.5.1 Explain the concept of scope as it relates to variables in functions.

9.5.2 Explain the difference between global and local variables.

9.5.3 Declare global and local variables.

9.5.4 Identify global and local variables in code and state best practices for their use.

9.5.5 Explain the use of the keyword `global`.

9.5.6 Explain the meaning of "pass by value" in the context of functions.

9.5.7 Explain the meaning of "pass by reference" in the context of functions.

9.1 Function Basics

Function Classifications (9.1.1)

Trivia night is a popular event at pizzerias (**Figure 9-1**), and players can brush up ahead of time with online games. Trivia's question-and-answer format provides a great use case for incorporating functions into your programs.

Figure 9-1   Pizza-night trivia

A function is a named block of program code that performs a specific task. Functions can be classified into three categories:

- *Built-in functions* are provided by a programming language, relieving you of the need to import modules. You've used Python's built-in `print()` function, but Python also includes basic math functions, such as `abs()` for finding the absolute value of a number. Built-in functions are colored `purple` in IDLE and throughout this text.
- *Imported functions* are packaged in modules. They are distributed with a programming environment but need to be explicitly added to a program using a statement, signaled by the keyword `import`. A random number generator is an example of an imported function that you can include in your programs.
- *Programmer-defined functions* are created by you, the programmer, to perform customized operations within a program. You can create these functions to modularize your programs and perform repetitive tasks.

Programmer-Defined Functions (9.1.2)

This module focuses on programmer-defined functions that you can create to perform a specific task, routine, operation, or process accessed by your main program. Suppose you're creating a trivia program. For each question, there is the user's answer and the correct answer. You could use a linear algorithm and check the answer after each question, like this:

```
score = 0

answer = input("Lake Chapala is the largest freshwater lake in which country? ")

if answer == "Mexico":

    print("Correct!\nYou earn 1 point.")

    score += 1

else:

    print("That is not correct.")
```

```
answer = input("Mac Gargan is the alter ego of what Spider-Man villain? ")
if answer == "Scorpion":
    print("Correct!\nYou earn 1 point.")
    score += 1
else:
    print("That is not correct.")
```

Notice that apart from the actual answers, "Mexico" and "Scorpion," the if-else logic to check the answers is the same pattern for each question. Eliminating that repetition is exactly where programmer-defined functions shine.

Flow of Execution (9.1.3, 9.1.4)

You can create a single function that is activated for every question to check the answer. The function can be triggered by a **function call** from multiple locations in a program. The flow of execution jumps to the function, performs the statements it contains, and then moves back to the previous execution path. **Figure 9-2** helps you visualize how functions affect the flow of program execution.

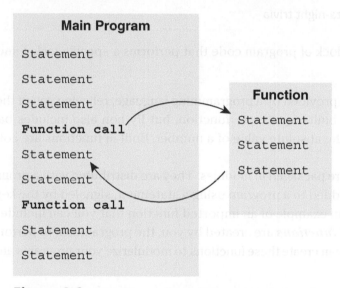

Figure 9-2   Function calls transfer execution to the specified function; flow returns to the previous execution path when the function is completed

Function Advantages (9.1.5, 9.1.6)

The trivia program is one use case for programmer-defined functions. Functions help you do the following:

- Modularize your code by grouping statements that perform each task.
- Simplify modifications because they are more likely to affect only the code in a function rather than statements scattered throughout the program.
- Reduce the amount of coding by creating blocks of code that can be reused multiple times in a program.
- Encapsulate code to simplify debugging.

Let's take a closer look at functions, starting with a simple example before working up to a more robust version that checks answers and scores trivia questions.

9.2 Void Functions

Void Function Basics (9.2.1, 9.2.2, 9.2.3, 9.2.4)

A **void function** is probably the simplest type of function because it performs a task, such as displaying a message or sum, without communicating with the main program. For example, you could create a void function for a trivia program that outputs a Welcome! message and rules at the start of the game. The keyword `def` signals to Python that the next section of code will be a function.

```
def welcome():

    print("Welcome to Trivia!")

    print("No fair looking online.")
```

This function, like all functions, begins with a one-line **function declaration** (or *function header*) that specifies its name and other essential descriptors. The **function name** is followed by parentheses and uses the same naming conventions as a variable. The **function body** is a block of statements that defines what the function does.

The two statements in the body of the `welcome()` function directly output messages. The messages are not returned to the main program. Because the function returns nothing to the main program, the function is void. **Figure 9-3** illustrates the components of a function.

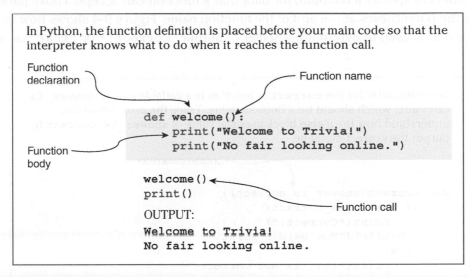

In Python, the function definition is placed before your main code so that the interpreter knows what to do when it reaches the function call.

Function declaration

Function name

```
def welcome():
    print("Welcome to Trivia!")
    print("No fair looking online.")
```

Function body

```
welcome()
print()
```

Function call

OUTPUT:
```
Welcome to Trivia!
No fair looking online.
```

Figure 9-3   Components of a function

Function Pseudocode (9.2.5)

Detecting functions in pseudocode can be tricky. The important thing to look for is behavior that is applied repeatedly to different data but behaves the same. Consider the following code outline:

```
Ask the first trivia question and obtain an answer.

Compare the inputted answer to the real answer and display an appropriate message.

Increase the score by 1 if the answer is correct.

Ask the second trivia question and obtain an answer.

Compare the inputted answer to the real answer and display an appropriate message.

Increase the score by 1 if the answer is correct.
```

The logic is the same between the first and second trivia questions. Note that two lines reference a "real answer," but the value of that real answer changes from one trivia question to the next. Sometimes you may need to write pseudocode that describes a function as "apply behavior on each item," indicating the same behavior should be repeated.

9.3 Functions with Parameters

Function Parameters (9.3.1)

What if you want to create a function that outputs **"Correct!"** when the answer is correct, but **"That is not correct."** when the answer is wrong? To output the appropriate message, the function needs to know if the answer is right or wrong. In this case, you can send data to a function. For example, you can send **True** to the function if the answer is correct but send **False** if the answer is wrong.

A function can use the data it receives to perform calculations, manipulate strings, control loops, output messages, and make decisions. A function with *parameters* uses data sent to the function as *arguments*. Let's explore the relationship between parameters and arguments.

Function parameters specify a template for data that a function can accept. Those parameters are listed as variables inside the parentheses at the end of the function name. **Figure 9-4** shows how to create a function with one parameter that is used to determine whether to output **"Correct!"** or **"That is not correct."**

The parameter for the **correct()** function is a variable named **answer_is_correct**, which should be a Boolean value. Trace the program so you understand how the if-else block uses the value of **answer_is_correct** to output the correct message.

Function parameter

```
def correct(answer_is_correct):
    if answer_is_correct:
        print("Correct!")
        print("You earn 1 point.")
    else:
        print("That is not correct.")
```

Figure 9-4   Function parameters

Q Is the function defined in Figure 9-4 a void function?

A Yes. A void function does not return information, but it can still receive information.

Function Arguments (9.3.2, 9.3.3)

How does a function get the value for a parameter? It receives the value from a function argument in the function call. A **function argument** is data that is *passed* to a function. For example, you could pass a Boolean value to the **correct()** function. Look for the function call and its argument in **Figure 9-5**.

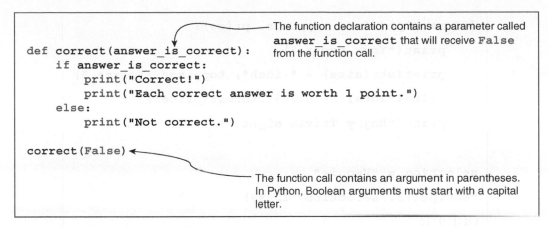

```
def correct(answer_is_correct):
    if answer_is_correct:
        print("Correct!")
        print("Each correct answer is worth 1 point.")
    else:
        print("Not correct.")

correct(False)
```

The function declaration contains a parameter called **answer_is_correct** that will receive **False** from the function call.

The function call contains an argument in parentheses. In Python, Boolean arguments must start with a capital letter.

Figure 9-5   Function arguments

Q What is the output of the program in Figure 9-5?

A The output is **"Not correct."**

The argument in the function call to **correct()** is a Boolean value, which is passed to the variable **answer_is_correct**. **Figure 9-6** can help you visualize this handoff.

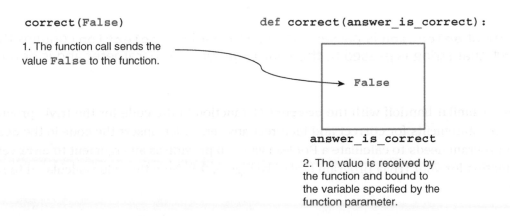

```
correct(False)                    def correct(answer_is_correct):
```

1. The function call sends the value **False** to the function.

False

answer_is_correct

2. The value is received by the function and bound to the variable specified by the function parameter.

Figure 9-6   The handoff copies the argument from the function call to the variable specified in the function declaration

The Handoff (9.3.4, 9.3.5)

The handoff between arguments and parameters is a powerful programming tool. Check out the function in **Figure 9-7** with its collection of parameters. Note that the function call can pass a variable, such as **topping**, as well as literals, such as **12** and **12.99**. When designing a parameter list, naming the parameters to represent their purpose, just like variables, is good coding practice.

```
def receipt(size, toppings, price):
    print("Your order:")
    print(str(size) + "-inch", toppings, "pizza.")
    print("Total ${:0.2f}".format(price))
    print("Enjoy Trivia night!")


selection = "Veggie"
receipt(12, selection, 12.99)
OUTPUT:
Your order:
12-inch Veggie pizza.
Total $12.99
Enjoy Trivia night!
```

Figure 9-7   Function with multiple parameters

Q In the program shown in Figure 9-7, which function argument is passed to the **toppings** function parameter?

A The argument **selection** is passed. Because the variable **selection** contains the string **"Veggie"**, that string is passed to the **toppings** function parameter and is printed on the receipt.

You can use a similar handoff with the **correct()** function in the code for the trivia program. Instead of writing the **print** statements for correct and incorrect answers twice, insert the code in the **correct()** function. The main program needs to calculate a Boolean value to provide as an argument to **correct()**. Using the **correct()** function for your trivia program looks like **Figure 9-8**. Note the value calculated to represent if the answer is correct.

```
def correct(answer_is_correct):
    if answer_is_correct:
        print("Correct!")
        print("Each correct answer is worth 1 point.")
    else:
        print("Not correct.")
```

Figure 9-8   Using **correct()** in the trivia program

```
score = 0
answer = input("Lake Chapala is the largest freshwater lake in which
country? ")
# Store the Boolean value representing if the answer is correct.
is_correct = answer == "Mexico"
correct(is_correct)
if is_correct:
    score += 1


answer = input("Mac Gargan is the alter ego of what Spider-Man
villain? ")
# Store the Boolean value representing if the answer is correct.
is_correct = answer == "Scorpion"
correct(is_correct)
if is_correct:
    score += 1
OUTPUT:
Lake Chapala is the largest freshwater lake in which country?
Mexico [Enter]
Correct!
Each correct answer is worth 1 point.
Mac Gargan is the alter ego of what Spider-Man villain? Doc Oc
[Enter]
Not correct.
```

Figure 9-8 Using `correct()` in the trivia program (Continued)

Q How many times does the code use the Boolean value stored in **is_correct** with each question asked?

A Twice—once outside of the function and once inside the **correct()** function call.

Testing the Boolean value twice means more work for you because you write the same if-statement in two locations. That is usually a signal that you could move some more code into the function. You could try moving the Boolean comparison into the **correct()** function, as shown in **Figure 9-9**.

```
def correct(answer_is_correct):
    if answer_is_correct:
        print("Correct!")
        print("Each correct answer is worth 1 point.")
        score += 1
    else:
        print("Not correct.")


score = 0
answer = input("Lake Chapala is the largest freshwater lake in which
country? ")
correct(answer == "Mexico")


answer = input("Mac Gargan is the alter ego of what Spider-Man
villain? ")
correct(answer == "Scorpion")
OUTPUT:
Lake Chapala is the largest freshwater lake in which country?
Mexico [Enter]
Correct!
Each correct answer is worth 1 point.
Traceback (most recent call last):
  File "9-9.py", line 11, in <module>
    correct(answer == "Mexico")
  File "9-9.py", line 5, in correct
    score += 1
UnboundLocalError:  local   variable   'score'   referenced   before
assignment
```

Figure 9-9   Cleaning up the code creates a problem

However, now there's a new problem. Within the function, an if-statement is used to increase the value of the **score** variable by 1. However, the **score** variable is defined outside of the function. This is a scope problem, which is explained in detail later. However, you can fix this without dealing with scope. You need to pass information back from the function, not just to it.

9.4 Return Values

Return Values (9.4.1, 9.4.2, 9.4.3)

In addition to passing data *to* a function, you can return data *from* a function. To do so, write a `return` statement at the end of the function. The data received, called a **return value**, can be used for calculations or other operations in the main program. You can think of return values like asking someone to find out something for you. You ask a person (function) to calculate the score and come back to you (return) the resulting score (return value).

With this in mind, the `correct()` function can be changed to both provide the output `"Correct!"` and return a `1` value to the main program if the answer is correct. If the answer is not correct, the program outputs `"That is not correct."` and returns a `0` value to the main program. The main program uses the return value to track the player's total score. **Figure 9-10** shows this revised code.

```
def correct(answer_is_correct):
    if answer_is_correct:
        print("Correct!")
        print("Each correct answer is worth 1 point.")
        return 1
    else:
        print("Not correct.")
        return 0


score = 0
answer = input("Lake Chapala is the largest freshwater lake
in which country? ")
score += correct(answer == "Mexico")


answer = input("Mac Gargan is the alter ego of what Spider-Man
villain? ")
score += correct(answer == "Scorpion")
OUTPUT:
Lake Chapala is the largest freshwater lake in which country?
Mexico [Enter]
Correct!
Each correct answer is worth 1 point.
Mac Gargan is the alter ego of what Spider-Man villain?
Doc Oc [Enter]
Not correct.
```

Figure 9-10   Using a return value

Trace through the code with the following walkthrough:

1. Suppose that the user answers **"Mexico"** to the first trivia question. **"Mexico"** is stored in the variable **answer**.
2. The statement **score += correct(answer == "Mexico")** calls the **correct()** function.
3. The function call passes one argument to the function: the Boolean comparison of **answer** and **"Mexico"**.
4. The function has one parameter: **answer_is_correct**.
5. **True** is stored in this parameter in this example.
6. Because the parameter stores **True**, the value **1** is returned.
7. The **1** is added to the value currently stored in **score**. Why? The statement **score += correct(answer == "Mexico")** adds the return value from the function to the variable called **score**.
8. In the main program, **1** is added to the score.

The concept embodied in the statement **score += correct(answer == "Mexico")** gets to the core advantage of functions. A function call that returns a value can be treated as if it were a value in the main program. The value **1** replaces the **correct(answer == "Mexico")** after the function call concludes with the **return** statement. If the Boolean value is **False**, then **0** is returned instead.

Now modify the code to display the correct answer if the user guesses wrong. You need more information inside **correct()**: the correct answer. The function will need two parameters, so change it to take the user's answer and the correct answer instead of one Boolean value. **Figure 9-11** details the code change.

```python
def correct(user_guess, correct_answer):
    if user_guess == correct_answer:
        print("Correct!")
        print("Each correct answer is worth 1 point.")
        return 1
    else:
        print("Not correct.")
        print("The correct answer was", correct_answer + ".")
        return 0


score = 0
answer = input("Lake Chapala is the largest freshwater lake in which
country? ")
score += correct(answer, "Mexico")


answer = input("Mac Gargan is the alter ego of what Spider-Man
villain? ")
score += correct(answer, "Scorpion")
```

Figure 9-11   Displaying the correct answer if the user's answer is wrong

```
print("Final score:", score)
```

OUTPUT:

Lake Chapala is the largest freshwater lake in which country?

Mexico [Enter]

Correct!

Each correct answer is worth 1 point.

Mac Gargan is the alter ego of what Spider-Man villain? Doc Oc

[Enter]

Not correct.

The correct answer was Scorpion.

Final score: 1

Figure 9-11   Displaying the correct answer if the user's answer is wrong (Continued)

Q To add another question to the trivia program, you can copy and paste the four lines of code for one of the current questions. What would you have to change in the pasted text?

A You would just have to change the text of the question and the correct answer.

In Python, every function returns something. Void functions return the value None, representing nothing returned. If you find you have a None value where you don't expect one, it may be that the function is missing a return statement.

Multiple Return Values (9.4.4)

Just as functions can have multiple inputs as a parameter list, you can also have multiple returned values. The syntax for returning multiple values is to separate them with commas in the return statement. Some examples:

```
return 5, 6
```

```
return price, tax, tip, total
```

To obtain the multiple returned values, assign variable names separated by commas to each return value in the same order they are returned. An example of the syntax:

```
first, second = returns_two_values()
```

In the context of a pizza parlor, suppose you want to make a function that, given a pizza type, returns the small, medium, and large prices. A small cheese pizza costs $7.99, a small veggie pizza costs $10.99, and any other small pizza costs $12.99. Upgrading to a medium adds $2 to the price, and upgrading to a large increases the price by $6. **Figure 9-12** shows one way to program this concept using multiple returned values.

```
def get_pizza_price(pizza_type):
    if pizza_type == "Cheese":
        small_price = 7.99
    elif pizza_type == "Veggie":
        small_price = 10.99
    else:
        small_price = 12.99

    medium_price = small_price + 2
    large_price = small_price + 6

    return small_price, medium_price, large_price

small, medium, large = get_pizza_price("Veggie")
print("Small:  ${:.2f}".format(small))
print("Medium: ${:.2f}".format(medium))
print("Large:  ${:.2f}".format(large))
OUTPUT:
Small:  $10.99
Medium: $12.99
Large:  $16.99
```

Figure 9-12 Multiple returned values

Function Signature (9.4.5, 9.4.6)

The **function signature** is what uniquely defines a function for the interpreter. The components of a function signature include the following:

- The keyword `def`
- The function name
- The function parameters (the **parameter list**)

As with variable names, you can't have two functions with the same name. Even if the parameter lists are different, each function needs a new name. **Figure 9-13** shows the keyword, name, and parameter of the function signature from Figure 9-12. The function name is `get_pizza_price` and the function parameter is `pizza_type`.

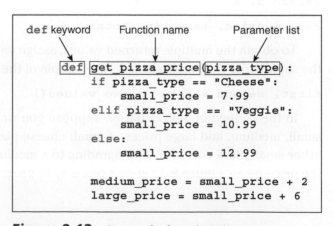

```
def keyword    Function name    Parameter list

def get_pizza_price(pizza_type):
    if pizza_type == "Cheese":
        small_price = 7.99
    elif pizza_type == "Veggie":
        small_price = 10.99
    else:
        small_price = 12.99

    medium_price = small_price + 2
    large_price = small_price + 6
```

Figure 9-13 Parts of a function signature

In the function signature's parameter list, you can provide values to use if the function is called without an argument for that parameter. For example, adding the medium price and large price increases to the `get_pizza_price()` function would make the function more useful, but increases programming overhead. To create a **default value** for a parameter, use the equals sign (=), similar to assignment. The value on the right of the equals sign is used only if the function is called without enough arguments. **Figure 9-14** shows this modification. It calls

```
def get_pizza_price(pizza_type, medium_increase=2, large_increase=6):

    if pizza_type == "Cheese":

        small_price = 7.99

    elif pizza_type == "Veggie":

        small_price = 10.99

    else:

        small_price = 12.99


    medium_price = small_price + medium_increase

    large_price = small_price + large_increase


    return small_price, medium_price, large_price

small, medium, large = get_pizza_price("Veggie")
print("Small:  ${:.2f}".format(small))
print("Medium: ${:.2f}".format(medium))
print("Large:  ${:.2f}".format(large))


small, medium, large = get_pizza_price("Veggie", 1, 2)
print("On Sale! Discount!")
print("Small:  ${:.2f}".format(small))
print("Medium: ${:.2f}".format(medium))
print("Large:  ${:.2f}".format(large))
OUTPUT:
Small:  $10.99
Medium: $12.99
Large:  $16.99
On Sale! Discount!
Small:  $10.99
Medium: $11.99
Large:  $12.99
```

Figure 9-14   Default parameters

`get_pizza_price()` for `"Veggie"` twice. The first function call uses the default values, and the second one overrides the default values by providing more arguments. Arguments are mapped left to right for each parameter in the parameter list. Any parameter without a default parameter has to come first in the parameter list, followed by any parameters with default values.

9.5 Scope

Scope Basics (9.5.1, 9.5.2, 9.5.3, 9.5.4, 9.5.5)

Here's a puzzler. Consider the following code snippet:

```
number = 5

def example(number):
    print(number)

example(12)

print(number)
```

What do you think the first output should be? Is it 5 or 12? What about the second number printed? The correct answer is that the output is 12, then 5. This is a conflict of scope. The parameter name **number** represents a different variable from the one named **number** outside of the function.

In the context of programming, **scope** refers to the visibility of program components, such as variables, to other parts of the program. In the **example()** function, the scope of the parameter **number** overwrote the outer variable with the same name.

Here's another scope problem. The following code will cause an error.

```
def example2():
    number = 5

example2()

print(number)
```

The variable **number** in the function **example2()** is only visible within that function. In general, variables and other components that are limited to a specific part of a program are referred to as having a local scope. The variable called **number** in the **example2()** function is a **local variable**.

In contrast, a **global variable** is accessible to an entire program. Global variables are defined outside of any function in the source code. Functions can access global variables without any hassle. **Figure 9-15** shows how code uses a global variable and crashes when it tries to use a local variable outside of its scope.

The following program contains a global variable called **external** and a local variable called **internal** in the function. The global variable can be accessed both inside and outside of the function **example()**. The local variable **internal** is defined in the function. If it is accessed outside of the function, it produces an error.

```
external = 1
```

Figure 9-15   Global and local variables

```
def example():

    internal = 2

    print(internal)

    print(external)


example()

print(external)

print(internal)


OUTPUT:

2

1

1

Traceback (most recent call last):

  File "9-13.py", line 10, in <module>

    print(internal)

NameError: name 'internal' is not defined
```

Rules and best practices:

- Global variables are defined at the beginning of a program, before functions, and before the main code of your program.
- Some programmers prefix global variables with **g** or **g_** to annotate that they are global.
- Variables declared within a function are automatically classified as local. No additional coding is necessary.
- Best practices avoid the use of global variables because they disrupt modularization, making programs more difficult to modify and debug.

Figure 9-15 Global and local variables (Continued)

It is possible to have two variables with the same name if they have different scopes. One variable could be global, but the other one local. Or the two variables could be declared in different functions. Local variables have the highest priority, then parameters, and then global variables, which have the lowest priority.

By default, Python assumes a variable is a new local-scope variable. If you try to modify a global variable and set it to a new value from within a function, the changes won't stick. See **Figure 9-16**.

```
external = 1


def example():

    internal = 2

    print("Internal inside function:", internal)

    external = 5

    print("External inside function:", external)


example()

print("External outside function:", external)

OUTPUT:

Internal inside function: 2

External inside function: 5

External outside function: 1
```

Figure 9-16   Incorrectly trying to modify a global variable within a function

Modifying a global variable inside a function requires some work. The keyword `global` followed by only the variable name signals to the interpreter that the variable identifier is global. **Figure 9-17** fixes the code from Figure 9-16.

```
external = 1


def example():

    internal = 2

    print("Internal inside function:", internal)

    global external

    external = 5

    print("External inside function:", external)


example()

print("External outside function:", external)

OUTPUT:

Internal inside function: 2

External inside function: 5

External outside function: 5
```

Figure 9-17   The keyword `global` signals the interpreter where to look

Pass by Value (9.5.6)

Consider the program in **Figure 9-18**. The program passes a number to a function, which then adds one to the parameter. What's weird is that this addition shows up inside the function, but after the function is over, so `number` contains the old value, **5**.

```
def add_one(number):

    print("Inside function, before addition:", number)

    number += 1

    print("Inside function, after addition:", number)


number = 5

print("Outside function, before function call:", number)

add_one(number)

print("Outside function, after function call:", number)
OUTPUT:
Outside function, before function call: 5

Inside function, before addition: 5

Inside function, after addition: 6

Outside function, after function call: 5
```

Figure 9-18 Two variables with different scopes though both are named `number`

In this case, the arguments passed to a function are copies of the data. In other words, when data is passed as an argument to a function, a copy of that data is assigned to the function's parameter, which can then be used within the function without affecting the original source of the data. The term **pass by value** refers to when data is passed as a copy of an argument to a function. The original variable retains its data. The variable in a function gets a copy of the data. Even if the main program variable and the function variable have the same name, any changes to the copy of the data only affect the variable in the function.

If you want to change the value of `number` in the main program, change the calling statement to include an assignment, and change `add_one()` to return the new value:

```
number = add_one(number)
```

The assignment statement explicitly changes the value of the variable `number` in the main program. To avoid confusion about the variables in the main program and the variables in a function, it is best to avoid using the same identifiers for arguments and parameters.

Pass by Reference (9.5.7)

Some variable types are not passed by value in Python. Instead, a variable is passed so that changes made to its internal structure persist after the function ends. The term **pass by reference** refers to when data is passed as a memory address into a function's argument. Rather than receive a copy of the data, the function receives a reference to the source of the data itself, and changing the data within the function will also change the data outside of the function. Lists are one type passed by reference, as well as any user-defined objects (covered in another module). **Figure 9-19** shows a program using a list as a parameter and changing its contents.

```
def add_one_to_first_number(number_list):
    print("Inside function, before addition:",
          number_list)
    number_list[0] += 1
    print("Inside function, after addition:",
          number_list)


number_list = [10,5,4,2,6]
print("Outside function, before function call:",
      number_list)
add_one_to_first_number(number_list)
print("Outside function, after function call:",
      number_list)
OUTPUT:
Outside function, before function call: [10, 5, 4, 2, 6]
Inside function, before addition: [10, 5, 4, 2, 6]
Inside function, after addition: [11, 5, 4, 2, 6]
Outside function, after function call: [11, 5, 4, 2, 6]
```

Figure 9-19   Changes to lists inside functions persist outside of the function due to pass by reference

Passing by reference saves memory space because a copy of the variable is not needed. Some computational time is also saved. In modern computers loaded with memory and equipped with fast processors, those savings are small compared to the potential for accidentally changing the value of a variable by calling a function. Passing by reference should be reserved for special situations in programs with clearly constrained algorithms.

Summary

- A function is a named block of program code that performs a specific task.
- Built-in functions are always available; you can use them without importing modules, libraries, packages, or other components.
- Imported functions are packaged in libraries and modules. They are typically distributed with a programming environment but need to be explicitly added to a program using the keyword `import`.
- Programmer-defined functions are created by you, the programmer, to perform customized operations within a program. Functions start with the keyword `def`.
- Functions help programmers modularize code by grouping statements that perform a specific task.
- Functions reduce coding overhead by creating blocks of code that can be reused multiple times in a program.
- Functions help programmers debug efficiently because code is encapsulated in discrete groups.

- A function declaration includes the function name and parameters.
- The body of a function contains the statements that define what the function does and may also include a `return` statement.
- Functions can be triggered by a function call from multiple locations in a program. A function call may include function arguments that are passed to the parameters of a function.
- Functions can send data back to the calling module by means of a `return` statement.
- Variables in a function have a different scope from the variables in the main program module or other functions. The scope of variables declared in a function have a local scope, making them visible only within the function. Variables with a global scope are visible throughout the entire program.
- In the context of functions, pass by value refers to a function call that passes a copy of an argument to a function.
- Pass by reference refers to a function call that passes a memory location to the variable that holds the argument.

Key Terms

default value	function parameters	pass by value
function argument	function signature	return value
function body	global variable	scope
function call	local variable	void function
function declaration	parameter list	
function name	pass by reference	

Module 10

Exceptions

Learning Objectives:

10.1 Defining Exceptions

Errors in Code (10.1.1, 10.1.2, 10.1.3)

A fact of life for you as a programmer is that you must debug code to find and fix errors. In fact, you have to debug a lot of code. When you do, look for logic errors and runtime errors. **Logic errors** are probably the most familiar to you: Part of the code is incorrect, but it still runs and produces output. For example, you might be checking for numbers greater than zero when you mean to check for numbers less than zero. You typically find logic errors by carefully reading the code.

Logic errors are different from semantic errors, which are errors caught by the compiler. As you know, a runtime error is a flaw in a program that causes it to fail during execution.

Another type of problem can interrupt a program as it is running. Suppose you are coding part of a video game that includes a character named Iceabella. She can make ice cream for you and other users, as long as you bring her enough ice and cream (see **Figure 10-1**). If you ask the character for ice cream before giving her any cream, what should she do? Should she try to create ice cream anyway? Should she close down her ice cream machine? Or should she tell you what's wrong so you can fix it?

home_sweet_home/Shutterstock.com
Volhah/Shutterstock.com

Figure 10-1   Ice cream making video game

Ideally, when a program can't perform a task as instructed, it should gracefully inform the user. If Iceabella can create ice cream only if she is given cream first, then the program must make sure those conditions are met before Iceabella attempts to make ice cream. For example, the program can display a message reminding you that Iceabella needs cream and then wait for you to supply it.

Code also has preconditions, or assumptions that need to be true for the code to work. If the preconditions aren't met, the code should fail gracefully instead of crashing, even in unusual situations.

In programming, an unusual situation is called an **exception**, an unexpected event that occurs as the program runs and prevents the program from completing execution. The unusual situation is said to trigger the exception and interrupt normal program flow.

Whereas an error is a design flaw that debugging should fix, an exception prevents part of a program from solving a problem on its own. The exception provides a way for one part of a program to ask for help from another part of the program. **Figure 10-2** shows the workflow communication between two program parts.

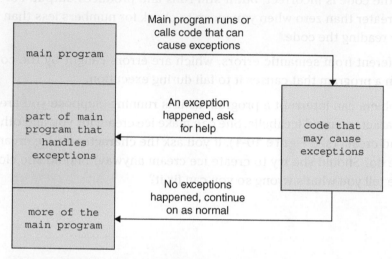

Figure 10-2 Communication between normal code and code with exceptions

When the main program encounters code that may cause an exception, the program flow can continue in the following two ways:

- If no exceptions occur, the flow can return a result to the main program, if one was requested.
- If an exception occurs, the code calls for help and is diverted to the part of the main program that handles exceptions. That part of the program resolves the exception, and the program continues running.

A robust, well-written program checks for exceptions in situations where it might not otherwise continue, and then responds to the exceptions appropriately. That means you as a programmer must check for possible exceptions and write code to handle them. The program can then detect unexpected errors and manage them without letting an unwanted situation bring the program to a halt.

Exception Types (10.1.4, 10.1.5, 10.1.6, 10.1.7)

Programmers talk about exceptions as events, but an exception can also be a package of information indicating what went wrong. This information can be as simple as a numerical code or string description, or more complicated bundles of information including the state of the program when the exception occurred and the exception type.

Programming languages provide general exceptions, which can be used for all problems, but don't provide context that would help solve the problems. These nonspecific exceptions are called **default exceptions**. Using default exceptions makes it easier to catch a problem but harder to know how to fix it. "Something bad happened" doesn't help you as much as "I have no cream for the ice cream." However, default exceptions can be useful to catch situations you may not realize will happen, such as operating system errors. When you receive an error message such as "Unknown error occurred," the program is using a default exception. The program detected the exception but did not correct it other than letting you know it happened.

Specific exception types represent specific kinds of errors. They tell programmers the type of problem that happened, allowing them to find solutions faster. For example, if you receive an error message such as "Invalid parameter type," the problem obviously has something to do with a parameter being the wrong type. To fix this problem, you need to examine the parameters.

For example, in the ice cream video game, Iceabella stating that she can't make ice cream doesn't help you understand how to fix the problem. If she tells you she needs cream first, you know you need to give her cream. Specific exception types narrow the possible ways to solve the problem and let the program return to its normal flow.

Many specific exceptions, which differ by programming language, are available to programmers. **Figure 10-3** shows some of the most common exception types you might need in Python.

Type	Situation	Example
`IndexError`	An index is outside an appropriate range	`numbers = []` `numbers[2]`
`NotImplementedError`	A function or method was not implemented but other program code attempts to run it	`nonexistent_function()`
`RuntimeError`	An error happens that does not fit any other exception type	`set_color("cat")`
`TypeError`	A function or method is given an argument that has an incorrect type	`square_root("cat")` `set_name(5)`
`ValueError`	A function or method is given an argument that has an incorrect value	`square_root(-5)` `set_age(-12)`
`ZeroDivisionError`	An attempt to divide by zero was made	`x = 4 / 0`

Figure 10-3 Common exceptions

Programming languages provide references, usually online, that define their exception types. It is the responsibility of a programmer to know, or know how to look up, the types of exceptions available in the language they use. Most programming languages also allow you to create your own exception types for special situations or to provide extra information about the error that happened. For example, with Iceabella, you might make a specific **NoIceCream** exception or provide a message to a **RuntimeError** exception.

Q Should you create a new exception or use one of Python's provided exceptions?

A Generally the exceptions Python provides work for any problem you run into. Creating your own exception is useful only rarely for situations specific to your program.

10.2 Dealing with Exceptions

Handling Others' Exceptions (10.2.1, 10.2.2)

When code causes an exception, programmers say the code "raises" or "throws" an exception. Programmers make their code **raise** exceptions when certain conditions are true. Handling the exception is more important than investigating why it was raised in the first place. If Iceabella has no cream, it doesn't matter if someone took the cream or that Iceabella used all the cream earlier. The problem is that Iceabella needs more cream before she can make ice cream. To handle raised exceptions, all you need to know is what is wrong so you can fix the problem.

Suppose you are trying to program an image editor, which needs to open image files. In Python, a module named Python Image Library (PIL) is designed to display images. The normal flow of a program assumes everything works correctly: The program loads an image to the screen, and then lets users modify the image and save it on a storage device.

What should your program do if it can't load the image for some reason? For example, the program might not be able to find the image file, or the file might not be in the correct format. You could take a few approaches to deal with the problem, depending on the tools available in the library of functions you are using, such as displaying an error message or a default image. Instead of dictating your approach, the programmer of the PIL module lets you control your program by raising an exception instead of trying to fix it for you. You can write code to detect the exception and handle it as you decide is best.

The code to detect an exception uses a logical control structure similar to an if-else block. The logical flow of the program changes depending on whether an exception occurs. Generally, to work with exceptions, programs **try** to do something and catch any exceptions that were raised in the code.

Try and Except Blocks (10.2.3, 10.2.4, 10.2.5, 10.2.6)

You can use a program flow control for trying and catching exceptions. The program flow control is called a **try-except block**. (Some languages refer to this program flow control as a *try-catch block*.) A try-except block has two parts: the **try** block and the **except** block. The **try** code attempts to proceed as if conditions are normal and nothing disrupts the program flow. If an exception is raised in the **try** block, the program flow moves to the **except** block. **Figure 10-4** shows a diagram of the flow for a try-except block.

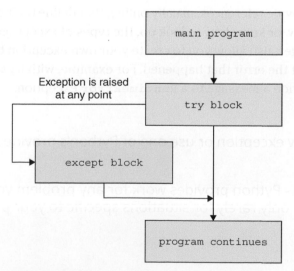

Figure 10-4 Try-except block logic flow

If no exception is raised, then the program executes normally through the `try` block. If an exception is raised in the `try` block, however, the program stops executing code in the `try` block and jumps to the start of the `except` block.

Unlike an if-else statement, a `try` block stops executing code when it detects an exception. The `except` block can fix the problem or stop the program entirely. Fixing the problem can take many forms, including using default values to fill in the missing information, displaying an error message, or logging the error in a file.

Figure 10-5 shows Python code for a simple example of calling two functions. Assume that the functions are programmed elsewhere, and each function might raise an exception. The arrows show what direction the program takes at each point.

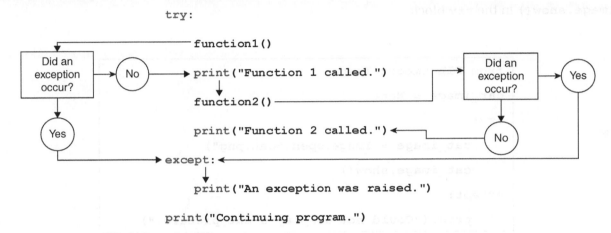

Figure 10-5   Python code flow example

In Figure 10-5, `function1` and `function2` can each raise an exception. If either function call triggers an exception event, then the logic jumps to the `except` block. When the code reaches the end of the `try` block or the `except` block, it jumps to the line after the try-except block, `print("Continuing program.")`, to continue the program.

The code in **Figure 10-6** attempts to load and display a cat image using the PIL module. The code uses a function from PIL named `Image.open()` to display `"cat.png"`, an image file. The function normally works correctly to display the image. However, the code is structured incorrectly to handle a situation where the image can't be displayed.

```
from PIL import Image
cat_image = None
try:
    cat_image = Image.open("cat.png")
except:
    print("Could not display a cat picture.")
cat_image.show()
```

Figure 10-6   A try-except block with a problem

Q Consider the example in Figure 10-6. What's wrong with the order of the statements?

A The last line, `cat_image.show()`, is placed outside of the try-except block. Displaying an image only works if the image loads successfully. The program could still crash at the last line if it tries to display an image that did not load correctly.

In the code shown in Figure 10-6, the `Image.open()` function can raise an exception if it can't display the cat. png file. However, because `cat_image.show()` works correctly only if `Image.open()` can find and retrieve the image file, the `cat_image.show()` statement belongs in the `try` block. You should include in the `try` block all the code that relies on the function that might raise an exception. **Figure 10-7** corrects this problem by including `cat_image.show()` in the `try` block.

```
from PIL import Image

cat_image = None

try:

    cat_image = Image.open("cat.png")

    cat_image.show()

except:

    print("Could not display a cat picture.")
```

Figure 10-7   Fixing the problem in the try-except block

When a statement in a `try` block fails and raises an exception, it signals the program to stop progressing through the block. If initializing the image fails (the program cannot find the file), or displaying the image fails (no display screen is connected), the code skips the `cat_image.show()` statement and jumps to the `except` block. If the `try` block completes without an exception being raised, it skips over the `except` block. If nothing was raised, the program does not have to deal with any exceptions.

Catching a general exception with a statement such as `except:` makes any exception in the `try` block jump to the `except` block. The generic message `"Could not display a cat picture."` fits a general exception, but a more specific message would be more helpful to users trying to solve the problem. Alternatively, you can program your code to only detect specific exceptions, as in **Figure 10-8**.

```
from PIL import Image

cat_image = None

try:

    cat_image = Image.open("cat.png")

    cat_image.show()

except FileNotFoundError:

    print("Could not find the cat picture file.")
```

Figure 10-8   Detecting specific exceptions

Using a specific built-in exception such as `FileNotFoundError`, you can display a more helpful message suited to the exception, such as `"Could not find the cat picture file."` The user can solve that problem by storing the file where the program can find it.

Additionally, you can include multiple `except` statements, one for each exception you expect the program to raise. **Figure 10-9** shows another error the `Image.open()` function can raise. Note that this exception is imported from the PIL module, as it is an exception specific to image-opening code.

```
from PIL import Image, UnidentifiedImageError
cat_image = None
try:
    cat_image = Image.open("cat.png")
    cat_image.show()
except FileNotFoundError:
    print("Could not find the cat picture file.")
except UnidentifiedImageError:
    print("Could not identify the picture format.")
```

Figure 10-9   Detecting more than one exception

The second `except` statement addresses a second exception: the program finds the specified file, but it is in the wrong format.

Now think about how you might program your interactions with Iceabella. Assume that the interactions are a series of functions you can call: `make_ice_cream()`, `add_cream()`, and `add_ice()`. A first start to the program would look like **Figure 10-10**.

```
choice = -1
amount = 0
print("Welcome to the Fantasy Ice Cream Shop! What do you want to
do?")
while choice != 0:
    print("   1: Make ice cream")
    print("   2: Add cream")
    print("   3: Add ice")
    print("   0: Quit")

    choice = int(input(">"))
```

Figure 10-10   Program to interact with Iceabella

```
        if choice == 1:
            make_ice_cream()
        elif choice == 2:
            amount = int(input("How much?> "))
            add_cream(amount)
        elif choice == 3:
            amount = int(input("How much?> "))
            add_ice(amount)
        print()
```

Figure 10-10   Program to interact with Iceabella (Continued)

The code in Figure 10-10 contains a loop that runs until the user inputs 0, indicating they are done interacting with Iceabella. The variable `choice` is set to -1 to indicate no choice has been made initially, and then is used as the flag for a `while` loop. The `choice` variable is set to the number the user enters via the command line. One of the three functions for interacting with Iceabella are called based on the number the user enters. Where could this program go wrong?

For simplicity's sake, assume that the only exceptions that could happen are the following:

- Adding a negative amount of cream
- Adding a negative amount of ice
- Trying to make ice cream when there's no cream
- Trying to make ice cream when there's no ice

Figure 10-11 shows one approach to handling these exceptions, though the approach is not ideal. All the code that relies on the function calls to Iceabella is within a `try` block, so that if an exception occurs within that code, the program will jump to the `except` block. However, the entire functionality, including parts that don't rely on Iceabella, are now within the `try` block.

```
choice = -1
amount = 0
print("Welcome to the Fantasy Ice Cream Shop! What do you want to
do?")
try:
    while choice != 0:
        print("   1: Make ice cream")
        print("   2: Add cream")
        print("   3: Add ice")
        print("   0: Quit")
```

Figure 10-11   Program with try-except block encompassing all code

```
        choice = int(input(">"))


        if choice == 1:
            make_ice_cream()
        elif choice == 2:
            amount = int(input("How much?> "))
            add_cream(amount)
        elif choice == 3:
            amount = int(input("How much?> "))
            add_ice(amount)
        print()
except:
    print("Something went wrong.")
```

Figure 10-11   Program with try-except block encompassing all code (Continued)

Q What would happen in the code shown in Figure 10-11 if Iceabella has no cream and you ask her to make ice cream?

A The entire interaction with Iceabella will stop working if anything goes wrong. An exception would stop all code in the **try** block and exit to the **except** block. In this case, that means the program stops entirely. However, you still want Iceabella to keep interacting with you, even if you make an impossible request.

Consider the alternative approach in **Figure 10-12**. This time, only the function call section of the code is surrounded by the **try** block, and the **except** block displays what went wrong.

```
choice = -1
amount = 0
print("Welcome to the Fantasy Ice Cream Shop! What do you want to do?")
while choice != 0:
    print("   1: Make ice cream")
    print("   2: Add cream")
    print("   3: Add ice")
    print("   0: Quit")


    choice = int(input("> "))
```

Figure 10-12   Program with the try-except block encompassing the exception-raising code

```
try:

    if choice == 1:

        make_ice_cream()

    elif choice == 2:

        amount = int(input("How much?> "))

        add_cream(amount)

    elif choice == 3:

        amount = int(input("How much?> "))

        add_ice(amount)

    print()

except:

    print("Something went wrong.")
```

Figure 10-12   Program with the try-except block encompassing the exception-raising code (Continued)

Q How does the change in the code shown in Figure 10-12 affect what happens if there's no cream?

A Iceabella will tell you something went wrong but will still wait for you to interact with her again.

Professional program design tries to keep only the lines of code that rely on exception-raising functions in the `try` block.

Figure 10-13 shows a general syntax for try-except blocks. A generic `except` statement (one that does not refer to a specific exception) must be the last option in the try-except block, similar to the `else` in an if-elif-else block. Also, you should have only one `except` statement per unique exception type.

```
try:

    # Code that might raise

    # exceptions somewhere...

except RuntimeError:

    print("A runtime error happened.")

except AttributeError:

    print("An attribute error happened.")

except:

    print("Any other exception ends up here.")
```

An `except` statement that does not specify an error type will catch any exception not caught by earlier `except` statements.

Figure 10-13   General syntax for try-except blocks

Q What happens if you place the general `except` statement before specific `except` statements?

A Because the general `except` statement works for all exceptions, none of the other `except` statements are triggered. Python's interpreter will notice this and instruct you to place it last.

10.3 Using Exceptions

Raising Exceptions (10.3.2, 10.3.4)

Like other programmers, you can raise your own exceptions. These `raise` statements act like a bailout: The program immediately stops your code and returns to where it was invoked with the exception information.

Recall that Iceabella has three functions you could call to interact with her. **Figure 10-14** shows what `make_ice_cream()`, `add_cream()`, and `add_ice` look like without exceptions.

```
cream_amount = 0
ice_amount = 0


def make_ice_cream():
    global cream_amount
    global ice_amount
    cream_amount -= 1
    ice_amount -= 1
    print("Ice cream was made!")


def add_cream(amount):
    global cream_amount
    cream_amount += amount
    print("Thanks for the", amount, "cups of cream!")

def add_ice(amount):
    global ice_amount
    ice_amount += amount
    print("Thanks for the", amount, "cups of ice!")
```

Figure 10-14   Program to simulate Iceabella's interactions

Two global variables, **cream_amount** and **ice_amount**, are initialized to zero, indicating that Iceabella starts out with no supplies. If either the **add_cream** or **add_ice** functions are called, the **cream_amount** or **ice_amount** variables are each increased by the **amount** parameter. Since these **amount** variables are global, the **global** keyword is used before referencing either variable to signal to Python which scope to use. Calling **make_ice_cream** decreases the **ice_amount** and **cream_amount** variables and signals that ice cream was made.

One of the exceptions you might expect Iceabella to raise is if you try to add a negative amount to either the **cream_amount** or **ice_amount** variables. **Figure 10-15** shows one way to modify the code from Figure 10-14 to handle these situations. It checks to see if the **amount** parameter is below 0 with an if-statement. If it is, the code raises a `ValueError`. Because both `add_cream` and `add_ice` can raise a `ValueError` exception, a more detailed message is added to the exception inside parentheses.

```
cream_amount = 0
ice_amount = 0

def make_ice_cream():
    global cream_amount
    global ice_amount
    cream_amount -= 1
    ice_amount -= 1
    print("Ice cream was made!")


def add_cream(amount):
    if amount < 0:
        raise ValueError("Cannot add negative amounts of
cream.")
    global cream_amount
    cream_amount += amount
    print("Thanks for the", amount, "cups of cream!")


def add_ice(amount):
    if amount < 0:
        raise ValueError("Cannot add negative amounts of
ice.")
    global ice_amount
    ice_amount += amount
    print("Thanks for the", amount, "cups of ice!")
```

Figure 10-15 Program that checks for positive amounts

You can have your code raise as many or as few exceptions as you see fit. Suppose the only requirements for starting to create ice cream is that both ice and cream are available to Iceabella in some amount greater than zero. If these requirements are not met, an exception should be raised. **Figure 10-16** shows how you might modify `make_ice_cream` to raise this exception.

```
cream_amount = 0
ice_amount = 0


def make_ice_cream():

    global cream_amount
    global ice_amount


    if cream_amount <= 0:

        raise RuntimeError("Not enough cream to make ice
cream.")

    elif ice_amount <= 0:

        raise RuntimeError("Not enough ice to make ice
cream.")


    cream_amount -= 1

    ice_amount -= 1

    print("Ice cream was made!")


def add_cream(amount):

    if amount < 0:

        raise ValueError("Cannot add negative amounts of
cream.")

    global cream_amount

    cream_amount += amount

    print("Thanks for the", amount, "cups of cream!")


def add_ice(amount):

    if amount < 0:

        raise ValueError("Cannot add negative amounts of
ice.")

    global ice_amount

    ice_amount += amount

    print("Thanks for the", amount, "cups of ice!")
```

Figure 10-16   Adding an exception to the `make_ice_cream()` function

The `make_ice_cream` function now has an `if` and an `elif` statement at the start. These conditions test for the ice and cream amounts before allowing Iceabella to state she has made ice cream. You do not need to wrap the remaining lines of the function code in an `else` block because once an exception is raised, the rest of the function will stop. In fact, in other situations, the raised exception may be anywhere in a function call chain. Any raised exception will be caught by the nearest try-except block.

To integrate the specific error messages back into the code from Figure 10-11, you need to use the keyword `as`. If you change the statement to `except Exception as e`, Python will create a variable with the identifier `e` that contains the exception information. **Figure 10-17** shows the main program, which needs the functions from Figure 10-16 to run.

```python
# Main program
choice = -1
amount = 0
print("Welcome to the Fantasy Ice Cream Shop! What do you want to
do?")
while choice != 0:
    print("   1: Make ice cream")
    print("   2: Add cream")
    print("   3: Add ice")
    print("   0: Quit")

    choice = int(input("> "))

    try:
        if choice == 1:
            make_ice_cream()
        elif choice == 2:
            amount = int(input("How much?> "))
            add_cream(amount)
        elif choice == 3:
            amount = int(input("How much?> "))
            add_ice(amount)
    except Exception as e:
        error_message = str(e)
        print(error_message)
    print()
```

Figure 10-17 Main Iceabella program

OUTPUT:

```
Welcome to the Fantasy Ice Cream Shop! What do you want to do?

    1: Make ice cream

    2: Add cream

    3: Add ice

    0: Quit

> 2 [Enter]

How much?> 10 [Enter]

Thanks for the 10 cups of cream!

    1: Make ice cream

    2: Add cream

    3: Add ice

    0: Quit

> 3 [Enter]

How much?> 12 [Enter]

Thanks for the 12 cups of ice!

    1: Make ice cream

    2: Add cream

    3: Add ice

    0: Quit

> 1 [Enter]

Ice cream was made!

    1: Make ice cream

    2: Add cream

    3: Add ice

    0: Quit

> 0 [Enter]
```

This output shows an input sequence that does not trigger any exceptions. How would you trigger all four **raise** statements from Figure 10-16?

Figure 10-17 Main Iceabella program (Continued)

When to Bail (10.3.1, 10.3.3)

Being able to hand off problems to someone else adds another decision layer to designing your program. Exceptions allow you to "bail out" of a piece of code that reaches a situation it can't complete. Bailing out is like an emergency break to stop and find someone else who knows more to fix the problem. When should you try to handle the problem yourself, and when should you bail out? This decision is a balancing act between strong code that handles all possible situations and exceptions to your code where it can't continue. If your program would have to make up a solution, let someone else handle it instead. If Iceabella tried to handle the lack of cream herself, she would need to somehow find the cream on her own, defeating the purpose of the interactions with her within the context of the game. Instead, she allows you to obtain the cream for her.

A general guideline is to think about what a function is requesting, such as "make ice cream." If the input provided makes that request impossible, raise an exception. Making ice cream assumes the ingredients are available to do so. When those assumptions are broken, a function should raise an exception instead of completing. However, if your functions are often raising exceptions, you may need to rethink your program design and change the assumptions.

Exceptions allow future users of your code libraries the control over how their program behaves. By raising exceptions only in cases where your code cannot continue, you keep your code focused on its own goals (making ice cream) while leaving other goals to other parts of the program (getting the cream). However, if you raise exceptions at any inconvenience, your library becomes tedious to use. It puts more responsibility on other programmers, which might reduce the usefulness of your library.

When to use an exception is generally up to the programmer. Is the problem something you can fix on your own? How much trouble does it cause if someone asks you to make ice cream but doesn't give you cream? The answers to those questions help you decide whether an exception is useful.

Q If you ask Iceabella to clean her shop when it is already clean, should she raise an exception?

A No, this is not a state in which Iceabella cannot continue. She should just reclean the shop or realize it is clean and do nothing.

Q If someone fills Iceabella's ice bucket with an angry ice-dragon instead of ice, should she raise an exception?

A Yes, Iceabella needs outside help to remove the angry ice-dragon from the ice bucket.

Summary

- In programming, an unusual situation is called an exception, an unexpected event that occurs as the program runs and prevents the program from completing execution. The unusual situation is said to trigger the exception and interrupt normal program flow because the program could not otherwise continue.
- A robust, well-written program checks for exceptions in situations where it might not otherwise continue, and then responds to the exceptions appropriately.
- Programming languages provide general exceptions, which can be used for all problems, but don't provide context that would help solve the problems. These nonspecific exceptions are called default exceptions.
- Specific exception types represent specific kinds of errors. They tell programmers the type of problem that happened, allowing them to find solutions faster. Many specific exceptions, which differ by programming language, are available to programmers.
- When code causes an exception, programmers say the code "raises" an exception. The code to detect an exception uses a logical control structure similar to an if-else block. The logical flow of the program changes depending on whether an exception occurs. Generally, to work with exceptions, programs try to do something and catch any exceptions that were raised in the code.
- You can use a program flow control called a try-except (or try-catch) block for trying and catching exceptions. The `try` code attempts to proceed as if conditions are normal and nothing disrupts the program flow. If an exception is raised in the `try` block, the program flow moves to the `except` block.
- A `try` block stops executing code when it detects an exception. The `except` block can fix the problem or stop the program entirely. Fixing the problem can take many forms, including using default values to fill in the missing information, displaying an error message, or logging the error in a file.
- Limit the amount of code inside a try-except block to only the code that relies on the part that might fail.

Key Terms

default exceptions	logic errors	try
exception	raise	try-except block

Module 11

File Operations

Learning Objectives:

11.1 File Input and Output

11.1.1 Describe directory structures.

11.1.2 Explain how to use the escape character in file paths.

11.1.3 Define absolute file path.

11.1.4 Define relative file path.

11.1.5 Identify the components of a file.

11.1.6 Recognize how a text file is represented in memory.

11.1.7 Define the term "file I/O."

11.1.8 List the operations available for file handling.

11.1.9 Describe the difference between handling a text file and a binary file.

11.1.10 List the file information that a programmer might request upon opening a file.

11.2 Processing a File

11.2.1 Define linear access as it applies to files.

11.2.2 Define random access as it applies to files.

11.2.3 Define buffered streams.

11.2.4 Explain how stream readers and writers work.

11.3 Reading from a File

11.3.1 Identify the generic syntax and permissions to open a file for reading.

11.3.2 Identify the default mode for opening a file for reading.

11.3.3 Explain how to verify that a file has been opened.

11.3.4 Identify an algorithm for reading an entire text file.

11.3.5 Explain how to read line by line from a text file.

11.3.6 Explain how to read a specific number of characters from a text file.

11.3.7 Identify common exceptions that occur when reading files.

11.3.8 Explain how to read records from a table in comma separated data format using `split()` and list comprehension.

11.4 Closing a File

11.4.1 Explain why it is good practice to close a file after using it.

11.4.2 Explain how to open and close a file using the keywords `with` and `as`.

11.5 Creating and Writing New Files

11.5.1 Identify the generic syntax for a statement to create a file.

11.5.2 Identify the generic syntax and permissions to open a file for writing.

11.5.3 Identify the default mode for opening a file for writing.

11.5.4 Explain the difference between append and write operations.

11.5.5 Describe the significance of including a newline argument in a write statement.

11.5.6 Identify an algorithm that writes multiple lines to a text file.

11.6 The os Module

11.6.1 Define the `os` module as a module with file manipulation behavior.

11.6.2 List the most useful and common functions in the `os` module for file I/O.

11.6.3 Explain how to use `os.path.join()` to create a file path.

11.6.4 Explain how to use functions from the `os` module to display all files within a directory.

11.6.5   Explain how to use functions from the **os** module to identify if a path is a file or directory.

11.6.6   Explain how to use functions from the **os** module to detect if a file or directory exists.

11.6.7   Explain how to use functions from the **os** module to remove files and directories.

11.1 File Input and Output

The Purpose of Files (11.1.1, 11.1.2, 11.1.3, 11.1.4)

Programs can request input from users and display output on the screen. Using input and output this way makes the most sense when manipulating small amounts of data, such as a single character, word, or sentence. To work with larger amounts of data, your programs can use files.

A **file** is a digital container that stores data such as text, settings, or program commands. A file can be a document, picture, video, or other type of information. You can also use files to supply data to your programs. For example, you can use a file to store a list of your favorite songs and their ratings, as shown in **Figure 11-1**.

GreenLandStudio/Shutterstock.com; Macrovector/Shutterstock.com

Figure 11-1   Personal song list

If you need to enter thousands of values and are not using files, you must type the values by hand and try to avoid making errors. Using a file to enter data is more efficient and less error prone.

Typically, when a program ends, its output data is lost. You can use files to permanently store data your code produces, no matter how much.

File handling is a way to read large amounts of data into your programs (more data than you'd reasonably expect a user to type) and to store data that your programs create.

You use a **folder**, also called a directory, as a storage space for organizing files into groups, similar to how you organize papers into physical folders, as shown in **Figure 11-2**. A folder can hold zero or more files. In fact, a folder can hold other folders.

corund/Shutterstock.com

Figure 11-2   Physical folders organizing files

Every operating system (OS) uses files to store and access data and programs. The OS stores the files in a hierarchy of folders called a *folder structure* or **directory structure**, an arrangement that reflects how the OS organizes files and folders. A typical directory structure resembles a tree. All files have a specific location on your computer. For example, in **Figure 11-3**, the file songs.txt is in the Playlists folder, two levels below the hard drive, along with other Music files.

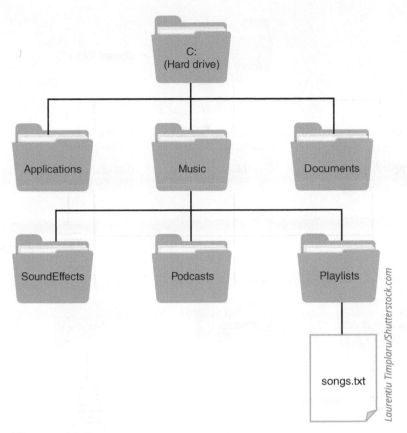

Laurentiu Timplaru/Shutterstock.com

Figure 11-3   Folders on a hard drive

When you want to use a file in a program, you have to refer to it by its name and location. You can describe a file's location in two ways: the **absolute file path** and the **relative file path**. The absolute path tells the exact location of a file on the computer starting from the hard drive, or your computer's main storage. The drive is usually represented as a letter (such as *C* in Windows) or a slash (/ in macOS and Unix systems) to indicate the topmost level of the directory structure. Depending on the OS, you use a forward slash (/) or a backslash (\) to separate the folder and file names at each level. The relative path provides the location of a file starting from another location in the file system. The differences are shown in **Figure 11-4**.

Suppose that you exported your playlist to a text file and stored it locally in the Music folder. You also created a playlist analysis program that needs to access data in the songs.txt file, which is stored in the Playlists folder. The absolute path to the songs.txt file looks like this:

C:\Music\Playlists\songs.txt

Because the current folder is the Music folder, the program can also access the songs.txt file by following a relative path. To do so, use the notation in Figure 11-4 to describe the file's position in relation to the current folder:

.\Playlists\songs.txt

In a relative path notation, a single dot with a backslash (.\) represents the current folder, and two dots and a slash (..\) represent the folder one level above the current one. The notation .\Playlists\songs.txt means "starting from the current folder, move down in the folder structure to the Playlists folder to find the songs.txt file."

You can think of an absolute path as the exact address of your home (123 Main Street, Sunny, Florida 32323) and the relative path as directions to your home from the grocery story (make a right on Orange Street, a left on Main Street, and stop at house #123).

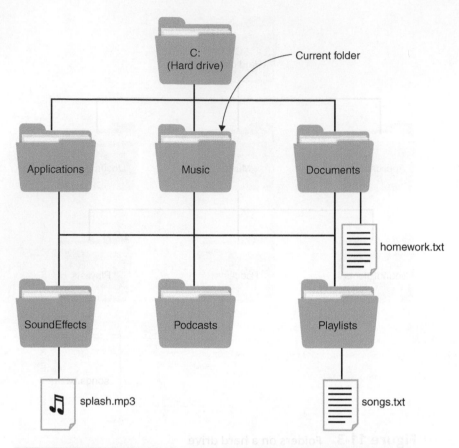

Figure 11-4 Relative and absolute paths to files and folders on a hard drive

Relative Paths	Absolute Paths
..\	C:\
..\Applications	C:\Applications
.	C:\Music
.\SoundEffects	C:\Music\SoundEffects
.\SoundEffects\splash.mp3	C:\Music\SoundEffects\splash.mp3
.\Podcasts	C:\Music\Podcasts
.\Playlists	C:\Music\Playlists
.\Playlists\songs.txt	C:\Music\Playlists\songs.txt
..\Documents	C:\Documents
..\Documents\homework.txt	C:\Documents\homework.txt

Laurentiu Timplaru/Shutterstock.com

Using the absolute file path in code assumes that the file will always be in the same location, even on different computers. Relative paths are more flexible because they remain relative to the current folder and are not affected if folders above the current one change name or location.

Q Suppose a user changes the name of the Music folder to Tunes. If the code contains an absolute file path to songs.txt, what happens when the program needs to access that file? What happens if the code contains a relative file path to songs.txt?

A When using an absolute path, the program would look for songs.txt starting at C: and then look for a folder named Music. However, the program would stop because no folder directly below C: is named Music. With a relative path, the program would look for the Playlists folder one level below the current folder and then find the songs.txt file.

When specifying the name of a file, it may be necessary to use **escape characters**, which act as alternate interpretations of characters that have another meaning. Because these characters have special meanings to the system, you may need to use escape characters with single quotations, double quotations, backslashes, and question marks when working with the file system, as shown in **Figure 11-5**.

Character	Name	Escape Character
'	Single Quotation Mark	\'
"	Double Quotation Mark	\"
\	Backslash	\\
?	Question Mark	\?

Figure 11-5   Escape characters

Anatomy of a File (11.1.5, 11.1.6)

In a computer, a file is treated as a named collection of uninterrupted data stored in memory, as shown in **Figure 11-6**. Each piece of information in the file is stored as a sequence of bytes in memory.

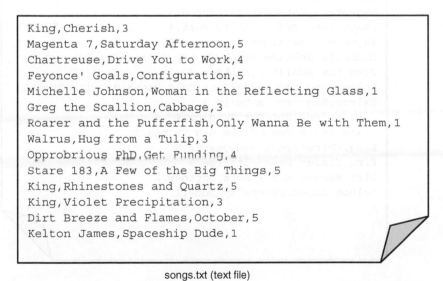

```
King,Cherish,3
Magenta 7,Saturday Afternoon,5
Chartreuse,Drive You to Work,4
Feyonce' Goals,Configuration,5
Michelle Johnson,Woman in the Reflecting Glass,1
Greg the Scallion,Cabbage,3
Roarer and the Pufferfish,Only Wanna Be with Them,1
Walrus,Hug from a Tulip,3
Opprobrious PhD,Get Funding,4
Stare 183,A Few of the Big Things,5
King,Rhinestones and Quartz,5
King,Violet Precipitation,3
Dirt Breeze and Flames,October,5
Kelton James,Spaceship Dude,1
```

songs.txt (text file)

| K | i | n | g | , | C | h | e | r | i | s | h | , | 3 | \n | M | a | g | e | n | t | a | | 7 | , | ... |

| ... | n | | J | a | m | e | s | , | S | p | a | c | e | s | h | i | p | | D | u | d | e | , | 1 | -1 |

songs.txt (in memory)

Figure 11-6   songs.txt represented in a text file and memory

A plain text file is the most basic type of data file used for input and output in programming. It arranges data in rows of text, which includes numbers and symbols. On a storage device, each character in a plain text file needs 1 byte of memory. For example, songs.txt has 449 characters and takes up 449 bytes of memory. As you know, a computer stores characters in memory using binary code, so A is stored as 01000001. The main advantage of text files is that they are simple to create and read and they don't require much storage space, even when they contain a lot of data.

When you create a file, the OS reserves a named location on a storage device for the file contents. Next, you add data to the file, which a program does by writing to the file. The file is stored on disk until it is explicitly erased by the operating system.

In general, a file can have the following components:

File name. The **file name** is the complete name of the file, including the extension, such as songs.txt. The file name extension identifies the type of file. For example, .txt indicates a plain text file, and .mp3 is an extension for music files in a compressed format.

Contents. The **contents** include the text or other data in the file.

Delimiter. A **delimiter** is a tab character or punctuation mark such as a comma used to separate information, such as an artist's name from a song title.

End of file. The **end of file (EOF)** is a special character or code that represents the last element in a file. The EOF follows the last character of a file and is often represented as the number 21.

Newline. A **newline** is a special character (**\n**) indicating the end of a line.

Access point. An **access point** keeps track of your current position in a file, similar to a cursor or insertion point.

Figure 11-7 shows the components of the songs.txt file.

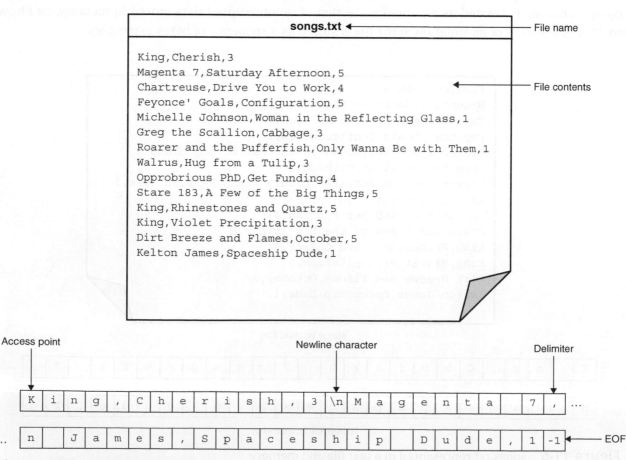

Figure 11-7 Elements of a file

Similar to escape characters used in file names, file contents can have escape characters. The newline character is represented as \n and shows that the following text will begin on the next line in the file. The tab escape code is represented as \t. When displayed on screen, \t begins the text that follows it after the next tab stop.

File Usage (11.1.7, 11.1.8, 11.1.9, 11.1.10)

When code reads information from a file, it is called **file input**. When your code writes information to a file, it is called **file output**. Together they are called file input and output, or **file I/O**. Some common file handling operations include opening a file, reading the contents, writing information into the file, and closing it.

Two types of data files include text files and binary files. A **text file** stores its contents as individual 8-bit (1 byte) ASCII characters, such as text and numbers that people can easily read. If you open the songs.txt text file in a text editor, for example, you can read the list of artist names, song titles, and ratings. Text files usually have a .txt extension and are created using a plain text editor. Text files that store programs or markup code have extensions such as .cpp, .java, .py, .csv, or .html.

Storing a text file using ASCII characters ensures that any type of operating system can handle the file. However, storing text as a series of 8-bit characters is a less efficient method that tends to consume memory.

In contrast, a **binary file** stores its contents in binary format, which you cannot easily read. The contents of binary files are not limited to ASCII text, but may contain byte patterns that do not print. For example, executable programs, music files, and images are binary files. If you open a binary file in a text editor, you will see symbols and other characters that do not form words except accidentally. Binary files can have a wide range of extensions such as .bin, .exe, .mp3, .pdf, and .doc.

The main advantage of binary files is that their encoding takes up less space than storing individual 8-bit ASCII characters, and computers can read them quickly. For example, a binary file can use a numeric format (such as IEEE 754) rather than text characters to store a value using less memory than ASCII.

Figure 11-8 compares text and binary files.

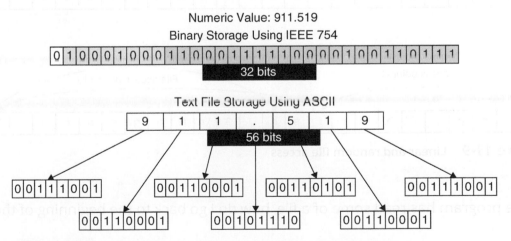

Figure 11-8 Binary versus text storage of the number 911.519

As you will see, your program needs to know whether it is using a text file or binary file to process it correctly. Binary files are encoded in a way that is specific to the type of file being read, so your program must read the code according to the encoding. Because text files simply store each character as its 8-bit ASCII representation, a program must only convert each character to its 8-bit set of binary codes.

Most programming languages have a **file handler**, a special built-in feature that allows you to interact with a file. You can use the file handler to request information about a file such as its size, type, location within the directory structure, the time it was created, and the time it was last modified. The file handler also provides features to enable file I/O, opening files, and closing files.

11.2 Processing a File

Accessing Files (11.2.1, 11.2.2)

Because files are stored in memory, consecutively, byte by byte, access is usually linear. A **file access point** is like a cursor—it indicates the current position in a file. You start at the first byte of the file and continue moving the file access point until the end of the file. Just as you are intended to read from a book, the computer reads each character or code in sequence, one by one, for the contents to have meaning. Reading a file this way is called **linear access** or sequential access.

In contrast, a program can also read a file using **random access**, which reads each character directly without first reading the character before it. Random file access is facilitated by changing the position of the file access point, a special variable that acts like a cursor indicating your position in a file. As a programmer, you can specify how many bytes to move the file access point from the current position. Positive values move the point toward the end of the file, and negative values move the point toward the beginning of the file. As you work with files, you must keep track of the file access point position to avoid attempting to move outside of the memory limits of the file. **Figure 11-9** compares linear and random file access.

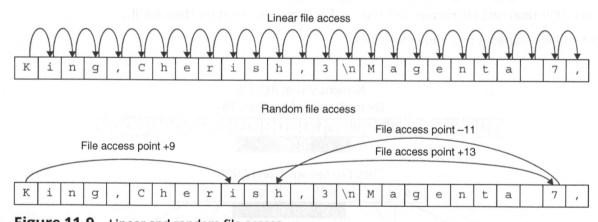

Figure 11-9   Linear and random file access

Q After the program has read some of a file, how do I go back to the beginning of the file?

A Each time you open a file, it places the file access point at the beginning of the file, allowing you to close and reopen the file. Alternatively, programming languages provide statements that reset the file access point to the beginning.

Streaming and Buffering (11.2.3, 11.2.4)

When your program uses file I/O, you are streaming information. The same way that you stream your favorite shows to binge-watch on your computer, you stream to read information at a fixed rate into your program. Essentially, a **stream** is a channel that allows you to interact with files stored on your computer or another drive. See **Figure 11-10**.

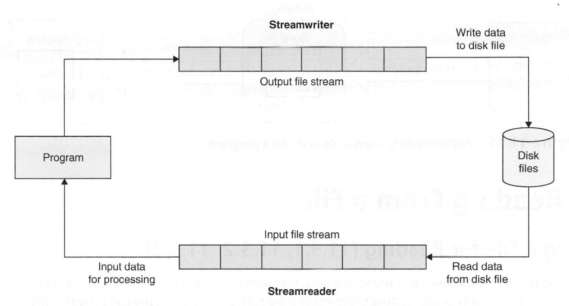

Figure 11-10   Streaming input and output streams using files

Some programming languages use a **streamwriter** to create a stream for writing text data to a file. The data from the text file is transferred to the stream and then written to the file. Similarly, a **streamreader** creates a stream for reading text from a file. The streamreader transfers the data from the file, into the stream, and then into your program.

Imagine that you are streaming a three-hour movie on your laptop. Previously, the laptop would need time to transfer the entire movie to your computer, and your computer would need a lot of space to hold the entire movie. Instead, your computer uses **buffering** to move data, bit by bit, into and out of a reserved part of memory (called a **buffer**) that your code can access.

Using a **buffered stream** can also improve performance when your program needs to read and write large amounts of data. Operating systems are constantly juggling many tasks. When reading a file, the OS does not read one byte at a time but reads a block of data and then switches to another task. While switching from one task to another, the OS needs to store the data somewhere, which is in a buffer. The advantages of buffering are shown in **Figure 11-11**.

The top part of Figure 11-11 shows an input file being read without using buffering. The program has to wait for the entire input file to be read before it can use the data. For large input files, this can involve significant delays. With buffering, shown in the bottom part of Figure 11-11, the buffer stores some data from the input file and sends it to the program, which can use the data immediately without waiting for the entire file to be read.

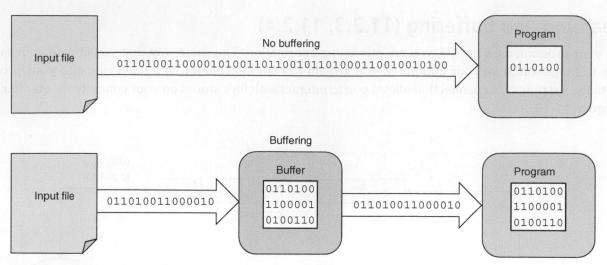

Figure 11-11   Buffering data from a file and into a program

11.3 Reading From a File

Opening a File for Reading (11.3.1, 11.3.2, 11.3.3)

The songs.txt file lists the artist's last name, the song title, and a rating of each song on a 1–5 scale. You can write code to perform tasks such as calculating the average song rating or counting the songs by the artist named King. Before your program can do that, it must open the file by accessing it on a storage device, such as a hard drive.

Opening a file for reading has the following syntax:

```
file_variable = open("songs.txt", access_mode)
```

In most programming languages, escape characters are not needed because the file name is enclosed in double quotes.

The following list breaks down the code piece by piece:

- The code starts with the variable **file_variable**.
- To indicate that **file_variable** should contain an open file, use the built-in function **open()**.
- Next, similar to passing arguments to a function, you specify the name of the file to open within parentheses. Enclose the file name in quotation marks, as in **"songs.txt"**.
- You can also include an **access_mode** argument that specifies how to access the file. The **access_mode** argument is optional and defines the purpose of opening the specified file. Common access modes are **"r"**, **"w"**, and **"a"** for read, write, and append, respectively. If you do not specify an **access_mode**, the program uses the default mode, **"r"**, to open a file stream for reading from a text file.

The preceding code snippet assumes that **"songs.txt"** is in the same folder as the program code. If the file is stored in a different folder, you must specify the relative or absolute path to the file so the program can find it.

You typically use the following **access_mode** arguments with text files:

Read. The **read** mode opens the specified file so that you can retrieve its contents. If the file does not exist, a file I/O error will be generated. Otherwise, the file is opened, and the file access point is positioned at the beginning of the file so you can begin retrieving the contents. Use the string **"r"** as the second argument to **open()**.

Write. The **write** mode opens the specified file so that you can add data to it. If the file does not exist, it is created. If the file does exist, the file access point is positioned at the beginning of the file and any existing information is overwritten. Use the string **"w"** as the second argument to open().

Append. The **append** mode opens the specified file so that you can add data to it. If the file does not exist, it is created. If the file does exist, the file access point is placed at the end and the new information is written after that point. Use the string **"a"** as the second argument to open().

Q How would you change the arguments of the line **file_variable = open("songs.txt", access_mode)** to open songs.txt for reading?

A You would write **file_variable = open("songs.txt", "r")**.

Most of the time, the code shown earlier opens **"songs.txt"** so your program can perform other tasks with it. What if another program accesses **"songs.txt"** at the same time (perhaps to add new songs) or the name of the file is changed to **"my_songs.txt"**? An error will occur, so you want to include code to check that the file has actually been opened. You can use a **try** block to catch exceptions that occur, as shown in **Figure 11-12**.

```
try:

    file_variable = open("songs.txt", "r")

except Exception as e:

    print(e)
```

Figure 11-12 Using exception handling to open a file for reading

The code in Figure 11-12 opens the songs.txt file and handles an exception, should one occur. As in the earlier code example, first a file variable is declared. Next, the code that opens the file is enclosed within a **try** block. If an exception occurs, it is caught in the **except** block. The detailed message contained within the exception is printed and the program exits. The printed message will reflect the type of exception that occurred, such as being unable to read from a file that does not exist.

Reading from a File (11.3.4, 11.3.5, 11.3.6, 11.3.7)

After your program opens **"songs.txt"**, it can read from it. Reading a file means that the OS starts at the beginning of the file (or wherever your file access point is currently placed) and delivers a copy of that information to your program. You use variables such as integers, characters, and strings to store the information given to your file. As the program reads each piece of data, the file access point updates and moves to the next item in the file.

Python lets you read from a file in a few ways. You can read the entire file at once, read one line at a time, or read a specified number of characters (bytes) at a time. The amount of data in a file is often unknown, so how to stop reading depends on the file method used.

A file is allocated a certain amount of space in memory. The EOF character keeps programs from accessing memory locations beyond the location of the file. A program cannot read past the EOF character because it violates file integrity and will crash the program. Python's file reading methods automatically detect the EOF for you and stop reading any new data at that point.

To read the entire contents of a file, you use the **read()** method with **file_variable**. This method reads every single bit of data from the file, including any escape characters. **Figure 11-13** shows reading the contents of **"songs.txt"** into a variable named **contents**. When **contents** is printed, it does not show the escape characters. Instead of including the **"\n"** codes, the printout includes actual newlines.

```
file_variable = open("songs.txt", "r")

contents = file_variable.read()

print(contents)

OUTPUT:
King,Cherish,3

Magenta 7,Saturday Afternoon,5

Chartreuse,Drive You to Work,4

Feyonce' Goals,Configuration,5

Michelle Johnson,Woman in the Reflecting Glass,1

Greg the Scallion,Cabbage,3

Roarer and the Pufferfish,Only Wanna Be with Them,1

Walrus,Hug from a Tulip,3

Opprobrious PhD,Get Funding,4

Stare 183,A Few of the Big Things,5

King,Rhinestones and Quartz,5

King,Violet Precipitation,3

Dirt Breeze and Flames,October,5

Kelton James,Spaceship Dude,1
```

Figure 11-13   Reading the entire contents of a file

Reading line by line from a file requires a flow control sequence, either a for-loop if you know how many lines are stored in the file or a while-loop if the number of lines is unknown. Most often you won't know how many lines are in a file, so the while-loop is best. The while-loop condition should remain **True** until the EOF is reached. The **readline()** method, when used on a file variable, will return each line in the file, including the newline escape character at the end. If the **readline()** method reaches the EOF, it returns the empty string **""**. **Figure 11-14** shows how you would read and append each line in songs.txt to a list. The escape characters are visible in this example because the strings are not printed, but the list containing them is.

```
file_variable = open("songs.txt", "r")

contents = []

line = file_variable.readline()

while line != "":

    contents.append(line)

    line = file_variable.readline()

print(contents)
```

OUTPUT:
```
['King,Cherish,3\n', 'Magenta 7,Saturday Afternoon,5\n', 'Chartreuse,Drive
You to Work,4\n', "Feyonce' Goals,Configuration,5\n", 'Michelle Johnson,Woman
in the Reflecting Glass,1\n', 'Greg the Scallion,Cabbage,3\n', 'Roarer and
the Pufferfish,Only Wanna Be with Them,1\n', 'Walrus,Hug from a Tulip,3\n',
'Opprobrious PhD,Get Funding,4\n', 'Stare 183,A Few of the Big Things,5\n',
'King,Rhinestones and Quartz,5\n', 'King,Violet Precipitation,3\n', 'Dirt
Breeze and Flames,October,5\n',  'Kelton James,Spaceship Dude,1']
```

Figure 11-14   Reading the entire contents of a file line by line

To read individual characters, use the **read()** method again but pass an integer argument representing how many characters you want to read. For example, **file_variable.read(1)** will return one character and **file_variable.read(5)** will return five. As with **readline()**, the EOF is when **read()** returns the empty string. **Figure 11-15** shows how to read all of the contents of songs.txt two characters at a time, appending each pair of characters to a list. Note that in the printout, the escape characters count as a character to **read()**, resulting in data like **"\nM"** stored in contents. Additionally, if there are not enough characters to read to satisfy the integer passed to **read()**, it will read however many characters are left in the file.

Following are common exceptions that can occur when reading files:

The input stream is not open. There was an error creating the file handler, so the stream is never created.

The file is empty. In this case, the file opens, but its only content is the EOF character.

The file does not exist. The file you attempted to open could not be found in the specified location.

The file is actually a folder. The file that you requested to open is not a readable file but is actually a folder.

The file is already open by another program. Multiple file handlers can open the same file for reading with no problem, but once a program begins writing to the file, a lock is placed on the file and no one can open it until the writing has finished and the lock has been released.

In each case, it's a good programming practice to try and catch any generated exceptions and use the file handler to check for unintended states, such as an empty file or a locked file.

```
file_variable = open("songs.txt", "r")

contents = []

two_characters = file_variable.read(2)

while two_characters != "":

    contents.append(two_characters)

    two_characters = file_variable.read(2)

print(contents)
```

OUTPUT:
```
['Ki', 'ng', ',C', 'he', 'ri', 'sh', ',3', '\nM', 'ag', 'en', 'ta', ' 7', ',S',
'at', 'ur', 'da', 'y ', 'Af', 'te', 'rn', 'oo', 'n,', '5\n', 'Ch', 'ar', 'tr', 'eu',
'se', ',D', 'ri', 've', ' Y', 'ou', ' t', 'o ', 'Wo', 'rk', ',4', '\nF', 'ey', 'on',
'ce', "' ", 'Go', 'al', 's,', 'Co', 'nf', 'ig', 'ur', 'at', 'io', 'n,', '5\n', 'Mi',
'ch', 'el', 'le', ' J', 'oh', 'ns', 'on', ',W', 'om', 'an', ' i', 'n ', 'th', 'e ',
'Re', 'fl', 'ec', 'ti', 'ng', ' G', 'la', 'ss', ',1', '\nG', 're', 'g ', 'th', 'e ',
'Sc', 'al', 'li', 'on', ',C', 'ab', 'ba', 'ge', ',3', '\nR', 'oa', 're', 'r ', 'an',
'd ', 'th', 'e ', 'Pu', 'ff', 'er', 'fi', 'sh', ',O', 'nl', 'y ', 'Wa', 'nn', 'a ',
'Be', ' w', 'it', 'h ', 'Th', 'em', ',1', '\nW', 'al', 'ru', 's,', 'Hu', 'g ', 'fr',
'om', ' a', ' T', 'ul', 'ip', ',3', '\nO', 'pp', 'ro', 'br', 'io', 'us', ' P', 'hD',
',G', 'et', ' F', 'un', 'di', 'ng', ',4', '\nS', 'ta', 're', ' 1', '83', ',A',
' F', 'ew', ' o', 'f ', 'th', 'e ', 'Bi', 'g ', 'Th', 'in', 'gs', ',5', '\nK',
'in', 'g,', 'Rh', 'in', 'es', 'to', 'ne', 's ', 'an', 'd ', 'Qu', 'ar', 'tz', ',5',
'\nK', 'in', 'g,', 'Vi', 'ol', 'et', ' P', 're', 'ci', 'pi', 'ta', 'ti', 'on', ',3',
'\nD', 'ir', 't ', 'Br', 'ee', 'ze', ' a', 'nd', ' F', 'la', 'me', 's,', 'Oc', 'to',
'be', 'r,', '5\n', 'Ke', 'lt', 'on', ' J', 'am', 'es', ',S', 'pa', 'ce', 'sh', 'ip',
' D', 'ud', 'e,', '1']
```

Figure 11-15   Reading the contents of a file two characters at a time

Comma-Separated Values (11.3.8)

The songs.txt file is formatted so that the data for each song is on its own line, with the artist, song title, and rating each separated by a comma, as shown in **Figure 11-16**.

Q   How could you use the information about songs.txt to read the file more efficiently than character by character?

A   Because you know that each line of the file has the same artist-song-rating format, you can read each line of the file, saving the information from the file in that order.

As Figure 11-16 shows, songs.txt is a **comma-delimited text file**, also known as **comma-separated values** (.csv extension), resembling records in a table in which each chunk of data is separated by a comma. Programs can read comma-delimited text files more efficiently than character by character. Each chunk of data up to a comma is a **field**. One line containing an artist, song, and rating is a **record**. Because the data is arranged in fields and records, it is structured as a **table**.

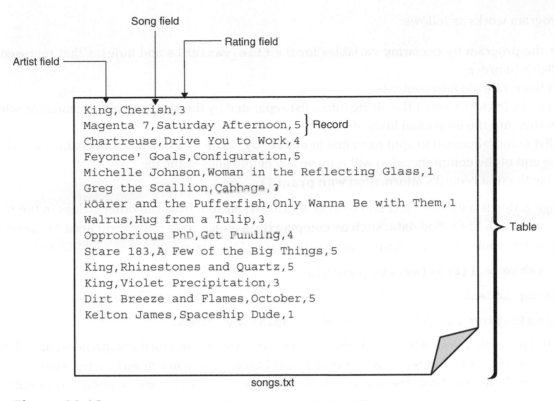

Artist field
Song field
Rating field

```
King,Cherish,3
Magenta 7,Saturday Afternoon,5  } Record
Chartreuse,Drive You to Work,4
Feyonce' Goals,Configuration,5
Michelle Johnson,Woman in the Reflecting Glass,1
Greg the Scallion,Cabbage,2
Roarer and the Pufferfish,Only Wanna Be with Them,1
Walrus,Hug from a Tulip,3
Opprobrious PhD,Get Funding,4
Stare 183,A Few of the Big Things,5
King,Rhinestones and Quartz,5
King,Violet Precipitation,3
Dirt Breeze and Flames,October,5
Kelton James,Spaceship Dude,1
```

Table

songs.txt

Figure 11-16   Fields and records in a comma-delimited file

In the program reading songs.txt, you can read the entire contents into **file_variable** and then use the Python string method **split()** and list comprehension to split the data into a two-dimensional list, as in **Figure 11-17**.

```python
file_variable = open("songs.txt", "r")


artist_index = 0
song_index = 1
rating_index = 2


contents = file_variable.read()


split_by_line = contents.split("\n")
split_by_comma = [x.split(",") for x in split_by_line if x != ""]


print("First Artist:", split_by_comma[0][artist_index])
print("First Song:", split_by_comma[0][song_index])
print("First Rating:", split_by_comma[0][rating_index])
```

Figure 11-17   Reading a comma-delimited text file

The program works as follows:

- Start the program by declaring variables for the **file_variable** and indexes that represent each of the fields in order.
- Read the entire file into contents.
- Use **split("\n")** to split the string into a list separated by the newline escape character, which splits the string into the individual lines of the file.
- Use list comprehension to split each line in **split_by_line** by a comma. The conditional **if x != ""** at the end of the comprehension will remove any empty lines in the file.
- Display the first record's information with **print()**.

Although rating is a number, it is still read as a string when split from the other strings in the record. If you plan to do math with the rating data, such as compute the average song rating, you need to convert the string to an integer. You could use list comprehension to map **int()** to the ratings:

```
final_table = [[line[artist_index],
line[song_index],
int(line[rating_index])] for line in split_by_comma]
```

You can think of this nested list comprehension in two parts: the inner list comprehension and the outer list comprehension. The outer comprehension creates a list based on each line in **split_by_comma**. Then, for each line that is visited, the inner comprehension creates an almost identical copy, mapping **int()** onto the rating.

The code in **Figure 11-18** reads the entire songs.txt file line by line (or song by song) and counts the number of songs in the file.

```
file_variable = open("songs.txt", "r")


artist_index = 0
song_index = 1
rating_index = 2


contents = file_variable.read()


split_by_line = contents.split("\n")
split_by_comma = [x.split(",") for x in split_by_line]
final_table = [[line[artist_index], line[song_index],
int(line[rating_index])] for line in split_by_comma]
song_count = len(final_table)


print("There are", song_count, "songs in the file.")
OUTPUT:
There are 14 songs in the file.
```

Figure 11-18   Reading the songs.txt file

11.4 Closing a File

Closing Files After Use (11.4.1)

After you have read a file and are finished using it, the program should close it. For example, suppose that when you finish reading the songs.txt file to calculate your average song rating, your program unexpectedly stops due to some unforeseen error. This can lead to file corruption and loss of data. In larger programs, having too many files open at once can detract from performance. Closing a file restores resources (such as buffers) to the system. For these reasons, it is a good practice to close files when you no longer need them.

After a file is closed, it becomes available to be opened by other code. To close the songs.txt file, include the following statement at the end of the program or when the file is no longer needed by your program:

`file_variable.close()`

Be sure to close a file only when you are sure that your code no longer needs to access it. Trying to read from an already closed file may cause an error while your code is running.

Using `with` and `as` Keywords (11.4.2)

Always remembering to open and close files can get tedious. Python has two keywords you use to open and close a file within a code block. You can use the keywords `with` and `as` to create a temporary file variable and close it immediately after you are done with it, signaled by the end of the code block. The calls to `open()` and `close()` are done for you. **Figure 11-19** shows the same code as Figure 11-18 but using `with` and `as` instead of `open()` and `close()`. Using `with` and `as` also acts like a try-except block should an exception occur and fail gracefully instead of crashing the program.

```
with open("songs.txt", "r") as file_variable:

    contents = file_variable.read()


    artist_index = 0
    song_index = 1
    rating_index = 2


    split_by_line = contents.split("\n")
    split_by_comma = [x.split(",") for x in split_by_line if x != ""]
    final_table = [[line[artist_index], line[song_index], int(line[rating_index])]
for line in split_by_comma]
    song_count = len(final_table)


    print("There are", song_count, "songs in the file.")
OUTPUT:
There are 14 songs in the file.
```

Figure 11-19   Using the keywords `with` and `as` to open and close a file

11.5 Creating and Writing New Files

Creating a File (11.5.1)

The same way that you use code to read information from a file, you can also create a new file. Suppose that you want to make another text file containing all of your favorite songs, ones you rated 4 or higher. In some programming languages, opening a file for writing with a unique name creates the file in the same folder as your program code. The new file is empty and contains only the EOF character, so you need to write data into the file before a program can use it. The following code snippet shows the general syntax for opening a file:

```
output_file = open("favorite_songs.txt", "w")
```

To create a new file, you assign a file what is returned by `open()`, but with `"w"` as the access mode. By using the file handler to open a file for writing that does not exist, your program will create a new empty file named `"favorite_songs.txt"` in the same directory as your code.

Using `open()` with the write access mode `"w"` will erase any existing file with the same name. To preserve the contents of the file when opening, use the append access mode `"a"`. Using the append access mode will still create the file if it doesn't exist.

Opening a File for Writing (11.5.2, 11.5.3, 11.5.4)

You open a file for writing after creating a new file or when you want to add data to an existing file. For example, suppose you created favorite_songs.txt to hold your top songs, those rated 4 or 5, and now want to add the top-rated songs from songs.txt to favorite_songs.txt. You also bought some music and want to add more songs to your list in songs.txt. In either case, you can use file I/O to write text into a file.

Q Would you use the `"w"` or `"a"` access mode to add new songs to songs.txt?

A Access mode `"a"` is the most appropriate in this case because you want to preserve the previous songs and add to the list.

Writing to and Appending a File (11.5.5, 11.5.6)

Suppose that your friends ask you to write code to help manage their music playlists as well. You can't give them your songs.txt file because they have different songs on their computer. You can, however, use a program to write files. The program asks your friends to enter their songs. It then creates a new text file named their_songs.txt. The program is shown in **Figure 11-20**.

```
with open("their_songs.txt", "w") as output_file:

    num_songs = int(input("Hello friend. How many songs would you like to enter? "))


    for i in range(num_songs):
        artist = input("Please enter the artist name. ")
        song = input("Please enter the song name. ")
        rating = input("Please enter the rating (1-5). ")


        output_file.write(artist + "," + song + "," + rating + "\n")


    print("Thanks! Your file has been written.")


OUTPUT:
Hello friend. How many songs would you like to enter? 1 [Enter]
Please enter the artist name. Rizzo [Enter]
Please enter the song name. Lies Hurt [Enter]
Please enter the rating (1-5). 4 [Enter]
Thanks! Your file has been written.
```

Figure 11-20   Writing a new file for a new song list

The program works by performing the following tasks:

- Create the file called **"their_songs.txt"** by using the keyword **with** to open the output file for writing.
- Use the keyword **as** to create a file variable named **output_file**.
- Prompt your friend to enter the number of songs to enter in the file and store the response in the variable **num_songs**.
- In a for-loop, iterate from 0 to the number of songs that your friend entered. Also prompt your friend to provide the artist name, song title, and rating for a song.
- Write the responses to the specified file. Because the file has to be formatted in a specific way, after the artist name is written, you write a comma followed by the song name, a comma, and then the rating.
- After the rating, you write the newline character to the file, indicating that the next piece of information (i.e., the next song) should start on the next line.
- Finally, you display a message stating that the file has been written and you close the output file.

If you want to go through your songs in songs.txt and write all of the favorites to a new file named favorite_songs.txt, you need to read and write at the same time. While you read each song from songs.txt, check the rating score. If the rating is 4 or higher, then write the song data to favorite_songs.txt.

To write one song per line, you also need to include a newline character, which works like pressing the Enter key so that the following text appears on the next line. You specify a newline character using **"\n"** as the newline argument in a **write()** statement, as in **Figure 11-21**.

```
with open("songs.txt", "r") as input_file,
open("favorite_songs.txt", "w") as output_file:


    artist_index = 0

    song_index = 1

    rating_index = 2


    contents = input_file.read()

    split_by_line = contents.split("\n")

    split_by_comma = [x.split(",") for x in split_by_line if x
!= ""]

    final_table   =   [[line[artist_index],   line[song_index],
int(line[rating_index])] for line in split_by_comma]


    for record in final_table:
        if record[rating_index] >= 4:

            output_file.write(record[artist_index] + ","
+ record[song_index] + "," + str(record[rating_index]) +
"\n")
```

Figure 11-21   Saving the favorite songs to a new file

Figure 11-22 shows the songs.txt and favorite_songs.txt files after running the program shown in Figure 11-21.

Now you have a list of your favorite songs. When it's time to add more favorite songs, you can update the favorite_songs.txt file. However, if you open favorite_songs.txt for writing with the access code **"w"**, the file access will start at the beginning of the file, and you'll write over the current contents of the file. Instead, use the **"a"** access mode argument, which keeps the current songs in the file and writes the new records at the end of the file. The code for appending resembles Figure 11-21, except you would change the line to open the output file from access mode **"w"** to **"a"**, as in the following code snippet:

```
open("favorite_songs.txt", "a")
```

Q Can I code a program to read and write to the same file at the same time?

A It depends. Some operating systems let you write to a file while other programs (including your own) are reading from it. Others place a lock on the file, restricting access until someone closes the file. In general, reading and writing to the same file at the same time is a bad practice and should be avoided. If a file is being read while another program is writing to it, the read information may be out of date.

songs.txt

```
King,Cherish,3
Magenta 7,Saturday Afternoon,5
Chartreuse,Drive You to Work,4
Feyonce' Goals,Configuration,5
Michelle Johnson,Woman in the Reflecting Glass,1
Greg the Scallion,Cabbage,3
Roarer and the Pufferfish,Only Wanna Be with Them,1
Walrus,Hug from a Tulip,3
Opprobrious PhD,Get Funding,4
Stare 183,A Few of the Big Things,5
King,Rhinestones and Quartz,5
King,Violet Precipitation,3
Dirt Breeze and Flames,October,5
Kelton James,Spaceship Dude,1
```

favorite_songs.txt

```
Magenta 7,Saturday Afternoon,5
Chartreuse,Drive You to Work,4
Feyonce' Goals,Configuration,5
Opprobrious PhD,Get Funding,4
Stare 183,A Few of the Big Things,5
King,Rhinestones and Quartz,5
Dirt Breeze and Flames,October,5
```

Figure 11-22   Contents of songs.txt and favorite_songs.txt

11.6 The os Module

Functions for Files and Directories (11.6.1, 11.6.2, 11.6.3, 11.6.4)

Python has the os (operating system) module available for import. The os module contains many useful file-related functions. **Figure 11-23** lists some functions that you might use while dealing with files in Python.

Function	Description	Code Example
os.path.join()	Joins any number of strings into a path using the appropriate separator based on your current OS	print(os.path.join("folder", "file.txt"))
os.path.isfile()	Given a path, returns True if the path points to a file (not a folder), False otherwise	os.path.isfile("songs.txt")
os.path.isdir()	Given a path, returns True if the path points to a directory (folder), False otherwise	os.path.isdir("top_50")
os.path.exists()	Given a path, returns True if the path points to a file or directory, False otherwise	os.path.exists ("folder\song.txt")
os.listdir()	Given a path to a directory, returns a list containing strings representing all files and directories within	os.listdir("poems")
os.remove()	Given a path to a file, removes the file; does not work with directories or folders	os.remove("songs.txt")
os.rmdir()	Given a path to a directory, removes the directory; does not work with files or nonempty directories	os.remove("poems")

Figure 11-23   Common useful functions in the os module

Recall that in a file path, the character used to separate folder and file names depends on the OS running the program. If you program your Python code to work on macOS and give the program to a friend who uses Windows, any "/" or "\" symbols in the program code will cause the code to not work. The os.path.join() function combines an iterative sequence of strings into a file path using the appropriate separator depending on the system at runtime. **Figure 11-24** shows how you might use this function.

```
import os

folder = input("Enter a folder name: ")
filename = input("Enter a filename: ")

filepath = os.path.join(folder, filename)

print(filepath)
OUTPUT:
Enter a folder name: top_50 [Enter]
Enter a filename: bye.mp3 [Enter]
top_50\bye.mp3
```

Figure 11-24   Using os.path.join() to create a file path

The program creates two variables, one named **folder**, which obtains input for the folder the user wants to use, and one named **filename** for the file the user wants to use. The two variables are passed to os.path.join() to create a string stored in the file path. Any number of arguments can be passed to os.path.join(), not just two as shown in Figure 11-24.

Given a path to a directory, the `os` module function `os.path.listdir()` will generate a list of strings of the files in the directory. This list is useful when you want to automate a file management process. For example, you might want to see how many .txt files a directory contains. **Figure 11-25** shows how you might do this in code. The code uses the string method `endswith()` to detect whether a file name ends with the correct extension.

```
import os


folder = input("Enter a folder name: ")
all_files = os.listdir(folder)
count = 0


for file in all_files:
    if file.endswith(".txt"):
        count += 1


print("There are", count, "files ending in .txt.")
OUTPUT:
Enter a folder name: poems [Enter]
There are 3 files ending in .txt.
```

Figure 11-25   Counting all files in a folder with the ending "`.txt`"

File Properties (11.6.5, 11.6.6)

You may want to detect the type of item a path is pointing to. Is it a file or a directory? The `os` module has a function for both situations. The `os.path.isfile()` function will return `True` if the path points to a file, regardless of the extension. The `os.path.isdir()` function will return `True` if the path points to a directory, even if the directory name is something silly like `"folder.txt"`. **Figure 11-26** shows how you could use `os.path.isdir()` to count the subfolders within a folder. The code in Figure 11-26 uses `os.path.join()` because it's not checking the string name of a file but the actual file path.

```
import os

folder = input("Enter a folder name: ")
all_files = os.listdir(folder)
count = 0


for file in all_files:
    file_path = os.path.join(folder, file)
    if os.path.isdir(file_path):
        count += 1


print("There are", count, "subfolders in", folder + ".")
OUTPUT:
Enter a folder name: poems [Enter]
There are 2 subfolders in poems.
```

Figure 11-26   Counting directories in a given folder

You can use the **os.path.exists()** function to detect whether a path points to an actual file or directory. The function will return **True** if the given path does point to a file or directory or it will return **False** if nothing exists at the path. **Figure 11-27** shows how you can use **os.path.exists()** to detect if a given folder and file name point to an actual file.

```
import os

folder = input("Enter a folder name: ")
filename = input("Enter a file name: ")
path = os.path.join(folder, filename)


if os.path.exists(path):
    print("The path", path, "exists.")
else:
    print("The path", path, "does not exist.")
OUTPUT:
Enter a folder name: poems [Enter]
Enter a file name: dawn.txt [Enter]
The path poems\dawn.txt exists.
```

Figure 11-27   Verifying a path

Removing Files and Directories (11.6.7)

Use `open()` to create files automatically by providing the **"w"** or **"a"** access mode. To delete files, you must use the `os` module function `os.remove()`. You can remove a directory with `os.rmdir()`, but the directory must be empty. **Figure 11-28** shows code that will delete any files in a directory that do not have the **".txt"** extension. The code uses the `os.path.isfile()` function so that it does not try to delete any directories.

```
import os

folder = input("Enter a folder name: ")
all_files = os.listdir(folder)
removed_files = 0

for file in all_files:
    file_path = os.path.join(folder, file)
    if os.path.isfile(file_path) and not file.endswith(".txt"):
        os.remove(file_path)
        removed_files += 1


print(removed_files, "files were removed.")
```
OUTPUT:
```
Enter a folder name: poems [Enter]

7 files were removed.
```

Figure 11-28   Removing files that do not have a `".txt"` extension

Summary

- A file is a named container of data stored in memory, such as a document, picture, or song. Use files as a way to read large amounts of data into your program or write large amounts of data from your program, also called file input/output (I/O).
- Folders contain and organize files into groups. An operating system stores files in an arrangement of folders called a folder structure or directory structure.
- The location of a file on your computer can be described by a relative path or an absolute path. The absolute path indicates the exact location of a file on the computer starting from the main storage device or drive. The relative path provides the location of a file starting from another location in the folder structure. Relative paths are more flexible than absolute paths because they are not affected if folders above the current one change name or location.

- Programs typically read two types of files: text files and binary files. Files can be read sequentially until the end-of-file character is reached, which is called linear access or sequential access.
- Buffering helps to stream large amounts of data into your program by moving data, bit by bit, into and out of a reserved part of memory called a buffer. Buffering can improve performance when your program needs to read or write a lot of data.
- Before a program can use a file, it must open the file by locating it on a storage device and then associating it with a file variable. To access the data in a file, a program reads from the file. The program can read unstructured data in a file character by character. In a structured file, such as a comma-delimited text file, the program can read the data field by field.
- In a delimited text file, you can use a loop to read a file efficiently. After reading a file, the program can process the file data to do operations such as performing calculations. You might need to convert string data to an integer or other numeric data type to use it for processing.
- A program writes to a file when it creates or opens a file and then adds data to it or when it appends new data to the end of an existing file. The file I/O mode depends on the data type and the desired operation, whether reading, writing, or appending to a file.
- To avoid system performance problems, programs should close files as soon as the files are no longer needed.
- Common exceptions when opening a file include not finding the specified file, trying to close a file that has already been closed, and encountering improper formatting in a comma-delimited text file.
- The keywords `with` and `as` open and close a file for you and are the best way to open and close files in Python.
- The `os` module contains many file-related functions, including `os.path.join()` and `os.remove()`.

Key Terms

absolute file path	end of file (EOF)	linear access
access point	escape characters	newline
append	field	random access
binary file	file	read
buffer	file access point	record
buffered stream	file handler	relative file path
buffering	file handling	stream
comma-delimited text file	file input	streamreader
comma-separated values	file I/O	streamwriter
contents	file name	table
delimiter	file output	text file
directory structure	folder	write

Module
12

Recursion

Learning Objectives:

12.1 Key Components of Recursion

12.1.1 Define recursion as a problem-solving approach.

12.1.2 Describe the purpose of recursion.

12.1.3 Explain the components of a recursive function.

12.1.4 List advantages and disadvantages of recursion.

12.2 Using Recursion To Solve Complex Problems

12.2.1 Explain the application of recursion.

12.2.2 Differentiate recursive algorithms from algorithms that use repetition control structures.

12.2.3 Define the "divide and conquer" approach to problem solving.

12.2.4 Analyze how to use a base case and a recursive case to implement recursion into an iterative programming solution.

12.2.5 Construct a procedural program using recursion.

12.3 Managing Memory During Recursion

12.3.1 Explain memory management and its importance with recursion.

12.3.2 Explain the use of a stack during recursion.

12.3.3 Explain tail-recursive functions.

12.1 Key Components of Recursion

The Recursive Mindset (12.1.1, 12.1.2)

Computer science, in general, is telling computers to solve problems. Similar to when you solve a problem, the computer can guess an answer randomly or it can try to be smarter about it. Suppose you are playing a guessing game where your friend is thinking of a number between 1 and 100, as in **Figure 12-1**. You say "27" as your first guess, and your friend responds, "No, my number is higher than that." You now know that the number must be between 27 and 100. How does your approach change? You use the response from your friend as a way to eliminate possibilities and arrive at the correct answer more quickly than randomly guessing.

The most efficient way to play this game is to start at 50. Guessing a number halfway between the smallest and largest numbers means that if you do not guess the correct answer, you still eliminate half of the options. If your friend responds "higher" to 50, you know the smallest possible value is 51. Your next guess is halfway

Figure 12-1 Numbers guessing game

between 51 and 100, 75. If your friend responds "lower," you have a new upper bound to the range of possible answers. You now know the number is greater than 50 and less than 75. Each time you guess, you update the range of possible numbers and perform the same task as when 1 and 100 were the boundaries. Your strategy is as follows:

1. Guess a number halfway between the smallest and largest number.
2. If told "higher," update the smallest number to this guess plus 1.
3. If told "lower," update the largest number to this guess minus 1.
4. Repeat steps 1–3 until you are correct.

When you use this strategy in the number guessing game, you are breaking down a large problem into smaller similar problems. Each piece can then be broken down until the problem is so small, it is easily solved. Eventually, the number guessing game eliminates all except one number to guess. **Figure 12-2** shows an example of the game, starting with 1 and 10 as the smallest and largest numbers.

Recursion is the problem-solving approach that divides large problems into smaller, identical problems. The same steps are applied to each smaller version of the problem, although with different restrictions, such as the upper and lower boundaries for the number game.

Recursion Basics (12.1.3)

The recursive mindset uses functions to solve problems. Following are brief reminders about functions:

- Functions are named blocks of code that perform a specific task.
- Functions can have information passed to them as parameters.
- Functions can return information as return values, which can be used for calculations and other operations.
- Functions can be "called" to execute the lines of code inside the function.
- Functions can call other functions.

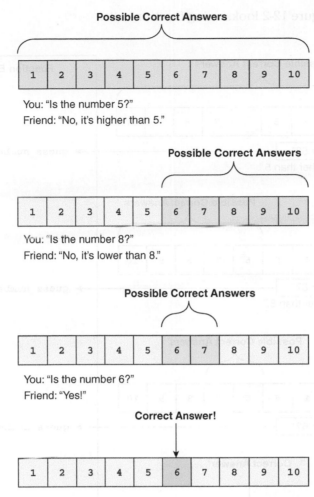

Figure 12-2   Guessing a number between 1 and 10

Take a moment to review that last point. Functions are like any other block of code. Anything you can do in one block of code, you can do in another. Therefore, functions can call other functions. This is one of the keys to elegant code design. A function can call any function in the scope of the code, including itself.

A **recursive function** calls itself at least once. At each function call, recursive functions use modified parameters to shrink the size of the problem. For the guessing game, the modified parameters are the lower and upper boundaries of the number range. If you don't modify the parameters for the recursive function, the recursive function does not stop; this is called **infinite recursion**.

Q What is the difference between an infinite loop and infinite recursion?

A With an infinite loop, the variable tested for stopping the loop isn't modified so that the conditional statement will be `False`. With infinite recursion, the problem size is never reduced. You need to make the problem smaller for recursion to find a solution.

Figure 12-3 shows how Figure 12-2 looks using function calls.

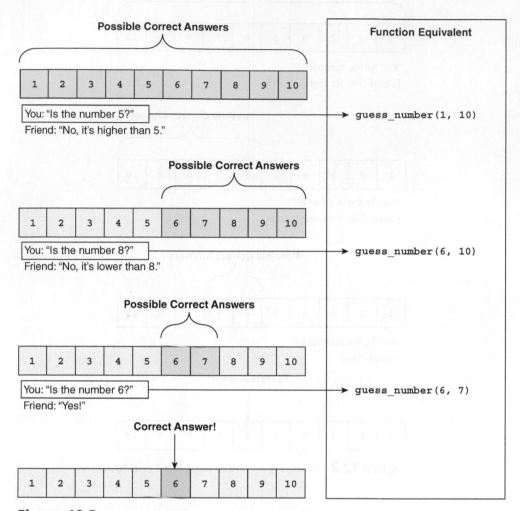

Figure 12-3 Guessing game using function calls

In the number game, you stop guessing when you guess the number correctly. This is an example of a **base case**, a condition where you should stop trying to solve the problem. One type of base case signals an early exit from the function. If you guess the right number in the guessing game, you can stop without updating the number range.

A base case can also represent a problem small enough to solve quickly. For example, if you run out of numbers to guess, you know that your friend made a mistake in answering, and that you need to tell the person so. Recursive functions can have more than one base case, such as one to exit the function early and another to solve the program when it is small enough.

As with normal functions, a recursive function can return a value. If the recursive function does not need to return information, then recursion is easy. A simple program to print the numbers from 1 to 10 using recursion could be designed as follows:

```
def display_numbers(n):
if n > 10:
```

```
return
else:
print(n)
display_numbers(n + 1)
```

Look over this program line by line to see how it works. The `def` statement in the first line indicates you are creating a function with the name **display_numbers**. Including the **n** in parentheses shows this function accepts one parameter. The if-else block sets the condition that if the parameter **n** is greater than **10**, the function returns without doing anything. Otherwise, the function displays the value stored in **n** and calls itself, this time with the value increased by **1**.

If the recursive function needs to return a value, it passes information in a chain. Think of a game of telephone, where people stand in a line and can only talk to two people: the person to their right and the person to their left. If the last person on the right has information to return to the first person, they have to tell the person to their left, who has to tell the person to their left, and so on until the information reaches the first person at the start of the line. The good news is that computers don't mix up the information along the way, as usually happens when playing telephone. For example, calculating the sum of numbers from 10 to 1 could be designed as follows:

```
def add_numbers(n):
if n < 1:
return 0
else:
total = n + add_numbers(n - 1)
return total
```

This function still has only one parameter, but now has a returned value.

Q What is the returned value if **n** is **0**?

A If **n** is **0**, the base case of **n** < **1** is met, so **0** is returned.

Q What is the returned value if **n** is **1**?

A If **n** is **1**, the function makes one recursive call, then adds **1** to the result. This recursive call passes **0** to **add_numbers**, which returns **0**. The returned value of the initial call is **1**.

The returned value is all values between **1** and **n** added together. Here, each function asks a recursive call for its result, and then adds the current value of **n** to the returned value and stores it in **total**.

Recursion can represent a single line of problem solving, as in the example of the number guessing game. This type of recursive function calls itself once and is called **linear recursion**. Linear recursion is the easiest to program; it is the most similar to for-loops. Other versions of recursion known as **branching recursion** do not limit themselves to one recursive call. **Figure 12-4** and **Figure 12-5** show how these two flows of recursion work.

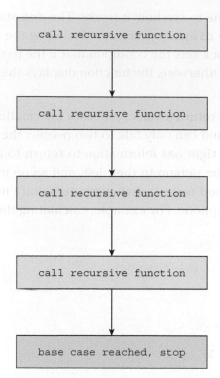

Figure 12-4 Linear recursive function calls (arrows represent actual function calls)

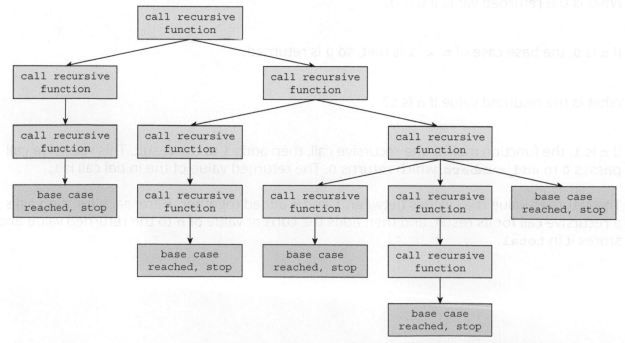

Figure 12-5 Branching recursive function calls (arrows represent actual function calls)

With the linear recursion shown in Figure 12-4, each time the code visits a function, the function calls itself at most once or stops when it reaches a base case.

With the branching recursion shown in Figure 12-5, each time the code visits a function, the function calls itself one or more times or stops when it reaches a base case.

When to Use Recursion (12.1.4)

Ask yourself the following key questions when deciding whether to use recursion to solve a problem:

- Can this problem be broken down into smaller problems?
- Are the smaller problems identical to the larger problems?
- Is there a way to divide the problem into smaller subproblems that are easy to solve?

While linear recursion and loops can be similar, keep a mental note of when it is easier to design a program with one or the other. The two are like a hammer and a saw. Technically, you could use a hammer to cut a piece of wood in half, but it would be easier if you used the appropriate tool.

Q When should you use loops? When should you use recursion?

A Use loops when you need to do the same thing without changing the situation. Use recursion when you need to reduce the problem to solve it.

Think of recursion as delegating tasks. How can you delegate smaller problems to other people? How can you put the pieces back together after receiving the results? What should the smallest task be, at which point you cannot delegate anymore?

12.2 Using Recursion To Solve Complex Problems

Designing Recursive Structures (12.2.1, 12.2.2, 12.2.3)

Use the following checklist when writing a recursive function:

1. Check for the base case.
2. Modify the parameters.
3. Invoke the function recursively.
4. Return the result to the calling function, if appropriate.

Checking for a base case is the same as asking yourself "When should I stop?" To modify the parameters, ask "How is the problem changing through the recursive calls?" Finally, if a value is returned, you can do something with it. This could be as simple as returning the information unchanged to the calling function or calculating a new value to return.

The number guessing game uses linear recursion. **Figure 12-6** shows a working program for the game.

```
def guess_number(low, high):
    # Comments are indicated with a # at the beginning.

    # Base case
    if low > high:

        return -1


    middle = (low + high) // 2
    hint = input("Is your number " + str(middle) + "? ")

    # Base case
    if hint == "correct":

        return middle

    # higher
    elif hint == "higher":

        return guess_number(middle + 1, high)

    # lower
    else:

        return guess_number(low, middle - 1)
print("Enter higher, lower, or correct.")
print("Think of a number between 1 and 10.")
number = guess_number(1, 10)
if number != -1:

    print("Your number is " + str(number) + "!")

else:

    print("You cheated :(")

OUTPUT:
Enter higher, lower, or correct.
Think of a number between 1 and 10.
Is your number 5? higher [Enter]
Is your number 8? lower [Enter]
Is your number 6? correct [Enter]
Your number is 6!
```

Figure 12-6   Program to play the guessing game

Q Is the base case checked in Figure 12-6? If so, how?

A The code in Figure 12-6 has two base cases: cheating and correct answers. Cheating is when the lower boundary is higher than the upper boundary. Correct is when your friend says you're right.

Q Are the parameters modified in Figure 12-6? If so, how?

A If your friend replies "higher," then the lower boundary is increased to the guessed number plus 1. If your friend replies "lower," then the upper boundary is decreased to the guessed number minus 1.

Q Is the function invoked recursively in Figure 12-6? If so, how?

A Based on your friend's answers, "higher" invokes the function with a new lower boundary, and "lower" invokes the function with a new upper boundary.

Q Is anything returned in Figure 12-6? If so, what?

A The correctly guessed number is returned. Otherwise, –1 is returned if cheating was involved.

Anything done in a loop (an algorithm that uses a repetition control) can be done with recursion. **Figure 12-7** compares the `display_numbers` code using a while-loop structure and its recursive equivalent. The goal of both approaches is to display all numbers from 1 to 10. With a loop executing based on the variable `current_number`, it starts with `current_number` set to 1 and ends when `current_number` is greater than 10. The base case is when the variable `current_number` goes beyond 10.

Some recursion modifies its parameters incrementally, like adding 1 in `display_numbers`. Another way to design recursive code is called "divide and conquer." As the name suggests, you divide the problem to conquer it. You took this approach in the number guessing game. Each time you guess, you divide the range of possible correct answers in half. Eventually, you conquer the problem by guessing the right number.

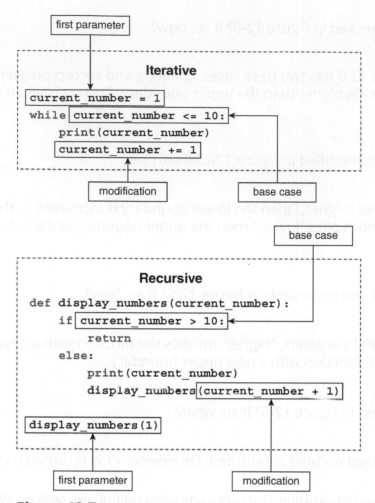

Figure 12-7   Loop and recursion to perform the same task

Linear Recursion (12.2.4, 12.2.5)

Identifying linear recursion problems is like knowing when you should use a loop. Can you solve a set of smaller problems in sequence? If so, use a loop or linear recursion. One example of an iterative problem is to add the numbers **1** to **10**. The following for-loop takes an iterative approach:

```
count = 0

for number in range(1, 11, 1):

    count += number

print(count)
```

Q How would you translate this code to recursion?

A Use the checklist. Start with the base case, which is the test case in the for-loop. A range in Python has a test case implied in the second argument. In this case, **number** will always be less than or equal to **10**. In the recursive code, you reverse the test case to check if **number** is greater than **10** (instead of less than or equal to **10**) because that is when you stop the sequence. The increment (last argument to **range**) is how you modify the parameters, and the start (first argument to **range**) is how you invoke the first recursive call.

Figure 12-8 shows how to use linear recursion to add the numbers 1 to 10.

```
def add_numbers(current_number):

    if current_number > 10:

        return 0

    else:

        next_number = current_number + 1

        count = add_numbers(next_number)

        return current_number + count

print(add_numbers(1))

OUTPUT:

55
```

Figure 12-8   Recursively adding the numbers from 1 to 10

Q Can you apply the recursive checklist to the linear recursion code?

A The base case is the line with `if current_number > 10`. The `next_number = current_number + 1` statement modifies the parameters. The recursive call stores the returned value in `count`. The returning value is calculated in the last line. The starting recursive call is the line outside of the function, `add_numbers(1)`.

To display the result, use the `print()` function to display the value returned by `add_numbers(1)`. The output is `55`, or the result of adding the numbers from `1` to `10`.

Branching Recursion (12.2.5)

Some problems are more complicated than an iterative design can handle. Think of a computer folder containing files and other folders. Suppose you want to count the files with a .txt extension in the folder and any subfolders (folders within folders). The following functions are already programmed in Python; you just need to import the `os` module for some of them:

- `os.listdir("folder")`: Given a folder name, this function returns a list of all files in the folder. A list is a way to store multiple strings in one variable, symbolized with square brackets. A list can also be used directly with a for-loop.
- `os.path.isdir("filename")`: Detects if the file name given is a folder. Returns `True` if the file name is a folder and returns `False` otherwise.
- `os.path.join(["folder","filename"])`: Given a series of strings, this statement returns a folder name and file name as a path. For example, `os.path.join(["folder", "subfolder", "example.txt"])` when used on a Windows machine returns the string `"folder\subfolder\example.txt"`.
- `"filename".endswith("extension")`: Given a file name and an extension, this function returns `True` if the file name ends with the extension or `False` otherwise. For example, `"example.txt".endswith(".txt")` returns `True`.

Can you solve this problem iteratively? You can use a for-loop to test each file and increase the count by 1 for each file with the extension .txt. **Figure 12-9** shows how this might look.

```
import os

folder = input("Enter a folder name: ")
count = 0
files = os.listdir(folder)

for filename in files:
    if filename.endswith(".txt"):
        count += 1

print(count)

OUTPUT:

Enter a folder name: exampleFolder [Enter]
2
```

Output will change depending on where you run the program and the files you have on your computer.

Figure 12-9   First attempt at iteratively counting files with a .txt extension

The input is the name of the folder. Using **os.listdir()**, the code collects the names of the files within that folder. The variable **count** is used to keep track of how many files are identified as ending with **.txt**. Using a for-loop, each file in the folder is examined for the **.txt** extension, and **1** is added to **count** if the file is a **.txt** file.

What happens if the file name stored in the variable **folder** contains another folder, which also contains **.txt** files? In that case, you need to count the files in the nested subfolder. You could try to fix this by adding another for-loop; see **Figure 12-10**.

```
import os

folder = input("Enter a folder name: ")
count = 0
files = os.listdir(folder)

for filename in files:
    file_path = os.path.join(folder, filename)
    if filename.endswith(".txt"):
        count += 1
    elif os.path.isdir(file_path):
        subfolder_files = os.listdir(file_path)
        for subfilename in subfolder_files:
            if subfilename.endswith(".txt"):
                count += 1

print(count)

OUTPUT:

Enter a folder name: exampleFolder [Enter]
5
```

Output will change depending on where you run the program and the files you have on your computer.

Figure 12-10   Second attempt at iteratively counting files with a .txt extension

Now the code has an else-if condition to detect a nested folder. In the else-if block, the code is nearly identical to the code in the main program. It counts each file in `file_path` that has a `.txt` extension. However, that still doesn't solve the problem. What if `file_path` also contains a folder? What if that new folder also contains a folder? You need an infinite number of nested ifs and loops to solve this problem with an iterative algorithm.

You can't solve this problem iteratively. Each new folder you find means you have to go into the folder to count its files. This is a perfect time to use a recursive algorithm. For each new folder, you perform the same action on a smaller problem.

The code in **Figure 12-11** shows how to solve the file-counting problem using recursion. Your base case is whether a file name in a folder is a `.txt` file. If it is, increase the count of files by 1. If the file name is a folder, then you count the `.txt` files it contains. You need to increase the total of `.txt` files by the result of counting the files in that subfolder. Each folder has its own count of `.txt` files, which must be summed to find the total in `count`.

```
import os

def count_txt_files(folder):
    count = 0
    files = os.listdir(folder)
    for filename in files:
        file_path = os.path.join(folder, filename)

        # Base case
        if filename.endswith(".txt"):
            count += 1

        # Branching recursive calls
        elif os.path.isdir(file_path):
            subcount = count_txt_files(file_path)
            count += subcount

    return count

starting_folder = input("Enter a folder name: ")
final_count = count_txt_files(starting_folder)
print(final_count)
```

OUTPUT:◄─────────────────────── Output will change depending on where you run the program and the files you have on your computer.

```
Enter a folder name: exampleFolder [Enter]
12
```

Figure 12-11   Recursively counting files with a .txt extension

This is an example of branching recursion, which includes more than one call to the recursive function, `count_txt_files`. It begins with a for-loop as in a standard iterative structure. Each time the code finds a folder instead of a file, it branches to the `count_txt_files` function to count the files in the folder. Although the code starts with a for-loop, it takes a recursive approach to perform a repetitive task and avoid impossible infinite code.

Another example of branching recursion is the computed list known as the Fibonacci sequence. The Fibonacci sequence is a weird series of numbers defined recursively, as follows:

- The first number is 1.
- The second number is 1.
- The third number is the second plus the first number.
- The fourth number is the third plus the second number.
- The nth number is the sum of $(n - 1) + (n - 2)$.

The sequence starts with the following 10 numbers:

1, 1, 2, 3, 5, 8, 13, 21, 34, 55

To find the next number in the Fibonacci sequence, you use recursion. The code in **Figure 12-12** defines a function named `fibonacci` with a parameter called `n`, which refers to the position in the sequence. You have two base cases: if the value passed in `n` to `fibonacci` is 1 or 2, they both return 1, as shown in the `if` block. If `n` is something other than 1 or 2, you can call the function recursively by subtracting 1 and then 2 from `n`. The result of `n - 1` is stored in the variable `n1`, and the result from `n - 2` is stored in `n2`. The program then returns the sum of the two recursive calls.

```
def fibonacci(n):

    # Base case
    if n == 1 or n == 2:
        return 1


    # Find the fibonacci number for n - 1
    n1 = fibonacci(n - 1)


    # Find the fibonacci number for n - 2
    n2 = fibonacci(n - 2)


    # Add together and return
    return n1 + n2


n = int(input("Enter a number: "))
fibonacci_n = fibonacci(n)
print("The Fibonacci number is", fibonacci_n)
OUTPUT:
Enter a number: 6 [Enter]
The Fibonacci number is 8
```

Figure 12-12   Code to program the Fibonacci sequence

Q If you write `fibonacci(2)`, how many times is the `fibonacci` function called recursively?

A None, because `fibonacci(2)` is one of the base cases.

Q If you write `fibonacci(4)`, how many times is the `fibonacci` function called recursively?

A The number **4** is not **1** or **2**, so `fibonacci(3)` and `fibonacci(2)` are called recursively. Calling `fibonacci(3)` calls `fibonacci(2)` and `fibonacci(1)`. Both **1** and **2** are base cases, so there are no more recursive calls. The total number of recursive calls is four.

Recall that the Fibonacci sequence starts with 10 numbers: 1, 1, 2, 3, 5, 8, 13, 21, 34, 55. How does the code calculate the 11th Fibonacci number? The `fibonacci` function takes **11** as its argument. That number is not **1** or **2**, so the `fibonacci` function is called recursively with arguments of **10** (which is **11 - 1**) and **9** (which is **11 - 2**). The first `fibonacci` function returns **55**, and the second returns **34**. Add the returned values to find the next number in the Fibonacci sequence, which is **89**.

12.3 Managing Memory During Recursion

Memory Management (12.3.1, 12.3.2)

A function that calls itself many times can require a lot of memory when the program runs. A computer reserves a block of memory to keep track of the current state of the program. This block contains the names of all the variables in your program along with the values stored in each variable.

The code in **Figure 12-13** sums the numbers from 1 to 10 using recursion.

```
def sum_numbers(current_number):
    if current_number == 0:
        return 0
    else:
        sum_total = sum_numbers(current_number - 1)
        return current_number + sum_total
print(sum_numbers(10))
```
OUTPUT:
55

Figure 12-13 Adding all numbers from 1 to 10

Q How many variables does the code in Figure 12-13 need to remember?

A The line `return current_number + sum_total` follows the recursive call to the `sum_numbers` function. That means the program must remember `current_number` after the recursive call comes back. Each time a function is called, another memory block is set aside for that function's lifetime, and then marked as no longer needed once the function returns. Calling `sum_numbers(10)` means the code needs to remember 11 variables.

Figure 12-14 outlines the memory the code needs to hold variables when it calls `sum_numbers(10)`.

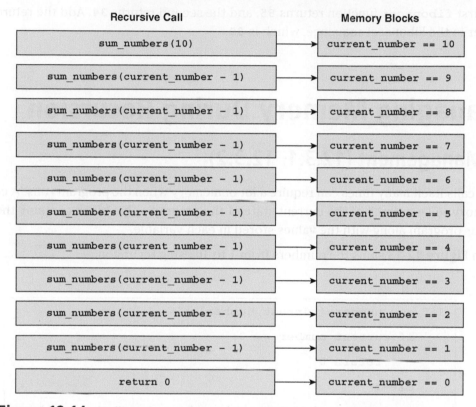

```
def sum(current_number)
    if current_number == 0:
        return 0
    else:
        sum_total = sum(current_number - 1)
        return current_number + sum_total

sum(10)
```

Recursive Call   **Memory Blocks**

sum_numbers(10)	→	current_number == 10
sum_numbers(current_number - 1)	→	current_number == 9
sum_numbers(current_number - 1)	→	current_number == 8
sum_numbers(current_number - 1)	→	current_number == 7
sum_numbers(current_number - 1)	→	current_number == 6
sum_numbers(current_number - 1)	→	current_number == 5
sum_numbers(current_number - 1)	→	current_number == 4
sum_numbers(current_number - 1)	→	current_number == 3
sum_numbers(current_number - 1)	→	current_number == 2
sum_numbers(current_number - 1)	→	current_number == 1
return 0	→	current_number == 0

Figure 12-14   Calling `sum_numbers(10)` needs 11 memory blocks

Each time a recursive function finishes, it needs to return to the memory state directly before it. Computers use data structures called **stacks** to store the memory blocks for recursive function calls. As with a stack of pancakes, you can only place new pancakes on top and can only remove pancakes from the top. Each time a recursive function is called, a new memory block is placed on top of the stack as in **Figure 12-15**.

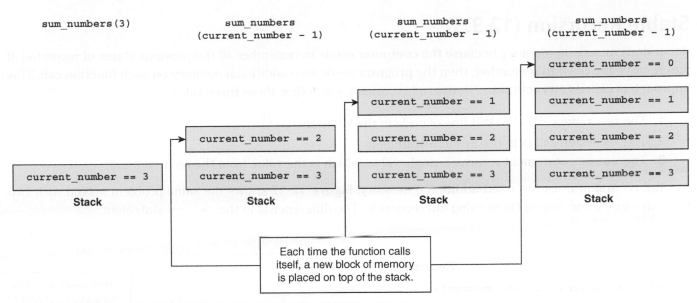

Figure 12-15   Memory stack for recursive function calls

Each time a function finishes, the top of the stack is removed, as in **Figure 12-16**.

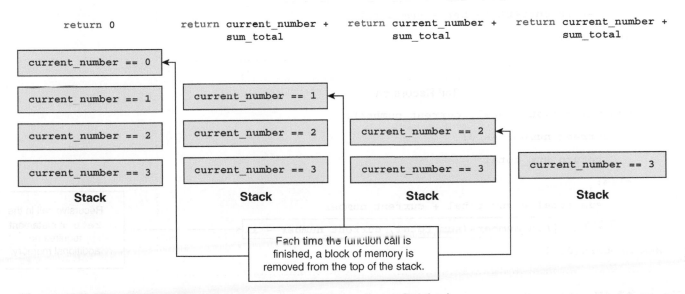

Figure 12-16   Memory stack when recursive function calls are finished

The longer a recursive chain of calls, the more memory is needed to keep track of what happened in the previous calls. In fact, the computer can run out of memory if the recursion goes on for too long. This is only a problem if you are working with exceptionally large datasets, such as a list of everyone who has ever lived on Earth. For a recursive algorithm to deal with loads of data, it needs to get smart about its memory management.

Stable Recursion (12.3.3)

Recursion can use up memory because the computer needs to remember all the previous states of recursion. If you remove the need to remember, then the program needs zero additional memory on each function call. This approach is called **tail recursion**. To use tail recursion, you follow these three rules:

1. The recursive call is the last line of code in the function.
2. The recursive call is in the **return** statement.
3. The **return** statement returns a single value, which is the value from the recursive call.

Tail recursion does not need additional memory. **Figure 12-17** shows the same problem solved with two recursive functions, one of them using tail recursion. The difference is in the **return** statement.

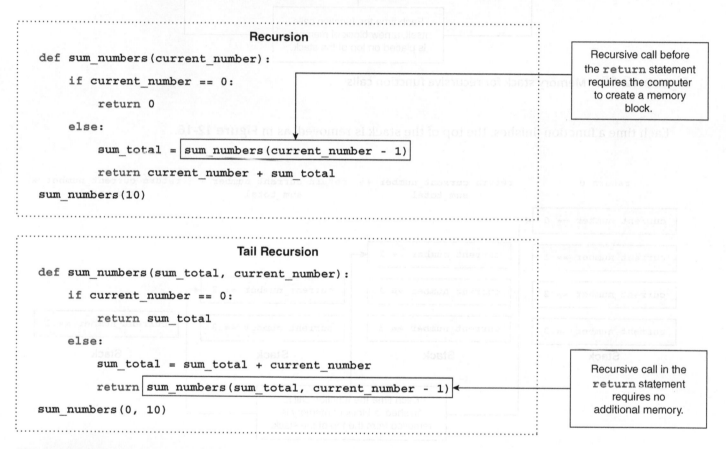

Recursion

```
def sum_numbers(current_number):

    if current_number == 0:

        return 0

    else:

        sum_total = sum_numbers(current_number - 1)

        return current_number + sum_total

sum_numbers(10)
```

Recursive call before the **return** statement requires the computer to create a memory block.

Tail Recursion

```
def sum_numbers(sum_total, current_number):

    if current_number == 0:

        return sum_total

    else:

        sum_total = sum_total + current_number

        return sum_numbers(sum_total, current_number - 1)

sum_numbers(0, 10)
```

Recursive call in the **return** statement requires no additional memory.

Figure 12-17 Using tail recursion

Both sets of code sum the numbers from **10** to **1**. The tail recursive code passes the **sum_total** variable to the recursive function call instead of using a local variable. With this approach, the computer does not need to remember anything, so it does not use additional memory.

Summary

- Recursion is a strategy for approaching large problems in computer science by breaking the problem down into smaller identical problems. The same steps are applied to each smaller version of the problem, although with different restrictions.
- A recursive function calls itself at least once. With each function call, a recursive function uses modified parameters to reduce the size of the problem.
- If the parameters of a recursive function are not modified, the recursive function does not stop, creating an infinite recursion.
- A base case is a condition that stops the recursion, such as guessing the correct number in a number guessing game. A base case can also represent a problem small enough that it can be solved quickly.
- A recursive function should check for the base case as its first step. Make sure the code also modifies the parameters, invokes the function recursively one or more times, and does something with any returned value.
- Linear recursion is a recursive function that calls itself once at most or stops when it reaches a base case.
- Branching recursion is a recursive function that calls itself more than once.
- Loops are similar to linear recursion, although you use each approach in different situations. Use loops when you need to do the same task without changing the conditions. Use recursion when you need to reduce the problem to solve it.
- Each recursive function call requires another block of memory from the computer unless the function is designed to use tail recursion.

Key Terms

base case

branching recursion

infinite recursion

linear recursion

recursion

recursive function

stacks

tail recursion

Module

13

Modules

Learning Objectives:

13.1 Storing Code in Modules

13.1.1 Explain the benefits of storing code in multiple files.

13.1.2 Describe module structures.

13.1.3 Define nested modules.

13.2 Importing Modules

13.2.1 Explain how the keyword `import` copies code from another module.

13.2.2 Explain how the keyword `from` copies code from another module.

13.2.3 Explain how the wildcard * modifies the `from` keyword import.

13.2.4 Identify the differences in a program with the different modes of import.

13.2.5 Recognize when to use `import` versus `from`.

13.2.6 Recognize how to use `import` with nested modules.

13.3 Creating Modules

13.3.1 Explain how to create a module in the same folder as another program.

13.3.2 Recognize that code within modules is no different than outside code.

13.3.3 Explain the significance of having a main function.

13.3.4 Explain the use of `__name__ == "__main__"`.

13.3.5 Define docstring.

13.3.6 Identify that the `help()` function displays the docstring in a module or function.

13.4 Creating Nested Modules

13.4.1 Explain how to create a module inside a folder.

13.4.2 Identify the `__init__.py` file as what converts a folder into a module.

13.4.3 Identify that `__init__.py` is needed in every folder in a nested module system.

13.4.4 Identify the change to `import` statements within a module to relative `import` statements.

13.5 Useful Modules in Python

13.5.1 Explain the purpose of the `math` module.

13.5.2 List some of the available functions in the `math` module.

13.5.3 Explain the purpose of the `random` module.

13.5.4 List some of the available functions in the `random` module.

13.5.5 Identify the `pip` command as the primary way to install new modules.

13.5.6 Recognize that `pip` will try to install dependent modules.

13.5.7 Use `pip` to uninstall modules.

13.1 Storing Code in Modules

Library of Previous Knowledge (13.1.1)

The number of functions and methods available to you in Python is vast. Other programmers have created code for other people to use. You can think of this code as a big library, as in **Figure 13-1**.

Figure 13-1   A library with resources for you to use

A library contains a lot of information, but you rarely need all of it. Sometimes you need a reference book on math; other times you may want to check out a recipe book or look at pictures of cats. Instead of taking every book or resource in the library home with you, you check out only the items you need at the time. This is how the available code for Python is designed. The Python code library includes extra **modules** created by other programmers that you can use to make your programs easier to build. Modules are pre-programmed pieces of code you can bring into a program as if you made them yourself.

Module Structure (13.1.2, 13.1.3)

A module contains Python code in a file stored in the same folder as the current project or in a special folder containing .py source code files. Python stores its default modules in a certain location, but you can keep new modules (ones you or others create) in any location. Because the modules are separate from other files, you use a keyword to tell Python which modules or parts of modules you want to include in your program. Using the keyword is like telling the librarian which books you want to check out.

Modules are organized by purpose. For example, the Python **math** module contains helpful math-related functions, like **math.pow()**. Instead of writing the code for this calculation yourself, you can use the Python **math** module, which offers error-free code. Because the modules are organized by purpose, you can check out only the modules that would be useful in your current programming task.

Just as some books have chapters or sections that break down a topic into easier-to-manage parts, Python modules can come in bite-sized pieces. **Nested modules** are modules stored within other modules. The **path** module is a nested module inside the **os** module, usually referenced as **os.path** when used in code. You can use nested modules on their own, just like a non-nested module. How you reference code within a module depends on how you bring it into the program.

13.2 Importing Modules

Using **import** (13.2.1)

Creating access to code from an external module is called **importing**. Use the keyword **import** to include code from another file. The following is the general syntax for importing from another module:

import <*module_name*>

Here, the *italics* and angle brackets **<>** indicate that **<*module_name*>** is a placeholder term to be replaced with the name of an actual module. You don't need the angle brackets when importing in your program, and there is no literal module called **module_name**.

When you import a module and use one of its functions, you reference the module name before the function name. For example, if you want to use the **factorial()** function from the **math** module, you reference it as **math.factorial()**, as in **Figure 13-2**.

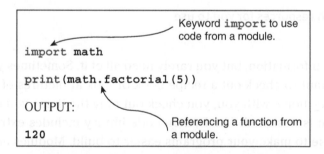

Figure 13-2 Using the **factorial()** function from the **math** module

Using **import** is like copying all the code from a module into your code. Because a module can contain many functions, Python syntax requires you to include the module name in the identifier reference for a function. This requirement prevents scope conflicts. If you program your own version of **factorial()**, you can still reference both functions, even after importing the **math** module. **Figure 13-3** shows how to reference an imported function and a function you created yourself.

```
import math
                            Programmer-defined
                            factorial().
def factorial(n):
    print("My Special Factorial")
    total = 1
    for i in range(1, n+1):
        total *= i
                            factorial()
    return total          function imported from
                            the math module.
print(math.factorial(5))

print(factorial(5))

OUTPUT:
120
My Special Factorial
120
```

Figure 13-3 Using two `factorial()` functions

Using `from` to Import (13.2.2, 13.2.3, 13.2.4, 13.2.5)

If you will use the code you're importing frequently in a program, typing the module name for every function could get tedious. In such cases, you can use the keyword `from` when importing a module. Using the keyword `import` by itself gives you access to all the code in the specified module. Use the keyword `from` with `import` to import only the parts of the module you specify. The following is the general syntax:

```
from <module_name> import <function_name>
```

To import more than one function from a module, write the statement on one line, separating each function by a comma:

```
from <module_name> import <function1>, <function2>
```

Figure 13-4 shows the change in code from Figure 13-2 if you use `from` to import from **math**.

```
from math import factorial
print(factorial(5))

OUTPUT:
120
```

Figure 13-4 Using `from` to import only `factorial()` from **math**

Q Why wouldn't you want to import all of the functions from a module?

A Modules can be very large and contain items that are not necessary for your code. Importing an entire module is inefficient, like taking the whole cooking section home from a library when you only need a book about making bread.

If you plan to frequently use many items from a module, you can use `from` and the asterisk (*) wildcard character to import all items from the module. Use the following syntax to import all the code in a module without repeating the module name in each reference:

```
from <module_name> import *
```

When to use the * wildcard instead of specific named imports depends on the situation. Generally, if you are importing more than five items from the same module, using the * wildcard saves coding time. Either approach produces the same result. The output from the code in Figure 13-4 would not change if you modified `from` `math` `import` `factorial` to `from` `math` `import *`.

Nested Module Imports (13.2.6)

Importing from nested modules is the same as importing from top-level modules. You can import the upper modules or only the nested module you need. If you import only from a nested module, such as `os.path`, then only `os.path` functions will be available, not functions or other code from the upper module `os`.

13.3 Creating Modules

Getting Started with Modules (13.3.1, 13.3.2)

To create a module, you place your own .py file in the same folder as the program that will use the module. Done! See **Figure 13-5**.

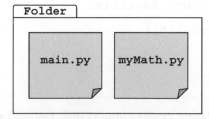

Figure 13-5   Creating a module by placing it in the same folder as the main program

The code in **myMath.py** is no different from code you would have programmed without making it a module. It might contain one variable, **pi**, and two functions, **factorial()** and **abs()**. Having this code in a module instead of the main program allows you or other programmers to reuse the code in other programs.

The `main()` Function (13.3.3, 13.3.4)

When programming **myMath.py**, you may want to include testing statements after the functions to make sure that everything works correctly. **Figure 13-6** shows how you might test the code when programming the module.

```
# Test code in the MyMath.py module
pi = 3.14159

def abs(x):
    if x < 0:
        return -x
    else:
        return x

def factorial(n):
    total = 1
    for i in range(1, n+1):
        total *= i
    return total

print("Testing math:")
print("Absolute value of -5:", abs(-5))
print("Absolute value of 5:", abs(5))          — Testing statements
print("Value of pi:", pi)
print("Factorial of 5:", factorial(5))
```

Figure 13-6   Adding test code to a module

However, if you import items from **myMath.py** into a new program now, the test code runs in the new program and produces the output shown in **Figure 13-7**.

```
from myMath import pi, factorial
print("Pi:", pi)
print("Factorial of 7:", factorial(7))

OUTPUT:
Testing math:
Absolute value of -5: 5
Absolute value of 5: 5          This printout
                                shouldn't be here!
Value of pi: 3.14159
Factorial of 5: 120
Pi: 3.14159
Factorial of 7: 5040
```

Figure 13-7   All module code including test code is imported and run

When importing, all code in the imported module is run. This includes any `print()` statements, calculations, and other items. If you want to reuse the code in the module elsewhere, you may want control over how and when the module contents are run. Placing code inside functions prevents it from running automatically. When creating modules, it's a good idea to place all code inside functions. This way, the code runs only when the function is called, leaving it to future programs to decide when to run the testing code. **Figure 13-8** moves the testing code inside a function named `test()`.

```
pi = 3.14159
def abs(x):
    if x < 0:
        return -x
    else:
        return x
def factorial(n):
    total = 1
    for i in range(1, n+1):
        total *= i
    return total
def test():
    print("Testing math:")
    print("Absolute value of -5:", abs(-5))
    print("Absolute value of 5:", abs(5))
    print("Value of pi:", pi)
    print("Factorial of 5:", factorial(5))
```

Figure 13-8 Moving the testing code into a function

Using a function such as `test()` fixes the problem from Figure 13-7, but if you run the code in Figure 13-8, the output from the test statements won't print. All your code is contained in a **main function**, in this situation called `test()`, but frequently called `main()`. You want the function to run in a specific situation, not when the module is imported, but when the module is run directly, such as by pressing F5 in IDLE.

Python creates hidden variables when it runs a program, one of which is the variable __name__. The double underscores before and after `name` mean this is a hidden identifier. This variable is given a string value representing the name of the current code location. If the code is an imported module, the name of the code location is the name of the module (for example, `"myMath"`). However, if the running code is the main code, the name of the code location is `"__main__"`. **Figure 13-9** shows how to program `myMath.py` so that it will run its tests only when running the module code on its own, not when the module is imported.

```
pi = 3.14159

def abs(x):
    if x < 0:
        return -x
    else:
        return x

def factorial(n):
    total = 1
    for i in range(1, n+1):
        total *= i
    return total

def test():
    print("Testing math:")
    print("Absolute value of -5:", abs(-5))
    print("Absolute value of 5:", abs(5))
    print("Value of pi:", pi)
    print("Factorial of 5:", factorial(5))

if __name__ == "__main__":
    test()
```
Run **test()** only when running the module code, not when the module is imported.

Figure 13-9   Using the __name__

Module Documentation (13.3.5, 13.3.6)

All built-in Python modules provide information for you to learn about them. Using the `help()` function on a module will tell you more about it. You can also use the `help()` function on functions. **Figure 13-10** shows the output of the `help(abs)` function. Note that the function name inside of `help()` is missing its set of parentheses. This is because you don't want the code in `abs()` to run, you want help on the function itself.

```
print(help(abs))

OUTPUT:

Help on built-in function abs in module builtins:


abs(x, /)

    Return the absolute value of the argument.
```

Figure 13-10   The help() function

When programming your own modules, you can use the docstring to provide help information. The docstring is a string enclosed by three quotation marks. When the `help()` function is called, the string in triple quotation marks is displayed. The placement of the docstring indicates which part of the module it corresponds to. Include the docstring for the entire module at the top of the .py file. Place the docstring inside a function signature to provide information about the function only. **Figure 13-11** shows how you might add docstrings to the `myMath.py` module and its functions.

```python
"""myMath.py

Author: Dr. Elizabeth Matthews

A module containing some math functions and
an approximation of pi."""
pi = 3.14159

def abs(x):
    """abs(x)

    Returns the absolute value of x."""
    if x < 0:
        return -x
    else:
        return x

def factorial(n):
    """factorial(n)

    Returns the factorial of n."""
    total = 1
    for i in range(1, n+1):
        total *= i
    return total

def test():
    """A test program for the module."""
    print("Testing math:")
    print("Absolute value of -5:", abs(-5))
    print("Absolute value of 5:", abs(5))
    print("Value of pi:", pi)
    print("Factorial of 5:", factorial(5))

if __name__ == "__main__":
    test()
```

Figure 13-11 Docstrings for `myMath.py`

13.4 Creating Nested Modules

Folders as Modules (13.4.1, 13.4.2, 13.4.3)

If you create many modules, you can organize them like files on a computer. You could save everything to the desktop, or you could create folders by category.

To convert a normal folder into a Python module, you need to place a special Python file named **__init__.py** in the folder. Doing so makes the folder a Python module you can import from. The file name must have two underscores on either side of the **init** text. **Figure 13-12** shows the contents of a folder containing a custom Python module. You can add code to the **__init__.py** file, but it also works as an empty file.

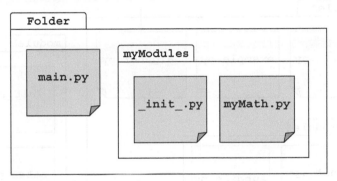

Figure 13-12   Creating a module folder requires **__init__.py**

To import from modules within a folder, you chain the folder name with the module source code name. For example, to import the **abs()** function in the **myMath.py** source code file stored in the **myModules** folder, write **from myModules.myMath import abs**. You can nest other module folders within an upper module folder, if necessary, though each folder needs its own **__init__.py** file.

Relative Imports (13.4.4)

Suppose one of the modules you created needs to import code from another module in the same folder. You can use a standard **import** statement, such as **import math** or **import myMath**. However, if you use a **from** statement in a module folder, you need to use a **relative import** path. For example, suppose you are creating a **circle.py** module in the **myModules** folder and want to import the value of **pi** from **myMath**. To import from another module within the same module folder, precede the module name by a dot (**.**). **Figure 13-13** shows what the **circle.py** module might look like.

```
from .myMath import pi

def area(radius):

    return pi * radius * radius

def circumference(radius):

    return 2 * pi * radius
```

Figure 13-13   Relative import within a module folder

To access a folder above the current module, you use two dots (**..**) to go up by one module folder, three dots (**...**) to go up by two folders, and so on. **Figure 13-14** is a diagram of how to access relative modules from the file named **example.py**.

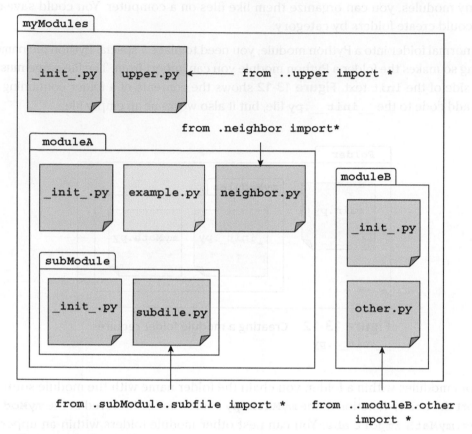

Figure 13-14   Relative imports within module folders

13.5 Useful Modules in Python

Built-In Modules (13.5.1, 13.5.2, 13.5.3, 13.5.4)

When you install Python on your computer, it provides built-in modules. You can use some built-in modules without expressly importing them, such as the **help()** function, which provides helpful information about a specified module.

Computer programs often require computation and mathematical manipulations. Simpler and more common functions, such as **abs()** and **sum()**, are also free to use without an **import** statement. However, importing from the **math** module gives you access to many functions related to more complex mathematical operations, such as calculating a square root. **Figure 13-15** lists some functions in the **math** module.

Function	Description	Example
`math.factorial()`	Returns the multiplicative sum of a number (5 * 4 * 3 * 2 * 1).	`math.factorial(5)`
`math.pow()`	Returns the value of the first parameter raised to the power of the second parameter.	`math.pow(4,3)`
`math.sqrt()`	Returns the square root of a number.	`math.sqrt(16)`
`math.cos()`	Returns the cosine of the parameter, assuming the parameter is in radians.	`math.cos(1.5)`
`math.pi`	The mathematical constant π.	`math.pi * radius * radius`

Figure 13-15 Functions from the `math` module

Another useful module you must import is the **random** module. You can use random numbers for generating test data or when creating basic artificial intelligence for a computer opponent in a game, for example. You can generate a random number between a smaller and larger value with **random.randint(smaller, larger)**. You also can shuffle a list into a random order with **random.shuffle(number_list)**. **Figure 13-16** shows some functions in the **random** module.

Function	Description	Example
`random.randint()`	Return a random integer between the first parameter and the second parameter, including the second parameter.	`random.randint(0,100)` `random.randint(0,1)`
`random.choice()`	Return a random selection from an iterative sequence like a list.	`random.choice(["red", "blue", "green"])`
`random.shuffle()`	Shuffles the values in an iterative sequence; does not return anything but changes the value in the variable.	`n = [x for x in range(10)]` `random.shuffle(n)`
`random.sample()`	Returns a random unique selection of multiple values from an iterative sequence.	`random.sample(["red", "blue", "green", "orange", "yellow"], 2)`

Figure 13-16 Functions from the `random` module

The `pip` Command (13.5.5, 13.5.6, 13.5.7)

The built-in Python modules are not the only ones available to you. You can download and install other modules, and then use them like the built-in modules.

You can use the **pip command** at the Python command line to have Python attempt to install modules for you. The **pip** command comes with newer downloads of Python and is the easiest way to install extra modules if you know the module name.

The **pip** command also has the benefit of downloading and installing auxiliary modules that the primary module relies on. For example, the **matplotlib** module provides functions for creating graphs but requires you to have installed the **NumPy** module. Using **pip** to install **matplotlib** will detect this dependency and install **NumPy** for you.

The following is the syntax for using the **pip** command in the command terminal:

```
python -m pip install <module_name>
```

The **-m** signals to Python that you are running the **pip** module. Including the word **install** tells **pip** to install the specified module. **Figure 13-17** shows the results of a user successfully importing and installing **matplotlib**. The **"Requirement already satisfied:"** statements indicate that the user has already installed the **cycler**, **pillow**, **numpy**, **pyparsing**, and **setuptools** modules, which **matplotlib** requires.

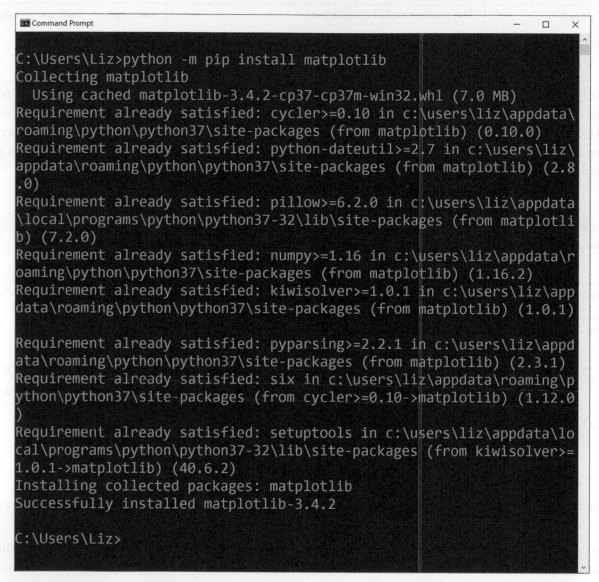

Figure 13-17 Using **pip** to install **matplotlib**

You can also use the **pip** command to uninstall modules using **uninstall** instead of **install**. See **Figure 13-18**. Python asks you to enter **y** or **n** to approve the removal of the module.

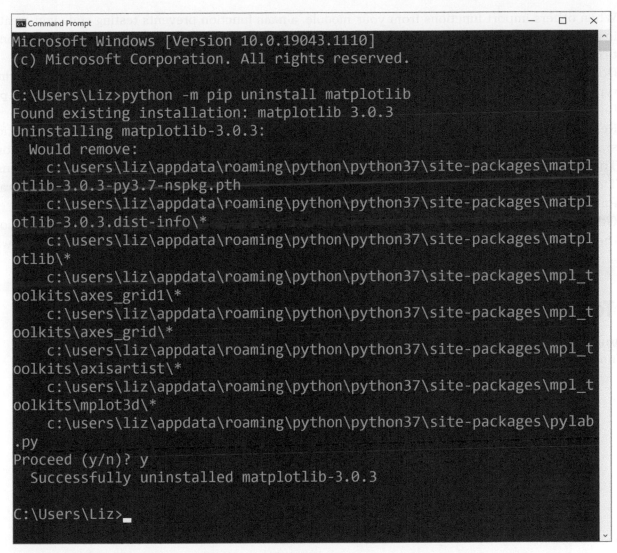

Figure 13-18 Using `pip` to uninstall `matplotlib`

Summary

- Modules contain information about previously created code. Python provides some modules as part of its installation, but you can download other modules from other programmers or create modules yourself. Using modules reduces error and streamlines your code.
- Modules can be stored in the same folder as the main program. Modules can also be stored in a separate folder, though the folder needs a file named `__init__.py` to be treated as a module.
- You use the keyword `import` to obtain code from other modules. When using `import` on its own, you must specify the module name with the name of any functions used from the module, as in `math.factorial()`. If you import using the keyword `from`, you can specify only the name of the function, as in `factorial()`.
- The wildcard `*` can be used with `from` and `import` to import everything from a module. It is not recommended to use the wildcard unless you are importing more than five items from a module.

- When others import functions from your module, a main function prevents testing code you created inside a module from being executed. The main function should be inside an if-statement with the condition `__name__ == "__main__"`.
- Docstrings are triple-quoted descriptions placed at the beginning of modules or functions. Docstrings typically provide information helpful to the programmer. When a programmer invokes the built-in `help()` function, the docstring is shown.
- Relative imports are like relative file paths. You can import from a nested module using relative notation, starting with `.` to represent the current module or `..` to specify the module containing the current one.
- The built-in `math` module is part of the Python installation and contains many helpful math functions.
- The built-in `random` module contains many helpful functions to create random choices for your program. Randomization is a quick way to test code.
- Other modules are recognized as standard, though they are not built into Python. You can download these modules with the `pip` command. The `pip` command can install or uninstall a module along with any other modules it depends on.

Key Terms

importing	modules	`pip` command
main function	nested modules	relative import

Module 14

Classes and Objects

Learning Objectives:

14.1 Classes In Object-Oriented Programming

14.1.1 Explain the difference between object-oriented programming (OOP) and procedural programming.

14.1.2 Define a class in OOP.

14.1.3 Explain how a class is similar to an architectural blueprint.

14.1.4 List the components that comprise a class.

14.1.5 Explain the function of the `class` keyword in creating a class.

14.2 Using Objects

14.2.1 Describe objects and OOP.

14.2.2 Explain instances and objects.

14.2.3 Compare an object as an instance of the blueprint.

14.2.4 Define complex data types.

14.2.5 Identify the similarities of implementing primitive data types to implementing objects from classes.

14.2.6 Explain how encapsulation can enhance coding structures.

14.2.7 Explain the concept of information hiding.

14.3 Using Static Elements in a Class

14.3.1 Explain how static variables are shared among instances of a class.

14.3.2 Explain the purpose of having static members of a class.

14.3.3 Define static methods.

14.4 Characteristics of Objects in Object-Oriented Programs

14.4.1 Define identity as it applies to OOP objects.

14.4.2 Define state as it applies to OOP objects.

14.4.3 Define behavior as it applies to OOP objects.

14.1 Classes in Object-Oriented Programming

Representing the Real World with Code (14.1.1)

Your code can represent ideas and concepts from everyday life. This can be done using **objects**, which are special kinds of variables that correspond to concrete objects in the real world. Programming that uses objects is aptly called **object-oriented programming (OOP)**. In OOP, you think in terms of key components, their data, the actions they can perform, and their interactions. When you collaborate with other coders, objects make your program more understandable.

In **procedural programming**, code is written step by step to create a set of instructions like a recipe for the computer to follow. When your program runs, it performs the exact steps in the same order as you wrote them. Procedural programming is useful for simple programs in which the algorithm has a finite number of steps, such as calculating the square root of a number. OOP is more appropriate when your program needs to model a complex, real-world system with many components, actions, and relationships, such as a banking application.

Procedural programming is usually the first programming paradigm that new coders learn, but it has limitations. For example, imagine that you are writing a procedural program to manage hundreds of cars at a dealership. The information you need to store in variables about each car includes the make, model, color, year, mileage, and many other details, as shown in **Figure 14-1**.

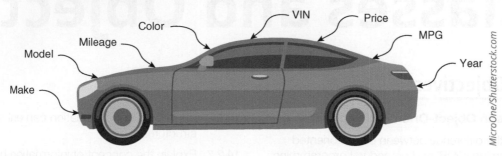

Figure 14-1 A car and its features

The amount of information for you and the program to keep track of would soon become overwhelming. If you need to change information, such as to add the vehicle identification number (VIN) to each car, you have to tediously modify every line of code corresponding to that change. As the number of changes increased, so would the difficulty of changing your code. OOP offers an alternative that allows you to easily modify the code in this scenario.

Using Classes (14.1.2, 14.1.3)

Classes make object-oriented programming possible. A **class** is a blueprint for creating an object. The same way that an architectural blueprint describes a building, a class describes an object. You use a class to create objects that share common characteristics, or properties, and build programs that use the objects. An architectural blueprint can be used to create many houses at different addresses, and a class can create many objects that share the same structure. The **Car** class is like a general model that can create objects such as a 2022 blue Honda Accord and a classic yellow Volkswagen Beetle.

A benefit of using classes is that it promotes code reuse. A programmer can reuse class code when making objects that have the same features. For example, if you want to store information about 500 cars in your dealership app, you could use one class file to describe all 500 cars.

Q How is the concept of a recipe (such as a cookie recipe) like a class?

A A recipe defines the characteristics of a cookie and you use it to create many cookies, which all have the same attributes, such as shape and crispiness, though the values of those attributes can vary.

Class Components (14.1.4, 14.1.5)

In many programming languages, `class` is a keyword that you use only to define a class. A class is generally made up of the following components:

- *Class name.* A **class name** identifies the class by a specific name. The class name is usually a noun, such as `Car`.
- *Initialization method.* The **initialization method** or **constructor** contains the starting instructions on how to set up the object. What is the object made of and what characteristics does it start with? You typically use the initialization method only once, when you create a new object.
- *Member variables.* The **member variables**, also called *attributes* or *properties*, make up the data stored in a class. These are defined in the initialization method.
- *Methods.* The **methods** describe the actions an object can perform. Methods are like functions that belong to the class. A method is usually a verb phrase, such as `test_drive()`.

A `Car` class (shown in **Figure 14-2**) has member variables to store a car's make, model, color, VIN, current price, miles per gallon (MPG), model year, and current mileage. Inside the class, member variables always start with the keyword `self`, representing the current object ("myself"). The class also includes methods to describe the actions that can be performed on a `Car` object. For example, the `give_discount()` method sets a discount of a specific percentage on a car, `increase_mileage()` allows a dealer to increase the car's stated mileage after a test drive to accurately reflect the car's current mileage, and `sell_car()` sets the sold variable as `True`, stores the final `self.price`, and sets `self.on_lot` to `False`. In the dealership database, the `test_drive()` method stores the `license_number` of the driver who took the car for a test drive, and then sets the value of `self.on_lot` to `False` in the code.

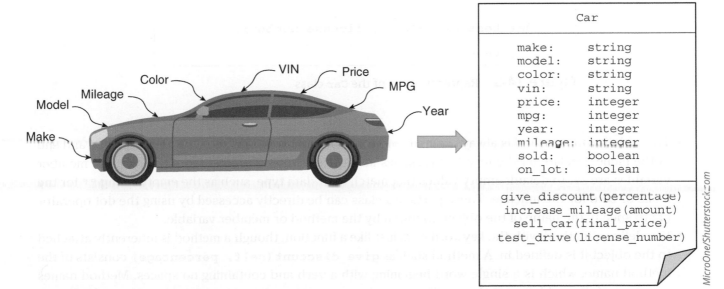

Figure 14-2 Features of a car represented as a class

Figure 14-3 shows the code to create the `Car` class.

- The code begins by using the `class` keyword to create a class named `Car`. Class names are capitalized by convention and are usually a noun (person, place, or thing). A class can have any name, except a reserved keyword. A class name follows similar rules as a variable name. It cannot begin with a number but can consist of letters, numbers, and the underscore character.

```
class Car():
    def __init__(self):
        self.make = ""
        self.model = ""
        self.color = ""
        self.vin = ""
        self.price = 0
        self.mpg = 0
        self.year = 0
        self.mileage = 0
        self.sold = False
        self.on_lot = False
    def give_discount(self, percentage):
        pass
    def increase_mileage(self, amount):
        pass
    def sell_car(self, final_price):
        pass
    def test_drive(self, license_number):
        pass
```

Figure 14-3   Representation of the Car class

- The initialization method is always named __init__(), with two underscores at the beginning and end of the name. Declare all the member variables inside the initialization method. Currently, the member variables are set to default empty values that match their data type, such as the empty string "" for the make or zero for the mileage. These parts of a class can be directly accessed by using the dot operator (.) to specify the name of the object, followed by the method or member variable.
- You define a method with the keyword def, just like a function, though a method is inherently attached to the object it is defined in. A method such as **give_discount(self, percentage)** consists of the method name, which is a single word beginning with a verb and containing no spaces. Method names are always followed by parentheses. The parentheses contain parameters to send to the method, such as a percentage value, which are required for the method to complete its action. The first parameter is always the keyword **self**, a property necessary for objects, followed by any other information needed. You use the keyword **pass** as a placeholder for the method contents, creating an essentially empty programming statement.
- An attribute such as **self.make** is a characteristic of a **Car**. Attributes are like normal variables except they are attached to an object. Attributes can consist of any value or data, including other objects.

14.2 Using Objects

Creating Objects (14.2.1, 14.2.2, 14.2.3)

An object-oriented program manipulates objects, and you make objects from classes. Each object is an **instance** of its class, a realized physical entity, while a class is a logical entity. If a class is the blueprint, each house created from the blueprint is an object.

In a program, a class is defined once, but an object can be created from that class many times. In the same way a blueprint is not an actual building, a class is not the actual object. As shown in **Figure 14-4**, the `Car` class reflects the general concept of a car, while an object in the `Car` class refers to an actual car in the dealership.

Class   **Objects**

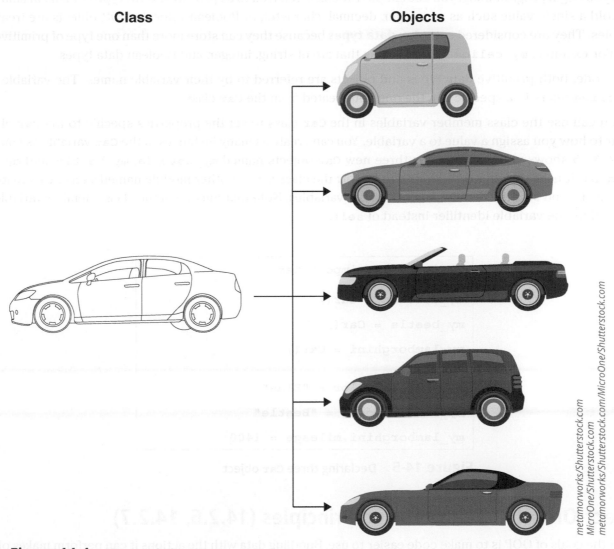

metamorworks/Shutterstock.com
MicroOne/Shutterstock.com
metamorworks/Shutterstock.com/MicroOne/Shutterstock.com

Figure 14-4   Class and objects

Assume you have a 2000 Toyota Celica. In Python, you invoke the class name like a function to create a new object. The following code creates an object named **my_celica** in the **Car** class:

```
my_celica = Car()
```

The code instantiates, or creates, a new object from the class **Car**. The parentheses on the right of the class name signals to Python to build an object from the class blueprint. The object is named **my_celica**. Code that refers to this specific car will reference the object by its name.

Q Fill in the blanks with the correct words: A class includes _____ to describe the actions an object can perform, and it includes _____, also called *attributes* or *properties*, that define the data the class can store. An instance of a class is an _____.

A methods; member variables; object

Objects as Variables (14.2.4, 14.2.5)

When you begin programming, you use simple variables, referred to as **primitive data types** or *built-in data types*, that hold a single value such as an integer, decimal, character, or Boolean value. In OOP, objects are treated as variables. They are considered **complex data types** because they can store more than one type of primitive data type. For example, **my_celica** has attributes that are of string, integer, and Boolean data types.

In code, both primitive data types and objects are referred to by their variable names. The variable name **my_celica** refers to a specific car, the one you created from the **Car** class.

You can use the class member variables in the **Car** class to set the properties specific to the **Car** objects, similar to how you assign a value to a variable. You can create as many instances of the **Car** variable as you need. **Figure 14-5** shows code that creates three new **Car** objects named **my_corolla**, **my_beetle**, and **my_lamborghini**. It uses the keyword **import** to import the class from another module named **vehicle**, creates the **Car** objects, and sets the data for some member variables. Note that outside of the class, member variables are accessed by the variable identifier instead of **self**.

```
from vehicle import Car

my_corolla = Car()

my_beetle = Car()

my_lamborghini = Car()


my_corolla.color = "Blue"

my_beetle.model = "Beetle"

my_lamborghini.mileage = 1400
```

Figure 14-5   Declaring three **Car** object

Object-Oriented Features and Principles (14.2.6, 14.2.7)

One of the goals of OOP is to make code easier to use. Bundling data with the actions it can perform makes objects easier to use, which is called **encapsulation**. A class encapsulates, or encloses, its attributes and methods into an object. That lets you treat an object's data and methods as a single entity.

Encapsulation enhances coding structures by emphasizing your code's member variables and their available actions. In other words, a **Car** object contains all of its attributes and abilities, just as a real-life car does. Encapsulation also gives you more control over how each object should function. For example, the **Car** class is a self-contained entity that bundles all of the data and actions that a **Car** object needs.

Encapsulation also aids with **information hiding**, which is concealing an object's data and methods from outside sources. An object can access its own data and methods, but other entities cannot. Also, users and other program components remain unaware of how an object's methods are carried out.

For example, the `test_drive()` method may initially only update the mileage of the car. Eventually the dealership changes the `test_drive()` method to also update the MPG attribute. Any code that needs to run `test_drive()` does not have to change, despite the internal behavior adjustment. Information hiding gives the maker of the `Car` class the freedom to change how the class works "under the hood" without users or other program components needing to know the details.

14.3 Using Static Elements in a Class

Static Member Variables (14.3.1, 14.3.2)

Suppose the owner of the dealership asks you to add a feature to your program. The dealer wants to keep a count of the cars in the dealership at any given time. To fulfill the request, you can add another attribute called `car_count` to the `Car` class. Each time the dealer receives a new car, `car_count` is incremented by one. Each time the dealer sells a car, `car_count` is decremented by one.

How should you modify the code to add the car-counting feature? Storing the same value in each `Car` object such as `my_celica`, `my_beetle`, and `my_lamborghini` takes up unnecessary space, especially as the number of `Car` objects increases. When a car is delivered to the dealership or sold, you'd also need to change the value of every `Car` object so that it has the correct value. It requires too many resources to store copies of the same thing when it needs constant updating. Instead, you can use a static variable to save resources and simplify the code.

A **static variable** is a member variable of a class and contains the same value in all instances of the class. You can think of it like a note written in the corner of the blueprint (class), rather than an attribute assigned to the created car (object). Essentially, all objects of the same class share the same static member variable, as shown in **Figure 14-6**. In the `Car` class, `my_celica`, `my_beetle`, and `my_lamborghini` can share the value of the `CAR_COUNT` static variable. Only one copy of the variable is stored in memory.

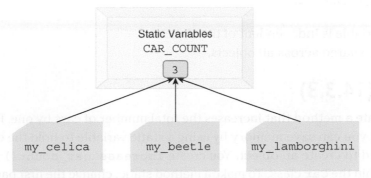

Figure 14-6   Each `Car` object shares the same static member variables

To create a static member of a class, declare the variable outside any method, typically before the `__init__()` method. The standard naming convention for static variables is to use all capital letters.

Figure 14-7 modifies the `Car` class to include a static member. To access static members of a class, use the class name instead of a variable identifier and the dot operator: `Car.CAR_COUNT`.

```
class Car():

    CAR_COUNT = 0  ←─────   New static
                            member
    def __init__(self):     variable

        self.make = ""

        self.model = ""

        self.color = ""

        self.vin = ""

        self.price = 0

        self.mpg = 0

        self.year = 0

        self.mileage = 0

        self.sold = False

        self.on_lot = False

    def give_discount(self, percentage):
        pass

    def increase_mileage(self, amount):
        pass

    def sell_car(self, final_price):
        pass

    def test_drive(self, license_number):
        pass
```

Figure 14-7   Adding a static variable

In the `Car` class, the value of `CAR_COUNT` needs to be updated only once. It then applies to every object in the `Car` class. Using a static member variable saves memory in your code. In general, consider using a static member variable in the following cases:

- The value of the variable is independent of the objects
- A value needs to be shared across all objects.

Static Methods (14.3.3)

Suppose you want to create a method that increases the total number of cars by one. Because `CAR_COUNT` does not refer to a specific car, you can save memory by using a static variable to hold the current number of cars. In this case, you do not need to create an object. You create `increase_car_count()` as a **static method** (also called a *class method*) within the `Car` class. To make a method static, change the first parameter from the keyword `self` to a parameter named `cls` (short for class) and add a line containing the `@classmethod` tag just before the method definition. **Figure 14-8** shows the static method `increase_car_count()` in code.

The static method is also independent of any specific object of the class and can be called without creating an instance of the object. A static method is called on the class itself and not on an instance of the class. The code would look like the following:

```
Car.increase_car_count()
```

```
class Car():

    CAR_COUNT = 0

    @classmethod
    def increase_car_count(cls):      ⎤ New static
        cls.CAR_COUNT += 1            ⎦ method

    def __init__(self):

        self.make = ""

        self.model = ""

        self.color = ""

        self.vin = ""

        self.price = 0

        self.mpg = 0

        self.year = 0

        self.mileage = 0

        self.sold = False

        self.on_lot = False

    def give_discount(self, percentage):
        pass

    def increase_mileage(self, amount):
        pass

    def sell_car(self, final_price):
        pass

    def test_drive(self, license_number):
        pass
```

Figure 14-8   Adding a static (class) method

Q When do I use static methods?

A Because static methods are not called on a specific object, you use them only to access static variables within a class and other static methods.

14.4 Characteristics of Objects in Object-Oriented Programs

Object Identity (14.4.1)

In OOP, although you can create many objects that use the same underlying class, they all have a unique **identity**, which is how you distinguish objects created using the same class. You provide unique identities by giving the object instances different variable names. For example, the identity of any **Car** object is the object's variable name, as shown in **Figure 14-9**.

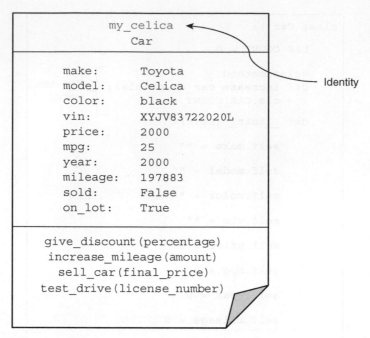

```
                      my_celica
                        Car

          make:        Toyota
          model:       Celica                        Identity
          color:       black
          vin:         XYJV83722020L
          price:       2000
          mpg:         25
          year:        2000
          mileage:     197883
          sold:        False
          on_lot:      True


         give_discount(percentage)
        increase_mileage(amount)
           sell_car(final_price)
         test_drive(license_number)
```

Figure 14-9   Identity of the my_celica object

In a **my_celica = Car()** statement, **my_celica** is the identity of the object. Any code that needs to reference this object will do so by using its variable name.

Q If two objects have the same values in all of their member variables, are they identical?

A Two objects can contain the same data, but it does not affect the object identity. They are separate instantiations of the same class, with different variable names representing different objects stored in separate areas of memory within the program.

Object State (14.4.2)

An object's **state** represents the data held in an object's member variables at any time. During the execution of your code, the state of an object can change frequently. In general, when the value of an attribute changes, so does the state of the object.

Methods are typically used to change the state of an object. For example, when a car is sold, the **price** is updated, the status of **on_lot** is changed to **False**, and **car_count** is decremented. An example of an object's state is shown in **Figure 14-10**.

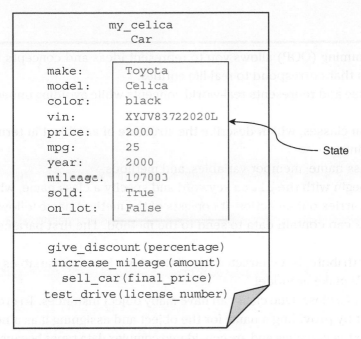

Figure 14-10 State of the `my_celica` object

Object Behavior (14.4.3)

As with people, an object's **behavior** describes what an object can do. Typically, behavior is thought of in terms of the methods or actions that an object can perform. The `Car` class can discount the price, increase the listed mileage after the car is taken out for test drives, set the car status to sold, and check it out for a test drive. These behaviors are shown in **Figure 14-11**.

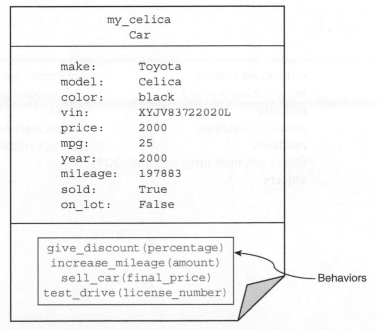

Figure 14-11 The behavior of the `my_celica` object

Summary

- Object-oriented programming (OOP) allows you to represent ideas and concepts from everyday life in your code using objects that correspond to real-life entities.
- OOP promotes code reuse and represents real-world concepts while avoiding unnecessary, complicated variable declarations.
- Objects are created from classes, which describe the structure of an object in terms of its features and capabilities, like blueprints.
- A class consists of a class name, member variables, and methods.
- To create a class, you begin with the `class` keyword and specify a class name, which is capitalized by convention. A method carries out an action. It consists of the method name followed by a set of parentheses. The parentheses can contain data to send to the method. The first parameter of all methods is the keyword `self`.
- A member variable, or attribute, is a characteristic of the class. Member variables describe the state of an object, such as a car's make or model.
- An object is an instance of a class. One class can have many object instances. To create an instance of an object, you instantiate it by providing a name for the object and assigning it as a new object in a class.
- In OOP, objects are treated as variables and are considered complex data types because they can store more than one type of primitive data. For example, an object can have string, integer, and Boolean attributes.
- OOP makes code easier to use and understand through encapsulation and information hiding. A class encapsulates, or encloses, its attributes and methods into an object, which lets you treat the object's data and methods as a single entity. Information hiding refers to how OOP conceals an object's data and methods from outside sources.
- Static variables within a class allow you to share a variable among all instances of the same class, without the need for multiple copies.
- Static methods allow you to access static variables in a class and do not require the use of an object. The tag `@classmethod` must appear before a static method.
- Objects are described in terms of their identity (such as the object's name), state (the data held in an object's member variables at any time), and behavior (what an object can do).

Key Terms

behavior	information hiding	primitive data types
class	initialization method	procedural programming
class name	instance	state
complex data types	member variables	static method
constructor	methods	static variable
encapsulation	object-oriented programming (OOP)	
identity	objects	

Module 15

Methods

Learning Objectives:

15.1 Using Methods

Why Use Methods? (15.1.1)

In object-oriented programming (OOP), classes have special programmer-defined functions called **methods**. A method consists of a block of code that performs some action related to its object. A method is like a function that belongs to an object and performs a specific task, routine, operation, or process. Methods help us organize repetitive tasks related to an object. You use methods to modify the behavior of objects because they make objects work. Without methods, objects would just be a collection of related data.

Suppose you are writing code to manage the cars in a car dealership called Zoe's Cars. You'll have a lot of cars to keep track of, and each car has a lot of properties, so you decide to use classes to organize their state. **Figure 15-1** shows some of the cars you might have on the lot at Zoe's Cars.

Figure 15-1   A dealership contains many kinds of cars

Once set up, the cars and the dealership have certain behaviors. You can test-drive a car, increase its mileage, sell a car, remove it from the dealership, add new cars to the dealership, and so on. The reasoning behind using objects to group together properties of a car or dealership also translates to grouping behaviors together with those objects. Test-driving requires a car, so instead of creating the logic in a disconnected function, you attach that logic to the **Car** object in a method.

As you may remember with functions, after the code in a function is run, it may or may not return a value to the line of code that called it. The same is true for methods. If the method returns a value, you set the value to be equal to the method call. Otherwise, you only need to call the method. An object can have an infinite number of defined methods that determine how it behaves. The more methods an object has, the more things it can do. To change a function into a method, it must be declared inside a class definition (indented) and it must take at least one parameter, the keyword **self**.

In a dealership, a **Car** object, for example, might have methods for discounting the price, increasing the mileage after a test drive, being sold, and registering a test drive. See **Figure 15-2**. Right now, the methods in the **Car** object are empty and do nothing, as indicated by the keyword **pass**.

You can use a **Dealership** class to hold the member variables and methods that are relevant to running a dealership. The methods in the **Dealership** class include actions a car dealer performs, such as selling cars, adding new cars into inventory, initiating a test drive, and checking in a car for service.

In code, the **Dealership** class would resemble **Figure 15-3**. The member variables in the **Dealership** object include the following along with other dealership details:

- **self.owner** is for the name of the owner. Initialize it to an empty string.
- **self.inventory** is for the cars in the dealership's inventory; a list of objects, each an instance of the **Car** class. Initialize it to an empty list.
- **self.address** is for the street address. Initialize it to an empty string.
- **self.capacity** is for the number of cars the dealership can hold. Initialize it to zero.

```
class Car():
    def __init__(self):
        self.make = ""
        self.model = ""
        self.color = ""
        self.vin = ""
        self.price = 0
        self.mpg = 0
        self.year = 0
        self.mileage = 0
        self.sold = False
        self.on_lot = False

    def give_discount(self, percentage):
        pass

    def increase_mileage(self, amount):
        pass

    def sell_car(self, final_price):
        pass

    def test_drive(self, license_number):
        pass
```

Member variables

Methods

Figure 15-2   Car class definition in Python

```
class Dealership():
    def __init__(self):
        self.owner = ""
        self.inventory = []
        self.address = ""
        self.capacity = 0

    def add_car(self, car):
        pass

    def sell_car(self, car, final_price):
        pass

    def test_drive(self, car, license_number):
        pass

    def check_in_car(self, car, services):
        pass
```

Figure 15-3   Dealership class definition in Python

The dealership is expecting some new cars this week. Zoe asks you to write code to add cars into the inventory. You can write a method called **add_car()** to help enter the new cars. The method has three components, labeled in **Figure 15-4**.

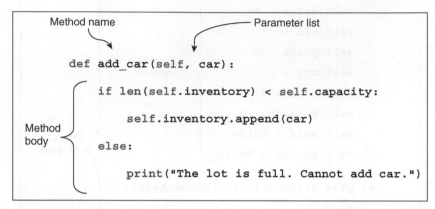

Figure 15-4   Method anatomy

In the first line in Figure 15-4, the code statement uses the keyword **def** as a signal that what follows is a method. The name of the method is **add_car()**. The **add_car()** method accepts the necessary **self** parameter and one additional parameter named **car**.

The rest of the code shows that **car** will be added to the **self.inventory**, which is an array of **Car** objects. First, the method checks to make sure that by adding this car, the dealership won't exceed its capacity. It checks the current number of cars in the dealership by using the built-in function **len()**, which returns the length of the **self.inventory** list. If the dealership has space for the car, it is added to the inventory. If not, the method prints an error message.

Anatomy of a Method (15.1.2)

A method includes the following components:

- **Method name.** The **method name** is the identifier to use when referring to the method in the code. The name is usually a verb followed by a noun, such as **add_car()**.
- **Parameter list.** The **parameter list** specifies the input given to the method so it can perform its task. A parameter list for a method always has **self** as its first parameter. For example, the parameter list for the **add_car()** method has two parameters, but only one represents actual input to the method: the **car** being added to the inventory.
- **Method body.** The **method body** is the list of statements or other code that the method executes to perform its actions.
- **Return statements.** The **return statement** indicates when to leave the method and what to return when doing so. These statements use the keyword **return**, optionally followed by the value to return, just like functions. In addition, if the method does not have a **return** statement, Python hides an implicit return with no value (the keyword **None**) at the end of the method. For example, the **add_car()** method has an implicit **return** statement at the end because no information needs to be returned.

A method must be defined before it can be used. Programmers define methods and can change them as necessary. For example, you may find a simpler way to perform the method's task. You can modify the behavior as appropriate for your context.

Using Methods (15.1.3, 15.1.4)

When you want a method to perform an action, it can be triggered by a **method call**. Like functions, the flow of execution jumps to the method, performs the statements it contains, and then returns to the previous execution path. To make a method call, use the following syntax if the method returns a value:

```
return_value = object.method(argument_1, argument_2, ...)
```

If the method does not return a value, use the following syntax:

```
object.method(argument_1, argument_2, ...)
```

Let's break down the syntax examples piece by piece:

- `object.method()`: Identify an object's identifier followed by the name of the method you want to call. Separate the variable and method names with a period. For example, `add_car()` is a method in the `Dealership` class, and `zoes_cars` represents an object of that class. Using `zoes_cars.add_car()` indicates that you are trying to call the method to add a car to the inventory of Zoe's Cars.
- `argument_1, argument_2`: You can pass zero, one, or more arguments to the object, which becomes the method's parameter list. Note, however, that the first parameter, `self`, is implied in the method call. The statement `zoes_cars.add_car()` will store the variable `zoes_cars` in `self` for you. The only arguments you need to provide are the ones that follow `self`. The `add_car()` method has one extra argument, an object of type `Car`.
- `return_value`: If the method has a result, it is returned to the variable specified in `return_value`. Like functions, if the method does not return a value, you can omit `return_value` from the method call. The `add_car()` method does not return a value, so you do not have to set a return value.

When a method is called, it starts executing the first statement in the method body and continues in order until the end of the method body. **Figure 15-5** shows the use of the `Dealership` and `Car` classes to create a `Dealership` and add cars with the `add_car()` method. The code requires you to have the `Car` class shown in Figure 15-2 in a module named **vehicle.py** and the `Dealership` class code shown in Figure 15-3 (with the `add_car()` method code from Figure 15-4 inside the `Dealership` class) in a module named **businesses.py**. The first two lines in Figure 15-5 import the classes from these modules and then the rest of the program behaves as if the classes were defined in the same file.

```
from businesses import Dealership

from vehicle import Car

dealer = Dealership()

dealer.owner = input("What is your name? ")

dealer.address = input("What is your address? ")

dealer.capacity = int(input("What is your lot's capacity? "))

num_new_cars = int(input("How many cars would you like to enter? "))

for i in range(num_new_cars):

    new_car = Car()

    new_car.make = input("Please enter the car's make: ")
```

Figure 15-5   Using the `add_car()` method to add a `Car` to a `Dealership` (*Continued*)

```
        new_car.model = input("Please enter the car's model: ")

        new_car.color = input("Please enter the car's color: ")

        new_car.vin = input("Please enter the car's vin: ")

        new_car.price = float(input("Please enter the car's price: "))

        new_car.mpg = float(input("Please enter the car's mpg: "))

        new_car.year = int(input("Please enter the car's year: "))

        new_car.mileage = int(input("Please enter the car's mileage: "))

    print()

    dealer.add_car(new_car)
```

OUTPUT:

What is your name? Zoe [Enter]

What is your address? 123 Main Street [Enter]

What is your lot's capacity? 10 [Enter]

How many cars would you like to enter? 2 [Enter]

Please enter the car's make: Honda [Enter]

Please enter the car's model: Fit [Enter]

Please enter the car's color: Green [Enter]

Please enter the car's vin: ABC123 [Enter]

Please enter the car's price: 15000 [Enter]

Please enter the car's mpg: 30 [Enter]

Please enter the car's year: 2010 [Enter]

Please enter the car's mileage: 15000 [Enter]

Please enter the car's make: Toyota [Enter]

Please enter the car's model: Celica [Enter]

Please enter the car's color: White [Enter]

Please enter the car's vin: XYZ987 [Enter]

Please enter the car's price: 50000 [Enter]

Please enter the car's mpg: 20 [Enter]

Please enter the car's year: 2015 [Enter]

Please enter the car's mileage: 20000 [Enter]

Figure 15-5   Using the add_car() method to add a Car to a Dealership

Q How do I decide if I should use a function or a method?

A It depends on the organization of your code. If you need to perform an action on an object, then you should use a method that belongs to the class. Otherwise, if the action does not need to be performed on the object, it should be a function.

Methods can also have default parameters, just like functions. For methods where an argument is optional or can have a default value to use when the programmer does not specify an argument, the syntax is the same as functions. Any parameter can have an equals sign followed by the default value. Parameters with default values must come after parameters without default values. Example syntax is as follows:

```
def method_name(self, param_1, param_2, optional_1=5, optional_2="hi"):
```

In the preceding syntax example, `param_1` and `param_2` do not have default values, and therefore must always be provided arguments when the method is called. In contrast, `optional_1` and `optional_2` both have default values. The method can be invoked with new arguments in those parameters but, if left empty, the values 5 and `"hi"` are used for `optional_1` and `optional_2`, respectively.

15.2 Changing the Default Behavior of an Object

The Double Underscore Methods (15.2.1, 15.2.2, 15.2.3)

Python's syntax and built-in functions have default behaviors for all classes, even if you don't define the behavior. **Figure 15-6** creates a `Car` object and then tries to use the built-in `print()` function.

```
from vehicle import Car

new_car = Car()

new_car.make = "Honda"

new_car.model = "Fit"

new_car.color = "Green"

new_car.vin = "ABC123"

new_car.price = 15999.99

new_car.mpg = 40.5

new_car.year = 2009

new_car.mileage = 15000

print(new_car)

OUTPUT:

<vehicle.Car object at 0x022DA070>
```

Figure 15-6 Default print behavior shows the type of object and its memory address

Notice the output includes angle brackets `<>` on either side of the text `"vehicle.Car object at"` and a series of numbers and letters starting with `0x`. The first part of the output indicates the type of object printed, and the numbers and letters are the memory address where this object is stored. The default behavior tells you some basics about the object but aren't terribly useful. You expect a statement like `print(new_car)` to show the state of the object, such as its color, MPG, and model year.

To change the default behavior for built-in functions, you need to use the double-underscore methods, or **dunder methods** for short. The function `print()` secretly calls a dunder method named `__str__()` for you, using a default `__str__()` if none is defined in your class. Adding a definition of `__str__` with no additional parameters other than `self` tells Python to use your version of the method instead of the default. The `__str__()` method expects a string returned and nothing printed. (The `print()` function will display what's returned to the screen.) Make sure you have exactly two underscores on either side of the dunder method name; otherwise, it won't work. **Figure 15-7** shows how you could add a `__str__()` method to the `Car` class, and how the output of Figure 15-6 would change.

```python
class Car():

    def __init__(self):

        self.make = ""

        self.model = ""

        self.color = ""

        self.vin = ""

        self.price = 0

        self.mpg = 0

        self.year = 0

        self.mileage = 0

        self.sold = False

        self.on_lot = False

    def __str__(self):

        string = "Make: " + self.make + "\n"

        string += "Model: " + self.model + "\n"

        string += "Color: " + self.color + "\n"

        string += "Vin: " + self.vin + "\n"

        string += "Price: " + str(self.price) + "\n"

        string += "MPG: " + str(self.mpg) + "\n"

        string += "Year: " + str(self.year) + "\n"

        string += "Mileage: " + str(self.mileage) + "\n"
```

Figure 15-7 Overriding the default print behavior with `__str__()` *(Continued)*

```
        string += "Is Sold: " + str(self.sold) + "\n"

        string += "Is On Lot: " + str(self.on_lot) + "\n"

        return string
```

OUTPUT: (From running code in Figure 15-6)

```
Make: Honda
Model: Fit
Color: Green
Vin: ABC123
Price: 15999.99
MPG: 40.5
Year: 2009
Mileage: 15000
Is Sold: False
Is On Lot: False
```

Figure 15-7   Overriding the default print behavior with __str__()

The overriding of dunder methods is called **operator overriding**, where the normal behavior of an operator is overridden. Programmers override operators to provide a concise, simple, and natural way to perform common operations on objects. Operators are overridden the same way that methods are defined.

Other dunder methods that can be overridden include, but are not limited to, all the mathematical operators, square bracket indexing like lists, and the `in` keyword. You should always create a dunder string method for complicated classes so it is easier to show the variable's state.

Equality Dunder Method (15.2.4, 15.2.5)

Suppose that in your car dealership program, you need a way to compare two cars to determine if they are the same car. For example, suppose that a customer wants to test-drive a blue Celica from 2009. How can you detect if the dealership has the right kind of car on the lot? If `Car` objects were primitive data types, you would use the equality operator (`==`) to make this comparison. This would look like the following:

```
car_comparison = car_1 == car_2
```

The variable `car_comparison` holds a Boolean (`True` or `False`) value, depending on whether `car_1` is equal to `car_2`. However, with anything but primitive types, the statement creates a problem. With objects (not primitives), this statement actually compares the memory locations storing the `car_1` and `car_2` variables, not the contents of the `car_1` and `car_2` objects, which is what you want to do. This subtle difference is shown in **Figure 15-8**.

The statement `car_1 == car_2` compares the memory locations `0xE2454516` and `0xE245451A`, finds they are different, and returns `False`. The default behavior for equality is to compare the **object identity**. If the two objects share the same memory location, they are exactly the same variable in the program, so they are equal. Otherwise, they are not. You need another approach to determine whether the `Car` objects' attributes are the same.

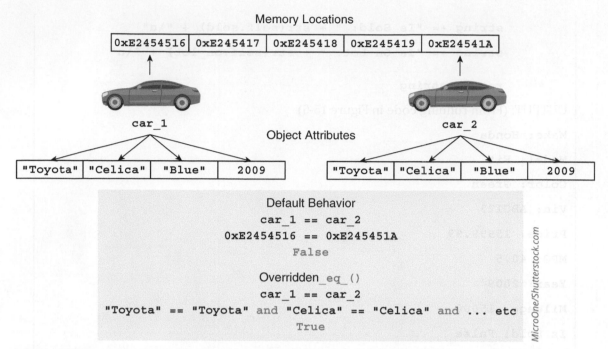

Figure 15-8   Default comparison operator compares memory addresses

In this example, the dealership is concerned with the make, model, color, and year for comparison. You could iterate over every car in the dealership and compare these properties by hand, as in **Figure 15-9**. This, however, will be annoying if you need to compare other cars in other situations.

```
from businesses import Dealership

from vehicle import Car

import random

import string

dealer = Dealership()

dealer.capacity = 20

# Options stored in a list for random choice later

make_and_model_options = [["Honda", "Fit"], ["Toyota", "Celica"], ["Ford", "F150"]]

colors = ["Blue", "Green", "Gray", "Black", "White", "Red"]

# Add 10 random cars

for i in range(10):

    car = Car()

    car.make, car.model = random.choice(make_and_model_options)

    car.year = random.randint(2009, 2010)

    car.color = random.choice(colors)
```

Figure 15-9   Manually comparing all properties for equality is tiresome (*Continued*)

```
          car.vin = "".join(random.choices(string.ascii_uppercase, k=3)) +
          "".join(random.choices("0123456789",k=5))

          car.price = random.randint(15000,200000)

          car.mpg = random.randint(15,50)

          car.on_lot = True

          dealer.add_car(car)

search_car = Car()
search_car.make = "Toyota"
search_car.model = "Celica"
search_car.color = "Blue"
search_car.year = 2009

print("You are looking for a", search_car.color,
        search_car.make, search_car.model, "from", str(search_car.year) + ".")

is_car_available = False

for car_on_lot in dealer.inventory:
    if car_on_lot.make == search_car.make and \
        car_on_lot.model == search_car.model and \
        car_on_lot.color == search_car.color and \
        car_on_lot.year == search_car.year:
        is_car_available = True
        break

if is_car_available:
    print("We have that car for sale!")
else:
    print("We don't have that car for sale, sorry!")
```

OUTPUT:

```
You are looking for a Blue Toyota Celica from 2009.
We have that car for sale!
```

Figure 15-9 Manually comparing all properties for equality is tiresome

Instead of object identity, the equality operator should check for **structural equality**. Structural equality means the contents or state of the objects are the same, not the memory addresses. Checking for structural equality doesn't have to evaluate all properties of an object, but only the parts relevant to the context's definition of equal. In this case, only the make, model, color, and year matter, not the VIN, price, MPG, and mileage. **Figure 15-10** shows how to override the equality operator with the dunder method __eq__().

```
class Car():
    def __init__(self):
        self.make = ""
        self.model = ""
        self.color = ""
        self.vin = ""
        self.price = 0
        self.mpg = 0
        self.year = 0
        self.mileage = 0
        self.sold = False
        self.on_lot = False

    def __eq__(self, other):
        if self.make == other.make and \
            self.model == other.model and \
            self.color == other.color and \
            self.year == other.year:
            return True
        else:
            return False

    # Other methods
```

Figure 15-10 Overriding the equality behavior with __eq__()

In the code, the first line—def __eq__(self, other)—states that you are about to define a new method in the class (that happens to be an overridden operator). In the method's parameter list, **other** is the parameter after **self** that is passed to the method. This parameter specifies which **Car** object to compare to the **Car** whose method was called. Consider the following statement:

```
car_comparison = car_1 == car_2
```

Here, **car_2** is the parameter that is being passed to the overridden __eq__() method of the **car_1** object. The result of the comparison is stored in the **car_comparison** variable. The preceding statement is structurally equivalent to **car_comparison = car_1.__eq__(car_2)**. You can call the dunder methods directly if so desired but it is considered poor style because it is harder to read.

The if-else block includes the code **self.make == other.make**, which compares the **make** of the car being passed to the **make** of the object whose __eq__() method was called. The conditional also compares the model, color, and year. If the condition is true, then __eq__() returns **True**; otherwise, it returns **False**.

By creating this method, you change the default behavior of the **==** operator. Now, if the **==** operator is called on two **Car** variables, the code will check the values instead of the memory locations. If the member variable values are the same, you can assume that the car matches the one being searched and return the value **True**. Otherwise, the car does not match what was being searched, so the code returns **False**. The changes to the earlier code are shown in **Figure 15-11**.

```
from businesses import Dealership
from vehicle import Car
import random
import string

dealer = Dealership()
dealer.capacity = 20

make_and_model_options = [["Honda", "Fit"], ["Toyota", "Celica"],
["Ford", "F150"]]
colors = ["Blue", "Green", "Gray", "Black", "White", "Red"]

# Add 10 random cars
for i in range(10):
    car = Car()
    car.make, car.model = random.choice(make_and_model_options)
    car.year = random.randint(2009, 2010)
    car.color = random.choice(colors)
    car.vin = "".join(random.choices(string.ascii_uppercase, k=3)) +
"".join(random.choices("0123456789",k=5))
    car.price = random.randint(15000,200000)
    car.mpg = random.randint(15,50)
    car.on_lot = True
    dealer.add_car(car)

search_car = Car()
search_car.make = "Toyota"
search_car.model = "Celica"
search_car.color = "Blue"
search_car.year = 2009
print("You are looking for a", search_car.color,
    search_car.make, search_car.model, "from", str(search_car.year)
+ ".")

is_car_available = False

for car_on_lot in dealer.inventory:
    if car_on_lot == search_car:  ←────── __eq__ is called by ==
        is_car_available = True
        break

if is_car_available:
    print("We have that car for sale!")
else:
    print("We don't have that car for sale, sorry!")
OUTPUT:
You are looking for a Blue Toyota Celica from 2009.
We have that car for sale!
```

Figure 15-11   Overriding equality cleans up code that uses your classes

You can override many types of operators besides the equality operator, including arithmetic, assignment, relational, and logical operators. It is not necessary to override all available operators. Overriding operators is left to your discretion as a programmer to simplify commonly used operations for your specific program. As a rule of thumb, overriding an operator should help make your code easier to write and easier to understand to others.

15.3 Using Constructors

Specifying How to Construct an Object (15.3.1)

So far, you've created a new **Car** object by using code in the following format:

```
new_car = Car()
```

Behind the scenes, your program calls a **constructor**, the **__init__**() initialization dunder method, which is a special method that creates an object called **new_car** and allocates enough memory to hold all of the information associated with a **Car**. Until now, the initialization dunder method set all of the object's member variables to default values, which you then had to override with the actual values, like **"Blue"**.

Creating an object frequently sets all the member variables; you can add a parameter list to the initialization method to reduce the code needed to create an instance of a class. What parameters to add depends on the class being designed. For example, suppose that when adding new cars to the inventory, the **mileage** is always 0, **on_lot** is always **True**, and **sold** is always **False**. It would make sense to create cars that have those initial values already set as the default. All other properties should be set by an input parameter. **Figure 15-12** shows a change to the **__init__**() method for the **Car** class to add **make**, **model**, **color**, **year**, **vin**, **price**, and **mpg** parameters.

```
class Car():
    def __init__(self, make, model, color, year, vin, price, mpg):
        self.make = make
        self.model = model
        self.color = color
        self.vin = vin
        self.price = price
        self.mpg = mpg
        self.year = year
        self.mileage = 0
        self.sold = False
        self.on_lot = True

    # Other methods
```

Figure 15-12   Parameter lists can be added to constructors

With this change, the code from Figure 15-11 can be rewritten as the code shown in **Figure 15-13**.

```python
from businesses import Dealership
from vehicle import Car
import random
import string


dealer = Dealership()
dealer.capacity = 20

make_and_model_options = [["Honda", "Fit"], ["Toyota",
"Celica"], ["Ford", "F150"]]
colors = ["Blue", "Green", "Gray", "Black", "White", "Red"]

# Add 10 random cars
for i in range(10):
    make, model = random.choice(make_and_model_options)
    dealer.add_car(Car(make, model, random.choice(colors),
                    random.randint(2009, 2010),
"".join(random.choices(string.ascii_uppercase, k=3)) +
"".join(random.choices("0123456789",k=5)),
                    random.randint(15000,200000),
                    random.randint(15,50)))

search_car = Car("Toyota", "Celica", "Blue", 2009, "", 0, 0)

# Searching is unchanged and omitted
```

Creating a `Car` is cleaner than in Figure 15-11.

Figure 15-13   Constructors with parameter lists clean up code for others

The code that creates **search_car** in Figure 15-11 has to provide placeholder arguments for parameters that do not matter in the terms of the search: the **vin**, the **price**, and the **mpg** are left as **""**, 0, and 0, respectively. To remove this requirement, you can use default values for your **__init__**() method, just like earlier. The signature of **__init__**() for **Car** then changes to the following:

```python
def __init__(self, make, model, color, year, vin="", price=0, mpg=0)
```

The code is further changed from Figure 15-13 to the code in **Figure 15-14**.

Q Can you define more than one constructor in an object?

A No. You can only have one **__init__**() method per class. You can, however, adjust the utility of your constructor with default parameters.

```
from businesses import Dealership
from vehicle import Car
import random
import string

dealer = Dealership()
dealer.capacity = 20

make_and_model_options = [["Honda", "Fit"], ["Toyota",
"Celica"], ["Ford", "F150"]]
colors = ["Blue", "Green", "Gray", "Black", "White", "Red"]

# Add 10 random cars
for i in range(10):
    make, model = random.choice(make_and_model_options)
    dealer.add_car(Car(make, model, random.choice(colors),
                    random.randint(2009, 2010),
"".join(random.choices(string.ascii_uppercase, k=3)) +
"".join(random.choices("0123456789",k=5)),
                    random.randint(15000,200000),
                    random.randint(15,50)))

search_car = Car("Toyota", "Celica", "Blue", 2009)
# Searching is unchanged and omitted
```

Unnecessary information can be omitted with default parameters.

Figure 15-14   Default parameter values clean up the code even more

Setting One Object to Equal Another (15.3.2)

Usually, you use the assignment operator (=) to set one variable equal to the value of another. Assume you have two variables, `car_1` and `car_2`, in your program. You want `car_1` to have the same properties as `car_2`. If you write `car_1 = car_2`, the default behavior happens. Because `car_1` and `car_2` are complex data types, the variable name is regarded as the object's address in memory. The statement `car_1 = car_2` stores the memory location of `car_2` in `car_1`, so now `car_1` is also referring to the same object as `car_2`.

The assignment statement makes the `car_1` object a **shallow copy** of `car_2`, meaning the copy is superficial and does not refer to a unique object that no other variable refers to. Shallow copies should be avoided. On the surface, the program appears to work as expected to add a transferred car to inventory. However, if `car_2` is modified in memory (perhaps by the code that created it), then `car_1` is also modified.

To avoid this problem, you can create a **clone method**. The clone method should create a new instance of the class and set all the properties to match. Creating a new instance guarantees that it will have a new memory address. **Figure 15-15** shows a `clone()` method for the `Car` class.

```
class Car():
    def __init__(self, make, model, color, year, vin="", price=0, mpg=0):
        self.make = make
        self.model = model
        self.color = color
        self.vin = vin
        self.price = price
        self.mpg = mpg
        self.year = year
        self.mileage = 0
        self.sold = False
        self.on_lot = True

    def clone(self):
        cloned_car = Car(self.make, self.model, self.color,
                         self.year, self.vin, self.price, self.mpg)

        return cloned_car

    # Other Methods
```

Figure 15-15 A clone method helps if you need an identical copy of an object

It is not always necessary to have a clone method. For example, in a **Dealership** object, you'd never have two of the exact same **Dealership** at the same address. The clone method achieves something called a **deep copy**, as it copies all properties of the object into a new memory location.

15.4 Getters and Setters

Visibility (15.4.1, 15.4.2)

Some member variables have specific properties you want to enforce, such as ensuring the year is a positive integer. Direct access to member variables places the responsibility of adhering to these properties on whoever might use your classes. While you can't prevent others from direct access, you can suggest certain properties are "private" by naming the member variables so that they start with a single underscore. **Figure 15-16** changes all of the member variables of the **Car** to suggest privacy.

Now that the properties of the **Car** class are private, you need more methods. Specifically, you need methods to define how to access the properties and how to change the properties.

```
class Car():
    def __init__(self, make, model, color, year, vin="", price=0, mpg=0):
        self._make = make
        self._model = model
        self._color = color
        self._vin = vin
        self._price = price
        self._mpg = mpg
        self._year = year
        self._mileage = 0
        self._sold = False
        self._on_lot = True

    # Other Methods
```

Figure 15-16   Suggesting privacy in Python with a single underscore

Getters (15.4.3, 15.4.4)

Methods that obtain properties of an object are called **getters** because they get values from the instance. Most getters can be simple. For example, the getter for the car's **vin** just needs to return the string. Some getters can get a property that is implied for the object. For example, **get_num_cars_on_lot()** for the **Dealership** class would get the number of cars on the lot. By convention, getter method names typically start with the word *get*, as in **get_vin()**. If the property being accessed by the getter is a Boolean value, then the method identifier should start with the word *is*, as in **is_sold()**.

The most important quality of a getter is that it only accesses properties. Otherwise, it is not considered a getter. Because of this, getter methods are also known as **accessor methods**. Getter methods never change anything about the object. **Figure 15-17** adds some getter methods.

```
class Car():
    def __init__(self, make, model, color, year, vin="", price=0, mpg=0):
        self._make = make
        self._model = model
        self._color = color
        self._vin = vin
        self._price = price
        self._mpg = mpg
        self._year = year
```

Figure 15-17   Some getter methods (*Continued*)

```
        self._mileage = 0

        self._sold = False

        self._on_lot = True

    def get_make(self):

        return self._make
    def get_model(self):

        return self._model
    def get_color(self):

        return self._color
    def get_vin(self):

        return self._vin
    def get_price(self):

        return self._price
    def get_mpg(self):

        return self._mpg
    def get_year(self):

        return self._year
    def get_mileage(self):

        return self._mileage
    def is_sold(self):

        return self._sold
    def is_on_lot(self):

        return self._on_lot

# Other Methods
```

Figure 15-17   Some getter methods

Setters (15.4.5, 15.4.6)

Methods that allow modification of an object's properties are called **setters** or **mutator methods**. It is good practice to use setters when data needs to have a specific form. By convention, names for setters start with the word *set*, as in **set_color()**. Setters that change Boolean variables usually take the form of a verb related to the property, such as **sell()**, which should change self._sold to **True**. **Figure 15-18** adds some setter methods to the **Car** class.

Simple setters, like **set_make()** or **set_model()** in Figure 15-18, should not be used in Python. In these cases, it is better to leave the member variable as "public" with no leading underscore.

```
class Car():

    def __init__(self, make, model, color, year, vin="", price=0, mpg=0):

        self._make = make

        self._model = model

        self._color = color

        self._vin = vin

        self._price = price

        self._mpg = mpg

        self._year = year

        self._mileage = 0

        self._sold = False

        self._on_lot = True

    # Mutators
    def set_make(self, make):

        self._make = make

    def set_model(self, model):

        self._model = model

    def set_color(self, color):

        self._color = color

    def set_vin(self, vin):

        self._vin = vin

    def set_price(self, price):

        if price > 0:

            self._price = price

    def set_mpg(self, mpg):

        if mpg > 0:

            self._mpg = mpg

    def set_year(self, year):

        if year > 1908:

            self._year = year

    def set_mileage(self, mileage):

        if mileage > 0:

            self._mileage = mileage

    def sell(self):

        self._sold = True
```

Figure 15-18   Adding setter methods to the Car class (*Continued*)

```
    def leave_lot(self):
        self._on_lot = False
    def return_to_lot(self):
        self._on_lot = True

    # Accessors
    def get_make(self):
        return self._make
    def get_model(self):
        return self._model
    def get_color(self):
        return self._color
    def get_vin(self):
        return self._vin
    def get_price(self):
        return self._price
    def get_mpg(self):
        return self._mpg
    def get_year(self):
        return self._year
    def get_mileage(self):
        return self._mileage
    def is_sold(self):
        return self._sold
    def is_on_lot(self):
        return self._on_lot

    # Other Methods
```

Figure 15-18   Adding setter methods to the Car class

Summary

- In object-oriented programming, methods are special programmer-defined functions that belong to a class and perform some action related to objects made from the class.
- Methods are similar to functions and consist of a method name, parameter list, and method body.
- Methods must be invoked (or called) to perform an action. When a method is called, it starts executing the first statement in the method body and continues in order until the end of the method body.

- You can use methods to customize the default behavior of an object. Most interactions in Python can be overridden with dunder (double-underscore) methods. Operator overriding allows you to specify how built-in operators should behave when operating on your objects. The default behavior often uses garbage data that can lead to errors in your program.
- You can make your code more usable with default values in the parameter list, which allows you to call the same method with optional arguments. Default values make your code easier to interpret and reuse.
- When using the assignment operator (=) to make an object equal to another object, the default functionality creates a shallow copy, a new object that refers to the same memory location as another object. It is good practice to create a clone method to ensure that you can create a deep copy of an object.
- Programs call constructors whenever a new object is instantiated. You can specify how a constructor sets the values of the member variables as an object is created. It is good programming practice to use constructors with default values in the parameter list to make it easier to create instances.
- Privacy of object member variables can be suggested by starting the variable name with an underscore. If a variable is suggested as private, then getter and setter methods are recommended. Getter and setter methods help control how others interact with your code, eliminating some possibility of error, such as a negative year.

Key Terms

accessor methods

clone method

constructor

deep copy

dunder methods

getters

method body

method call

method name

methods

mutator methods

object identity

operator overriding

parameter list

return statement

setters

shallow copy

structural equality

Module
16

Encapsulation

Learning Objectives:

16.1 Components of Class Structure

16.1.1 Explain how encapsulation can enhance coding structures.

16.1.2 Explain the concept of information hiding.

16.1.3 Explain the purpose of instance fields in classes.

16.1.4 Explain the purpose of methods in classes.

16.1.5 Explain the purpose of properties in classes.

16.1.6 Explain how to use a keyword to reference the current instance in OOP ("`self`").

16.2 Accessor and Mutator Context

16.2.1 Explain the purpose of an accessor in encapsulation.

16.2.2 Explain the purpose of a mutator in encapsulation.

16.3 Using Constructors

16.3.1 Explain the function of parameters in OOP.

16.3.2 Explain the function of arguments in OOP.

16.3.3 Define a default parameter as it applies to OOP.

16.4 Interfaces

16.4.1 Explain the purpose of interfaces.

16.4.2 Explain the function of method signatures in OOP.

16.1 Components of Class Structure

Data Hiding (16.1.1, 16.1.2)

When driving a car, as in **Figure 16-1**, you understand that operating the car changes its behavior. Pressing the accelerator makes the car speed up, and pressing the brake slows it down. If you don't know anything else about how cars work, you could still use a car comfortably. It doesn't matter if pressing the accelerator adds gasoline to the combustion engine or increases the electrical signal to your electric car's engine; pressing the accelerator makes the car go forward.

guteksk7/Shutterstock.com

Figure 16-1   Driving a car does not require understanding how the car works

You use a computer in the same way. You don't need to know how a computer was programmed in order to use it. You only need to know what it expects from you to provide output. When you move the mouse on your desk, you expect the output will be the computer updating the mouse pointer on the screen. In fact, hiding how the computer or car works makes it easier to use.

The details of how a car or a computer works depends on many properties and abilities bundled into one package. When you hear the word "car," you probably imagine an entire car. However, a car is made up of many independent parts, such as an engine, windows, wheels, doors, and seats, as shown in **Figure 16-2**. Each part has expectations and output. If you were to simulate a car for a simulation game, you would design each of these interworking parts according to its properties and abilities.

Digital Genetics/Shutterstock.com

Figure 16-2   A car has many parts

The bundling and hiding of information in computer science is called **encapsulation**. You use encapsulation to prevent trouble when designing and implementing classes and objects. Writing programs is like making a meal. Encapsulation is being tidy in your workspace. Being tidy does not achieve the goal of making dinner, but it is still a good habit to build because tidiness makes it easier for someone else to use your workspace, less likely to use salt instead of sugar, or easier to move to other projects. In a similar way, using encapsulation properly creates code that is sturdier and easier to use.

Although the term "encapsulation" may be new to you, you've already used encapsulated features in your programs. For example, output to the screen is built into any programming language. You do not need to understand how a program produces output to display text. You only need to know that the `print()` function displays text to the command line. If the compiler changes how it processes the statement to print text, your program would continue to work as you wrote it.

Designing Objects (16.1.3, 16.1.4, 16.1.5)

Classes are a fundamental part of object-oriented programming (OOP), which treats programs as objects, similar to real-world objects. A rubber ball is an object with specific attributes you can use to describe it. For example, the ball has a radius, color, and bounciness factor. These attributes are called the **properties** of an object. The possible properties of an object are stored in the class definition as member variables (also known as **instance variables**). Using the term "member variable" is a way to describe variables that are part of an object, rather than independent variables.

When designing an object in OOP, you start by identifying its properties. What are the defining features of this object that you, or another programmer, need to know about? Suppose you are a programmer at a company and your boss asks you to program a basic **Car** class. Your boss also tells you that someone else will be using this class in their project without your help. The **Car** class needs to have a paint color, a year of manufacture, mileage, oil level, and current speed. (A real-life car would have many more properties.)

You use these properties to start to program a **Car** as a class, as shown in **Figure 16-3**. The code starts by defining the name of the class to be **Car**. It then sets up the property variables of `self.paint_color`, `self.year`, `self.mileage`, `self.oil_level`, and `self.current_speed`.

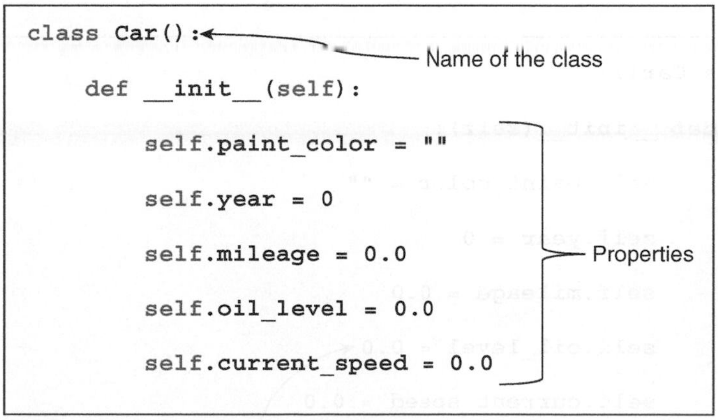

```
class Car():◄──────────────── Name of the class

    def __init__(self):

        self.paint_color = ""

        self.year = 0

        self.mileage = 0.0                ─── Properties

        self.oil_level = 0.0

        self.current_speed = 0.0
```

Figure 16-3   Properties of a car

Q **Figure 16-4** shows multisided gaming dice. These dice can have any number of sides, with the smallest number of sides being four. On each side is a number. When a die is rolled, one of the sides is considered "up." What do you think the properties of this object should be?

Mine Eyes Design/Shutterstock.com

Figure 16-4   Multisided gaming dice

A The number of sides should be a property (such as `self.num_sides`) so that you need only one class to represent all die types. The side facing up should also be a property (`self.face_up`) as it represents the state of the die.

Some properties of an object are important to the object itself but do not need to be known by others. These properties are called instance fields. An **instance field** of an object is an internal variable not meant to be seen from the outside. The object itself may modify it, or leave it alone, but any outside code should not access it. An example of an instance field for a `Car` object would be the oil level. A dashboard does not typically display the amount of oil in the car; it displays a "change oil" indicator light when the oil level is low. **Figure 16-5** shows the code for using a `self.oil_level` instance field.

The code in Figure 16-5 shows a method that interacts with an instance field. Other implemented parts of the car are omitted for brevity. A method named **should_change_oil()** will return a Boolean **True** or **False** value indicating whether the oil needs changing. It returns **True** if the `self.oil_level` of the car is less than 0.5, or **False** otherwise.

```python
class Car():

    def __init__(self):

        self.paint_color = ""

        self.year = 0

        self.mileage = 0.0

        self.oil_level = 0.0

        self.current_speed = 0.0


    def should_change_oil(self):

        return self.oil_level < 0.5
```

Instance field: other code cannot access it

Figure 16-5   Oil level is an instance field of a `Car` object

Q Consider the dice in Figure 16-5 again. What would be an instance field for a `Die` object?

A Recall that instance fields are properties of objects that cannot be seen from the outside but are used internally. One possible instance field for a `Die` object could be whether it is a weighted die that allows the user to cheat. If you are cheating, you do not want others to know you are being sneaky. So, if your dice need a cheating property to always land as "6" on a six-sided die, this property should be completely hidden from the outside.

Properties and instance fields describe the object's state. For example, the `self.current_speed` and `self.oil_level` properties describe a `Car` object's state. Actions are behaviors objects can use to change their state. A car can increase its speed or turn on its headlights. Recall that these actions are represented in code as methods. For example, a `Car` object can have an `accelerate()` method.

Another way to think about methods is as functions that are so useful to an object, they should always be included with an instance of that object. For example, all running cars can change speed, so all `Car` objects should have an `accelerate()` method. Each time you add a parameter to a function, you increase the requirements placed on others to use the function. If a function must always pass a `Car` object as an argument, then another programmer must always pass a `Car`. Making the behavior a method instead removes the possibility of the other programmer forgetting to include the `Car` argument.

Q Return to Figure 16-4 again. What action should a `Die` object have?

A When interacting with dice, you can roll them to change which value faces up. The die in the upper-left corner of Figure 16-4 has four sides. A method such as `roll()` should randomly change the `self.face_up` value to any number from 1 to 4 for this instance of the `Die` object.

Figure 16-6 contains code to use a function to accelerate a car, and **Figure 16-7** contains the method equivalent. Compare the code between the figures: the `accelerate()` method has less opportunity to fail because you're required to call it on a `Car` object.

```
from vehicle import Car

def accelerate(car, amount):

    car.current_speed += amount

my_car = Car()

accelerate(my_car, 50)

print("Current speed:", my_car.current_speed, "MPH.")

OUTPUT:

Current speed: 50.0 MPH.
```

The car variable always has to be passed, leaving room for error.

Figure 16-6 Code for an `accelerate()` function

```
class Car():
    def __init__(self):
        self.paint_color = ""
        self.year = 0
        self.mileage = 0.0
        self.oil_level = 0.0
        self.current_speed = 0.0

    def should_change_oil(self):
        return self.oil_level < 0.5

    def accelerate(self, amount):
        self.current_speed += amount
```

You can't call `accelerate()` without a `Car` object, removing error opportunities.

```
if __name__ == '__main__':
    my_car = Car()
    my_car.accelerate(50)
    print("Current speed:", my_car.current_speed, "MPH.")
OUTPUT:
Current speed: 50.0 MPH.
```

Figure 16-7   Code for an `accelerate()` method

Self-Reference (16.1.6, 16.1.7)

When talking about objects, context matters. "A car is red" doesn't mean much if you have five cars. However, "this car is red" tells you something about a specific car. To refer to the current object's properties and fields, use a **self-reference keyword**. In Python, the keyword is `self`. Python must always use the self-reference keyword explicitly, otherwise Python will look for a local variable instead. The variables `self.current_speed` and `current_speed` are different variables with different memory addresses.

Figure 16-8 shows a code snippet that first references a local variable and then references a class variable with the same identifier. In this sample code, an object has the property `self.current_speed`, and a local variable is also declared with the identifier `current_speed`.

The code in Figure 16-8 has two variables with similar identifiers, both essentially named `.current_speed`. The program can use a local and class variable with the same name because the instance variable `self.current_speed` is defined with a self-reference keyword, making it an explicit self-reference.

Explicit referencing can make your code easier to read as well as easier to match parameter identifiers, as shown in **Figure 16-9**. The code in Figure 16-9 sets a member variable to the value passed in as a parameter. To make it clear what the parameter matches, the parameter and the class property have a similar identifier: `self.year` and `year`.

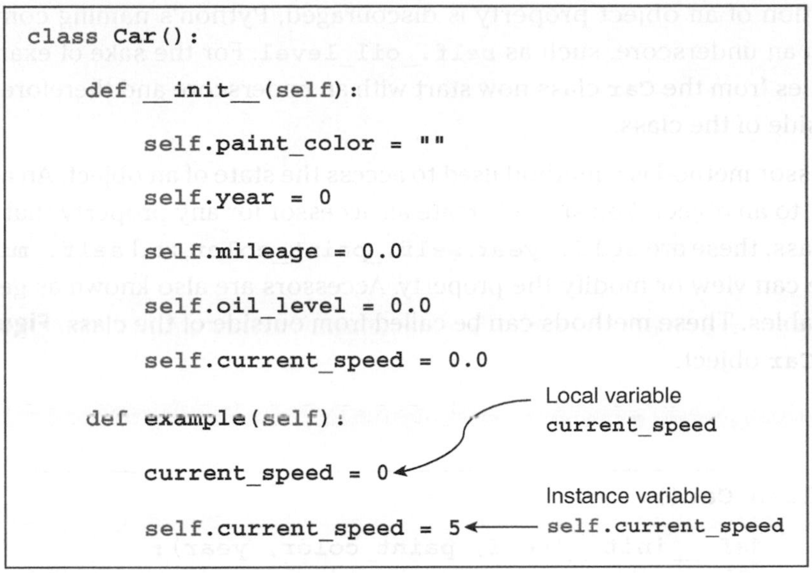

```
class Car():

    def __init__(self):

        self.paint_color = ""

        self.year = 0

        self.mileage = 0.0

        self.oil_level = 0.0

        self.current_speed = 0.0

    def example(self):

        current_speed = 0

        self.current_speed = 5
```

Local variable
current_speed

Instance variable
self.current_speed

Figure 16-8   Local and instance variables with similar identifiers

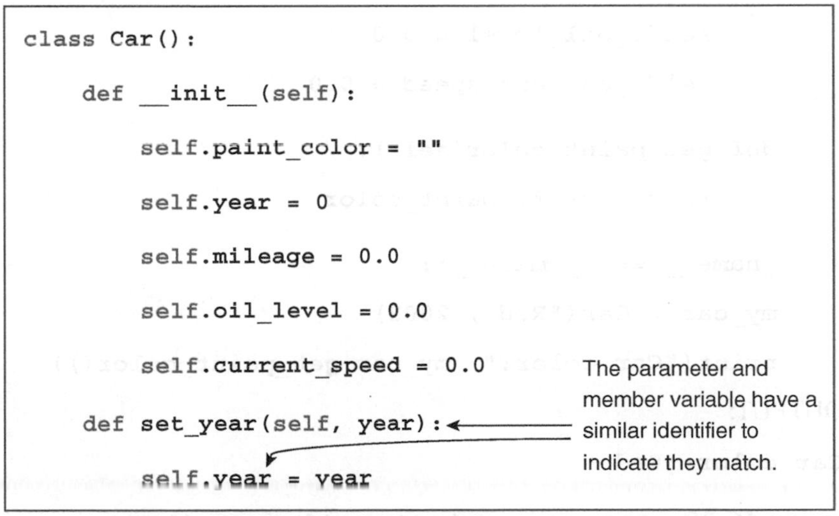

```
class Car():

    def __init__(self):

        self.paint_color = ""

        self.year = 0

        self.mileage = 0.0

        self.oil_level = 0.0

        self.current_speed = 0.0

    def set_year(self, year):

        self.year = year
```

The parameter and
member variable have a
similar identifier to
indicate they match.

Figure 16-9   Matching parameters to the instance identifier

16.2 Accessor and Mutator Context

Viewing Data from an Object (16.2.1)

Limiting how someone interacts with an object reduces the chance for an error. Imagine a calculator with the standard set of numbers plus buttons labeled A, B, and so on. What if pressing a lettered button caused an error? You would wonder why the calculator had letter buttons in the first place. By allowing only access or changes to an object in certain situations, you make the code less prone to error. Instead of relying on direct manipulation of the state of the object, you use accessors (getters) and mutators (setters) to guide the interactions.

If direct manipulation of an object property is discouraged, Python's naming convention is to start the variable identifier with an underscore, such as `self._oil_level`. For the sake of examples moving forward, assume all the properties from the `Car` class now start with an underscore and therefore should not be directly manipulated from outside of the class.

Recall that an accessor method is a method used to access the state of an object. An accessor does not allow changes, or mutations, to an object. You should create an accessor for any property that should be visible from outside. For the `Car` class, these are `self._year`, `self._paint_color`, and `self._mileage`. Being "visible" means that other code can view or modify the property. Accessors are also known as getters because they get values of member variables. These methods can be called from outside of the class. **Figure 16-10** shows a possible accessor for the `Car` object.

```
class Car():
    def __init__(self, paint_color, year):
        self._paint_color = paint_color
        self._year = year
        self._mileage = 0.0
        self._oil_level = 0.0
        self._current_speed = 0.0

    def get_paint_color(self):
        return self._paint_color

if __name__ == '__main__':
    my_car = Car("Red", 2002)
    print("Car color:", my_car.get_paint_color())
OUTPUT:
Car color: Red
```

Figure 16-10   An accessor method (getter) for a `Car` object

Accessors usually do not require more than a single line of code in the method. At the bottom of Figure 16-10, the `print()` statement uses the getter method instead of accessing the `self._paint_color` property directly. Because direct variable access allows many mistakes, such as setting the `self._paint_color` to "lizard," you don't want someone else to access `self._paint_color`, even to print its value.

Changing Data in an Object (16.2.2)

Recall that a mutator method is a method used to change data. With encapsulation, you use mutators to control changes to your object by other users. By having other programmers use a mutator method instead of directly changing the property, you can limit how the property is changed. Mutators are also known as setters because they set the value for member variables. Imagine you are creating a method that sets the year a car was made.

The earliest mass-manufactured car was the Ford Model T in 1908. The mutator shouldn't let anyone set the year to a value earlier than 1908. The paint color should also be limited, to prevent colors such as "lizard." **Figure 16-11** shows mutators for the `Car` object.

```
AVAILABLE_COLORS = ["Blue", "Red", "Green", "Black", "White", "Gray"]

class Car():
    def __init__(self, paint_color, year):
        self.set_paint_color(paint_color)

        self.set_year(year)

        self._mileage = 0.0

        self._oil_level = 0.0

        self._current_speed = 0.0

    def set_paint_color(self, paint_color):
        for color in AVAILABLE_COLORS:
            if color == paint_color:
                self._paint_color = paint_color

                return

        self._paint_color = AVAILABLE_COLORS[0]

    def set_year(self, year):
        if year >= 1908:
            self._year = year

        else:
            self._year = 1908
```

Figure 16-11   Setters for a `Car`

The two mutators shown in Figure 16-11 check for invalid values in their parameters. First, `set_paint_color()` uses a loop to iterate over all possible colors, which are listed in the `AVAILABLE_COLORS` variable. If the parameter contains a color in `AVAILABLE_COLORS`, then it sets the member variable and returns. If the method reaches the end of the loop and has not quit, that means the value provided is not a valid color, so the method sets the value to the first valid color. Next, `set_year()` checks if the value given for a year is later than 1908. If the year is valid, the member variable is set; otherwise, it uses the default year of 1908.

Using getter and setter methods instead of directly modifying the object properties ensures that your code can make assumptions about the object's state. For example, you can be sure the `Car` object can't have a year earlier than 1908, and the paint is a valid color. Notice that the initialization of the `Car` object now calls these setter methods, too. Now the only way that the year or paint color is changed is by these setters, guaranteeing no errors.

A class that does not have any mutators and marks all properties as private are called **immutable**. These objects will not change once they are created.

16.3 Using Constructors

Parameters and Arguments (16.3.1, 16.3.2)

Figure 16-11 has an initialization method, named __init__(), which is the class's constructor. Recall that a constructor is a special method that creates an object and allocates enough memory to hold the information associated with the object. Programs usually call constructors when a new object is created to initialize objects of their class type. You can use constructors for data hiding with encapsulation. When you create an object, you are the expert on the object and know the best way to set it up. The constructor is like a setup wizard you can use for installing a new program. The constructor handles the complicated parts of an object and asks you only for the parts that might change. A car may have different paint colors, but the paint is still applied in the same way regardless of the color.

The **Car** constructor has two parameters, **year** and **paint_color**, which are passed to the two setter methods **set_paint_color()** and **set_year()**. Using setters ensures that the limitations created within the setters are enforced in the constructor. The remaining lines of code set all properties of the **Car** object to starting values, such as the **self.mileage** property starting at **0**.

Designing your object requires you to decide which parameters are important. What aspects of the object would someone want to change when setting up an instance of the object? What parts can be left alone? Address the aspects to change as parameters to the constructor. Each aspect is one parameter in the constructor, which in turn can be passed an argument to set that aspect to a value.

Q If someone is making a new **Car** object, what parts should they be allowed to set? Which parts should be off limits?

A They should be able to set the paint color and year because those properties are aspects of the car that you can change when building the car. The mileage shouldn't be changed because the car determines the mileage. A newly created car can be red, blue, or green, but it always has zero miles.

The parameters are the variables provided in the method signature. The **arguments** are the values provided to those parameters. The number of parameters you define for an object corresponds to the number of arguments to supply.

In Figure 16-11, the **Car** class has a constructor with two parameters of **year** and **paint_color**. A **Car** object can be created later with two unique arguments such as **2020** and **"Blue"**.

Default Parameters (16.3.3)

As objects become more complicated, you might not want or need to supply all arguments to an object's constructor. You can specify **default parameters** to use if the constructor omits parameters for the object.

For example, because every new **Car** object needs to have a paint color, **paint_color** could be a default parameter with a color of **"Black"**. List the default parameters after the parameter identifier in the parameter list.

Figure 16-12 shows how you could design the **Car** constructor so the user does not need to provide the color or year argument. Using **"Black"** as the default color is arbitrary. You can assume that the other programmer will select the colors for each car. However, if the color does not matter to the final program, being able to write less code when creating cars is helpful.

```
AVAILABLE_COLORS = ["Blue", "Red", "Green", "Black", "White", "Gray"]

class Car():

    def __init__(self, paint_color="Black", year=1908):
        self.set_paint_color(paint_color)
        self.set_year(year)
        self._mileage = 0.0
        self._oil_level = 0.0
        self._current_speed = 0.0

    def set_paint_color(self, paint_color):
        # See if the color is in the AVAILABLE_COLORS list
        for color in AVAILABLE_COLORS:
            if color == paint_color:
                # If the color is in the list, then it's valid
                self._paint_color = paint_color
                return
        # If the code reaches this point, it is not a valid color
        # Defaults to the first color in the AVAILABLE_COLORS list
        self._paint_color = AVAILABLE_COLORS[0]

    def set_year(self, year):
        if year >= 1908:
            self._year = year
        else:
            self._year = 1908
```

Figure 16-12 A constructor with a default parameter

The code in Figure 16-12 shows a constructor with two parameters, **year** and **paint_color**. The use of the assignment syntax in the parameter list shows how to specify a default value. Assigning **paint_color** to **"Black"** means that if not enough parameters are provided to the constructor, then the computer fills in the missing argument for **paint_color** with **"Black"**. The same happens with **year** and 1908.

16.4 Interfaces and Headers

Interfaces (16.4.1)

When using code created by someone else, programmers only need to know the expected input and result. You can provide a shorthand guide to the expected input and output with **interfaces**, which are the minimum amount of information needed to interact with code. If an interface stays the same but the implementation changes, the outside programmer can still use the code.

Consider the following function, which calculates the minimum of three numbers.

```python
def min(x, y, z):
    if x <= y and x <= z:
    return x
    elif y <= x and y <= z:
    return y
    else:
    return z
```

This function starts by comparing x to y and z, and if x is less than or equal to both, it returns x. Then it compares y to x and z, returning y if y is less than or equal to both. Finally, it returns z if it reaches the else part of the conditional block because by this point z has to be the minimum. If you ran the min() function with the values 5, 10, and 2, the function would return 2. The function interface expects three numbers as parameters, called by the identifier min(), and returns the minimum of the three values passed to it. Code to use this function could look like the following:

```python
x = int(input("Enter x: "))
y = int(input("Enter y: "))
z = int(input("Enter z: "))
print("The smallest number is:", min(x, y, z))
```

Now consider the following alternative implementation for min():

```python
def min(x, y, z):
    min_guess = x
    if y < min_guess:
    min_guess = y
    if z < min_guess:
    min_guess = z
    return min_guess
```

This version of min() starts by creating a variable called min_guess, which it initializes to the value in x. Next, it checks to see if y is less than the current value in min_guess. If y is less than min_guess, it updates min_guess to contain the value from y. It repeats this check with z. If you ran the min() function with the values 5, 10, and 2 in this implementation, the function would return 2 as before.

Q Does the code to use the min() function have to change when the implementation changes?

A Although the implementation changed, the input, expected behavior, and output did not. Externally, it's as if the function hadn't changed at all. If all you knew about min() was that it expects three numbers and will return the minimum of those three, you do not need to know how it is implemented in order to use it. Both implementations, given 5, 10 and 2 as arguments, return 2.

Programming an Interface (16.4.2)

You use interfaces to quickly show how to interact with a piece of code. As you saw earlier, you only need to know certain things to use code. Knowing how it is implemented is optional. If you are creating code for another programmer, as your boss requested, creating an interface is a way to provide your coworker with all that is needed to succeed. To be useful, interfaces need to identify the following elements:

- How to invoke the function or method.
- What the function or method will do.
- What the function or method will return.

Some interfaces are meant for humans only. This means that the interface conveys knowledge to people but doesn't provide any enforceable code. For example, the docstring returned by `help()` is a human-only interface. It counts on a person to remember everything about the interface. In contrast, some programming languages provide a way to enforce the interface in the code.

Suggesting an interface using code lets you create a program that does not run if the interface is used incorrectly. It can also remove human error when the code is used and reduces how much the programmer must memorize. Similar to how a compiler does not allow you to use the incorrect syntax in a `for` loop, neither does a programming language let you use an interface incorrectly. Both will point to the exact place where the error occurred. Python can simulate interfaces but not enforce them, like how it simulates private variables.

Figure 16-13 shows how you could program the interface for the `Car` class. A new class is defined as `Car_Interface` and all the methods are created. However, each method body contains an exception raised: `NotImplementedError`. This means that the user of your code will get this error when trying to invoke the methods if they are not overwritten in the `Car` class. These method signatures contain the three items listed earlier for indicating a useful interface: how to invoke the method, what it will do, and what it will return. The only thing not contained is how it will do what it does.

```
class Car_Interface():

    # Accessors
    def get_year(self):
        raise NotImplementedError("get_year must be implemented.")
    def get_paint_color(self):
        raise NotImplementedError("get_paint color must be implemented.")
    def get_mileage(self):
        raise NotImplementedError("get_mileage must be implemented.")
    def get_speed(self):
        raise NotImplementedError("get_speed must be implemented.")
    def should_change_oil(self):
        raise NotImplementedError("should_change_oil must be implemented.")

    # Mutators
    def set_paint_color(self, paint_color):
        raise NotImplementedError("set_paint_color must be implemented.")
```

Figure 16-13   Interface for the `Car` class (*Continued*)

```
    def set_year(self, year):

        raise NotImplementedError("set_year must be implemented.")

    def increase_miles(self, amount):

        raise NotImplementedError("increase_miles must be implemented.")

    def accelerate(self, amount):

        raise NotImplementedError("accelerate must be implemented.")

    def travel(self, time_in_seconds):

        raise NotImplementedError("travel must be implemented.")
```

Figure 16-13　Interface for the `Car` class

Note the difference between the interface and the implementation. The interface is only the method signature, while the implementation is the code within the method. An interface does not provide code you can run or show you how to achieve the end result. Interfaces are limited to method signatures that tell you how to interact with the code and what to expect back. An interface is usually stored in a separate file and defines the behavior only.

The implementation is the part of the code that actually does something. Implementations include `for` loops, `if` statements, and input commands, for example, that tell the computer what to do. You've primarily been working with implementations when you think of code. Implementations are stored in a file separate from the interface.

When the implementation is stored in another file, Python needs to signal to which class these behaviors belong. Place the `Car_Interface` class name inside the parentheses that follow the `Car` class name. **Figure 16-14** shows how the `Car` class implementation changes by including the interface from Figure 16-13.

```
from interfaces import Car_Interface

class Car(Car_Interface):

    def __init__(self):
        self.paint_color = ""

        self.year = 0

        self.mileage = 0.0

        self.oil_level = 0.0

        self.current_speed = 0.0

    def set_year(self, year):

        if year >= 1908:

            self._year = year

        else:

            self._year = 1908

    # Implementation of other methods from the interface omitted
```

Figure 16-14　Signaling the use of an interface in Python

The implementation is not shown in full in Figure 16-14, but the implementation should override all of the methods in the **Car_Interface** class. The **Car_Interface** class defines the kinds of behavior that a **Car** object should have. By writing the **Car** class so that it implements this interface, you are committing the **Car** class to implementing those behaviors, although it may also include other behaviors as well. However, the specific details of each behavior are worked out in the **Car** class itself. Another class, such as an **Electric_Car** class, might also implement the **Car_Interface**. In that case, the **Electric_Car** class will also be committed to implementing the behaviors defined by the **Car_Interface**. However, the specific details of its implementation, or how the interface methods are overridden, may differ from the **Car** class.

Summary

- Encapsulation is the practice of bundling and hiding information in one object. Using encapsulation allows you to design code for other programmers to use while still controlling your program design.
- When you design an object, you identify its properties and actions. The properties become variables within a class, while the behaviors and actions become methods. Instance fields are variables the class might use but are never accessed from outside the class.
- To reference the current object instance, you use a self-reference keyword, **self**. Python requires you to always use explicit referencing, so any member variable must be accessed as **self.variable_name**.
- Encapsulation is enforced by programming accessors and mutators, or getters and setters. These methods restrict how outside code can interact with your code by allowing access or mutation within certain parameters, such as never allowing a decrease in car mileage.
- Constructors set up an object to be used by other code. The parameters of a constructor indicate how much control outside code has over objects you've designed. Default parameters give other programmers a shorthand way to initialize objects instead of detailing all the properties in the construction.
- Naming instance variables with an underscore at the start suggests that they are "private" and should not be accessed directly. Prefixing instance variable names suggests privacy but does not actually make the variables private; they can be accessed by outside code. Proper convention relies on understanding that if a variable starts with an underscore, you should treat it as if you cannot access it, even though you could.
- Interfaces are the minimal set of instructions a programmer needs to know about a piece of code to interact with it. The interface provides the input, output, and expected behavior to other programmers.

Key Terms

arguments	immutable	interfaces
default parameters	instance field	properties
encapsulation	instance variables	self-reference keyword

Module
17

Inheritance

Learning Objectives:

17.1 Using Inheritance

Creating Classes from Other Classes (17.1.1, 17.1.2)

Zoe's dealership has enjoyed success since you began writing code to manage the cars. The owner now has room to expand the dealership's capacity. With this new expansion, the inventory will include cars (gas, hybrid, and electric), motorcycles, trucks, and vans. Now is a good time to identify ways to better structure your code. Code reuse is a programming fundamental that you should strive to maintain in all of your programs.

The concept of inheritance will help you to write code for the dealership's expansion. In programming, **inheritance** is a way of creating a new class from an existing class. In the same way that children inherit genetic features from their biological parents (eyes, hair, and height, for example), classes can inherit the methods (including constructors) and member variables of other classes. Inheritance allows you to use the common properties of one class to define other classes, creating a hierarchy. Generally, a class created through inheritance is a more specialized or specific version of the original class.

As a rule of thumb, if you have logically related classes with common features, inheritance will likely make your code simpler. Inheritance is a useful tool when the same code uses related classes and needs to treat them similarly. Using inheritance also helps you to avoid duplicating code. For example, the code for checking out a motor vehicle for a test run is the same, regardless of whether it is a car, truck, motorcycle, or van. See **Figure 17-1**.

Figure 17-1   Car, truck, motorcycle, and van

MicroOne/Shutterstock.com, Ivengo/Shutterstock.com, iman fanani/Shutterstock.com

The new version of the dealership code needs to manage cars, motorcycles, trucks, and vans in three categories: gas vehicles, electric vehicles, and hybrid vehicles. They are all logically related because they are all motor vehicles and sold in the dealership. You can create a new class called **MotorVehicle** to cover all of the inventory sold in the dealership (see **Figure 17-2**). If the owner decides to sell another type of motor vehicle in the future (such as a golf cart), you can add that object to the program with a minimal amount of code because it can inherit from **MotorVehicle**.

```
                MotorVehicle

            make : string
            model : string
            color : string
             vin : string
            price : integer
             mpg : integer
            year : integer
          mileage : integer
        fuel_level : double
     tank_capacity : double
            sold : boolean
          on_lot : boolean

      give_discount(percentage)
      increase_mileage(amount)
      sell_vehicle(final_price)
          refuel(amount)
```

Figure 17-2   **MotorVehicle** class description

As shown in Figure 17-2, inheritance allows you to create a more general class with all the common features found in the objects of that type. For example, all motor vehicles have a make, model, color, VIN, price, MPG, year, mileage, fuel level, and fuel tank capacity. In the dealership, motor vehicles also have a status to indicate if they are sold or on the lot. They also have similar actions that need to be performed, including discounting the price, increasing the mileage after a test drive, selling the vehicle, checking the vehicle out for a test drive, and refueling the vehicle.

Family Trees in OOP (17.1.3)

In a family tree linking family members, children inherit from parents and grandparents. The same terminology is used in inheritance for OOP. The diagram of the inheritance relationship between classes is called an **inheritance hierarchy**, or class hierarchy. Building an inheritance hierarchy starts when a class inherits from another class. **Figure 17-3** shows three classes inheriting from the `MotorVehicle` class: `GasVehicle`, `HybridVehicle`, and `ElectricVehicle`. Each of these three classes is represented by a box containing the class name with an arrow pointing to the class from which it inherits.

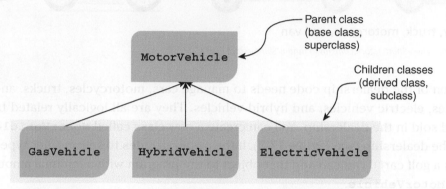

Figure 17-3 Inheritance class hierarchy for `MotorVehicles` sold in a dealership

The top class in the hierarchy is the **parent class**, also called the *base class* or `super` *class*. It refers to the class from which all the other classes are created. For example, `MotorVehicle` is the parent class of the `GasVehicle` class. The types of motor vehicles, such as gas, hybrid, and electric vehicles, are created (or derived) from the parent class. A `GasVehicle` is called a **child class**, or *derived class*, because it inherits the behavior and data members from the parent class.

The same way that each human parent is someone's child, a child class can also be a parent class. This feature is useful in the case of the `GasVehicle` class hierarchy. Three kinds of vehicles are sold at the dealership: gas-powered, electric-powered, and hybrid. Logically, each is a specialized version of a `MotorVehicle`. You can create those classes so that they inherit from the `MotorVehicle` class, making the hierarchy shown in Figure 17-3. Inheritance isn't limited to a single parent–child relationship. Any class can be a parent, even one that has its own parents.

Inheritance creates a hierarchy of classes, where the top class is the class from which all the other classes are created. For example, `GasVehicle`, `HybridVehicle`, and `ElectricVehicle` are types of motor vehicles, so they inherit directly from the `MotorVehicle` class. If programmed a `GasCar` and `GasTruck`, your inheritance diagram might look like that in **Figure 17-4**.

`GasVehicle`, `HybridVehicle`, and `ElectricVehicle` have methods from `MotorVehicle`. `GasCar` and `GasTruck` have methods from `GasVehicle`. `GasVehicle` and `MotorVehicle` are the **ancestors** of `GasCar` and `GasTruck`. In the hierarchy, any class that has one or more classes derived from it is an ancestor. Any class that is derived from a parent class is called a **descendant**.

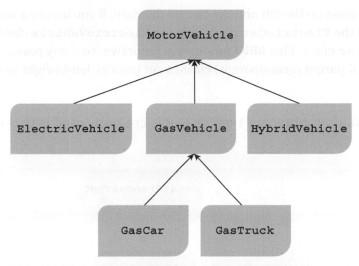

Figure 17-4 Classes inheriting from the `GasVehicle` class

The Method Resolution Order (17.1.4, 17.1.5, 17.1.6)

In Python, a child class can be derived from more than one parent class. This concept is called **multiple inheritance**. If a child class inherits from more than one parent, it receives all the accessible methods and member variables of the parent. An example of multiple inheritance is shown in **Figure 17-5**.

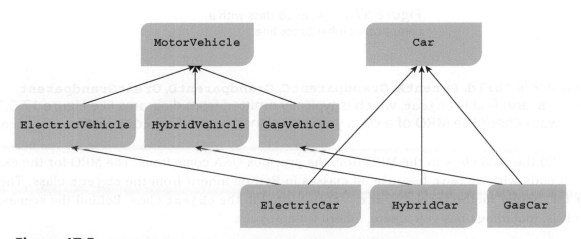

Figure 17-5 Multiple inheritance for some car-shaped classes

As shown in Figure 17-5, **ElectricCar** inherits from both **ElectricVehicle** and **Car**. **ElectricCar** inherits all of the features of **ElectricVehicle** as well as features that are specific to **Car**, such as a hatchback-style trunk. Multiple inheritance provides an easy way to create rich, complex objects by combining the features of preexisting related objects.

With inheritance, child classes inherit the properties of their parents. In Python, that means that when you invoke a property or method on an object, it follows a searching order as it looks for that property or method. This order is called the **Method Resolution Order (MRO)** and is defined by the order in which you list the parent classes for a child class. The parents have precedence from left to right. An **ElectricCar** object has the

`ElectricVehicle` parent class on the left and the `Car` on the right. If you invoke a method on an `ElectricCar` object, Python looks first in the `ElectricCar` class, then the `ElectricVehicle` class, then the `MotorVehicle` class, and then finally the `Car` class. This MRO property is recursive, so if any parent classes also have parents of their own, these parent of parent (grandparent) classes get priority left-to-right as well.

Q Examine **Figure 17-6**. If an object of type `Child` is created, what is that object's MRO?

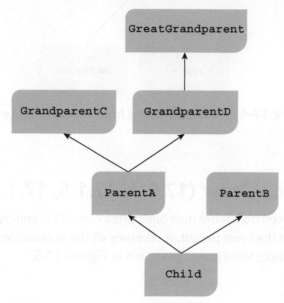

Figure 17-6   A `Child` class with a complicated inheritance line

A The order is **Child**, **ParentA**, **GrandparentC**, **GrandparentD**, **GreatGrandparent**, **ParentB**, and finally `object`, which is typically omitted from diagrams like Figure 17-6. You can always check the MRO of a class you've designed by printing `<ClassName>.__mro__`.

Where did the final class in the MRO from the previous Q&A come from? The MRO for the example in Figure 17-6 ends with `object` because all classes in Python inherit from the `object` class. The default behavior for dunder methods, like `__str__()`, is stored in the `object` class. Behind the scenes, Python has any class, including ones you create, inherit from `object`.

17.2 Necessary Components for Inheritance

Defining a Parent Class (17.2.1)

After setting the inheritance hierarchy for the new dealership code, you can begin thinking about the inner structure. As a rule of thumb, a parent class should consist of all the common features (methods and member variables) of the anticipated children. In the dealership example, you want to define a general `MotorVehicle` parent class, so you must identify all the shared features.

All motor vehicles in the dealership, regardless of the type, have similar methods and member variables, as listed in the previous section. These features provide a start for creating **MotorVehicle** as a base class, as shown in **Figure 17-7**. You should aim to create the base class with as many common features as possible to avoid duplicating code across the children of the parent class. This will not affect the functionality of your code, but it will enhance the reuse, readability, and underlying logic.

```
            MotorVehicle

        make : string
        model : string
        color : string
        vin : string
        price : integer
        mpg : integer
        year : integer
        mileage : integer
        fuel_level : double
        tank_capacity : double
        sold : boolean
        on_lot : boolean

    give_discount(percentage)
    increase_mileage(amount)
    sell_vehicle(final_price)
    refuel(amount)
```

```python
class MotorVehicle():
    def __init__(self):
        self.make = ""
        self.model = ""
        self.color = ""
        self.vin = ""
        self.price = 0
        self.mpg = 0
        self.year = 0
        self.mileage = 0
        self.fuel_level = 0.0
        self.tank_capacity = 0.0
        self.sold = False
        self.on_lot = True

    def give_discount(self, percentage):
        self.price -= self.price * percentage

    def increase_mileage(self, amount):
        self.mileage += amount

    def sell_vehicle(self, final_price):
        self.sold = True
        self.price = final_price

    def refuel(self, amount):
        self.fuel_level += amount
        if self.fuel_level > self.tank_capacity:
            self.fuel_level = self.tank_capacity
```

Figure 17-7 Defining a parent class

Because any class can become a parent class, the syntax for defining a parent class does not differ from the normal syntax for creating a class.

Defining a Child Class (17.2.2, 17.2.3, 17.2.4)

As previously described, a child class inherits the features of one or more of its parents. You can think of a child class as a customized version of the parent class. Not only does it contain the methods and member variables of the parent class, as specified by the inheritance settings, the child class can also include its own methods and member variables that are specific to the object. The following lines of code show the general syntax of defining such a class. First, the syntax for inheriting from one parent:

```
class <ChildClass>(<ParentClass>):
```

The syntax for inheriting from more than one parent:

```
class <ChildClass>(<ParentClass1>, <ParentClass2>, ...<etc.>):
```

As displayed, the code for defining a child class does not differ much from defining a normal class. The only change is the list of the parent classes from which the child class should inherit. List the parents inside the parentheses that follow the class name. The MRO still selects from left to right in order.

One more important change isn't to the syntax but to the contents of the initialization method. Because all member variables are set up in the __init__() method, a parent's member variables are only set up if that parent's __init__() method is somehow called in the child's __init__() method. Instead of calling each parent class's __init__() method, Python has an easier way to call all parents' initializations. You add it to the very first line of code in the initialization method using the built-in function super():

```
class Child(Parent):
    def __init__(self):
        super().__init__()
```

The initialization call with super() can go anywhere in the child class's __init__() method. It's standard practice to place it at the start. The super() call to __init__() will call __init__() on all parents of the child class.

Q Do I have to add methods and attributes when creating a child class from a parent class?

A No, but it is common to add class-specific variables to further customize the class. It's perfectly fine to create a child class that is identical to the parent class, though this practice is not useful because it does not take advantage of the opportunities that inheritance provides for customizing.

For example, to create the GasTruck class that inherits from the GasVehicle class, you would include attributes specific to the GasTruck class, which differentiate it from a general GasVehicle, such as the width and length of the flatbed in the back of the truck. The code for customizing the class would resemble the following:

```
class Truck(GasVehicle):
    def __init__(self):
        super().__init__()
        self.flatbed_width = 0.0
        self.flatbed_length = 0.0
```

The compiler runs the super().__init__() method, which runs the code in the GasVehicle class's __init__() method, adding all the properties from that initialization. The GasVehicle class's MRO is now [GasTruck, GasVehicle, MotorVehicle, object]. A child class can have additional methods and variables that are not included in the parent class. This is how the child class becomes a more specific, customized version of the parent.

17.3 Creating a Child Class that Inherits from a Parent Class

Inheritance Syntax (17.3.1, 17.3.2, 17.3.3)

Now that you are familiar with the concept of inheritance and its components, you can create an inherited class. The syntax for writing code for a child class that inherits from a parent class differs from language to language. **Figure 17-8** shows the Python code you would write to begin the `MotorVehicle`, `GasVehicle`, `GasTruck` class hierarchy. You start with the `MotorVehicle` class.

```python
class MotorVehicle():
    def __init__(self):
        self.make = ""
        self.model = ""
        self.color = ""
        self.vin = ""
        self.price = 0
        self.year = 0
        self.mileage = 0
        self.fuel_level = 0.0
        self.tank_capacity = 0.0
        self.sold = False
        self.on_lot = True

    def give_discount(self, percentage):
        self.price -= self.price * percentage

    def increase_mileage(self, amount):
        self.mileage += amount

    def sell_vehicle(self, final_price):
        self.sold = True
        self.price = final_price

    def refuel(self, amount):
        self.fuel_level += amount
        if self.fuel_level > self.tank_capacity:
            self.fuel_level = self.tank_capacity
```

Figure 17-8 The `MotorVehicle` parent class

Figure 17-8 shows the definition of the `MotorVehicle` class containing properties relevant to all `MotorVehicle` objects, such as the VIN. **Figure 17-9** shows the code that extends this parent class to make the `GasVehicle` class and the `Truck` class. The `GasVehicle` class inherits all the properties and methods of `MotorVehicle` and adds its own property of `self.mpg`. The `GasTruck` adds more properties that define the length and the width of the flatbed.

```python
class GasVehicle(MotorVehicle):
    def __init__(self):
        super().__init__()
        self.mpg = 0

class GasTruck(GasVehicle):
    def __init__(self):
        super().__init__()
        self.flatbed_length = 0.0
        self.flatbed_width = 0.0
```

Figure 17-9   `GasTruck` inheriting from `GasVehicle`, which inherits from `MotorVehicle`

Figure 17-10 shows how to use the child `GasTruck` class. First, the definition of `GasTruck` is imported from a module named `vehicles.py`. Next, a `GasTruck` object is declared. All the member variables of the `GasTruck` object, including those inherited from `MotorVehicle` and `GasVehicle`, are initialized. At the end, some of the member variables are written to the screen.

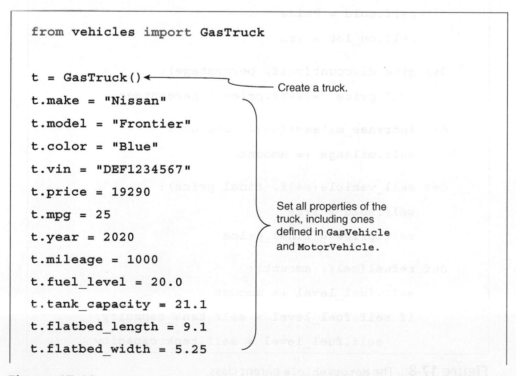

```python
from vehicles import GasTruck


t = GasTruck()          ← Create a truck.
t.make = "Nissan"
t.model = "Frontier"
t.color = "Blue"
t.vin = "DEF1234567"
t.price = 19290
t.mpg = 25
t.year = 2020
t.mileage = 1000
t.fuel_level = 20.0
t.tank_capacity = 21.1
t.flatbed_length = 9.1
t.flatbed_width = 5.25
```

Set all properties of the truck, including ones defined in `GasVehicle` and `MotorVehicle`.

Figure 17-10   Code to showcase the inheritance of the `Truck` class (*Continued*)

```
print("Truck features:")
print("Make:", t.make)
print("Model:", t.model)
print("Color:", t.color)
print("Year:", t.year)
print("Price:", t.price)
print("Flatbed Length:", t.flatbed_length)
print("Flatbed Width:", t.flatbed_width)
OUTPUT:
Truck features:
Make: Nissan
Model: Frontier
Color: Blue
Year: 2020
Price: 19290
Flatbed Length: 9.1
Flatbed Width: 5.25
```

Display the truck properties.

Figure 17-10 Code to showcase the inheritance of the `Truck` class

Customizing Behavior (17.3.4)

As written, the `MotorVehicle` class includes a method to refuel the vehicle. The `refuel()` method is inherited from `MotorVehicle` by any children classes. The `GasVehicle`, `HybridVehicle`, and `ElectricVehicle` class each has a copy of the `refuel()` method. In the `MotorVehicle` class, the `refuel()` method specifies the number of gallons of gas to add to the tank. An electric vehicle does not have a gas tank, so this version of the `refuel()` method inherited from `MotorVehicle` does not apply. Neither does the `self.tank_capacity` nor `self.fuel_level` properties. In this situation, refactoring will help.

Refactoring is the process of reexamining your code for better organization. Refactoring isn't limited to objects, but frequently happens when trying to design an inheritance hierarchy for your program. Initially, it was assumed that all `MotorVehicle` objects would have a fuel-based energy source, but now you need to create an `ElectricVehicle`. A better design for this situation would have another class called `GasVehicle` that inherits from `MotorVehicle`. **Figure 17-11** shows a refactoring option for the `MotorVehicle` class.

```
class MotorVehicle():
    def __init__(self):
        self.make = ""
        self.model = ""
        self.color = ""
        self.vin = ""
```

Figure 17-11 Refactoring the `MotorVehicle` class (*Continued*)

```
                self.price = 0

                self.year = 0

                self.mileage = 0

                self.sold = False

                self.on_lot = True

        def give_discount(self, percentage):

                self.price -= self.price * percentage

        def increase_mileage(self, amount):

                self.mileage += amount

        def sell_vehicle(self, final_price):

                self.sold = True

                self.price = final_price

    class GasVehicle(MotorVehicle):

        def __init__(self):

                super().__init__()

                self.mpg = 0

                self.fuel_level = 0.0

                self.tank_capacity = 0.0

        def refuel(self, amount):

                self.fuel_level += amount

                if self.fuel_level > self.tank_capacity:

                        self.fuel_level = self.tank_capacity

    class ElectricVehicle(MotorVehicle):

        def __init__(self):

                super().__init__()

                self.mpge = 0 # miles per gallon equivalent

                self.battery_percent = 0.0

        def refuel(self, amount):

                self.battery_percent += amount

                if self.battery_percent > 100.0:

                        self.battery_percent = 100.0
```

Figure 17-11   Refactoring the MotorVehicle class

The `self.fuel_level`, `self.tank_capacity`, and `self.mpg` are now moved to a new class, `GasVehicle`. The behavior for the `refuel()` method is also moved into `GasVehicle`. The `ElectricVehicle` class contains the properties `self.battery_percent` and `self.mpge` (miles per gallon equivalent). The refuel method increases the `self.battery_percent` by the amount compared to a maximum of 100 percent, in contrast to the `GasVehicle` class, which uses `self.tank_capacity` as a maximum.

However, now the `MotorVehicle` class has no guarantee that the child classes will be able to refuel, which is vital for a vehicle. Further refactoring should include a placeholder method in the `MotorVehicle` class and then override the method in the child classes. **Method overriding** allows a child class to provide its own implementation of a method that is already inherited from one of its ancestors. Method overriding is useful when you need to ensure that a method will exist in all child classes, but the implementation of the method may differ across those child classes. Any method can be overridden to provide customized behavior. You can customize the `refuel()` method to fit the `ElectricVehicle` or `GasVehicle` class.

Figure 17-12 shows a `refuel()` method added to `MotorVehicle` that raises the `NotImplementedError` exception with a message stating that all child classes of `MotorVehicle` must be able to refuel. **Figure 17-13** shows how the children classes can override the not implemented method inherited from the parent class (with `MotorVehicle` omitted for brevity).

```
class MotorVehicle():

    def __init__(self):
        self.make = ""
        self.model = ""
        self.color = ""
        self.vin = ""
        self.price = 0
        self.year = 0
        self.mileage = 0
        self.sold = False
        self.on_lot = True


    def give_discount(self, percentage):
        self.price -= self.price * percentage


    def increase_mileage(self, amount):
        self.mileage += amount


    def sell_vehicle(self, final_price):
        self.sold = True
        self.price = final_price


    def refuel(self, amount):
        raise NotImplementedError("Child classes of
MotorVehicle must implement a refueling method.")
```

refuel() method with NotImplementedError exception.

Figure 17-12 Adding a placeholder `refuel()` method to `MotorVehicle`

```
class GasVehicle(MotorVehicle):
    def __init__(self):
        super().__init__()
        self.mpg = 0
        self.fuel_level = 0.0
        self.tank_capacity = 0.0

    def refuel(self, amount):          ◄
        self.fuel_level += amount
        if self.fuel_level > self.tank_capacity:
            self.fuel_level = self.tank_capacity

class ElectricVehicle(MotorVehicle):          refuel() is defined
    def __init__(self):                        in all child classes.
        super().__init__()
        self.mpge = 0 # miles per gallon equivalent
        self.battery_percent = 0.0

    def refuel(self, amount):          ◄
        self.battery_percent += amount
        if self.battery_percent > 100:
            self.battery_percent = 100.0
```

Figure 17-13 Overriding the placeholder `refuel()` method inherited from `MotorVehicle`

Another application for method overriding is a `HybridVehicle` class. A `HybridVehicle` has a combustion gas engine and an electric battery. It needs the behavior of both the `GasVehicle` and `ElectricVehicle` classes. The approach is to call either the `GasVehicle refuel()` method or the `ElectricVehicle refuel()` method, depending on a `fuel_type` parameter given to the `refuel()` method in the `HybridVehicle` class.

Suppose you decide to use multiple inheritance and call one of the two inherited `refuel()` behaviors. The `super()` method will let you search your MRO for the specific method, skipping the first class in the MRO, but will find the first occurrence of a method, even if another class has the same method name, as it steps through the MRO. For example, if you define the `HybridVehicle` class to inherit from both `GasVehicle` and `ElectricVehicle`, in that order, then `super().refuel()` will always find the `refuel()` method in the `GasVehicle` class. To call the `refuel()` method in the `ElectricVehicle` class, or any other parent's method, you can use a direct method call with the class name to override the MRO.

To make a direct call to a method you've inherited, use the syntax `<ClassName>.method(self, <any arguments>)`. Note that this time the method call requires you to pass the keyword `self`. Look at **Figure 17-14**, specifically the new `HybridVehicle` class. (The `MotorVehicle` class from Figure 17-12 is omitted again.)

The `refuel()` method uses the new `fuel_type` parameter to create an if-else condition. Next, it calls either `GasVehicle.refuel(self, amount)` or `ElectricVehicle.refuel(self, amount)`.

```
class GasVehicle(MotorVehicle):
    def __init__(self):
        super().__init__()
        self.mpg = 0
        self.fuel_level = 0.0
        self.tank_capacity = 0.0


    def refuel(self, amount):
        self.fuel_level += amount
        if self.fuel_level > self.tank_capacity:
            self.fuel_level = self.tank_capacity


class ElectricVehicle(MotorVehicle):
    def __init__(self):
        super().__init__()
        self.mpge = 0 # miles per gallon equivalent
        self.battery_percent = 0.0


    def refuel(self, amount):
        self.battery_percent += amount
        if self.battery_percent > 100:
            self.battery_percent = 100.0


class HybridVehicle(GasVehicle, ElectricVehicle):
    def __init__(self):
        super().__init__()


    def refuel(self, amount, fuel_type):
        if fuel_type == "gas":
            GasVehicle.refuel(self, amount)
        else:
            ElectricVehicle.refuel(self, amount)
```

HybridVehicle class

Figure 17-14   Creating a `HybridVehicle` class

Overriding and Reuse (17.3.5)

Code can be simplified by calling behavior from a parent class while adding new behavior in the child class, as in the `HybridVehicle` `refuel()` method. The `__str__()` method also should use the combination of overriding a method while still using the overridden behavior. Consider the variables a `GasVehicle` and `ElectricVehicle` would have to display for their `__str__()` methods. Some are different, such as `self.tank_capacity` or `self.battery_percent`, but some are the same, such as `self.sold` or `self.price`. If programmed standalone `__str__()` methods in both child classes, you'd have duplicate code, which usually is a sign you may want to refactor again.

Start with the `__str__()` method for `MotorVehicle`. Create a string that contains all the properties shared by any child class and return it as you would normally. **Figure 17-15** shows this dunder method.

```python
class MotorVehicle():
    def __init__(self):
        self.make = ""
        self.model = ""
        self.color = ""
        self.vin = ""
        self.price = 0
        self.year = 0
        self.mileage = 0
        self.sold = False
        self.on_lot = True

    def give_discount(self, percentage):
        self.price -= self.price * percentage

    def increase_mileage(self, amount):
        self.mileage += amount

    def sell_vehicle(self, final_price):
        self.sold = True
        self.price = final_price

    def refuel(self, amount):
        raise NotImplementedError("Child classes of
MotorVehicle must implement a refueling method.")

    def __str__(self):    ←———— Dunder method
        result = ""
        result += "{:>10s}: {:s}\n".format("Make",
self.make)
        result += "{:>10s}: {:s}\n".format("Model",
self.model)
        result += "{:>10s}: {:s}\n".format("Color",
self.color)
```

Figure 17-15 The start of a `__str__()` method (*Continued*)

```
        result += "{:>10s}: {:s}\n".format("VIN",
self.vin)
        result += "{:>10s}: ${:0.2f}\n".format("Price",
self.price)
        result += "{:>10s}: {:d}\n".format("Year",
self.year)
        result += "{:>10s}: {:d}\n".format("Mileage",
self.mileage)
        result += "{:>10s}: {:s}\n".format("Sold",
str(self.sold))
        result += "{:>10s}: {:s}\n".format("On Lot",
str(self.on_lot))
        return result


car = MotorVehicle()
car.make = "Temporary"
car.model = "Example"
car.color = "Blue"
car.vin = "ABC123"
car.price = 15000
car.year = 1980
print(car)
```

OUTPUT:

```
      Make: Temporary
     Model: Example
     Color: Blue
       VIN: ABC123
     Price: $15000.00
      Year: 1980
   Mileage: 0
      Sold: False
    On Lot: True
```

Figure 17-15   The start of a `__str__()` method

The overriding of the `__str__()` method's behavior in the child classes can use the string created by this method in the parent class. Use a call to `super().__str__()` to obtain the string created by the `MotorVehicle` class, then append onto the returned value any further variables that need to be shown. **Figure 17-16** shows the `GasVehicle` and `ElectricVehicle` classes using inheritance along with method overriding in the `__str__()` methods. (The `MotorVehicle` class is again omitted for brevity.) **Figure 17-17** includes the code showcasing the new dunder method in action.

```
# MotorVehicle class omitted for brevity #

class GasVehicle(MotorVehicle):
    def __init__(self):
        super().__init__()
        self.mpg = 0
        self.fuel_level = 0.0
        self.tank_capacity = 0.0

    def refuel(self, amount):
        self.fuel_level += amount
        if self.fuel_level > self.tank_capacity:
            self.fuel_level = self.tank_capacity

    def __str__(self):
        result = super().__str__()
        result += "{:>10s}: {:.2f}\n".format("Fuel Level", self.fuel_level)
        result += "{:>10s}: {:.2f}\n".format("Tank Cap", self.tank_capacity)
        return result

class ElectricVehicle(MotorVehicle):
    def __init__(self):
        super().__init__()
        self.mpge = 0 # miles per gallon equivalent
        self.battery_percent = 0.0

    def refuel(self, amount):
        self.battery_percent += amount
        if self.battery_percent > 100:
            self.battery_percent = 100.0

    def __str__(self):
        result = super().__str__()
        result += "{:>10s}: %{:.2f}\n".format("Battery", self.battery_percent)
        return result
```

Figure 17-16 Creating the `__str__()` method for `GasVehicle` and `ElectricVehicle`

```
gas_car = GasVehicle()
gas_car.make = "Honda"
gas_car.model = "Fit"
gas_car.color = "Gray"
gas_car.vin = "ABC123"
gas_car.price = 15000
gas_car.year = 2014
gas_car.tank_capacity = 10
gas_car.refuel(6)

electric_car = ElectricVehicle()
electric_car.make = "Tesla"
electric_car.model = "Model 3"
electric_car.color = "Green"
electric_car.vin = "DEF456"
electric_car.price = 30000
electric_car.year = 2018
electric_car.refuel(87)

print(gas_car)
print(electric_car)
```

OUTPUT:

```
      Make: Honda
     Model: Fit
     Color: Gray
       VIN: ABC123
     Price: $15000.00
      Year: 2014
   Mileage: 0
      Sold: False
    On Lot: True
Fuel Level: 6.00
  Tank Cap: 10.00

      Make: Tesla
     Model: Model 3
     Color: Green
       VIN: DEF456
     Price: $30000.00
      Year: 2018
   Mileage: 0
      Sold: False
    On Lot: True
   Battery: %87.00
```

Figure 17-17   Using the `__str__()` method for `GasVehicle` and `ElectricVehicle`

How do I know when to refactor code?

 When you find the same code in two locations, you should refactor. If the code is similar but not exactly the same, ask yourself if you could use a parameter, as with the **refuel()** method in the **HybridVehicle** class, to make the code more flexible.

Summary

- In programming, inheritance is a way of creating a new class from another existing class. Inheritance builds a class hierarchy resembling a family tree, displaying which class has inherited from another class.
- A parent is the class that is being inherited from, a child is the class that is inheriting, and an ancestor is any parent or grandparent in a class hierarchy.
- A child can inherit from more than one parent.
- The Method Resolution Order represents the order in which Python will look for methods called on a class.
- All Python classes inherit from the built-in **object** class, which contains the default behaviors for some of the dunder methods.
- Because any class can become a parent class, the syntax for defining a parent class does not differ from the normal syntax for creating a class.
- Defining a child class does not differ much from the code for defining a normal class. The two additions are passing the parent class(es) inside the parentheses after the child class's name and invoking **super().__init__()** in the initialization method.
- Refactoring is the process of reevaluating your code structure to see if there's a better way. If you have the same code in multiple locations, try to refactor to a better design.
- Method overriding is useful when the way that the parent class has implemented a method doesn't apply to the child class and needs to change. Any method can be overridden to provide customized behavior.

Key Terms

ancestors
child class
descendant
inheritance

inheritance hierarchy
method overriding
Method Resolution Order (MRO)

multiple inheritance
parent class
refactoring

Module
18

Polymorphism

Learning Objectives

18.1 Polymorphism Basics

Flexibility While Coding (18.1.1)

As a programmer, in addition to striving to write code that can handle any possible user input, you should also aim to create code that can handle any change in requirements. To provide this flexibility, many programming languages adopt the concept of **polymorphism**, a word combining the prefix *poly*, which means "many," and *morph*, which means "shape or form." In other words, polymorphism refers to an object that can take on many forms.

Simply put, polymorphism means that you can treat any descendant of a class as if it were the parent class. If you are programming for a car dealership, for example, you are coding a system to help the owner sell many kinds of motorized vehicles, as shown in the class hierarchy in **Figure 18-1**.

All objects in the dealership inherit from the **MotorVehicle** class. Because of polymorphism, if you define a method or function that takes any descendant of a **MotorVehicle** variable as a parameter, then that method or function can treat all arguments passed in as if they were the same, provided that the behavior applied can treat the arguments the same.

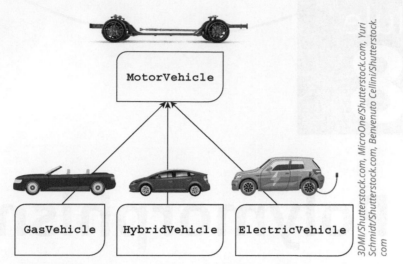

Figure 18-1 MotorVehicle inheritance hierarchy

The **add_vehicle()** method in the following code adds a vehicle to the car dealer's inventory. The parameter can be a **GasVehicle**, **HybridVehicle**, or **ElectricVehicle**. The code works no matter which descendant of **MotorVehicle** is added.

```python
def add_vehicle(self, motor_vehicle):
    if len(self.inventory) < self.capacity:
        self.inventory.append(motor_vehicle)
    else:
        print("The lot is full. Cannot add vehicle.")
```

This code takes as a parameter any **MotorVehicle** (or child of **MotorVehicle**) into the **add_vehicle()** method. If the inventory has space, the **MotorVehicle** is added. If the inventory does not have space, an error message is printed. By creating the **add_vehicle()** method like this, any other part of the code can add a **MotorVehicle** (or any child of **MotorVehicle**) to the inventory.

The following code declares three vehicles as objects of each class that is a child of **MotorVehicle**: **HybridVehicle**, **GasVehicle**, and **ElectricVehicle**. It also uses the **add_vehicle()** method to add the three vehicles to the inventory.

```python
zoes_zippy_cars = Dealership()

prius = HybridVehicle()

tundra = GasVehicle()

tesla = ElectricVehicle()

zoes_zippy_cars.add_vehicle(prius)

zoes_zippy_cars.add_vehicle(tundra)

zoes_zippy_cars.add_vehicle(tesla)
```

Any object that has been created from a class that inherits from the **MotorVehicle** class can be used with the **add_vehicle()** method to add vehicles to the inventory. In this case, you add **prius**, **tundra**, and **tesla** to the inventory.

A benefit of polymorphism is that if you need to add any other motor vehicles to the dealership and the class you are adding inherits from the parent class, you don't have to change much code.

Q Can I make an object from the `MotorVehicle` class type?

A Yes, in theory you could. However, it would not make much sense in this context. It is impossible to go to a car dealership and purchase a generic motor vehicle. You would need to specify which kind.

In Python, you can check the inheritance relationship of a variable using the built-in `isinstance()` function. The `isinstance()` function takes two arguments: the object you want to check and the class name that might be its ancestor. The function returns `True` if the object is a direct instance or a descendant of the given class. The following adjustment to the `add_vehicle()` method allows only objects that are classes inheriting from `MotorVehicle`.

```python
def add_vehicle(self, motor_vehicle):

    if not isinstance(motor_vehicle, MotorVehicle):

        print("Can only add motor vehicle objects to a dealership.")

    elif len(self.inventory) <self.capacity:

        self.inventory.append(motor_vehicle)

    else:

        print("The lot is full. Cannot add vehicle.")
```

The `Dealership` class represents the `self.inventory` object as a list. However, any type of element can be stored in a list, and the elements do not have to be the same type. The same `self.inventory` list can hold `ElectricVehicle`, `HybridVehicle`, and `GasVehicle` objects. The structure for the `Dealership` class is shown in **Figure 18-2**.

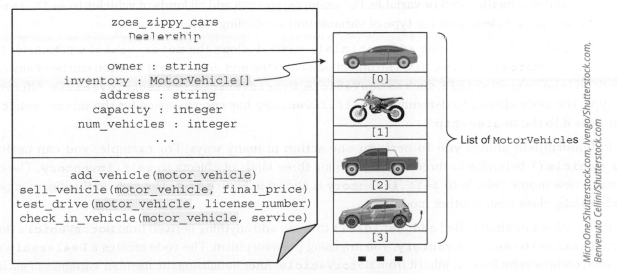

Figure 18-2 Defining the `Dealership` class using polymorphism

If you didn't use inheritance and polymorphism, related objects would have a lot of duplicate code. For example, the `self.inventory` object would have three lists (one for each type of motor vehicle). You would also have three of each method that the `Dealership` performs. This extra code adds unnecessary overhead. The code for defining the `Dealership` class is shown in **Figure 18-3**.

```
from vehicles import *

class Dealership():

    def __init__(self):

        self.owner = ""

        self.inventory = []

        self.address = ""

        self.capacity = 0


    def add_vehicle(self, motor_vehicle):

        if not isinstance(motor_vehicle, MotorVehicle):

            print("Can only add motor vehicle objects to a dealership.")

        elif len(self.inventory) < self.capacity:

            self.inventory.append(motor_vehicle)

        else:

            print("The lot is full. Cannot add vehicle.")
```

Figure 18-3   Defining a `Dealership` class

Now you can invoke any method in the `Dealership` class without being concerned about what type of motor vehicle is used in a method call or variable. For example, you can add all kinds of vehicles to `self.inventory` without needing to remember what type of variable you are dealing with.

In the code in Figure 18-3, the `add_vehicle()` method allows the `motor_vehicle` parameter to be an instance of the `MotorVehicle` class. The object passed to the `add_vehicle()` method can be of any type that is derived from `MotorVehicle`, such as `GasVehicle`, `HybridVehicle`, or `ElectricVehicle`. After enforcing the type, the code checks to determine if `self.inventory` has enough space for the `motor_vehicle`, and then adds it to the `Dealership`.

Polymorphism allows you to perform one action in many ways. For example, you can perform the `add_vehicle()` behavior in three ways by adding three kinds of objects to `self.inventory`. The code for adding a new motor vehicle to `self.inventory` is shown in **Figure 18-4**. The code in this figure imports the `Dealership` class from another module.

By creating a method called `add_vehicle()` that can add anything derived from `MotorVehicle` (including `MotorVehicle`) to `self.inventory`, you are using polymorphism. The code creates a `Dealership` variable and then creates vehicles that inherit from `MotorVehicle`. After initializing the member variables of each object, you can use the `add_vehicle()` method to add the object to the `self.inventory` of `zoes_zippy_cars`. The output shows that the behavior was successfully executed.

```
from businesses import Dealership

from vehicles import *


zoes_zippy_cars = Dealership()          ← Create a Dealership variable.

zoes_zippy_cars.capacity = 100

# Other code to initialize properties of the Dealership


corolla = GasVehicle()

tesla = ElectricVehicle()               Create different kinds of vehicles
                                        that inherit from MotorVehicle.
prius = HybridVehicle()


zoes_zippy_cars.add_vehicle(corolla)

zoes_zippy_cars.add_vehicle(tesla)      Call add_vehicle() to add
                                        each vehicle to the inventory.
zoes_zippy_cars.add_vehicle(prius)


print("Total vehicles on lot:",

len(zoes_zippy_cars.inventory))
OUTPUT:

Total vehicles on lot: 3
```

Figure 18-4 Method for adding a vehicle

Classes within Classes (18.1.2, 18.1.3)

Classes can have different kinds of relationships with each other to solve a problem. Inheritance makes the **is-a relationship** possible. The is-a relationship occurs between a parent and a child class where one class is a subclass of another class. In the **Dealership**, the **MotorVehicle** class (parent) has "is-a" relationships with the **ElectricVehicle**, **GasVehicle**, and **HybridVehicle** (children) classes. In an is-a relationship, you can treat a child class as an instance of the parent class. This is when **isinstance()** will return **True**.

The second kind of relationship is called a **has-a relationship**, where a class is a member variable in another class. Composition makes the has-a relationship possible. Just because a class contains another class, it does not inherit the capabilities of the class it contains. For example, the **Dealership** class contains an array of **MotorVehicle** objects. This is a has-a relationship because a **Dealership** has **MotorVehicles**. The **Dealership** is not a **MotorVehicle**, nor does it inherit the capabilities of the **MotorVehicle** class. **Figure 18-5** shows an example of the difference between the is-a and has-a relationship.

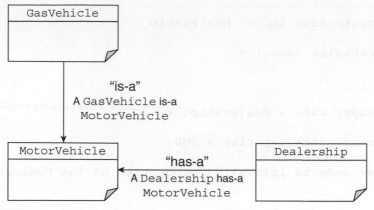

Figure 18-5   The has-a and is-a relationships

18.2 Virtual Methods

Anticipating Customization (18.2.1, 18.2.2, 18.2.3)

If you review the code for the dealership, you might realize that there is no such thing as a generic **MotorVehicle**. A **MotorVehicle** should not implement some methods because its behavior varies depending on what type of **MotorVehicle** is being used. For example, suppose the **MotorVehicle** class implements a method called **calculate_fuel_consumption()** that returns an estimated dollar amount for the car to travel a given number of miles.

This price calculation depends on whether the **MotorVehicle** is a **GasVehicle**, **HybridVehicle**, or **ElectricVehicle**. A **GasVehicle** calculates the price based on the car's average MPG, the **HybridVehicle** calculates the price using the car's MPG and estimated battery usage, and the **ElectricVehicle** bases the price on the cost of the electricity to travel the distance. See **Figure 18-6**.

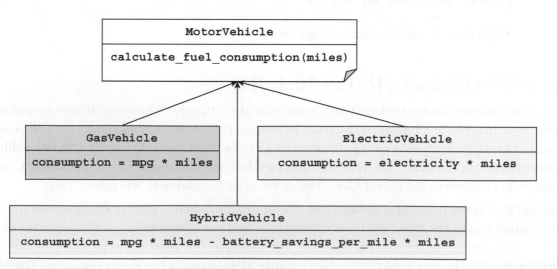

Figure 18-6   Differing method implementations

Because a `MotorVehicle` is not a specific type of vehicle, it makes sense to require each kind of `MotorVehicle` to indicate how it will implement the `calculate_fuel_consumption()` method. You can use a **pure virtual method** to specify that the derived class will define the method inherited from the parent class.

Pure virtual methods are not defined in the base class because any class derived from it should define its own version of the method. For example, `MotorVehicle` does not define the behavior of the `calculate_fuel_consumption()` method. Instead, any object derived from `MotorVehicle` (`GasVehicle`, `HybridVehicle`, or `ElectricVehicle`) will create its own implementation of the method.

In Python, you can't force a virtual method, but you can suggest it in your code design. In any method, you can raise the `NotImplementedError` so that any child classes that inherit from your parent class must override the method to use it. This suggests that a derived class will create its implementation of this method. Code for defining and using a pure virtual method is shown in **Figure 18-7**. Note that the method calls for all objects to be identical regardless of the type of object. Polymorphism in action!

```python
class MotorVehicle():
    def __init__(self):
        self.make = ""
        self.model = ""
        self.color = ""
        self.vin = ""
        self.price = 0
        self.year = 0
        self.mileage = 0
        self.sold = False
        self.on_lot = True

    def calculate_fuel_consumption(self, miles):
        raise NotImplementedError("All child classes of MotorVehicle must
implement calculate_fuel_consumption.")

    # Other methods omitted

class GasVehicle(MotorVehicle):
    def __init__(self):
        super().__init__()
        self.mpg = 0
        self.fuel_level = 0.0
        self.tank_capacity = 0.0
    def calculate_fuel_consumption(self, miles):
        return self.mpg * miles
```

Figure 18-7 Pure virtual methods in Python (*Continued*)

```
        # Other methods omitted

class ElectricVehicle(MotorVehicle):
    def __init__(self):
        super().__init__()
        self.battery_percent = 0.0
        self.electricity_cost = 0.0

    def calculate_fuel_consumption(self, miles):
        return self.electricity_cost * miles

    # Other methods omitted

class HybridVehicle(GasVehicle, ElectricVehicle):
    def __init__(self):
        super().__init__()
        self.battery_savings_per_mile

    def calculate_fuel_consumption(self, miles):
        return self.mpg * miles - self.battery_savings_per_mile * miles

    # Other methods omitted

tesla = ElectricVehicle()
tesla.electricity_cost = 13.0
honda = GasVehicle()
honda.mpg = 30.0
prius = HybridVehicle()
prius.battery_savings_per_mile = 4.0
prius.mpg = 25.0

print("Fuel consumption for 10 miles")
print("Tesla:", tesla.calculate_fuel_consumption(10))
print("Honda:", honda.calculate_fuel_consumption(10))
print("Prius:", prius.calculate_fuel_consumption(10))

OUTPUT:

Fuel consumption for 10 miles
Tesla: 130.0
Honda: 300.0
Prius: 210.0
```

Figure 18-7   Pure virtual methods in Python

Abstract Classes (18.2.4, 18.2.5)

When you create a pure virtual method, you are also creating an **abstract class**, which is any class that has one or more pure virtual methods. If a class has pure virtual methods, it should not be instantiated, so you should not create a variable of type `MotorVehicle`. A car represented in the dealership must be a `GasVehicle`, `HybridVehicle`, or `ElectricVehicle`. An abstract class is generally used to represent a generic concept in a class hierarchy, such as a `MotorVehicle`, rather than a specific object, such as a `GasVehicle`.

As a rule of thumb, you should use an abstract class if you have closely related classes that need to implement multiple versions of the same method, as with the types of vehicles. Abstract classes are a good programming choice if you want to use inheritance but do not want to create an object with the same functionality as the base class. An abstract class often represents such an abstract idea that its instantiation does not make sense in the context of the program. For example, `MotorVehicle` is an abstract idea that must be defined as a `GasVehicle`, `HybridVehicle`, or `ElectricVehicle` to have meaning within the program. A generic `MotorVehicle` is not meaningful in this context.

Summary

- Polymorphism is a concept in object-oriented programming in which an object can have many types. Inheritance is the main driver of polymorphism because a class derived from another class can be treated as the base class.
- Polymorphism means that an object of a child class can be treated as though it were an object of its parent class. Inheritance and polymorphism help to avoid duplicate code within related objects.
- The is-a relationship enables objects of a child class to be treated as an object of the parent or ancestor class. Inheritance fuels this relationship in OOP.
- The has-a relationship describes when a class has an object of another class as a member variable. In this type of relationship, the class does not inherit the capabilities of the class it contains.
- In some programming scenarios, it makes sense to require the children of a base class to provide their own implementation of a method, especially if the functionality significantly varies between classes. This is called a pure virtual method.
- Any class with one or more pure virtual methods is called an abstract class. An abstract class cannot be instantiated and is generally used to represent a generic concept in a class hierarchy, rather than a specific object.

Key Terms

abstract class	is-a relationship	pure virtual method
has-a relationship	polymorphism	

Module
19

Linked List Data Structures

Learning Objectives:

19.1 Linked List Structures

19.1.1 Explain the purpose of data structures, such as linked lists.

19.1.2 List commonly used data structures.

19.1.3 Classify data structures as linear or nonlinear.

19.1.4 List the operations associated with data structures.

19.1.5 Classify data structures as built-in, imported, or programmer-defined.

19.1.6 Identify the components of a linked list.

19.1.7 Illustrate the physical layout of a linked list in memory.

19.2 Types of Linked Lists

19.2.1 Draw a conceptual diagram of a singly linked list.

19.2.2 Characterize and identify use cases for a singly linked list.

19.2.3 Draw a conceptual diagram of a doubly linked list.

19.2.4 Characterize and identify use cases for a doubly linked list.

19.2.5 Draw a conceptual diagram of a circular linked list.

19.2.6 Characterize and identify use cases for a circular linked list.

19.2.7 Compare and contrast the characteristics of linked lists with Python lists.

19.3 Code a Linked List

19.3.1 Express the high-level algorithm for creating a linked list based on a **Node** class and a **LinkedList** class.

19.3.2 State the purpose of the **Node** class.

19.3.3 Identify pointer declarations.

19.3.4 Identify elements of the **LinkedList** class.

19.3.5 Express the algorithm for appending a node to a linked list.

19.3.6 Express the algorithm for traversing a linked list.

19.3.7 Explain the use of a temporary pointer for traversing a linked list.

19.3.8 Express the algorithm for prepending a node to a linked list.

19.3.9 Identify code that finds a specific element in a linked list.

19.3.10 Diagram the way pointers shuffle when inserting an element in a linked list.

19.1 Linked List Structures

Data Structure Selection (19.1.1, 19.1.2, 19.1.3, 19.1.4)

A musical composition is a series of notes. In the classical music of India, the notes of a basic scale are Sa, Re, Ga, Ma, Pa, Dha, and Ni, as shown in **Figure 19-1**. These notes can be arranged in many ways to form songs.

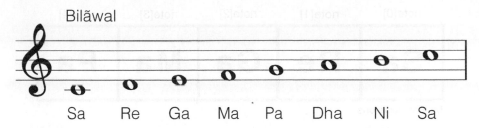

Figure 19-1   A basic scale for classical music in India

When composing a song, songwriters add, change, and delete notes. If you were coding a songwriting app, how would you organize the song data in memory so that it is easy to access and modify during runtime?

Computer scientists have devised many methods for organizing data in memory. These methods are referred to as data structures. More specifically, a **data structure** is a specific layout of data values in memory and a set of operations that can be applied to those values.

Figure 19-2 illustrates six data structures commonly used by programmers.

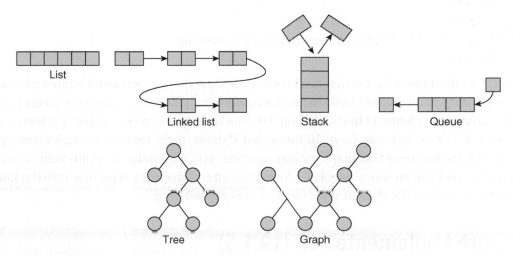

Figure 19-2   Common data structures

Python lists, linked lists, stacks, and queues are examples of linear data structures. A **linear data structure** arranges data elements in a sequential chain. A **nonlinear data structure** arranges data as hierarchies or webs in which there can be multiple links between data elements.

Q   Which data structures in Figure 19-2 are nonlinear?

A   Trees and graphs are nonlinear data structures because they connect a hierarchy or network of data elements rather than a linear sequence of elements.

The data structure you select for a set of data depends on how that data will be used. For example, for a music composition app, users create compositions that contain a varying number of notes. Notes need to be added, deleted, and changed. The final composition, though, is played sequentially.

You could use a Python list to work with the notes of a musical composition. Is that the best data structure you could select? A Python list holds data in consecutive memory locations. Each element has a corresponding index, such as 0, 1, or 2. See **Figure 19-3**.

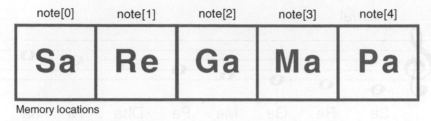

Figure 19-3 A Python list holds data in consecutive memory locations

You can access the data in a Python list using a statement such as `first_note = note[0]`. You can also change a note with a statement such as `note[4] = "Dha"`. Efficiently traversing a Python list can be accomplished using a loop.

When selecting a data structure, you should consider the efficiency of the following operations:

Accessing an individual element.
Appending a new element to the end of the structure.
Inserting an element within the structure.
Deleting an element.
Modifying an element.
Traversing the structure to display or manipulate each element.
Sorting the elements.

Considering the limitations, a Python list might not be the best data structure for a musical composition app. Python hides its memory management tasks when you modify a Python list, especially when you're increasing or decreasing the number of elements in the Python list. One task Python hides is that it reserves more memory than you need for a list. Your list may have 10 items, but Python might reserve enough memory for 16 items. Because you have no control over this memory management, you may want to create your own data structure so you have final say over the memory use. Let's look at an alternative data structure called a linked list to see if it would be better suited for the data in your musical composition app.

Data Structure Implementation (19.1.5)

Python includes many data structures for you to use, but a linked structure is one you can design yourself. You can create programmer-defined data structures by coding relationships among primitive data types, such as integers, floats, and Booleans.

You can use several algorithms for coding a data structure. For example, you might code a linked list using a function or a class. Coding a linked list as a class is a common implementation, but first let's explore some basic information on how linked lists work.

Linked List Basics (19.1.6, 19.1.7)

A **linked list** is a collection of data that can be stored in nonconsecutive memory locations. In a simplified memory layout, assume that memory locations are boxes that can store an integer, string, or any other chunk of data. In **Figure 19-4**, the string `"Sa"` is stored in Box 6 of memory. This is the first element in the list, sometimes referred to as the **head** of the list.

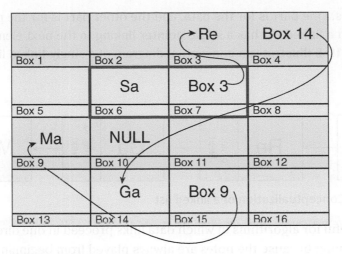

Figure 19-4   Linked list memory layout

Q Where is the second item of the list?

A The second element in the list, `"Re"`, is not stored in Box 7 or Box 8, which are the next consecutive memory locations. In a linked list, `"Re"` can be stored just about anywhere in memory. In this example, it is stored in Box 3.

To connect the elements in a linked list, each data element is associated with a link to the next address. These links connect the data elements into a linear structure in which each element links to the next element. In a doubly linked list (discussed later), each element also links to the previous element.

The link between two data elements is generally referred to as a pointer, though some programming languages call it a reference. Technically, a **pointer** is a variable that holds the memory address of another variable. A **reference** accomplishes a similar goal by referring to the memory location of a variable or other object. In Python, to be brief, pointers and references are used to describe a variable that contains another instance variable of a class.

Q Look back at Figure 19-4. What is in Box 7?

A Box 7 contains "Box 3," which is a pointer that points to `"Re"` in Box 3.

`"Sa"` and the pointer to Box 3 are two parts of a **node**. The first node in the linked list carries a pointer to Box 3, which is the location of `"Re"`, the second element in the list. The last element in a linked list typically points to None. None represents the abstract concept of "nothing" or "nowhere": There is no memory address to go to.

19.2 Types of Linked Lists

Singly Linked Lists (19.2.1, 19.2.2)

Conceptually, a linked list is often diagrammed as a sequence of nodes connected with arrows. The pointer called **head** references the first node in the linked list.

Each node has two parts. One part is for the data, and the other part is for the pointer to the next data element. When each element in a linked list has a single pointer linking to the next element, the structure is called a **singly linked list**. **Figure 19-5** illustrates a conceptual diagram of a singly linked list.

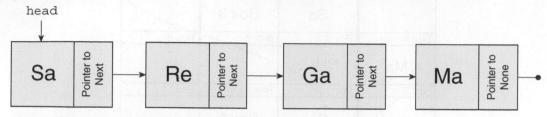

Figure 19-5   Conceptualization of a linked list

A singly linked list is useful for algorithms in which data links proceed in one direction. It is an efficient data structure for the notes in a song because the notes are always played from beginning to end.

Q What other activities can be represented by a singly linked list?

A Here are a few:

- Storing the frames for a video file that is played from beginning to end.
- Processing the people in a telephone queue as the person at the **head** of the list leaves and newcomers are added to the end.
- A navigation system that stores a list of directions that are followed in sequence from beginning to end.
- Storing a game character's path through a dungeon.

Doubly Linked Lists (19.2.3, 19.2.4)

What if you're coding an app for a playlist of songs? Users might want to scroll forward or backward through the list of songs using controls such as those shown in **Figure 19-6**.

Figure 19-6   Playlist controls for cueing up the next or previous song

A **doubly linked list** has two pointers for each element. One pointer links to the next element, and the other pointer links to the previous element, as shown in **Figure 19-7**.

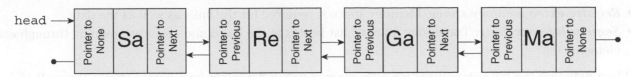

Figure 19-7   Conceptualization of a doubly linked list

A doubly linked list shines for algorithms that require traversing a list from beginning to end or from the end to the beginning.

Q In addition to a playlist app, can you think of other use cases for doubly linked lists?

A You might have thought of the following use cases:

- Using the Back and Next buttons in a browser to traverse a list of webpages.
- Storing the coordinates of a GPS tracker so that you can retrace your steps and find your way home.
- Tracking key presses for the Undo and Redo operations in a text editor.

Circular Linked Lists (19.2.5, 19.2.6)

For some algorithms, the list of data has no clear beginning or end. In a **circular linked list**, the last node points back to the first node, as shown in **Figure 19-8**.

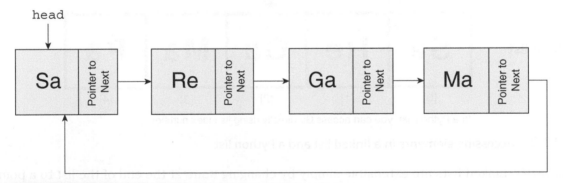

Figure 19-8   Conceptualization of a circular linked list

A circular list can be singly or doubly linked. You can use a circular linked list for algorithms in which data is cycled through repeatedly. You could use a circular linked list to store a list of players in a multiplayer game and use that list to rotate through each player's turns. Systems programmers might use a circular linked list to store a series of processes that the computer executes partially on a first pass, then continues to execute on subsequent passes.

Linked List Characteristics (19.2.7)

Singly, doubly, and circular linked lists have the following characteristics:

- ***Extensible.*** Elements can be easily appended to the end of the list.
- ***Modifiable.*** Elements can be efficiently inserted and deleted because to move a node, only the pointers to the data have to change.

- ***Require extra memory space.*** Memory space is required for the links as well as the data.
- ***Sequential searching.*** Traversing a linked list begins at the **head** and requires stepping through each element.

When planning the data structures for a program, a linked list might be a better choice than a Python list. Understanding the differences can help you choose the most efficient structure for your programs. Let's compare linked lists to Python lists.

Access. Linked lists support sequential access, whereas Python lists support random access. To access an element in a linked list, you must always begin at the **head** of the list and follow the links one by one until you reach the target element. In contrast, a Python list element can be reached simply by specifying its index number. See **Figure 19-9**.

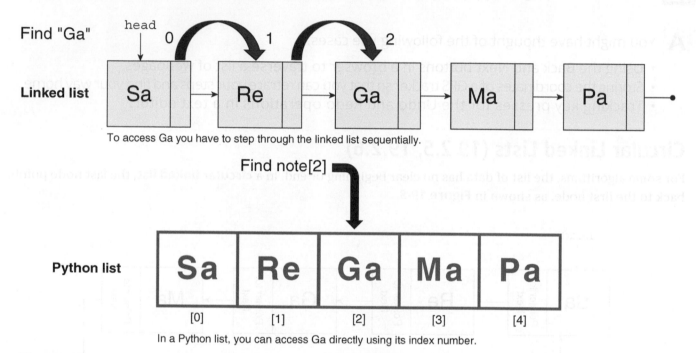

Figure 19-9   Accessing elements in a linked list and a Python list

Extensibility. Linked lists are extensible simply by changing **None** at the end of the list to a pointer to the new element. In contrast, the size of a Python list is fixed when it is declared. Python handles this memory management for you behind the scenes, but it can still affect your program. If a Python list is full and has no extra memory nearby, adding an element requires Python to copy the contents of the original Python list into a second, larger Python list before adding a new element. See **Figure 19-10**.

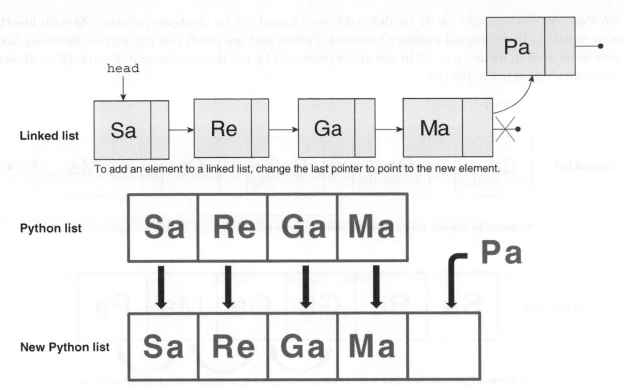

To add an element to a linked list, change the last pointer to point to the new element.

To add an element to a Python list that has no memory next to it, Python must first create a new, larger Python list.

Figure 19-10   Appending elements to a linked list and a Python list

Insertion. A new element can be inserted anywhere in a linked list by changing two pointers. Items in the original list remain in their current memory locations. In contrast, to insert an element into a Python list, multiple elements may need to shift to other memory locations to make space for the new element. See **Figure 19-11**.

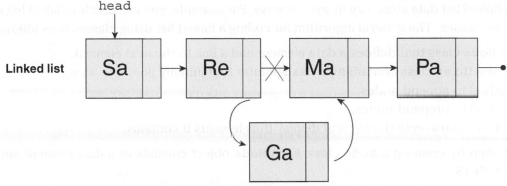

To insert an element into a linked list, you can adjust two pointers.

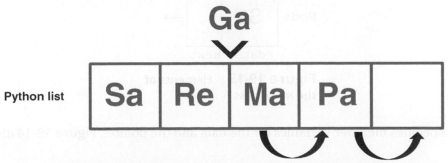

To insert an element in a Python list, Python has to move all of the subsequent elements to create a space for the new element.

Figure 19-11   Inserting elements into a linked list and a Python list

Deletion. An element can easily be deleted from a linked list by changing pointers. As with insertions, elements remain in their original memory locations. Python lists are much less efficient for deletions because elements must shift in memory to fill in the space produced by the deleted element. **Figure 19-12** shows two **"Ga"** elements; one is to be deleted.

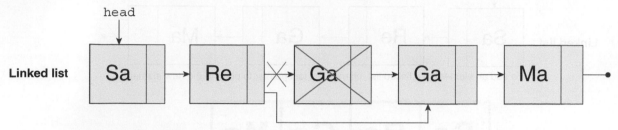

To delete an element from a linked list, simply change the pointer to the subsequent next element.

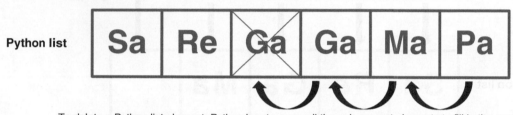

To delete a Python list element, Python has to move all the subsequent elements to fill in the gap.

Figure 19-12   Deleting elements in a linked list and a Python list

19.3 Code a Linked List

The Node Class (19.3.1, 19.3.2, 19.3.3)

You can code a linked list data structure in several ways. For example, you can create a linked list based on functions or based on classes. The general algorithm for coding a linked list using classes is as follows:

Construct a **Node** class that defines a data element and a link to the next element.

Create a **LinkedList** class containing a **head** pointer that initially points to **None**.

Create a method to append nodes.

Create a method to prepend nodes.

Create a method to traverse the list and display the elements it contains.

Let's get started by creating a **Node** class. Each **Node** object consists of a data element and a pointer, as shown in **Figure 19-13**.

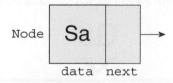

Figure 19-13   Elements of the **Node** class

The **Node** class specifies member variables for the data and the pointer. **Figure 19-14** displays the code for the **Node** class.

```
class Node():
    def __init__(self, data):
        self.data = data
        self.next = None
```

Figure 19-14   Code for the `Node` class

The `Node` class has two member variables: `self.data`, a string, and `self.next`, a pointer to the next node of the list. The `self.next` variable should contain only another `Node` object or, if empty, the void value `None`.

The constructor initializes a `Node` object with one input parameter. The `self.data` variable is set to the value in the data parameter, and the `self.next` variable is set to `None`.

The `LinkedList` Class (19.3.4)

The `LinkedList` class creates a pointer to the **head** of the list and initially sets it to `None`. The `LinkedList` class will also include methods that manipulate the linked list. **Figure 19-15** displays the code that creates the `LinkedList` class.

```
from node import Node
class LinkedList():
    def __init__(self):
        self.head = None
```

Figure 19-15   Code for the `LinkedList` class

In the `LinkedList` class, the `self.head` variable is a pointer to the **head** of the list. The `self.head` pointer is initially set to `None` because the list is empty.

The `append()` Method (19.3.5, 19.3.6, 19.3.7)

A linked list is populated by appending elements, such as `"Sa"`, `"Re"`, and `"Ga"`, to the end of the data structure. When the list is empty, the element being appended becomes the **head** of the list. Otherwise, a loop traverses the list to the last element where you can append the new node. To populate the linked list class, you create the `append()` method. The pseudocode for the algorithm of the `append()` method goes like this:

```
Create an instance of a Node that contains the data to append

If the linked list is empty:

    Set the start of the linked list to the new node

Otherwise:

    Create a searcher pointer that starts at the head of the linked list

    While the searcher pointer does not point to the end of the list:

    Advance the searcher pointer to the next node

    At the end of the list, set the last pointer to reference the same node as the new

Node pointer so that the new Node is linked to the list
```

Q How can you tell if a list is empty?

A The **head** points to **None**.

Figure 19-16 details the code for appending a new element to the end of the linked list.

```
from node import Node
class LinkedList():
    def __init__(self):
        self.head = None

    def append(self, data):
        new_node = Node(data)

        if self.head == None:
            self.head = new_node

        else:
            searcher = self.head
            while searcher.next != None:
                searcher = searcher.next
            searcher.next = new_node
```

Figure 19-16 Code for the **append()** method

The **append()** method begins with **new_node = Node(data)**, which creates a new node containing a data value and an associated variable called **new_node**.

If **self.head == None**, the list is empty, and the **self.head** pointer takes on the value of **new_node** to make the new node the **head** of the list. Otherwise, **searcher = self.head** creates a pointer called **searcher** that references the same node as the **self.head** pointer where the traversal begins.

A while-loop handles the traversal. If **searcher.next** is not **None**, it is not the end of the list, so the next pointer is loaded into **searcher** using the statement **searcher = searcher.next**. When the value in **searcher.next** is **None**, it is the end of the list and the new node can be added using the statement **searcher.next = new_node**. The loop stops before it falls off the end of the list.

You can use a driver program (a program to showcase the code you just created) to create an instance of a linked list that calls the **append()** method. The code in **Figure 19-17** creates a linked list called **my_list** and appends three nodes for strings **"Sa"**, **"Re"**, and **"Ga"**.

```
from linkedList import LinkedList
my_list = LinkedList()
my_list.append("Sa")
my_list.append("Re")
my_list.append("Ga")
```

Figure 19-17 Driver code to append elements to the linked list

You'll want to see the results of the append operation by displaying the list. For that, you can create a method called __str__(). This method begins at the **head** of the list and uses a while-loop to traverse the list by following the pointers from one element to the next until it reaches the **None** pointer at the end of the list. Here is the pseudocode for the algorithm:

```
If the list is empty:

    display the message "The list is empty."

Otherwise:

    Create a pointer to traverse the list and start it at the first node

    While the pointer points to a node object and has not fallen off the end of the list

        Display the data pointed to by the pointer

        Advance the pointer to the next node
```

Trace through the code in **Figure 19-18** and look for the statement that moves the pointer along.

```python
from node import Node

class LinkedList():

    def __init__(self):

        self.head = None

    def __str__(self):

        string = ""

        if self.head == None:

            string += "The list is empty!"

        else:

            traverser = self.head

            while traverser != None:

                string += traverser.data + "\n"

                traverser = traverser.next

        return string

    def append(self, data):

        # code omitted
```

Figure 19-18   Code for traversing the list to output of the data for each node in the `LinkedList`

The __str__() method begins by checking if the list is empty. If the list contains elements, **traverser = self.head** creates a pointer called **traverser** that references the same node as the **self.head** pointer.

The reference **traverser.data** holds the data for the first node and the statement appends it to the string to return. Then **traverser = traverser.next** loads **traverser** with the pointer to the next node.

Q If the list contains **"Sa"** **"Re"** **"Ga"** **"Ma"**, what is the output when a program calls **__str__()**?

A The output is:

Sa

Re

Ga

Ma

The prepend() Method (19.3.8)

Adding to the end of a linked list requires the algorithm to walk all the way to the end before adding the data. Linked list data structures are much better at adding data to the beginning, or prepending the data. Because of the pointer style structure in a linked list, the start of the list is an arbitrary memory location and can be changed. New nodes can be inserted at the start without walking the entire chain, which is great when the list contains a lot of data. To add data to the beginning of a linked list class, you create the **prepend()** method.

Whatever is at the start of the list becomes the data in the **next** pointer, and the new node becomes the **head** of the list. Even if the list is empty, the same code is run. If the list is empty, then the **head** pointer contains **None**. Setting the new node's **next** pointer to **None** is the correct behavior if the list is empty. The pseudocode outline for prepending is straightforward:

Create a new node with the new data

Set the new node's next to point to the current head of the list

Point the list's head to the new node

Figure 19-19 shows the code of the **prepend()** method.

```
from node import Node
class LinkedList():
    def __init__(self):
        self.head = None
    def __str__(self):
        # Omitted
    def prepend(self, data):
        new_node = Node(data)
        new_node.next = self.head
        self.head = new_node
    def append(self, data):
        # Omitted
```

Figure 19-19   Code for prepending an element to a linked list

Finding an Element in a Linked List (19.3.9)

You can use the general algorithm for traversing a linked list to look at each element and determine if it matches a specified target value. The pseudocode for the algorithm goes like this:

```
Start a pointer at the beginning of the list

While the pointer is pointing to a Node variable:

    If the node at that pointer has data which matches the target value:

        return True

    Otherwise:

        Advance the pointer to the next node

Return False if the pointer reaches this point because no node matched the target
```

In Python, you can use the keyword in to detect if an object contains a value. The statement 5 in [1, 2, 3, 4, 5] returns True. The dunder method called by in is __contains__(), which has one input parameter (the value for which you are searching). **Figure 19-20** illustrates the code for the __contains__() method for the LinkedList class.

```
from node import Node
class LinkedList():
    def __init__(self):
        self.head = None
    def __str__(self):
        # Omitted
    def __contains__(self, target):
        traverser = self.head
        while traverser != None:
            if traverser.data == target:
                return True
            traverser = traverser.next
        return False
    def prepend(self, data):
        # Omitted
    def append(self, data):
        # Omitted
```

Figure 19-20   Code for finding an element in a linked list

The __contains__() method accepts one argument for the target value. If the list is empty, the target is not in the list. The traverser = self.head statement sets a pointer to the first item in the list. While the pointer is pointing to a Node object and not to None, the value at traverser needs to be checked. If traverser.data is the target value, `True` is returned. Otherwise, `traverser` is set to the `traverser.next` pointer and the loop iterates to the next list element. If the while-loop finishes, then the target is not in the list, and `False` is returned.

Figure 19-21 shows the use of `prepend()`, `__contains__()`, and `__str__()`.

```
from linkedList import LinkedList
my_list = LinkedList()
my_list.prepend("Ma")
my_list.prepend("Ga")
my_list.prepend("Re")
my_list.prepend("Sa")
print(my_list)
if "Ga" in my_list:
    print("Ga is in the list!")
else:
    print("Ga is not in the list!")
OUTPUT:
Sa
Re
Ga
Ma
Ga is in the list!
```

Figure 19-21 Explicitly using `prepend()` and implicitly using `__str__()` and `__contains__()`

The `insert()` Method (19.3.10)

Inserting an element into a linked list requires you to shuffle pointers. The general pseudocode for the algorithm is:

`Start a temporary pointer variable at the front of the linked list`

`Walk the pointer to the location to insert the new element by advancing the pointer to the next node`

`Create a new node with the new data and have its next pointer point to the temporary variable's next`

`Point the temporary variable's next to the new node`

Figure 19-22 shows the three steps of inserting an element after identifying where to insert the element.

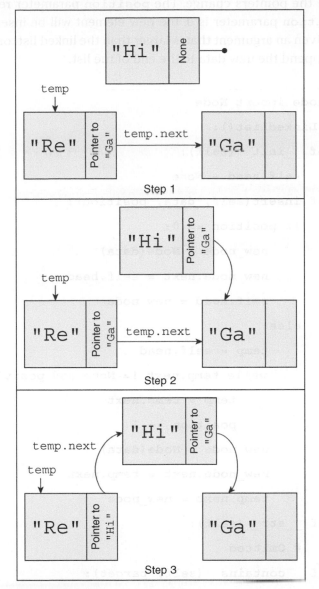

Figure 19-22   Pointer shuffling for inserting a new node between "Re" and "Ga" in a linked list

1. Step 1 shows the **Node** objects when the **temp** pointer is pointing to the **Node** after which the new **Node** should be inserted. No pointers in the linked list structure have been changed yet. The new **Node** has been created to contain **"Hi"**, but its **next** pointer is not pointing anywhere yet.

2. Step 2 shows connecting the new **Node**'s next pointer to the list. It points to the **Node** after **temp**, or **temp.next**. The new **Node** now points to the continuation of the linked list as its **next**, but the linked list does not contain the new **Node** yet.

3. Step 3 adds the new **Node** by changing where **temp** points to as the next element. The **temp.next** pointer is redirected to point to the new **Node**, which points to the rest of the list as its next element (step 2).

The variable **temp** already points to the **Node**, which is the one before where the new node needs to be inserted. Pay attention to the pointers in the figure compared to the description of the steps earlier.

To insert an element into a linked list, you program the **insert()** method. Trace through the code in **Figure 19-23** and find where the pointers change. The **position** parameter represents where to insert the new **Node** object. If the **position** parameter is 0, the new element will be inserted at the start of the list. If the **position** parameter is given an argument that is larger than the linked list, or if the linked list is empty, the **insert()** method will just append the new data to the end of the list.

```python
from node import Node
class LinkedList():
    def __init__(self):
        self.head = None
    def insert(self, data, position):
        if position == 0:
            new_node = Node(data)
            new_node.next = self.head
            self.head = new_node
        else:
            temp = self.head
            while temp.next != None and position > 1:
                temp = temp.next
                position -= 1
            new_node = Node(data)
            new_node.next = temp.next
            temp.next = new_node
    def __str__(self):
        # Omitted
    def __contains__(self, target):
        # Omitted
    def prepend(self, data):
        # Omitted
    def append(self, data):
        # Omitted
```

Figure 19-23   Code for inserting a node in a linked list

The **insert()** method begins by checking to see if the **position** parameter has the value 0. If the value is 0, then the new node needs to be inserted at the start of the linked list. The code inside the code block after the if-statement is identical to the code from **prepend()** because inserting at the start of a list is the same as prepending to a list.

If the value is not 0, a temporary variable named `temp` is set to start at the `head` of the list. A while-loop steps through the list. The `while` conditional statement has two parts combined with the Boolean operator `and`. If the `temp` variable is at the end of the list or the insertion location has been reached, the while-loop ends. Otherwise, the `temporary` pointer is advanced with `temp = temp.next`.

Once the loop finishes, the `new_node.next = temp.next` statement links the new node to the next node in the list. Then `temp.next = new_node` links the target to the new node.

After you've defined the `Node` class, the `LinkedList` class, and methods for appending, traversing, finding, and inserting elements, you can use a driver program such as the one in **Figure 19-24** to experiment with linked lists.

```
from linkedList import LinkedList
my_list = LinkedList()
my_list.append("Sa")
my_list.append("Re")
my_list.append("Ga")
print("The original list:")
print(my_list)
if "Sa" in my_list:
    print("Found Sa in the list!")
else:
    print("Did not find Sa in the list.")
print()
my_list.insert("Hi", 2);
print("The list after the insertion:")
print(my_list)
OUTPUT:
The original list:
Sa
Re
Ga
Found Sa in the list!
The list after the insertion:
Sa
Re
Hi
Ga
```

Figure 19-24   Linked list driver code to append, traverse, find, and insert

Summary

- A linked list is a linear data structure. A data structure is a specific layout of data values in memory and a set of operations that can be applied to those values. Other data structures include Python lists, stacks, queues, trees, and graphs. Data structures are used to hold data in memory during program execution.
- A linked list is a collection of data that can be stored in nonconsecutive memory locations. Each element in a linked list is called a node. Each node consists of data and a pointer to the next node. The first node in a linked list is referred to as the **head**.
- When each element in a linked list has a single pointer linking to the next element, the structure is called a singly linked list. A doubly linked list has two pointers for each element. One pointer links to the next element; the other pointer links to the previous element. In a circular linked list, the last node points back to the first node.
- Linked lists are easy to extend and modify. However, they require extra memory for the pointers and must be accessed sequentially beginning at the **head** of the list.
- You can use a variety of algorithms for coding linked lists. One popular way is to create a **Node** class for each data element and a **LinkedList** class with methods for appending elements, traversing the list, inserting elements, finding elements, displaying elements, and other operations.
- Coding a linked list is one of the challenges you might experience in a technical interview when seeking a programming job, so you'll want to keep linked lists in your programming skill set.

Key Terms

circular linked list	linear data structure	pointer
data structure	linked list	reference
doubly linked list	node	singly linked list
head	nonlinear data structure	

Stacks and Queues

Learning Objectives:

20.1 Stacks

20.1.1 Explain why stacks are considered limited access, linear data structures.

20.1.2 Explain the meaning of LIFO in the context of stacks.

20.1.3 Use the terms "push" and "pop" in the context of stacks.

20.1.4 State the efficiency of push, pop, and search operations performed on a stack.

20.1.5 Provide examples illustrating the use of stacks in computer programs.

20.1.6 Identify the classes that are used when implementing a stack based on a linked list.

20.1.7 Diagram the processes for pushing and popping elements from a linked list stack.

20.1.8 Create a __str__() method for a stack.

20.2 Queues

20.2.1 Classify a queue as a linear, limited access data structure that is accessed as FIFO.

20.2.2 Contrast the FIFO operation of a queue with the LIFO operation of a stack.

20.2.3 Apply the terms "enqueue" and "dequeue" in the context of queues.

20.2.4 Label the elements of a queue.

20.2.5 State the efficiency of queuing operations, such as enqueue and dequeue.

20.2.6 Provide examples illustrating the use of queues in computer programs.

20.2.7 Describe the classes that are used when coding a queue based on a linked list.

20.2.8 Recall the algorithms for enqueuing and dequeuing elements from a linked list queue.

20.2.9 Create a __str__() method for a queue.

20.1 Stacks

Stack Basics (20.1.1, 20.1.2, 20.1.3, 20.1.4)

Cafeteria food. It's not always great, but after queuing up in a line, you can quickly grab a tray off the stack, slide it down the rails, and pile it up with food. See **Figure 20-1**. That experience provides a foundation for understanding two important data structures: stacks and queues. Let's start with stacks.

Claudio Divizia/Shutterstock.com

Figure 20-1   A cafeteria has stacks and queues

In programming, a **stack** is a limited-access, linear data structure in which the last data element added is the first element removed. As an analogy, visualize a busy cafeteria. The trays are stacked one on top of another. The top tray on the stack (the last one added) is the first one that can be removed. To reach the tray at the bottom of the stack, all the other trays must be removed first.

The data in a stack is controlled by a last-in, first-out algorithm referred to as **LIFO** (pronounced "LIE foh"). Adding a data element to the top of the stack is accomplished with a **push** operation. Deleting an element from the top of a stack is accomplished with a **pop** operation.

Stacks may also support a **peek** operation that retrieves the value of the top element without removing it from the stack. **Figure 20-2** shows a conceptual diagram of a stack, along with its push and pop operations.

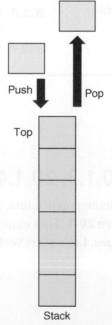

Push   Pop

Top

Stack

Figure 20-2   Stack data structure

The characteristics of a stack data structure include the following:

Linear. Elements in a stack are related linearly, not hierarchically. Each element is chained to one previous element and one next element.

Homogeneous. Typically, the elements in a stack are all the same data type. With Python, you can add elements of any type to a stack, but it is not recommended.

Efficient addition and removal. No matter how many elements a stack contains, adding or removing an element from the stack can be accomplished in a single operation. Push and pop can only be applied to the top element of the stack, so theoretically the number of additional elements in the stack has no effect on the efficiency of the push and pop operations.

Extensible. Stacks allocate memory dynamically as elements are added. Unlike arrays, the length of a stack does not need to be declared.

Limited access. Only the top element in a stack can be accessed. The elements further down the stack cannot be accessed directly. There is no easy way to iterate through all the elements in a stack. To search for an element in a stack, you have to remove elements one by one until the target element is found. If you want to keep the original stack, you have to store all of the elements that you pop off, then push them back to the stack when you are done.

Q Why would you want to make it harder to access data when a Python list is easy to use?

A Sometimes more rules ensure less error. As you will see later, certain use cases work great with stacks, and stacks prevent interaction except in a very specific way, thus eliminating errors. You could use a Python list to complete any of the examples in this chapter, but would have to work harder, mentally, to keep everything straight.

Stack Use Cases (20.1.5)

Stacks are a handy tool for your programming toolkit. Consider using a stack when you are working with data that requires operations such as the following:

Reversing order. Stacks work well for algorithms that reverse words or other objects. **Figure 20-3** can help you visualize how to use a stack to reverse the letters in a word. You push each letter onto the stack. The first letter ends up at the bottom. The last letter ends up at the top. As you pop off each letter, the word is spelled backward.

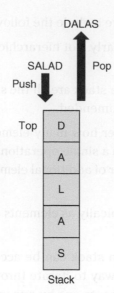

Figure 20-3   Reversing a word using a stack

Q If you push BURRITO onto a stack, in what sequence will the letters pop off?

A The letters will pop off in reverse order: OTIRRUB.

Undo and redo. Stacks are also useful for undo and redo operations. For example, a word processing program can use a stack to collect each keystroke and command the user makes. Suppose the user deletes a word. That operation is pushed to the top of the stack. The user decides that the word should not have been deleted and selects Undo. The word processing program pops the delete operation off the stack. Presto! The word is undeleted.

Retracing steps. A stack might also be used to keep a list of websites visited by a browser. Every new page pushes a link onto the stack. The Prev button pops a link off the stack and goes back to the previous page that the browser displayed. This aspect of stacks is also handy for solving maze problems in which choosing the wrong path requires you to reverse to an intersection to try a different path.

Testing symmetry. Stacks are useful for testing symmetry. For example, word processing programs use the " symbol for opening a quotation, but the " symbol for closing a quotation. How does the program know which to use? When the quotation symbols are stored on a stack, popping the top element indicates whether the last one was an opening or closing quotation mark.

Code a `Stack` Class (20.1.6, 20.1.7)

Python does not have built-in support for a stack class, so you program one yourself. You can implement a stack based on a linked list. As a quick review, recall that a linked list is a chain of nodes, each with a pointer to the next node. The diagram in **Figure 20-4** illustrates a linked list in a vertical orientation that resembles a stack.

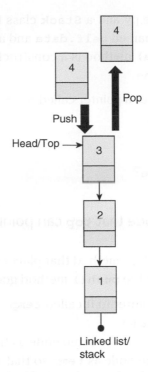

Figure 20-4   A linked list can be used to implement a stack

Q What part of a linked list is equivalent to the top of a stack?

A The head of a linked list is equivalent to the top of a stack. When you picture the head of a linked list as the top of a stack, then you can see how the two structures are related.

You can implement a stack as a linked list with methods to push and pop data elements. The code for a linked list stack begins by defining a **Node** class and a **Stack** class, as shown in **Figure 20-5**. The **Node** class defines a node as having data and a link to the next node, just like the **Node** class used for **LinkedList**. The **Stack** class creates a pointer called **top** that initially points to **None**.

```
node.py:
class Node():

    def __init__(self, data):

        self.data = data

        self.next = None
stack.py:
from node import Node

class Stack():

    def __init__(self):

        self.top = None
```

Figure 20-5   Code for the **Node** and **Stack** classes

The code declares a **Node** class in node.py and a **Stack** class in stack.py, which imports the **Node** class. The **Node** class has two attributes: a value named **self.data** and a pointer called **self.next** that references the next node. The **__init__(self, data)** method is a constructor for a **Node** object containing data set to **data** and the **self.next** pointer set to **None**.

In the **Stack** class, the constructor creates a pointer called **self.top**, and the **self.top = None** statement initially sets the **self.top** pointer to **None**.

Q Why does **top** initially point to **None**?

A The stack does not yet include a node that **top** can point to.

Push(). The **Stack** class includes a **push()** method that places an element at the top of the stack, which is the head of the linked list. The algorithm for the **push()** method goes like this:

Create a new node with an associated pointer to it called **temp**.
Load data into the node referenced by **temp**.
Change the **temp.next** pointer to reference the same node as the **top** pointer.
Set the **top** pointer to reference the same node as **temp** so that **top** points to the top node in the stack.

The diagram in **Figure 20-6** illustrates what happens when an element is pushed to the top of the linked list stack.

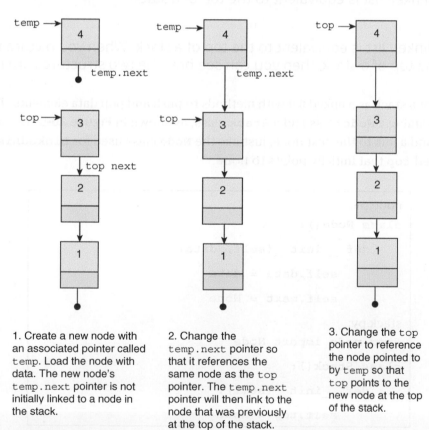

1. Create a new node with an associated pointer called temp. Load the node with data. The new node's temp.next pointer is not initially linked to a node in the stack.

2. Change the temp.next pointer so that it references the same node as the top pointer. The temp.next pointer will then link to the node that was previously at the top of the stack.

3. Change the top pointer to reference the node pointed to by temp so that top points to the new node at the top of the stack.

Figure 20-6   Conceptual diagram for pushing elements onto the linked list stack

Q To which node does `temp.next` link during the `push()` method?

A The `temp.next` pointer initially points to `None`, but then links to the `top` node.

The code for pushing an element to the top of the stack is detailed in **Figure 20-7**.

```
from node import Node
class Stack():
    def __init__(self):
        self.top = None
    def push(self, data):
        temp = Node(data)
        temp.next = self.top
        self.top = temp
```

Figure 20-7 Code for the `push()` method

The statement `temp = Node(data)` creates a new node referenced by a pointer called `temp` and populates the node with the value from `data`. Then `temp.next = self.top` links the new node's `next` pointer to the current `top` of the stack. The statement `self.top = temp` changes the `self.top` pointer so it references the new node that is now the `top` node of the stack.

Pop(). The `Stack` class should also include a method to pop an element off the top of the linked list stack. If the stack contains data, the code assigns the `top` node to a pointer called `temp`. It then makes the next node the `top` node of the list. Finally, it returns the value that was removed from the stack. Here is the algorithm:

If the stack is empty, then display "Empty stack."
Otherwise, do the following:

> Create a pointer called `temp` that references the same node as the pointer called `top`.
> Set the `top` pointer to reference the same node as the `top.next` pointer.
> Return the data stored in `temp`.

Figure 20-8 illustrates the algorithm visually.

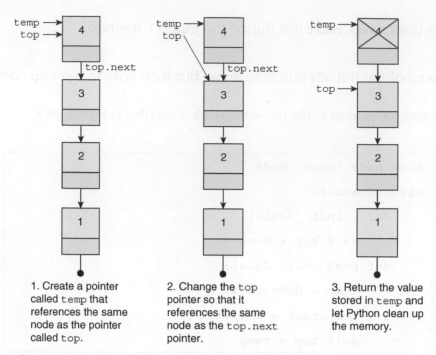

1. Create a pointer called `temp` that references the same node as the pointer called `top`.

2. Change the `top` pointer so that it references the same node as the `top.next` pointer.

3. Return the value stored in `temp` and let Python clean up the memory.

Figure 20-8   Conceptual diagram for popping elements off the linked list stack

Q Why do you have to create a `temp` pointer instead of just modifying the `self.top` pointer?

A If you do not create a `temp` pointer, the value at the top of the stack would be lost and could not be returned.

In the linked list implementation, you'll first check whether the stack is empty and display "Empty stack" If that is the case. If the stack contains elements, the `pop()` method proceeds according to the algorithm. The code for popping the `top` element from a stack is detailed in **Figure 20-9**.

```python
from node import Node

class Stack():
    def __init__(self):
        self.top = None
    def push(self, data):
        # Omitted
    def pop(self):
        if self.top == None:
            print("Empty stack.")
        else:
            temp = self.top
            self.top = self.top.next
            return temp.data
```

Figure 20-9   Code for the `pop()` method

The if-clause checks if the stack is empty. Otherwise, the stack contains nodes and the `temp = self.top` statement creates a pointer called `temp` that references the `top` node of the stack. The statement `self.top = self.top.next` points `top` to the second (next) node in the stack. Finally, `return temp.data` returns the value that was at the `top` node of the stack.

After you have defined the `push()` and `pop()` methods, you can use them in programs. Remember to create the `Stack` object in your driver code. In **Figure 20-10**, the driver code creates a `Stack` object called `my_stack`. It pushes first 1, then 2 onto the stack. After that, the code attempts to pop off three items. Because the stack contains only two items, the last `pop()` method produces the "Empty stack" message.

```
from stack import Stack

my_stack = Stack()

my_stack.push(1)

my_stack.push(2)

for i in range(3):

    print("Attempting to pop.")

    value = my_stack.pop()

    print("Value returned:", value)

OUTPUT:

Attempting to pop.

Value returned: 2

Attempting to pop.

Value returned: 1

Attempting to pop.

Empty stack.

Value returned: None
```

Figure 20-10   Driver code for the linked list stack

Stack Printing (20.1.8)

While there is limited access to a stack, it can be useful to print its contents when debugging. The way to move through the stack is the same as through a `LinkedList`. The following pseudocode is for the printing algorithm:

`Start a temporary traversing pointer at the top of the stack.`

`While the traverser is pointing to a node and hasn't fallen off the bottom of the stack:`

> `Add the data at the node to the string.`

> `Move the traverser to the next node.`

Figure 20-11 shows the code to override the dunder method used by `print()` for a `Stack` object, and **Figure 20-12** shows the use of `print()` with this new overridden method.

```
from node import Node
class Stack():
    def __init__(self):
        self.top = None
    def __str__(self):
        string = "Top of stack - "
        traverser = self.top
        while traverser != None:
            string += str(traverser.data) + " "
            traverser = traverser.next
        string += "- Bottom of stack"
        return string
    def push(self, data):
        # Omitted
    def pop(self):
        # Omitted
```

Figure 20-11   Implementing a __str__() method for the Stack class

```
from stack import Stack
my_stack = Stack()
my_stack.push("B")
my_stack.push("U")
my_stack.push("R")
my_stack.push("R")
my_stack.push("I")
my_stack.push("T")
my_stack.push("O")
print(my_stack)
OUTPUT:
Top of stack - O T I R R U B - Bottom of stack
```

Figure 20-12   Implicitly using the __str__() method with a Stack

20.2 Queues

Queue Basics (20.2.1, 20.2.2, 20.2.3, 20.2.4, 20.2.5)

A **queue** is a limited-access, linear data structure in which elements are removed from the front and added to the rear. The people in line at a cafeteria form a queue. The first person in line is the first person to be served and leave the line. New arrivals are added to the end of the line.

Like a line of people, the data in a queue is controlled by a first-in, first-out algorithm referred to as **FIFO** (pronounced "FI foh"). Adding a data element to the rear of a queue is accomplished with an **enqueue** operation. Deleting an element from the front of the queue is accomplished with a **dequeue** operation.

Queues may also support a peek operation that retrieves the value of the front element without removing it from the queue.

Figure 20-13 illustrates a conceptual diagram of a queue, along with its enqueue and dequeue operations.

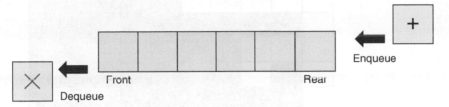

Figure 20-13   Queue data structure

Data in a queue can be efficiently enqueued and dequeued, but as with stacks, traversal is less efficient. Additional characteristics of queue data structures are similar to those of a stack.

- Homogeneous (typically)
- Linear
- Efficient addition and removal
- Extensible
- Limited access

Queue Use Cases (20.2.6)

The basic characteristic of a queue is that it can hold data and eventually release it in sequential order. Queues shine for algorithms that represent a sequence of tasks that must be processed in the order in which they occur. Here are some examples:

Scheduling. Operating systems track and schedule the processes from multiple programs that all require CPU processing time.

Asynchronous data transfer. Data that cannot always flow freely may be held in a buffer and then released. Keyboards include buffers that store keypresses until they can be handled by a software application. Print spoolers hold character data until a printer is ready to receive it.

Flood fill algorithms. Games such as Go and Minesweeper use queues to determine which squares are cleared. In paint software, a queue controls the bucket tool that fills connected, similarly colored areas with a specified new color. See **Figure 20-14**.

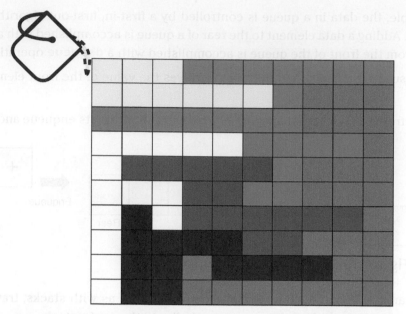

Figure 20-14 Flood fill algorithms are based on queues

First come, first served. Applications that control commercial phone systems place callers on hold and connect them to agents on a first-come, first-served basis. Print queues hold a series of documents and print them out in the order that they were received.

Traversal algorithms. Queues are used to follow a path through a hierarchical structure called a tree. A queue is a good way to keep track of the locations you've traversed and the order in which they are traversed.

Shortest path. A queue is a key part of the solution to mapping problems such as the classic Chess Knight Problem to find the minimum number of steps taken by the Knight to move from point A to point B on a chessboard. See **Figure 20-15**.

Figure 20-15 The algorithm for the Chess Knight Problem is based on a queue data structure

Code a Queue Class (20.2.7, 20.2.8)

Although most programming languages provide a variety of built-in functionality for queues, you have the most control if you create a linked list and provide it with methods for enqueueing and dequeuing.

Conceptually, a queue can be a linked list in which the head of the list is designated as the front of the queue where data elements are removed. The tail of the linked list becomes the rear of the queue where data elements are added, as shown in **Figure 20-16**.

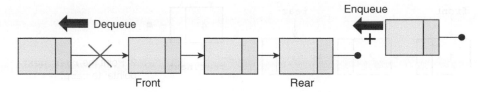

Figure 20-16   A linked list can be used to implement a queue

Q   Is the head of a linked list equivalent to the front or rear of a queue?

A   The head of a linked list is equivalent to the front of a queue.

The code for a linked list queue begins by creating a **Node** class and a **Queue** class, as shown in **Figure 20-17**.

```
from node import Node
class Queue():
    def __init__(self):
        self.front = None
        self.rear = None
```

Figure 20-17   Code for the **Queue** class

The **Queue** class uses the same **Node** class as the **Stack** class, stored in node.py. The **Queue** class tracks both the front and rear of the queue with those pointers initially set to **None** in the **Queue** constructor.

Q   In a queue, which pointers are initially set to **None**?

A   The front and rear nodes are initially empty, so the front and rear pointers are set to **None**.

Enqueue(). The **enqueue()** method is designed to add a data element to the rear of the linked list queue, as shown in **Figure 20-18**.

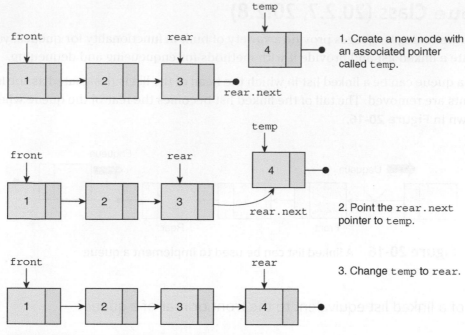

Figure 20-18   Enqueueing a node

Q Initially, what is the value of the **rear.next** pointer?

A The **rear.next** pointer is initially **None**.

The enqueue algorithm goes like this:

Create a new node with a pointer to it called **temp**.

Load data into the node referenced by **temp**.

If the queue is empty, the new node becomes the front and the rear of the queue.

Otherwise, point the **rear.next** pointer to the node referenced by **temp** and then change **temp** to **rear**.

The code for the **enqueue()** method is detailed in **Figure 20-19**.

```python
from node import Node
class Queue():
    def __init__(self):
        self.front = None
        self.rear = None
    def enqueue(self, data):
        temp = Node(data)
        if self.rear == None:
            self.front = self.rear = temp
        else:
            self.rear.next = temp
            self.rear = temp
```

Figure 20-19   Code for the **enqueue()** method

The statement `temp = Node(data)` creates a new node containing the value from `data` with an associated pointer called `temp`. The if-clause makes the new node the front and rear of the queue if the queue is empty. If the queue contains nodes, `self.rear.next = temp` points the last node in the queue to the new node. The statement `self.rear = temp` moves the `self.rear` pointer to the newly enqueued node.

Dequeue(). The `dequeue()` method removes a data element from the front of the linked list queue. This method is like the `pop()` method in a stack and uses a similar algorithm. Here's the algorithm:

If the queue is empty, then display "Empty queue."
Otherwise, do the following:

> Create a pointer called `temp` that references the same node as the pointer called `front`.
> Set the `front` pointer to reference the same node as the `temp.next` pointer.
> Return the data now stored in `temp`.

The code for the `dequeue()` method is in **Figure 20-20**.

```
from node import Node
class Queue():
    def __init__(self):
        self.front = None
        self.rear = None
    def dequeue(self):
        if self.front == None:
            print("Empty queue.")
        else:
            temp = self.front
            self.front = temp.next
            return temp.data
    def enqueue(self, data):
        # Omitted
```

Figure 20-20   Code for the `dequeue()` method

The if-clause checks if the queue is empty. If the queue is not empty, the `temp = self.front` statement creates a pointer called `temp` that refers to the same node as the `self.front` pointer. The statement `self.front = temp.next` points `self.front` to the second node in the queue, making that node the front of the queue. Then the code returns the value stored in `temp`, which was previously at the front of the queue.

Q Which pointers reference the same node when the dequeue operation begins?

A The `self.front` and `temp` pointers both reference the front node when the dequeue operation begins.

Queue Printing (20.2.9)

The printing algorithm for a `Queue` class is identical to that of a `Stack`. Start at the front of the pointer chain and add each node until none remain. The code for overriding the `__str__()` method for a `Queue` class is shown in **Figure 20-21**.

```python
from node import Node

class Queue():

    def __init__(self):

        self.front = None

        self.rear = None

    def __str__(self):

        string = "Front of queue - "

        traverser = self.front

        while traverser != None:

            string += str(traverser.data) + " "

            traverser = traverser.next

        string += "- Rear of queue"

        return string

    def dequeue(self):

        # omitted

    def enqueue(self, data):

        # omitted
```

Figure 20-21   Creating a `__str__()` for the `Queue` class

Your driver code can create an instance of the `Queue` class such as `my_queue` and use the `enqueue()` and `dequeue()` methods to add or remove elements from the queue. The driver code in **Figure 20-22** enqueues two elements, prints the queue, then dequeues both elements.

```
from queue import Queue

my_queue = Queue()

my_queue.enqueue(1)

my_queue.enqueue(2)

print(my_queue)

print("Removing from queue:", my_queue.dequeue())

print("Removing from queue:", my_queue.dequeue())

OUTPUT:

Front of queue - 1 2 - Rear of queue

Removing from queue: 1

Removing from queue: 2
```

Figure 20-22   Driver code for the linked list queue

Summary

- A stack is a limited-access, linear data structure in which the last data element added is the first element removed. The data in a stack is controlled by a last-in, first-out algorithm referred to as LIFO.
- Adding a data element to the top of the stack is accomplished with a push operation. Deleting an element from the end of a stack is accomplished with a pop operation. Stacks may also support a peek operation that retrieves the value of the top element without removing it from the stack.
- Stacks are linear, (typically) homogeneous, and extensible. Adding and removing elements from the top of a stack is very efficient. Stacks are limited access, however, so traversing the data is less efficient because it requires popping elements off the stack one by one.
- Stacks are a handy tool for algorithms that rely on reversing, retracing, undoing, or testing symmetry.
- Most programming languages have built-in stack support. An alternative is to implement a stack based on a linked list. The code for a linked list stack typically includes a **Node** class, a **Stack** class, a **push()** method, and a **pop()** method.
- A queue is a limited-access, linear data structure in which elements are removed from the front and added to the rear. The data in a queue is controlled by a first-in, first-out algorithm referred to as FIFO.
- Adding a data element to the rear of a queue is accomplished with an enqueue operation. Deleting an element from the front of the queue is accomplished with a dequeue operation. Queues may also support a peek operation that retrieves the value of the front element without removing it from the queue.
- Queues have characteristics similar to those of a stack. They are (typically) homogeneous, linear, and extensible. Enqueuing and dequeuing are efficient, but limited access makes traversal activities less efficient.
- Queues are useful tools for algorithms that represent a sequence of tasks that must be processed in the order in which they occur.
- As with stacks, queues can be implemented based on linked lists. A linked list queue includes a **Node** class, a **Queue** class, an **enqueue()** method, and a **dequeue()** method.

Key Terms

dequeue	LIFO	push
enqueue	peek	queue
FIFO	pop	stack

Module
21

Trees and Graphs

Learning Objectives:

21.1 Nonlinear Data Structures

21.1.1 Describe the difference between linear and nonlinear data structures.

21.1.2 Explain the design of nonlinear data structures.

21.1.3 Define "nodes" and "edges" in nonlinear data structures.

21.2 Tree Structures

21.2.1 Classify trees as nonlinear abstract data structures.

21.2.2 Identify the key elements of a tree data structure.

21.2.3 Associate the term "hierarchical" with tree data structures.

21.2.4 Identify the height and depth of a tree data structure.

21.2.5 Explain why a tree structure can be described as recursive.

21.3 Solving Problems Using Trees

21.3.1 Provide examples that use trees to represent hierarchical data.

21.3.2 State the key characteristic of a binary tree.

21.3.3 Differentiate between a binary tree and a binary search tree.

21.3.4 Define the term "traversal" as it relates to tree data structures.

21.3.5 Trace the path of a depth first traversal.

21.3.6 Trace the path of a breadth first traversal.

21.4 Graph Structures

21.4.1 Classify a graph as a nonlinear abstract data structure.

21.4.2 Compare diagrams of graphs to diagrams of trees.

21.4.3 State four characteristics that differentiate graphs from trees.

21.4.4 Explain the difference between directed and undirected graphs.

21.5 Solving Problems with Graphs

21.5.1 Provide examples of using graph data structures to represent data.

21.5.2 Associate the term "network model" with graph data structures.

21.5.3 Define the term "shortest path" as it relates to graphs.

21.5.4 Provide examples of using shortest paths in the real world.

21.5.5 Trace Floyd's Algorithm.

21.1 Nonlinear Data Structures

Linear versus Nonlinear Structures (21.1.1, 21.1.2)

The easiest information for a computer to manage is a linear data structure where data elements are arranged sequentially and each element is connected to the previous and next one, such as the guest list for a party or the high scores on a video game.

Not all data is linear, however, but is arranged as a hierarchy or a web with one or more links between data elements. Examples of nonlinear data include an organizational chart, a family tree, and a website map that shows how each webpage connects to the home page.

Imagine you are in a hedge maze, shown in **Figure 21-1**. Consider a path through the maze as a series of choices. At each intersection, you choose a direction to continue through the maze or exit.

Gordon J A Dixon/Shutterstock.com

Figure 21-1   Hedge maze

Figure 21-2 shows a simpler maze with each decision point labeled with a letter from A through G. The entrance is shown with a blue arrow pointing into the maze, and the exit is shown with a blue arrow pointing out of the maze.

Suppose you want to display all possible routes through the maze, including paths that result in a dead end. You could represent each route as a list of instructions, which is a linear data structure. For example, how would you describe traveling to the D intersection? Take the path south to intersection A, then west to intersection B, then west again to reach intersection D. How would you describe the path to intersection E? Go south, west, and south to reach E. The first two instructions to intersections D and E create overlapping paths (first go south, then go west) because the paths to D and E each pass through intersection B. Listing all possible routes creates many redundant instructions.

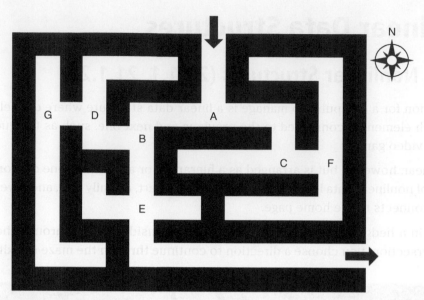

Figure 21-2   Computer-friendly maze

Mazes are weblike structures that are best represented nonlinearly. A linear description of the maze is possible but is tedious and repetitive.

Nonlinear Building Blocks (21.1.3)

Recall that in a linear data structure, a node stores a piece of information and a pointer to another node somewhere else in the computer's memory. Nonlinear structures use the same idea of nodes, except the number of connections is not limited to a single link. Instead, each node can have one or more connections. **Figure 21-3** compares a linear structure and a nonlinear structure.

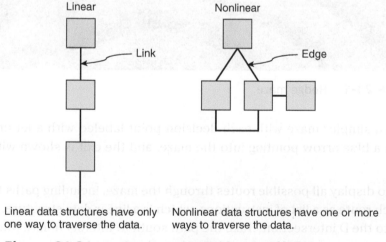

Figure 21-3   Linear versus nonlinear data structures

In a nonlinear data structure, the connections between nodes are called **edges**. An edge can be directed, which means it is like a one-way street. A directed edge can go from A to B, but not in reverse. An edge can also be undirected, which means it can be taken in either direction: A to B or B to A. How edges are restricted affects the design of each data structure.

21.2 Tree Structures

Tree Basics (21.2.1, 21.2.2, 21.2.3)

A **tree** is a hierarchical nonlinear data structure. As with a linked list, a tree has a starting point and a connection from one data element to the next. Unlike linked lists, each node in a tree can have more than one connection to other data elements.

Imagine a tree with branches that split into leaves. Now imagine a piece of information at each point where the tree splits. The splitting points are nodes. Although trees grow and branch out upward, traditionally coding trees are drawn upside down so the starting point appears at the top of the diagram. **Figure 21-4** shows the nodes in a tree data structure. The image on the right shows how trees are traditionally diagrammed in computer science.

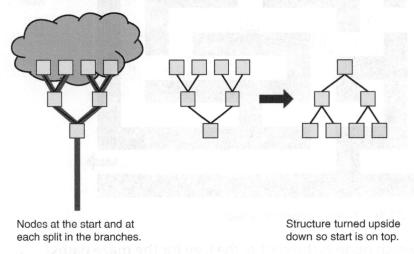

Nodes at the start and at each split in the branches.

Structure turned upside down so start is on top.

Figure 21-4 Nodes in a tree structure

The edges in a tree structure represent the branches and connect one node to other nodes. **Figure 21-5** shows nodes and edges in a tree diagram.

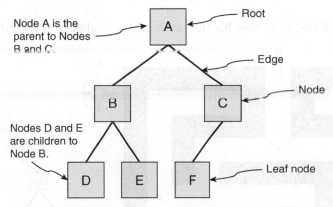

Node A is the parent to Nodes B and C.

Root

Edge

Node

Nodes D and E are children to Node B.

Leaf node

Figure 21-5 Nodes and edges in a basic tree

Two nodes are related if they are connected by an edge, such as Node A and Node C in Figure 21-5. Each node can have only one edge connecting it to another node. That means the number of edges in a tree equals the number of nodes minus one. The tree in Figure 21-5 has six nodes and five edges.

One node can be a **parent** or **child** of another node. In Figure 21-5, Node A is the parent of Node B and Node C. The children of Node B are Nodes D and E. A tree is hierarchical because of these parent–child relationships, with nodes above or below one another.

The nodes at the top and bottom of a tree have special names. The **root** node is at the top of the tree and has no parent node. The nodes at the bottom, which have no children, are called **leaf nodes**. In Figure 21-5, the root is Node A, and the leaf nodes are Nodes D, E, and F. A tree can have only one parent node. A node may have zero or more children, but only one parent. The only exception to this rule is the root node, which does not have a parent.

In the maze example, you could represent the choices at each intersection as a tree. Each intersection is a node, and the paths are edges. See **Figure 21-6**. From intersection A, you have two choices: West takes you to intersection B, and east takes you to intersection C.

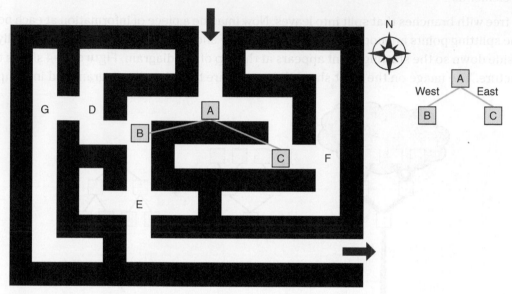

Figure 21-6   Tree structure in a maze

Q In Figure 21-6, which node is the root of the tree for the maze paths?

A The starting point of the maze, intersection A, is the root because it has no parent node. There is no decision to make before intersection A.

Figure 21-7 shows the full decision tree for the maze paths. Nodes with no letters represent dead ends.

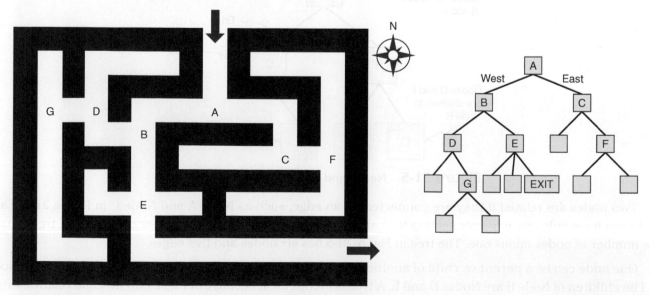

Figure 21-7   Full tree structure for the complete maze

Tree Properties (21.2.4)

A tree's shape can be described by its size, height, and width.

Size. The size refers to the number of nodes in the tree.

Height. The height is determined by the number of node rows in a tree, including the root node. A row in a tree contains all nodes that are an equal number of edges away from the root. A tree's height cannot be greater than its size.

Width. The width is determined by the number of children in the largest row of the tree. This row is not always the bottom of the tree.

Q What are the size, height, and width of each tree shown in **Figure 21-8**?

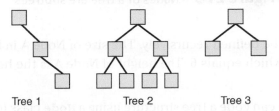

Tree 1   Tree 2   Tree 3

Figure 21-8   Several different trees

A Tree 1 has a size of 3, a height of 3, and a width of 1; tree 2 has a size of 7, a height of 3, and a width of 4; and tree 3 has a size of 3, a height of 2, and a width of 2.

You describe the location of a node by its depth into the tree. To calculate a node's depth, start at the root, which has a depth of 0. Add 1 to the depth each time you follow an edge to a child node. Note the difference between height and depth: a tree has a height, and a node has a depth. The smallest tree has a height of 1, which means it has only one row of nodes and a single node in that row. The shallowest node has a depth of 0, which means it is the root node.

Q What are the depths of Nodes A, C, and E in Figure 21-5?

A The depths of Nodes A, C, and E are 0, 1, and 2, respectively.

In a maze, the height of a tree represents the number of intersections you must pass through to find your way out or to reach a dead end. The taller the tree, the more directions you select along the path. The size of the tree represents how many paths the maze contains.

Trees as Recursive Structures (21.2.5)

Recall that recursion is the act of dividing a problem into smaller copies of the same problem to solve it. Trees are recursive structures in that every node in a tree is also arranged as a tree, creating a subtree. To solve the problem posed by a tree data structure, you solve each subtree.

Although each tree has only one root, any other node is a tree, disregarding the parent of that node. In **Figure 21-9**, Node B is a subtree attached to Node A. The other nodes are also tree structures.

Each node, even nodes without children, are subtrees. This means that a tree has a recursive definition. A tree or subtree is one of the following:

- A single node, or a tree of height 1
- A node with children subtrees of smaller heights

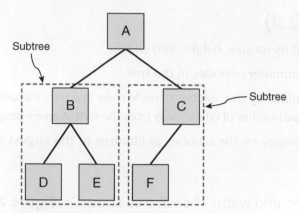

Figure 21-9 Nodes of a tree are subtrees

Properties of a tree can also be defined recursively. The size of Node A in Figure 21-9 is the size of subtrees B and C added together, plus 1, which equals 6. The height of Node A is the height of the tallest subtree plus 1, which is 3.

Figure 21-10 shows how you can code a tree structure using a `Node` class for a nonlinear data structure. The code is for a specific type of nonlinear `Node`, a tree with only two children, labeled `left` and `right`.

```
class Node():

    def __init__(self, data, left=None, right=None):

        self.data = data                  ⎫  left and right are the paths to
        self.left = left                  ⎬  take for a binary tree.
        self.right = right                ⎭

    def print_tree(self, level=0):

        # Recursive string creation for a tree node
        # Prints the tree rotated 90 degrees to the left

        s = ""

        # If there is a right subtree, print it first
        if self.right != None:
            s += self.right.print_tree(level + 1)

        # Add space to the left before printing the
        current node's data
        for i in range(level):
            s += "| "

        s += str(self.data) + "\n"
```

Figure 21-10 Modifying the `Node` class and adding a `__str__()` method for trees *(Continued)*

```
                    # If there is a left subtree, print it last
                    if self.left != None:
                        s += self.left.print_tree(level + 1)

                    return s

            def __str__(self):
                # Override the print() dunder method
                return self.print_tree(0)

    if __name__ == '__main__':
        tree = Node(5)

        # Depth 1
        tree.left = Node(2)
        tree.right = Node(8)

        # Depth 2
        tree.left.left = Node(1)
        tree.left.right = Node(3)
        tree.right.left = Node(7)
        tree.right.right = Node(10)

        print(tree)
    OUTPUT:
    |   |   10
    |   8
    |   |   7
    5
    |   |   3
    |   2
    |   |   1
```

Figure 21-10   Modifying the `Node` class and adding a `__str__()` method for trees

21.3 Solving Problems Using Trees

Tree Applications (21.3.1, 21.3.2)

You can use trees to solve many hierarchical problems beyond mazes. A video game often has moments in the story when the player can make choices. Each choice leads the story down one of many possible paths. A tree is a perfect way to organize these choices, as shown in **Figure 21-11**.

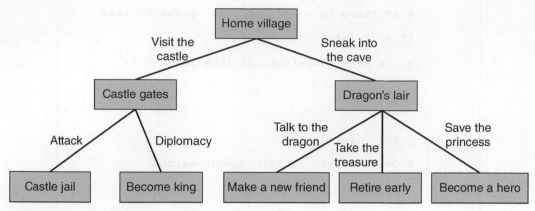

Figure 21-11 Tree for a story-driven game

Translating Morse code is also a good time to use a tree. Morse code is a communication method that uses short and long sounds to represent letters. For example, "dot dot dash dot" means the letter "F." The tree in **Figure 21-12** shows how to translate Morse code into letters. Each node has a left edge for dot (.) and a right edge for dash (-). You follow the left path for each dot in the code, and you follow the right path for each dash to arrive at the node containing the translated letter. To translate "dot dot dash dot," you go left, left, right, and left through the tree to end up at the leaf node containing "F."

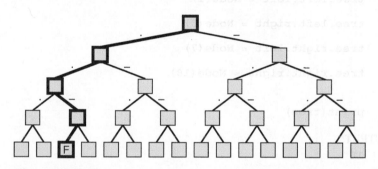

Figure 21-12 Morse code tree with "F" highlighted

Most often, trees are used in a binary format, where each node has up to two options, similar to the Morse code tree in Figure 21-12. **Binary trees** have no more than two children per node. In other words, a node in a binary tree can have zero, one, or two children, as shown in **Figure 21-13**.

Each new row in a binary tree has room for twice as many children as the previous row because each node can have two children. In a complete (or full) binary tree, each node except a leaf node has two children. In Figure 21-13, Tree A is a complete tree. Its size is 7 and its height is 3. In a complete binary tree, the height is $\log2(n)$ rounded up, or equal to how many times you can divide the size by 2 until the result is less than 1. You can calculate that a binary tree containing 7 items has a height of 3 as follows:

$$7 / 2 = 3.5$$
$$3.5 / 2 = 1.75$$
$$1.75 / 2 = 0.875$$

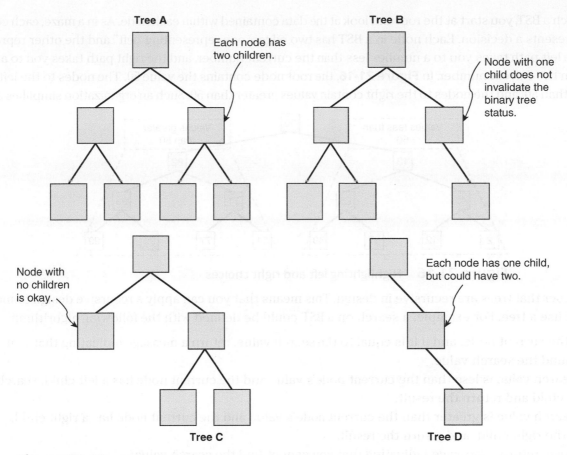

Figure 21-13   Binary trees

Data Storage in Trees (21.3.3, 21.3.4, 21.3.5, 21.3.6)

Each node in a tree can contain data or information. In Morse code, the letter "U" translates to "dot dot dash." This translation follows the same path as "F" in a Morse code tree, but stops one node above "F," where the letter "U" is stored. See **Figure 21-14**.

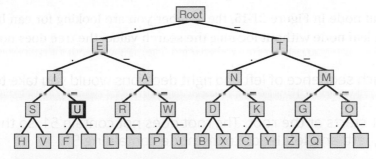

Figure 21-14   Morse code tree with "U" highlighted

A commonly used tree is a **binary search tree (BST)**, a binary tree used to search for a specific value. Each node in a BST contains one piece of searchable information. **Figure 21-15** shows a possible BST with a number in each node.

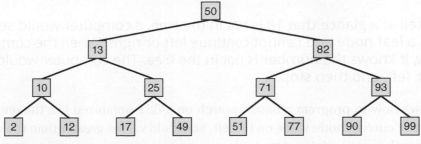

Figure 21-15   Binary search tree

To search a BST, you start at the root and look at the data contained within each node. As in a maze, each edge from a node represents a decision. Each node in a BST has two edges, one representing "left" and the other representing "right." The left path takes you to a number less than the current number, and the right path takes you to a number greater than the current number. In **Figure 21-16**, the root node contains the value 50. The nodes to the left contain values less than 50, and the nodes to the right contain values greater than 50. Such an organization simplifies a search.

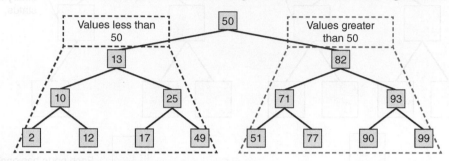

Figure 21-16   Highlighting left and right choices

Remember that trees are recursive in design. This means that you can apply a recursive design to most algorithms that use a tree. For example, a search on a BST could be defined with the following algorithm:

Check the current node, and if it is equal to the search value, return a message indicating that you have found the search value.

If the search value is less than the current node's value and the current node has a left child, search the left child and return the result.

If the search value is greater than the current node's value and the current node has a right child, search the right child, and return the result.

Otherwise, return a message indicating that you cannot find the search value.

You can use this algorithm to find a number in a tree. Suppose you want to find the number 17 in the BST shown in Figure 21-15. First look at the data stored in the root node, which contains 50. That number is not 17, so you need to keep looking. Because 17 is less than 50, follow the edge on the left to the node containing 13. Because 17 is greater than 13, follow the edge on the right to the node containing 25. Because 17 is less than 25, follow the node on the left to the node containing 17, the number you want to find.

Although 17 is in a leaf node in Figure 21-15, the number you are looking for can be in any node, including a leaf node. If you reach a leaf node without locating the search value, the tree does not include that number.

Q In Figure 21-15, which sequence of left and right decisions would you take to find the number 51?

A The path to find 51 starts at the root. The root does not contain 51, so the search continues. Taking paths right, left, and left leads to the node containing 51.

Q In Figure 21-15, which sequence of left and right decisions would you take to find the number 18?

A While you can tell at a glance that 18 is not in the tree, a computer would search for the value until it reaches a leaf node and cannot continue left or right. When the computer runs out of edges to follow, it knows the number is not in the tree. The computer would search the BST by going left, right, left, and then stop.

Figure 21-17 shows how to program a binary search on a BST organized like the one in Figure 21-15, with child values less than the current node value on the left, and child values greater than the current node value on the right. The code uses the earlier defined **Node** class.

```
from node import Node          ◄————————————  The Node class is from Figure 21-10.

def binary_search(tree, data):
                                              If the current node to search doesn't
    if tree == None:  ◄—————————————————      exist, then the value is not in the tree.

        print("The item", data, "is NOT in the tree!")

    else:                                        If the current node has
                                                 data equal to the search
        if tree.data == data:  ◄—————————        value, then it is in the tree.

            print("The item", data, "IS in the tree!")

        elif tree.data > data:

            binary_search(tree.left, data)◄
                                              Otherwise, go left or right depending
        else:                                 on if the search value is less than
                                              or greater than the current data,
            binary_search(tree.right, data)   respectively.


if __name__ == '__main__':

    tree = Node(5)

    # Depth 1

    tree.left = Node(2)

    tree.right = Node(8)


    # Depth 2

    tree.left.left = Node(1)

    tree.left.right = Node(3)

    tree.right.left = Node(7)

    tree.right.right = Node(10)


    print(tree)

    binary_search(tree, 7)

    binary_search(tree, 3)

    binary_search(tree, 12)

OUTPUT:
|  |  10
|  8
|  |  7
5
|  |  3
|  2
|  |  1

The item 7 IS in the tree!
The item 3 IS in the tree!
The item 12 is NOT in the tree!
```

Figure 21-17   Programming a binary search on a BST

The path to find the number 17 in the BST shown in Figure 21-15 and the path from the start to the exit in the maze are both instances of a single path in a tree. In contrast, a **traversal** must visit every node, not take a single path through the branches. A traversal requires some backtracking as each node includes multiple choices that need to be explored to make a complete traversal. All traversals start at the root node.

There are two common ways to traverse a tree. The first traversal is called a **depth first (DF) traversal**, which begins at the root and charges ahead with its decisions along a branch, backtracking only if it has nowhere else to go.

Figure 21-18 shows a simple binary tree where each node has a color and two edges, left and right.

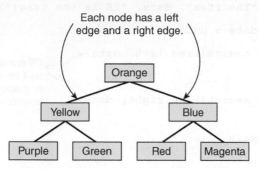

Figure 21-18 Binary tree with color values

A DF traversal explores the binary tree as follows:

1. The first node is the orange node. At this point you select a preference for decisions, such as continuing left before right.
2. The next node on the left contains yellow.
3. The next node on the left contains purple.
4. The traversal has nowhere to go, so it backs up to the previous node, which contains yellow.
5. One decision at the yellow node has not been traversed yet, so the traversal continues to the right node, which contains green.
6. The traversal has nowhere to go, so it backs up to yellow.
7. The yellow node offers no more choices, so the traversal backs up to orange.
8. The remaining decision is to continue to the right, so the traversal follows the path to blue.
9. The pattern continues to visit the red node, and then the magenta node. The final DF traversal order of colors is orange, yellow, purple, green, blue, red, and magenta.

In contrast to a DF traversal is a **breadth first (BF) traversal**. Instead of committing to a decision path and backtracking when all options are exhausted, a BF traversal visits each node at a level within the tree before moving on.

To use a BF traversal with the color tree in Figure 21-18, you again start at orange, and then visit yellow. Although a DF traversal visits the purple node next, a BF traversal visits the blue node next because the blue node is on the same level (or row) as the yellow node. The current level does not contain other nodes, so the BF traversal continues to the next row and visits purple, green, red, and then magenta. The final BF traversal is orange, yellow, blue, purple, green, red, and magenta.

To program these two traversals, you need to use two linear data structures: a queue and a stack. **Figure 21-19** shows a simplistic (but not efficient) implementation of each using a Python list. As a brief review: a stack can only add and remove at one end, like a stack of pancakes, while a queue adds to one end and removes from the opposite, like a checkout lane.

```
class Stack():
    def __init__(self):
        self.contents = []
    def push(self, data):
        self.contents.append(data)
    def pop(self):
        if len(self.contents) == 0:
            print("Empty stack")
        else:
            return self.contents.pop(-1)
    def __len__(self):
        return len(self.contents)
class Queue():
    def __init__(self):
        self.contents = []

    def enqueue(self, data):
        self.contents.append(data)
    def dequeue(self):
        if len(self.contents) == 0:
            print("Empty queue.")
        else:
            return self.contents.pop(0)
    def __len__(self):
        return len(self.contents)
```

Figure 21-19 Simple `Stack` and `Queue` classes using a Python list implementation

Figure 21-20 uses the earlier defined **Node** class to demonstrate both depth first and breadth first traversals. Note how similar the code is for the two traversals. The logic for the traversals is mostly handled by the queue and stack data structures. The only difference between the two traversals is the node to visit next, which the queue and stack keep track of for you.

```
from node import Node
from linearStructures import Stack, Queue
def depth_first_traversal(tree):
    node_stack = Stack()
    node_stack.push(tree)
```

Figure 21-20 Programming depth and breadth first traversals (*Continued*)

```
        while len(node_stack) > 0:

            visiting_node = node_stack.pop()

            print(visiting_node.data, end=" ")

            if visiting_node.right != None:

                node_stack.push(visiting_node.right)

            if visiting_node.left != None:

                node_stack.push(visiting_node.left)

        print()

def breadth_first_traversal(tree):

    node_queue = Queue()

    node_queue.enqueue(tree)

    while len(node_queue) > 0:

        visiting_node = node_queue.dequeue()

        print(visiting_node.data, end=" ")

        if visiting_node.right != None:

            node_queue.enqueue(visiting_node.right)

        if visiting_node.left != None:

            node_queue.enqueue(visiting_node.left)

    print()

if __name__ == '__main__':

    tree = Node(5)

    # Depth 1

    tree.left = Node(2)

    tree.right = Node(8)

    # Depth 2

    tree.left.left = Node(1)

    tree.left.right = Node(3)

    tree.right.left = Node(7)

    tree.right.right = Node(10)

    print(tree)

    depth_first_traversal(tree)

    breadth_first_traversal(tree)
```

Figure 21-20 Programming depth and breadth first traversals (*Continued*)

```
OUTPUT:
| | 10
| 8
| | 7
5
| | 3
| 2
| | 1
5 2 1 3 8 7 10
5 8 2 10 7 3 1
```

Figure 21-20   Programming depth and breadth first traversals

21.4 Graph Structures

Graph Basics (21.4.1, 21.4.2, 21.4.3)

Graphs are another variant of nonlinear abstract data structure. The difference between graphs and trees is that graphs have no enforced hierarchy. The nodes in a graph are connected to other nodes, but no one node is the start of the structure. Think of a map of your town, with blocks of buildings and the streets connecting them. When trying to figure out directions from one place to another, the starting and ending points are relative to your current location.

Figure 21-21 shows three graphs. Note that trees and graphs can look quite similar. Unlike trees, however, graphs have no root nodes, no limit on edges between nodes, no parent–child relationships, and possibly more than one path between nodes.

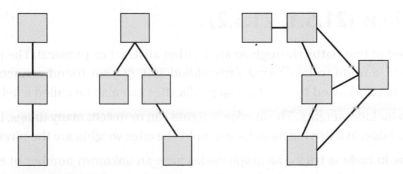

Figure 21-21   Basic graphs

Types of graphs include the following:

Sparse graph. A **sparse graph** does not contain many edges between the nodes.
Complete graph. In a **complete graph**, every node has an edge to every other node.
Connected graph. In a **connected graph**, all nodes are connected by at least one edge to a group of nodes.
Unconnected graph. An **unconnected graph** has islands of nodes not connected to the main group.

Figure 21-22 shows examples of each type of graph.

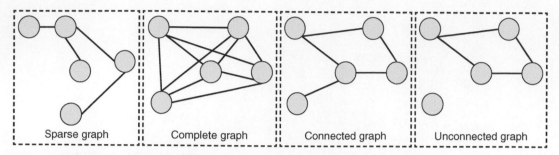

Figure 21-22 Types of graphs

Directed and Undirected Graphs (21.4.4)

Sometimes roads are one-way only, so that they must be traveled in only one direction. A **directed graph** has edges like one-way roads. A directed edge can link from Node A to Node B, but not from Node B to Node A. An **undirected graph** does not restrict the direction of any edge. **Figure 21-23** shows directed and undirected graphs, with arrows indicating a directed edge.

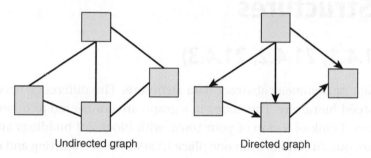

Figure 21-23 Directed versus undirected graphs

21.5 Solving Problems with Graphs

Graph Applications (21.5.1, 21.5.2)

Graphs are typically used to find paths through an area, either abstract or physical. The paths could be the way to find the exit to a maze, a route to take using a navigation app, or your friend connective network on social media. This connective network used by most social media sites can also be called a network model.

In graphs, edges can include weights. These **edge weights** can represent many things, but typically are related to the "cost" to take that edge. In a driving map, for example, the edge weights are the physical distances in miles.

Representing graphs in code is tricky, as graph nodes have an unknown number of edges. Instead of representing the graph as a series of edges attached to nodes, you can use an **adjacency matrix**. This matrix is a two-dimensional grid, with a row and column for each node. The value at the intersection of two nodes represents the edge weight.

Figure 21-24 shows an adjacency matrix. If a node has no edge, then it has an edge weight of 0. Otherwise, the matrix contains a positive number. The labels in the left column are the starting nodes, and the labels in the top row are the destination nodes. In Figure 21-24, you read the cell containing "5" as "the edge from A to B has a weight of 5."

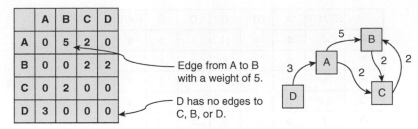

	A	B	C	D
A	0	5	2	0
B	0	0	2	2
C	0	2	0	0
D	3	0	0	0

Edge from A to B with a weight of 5.

D has no edges to C, B, or D.

Figure 21-24 Adjacency matrix and graph it represents

Q Does the adjacency matrix in Figure 21-24 describe a directed graph or an undirected graph? How can you tell?

A The matrix includes an edge from A to B, but not from B to A, creating a one-way path. Therefore, the matrix describes a directed graph. An undirected graph would not have any one-way paths.

Computing Paths (21.5.3, 21.5.4, 21.5.5)

When driving somewhere or exploring a maze, you typically want the **shortest path** to the destination. In a graph, you find the shortest path by adding the edge weights of the nodes. The minimum sum of edges is the shortest path.

Figure 21-25 shows a maze and its graph. You can find the exit easily by looking at the graph, but a computer can't. A computer has to compare nodes and paths one by one.

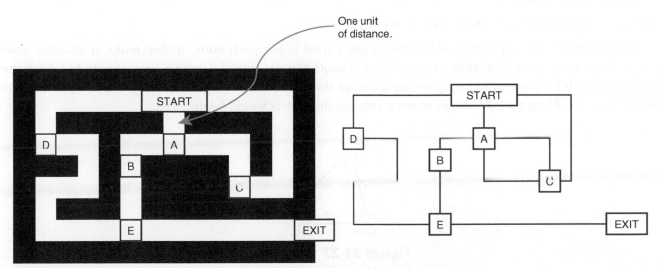

One unit of distance.

Figure 21-25 Maze and its graph

To have a computer solve the maze and find the exit, you need to convert the maze into an adjacency matrix. The size of the square containing a letter represents 1 unit of distance. For example, the distance between START and A is 2, as it takes two squares to arrive at A. **Figure 21-26** shows the adjacency matrix for the maze in Figure 21-25.

	START	A	B	C	D	E	EXIT
START	0	2	0	11	7	0	0
A	2	0	3	5	0	0	0
B	0	3	0	0	0	3	0
C	11	5	0	0	0	0	0
D	7	0	0	0	0	12	0
E	0	0	3	0	12	0	8
EXIT	0	0	0	0	0	8	0

Figure 21-26   Adjacency matrix for the maze

Q Does the adjacency matrix in Figure 21-26 describe a directed graph or an undirected graph?

A The matrix does not indicate any one-way paths, so it describes an undirected graph.

To calculate the shortest path from a starting point to a destination, you can use an algorithm called **Floyd's Algorithm**. It calculates the shortest distance between two nodes and the shortest distance between all nodes in the graph. Given an adjacency matrix like the one in Figure 21-26, Floyd's Algorithm creates a new matrix where the values are the shortest distance between two nodes, not just edges. The pseudocode outline for Floyd's Algorithm is as follows:

```
for each node index i
for each node index r
for each node index c
A[r][c] = min(A[r][c], A[r][i] + A[i][c])
```

The algorithm looks at each node in the graph, called **i**. For each node, it then looks at all other nodes, called **r**. For each node **r**, it checks to see if there is another node, called **c**, with a shorter path to take. If there is a shorter path between **r** and **c** by taking a detour through node **i**, then the path matrix is updated to this shorter distance. **Figure 21-27** shows when a value in the matrix would be updated.

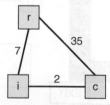

Figure 21-27   The path from r to c is longer than from r to i to c

Figure 21-28 shows a program for applying Floyd's Algorithm. To interpret the results, consider that each entry in the matrix now has the shortest possible path between the two nodes. For example, the output in Figure 21-28 shows first the adjacency matrix and then Floyd's results. If you look at the row labeled START and read across to the column labeled EXIT, the shortest path out of the maze takes 16 steps.

```python
def print_matrix(matrix, node_names):

    print("{:>10s}".format(" |"), end="")

    for column in range(len(matrix[0])):

        print("{:>8s}".format(node_names[column] + " |"), end="")

    print()

    print("-" * (len(matrix) * 10))

    for row in range(len(matrix)):

        print("{:>10s}".format(node_names[row] + " |"), end="")

        for column in range(len(matrix[row])):

            print("{:>8s}".format(str(matrix[row][column]) + " |"), end="")

        print()

    print()

def floyds(matrix):

    for i in range(len(matrix)):

        for r in range(len(matrix)):

            for c in range(len(matrix)):

                if r != c and matrix[r][i] != 0 and matrix[i][c] != 0:

                    if matrix[r][c] == 0:

                        matrix[r][c] = matrix[r][i] + matrix[i][c]

                    else:

                        matrix[r][c] = min(matrix[r][c], matrix[r][i] +
matrix[i][c])

if __name__ == '__main__':

    node_names = ["START", "A", "B", "C", "D", "E", "EXIT"]

    matrix = [[0, 2,0,11,7, 0, 0],

              [2, 0,3,5, 0, 0, 0],

              [0, 3,0,0, 0, 3, 0],

              [11,5,0,0, 0, 0, 0],

              [7, 0,0,0, 0, 12,0],

              [0, 0,3,0, 12,0, 8],

              [0, 0,0,0, 0, 8, 0]]

    print_matrix(matrix, node_names)

    floyds(matrix)

    print("\nFloyd's:")

    print_matrix(matrix, node_names)
```

Figure 21-28   Program to apply Floyd's Algorithm (*Continued*)

OUTPUT:

	START	A	B	C	D	E	EXIT
START	0	2	0	11	7	0	0
A	2	0	3	5	0	0	0
B	0	3	0	0	0	3	0
C	11	5	0	0	0	0	0
D	7	0	0	0	0	12	0
E	0	0	3	0	12	0	8
EXIT	0	0	0	0	0	8	0

Floyd's:

	START	A	B	C	D	E	EXIT
START	0	2	5	7	7	8	16
A	2	0	3	5	9	6	14
B	5	3	0	8	12	3	11
C	7	5	8	0	14	11	19
D	7	9	12	14	0	12	20
E	8	6	3	11	12	0	8
EXIT	16	14	11	19	20	8	0

Figure 21-28   Program to apply Floyd's Algorithm

Summary

- Use a nonlinear data structure for data arranged as a hierarchy or web with one or more connections between data elements.
- In a nonlinear data structure, each node can have one or more connections, called edges.
- A tree is a hierarchical nonlinear data structure with a starting point and nodes where each node is connected by an edge to another node. A tree is hierarchical because it establishes parent–child relationships between nodes. The root node at the top of the tree has no parent node, and the leaf nodes at the bottom of the tree have no children.
- A tree's shape is described by the size, height, and width of the tree. You describe the location of a node by its depth in the tree.
- Trees are recursive structures because every node in a tree is also arranged as a tree, creating a subtree.
- A binary tree has no more than two children per node. A tree that translates Morse code is a binary tree. You use a binary search tree (BST) to search for a specific value. Each node in a BST contains one piece of searchable information.
- The route from the start to the exit in a maze is a single path in a tree. A traversal, on the other hand, visits every node in the tree, starting from the root node. A depth first (DF) traversal begins searching

at the root and continues along a branch, backtracking after it reaches a leaf node. A breadth first (BF) traversal visits each node at a level (or row) within the tree before continuing to the next level.

- Graphs are nonlinear data structures similar to trees, but do not arrange nodes in a hierarchy. In addition, graphs have no root nodes and allow more than one path between nodes.
- Graphs can be directed or undirected. A directed graph has edges like one-way roads, where an edge links Node A to Node B, but does not link Node B to Node A. An undirected graph does not restrict the direction of its edges.
- Graphs are typically used to find paths through an abstract or physical area, such as a city or maze. Edges in a graph can include weights that might indicate the cost to take that edge. In a driving map, for example, the edge weights are the distances between locations.
- An adjacency matrix represents a graph as a grid instead of a series of edges attached to nodes. The matrix includes a row and column for each node, and the value at the intersection of two nodes indicates the edge weight.
- To calculate the shortest path from a starting point to a destination, you can use Floyd's Algorithm.

Key Terms

adjacency matrix	directed graph	shortest path
binary search tree (BST)	edge weights	sparse graph
binary trees	edges	traversal
breadth first (BF) traversal	Floyd's Algorithm	tree
child	graphs	unconnected graph
complete graph	leaf nodes	undirected graph
connected graph	parent	
depth first (DF) traversal	root	

Module
22

Algorithm Complexity and Big-O Notation

Learning Objectives:

22.1 Big-O Notation

22.1.1 Explain why programmers are interested in algorithm performance.

22.1.2 Name two factors that affect algorithm efficiency.

22.1.3 Differentiate runtime from time complexity.

22.1.4 Identify asymptotic analysis as a way to evaluate the performance of an algorithm as the size of its input grows.

22.1.5 Identify the three asymptotic notations that apply to algorithm performance.

22.2 Time Complexity

22.2.1 State the purpose of Big-O notation.

22.2.2 State that Big-O is expressed based on the size of the input n.

22.2.3 Identify the general format for Big-O notation.

22.2.4 Identify the Big-O notation and graph for constant time and provide an example of an algorithm that has linear time complexity.

22.2.5 Identify the Big-O notation and graph for linear time and provide an example of an algorithm that runs in quadratic time.

22.2.6 Identify the Big-O notation and graph for quadratic time and provide an example of an algorithm that runs in logarithmic time.

22.2.7 Identify the Big-O notation and graph for logarithmic time.

22.2.8 Correctly identify that the order of efficiency is O(C), O(log n), O(n), O(n^2).

22.3 Space Complexity

22.3.1 State that space complexity is the amount of memory space required by an algorithm to execute an algorithm.

22.3.2 Differentiate instruction space, data space, and auxiliary space.

22.3.3 State that the calculation for space complexity can be based on data space, auxiliary space, or both.

22.3.4 Identify algorithms that have constant space complexity.

22.3.5 Identify algorithms that have O(n) space complexity.

22.3.6 Associate appending elements to an array as an algorithm that requires linear space complexity.

22.3.7 Identify an example of a loop that does not have O(n) space complexity, but has O(n) time complexity.

22.4 Complexity Calculations

22.4.1 Determine the Big-O time complexity for each line of a program.

22.4.2 Determine the time complexity of loops.

22.4.3 Combine Big-O terms.

22.4.4 Simplify Big-O terms.

22.4.5 Determine the overall Big-O for the code representing an algorithm.

22.1 Big-O Notation

Algorithm Complexity (22.1.1, 22.1.2, 22.1.3)

A Big Mac (**Figure 22-1**) is a double-decker hamburger, the flagship product of a popular fast-food restaurant chain. But what's a Big-O? It is not something to eat, but it does relate to computer programming.

Figure 22-1   Big Mac or Big-O?

Many programming problems can be solved with more than one algorithm. How do you know which algorithm is best?

For many programming problems, the best solution is the most efficient one. Programmers and computer scientists are interested in ways to make programs most efficient so that applications run quickly and use a minimal amount of system resources. But exactly what makes one algorithm more efficient than another? Let's find out.

Algorithm efficiency can be measured by time and by space.

- **Time complexity** refers to the amount of time required to run an algorithm as its data set grows. In general, algorithms that execute most quickly are most time efficient. Algorithms that require more time as the data set grows have more time complexity.
- **Space complexity** refers to the amount of memory required by an algorithm as its data set grows. Algorithms that require the least memory space are likely to be the most space efficient. Algorithms that require more space as the data set grows have more space complexity.

In computing, the concept of time is slippery. Time could refer to runtime—the number of microseconds required for an algorithm to complete execution. But runtime on what hardware platform and with what data set? Exactly what is included in runtime? File access time? Transmission time? Build time?

Q Why might runtime not be a good metric of program efficiency?

A Runtime is hardware dependent. It is not a good metric for efficiency because an algorithm might require more time to run on a cloud-based hardware platform than on a local hardware platform.

Asymptotic Analysis (22.1.4)

A set of metrics can be used as objective measures of an algorithm's time efficiency or space efficiency. **Asymptotic analysis** provides programmers with a way to evaluate the performance of an algorithm as the size of its dataset grows.

Q Suppose you have two different algorithms for sorting data. One algorithm sorts 10 items in 10 ms, but takes 100 ms to sort 100 items. The other algorithm sorts the 10 items in 20 ms, but takes 40 ms to sort 100 items. Which algorithm is more efficient for large data sets?

A You can hypothesize that the second algorithm is much more efficient for large data sets. Although the first algorithm sorts a small amount of data quickly, processing time increases linearly as the data set grows. The second algorithm takes longer to sort 10 items, but less time to sort a larger data set.

Figure 22-2 shows graphs of these two algorithms. You can see that the time complexity of the first algorithm continues to increase as the data set grows. In contrast, the time complexity of the second algorithm levels off for larger data sets.

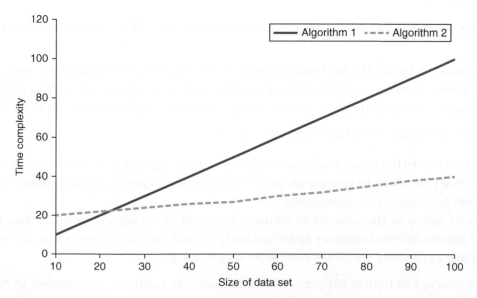

Figure 22-2   Time complexity varies for different algorithms and data set size

Asymptotic analysis reveals the efficiency of algorithms. You can use it to compare various algorithms before selecting the one to use.

Asymptotic Notation (22.1.5)

The performance of an algorithm can be expressed in **asymptotic notation**. Three of these notations are commonly applied to programming.

Big-O notation is used to express the worst-case time complexity or space complexity of an algorithm. Worst-case is sometimes referred to as upper bounds because it measures the maximum complexity of an algorithm.

Big-Omega notation (Big-Ω) is used to express the best-case time complexity or space complexity. Because an algorithm will never perform faster or take less space than its Big Omega, this metric delineates the lower bound.

Big-Theta notation (Big-θ) encompasses both the upper and lower bounds of an algorithm, a situation sometimes referred to as a tight bound.

Of these three notations, Big-O is most frequently used to measure the efficiency of algorithms. Familiarity with Big-O notation is not only useful for evaluating algorithms for your programs, but also an important concept to have in hand for job interviews. Note that Big-Ω <= Big-θ, and Big-θ <= Big-O.

22.2 Time Complexity

Big-O Metrics (22.2.1, 22.2.2, 22.2.3)

Programmers are primarily concerned with the worst-case scenarios for time and space complexity because it is important to know the maximum amount of time or space an algorithm might require when it is executed. Big-O notation allows programmers to quantify and express that maximum.

Big-O notation takes into consideration the time complexity as a data set increases in size. That data might be accessed from a file, dimensioned as an array, stored as a list, or input during runtime.

The letter O is used for Big-O notation because the rate of growth of a function is also called its *order*. The general format for Big-O notation is O(*complexity*), where *complexity* indicates the time or space requirements of an algorithm relative to the growth of the data set *n*.

Q What do you think *n* stands for in Big-O notation?

A In Big-O notation, *n* indicates the number of elements in a data set.

The following Big-O metrics are most commonly used to measure the time complexity of algorithms.

O(C) Constant time
O(*n*) Linear time
O(n^2) Quadratic time
O(log *n*) Logarithmic time

Let's take a quick look at each of these metrics and the kinds of algorithms to which they apply.

Constant Time (22.2.4)

Suppose you have a list of fast-food restaurants sorted in order by the date they were first established. The first element in the list is White Castle because it was established in 1921. You write a program to find the first element in this list.

Finding the first element in a list requires one line of code that specifies one operation: get the item at index [0].

```
first_item = fast_food_list[0]
```

It does not matter how many fast-food restaurants are in the data set. It could contain five or five million. The algorithm to find the first one will operate in the same amount of time. In Big-O notation, this type of algorithm executes in **constant time** because it does not change as the data set becomes larger.

A line plot with the number of data elements on the x-axis and the number of operations on the y-axis is a flat line for constant time, as shown in **Figure 22-3**.

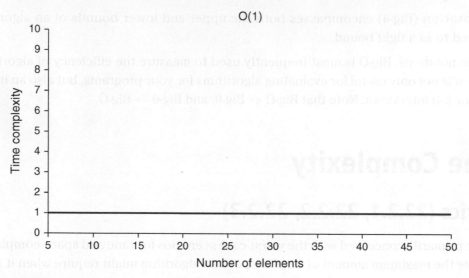

Figure 22-3 The graph of constant time is a flat line

The Big-O notation for constant time is **O(C)**, where C is the number of operations required to complete the algorithm.

Q Finding the first element in a list requires only one operation in constant time. What is the Big-O notation for this operation?

A For finding the first element in a list, the time complexity is a single operation, so the Big-O notation would be O(1).

Linear Time (22.2.5)

What about an algorithm to find any specific fast-food restaurant in the list? Is Jollibee in the list of fast-food restaurants? To search the list, you need to loop through the list to examine each item, as in the following Python code.

```
i = 0

while i < len(fast_food_list):

    if fast_food_list[i] == "Jollibee":

        print("Found it!")

        break

    else:

        i += 1
```

The worst case for this search would be when Jollibee is the last item in the list. If it is the last item in a list of 10 fast-food restaurants, the algorithm requires 10 loops. If the list contains 50 fast-food restaurants, the algorithm requires 50 loops. As the data set of items in the list grows, the time complexity increases at a linear rate shown in **Figure 22-4**.

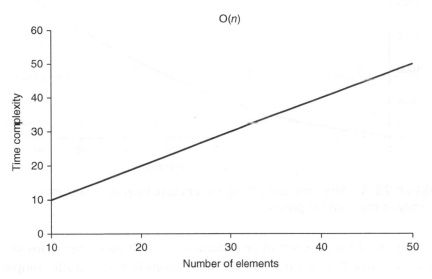

Figure 22-4   The time complexity for a loop is a linear slope

This type of time complexity is referred to as **linear time**. It relates directly to the number of items in a data set. If the number of items is n, then the time complexity is expressed in Big-O notation as **O(n)**.

Q Which is more efficient, constant time or linear time?

A Algorithms of linear complexity are less efficient than algorithms that run in constant time. O(n) algorithms require more and more processing time as the size of the data set increases.

Algorithms based on iterative structures, such as finding an item in an unsorted list, typically have linear time complexity. Inserting, deleting, and searching array elements, searching a stack or linked list, and hash table operations are also typical examples of algorithms with linear complexity.

Quadratic Time (22.2.6)

White Castle is the first item in the list of fast-food restaurants because it was the first one established. To sort the list in alphabetical order, you can use an insertion sort based on nested loops.

In the worst-case scenario, both loops execute for all of the items in the list. If the list contains five items, the outer loop executes five times and each of those iterations executes five times. That's 5^2, or 25, iterations. If the list contains 50 fast food restaurants, the time complexity is 50^2, or 2500 iterations. Wow! Increasing the number of items in the list significantly increases the time complexity of the insertion sort, as shown in **Figure 22-5**.

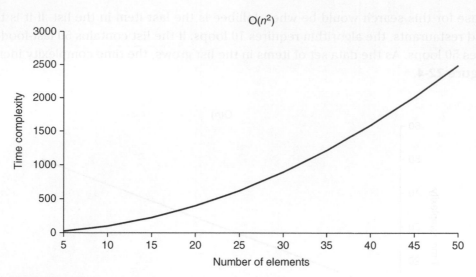

Figure 22-5   The time complexity for a nested loop increases more sharply as the data set grows

This type of time complexity is referred to as **quadratic time**. It increases more sharply than linear time complexity as the data set grows. Because the number of iterations is n^2, quadratic complexity in Big-O notation is expressed as **O(n^2)**.

Simple sorting algorithms, such as quick sort, bubble sort, selection sort, and insertion sort, have quadratic time complexity. They are best avoided when working with large datasets. You can use alternative, more efficient sorting algorithms in your programs.

Q Suppose you have a program that searches through a data set one element at time and another program that uses an insertion sort to put the elements in alphabetical order. Which program has the better time efficiency?

A The search has O(n) complexity. The sort has O(n^2) efficiency. That means the search is more efficient.

Logarithmic Time (22.2.7, 22.2.8)

Computer scientists and programmers are always looking for clever algorithms that divide and conquer. Using a binary search to find items in a sorted list is an example of this divide-and-conquer strategy.

Suppose you have a list of 11 fast-food restaurants sorted alphabetically. You can simplify this list as [A, B, C, D, E, F, G, H, I, J, K]. A binary search locates the middle item in the list and checks to see if it is the target. If not, half of the list is discarded based on whether the target is greater than or less than the middle item. This process of discarding half the list continues until the target is found. See **Figure 22-6**.

Q How many iterations are required to find J in the list of 11 items?

A Three iterations are required. The first uses F as the midpoint in the whole list. The second uses I as the midpoint in the sublist. The third uses J as the midpoint of the sublist. J is found in the third iteration.

| A | B | C | D | E | F | G | H | I | J | K |

1. To check if J is in the list, look at the midpoint. If the midpoint is not what you're looking for and it is less than the target value, throw out half the list that is less than or equal to the midpoint.

| G | H | I | J | K |

2. Check the midpoint in the sublist. If that midpoint is not the target and it is less than the target value, discard half of the sublist that is less than or equal to the target.

| J | K |

3. With only two elements left, use the first one as the midpoint. That is the target value. You found it in three steps.

Figure 22-6   A binary search uses a divide-and-conquer algorithm to reduce time complexity

In a binary search, the iterations do not grow dramatically with the size of the list because with each iteration, half of the list is eliminated. **Figure 22-7** illustrates this growth pattern that decreases in slope as the data set grows.

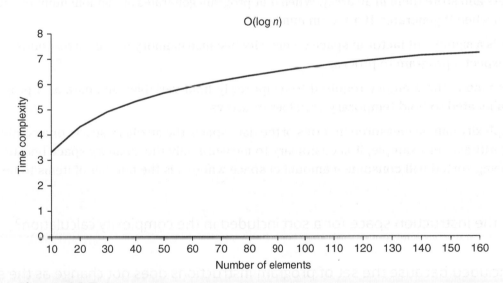

Figure 22-7   The graph of logarithmic time decreases in slope as the number of data elements increases

At most, four iterations are required for a binary search to find an item in a 10-item list. A maximum of five iterations are required for a 20-item list, seven iterations for a 100-item list. This trend is characteristic of logarithms.

A logarithm is the opposite of exponentiation. Whereas an exponent multiplies, a logarithm divides. Binary searches and operations on binary trees run in **logarithmic time** characterized by the ratio of operations decreasing as the size of the data set grows.

Because the number of iterations is log *n*, logarithmic time in Big-O notation is expressed as **O(log *n*)**. Logarithmic time is considered to be more efficient than either linear or quadratic time. Algorithms that run in logarithmic time are your buddies.

22.3 Space Complexity

Memory Space (22.3.1, 22.3.2, 22.3.3)

As a programmer, you should be aware of the memory requirements for the programs that you code. Today's computers have lots of memory but may be called upon to process huge data sets. Using asymptotic analysis to get a handle on the space complexity of your algorithms can help you understand memory requirements as your programs scale up to large data sets.

Computer programs require three types of memory space to hold instructions and data.

Instruction space is the memory used to store the code for a program. When a program runs, memory space is used to store the compiled version of a program, its bitcode, or the source code that will be processed by an interpreter. Writing efficient code can reduce the amount of instruction space required to execute an algorithm.

Instruction space is not affected by the size of the data set. For example, the set of instructions to sort a list doesn't change if the list contains 10 items or 10,000 items. Because time complexity metrics are tied to the size of the data set, the size of the instruction set does not play a role in determining space complexity.

Data space is the memory required to hold data that is accessed by a program, input to a program, or generated by the program. As that data grows, more memory is required. Suppose you write a program to generate random numbers and store them in an array. When that program generates 50 random numbers, it requires more data space than when it generates 10 random numbers.

Data space is a significant factor in space complexity because memory usage corresponds to the size of the data sets you expect a program to process.

Auxiliary space is the memory required to temporarily hold variables and data as a program runs. This space may be allocated to hold temporary variables or arrays.

Space complexity can be measured in terms of the data space, the auxiliary space, or a combination of both. For sorting algorithms, for example, it is customary to measure only the auxiliary space because it is assumed that the data being sorted will consume n amount of space where n is the number of items to be sorted.

Q Why isn't the instruction space for a sort included in the complexity calculation?

A It's not included because the set of program instructions does not change as the size of the data set changes.

Programs typically exhibit two types of space complexity:

O(1) Constant space
O(n) Linear space

Constant Space Complexity (22.3.4)

Algorithms with **constant space complexity** require the same amount of memory regardless of the size of the data set. A bubble sort is an example of an algorithm that uses constant space.

To code a bubble sort, begin by comparing the first two elements. If the first element is larger than the second element, put the first element in a temporary variable, move the second element into the first position, and then move the value in the temporary variable to the second position, as shown in **Figure 22-8**.

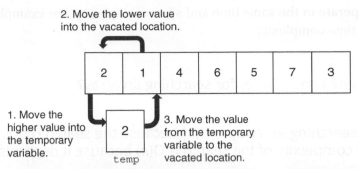

2. Move the lower value into the vacated location.

1. Move the higher value into the temporary variable.

3. Move the value from the temporary variable to the vacated location.

temp

If a pair of numbers is out of order, switch them by rotating through a temporary variable.

Figure 22-8   A bubble sort uses one temporary memory location regardless of the number of elements in a data set, so the space complexity is constant O(1)

The bubble sort continues to compare pairs of elements and swap them as necessary. After several passes, the elements are sorted. This algorithm requires only one temporary variable for the sort, regardless of how many elements are to be sorted. Because the auxiliary space requirements do not change as the data set grows, the algorithm runs in constant space, O(1).

Bubble sorts, heap sorts, insertion sorts, selection sorts, and shell sorts all operate in constant space. These algorithms are sometimes referred to as *in-place sorts* because they essentially overwrite the data in the original array, rather than creating a new array to hold the sorted data.

Linear Space Complexity (22.3.5, 22.3.6, 22.3.7)

Algorithms with **linear space complexity** require more space as the size of the data set grows. A brute force sorting algorithm is an example of linear space complexity. It uses two arrays: the original unsorted array and a new array to hold sorted elements.

To carry out the sort, your program looks through the unsorted array to find the smallest element and puts it in the first position of the new array. The program then looks through the unsorted list to find the next smallest element and puts it in the second position of the new array. This process repeats for every item in the unsorted array. See **Figure 22-9**.

Original list

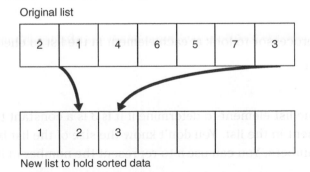

New list to hold sorted data

Figure 22-9   A brute force sort uses two lists, so the space complexity O(*n*) increases as the data set grows

Because this code generates a second array of the same size as the unsorted list, the algorithm's space complexity is O(*n*). The complexity increases as the size of the dataset increases.

Merge sorts and tree sorts operate in linear space. They are less space efficient than in-place sorts, so they may not be suitable for large data sets.

Algorithms do not have to operate in the same time and space complexity. For example, a bubble sort has O(1) space complexity, but O(n) time complexity.

Q What are the space and time complexities for searching an array?

A The space complexity of searching an array is O(1) because the search requires no additional memory space. The time complexity of the search is O(n) because it depends on the number of elements in the array.

22.4 Complexity Calculations

Line-by-Line Time Complexity (22.4.1, 22.4.2)

Suppose that you have a list of numbers, such as 1, 2, 3, 4, 5 or 5, 4, 3, 2, 6, 3, 2, 9, 2. The list could be any length. You've devised the following algorithm that looks through the list to count the number of 3s it contains:

```
total = 0

for element in the_list:
    if element == 3:
        total += 1
```

Q What do you think is the time complexity of this algorithm?

A It is linear time, O(n). Let's find out why.

The first line of the program is an assignment statement. Within the processor, this statement requires a single step that takes place in constant time. So far, the algorithm has a time complexity of O(1).

```
total = 0
```

The for-loop requires the processor to look at each element in the list to check if it is a 3:

```
for element in the_list:
    if element == 3:
```

The process of checking one list element to determine if it is 3 is a constant time operation, but this operation takes place for every element in the list. You don't know the size of the list because this general algorithm could be used for any list of numbers. You can use n to represent the number of items in the list.

The time complexity of stepping through the list to check each number is O(n): one step for each item in the list. Including the O(1) time complexity for the initialization step of the algorithm, your time complexity so far is O(1 + n).

```
total = 0                          O(1)
for element in the_list:
    if element == 3:               O(n)
                                   Total: O(1 + n)
```

Incrementing the total with `total += 1` also takes place within the loop. Potentially, every element in the list could be 3. Therefore, this operation also depends on the number of items in the list. You can add this to the list of time complexities as another n.

```
total = 0                            O(1)
for element in the_list:
    if element == 3:                 O(n)
        total += 1                   O(n)
                                     Total: O(1 + n + n)
```

So far, the complexity is $1 + n + n$, based on the initial assignment statement and the two statements within the loop. Mathematically, this is the same as $1 + 2n$.

Q How would you express this in Big-O notation?

A It is $O(1 + 2n)$.

Combine and Simplify (22.4.3, 22.4.4)

Now things get interesting. Although you have calculated the number of steps for the algorithm, Big-O time complexity is only focused on the upper bounds of a program's runtime. You can simplify $O(1 + 2n)$.

The limiting factor is not the constant operation, so you can simply eliminate the 1. You can also eliminate the 2 from the $2n$ notation. Why? Because $2n$ and n are both linear functions. They indicate the same *type* of growth, even if the *rate* of growth is different. As the number of elements in the list increases, the rate of growth is the same for n as for $2n$. **Figure 22-10** illustrates this somewhat nonintuitive concept.

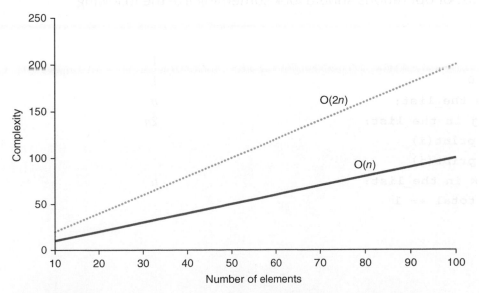

Figure 22-10   Algorithms with $O(n)$ and $O(2n)$ time complexities both increase linearly

For the purposes of Big-O notation, O($2n$) is the same as O(n). As a result, the algorithm for counting the number of 3s in a list is bounded by linear time complexity, which you can express in Big-O notation as O(n).

To summarize, when you want to determine the time complexity of an algorithm, do the following:

1. List the complexity for each line of code.
2. Mathematically combine terms.
3. Select the most time-complex term, such as O(C), O($\log n$), O(n), or O(n^2).

A Mystery Algorithm (22.4.5)

Let's take a look at one more example to make sure that you've got the hang of these Big-O calculations.

Suppose that you have a list called **the_list**, which could be any length. Here is the Python code for a mystery algorithm designed to process the list. The algorithm is a mystery because its purpose doesn't matter. You're only concerned with its time complexity.

```
a = 5

total = 0

for i in the_list:
    for j in the_list:
        print(i)
        print(j)
    for k in the_list:
        total += 1
```

Q Take a moment to jot down the time complexity for each operation of the mystery function. What is the extended expression for all of the operations in this algorithm?

A Your initial list of operations should look something like the following.

```
a = 5                               1
total = 0                           1
for i in the_list:                  n
    for j in the_list:              2n
        print(i)
        print(j)
    for k in the_list:              n
        total += 1
```

Q What is the expanded expression for all of the operations in this algorithm?

A It is $2 + n * 2n + n$.

The 2 is derived from the first two assignment statements.

n is derived from the "i" loop.

$2n$ is derived from the "j" loop's two print statements.

The final n is derived from the addition operation within the "k" loop.

You might wonder where the multiplication comes from. Notice the nested for-loops. The outside for-loop begins with the first number in the list, but then the inner for-loop steps through each element in the list. If the list contains four elements, the two loops will not execute $4 + 4$ times. They will execute 4×4 times. Aha! That is the source of the multiplication.

Next, simplify the expression. $2 + n * 2n + n$ simplifies to $2 + 2n^2 + n$.

Q What is the result when you eliminate the constants?

A It is $n^2 + n$.

Finally, all you have to do is choose the term that represents the fastest growing time complexity and convert it into Big-O notation. Of n^2 and n, n^2 is the fastest growing time complexity. In Big-O notation, the time complexity for the mystery algorithm is $O(n^2)$.

To recap, you can figure the time complexity of a function by listing the complexity of the operations required for each line of code. You can mathematically combine the terms and eliminate any coefficients. Finally, select the most time-complex term as the boundary to use in the Big-O expression.

Summary

- Time complexity refers to the amount of time required to execute an algorithm as its data set grows. In general, algorithms that execute most quickly are most time efficient. Algorithms that require more time as the data set grows have more time complexity.
- Space complexity refers to the amount of memory required by an algorithm as its data set grows. Algorithms that require the least memory space are likely to be the most space efficient. Algorithms that require more space as the data set grows have more space complexity.
- A set of metrics can be used as objective measures of an algorithm's time efficiency or space efficiency. Asymptotic analysis provides programmers with a way to evaluate the performance of an algorithm as the size of its data set grows.
- Asymptotic notations include Big-O, Big-Omega, and Big-Theta. Of these three notations, Big-O is most frequently used to measure the efficiency of algorithms.
- Big-O notation is used to express the worst-case time complexity or space complexity of an algorithm. Worst-case is sometimes referred to as upper bounds because it measures the maximum complexity of an algorithm.
- The efficiency of algorithms that execute in constant time do not change as the data set becomes larger. The Big-O notation for constant time is $O(C)$, as in $O(1)$.

- Algorithms that increase linearly as the data set becomes larger execute in linear time, expressed as $O(n)$. Algorithms of linear complexity, such as those containing a loop, are less efficient than algorithms that run in constant time.
- Algorithms, such as those containing nested loops, that require multiple passes through a data set execute in quadratic time, expressed as $O(n^2)$.
- Divide-and-conquer algorithms, such as a binary search, execute in logarithmic time, expressed as $O(\log n)$.
- Space complexity may measure data space, auxiliary space, or both and is typically either $O(1)$ or $O(n)$. Computer scientists typically use space complexity when evaluating the efficiency of sorting algorithms.
- To determine the complexity of an algorithm, you can perform a line-by-line asymptotic analysis by listing the complexity for each line of code, mathematically combining terms, and selecting the most complex term.

Key Terms

asymptotic analysis	constant time	$O(\log n)$
asymptotic notation	data space	$O(n)$
auxiliary space	instruction space	$O(n^2)$
Big-O notation	linear space complexity	quadratic time
Big-Omega notation	linear time	space complexity
Big-Theta notation	logarithmic time	time complexity
constant space complexity	$O(C)$	

Module 23

Search Algorithms

Learning Objectives:

23.1 Using Search Algorithms

23.1.1 State the purpose of a search algorithm.

23.1.2 Define the term "search space."

23.2 Performing a Linear Search

23.2.1 Identify the algorithm for a linear search.

23.2.2 Identify data structures that can be searched linearly.

23.2.3 State the time complexities of a linear search.

23.2.4 Explain why linear search is rarely used.

23.3 Performing a Binary Search

23.3.1 Categorize binary search with the computational thinking concept of divide and conquer.

23.3.2 Identify the characteristics of data structures that support a binary search.

23.3.3 List examples of databases that have the characteristics required for a binary search.

23.3.4 Distinguish between the iterative and recursive algorithms for the binary search of a list.

23.3.5 Identify the following in a binary search algorithm: min index, max index, middle index.

23.3.6 Analyze what happens if the search space contains more than one target value.

23.3.7 State the time and space complexities for a binary search.

23.4 Using Regular Expressions in Search Algorithms

23.4.1 Define a regular expression as a sequence of characters that define a search pattern.

23.4.2 Associate "regex," "re," and "regexp" with the term "regular expression."

23.4.3 Identify algorithms that use regular expressions.

23.4.4 Match regex metacharacters to their operations.

23.4.5 Analyze regular expressions that use [] , * , ? , | , ! , and + .

23.1 Using Search Algorithms

Search Basics (23.1.1, 23.1.2)

Computers can store large amounts of information represented as text, images, spreadsheets, music, and many other formats. All this information exists as a collection of ones and zeros in your system's memory, which can hold terabytes of data. To make this information useful to you, the computer must be able to search for and retrieve the information you need. Special algorithms called **search algorithms** find a specific piece of information within a large set of data as efficiently as possible. Search algorithms are typically evaluated based on how fast they return the desired result.

You can think of searching for information on a computer as like searching for a contact in a phone book. The contact information is sorted alphabetically to help you to find a phone number faster. For example, imagine that your cell phone lists contacts in random order, as in **Figure 23-1**.

Figure 23-1   Contacts in a cell phone

To find a specific contact name such as Sandra Taylor in a random list, you would need to look through the list of contact names. If you have a short list of contacts in your phone, then looking for Sandra Taylor is easy. However, as you add contacts to the list, the task gets more difficult because the **search space**, or the amount of data you are searching, gets larger.

23.2 Performing a Linear Search

Looking for a Needle in a Haystack (23.2.1, 23.2.2)

Sometimes, searching for data seems like you are looking for a needle in a haystack. The search space contains a huge amount of information, and you need to find the one value that you need. Consider the unordered list of contacts shown in **Figure 23-2**.

Figure 23-2   Unordered contact list

Using object-oriented programming, you decide to create a class to store information about your phone contacts. This class needs to store the person's first name, last name, and mobile number. You then create the code in **Figure 23-3**. You also create an object for each of your contacts and store them in a list variable named `contact_list`.

```python
class Contact():
    def __init__(self, first_name, last_name, mobile_number):
        self.first_name = first_name
        self.last_name = last_name
        self.mobile_number = mobile_number


person1 = Contact("Riah", "Justice", "202-345-8643")

person2 = Contact("George", "Castile", "301-753-4543")

person3 = Contact("Amauhd", "McClain", "240-243-6532")

person4 = Contact("Sandra", "Taylor", "443-567-6950")

person5 = Contact("Floyd", "Garner", "734-546-6950")

person6 = Contact("Elijah", "Arbery", "313-809-6352")

person7 = Contact("Pamela", "Sterling", "864-754-3227")

person8 = Contact("Breonna", "Bland", "352-429-4372")


contact_list = [person1, person2, person3, person4,
                person5, person6, person7, person8]
```

Figure 23-3 Code for a `Contact` class and how you might store your `contact_list` as a Python list

Suppose you need to call Sandra Taylor but you have no idea where her name is located within your unordered list of contacts. Your first instinct might be to scroll through the entire list, looking at each name one at a time to find Sandra Taylor. This type of search algorithm is called **linear search**, where you look at each item in a list one by one to find what you are looking for. Linear search is the simplest search algorithm when the information you are searching is in a random order.

You typically use a linear search algorithm when your data is stored in a list. Generally, linear search can be used for any contiguous data structure. When coding a linear search algorithm, a loop is often used. Following is the algorithm for linear search:

Specify a cursor variable to start searching at the beginning of the search space.
Inspect the current element at the cursor and determine if it is the value you are looking for.
If the current element is the item that you are looking for, return the index of the item, the item itself, or the value `True` and end the search.
Otherwise, do the following:

Iterate to the next element and begin the inspection process again.

If you have reached the end of the search space, end the search.
Return a sentinel value to indicate that the search has terminated without finding the element.

In coding, a **sentinel value** (or flag value) is a special value used to indicate that a search should end. The sentinel should not be a valid value that you'd expect to find within the search space. For example, −1 is an appropriate sentinel value to put at the end of a list of positive integers to show that the end of the list has been reached. Within objects, you can create sentinel values by manipulating the values of the data members.

Figure 23-4 illustrates the code for the `linear_search()` method.

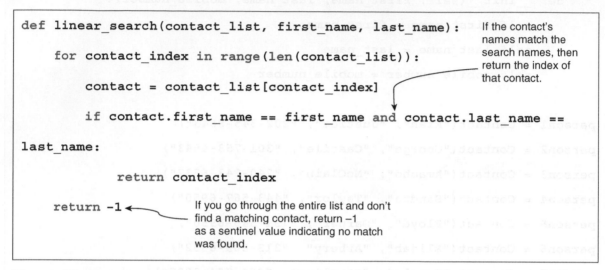

Figure 23-4 contents:

```
def linear_search(contact_list, first_name, last_name):

    for contact_index in range(len(contact_list)):

        contact = contact_list[contact_index]

        if contact.first_name == first_name and contact.last_name ==
last_name:

                return contact_index

    return -1
```

If the contact's names match the search names, then return the index of that contact.

If you go through the entire list and don't find a matching contact, return −1 as a sentinel value indicating no match was found.

Figure 23-4   Code for a `linear_search()` function

Q   How do I know if my search algorithms should return the index of the data I am searching for, the data itself, or `True`?

A   The value that should be returned depends on the context and purpose of the search. If you need to know only the location of the information, return the index. If you need to manipulate the data, return the data item itself. If you just need to verify that the desired value is in the search space, it is appropriate to return the value `True`.

Figure 23-5 uses the `linear_search()` to look for Sandra Taylor. If the value −1 is returned (the sentinel value), then Sandra is not listed in your `contact_list`. Otherwise, Sandra's contact is in the index returned by `linear_search()`.

Riah Justice   George Castile   Amauhd McClain   Sandra Taylor   Floyd Garner   Elijah Arbery   Pamela Sterling   Breonna Bland

Sapann Design/ Shutterstock.com

Figure 23-5   Using linear search with some `Contact` objects in a list *(Continued)*

```
from phone_information import Contact
from search_algorithms import linear_search


person1 = Contact("Riah", "Justice", "202-345-8643")
person2 = Contact("George", "Castile", "301-753-4543")
person3 = Contact("Amauhd", "McClain", "240-243-6532")
person4 = Contact("Sandra", "Taylor", "443-567-6950")
person5 = Contact("Floyd", "Garner", "734-546-6950")
person6 - Contact("Elijah", "Arbery", "313-809-6352")
person7 = Contact("Pamela", "Sterling", "864-754-3227")
person8 = Contact("Breonna", "Bland", "352-429-4372")


contact_list = [person1, person2, person3, person4,
                person5, person6, person7, person8]


found_index = linear_search(contact_list, "Sandra", "Taylor")


if found_index != -1:
    print("Sandra Taylor is located at index:", found_index)
else:
    print("Sandra Taylor is not in the contact list.")
OUTPUT:
Sandra Taylor is located at index: 3
```

Figure 23-5 Using linear search with some `Contact` objects in a list

Evaluating Search Time (23.2.3, 23.2.4)

The linear search found the Sandra Taylor contact quickly because the name was near the beginning of the list. Suppose the contact you were looking for happened to be at the end of the list. A linear search would take longer because it examines everything within the search space before it can find the solution. If the item you're looking for is not in the search space, a linear search also examines every item before determining that the item cannot be found. As you may imagine, linear search is considered the slowest search method.

In the worst-case scenario, a linear search looks through an entire list before it can find the desired object. As the size of the list grows, search performance can decrease significantly because it takes longer to find the target data. For this reason, linear search is rarely used. You can use other strategies to reduce the time necessary to search for an item in a list.

23.3 Performing a Binary Search

Shrinking the Search Space (23.3.1, 23.3.2, 23.3.3)

As the size of the search space increases, the amount of time that it takes to find a solution also increases. For example, an unordered list of contacts would take a long time to search one by one. Now, imagine that the list is sorted. Each contact is listed alphabetically by first name, as shown in **Figure 23-6**.

| Riah Justice | George Castile | Amauhd McClain | Sandra Taylor | Floyd Garner | Elijah Arbery | Pamela Sterling | Breonna Bland |

| Amauhd McClain | Breonna Bland | Elijah Arbery | Floyd Garner | George Castile | Pamela Sterling | Riah Justice | Sandra Taylor |

Sapann Design/Shutterstock.com

Figure 23-6   List of contacts in alphabetical order by first name

Suppose you want to find contact information for Breonna Bland. In an unordered search, you'd need to look through every contact until you reached Breonna's contact information at the end of the list. The search takes a long time because as the amount of information increases, you lose time examining many contacts until you find the one you want.

If your data is ordered, the search becomes easier. You can take advantage of the inherent ordering system for letters (A to Z) and for numbers (0 to 9). Suppose you are looking up the word *dog* in the dictionary. If you open the dictionary to a page with words that begin with the letter *m*, then you know that the definition of dog is listed before this page. You do not need to look at any words that come after the letter *m* because you know the first letter in *dog* comes before *m*. In essence, you have reduced the search space by 50 percent.

Search becomes easier when you can eliminate part of the search space. To take advantage of the ordering of data, you can use a **binary search algorithm**, which divides the search space in half until the target value is located. This approach is typically referred to as a **divide-and-conquer technique** because each step divides the search space and eliminates part of it on the path to a solution.

Any data structure that uses binary search must have the data in the search space in sorted order. Binary search algorithms do not work on unsorted data or data with duplicate values. An ordered collection of data, such as a dictionary, has the characteristics necessary for binary search. In general, any collection of data that consists of unique values that can be ordered is required for binary search.

When coding a binary search algorithm, you use recursion or iteration. The algorithm for binary search is the following:

1. Specify a cursor variable called `lower_index` to point to the first element in the search space.
2. Specify a cursor variable called `upper_index` to point to the last element in the search space.

3. Specify a cursor variable called `midpoint_index` to begin at the middle of the search space, the size of the search space divided by 2.

4. If the current element is the item that you are looking for, return the index of the item, the item itself, or the value `True` and end the search.

5. Otherwise, do the following:

   Determine if the target you are looking for comes before or after the current element.

   If the target comes before the current element:

   • Move `upper_index` to the item before `midpoint_index`.
   • Move `midpoint_index` to the middle of the new list formed between `lower index` and `upper index`.
   • Start again at step 4 (recursively).

   If the target comes after the current element:

   • Move `lower_index` to the item after `midpoint_index`.
   • Move `midpoint_index` to the middle of the new list formed between `lower_index` and `upper_index`.
   • Start again at step 4 (recursively).

6. If the `lower_index` and `upper_index` cross each other (i.e., `lower_index` is on the right, and `upper_index` is on the left), then return −1 and end the search.

Implementing Binary Search (23.3.4, 23.3.5, 23.3.6, 23.3.7)

At the beginning of the binary search algorithm for finding Breonna Bland's contact information in a sorted list, `lower_index` is set at index 0, `upper_index` is index 7, and `midpoint_index` is index 3, as shown in **Figure 23-7**.

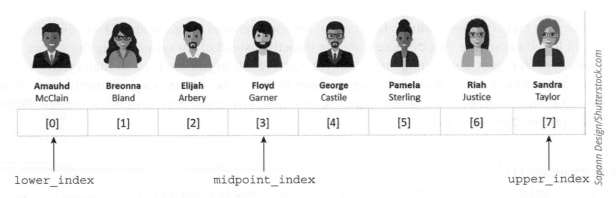

Sapann Design/Shutterstock.com

Figure 23-7   Binary search, stage 1

The `midpoint_index` is not pointing to Breonna Bland, so you update `upper_index` to point to the index to the left of `midpoint_index` (index 2) and update `midpoint_index` to point to the index between `lower_index` and `upper_index` (index 1). Now `midpoint_index` is pointing to index 1, which is the location of the target. See **Figure 23-8**.

As you may have noticed, the binary search algorithm requires each value in the search space to be unique. What would happen if the search space contained duplicate values? Suppose index 2 held a contact identical to index 1 so that both contacts had the name Breonna Bland. The algorithm would still work the same and return index 1 as the result. Index 2 would be ignored as a possible solution. Depending on the context of your problem and the solution requirements, this behavior may be undesirable. For example, suppose you need to count the number of times a certain value appears within your ordered search space. Ignoring duplicates would be a problem in this case.

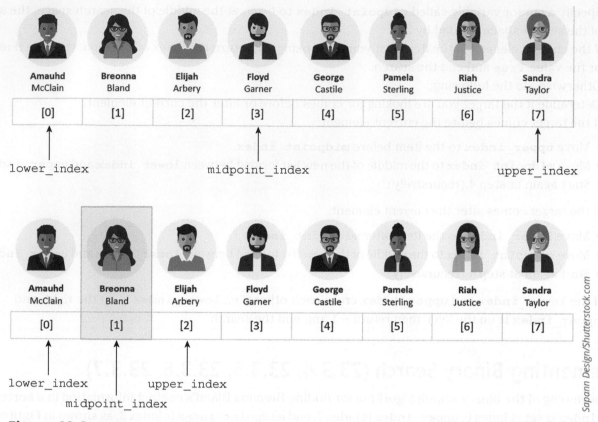

Figure 23-8   Binary search, stage 2

To make your code cleaner, adding a few dunder method overrides is a good idea. Overriding the **__eq__()** method will let you compare two **Contact** objects directly instead of always checking the **first_name** and **last_name** of each object. Overriding the **__lt__()** method will let you use the less than symbol (<) with two objects of the **Contact** class, again reducing the need to check the **first_name** property of an object. The same benefit comes from overriding the **__gt__()** method, giving you access to the > symbol. **Figure 23-9** shows the updated **Contact** class.

```python
class Contact():
    def __init__(self, first_name, last_name, mobile_number):
        self.first_name = first_name
        self.last_name = last_name
        self.mobile_number = mobile_number


    def __eq__(self, other):
        if self.first_name == other.first_name and self.last_name == other.last_name:
            return True
        return False
```

Figure 23-9   Adding comparison dunder methods to the **Contact** class *(Continued)*

```
        def __lt__(self, other):
            if self.first_name < other.first_name:
                return True
            return False


        def __gt__(self, other):
            if self.first_name > other.first_name:
                return True
            return False
```

Figure 23-9   Adding comparison dunder methods to the `Contact` class

A binary search algorithm can be correctly implemented using recursion or iteration. The recursive algorithm is simpler to code, but the iterative solution takes up less computer memory to use. This is because recursion adds multiple function calls to the call stack as it copies subsections of the data in each recursive call. Regardless, both algorithms can successfully return a solution. The code for implementing a binary search recursively is shown in **Figure 23-10**.

```
def binary_search(contact_list, lower_index, upper_index, target_contact):

    if lower_index <= upper_index:

        midpoint_index = (lower_index + upper_index) // 2


        print("Lower index:", lower_index)
        print("Upper index:", upper_index)
        print("Midpoint index:", midpoint_index)


        if contact_list[midpoint_index] == target_contact:
            return midpoint_index


        elif (contact_list[midpoint_index] > target_contact):
            return binary_search(contact_list, lower_index, midpoint_index - 1,
target_contact)


        else:
            return binary_search(contact_list, midpoint_index + 1, upper_index,
target_contact)


    return -1
```

Figure 23-10   Recursive code for binary search

Updating the code from Figure 23-5 to use the new dunder methods and binary search is shown in **Figure 23-11**. The output does not change much because the purpose of both the `linear_search()` algorithm and `binary_search()` algorithm are the same. However, the index that is actually returned is different because the `contact_list` has the `Contact` objects in a new order. The most important change is how the result is achieved. The `Contact` objects are now created in sorted order, which is something `binary_search()` requires.

```
from phone_information import Contact

from search_algorithms import binary_search


person1 = Contact("Amauhd", "McClain", "240-243-6532")

person2 = Contact("Breonna", "Bland", "352-429-4372")

person3 = Contact("Elijah", "Arbery", "313-809-6352")

person4 = Contact("Floyd", "Garner", "734-546-6950")

person5 = Contact("George", "Castile", "301-753-4543")

person6 = Contact("Pamela", "Sterling", "864-754-3227")

person7 = Contact("Riah", "Justice", "202-345-8643")

person8 = Contact("Sandra", "Taylor", "443-567-6950")


contact_list = [person1, person2, person3, person4,

                person5, person6, person7, person8]

found_index = binary_search(contact_list, 0,

len(contact_list)-1, person2)


if found_index != -1:

    print("Breonna Bland is located at index:",

found_index)

else:

    print("Breonna Bland is not in the contact list.")
OUTPUT:
Lower index: 0

Upper index: 7

Midpoint index: 3

Lower index: 0

Upper index: 2

Midpoint index: 1

Breonna Bland is located at index: 1
```

> Add the `Contact` objects in sorted order for binary search to work.

Figure 23-11 Testing `binary_search()` on a sorted `contact_list`

The code for implementing a binary search iteratively is shown in **Figure 23-12**. If you use this function with the code in Figure 23-11, the output will not change.

```python
def binary_search(contact_list, lower_index, upper_index, target_contact):

    while lower_index <= upper_index:

        midpoint_index = (lower_index + upper_index) // 2


        print("Lower index:", lower_index)
        print("Upper index:", upper_index)
        print("Midpoint index:", midpoint_index)


        if contact_list[midpoint_index] == target_contact:
            return midpoint_index


        elif (contact_list[midpoint_index] > target_contact):
            upper_index = midpoint_index - 1


        else:
            lower_index = midpoint_index + 1

    return -1
```

Figure 23-12   Iterative code for binary search

A binary search reduces the search space by half on each iteration. This behavior reduces the number of evaluations needed to find your target. For this reason, if the search space contains n items, binary search takes $\log_2(n)$ comparisons at most to determine the answer. For example, the contact list has eight contacts. A linear search needs up to eight evaluations to find a match. However, using a binary search, you only need to perform two comparisons (index 3 and index 1) to find the target. The expression $\log_2(8)$ results in 3, so the binary search performed less than the maximum of eight evaluations with a linear search.

23.4 Using Regular Expressions in Search Algorithms

Specifying a Search Pattern (23.4.1, 23.4.2, 23.4.3)

In a search scenario (such as a search engine), after you optimize the underlying search algorithm, you need a way to locate the information you want. Suppose you have a database full of contact information. The database grows as you add contacts over time. You recall the exact name of only some contacts. For other contacts, you remember partial names. In these cases, you can use a **regular expression** to search for a desired contact. A regular expression is a string of characters that describes the pattern of the text you are searching for. Regular expression is sometimes abbreviated as "regex," "re," or "regexp."

Regular expression algorithms are used in text editors (such as in the find operation), search engines, and lexical analysis, as shown in **Figure 23-13**.

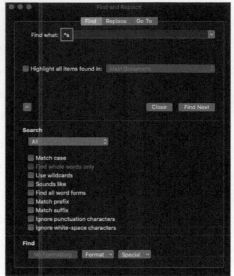

wwwebmeister/Shutterstock.com

Figure 23-13　Examples of regular expressions in a search engine and text editor

Regular Expression Search Operators (23.4.4, 23.4.5)

To create a regular expression, you use a string of characters that describes the pattern of the information you are seeking. The characters that describe the patterns used in regular expressions are called **metacharacters**. Metacharacters can be used alone or in combination with other metacharacters to describe patterns, such as those shown in **Figure 23-14**. Although metacharacters in regular expressions can vary from one programming language to another, the available features usually remain the same.

Metacharacters	Description	Usage
\d	Any single digit number from 0–9	\d\d\d matches
		202
		123
		555
\w	Any single letter (a–z, A–Z) or number (0–9)	\w\w\w matches
		313
		abc
		Ax3
\W	Any single symbol	\W\W matches
		@@
		@$

Figure 23-14　Regular expression metacharacters, meanings, and examples *(Continued)*

Metacharacters	Description	Usage
`[a-z]`	A set of characters where exactly one must match	`Ta[iy]lor` matches `Tailor` `Taylor`
`[0-9]`	A set of numbers where exactly one must match	`1[028]` matches `10` `12` `18`
`(abc)`	A set of characters that must be matched in this exact order	`Tay(lor)` matches `Taylor`
`(123)`	A set of numbers that must be matched in this exact order	`Tay(123)` matches `Tay123`
`|`	Logical OR; allows alternate patterns to be matched	`Ste(ph|f)en` matches `Stephen` `Stefen`
`?`	The character immediately before the question mark occurs 0 or 1 time only	`Breon?a` matches `Breona` `Breoa`
`*`	The character immediately before the asterisk occurs 0 or more times	`fre*` matches `fr` `fre` `free` `freee` `freeee`
`+`	The character immediately before the + occurs 1 or more times	`fre+` matches `fre` `free` `freee` `freeee`
`.`	The period matches any single letter, number, or symbol	`fre.` matches `free` `fred` `fre#` `fre!`
`{n}`	A quantifier that matches when the specified character or group of characters occurs exactly *n* times	`\d{4}` matches `2945` `1738` `0525` `1229` `fr[et]{2}` matches `free` `fret` `frte` `frtt`

Figure 23-14   Regular expression metacharacters, meanings, and examples *(Continued)*

Metacharacters	Description	Usage
{n,m}	A quantifier that matches when the specified character or group of characters occurs at least *n* times, but no more than *m* times	\d{2,4} matches 68 678 6789 12 123 1234

Figure 23-14   Regular expression metacharacters, meanings, and examples

Q How would you search for any 10-digit phone number (no dashes)?

A [0–9]{10}

Q How would you search for any year in this millennium (2000–2999)?

A 20/d/d/d

Q Which contact's first name would match the regular expression Br(e|i)(o|a)nna?

A Breonna Bland

Python has a built-in module you can import for matching regular expressions. The module **re** contains regular expression matching given a string. The general syntax is to first create a regular expression object with **re.compile("regex string")**. Creating a regular expression object to check for a 10-digit phone number with no dashes would be:

```
compiler = re.compile("[0-9]{10}")
```

Next, the compiler can create a match object given the string you want to check for the regular expression. To check the string **"234152"** as a valid 10-digit number, for example, create the match object with the following syntax:

```
matcher = compiler.match("234152")
```

Finally, you need code to check whether the string given to the **match()** method detected a pattern matching the regular expression. If the value returned is **None**, then there was no match. Otherwise, use the **matcher.group()** method to display all matches within the string (typically just one match, but could be more):

```
if matcher == None:

    print("No matches found")

else:

    print("Matches found:", matcher.group())
```

Summary

- To make the large amounts of information that computers store useful to you, a computer needs to efficiently search for desired information. Search algorithms are special algorithms that describe how to find a specific or target piece of information.
- The search space defines the amount of data that needs to be examined to find the target. Generally, as the search space increases, the time needed to find the target also increases.
- Linear search is the simplest search algorithm. Each element in the search space is examined until the target is located.
- Linear search can be performed on any contiguous data structure such as a list or a linked list.
- In the worst-case scenario, linear search requires you to look at every item in the search space before you find the solution, which is why linear search is rarely used.
- A binary search algorithm consecutively divides the search space in half until the target value is located. This approach is typically referred to as a divide-and-conquer technique because each step divides the search space on the path to a solution.
- Binary search reduces the search space by half on each iteration. This behavior reduces the number of times you have to evaluate an item to determine if it is equal to your target. If the search space contains n items, binary search takes at most $\log_2(n)$ comparisons to determine the answer.
- In a search scenario (such as a search engine), when you have optimized the underlying search algorithm, you need a way to specify the information you are seeking. When searching, you can use a regular expression to search for an item, such as a desired contact. A regular expression is a string of characters that describe the pattern of the text for which you are searching.
- The characters that describe the patterns used in regular expressions are called metacharacters. You can use metacharacters alone or in combination with other metacharacters to describe patterns.
- Python has a module, re, that provides regular expression matching. First a regular expression object is made, then a match object. If the match object is None, there was no match. Otherwise, using the matcher.group() method will show all matching substrings.

Key Terms

binary search algorithm

divide-and-conquer technique

linear search

metacharacters

regular expression

search algorithms

search space

sentinel value

Module 24

Sorting Algorithms

Learning Objectives

24.1 Qualities of Sorting Algorithms

Ordering Items (24.1.1)

Imagine you have a contacts book like the one in **Figure 24-1**, with one contact per page. Typically, the contact pages are organized alphabetically, but what if the pages fell out of the book when the binder rings were open? Finding someone's contact information would be tedious, as you would have to look at each page in a random order until you found the right one. If the contact pages were in alphabetical order, however, you could find information more easily. Instead of bundling all the pages together in random order, you would sort the pages before returning them to the contacts book.

Figure 24-1 Contacts book, organized by name

Sorting is an important topic in computer science as it makes data easier to find. Because computers commonly deal with large sets of data, you should know how to sort data (to find things more easily) and understand how the computer sorts. You can approach the task in a few ways using **sorting algorithms**.

To sort data items, a computer needs to know how the items relate to each other, such as whether one item is the same, less than, or greater than another item. Computers are set up to make numerical and alphabetical sorting easy, so that when you compare two numbers or letters, the computer knows how to order them. The character "a" is less than the character "b," and so on. The ability to use comparison operators, such as less than (<), is built into most programming languages.

Time Complexity in Sorting Algorithms (24.1.2)

How would you put the pages of your contacts book back in order? You could use many strategies to sort the contact pages. You could spread out the contact pages and look for patterns, or you could put a few pages in alphabetic order and then insert each other page in its correct place. The strategy a computer takes is determined by the sorting algorithm it uses. Each algorithm has advantages and disadvantages.

Picking up a contact page is considered one unit of work. Comparing one page to another page is also one unit of work. The total amount of work you must do to sort the contact pages depends on how many pages you have and the strategy you're using. The total amount of work a computer does to complete a task is known as the **runtime** of an algorithm. Runtimes are described in terms of the variable n, where n represents the number of items to sort. (In this case, "variable" refers to a letter or symbol that represents a value.)

Assume your sorting approach requires you to compare each contact page to every other contact page, as shown in **Figure 24-2**. If you have one stack of 10 items to sort and another stack of 100 items to sort, the overall time is greater for sorting the 100 items. The same is true for the runtime of an algorithm—it is the same proportionally compared to its input.

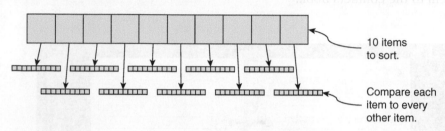

10 items to sort.

Compare each item to every other item.

Figure 24-2   Ten items with 10 work units per item

Q   What is the runtime of the strategy that requires you to look at every page as you sort each page?

A   If you have n contact pages, and each page requires n comparisons, the runtime is $n * n$, or n^2. Sorting 10 contact pages results in 10 * 10 = 100 comparisons, while sorting 100 contact pages results in 100 * 100 = 10,000 comparisons.

Recall that describing an algorithm's runtime in terms of a mathematical variable is known as **Big-O** runtime. The n^2 runtime is $O(n^2)$ in Big-O syntax. Big-O time complexity is focused only on the upper bounds of a program's runtime. If a full polynomial expression such as $n^3 + 2n^2 + n + 10$ describes a runtime, you would write the runtime as $O(n^3)$ instead of the full polynomial. **Figure 24-3** shows how, as n increases, the other parts of the polynomial equation matter less. In other words, n^2 and $n^2 + n$ are close in value as n increases.

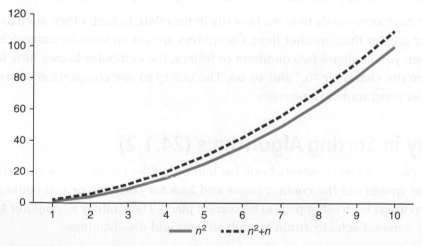

Figure 24-3   Comparing n^2 and $n^2 + n$

The runtime of an algorithm can be described in three ways: the best case, the worst case, and the average case. The **best-case runtime** is the fastest an algorithm can possibly run. Suppose you pick up all your contact pages, look through them once, and realize they're already in sorted order. This is the best-case scenario because no more work is needed. The **worst-case runtime** is the longest an algorithm can possibly run. Provided a sorting algorithm doesn't rely on luck to sort the items, eventually the algorithm stops; the worst-case runtime is how long that takes. The **average-case runtime** is how long the algorithm takes on average, given the unsorted items are shuffled an average amount.

Typically, the average case is the most useful information about a sorting algorithm. However, also knowing the worst-case and best-case runtimes and how those cases occur helps you select an algorithm. If you know that the worst case is likely to happen often when you use an algorithm, then you can select a different algorithm.

Sorting Properties (24.1.3, 24.1.4)

Other properties to consider when selecting a sorting algorithm include memory requirements and stability. Some sorting algorithms require extra memory. If memory is scarce or you are working with a very large data set, you need to conserve memory anywhere you can.

One way to conserve memory is to use an **in-place algorithm**, which uses zero extra memory. If you have 10 items to sort, an in-place algorithm uses only the memory already available and no more. An example of an in-place algorithm is a bubble sort, which you'll examine shortly.

Another property of an algorithm is whether it is stable. A **stable algorithm** means that the items to sort are not rearranged during the sorting process. For example, suppose two of the contacts you are sorting are named Sarah B. A stable algorithm sorts the two contacts after the "A" contacts and before the "C" contacts but keeps the two Sarah B contacts in their original order. If Sarah B with the birthday in June is listed before Sarah B with the birthday in August in your book, then after the sorting is complete, Sarah B with the June birthday still comes first.

Recall that a common algorithmic tactic for computers is to use a **divide-and-conquer technique**. This means the algorithm splits the problem, usually in half, to solve it. If you're looking for a contact whose last name starts with *J*, for example, you start in the middle of the contact book. If the middle page contains names starting with *M*, you know your contact is on a page in the previous part of the book. The divide-and-conquer approach has a runtime equivalent to how many times you can divide the total search space in half. If you have 16 contacts and check the middle, then you eliminate eight contacts you don't have to check. If you check the middle of the remaining contacts, you eliminate four, then two, and then one. Using a divide-and-conquer approach results in less work for you or the computer.

The "divide by 2 until you can't" approach can be mathematically expressed as a logarithm. The log base 2 of a number is how many times you can divide that number in half. In Big-O terms, it is $O(\log^2 n)$, or sometimes simplified to $O(\log n)$ because you are almost always dividing in half, so the 2 can be implied.

Of the many sorting algorithms you can use, this module introduces those that help you understand how runtimes come into play when you are using a program to sort data. The sorting algorithms covered are bubble sort, quicksort, and merge sort.

To test and visualize these sorting algorithms, you can import the Python `random` module and use `random.shuffle()` to mix up items in a list.

24.2 Bubble Sort

Defining the Bubble Sort Algorithm (24.2.1, 24.2.2)

Bubble sort is an easy-to-program but inefficient sorting algorithm. The bubble sort algorithm has two parts: a pass and a swap. A pass is a loop that traverses over all the items to sort. For each item, the loop checks to see if a swap needs to be made. A swap is made when the two neighboring items are out of order. Python can swap two variables with the syntax `x, y = y, x`.

If the number at the current index is greater than the number one spot to the right, then the numbers are out of order. The value in the current index is stored in a temporary variable, the number to the right is placed in the current index, and then the value originally in the current index is placed in the index one to the right.

The pseudocode for one pass in a bubble sort algorithm is as follows:

```
For all indexes in the list except for the last:

    If the adjacent numbers are out of order:

        Swap the two numbers
```

The description of indexes for the for-loop stops at one position less than the end position. This is different from a normal for-loop because a swap checks the current index and the index one to the right; this is not possible for the last index. Inside the loop body is the code for a swap.

Q   Why does the for-loop need to stop one index position earlier than normal for-loops?

A   All indexes need to be valid when used to access items in a list. The item "one place to the right" of an index would be `index + 1`. If the loop continued to the last index, then `index + 1` would be an invalid index.

One pass of a bubble sort visits each item in the list once and swaps it as necessary to arrange the items in ascending order (A–Z or 0–9). **Figure 24-4** shows one pass through an unsorted list.

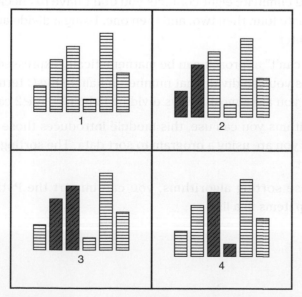

Figure 24-4   One pass of bubble sort (*Continued*)

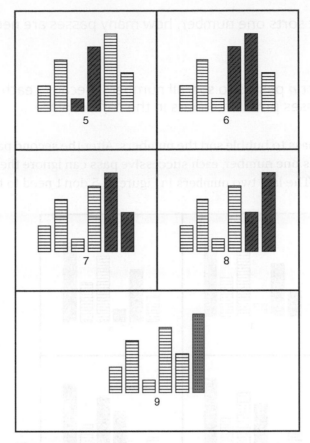

Figure 24-4   One pass of bubble sort

Each bar in Figure 24-4 represents a number, with the height of the bar corresponding to the number. The first pass of this bubble sort of 10 items takes nine steps:

- Step 1 shows the entire list of numbers as unsorted (white bars with horizontal stripes).
- Step 2 compares the two numbers highlighted in red with diagonal stripes. The two numbers are not out of order, so they are not swapped.
- The numbers in step 3 are also not out of order, so they are not swapped.
- Step 4 compares two numbers that are out of order.
- Step 5 swaps the numbers.
- Step 6 does not swap numbers because they are already in order.
- Step 7 compares two numbers that are out of order.
- Step 8 swaps the numbers.
- Step 9 shows the final list after one pass, with the rightmost number highlighted in blue.

Q What can you claim about the numbers in the last step of Figure 24-4? What has one pass achieved? What is true about the blue highlighted number?

A One pass has sorted ("bubbled") one item to the last index. The item that is sorted to the end is the largest value in the entire list of numbers, and therefore must be placed at the last index. One pass of bubble sort puts exactly one number in its sorted location.

Q If one pass of bubble sort sorts one number, how many passes are needed to sort all *n* numbers?

A Bubble sort needs at most *n* passes to sort all numbers. Because each pass puts one number in the correct place, *n* passes puts *n* numbers in the correct place.

Figure 24-5 shows a second pass to bubble sort the numbers. After the second pass, two numbers are sorted correctly. Because each pass sorts one number, each successive pass can ignore the sorted locations instead of checking all positions for swaps. The last two numbers in Figure 24-5 don't need to be compared.

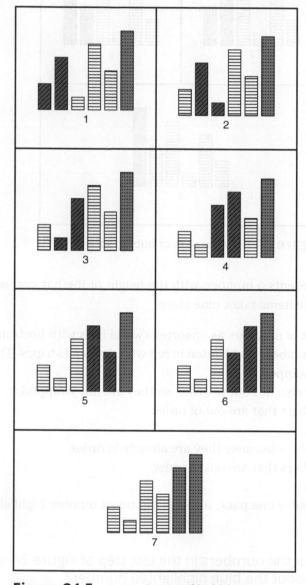

Figure 24-5 Second pass of bubble sort

Figure 24-6 shows the list after the remaining passes are completed.

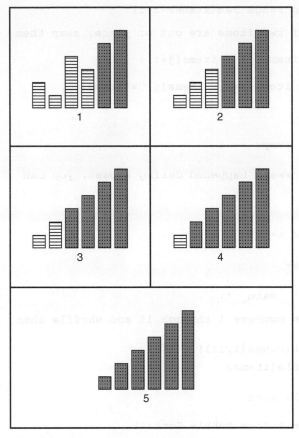

Figure 24-6   All passes of bubble sort

Although the items are sorted in step 4, the bubble sort continues to do a final comparison in step 5. You can program a bubble sort and stop as soon as the items are sorted. If no swaps are made during a pass, then the numbers are in sorted order and no more passes need to be made. **Figure 24-7** shows how to code a bubble sort.

```
import random

def bubble_sort(items):

    # Do n passes
    for i in range(len(items)):

        # Keep track of how many swaps for early exit
        swaps = 0

        # Look at each item except the last items that
would be sorted

        # (i items)
```

Figure 24-7   Bubble sort code (*Continued*)

```
        for j in range(len(items)-1-i):
            # If two items are out of place, swap them
            if items[j] > items[j+1]:
                items[j+1], items[j] = items[j],
items[j+1]

                swaps += 1
        # If no swaps happened during a pass, you can
stop early

        if swaps == 0:

            break

if __name__ == '__main__':
    # Create the numbers 1 through 11 and shuffle them
    items = list(range(1,11))
    random.shuffle(items)

    # Test bubble sort
    print("Items before Bubble Sort:")
    print(items)

    bubble_sort(items)

    print("Items after Bubble Sort:")
    print(items)
```

OUTPUT:
```
Items before Bubble Sort:
[10, 6, 3, 7, 1, 8, 5, 2, 9, 4]
Items after Bubble Sort:
[1, 2, 3, 4, 5, 6, 7, 8, 9, 10]
```

Your output may be different, due to the use of `random.shuffle()`.

Figure 24-7 Bubble sort code

Bubble Sort Properties (24.2.3, 24.2.4, 24.2.5, 24.2.6, 24.2.7)

When you program bubble sort to stop if it makes no swaps during a pass, then its best-case scenario is starting with an already sorted list. The program checks each item once on a pass, makes no swaps, and then stops. The best-case runtime of bubble sort of n items is $O(n)$.

The worst-case scenario is that the program needs to make all n passes to sort n items. If bubble sort does not stop early, then it has to make n passes, with each pass taking n comparisons. The worst-case runtime is $O(n^2)$. The worst-case scenario is triggered when the items are in reverse order, which is the opposite of the best case.

The average case is more difficult to figure out. Consider the "stopping early" part of bubble sort. To calculate an average of six numbers, for example, you add all the numbers and then divide by six. Bubble sort could stop early after one, two, or three passes, each equally likely assuming a random shuffle of the numbers. To find an average runtime, you can add the runtimes of all possible stopping-early situations, and then divide by n, as in the following:

$$\frac{1\ pass + 2\ passes + 3\ passes + \ldots + n\ passes}{n}$$

The summation pattern of $1 + 2 + 3$ up to some n is the following known summation:

$$1 + 2 + 3 + \ldots + n = \frac{n(n+1)}{2}$$

Apply this formula into the original summation and simplify the fractional on the right as follows:

$$\frac{\frac{n(n+1)}{2}}{n} = \frac{n+1}{2}\ passes$$

Each pass takes n work, so you rewrite the equation as follows:

$$n\left(\frac{n+1}{2}\right) = \frac{n^2 + n}{2}\ works$$

Remember that in Big-O notation, you can retain only the largest part of the polynomial and drop constant multipliers or divisors. As a result, even on average, bubble sort is still $O(n^2)$ work.

Bubble sort swaps items many times to order them, so it does not need additional memory to store items. Therefore, bubble sort is an in-place sort. Bubble sort swaps items only when they are strictly out of order. Because it does not swap identical items, bubble sort is also a stable algorithm.

Bubble sort is not the best option for most data sets. Instead, it is a simple and easy-to-program approach to sorting and provides a good introduction to how computers can sort items. If the data set is small enough that the runtime does not matter, then you could use bubble sort, though it is not the best sorting algorithm. If your data set is already mostly sorted, bubble sort has the best-case runtime of $O(n)$ because it can stop early. Otherwise, use a different sort.

24.3 Quicksort

Defining the Quicksort Algorithm (24.3.1, 24.3.2, 24.3.4)

Quicksort approximates an efficient sort. It relies on probabilities to ensure it generally performs well, despite having an undesirable worst-case scenario. Quicksort uses a divide-and-conquer approach. Like bubble sort, quicksort has two parts: a partitioning step and a recursive step.

In effect, the partitioning step picks a random item as a pivot, then figures out where that one item belongs in the sorted order. Imagine that to sort your unordered contact pages, you pick the page for your friend Megan Lee. You put Megan's page aside and create two piles: one for contact pages that should come before Megan's page, and another pile for contact pages that should come after Megan's page. After you have two piles, then you know that Megan's page goes between the two piles, as in **Figure 24-8**.

Figure 24-8   Divide and conquer to place a contact page

A quicksort algorithm selects the middle item as the pivot and then moves the pivot out of the way, as in **Figure 24-9**.

Figure 24-9   Quicksort pivot selection and movement

Next, to partition the values into two piles, the quicksort algorithm keeps track of a boundary index. The boundary index indicates that everything to the left is less than the pivot and everything to the right is greater than the pivot. The boundary index starts at the leftmost index and then iterates over all values other than the pivot (which is conveniently out of the way). If a value at an index is less than the pivot, it is moved to the boundary index and the boundary index is increased by one. If the value at an index is greater than the pivot, then both that value and the boundary index are left alone.

Figure 24-10 shows how the quicksort algorithm works with a boundary index. The boundary index is indicated by a black arrow below the number bars.

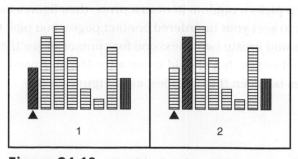

Figure 24-10   Partitioning for quicksort (*Continued*)

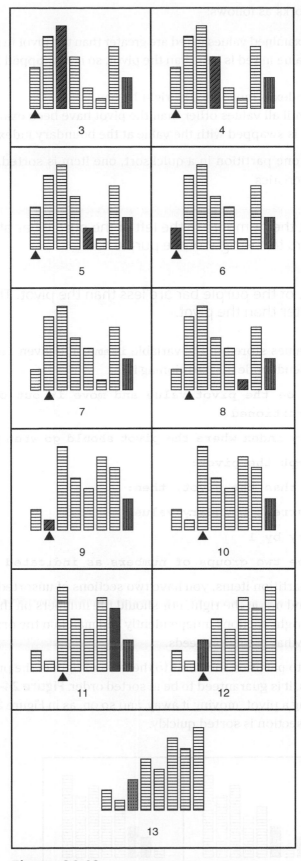

Figure 24-10   Partitioning for quicksort

The quicksort algorithm works as follows:

- In steps 1 through 4, the examined values in red are greater than the pivot in purple, so nothing is changed.
- In step 5, the examined value in red is less than the pivot, so it is swapped in step 6 with the value at the boundary index.
- In step 7, the boundary index is moved to the right by one.
- The process continues until all values other than the pivot have been examined.
- In the last step, the pivot is swapped with the value at the boundary index.

As with bubble sort, after one partition in a quicksort, one item is sorted. In addition, the left and right sections have different characteristics.

Q What can you say about the numbers to the left of the purple bar after step 13 in Figure 24-10? What about the numbers to the right of the purple bar?

A The numbers to the left of the purple bar are less than the pivot. The numbers to the right of the purple bar are greater than the pivot.

Given a list of numerical values stored in the variable `items`, and given `left` and `right` index variables indicating a sublist area, the pseudocode for partitioning is:

```
Pick the middle item to be the pivot value and move it out of the way, to the right
of the sublist to be partitioned

Keep track of the boundary index where the pivot should go when partitioning is finished

For all other items except the pivot:

    If the item is less than the pivot, then:

        Swap with the current boundary value

        Increase boundary by 1

Move pivot to between the two groups of numbers as indicated by the boundary index
```

After using a quicksort to partition items, you have two sections of unsorted numbers. The numbers to the left of the pivot should never end up on the right, nor should the numbers on the right end up to the left of the pivot. You can sort the left and right sections independently and maintain the order. You've created two smaller subproblems, which is exactly what recursion needs.

Quicksort recursively tries to partition the items to the left and right of the pivot until only one item remains to sort. If only one item remains, it is guaranteed to be in sorted order. **Figure 24-11** shows how quicksort works recursively on the left by picking a pivot, moving it away, and so on, as in Figure 24-10. Only two items remain to the left of the pivot, so the left section is sorted quickly.

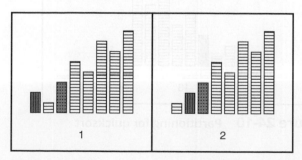

Figure 24-11   Recursive partitions in the left section (*Continued*)

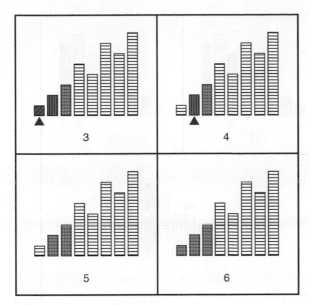

Figure 24-11   Recursive partitions in the left section

Figure 24-12 shows the progress continued with the numbers to the right of the pivot.

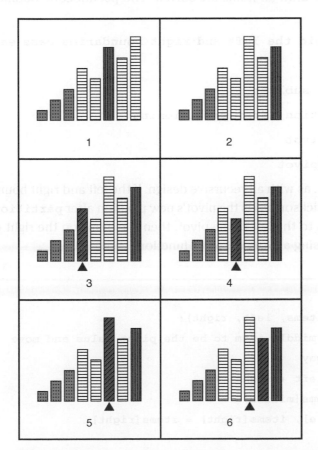

Figure 24-12   Recursive partitions in the right section
(*Continued*)

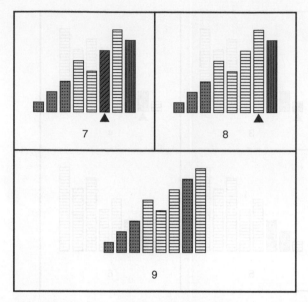

Figure 24-12 Recursive partitions in the right section

Quicksort continues this way until all items are sorted. The pseudocode outline for the recursive step in quicksort is:

```
Check for the base case: Did the left and right boundaries pass each other? Then stop.
Otherwise:
    Partition the current sublist
    Find the pivot's position after partitioning
    Recurse left of the pivot
    Recurse right of the pivot
```

First the base case is checked, as with all recursive design. If the left and right boundaries have crossed, then recursion stops. If it continues, quicksort finds the pivot's new position after **partition()** is called. The function is called recursively on the items to the left of the pivot, then the items on the right of the pivot. **Figure 24-13** shows the code for a quicksort using a **partition()** function.

```python
import random

def partition(items, left, right):
    # Pick the middle item to be the pivot value and move
it out of the way
    middle = (left + right) // 2
    pivot = items[middle]
    items[middle], items[right] = items[right],
items[middle]

    # Keep track of the boundary index
    boundary = left
```

Figure 24-13 Quicksort code (*Continued*)

```
        # Look at all other items
        for index in range(left, right):
            # If the item is less than the pivot, then the
boundary has to move
            if items[index] < pivot:

                # Swap with the current boundary value and
increase boundary by 1
                items[index], items[boundary] =
items[boundary], items[index]
                boundary += 1

        # Move pivot to between the two groups of numbers as
indicated by the boundary index
        items[right], items[boundary] = items[boundary],
items[right]

        # Return the boundary to inform quicksort how to
recurse
        return boundary

def quick_recurse(items, left, right):
    # Check for base case
    # Did the left and right boundaries pass each other?
Then stop.
    if left >= right:
        return

    # Find the pivot's position after partitioning
    pivot_position = partition(items, left, right)

    # Recurse left and right of pivot
    quick_recurse(items, left, pivot_position - 1)
    quick_recurse(items, pivot_position + 1, right)

def quick_sort(items):
    # Start the recursion to include all valid indexes
    # (length - 1 instead of length)
    quick_recurse(items, 0, len(items) - 1)

if __name__ == '__main__':
    # Create the numbers 1 through 11 and shuffle them
    items = list(range(1,11))
    random.shuffle(items)
```

Figure 24-13 Quicksort code (*Continued*)

```
    # Test quick sort
    print("Items before Quick Sort:")
    print(items)

    quick_sort(items)

    print("Items after Quick Sort:")
    print(items)
OUTPUT:
Items before Quick Sort:
[9, 4, 7, 6, 3, 8, 2, 5, 1, 10]
Items after Quick Sort:
[1, 2, 3, 4, 5, 6, 7, 8, 9, 10]
```

This may be different for you, due to the use of `random.shuffle()`.

Figure 24-13   Quicksort code

Quicksort Properties (24.3.3, 24.3.5, 24.3.6, 24.3.7, 24.3.8)

The runtime of a quicksort algorithm depends on how partitioning works out. Each partition requires O(n) work, where n is the total number of values to compare to the pivot. Even during recursive steps, considering all partitions at the same recursive depth requires O(n) work. See **Figure 24-14**.

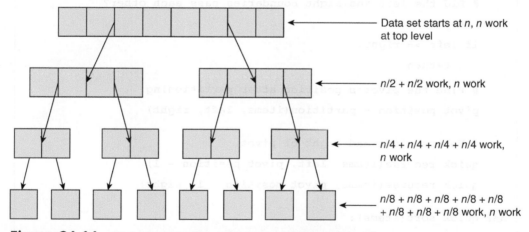

Data set starts at n, n work at top level

$n/2 + n/2$ work, n work

$n/4 + n/4 + n/4 + n/4$ work, n work

$n/8 + n/8 + n/8 + n/8 + n/8 + n/8 + n/8 + n/8$ work, n work

Figure 24-14   Dividing in half results in n work at each level

Quicksort's runtime is n multiplied by the number of times **partition()** is called. The best runtime is when quicksort evenly divides a list of numbers into two equal piles, similar to starting in the middle of a dictionary to find a word. In this case, each section of the list is about half the size of the starting list. Each section repeats the partition, which in the best case divides each section in half again.

Assuming that each partition is divided exactly in half, how many times can `partition()` be called? The log mathematical function represents the concept of "how many times can something be divided in half." Log base 2, also written as log2, or simplified to log in Big-O notation, returns the "how many times you can divide in half" value for a number, stopping when it reaches a value of 1 or lower. Log(2) is 1, log(4) is 2, log(8) is 3, and so on. Therefore, the best-case runtime for a quicksort algorithm is $O(n \log(n))$.

Quicksort has problems when it does not divide unsorted values equally. Consider the pivot picking: What happens if the largest value is selected as the pivot? What about when it recursively calls `partition()` and selects the second largest value as the pivot?

Q If quicksort picks each value in descending order from largest to smallest for its pivots, how many times is `partition()` called?

A Each partition would sort one value in the correct location, but leave most items unsorted to the left. This could happen *n* times.

If quicksort uses each value in descending order for its pivots, the runtime is $O(n^2)$. Despite this worst-case scenario requiring too much runtime (more than $O(n \log(n))$), quicksort is considered the best general-purpose sorting algorithm. This is because the worst case is unlikely. The probability that the worst pivot is picked at each `partition()` call is 1 in *n*, meaning that the chance of the worst-case scenario occurring is about $1/n^n$, which is very unlikely, especially if *n* is large. On average, quicksort has a runtime of $O(n \log(n))$.

Quicksort is an in-place algorithm because it uses no additional memory. However, quicksort is not stable, as moving pivots and partitioning values can swap the positions of identical values. In general, quicksort is a fast and memory-efficient sorting algorithm to use in any situation. You might consider a different algorithm if you need to guarantee the $O(n \log(n))$ runtime.

24.4 Merge Sort

Defining the Merge Sort Algorithm (24.4.1, 24.4.2, 24.4.4)

Merge sort is another divide-and-conquer algorithm. The two parts of merge sort are partitioning and merging. Effectively, the algorithm splits a list of numbers in half recursively so that the initial list is split into multiple sublists, each containing one element. The base case for the recursive call is when the list contains only one item, meaning that each such list is sorted. A function such as `merge()` is then used to merge pairs of sublists together so that the resulting list contains the elements of both in sorted order. The sublists are merged in this way until the initial list has been rebuilt, but now with its elements in sorted order. See **Figure 24-15**.

Splitting   Merging

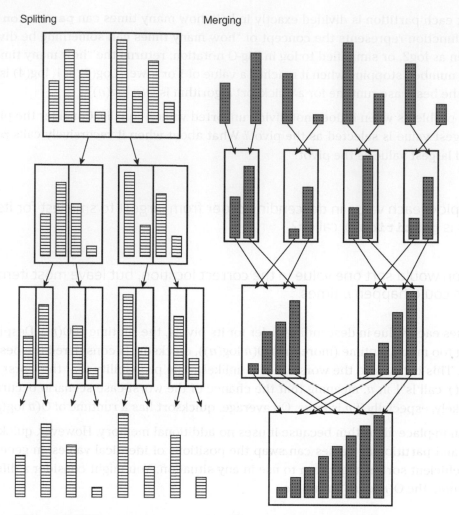

Figure 24-15   Merge sort always divides in half

With recursion, you first figure out when the base case occurs. In merge sort, the base case occurs when the list can no longer be split in half. The left and right indexes will mark the sublist. If the two indexes reach the same value, then only one value remains in the sublist. If the sublist has only one value, it can't be split anymore. The recursive merge sort pseudocode logic is as follows:

```
If the left and right indexes pass or equal each other, it is the base case and return
Otherwise:
    Find the middle
    Recurse left of the middle point
    Recurse right of the middle point
    Merge the sorted left and right sections
```

Assuming it works correctly, the **merge_recurse()** function splits the given list into two halves, indicated by the indexes from **left** to **middle** and from **middle + 1** to **right**. Next, you must use **merge()** to merge the two halves. Consider the lists in **Figure 24-16**.

Q Which number from the sorted `left` and `right` lists should be the first item in the `storage` result? How do you find it?

A After partitioning the list, the list is rebuilt by merging sublists so that the elements of the resulting list are sorted. Because of this, when merging two sub-lists, you know the two lists of numbers are already sorted. The smallest number (the number that must come first in the merged result) must be either the first number in `left` or the first number in `right`. You can move the smallest of those two numbers to the first index of `storage`. In Figure 24-16, the smallest number is 3.

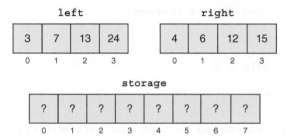

Figure 24-16   `left` and `right` can be merged into `storage`

The second number for the merged result is either the smallest remaining number from `left` or the smallest remaining number from `right`. After comparing those two numbers, 4 can be identified as the correct number to place in index 1 of `storage`. Next, 6, 7, 12, 13, 15, and then 24 are merged into `storage`. At each step, the code only needs to compare the smallest value from `left` with the smallest value from `right`. When one list is empty, no further comparisons are needed.

The pseudocode logic for merge sort is as follows:

```
Create enough storage to merge the two sections of the items list
Create three indexes to keep track of the place being accessed in the left section,
right section, and merged storage
While there is something in both the left and right sections:
    If the smallest number in the left section is smaller than the smallest number in
the right section:
        Copy it to the storage
    Otherwise copy the smallest number from the right section to storage
Check to see if there are any numbers in the left section and copy them to storage
Check to see if there are any numbers in the right section and copy them to storage
Copy the merged numbers back into the correct place in the items list
```

Figure 24-17 shows the code for a merge sort.

```
import random

def merge(items, left, middle, right):

    # Create enough storage to merge the two sections of
the items list
    storage = [None for x in range(right - left + 1)]

    # Three indexes to keep track of the place being ac-
cessed in the left section,
    # right section, and merged storage.
    left_index = left
    right_index = middle + 1
    storage_index = 0

    # While there is something in both the left and right
sections
    while left_index <= middle and right_index <= right:

        # If the left section has a number smaller than
the right section copy it to storage
        if items[left_index] <= items[right_index]:

            storage[storage_index] = items[left_index]
            storage_index += 1
            left_index += 1

        # Otherwise copy the number from the right sec-
tion to storage
        else:

            storage[storage_index] = items[right_index]
            storage_index += 1
            right_index += 1
```

Figure 24-17   Merge sort code (*Continued*)

```
            # Check to see if there are any numbers in the left
    section and copy them to storage
            # Numbers would only remain in the left section if
    the right section has no numbers
        while left_index <= middle:
            storage[storage_index] = items[left_index]
            storage_index += 1
            left_index += 1

            # Check to see if there are any numbers in the right
    section and copy them to storage
            # Numbers would only remain in the right section if
    the left section has no numbers
        while right_index <= right:
            storage[storage_index] = items[right_index]
            storage_index += 1
            right_index += 1

            # Copy the merged numbers back into the correct place
    in the items list
        for i in range(left, right + 1):
            items[i] = storage[i - left]

def merge_recurse(items, left, right):
    # If the left and right indexes pass each other, it
is the base case
    if left >= right:
        return
```

Figure 24-17   Merge sort code (*Continued*)

```
        # Find the middle

        middle = (left + right) // 2

        # Recurse left and right

        merge_recurse(items, left, middle)

        merge_recurse(items, middle + 1, right)

        # Merge the sorted left and right sections

        merge(items, left, middle, right)

def merge_sort(items):

    # Start the recursion with all valid indexes

    # (length - 1 instead of length)

    merge_recurse(items, 0, len(items)-1)

if __name__ == '__main__':

    # Create the numbers 1 through 11 and shuffle them

    items = list(range(1,11))

    random.shuffle(items)

    # Test quick sort

    print("Items before Merge Sort:")

    print(items)


    merge_sort(items)


    print("Items after Merge Sort:")

    print(items)
```

OUTPUT:

Items before Merge Sort:

[3, 6, 4, 9, 10, 1, 7, 8, 5, 2] ◄—— This may be different for you, due to the use of `random.shuffle()`.

Items after Merge Sort:

[1, 2, 3, 4, 5, 6, 7, 8, 9, 10]

Figure 24-17　Merge sort code

Merge Sort Properties (24.4.3, 24.4.5, 24.4.6, 24.4.7)

Unlike bubble sort, merge sort cannot stop early. The best, worst, and average runtimes for merge sort are the same because it always takes the same amount of work to complete the sort. Merging takes n work for the same reason partitioning did in Figure 24-14. Splitting a list of values in half takes $O(\log(n))$ work, as it does for quicksort. Merge sort always takes $O(n \log(n))$ work.

Merge sort needs extra memory for the recursive steps. Whenever you make a temporary copy of information in a computer, it requires more memory. Therefore, merge sort is not an in-place sorting algorithm. However, merge sort is stable because it favors the left side in ties in the merge code.

Merge sort guarantees the fast runtime of $O(n \log(n))$, which is important to consider when selecting a sorting algorithm. Merge sort, with a bit of modification, is also good for sorting linked lists. Recall that linked lists have poor random access, so sorts like quicksort are inefficient.

Summary

- Sorting algorithms try to efficiently organize items in a sorted order.
- You express the runtime of a sorting algorithm in terms of n, where n is the number of items to be sorted. Computer scientists use Big-O analysis, which includes only the largest part of a polynomial expression of n as the overall runtime. Algorithms can have best, worst, and average runtime cases.
- In-place algorithms do not need additional memory to run. Stable algorithms do not change the order of identical items, such as two contacts with the same name.
- A common tactic for computers is to divide and conquer, which tries to reduce the problem into two equal halves to make the runtime logarithmic.
- The bubble sort algorithm is easy to program but slow to run. Bubble sort uses passes to swap adjacent items if they are out of order, setting one item as sorted after one pass. After n passes, bubble sort is complete. Bubble sort can stop early if it makes a pass and no swaps occur. Bubble sort's runtimes are $O(n^2)$ for worst and average cases and $O(n)$ for the best case.
- The quicksort algorithm relies on probability to perform well. Quicksort uses partitioning and recursion to divide and conquer an unsorted list. Partitioning picks the middle item as a pivot and moves it out of the way. Quicksort then places all items less than the pivot on the left and all items greater than the pivot on the right before moving the pivot between these two groups. Quicksort next performs two smaller quicksorts on the left and right groups. Quicksort's runtimes are $O(n^2)$ in the worst case, which happens infrequently, and $O(n \log(n))$ for its average and best cases.
- The merge sort algorithm uses extra memory to guarantee a fast runtime. Merge sort splits an unsorted list in half to sort two smaller lists and then merges the two sorted results together. Merge sort has the same runtime for the best, worst, and average cases: $O(n \log(n))$.

Key Terms

average-case runtime	in-place algorithm	sorting algorithms
best-case runtime	merge sort	stable algorithm
Big-O	quicksort	worst-case runtime
bubble sort	runtime	
divide-and-conquer technique	sorting	

Module 25

Processor Architecture

Learning Objectives:

25.1 Processor Organization

25.1.1 List the key components of an integrated circuit.

25.1.2 Identify transistors as one of the most important components of an integrated circuit.

25.1.3 State Moore's law.

25.1.4 Analyze the current relevance of Moore's law.

25.1.5 Diagram the foundational computer components now referred to as von Neumann architecture.

25.1.6 Illustrate how von Neumann architecture maps to the components of a CPU.

25.1.7 Explain the function of a CPU.

25.1.8 Associate CPUs with microprocessors.

25.1.9 Classify a microprocessor as a type of integrated circuit.

25.2 Low-Level Instruction Sets

25.2.1 List the most common operations in a microprocessor instruction set.

25.2.2 Differentiate between CISC and RISC architectures.

25.2.3 Associate machine language with the instruction set of a CPU.

25.2.4 Differentiate between an op code and an operand.

25.2.5 Classify machine language as a low-level programming language.

25.2.6 List the characteristics of machine language.

25.2.7 Define assembly language as a low-level programming language with instructions that have a strong correspondence to machine language instructions.

25.2.8 Differentiate a machine language instruction from an assembly language instruction.

25.2.9 State advantages and disadvantages of low-level languages for creating software.

25.3 Microprocessor Operations

25.3.1 Identify the roles that registers, the instruction pointer, the ALU, and the control unit play in processing an instruction.

25.3.2 Identify the three phases of the instruction cycle: fetch, decode, execute.

25.3.3 Trace the execution of a short assembly language program that loads data into registers.

25.4 High-Level Programming Languages

25.4.1 Define the term "high-level programming language."

25.4.2 Provide examples of early high-level programming languages.

25.4.3 Provide examples of high-level programming languages that are currently in widespread use.

25.4.4 List the key characteristics of high-level programming languages.

25.4.5 List the advantages of high-level programming languages.

25.4.6 List the disadvantages of high-level programming languages.

25.1 Processor Organization

Integrated Circuits (25.1.1, 25.1.2)

The computing devices that you use come in all shapes and sizes. They include tiny smart sensors, digital watches and smartphones, portable tablets and laptops, desk-sized workstations, and room-sized server farms.

Regardless of the shape, size, function, or cost of these devices, they all contain integrated circuits. An **integrated circuit**, similar to those in **Figure 25-1**, contains microscopic electronic circuitry and components, such as transistors, capacitors, and resistors, etched onto a flat slice of silicon.

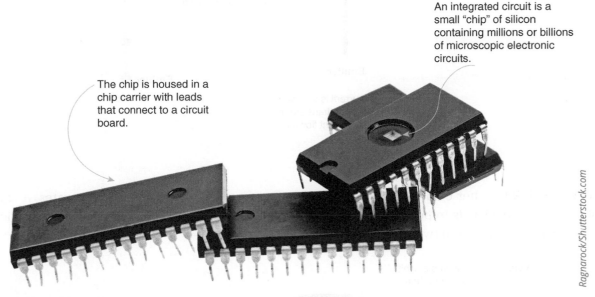

An integrated circuit is a small "chip" of silicon containing millions or billions of microscopic electronic circuits.

The chip is housed in a chip carrier with leads that connect to a circuit board.

Ragnarock/Shutterstock.com

Figure 25-1   Integrated circuits

Integrated circuits are sometimes referred to as "computer chips" or just "chips." Some integrated circuits are designed to carry out processing activities, while other chips are designed to handle memory, storage, input, or output.

A **transistor** is an electronic circuit that controls the flow of current. Transistors are one of the most important components in an integrated circuit because they perform two essential tasks:

Amplify signals. Transistors can make a signal stronger so that it has enough "juice" to travel through a circuit.

Act as switches. Transistors act as switches to control the flow of electronic signals. **Figure 25-2** shows how a transistor controls the flow of current from a collector to an emitter.

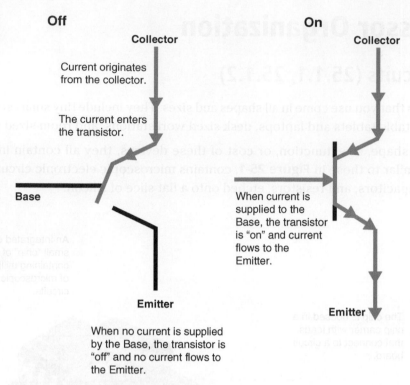

Off

Collector

Current originates from the collector.

The current enters the transistor.

Base

Emitter

When no current is supplied by the Base, the transistor is "off" and no current flows to the Emitter.

On

Collector

When current is supplied to the Base, the transistor is "on" and current flows to the Emitter.

Emitter

Figure 25-2 Transistors

Transistors link to other components, such as capacitors and resistors, to form logic gates. A **logic gate** manipulates electrical signals to perform logical and arithmetic operations. For example, the XOR logic gate in **Figure 25-3** can be used to add two bits.

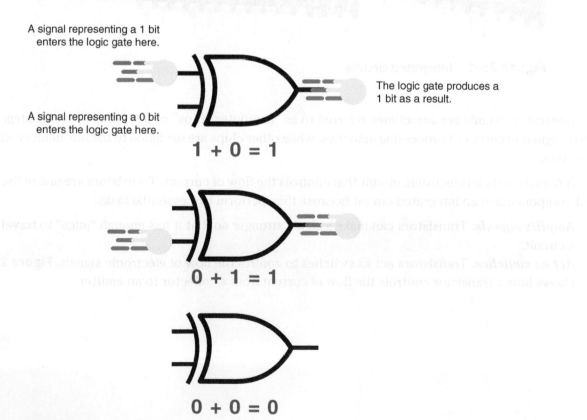

A signal representing a 1 bit enters the logic gate here.

A signal representing a 0 bit enters the logic gate here.

The logic gate produces a 1 bit as a result.

1 + 0 = 1

0 + 1 = 1

0 + 0 = 0

Figure 25-3 XOR logic gates

Q What will the logic gate in Figure 25-3 produce when both inputs are 1?

A It will produce 0. Remember that in binary, there is no "2." When this circuit gets 1 + 1 as the input, it has only one output, so it produces 0. A more complex set of circuits is needed for the operation that carries the 1 bit to complete the binary addition 1 + 1 = 10.

Logic gates can be used to achieve simple Boolean logic, similar to when you use the keywords `and` and `or`. AND gates combine 2 bits to be 1 if both bits are 1, and OR gates combine 2 bits to be 1 if either bit is 1.

Moore's Law (25.1.3, 25.1.4)

Today, integrated circuits contain billions of transistors and other microscopic components, but that wasn't always the case. The first integrated circuits invented in the 1950s had only a handful of components. Since then, the number of integrated circuit components, such as transistors, has doubled every two years. This phenomenon is based on a prediction made by an engineer named Gordon Moore and came to be known as **Moore's Law**.

Moore's law is important because as components become smaller, the distance between them decreases. Signals travel faster, which means that computers can operate with more speed.

Experts question whether Moore's Law will continue to hold true after 2025. With current silicon technology, miniaturization can only go so far. As electrons move faster through smaller and smaller circuits, they generate more and more heat. At some point, it may not be possible to prevent overheating.

CPUs (25.1.5, 25.1.6, 25.1.7, 25.1.8, 25.1.9)

A **computer** can be defined as a multipurpose device that accepts input, processes that input based on a stored set of instructions, and produces output. Abstracting away the details of circuit boards, silicon, integrated circuits, and transistors, **Figure 25-4** illustrates the core components of a computer.

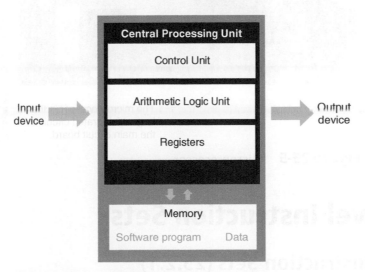

Figure 25-4   Core computer components of the von Neumann architecture

This abstract view of computers was first proposed by physicist John von Neumann in 1945. It is referred to as "von Neumann architecture" and still applies to the computers that you use today.

- Your computer's **central processing unit (CPU)** processes input and produces output according to the instructions supplied by a software program stored in memory.
- The CPU contains a control unit, an arithmetic logic unit, and registers.
- The **control unit** manages processing activities by collecting instructions and data, then sending them to the ALU.
- The **arithmetic logic unit (ALU)** performs arithmetic and logical operations.
- **Registers** are temporary areas for holding data.
- Computer programs and data are stored in memory where they can be accessed by the CPU.

The CPU for each of your digital devices is housed in a single integrated circuit called a microprocessor. A **microprocessor** is a complex integrated circuit containing billions of components designed to process data. On the circuit board of any digital device, you can easily identify the microprocessor because it is typically the largest integrated circuit. See **Figure 25-5**.

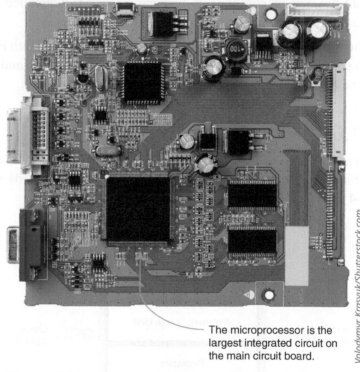

The microprocessor is the largest integrated circuit on the main circuit board.

Volodymyr Krasyuk/Shutterstock.com

Figure 25-5   Microprocessor

25.2 Low-Level Instruction Sets

Microprocessor Instruction Sets (25.2.1)

Computers perform billions of operations each second to accomplish relatively simple tasks, such as calculating your daily fitness activity or inserting an address in an email message. The reason for all this processing activity is that microprocessors are hard-wired to perform a limited set of operations for processing data.

A collection of preprogrammed microprocessor operations is called an **instruction set**. Each operation corresponds to a seemingly insignificant task, such as comparing two numbers to see if they are the same or moving a number from memory into the arithmetic logic unit. Here is a set of very basic microprocessor operations:

LOAD: Place a value in a CPU register.

MOVE: Copy a value from memory into a CPU register.

ADD: Add the values in two CPU registers.

SUBTRACT: Subtract the value in one CPU register from the value in another register.

MULTIPLY: Multiply the values in two CPU registers.

DIVIDE: Divide the value in one CPU register by the value in another register.

STORE: Copy a value from a CPU register into memory.

COMPARE: Check if the values in two registers are the same.

JUMP: Go to a different instruction.

END: Stop executing instructions.

Q Suppose the processor completed an ADD operation. Which operation would copy the result to a location in memory?

A The STORE operation would copy the result from a register and place it in memory.

RISC and CISC (25.2.2)

Although all microprocessors perform similar operations, the instruction set for the microprocessor in your phone is different from the instruction set for the microprocessor in a desktop computer optimized for gaming.

Some microprocessors have instruction sets consisting of hundreds of operations. These processors are classified as **complex instruction set computers (CISC)**. Microprocessors with small instruction sets are classified as **reduced instruction set computers (RISC)**.

As you might imagine, a RISC processor has to perform many more operations than a CISC processor to accomplish the same task, but each RISC instruction executes more quickly than a CISC instruction. **Figure 25-6** compares CISC and RISC.

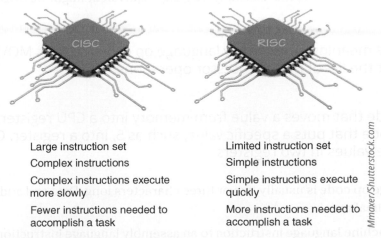

Large instruction set

Complex instructions

Complex instructions execute more slowly

Fewer instructions needed to accomplish a task

Limited instruction set

Simple instructions

Simple instructions execute quickly

More instructions needed to accomplish a task

Figure 25-6   RISC and CISC

In their simplicity, RISC processors use less power and require less cooling, which makes them ideal for mobile devices and high-performance servers. The ARM processor in your mobile phone is an example of a RISC processor.

The IBM PC that your grandmother used back in 1985 contained an x86 CISC processor, and the descendants of these microprocessors are still preferred for general-purpose computing devices such as desktop computers.

Machine Language (25.2.3, 25.2.4, 25.2.5, 25.2.6)

Each operation that a microprocessor performs has a corresponding instruction in **machine language** that is coded as a string of 0s and 1s. A machine language instruction has an **op code** that specifies an operation, such as load, add, move, or compare.

A machine language instruction can also have one or more **operands** that specify the data to process, its location in memory, or its destination in a register. The long strings of 0s and 1s in **Figure 25-7** contain an op code and operands that instruct the processor to load 5 into Register 1.

Op code	Operands	
10000101	00000101	00000001
LOAD	5	Register 1

Figure 25-7   Op codes and operands in machine language instructions

Machine language is classified as a **low-level programming language** because it provides very little abstraction from the binary operation of computer circuits. If you were programming in machine language, you would have to understand many details about microprocessor operations and remember the op codes corresponding to long sequences of 0s and 1s.

Assembly Language (25.2.7, 25.2.8, 25.2.9)

To avoid dealing with perplexing strings of 0s and 1s, programmers turned to **assembly language**, which uses text abbreviations for op codes that directly correspond to the op codes of machine language. Where a machine language op code might be 0000 0000, the assembly language equivalent might be ADD.

Q Can you guess the meaning of assembly language op codes such as MOV, LDI, and CMP? Hint: Look back at the list of microprocessor operations.

A MOV is the op code that moves a value from memory into a CPU register. LDI is the "load immediate" op code that puts a specific value, such as 5, into a register. CMP is the op code for comparing the values in two registers.

An assembly language op code is usually two or three characters long. Data and addresses used as operands are specified as hexadecimal numbers.

By comparing the machine language instruction to an assembly language instruction in **Figure 25-8**, you can see how the op codes and operands correspond.

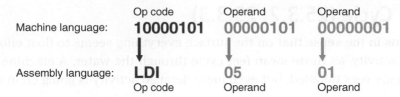

Figure 25-8   Compare a machine language instruction to its assembly language equivalent

If your interests lean toward programming controllers, device drivers, and operating systems, then you'll need assembly language skills. With assembly language, you can work directly with registers and memory addresses to optimize code so that it runs swiftly and efficiently. Hackers use lower-level languages such as assembly language to create and modify viruses. To thwart hackers, assembly language is also an important tool for security professionals.

25.3 Microprocessor Operations

Processing an Instruction (25.3.1)

In von Neumann's CPU architecture, a control unit and ALU work together to process instructions. The control unit has an **instruction register** that holds the instruction being processed.

The ALU has registers that hold the data being processed and the data that is produced. **Figure 25-9** shows how the CPU sets up an instruction to add the contents of two registers.

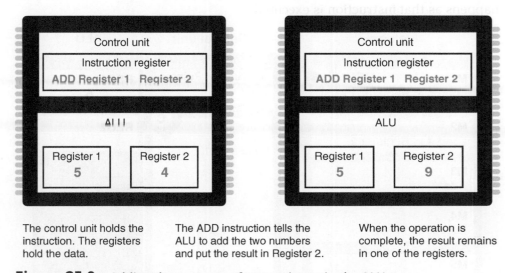

The control unit holds the instruction. The registers hold the data.

The ADD instruction tells the ALU to add the two numbers and put the result in Register 2.

When the operation is complete, the result remains in one of the registers.

Figure 25-9   Adding the contents of two registers in the ALU

The Instruction Cycle (25.3.2, 25.3.3)

Computers are like swans in the sense that on the surface everything seems to float effortlessly, but under the surface there is lots of activity, as those swan feet cycle through the water. A machine language or assembly language instruction seems very detailed, but even more detailed activity is going on in the microprocessor.

The execution of a machine language or assembly language instruction happens in three phases referred to as an **instruction cycle**, shown in **Figure 25-10**.

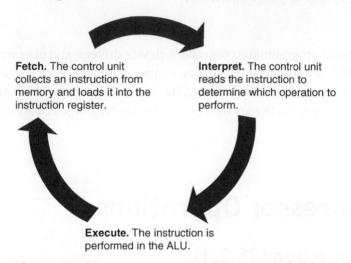

Fetch. The control unit collects an instruction from memory and loads it into the instruction register.

Interpret. The control unit reads the instruction to determine which operation to perform.

Execute. The instruction is performed in the ALU.

Figure 25-10   The instruction cycle

The machine language instructions for a program are held in a sequence of memory locations. To keep track of the instruction being executed, the control unit uses an **instruction pointer**. When the program begins, the instruction pointer holds the memory address of the first instruction. At the end of the instruction cycle, the instruction pointer is updated to point to the memory location that holds the next instruction.

Suppose a program begins with an instruction to load the value 5 into Register 1 of the ALU. **Figure 25-11** illustrates what happens as that instruction is executed.

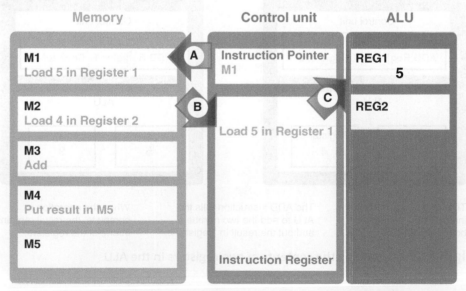

(A) The instruction pointer indicates M1 as the memory location of the first instruction.
(B) The control unit fetches the instruction and copies it to the instruction register.
(C) The instruction is interpreted and then executed by placing 5 in Register 1 of the ALU.
    Then the instruction pointer advances to M2 to fetch the next instruction.

Figure 25-11   Adding the contents of two registers in the CPU

Q Now that you know the basics of the instruction cycle, trace through the short assembly language program in **Figure 25-12**. What is the result of execution? Where does that result end up? What is in the instruction pointer? What is in the instruction register?

A The value 9 is in Register 2 and at memory location M5. The instruction pointer holds M5. The instruction register contains the last instruction: "Move Register 2 to M5."

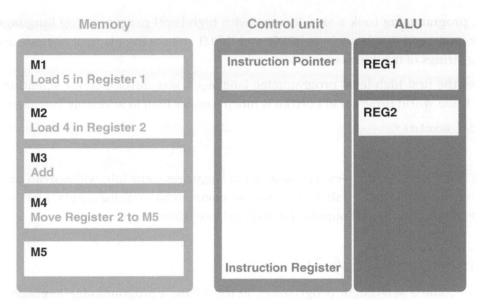

Figure 25-12   What is the result of executing the instructions in memory?

25.4 High-Level Programming Languages

Evolution (25.4.1, 25.4.2)

If you were a programmer working with early prototype computers in the 1940s, you might have struggled with machine languages and assembly languages. The first program that every programmer learns to write is "Hello World," a program that—you guessed it—displays or prints the message "Hello World!"

In assembly language, the Hello World program looks rather cryptic:

```
Dosseg

.model small

.stack 100h

.data

hello_message db 'Hello World!',0dh,0ah,'$'

.code

main proc

mov ax,@data

mov ds,ax

mov ah,9
```

```
mov dx,offset hello_message
int 21h
mov ax,4C00h
int 21h
main endp
end main
```

By the 1950s, programming took a step forward with **high-level programming languages** that provided easy-to-remember command words such as PRINT and INPUT to take the place of obscure assembly language op codes and long strings of machine language 0s and 1s.

Fortran, one of the first high-level programming languages, was developed for scientific and engineering applications. The Hello World program in Fortran is much simpler than in assembly language:

```
PRINT *, "Hello World!"
END
```

In the Fortran era, two other high-level programming languages came into widespread use. COBOL became the language for business data processing in banks and commercial establishments. LISP presented a unique approach to programming and is still popular for artificial intelligence applications.

Teaching Languages (25.4.2)

If you wanted to become a self-taught programmer in the 1980s, a programming language called BASIC was included with every personal computer. In BASIC, each instruction is numbered, usually beginning with line 100. The Hello World program in BASIC looks like this:

```
100 PRINT "Hello World!"
```

At universities, the prevailing teaching language was Pascal. In elementary schools, students used Logo to program an on-screen turtle robot to create geometric patterns, as shown in **Figure 25-13**.

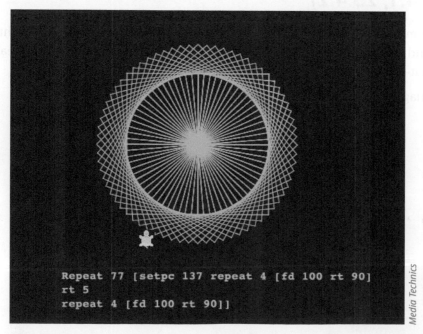

Figure 25-13 Logo program

The C Family (25.4.2, 25.4.3)

In the 1970s, the C programming language was an important development in high-level languages. Originally designed for creating utilities and operating systems, C became the parent for several of today's popular languages, such as C++, C#, and Objective-C.

C and its derivatives use extensive punctuation, such as parentheses, curly brackets, and semicolons, to ensure that each instruction is clear and unambiguous. The following program is written in C++ and prints the message **"Hello World!"**.

```
#include <iostream>

using namespace std;

int main()

{

    cout << "Hello World!" << endl;

    return 0;

}
```

Web Programming Languages (25.4.3)

With the popularity of the web in the 1990s came languages such as JavaScript, Java, Python, Ruby, and PHP. If you are interested in creating online apps, these programming languages are in demand.

In Java, the Hello World program looks like this:

```
public class Hello {

    public static void main(String[] args) {

        System.out.println("Hello World!");

    }

}
```

Q What are some similarities that you recognize between C and Java?

A Both C and Java make extensive use of punctuation, such as curly brackets and semicolons.

The Python programming language was created by a team of programmers whose philosophy was "simple is better than complex." The language has the simplicity of BASIC with minimal punctuation. You are familiar with how to create the Hello World! program in Python with a single line:

```
print ("Hello World!")
```

New programming languages are still being developed. In 2014, Apple introduced the Swift programming language, designed for creating applications that run on iPhones, iPads, iMacs, and other Apple devices.

Characteristics (25.4.4)

From the Hello World examples, you can see that high-level programming languages use familiar words to formulate sentence-like instructions, such as `print("Hello World!")`. Like natural languages, these programming languages also have basic grammar rules for structure and punctuation.

For computer scientists, the key characteristic of a high-level language is the level of abstraction that differentiates it from machine language. Few elements of a high-level language have a one-to-one correspondence to machine language instructions. Instead, a single high-level language command such as `print()` takes the place of a whole list of detailed assembly or machine language op codes. See **Figure 25-14**.

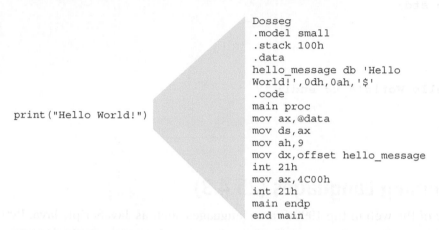

```
                               Dosseg
                               .model small
                               .stack 100h
                               .data
                               hello_message db 'Hello
                               World!',0dh,0ah,'$'
                               .code
                               main proc
   print("Hello World!")       mov ax,@data
                               mov ds,ax
                               mov ah,9
                               mov dx,offset hello_message
                               int 21h
                               mov ax,4C00h
                               int 21h
                               main endp
                               end main
```

Figure 25-14   A single instruction in a high-level programming language requires multiple instructions in a low-level language

The abstraction of high-level languages decouples programmers from the digital and binary aspects of physical devices. Using a high-level language, you rarely have to deal directly with registers within the microprocessor or addresses within RAM chips. When coding a print command, you don't need to know which display device or printer will be used. Your programming language manages the details of arranging pixels on a screen display or controlling the printer ink dispenser.

Advantages and Disadvantages (25.4.5, 25.4.6)

As you might expect, high-level languages have many advantages over low-level languages, but they have a few disadvantages, too. Here are the significant pros and cons.

+ ***Easy to understand.*** Imagine having to memorize strings of 0s and 1s that correspond to op codes. Commands such as `print`, `continue`, `return`, and `try` are easy to learn and remember. The sentence-like structure of high-level code makes it easy to understand and share with other programmers on your team.

+ ***Error detection.*** In 1947 a programmer named Grace Hopper was troubleshooting a computer error and discovered a moth in one of the relay mechanisms. Removing the "bug" got the computer running properly. Since then, coding errors have been referred to as "bugs," and correcting those errors is called debugging. Programs written in high-level programming languages are relatively easy to debug because they use command words and punctuation similar to natural languages.

+ ***Machine independent.*** The programs that you code using a high-level programming language are portable. You can write a program on one computer and distribute it for use on other computers.

— *Require translation.* Programs written in high-level languages cannot be directly executed by a microprocessor. The program code has to be converted into machine language. The conversion requires an extra step when coding or when the program runs.

— *Abstraction penalty.* Because high-level programming languages are separated from machine code by levels of abstraction, they may not be able to optimize processing tasks by taking advantage of low-level, machine-specific shortcuts. Programs coded in high-level languages typically run somewhat slower and require more memory than their machine-language or assembly-language counterparts.

Summary

- A computer can be defined as a multipurpose device that accepts input, processes that input based on a stored set of instructions, and produces output.
- The key components of today's computers are integrated circuits, which contain millions or billions of microscopic transistors, resistors, capacitors, and circuitry. Transistors are important because they amplify signals, act as switches, and form logic gates.
- Moore's Law states that the number of components manufactured in integrated circuits doubles every two years, producing faster computing devices.
- Modern computers are based on von Neumann architecture with a central processing unit that contains a control unit, an arithmetic logic unit, and registers. These elements are integrated into microprocessors that perform the operations contained in an instruction set.
- Microprocessors can be programmed using a low-level machine language and assembly language or a high-level programming language.
- Low-level programming language statements consist of an op code and an operand that correspond directly to the microprocessor's instruction set.
- High-level programming languages, such as BASIC, C++, Java, and Python, use natural language commands and offer a level of abstraction that distances programmers from the detailed instruction set.

Key Terms

arithmetic logic unit (ALU)	instruction cycle	microprocessor
assembly language	instruction pointer	Moore's Law
central processing unit (CPU)	instruction register	op code
complex instruction set computers (CISC)	instruction set	operands
computer	integrated circuit	reduced instruction set computers (RISC)
control unit	logic gate	registers
high-level programming languages	low-level programming language	transistor
	machine language	

Module
26

Data Representation

Learning Objectives:

26.3.11 Identify which notation has better readability: binary or hexadecimal.

26.4   ASCII and Unicode

26.4.1 Define the term "ASCII" as a standard method of representing non-numeric data using seven bits.

26.4.2 Understand why 7-bit ASCII can represent 128 characters.

26.4.3 Use an ASCII table to find the binary or decimal representation of a letter or symbol.

26.4.4 Define "control characters" as non-printable data such as line feeds or backspaces.

26.4.5 Identify Extended ASCII as a notation for representing 256 characters.

26.4.6 Define the term "Unicode" as the use of multiple bytes to represent characters included in most modern languages.

26.4.7 Associate UTF-8 with Unicode.

26.5   Memory Allocation

26.5.1 Explain the difference between memory and storage.

26.5.2 Differentiate between online and offline storage.

26.5.3 Explain the term "volatile" in the context of computer memory.

26.5.4 Explain the difference between read-only and read-write.

26.5.5 Classify memory and storage devices according to their technology: solidstate, magnetic, or optical.

26.5.6 Differentiate bits, bytes, and words.

26.5.7 Identify RAM as the type of memory used to temporarily hold the operating system, programs that are being executed, and the data needed by those programs.

26.5.8 Explain that memory consists of multiple storage locations that typically each hold one byte of data.

26.5.9 Define a "memory address" as a unique identifier for a memory location, usually represented by a hexadecimal number such as 0x9FFF.

26.1 Bits and Bytes

Digital Data (26.1.1, 26.1.2)

Q Here's a puzzler. What do each of the diagrams in **Figure 26-1** have in common?

A Each diagram is a digital, binary pair that represents two unique states. For example, an uncharged circuit is one state. A charged circuit is the other state.

Surprisingly, any of the digital, binary pairs in Figure 26-1 can be used to represent all kinds of data, such as letters, symbols, numbers, and even colors.

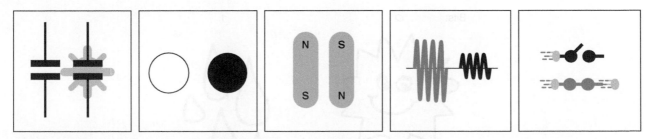

Figure 26-1   What do these diagrams have in common?

Digital data is discrete and chunky. The data shown by a digital clock can be 10:52 or 10:53, but the clock can't show the split seconds in between. In contrast, **analog data** is continuous. For example, the second hand on an analog clock sweeps through a continuous range of time.

Computers store and manipulate many types of digital data, such as words, numbers, symbols, colors, sounds, images, and video. That data is processed within electronic circuits, sent as wired and wireless signals all over the world, stored as microscopic dots on CDs, saved as magnetic particles on hard drives, and held in electronic gates within flash drives.

Data representation refers to the way data is abstracted or modeled. When data is abstracted into a series of units that can have one of two states, the data representation is **binary**. The exact mechanism for data representation may vary from one device to another but, as shown in **Figure 26-2**, the data retains two important characteristics: It is digital and it is binary.

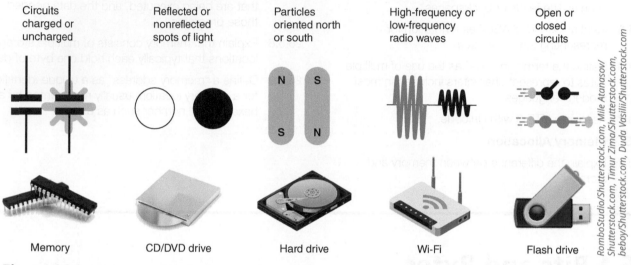

Circuits charged or uncharged	Reflected or nonreflected spots of light	Particles oriented north or south	High-frequency or low-frequency radio waves	Open or closed circuits
Memory	CD/DVD drive	Hard drive	Wi-Fi	Flash drive

RomboStudio/Shutterstock.com, Mile Atanasov/Shutterstock.com, Timur Zima/Shutterstock.com, beboy/Shutterstock.com, Duda Vasilii/Shutterstock.com

Figure 26-2   Computer data is digital and it is binary

Bits (26.1.3, 26.1.4, 26.1.5, 26.1.6, 26.1.7, 26.1.8, 26.1.9)

Although computers might use on/off signals, frequencies, colored dots, or magnetized particles to physically represent data, you can envision those two states as the **binary digits** 0 and 1.

A binary digit is commonly referred to as a **bit**, abbreviated as a lowercase *b*. A bit is the smallest unit of data manipulated by a digital device.

A single bit can be either a 0 or 1—that's two possibilities. A single bit could represent true or it could represent false. Or, a single bit could represent yes or no. As shown in **Figure 26-3**, one bit can be used to represent either of two units of information.

Bits: O   1

Sunny   Rainy

Figure 26-3   One bit can represent two units
of information

To represent any one of four pieces of information, you need two bits. To represent any one of eight pieces of information, you need three bits. **Figure 26-4** provides examples.

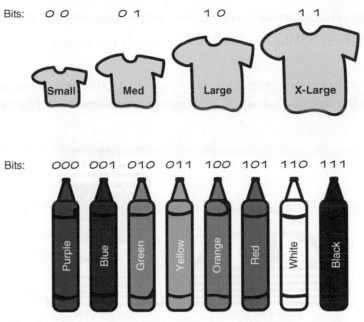

Figure 26-4   Two bits can represent four different units of information, and three bits can represent eight units of information

One bit: 2 possible units of information. Two bits: 4 possible units of information. Three bits: 8 possible units of information. You might be noticing a pattern. Each additional bit doubles the amount of information that can be represented.

Bits are based on the binary number system and correspond to powers of 2. To figure out how many units of information can be represented by any number of bits, simply plug in the number as the power of 2. One bit represents 2^1 units of information. For two bits, it is 2^2, for three bits it is 2^3.

Q How many different units of information can be represented using 5 bits?

A Five bits can be used to represent 32 different units of information. You can use a scientific or programming calculator to find the value of 2^5 or multiply 2 five times: $2 \times 2 \times 2 \times 2 \times 2$.

Bytes (26.1.10, 26.1.11, 26.1.12, 26.1.13, 26.1.14, 26.1.15)

Computers work with groups of eight bits called a **byte**. Here are the must-know basics about bytes:

- Byte is abbreviated as an uppercase *B*.
- Bytes are sometimes called "octets."
- 00001010 is a byte of data.
- Each byte can represent one of 2^8, or 256, different units of data.
- A byte of data is commonly used to store text: a letter, symbol, or punctuation mark.

Bits and bytes are used to measure transmission speed and storage capacity of digital devices. Bits for speed, bytes for capacity. These measurements can get quite large. For example, the speed of an Internet connection might be clocked at more than 50 million bits per second. A flash drive might store several billion bytes of data.

Such large numbers are often expressed using terms such as megabits and gigabytes.

The tricky thing about these numbers is that they commonly use **binary measurements** based on powers of 2, not powers of 10.

For example, in the world of computers, a kilo is 2^{10}, which is 1,024. But in everyday life, a kilo is just 1,000 because it is derived from the decimal value 10^3. You can see the difference in **Figure 26-5**.

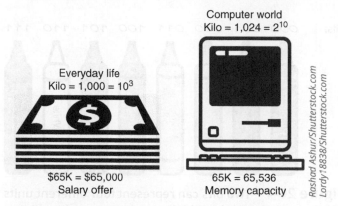

Figure 26-5   Measurements that relate to computers are based on powers of 2

Q Suppose your Visa chip card has 2K memory capacity. How many bytes of data can your card store?

A 2K is 1,024 × 2, which equals 2,048 bytes.

Figure 26-6 lists commonly used prefixes and abbreviations for binary measurements of bits and bytes.

Prefix	Abbreviation for bits	Abbreviation for bytes	Number of bits or bytes
Kilo	Kb	KB	$2^{10} = 1,024$
Mega	Mb	MB	$2^{20} = 1,048,576$
Giga	Gb	GB	$2^{30} = 1,073,741,824$
Tera	Tb	TB	$2^{40} = 1,099,511,627,776$
Peta	Pb	PB	$2^{50} = 1,125,899,906,842,624$
Exa	Eb	EB	$2^{60} = 1,152,921,504,606,846,976$
Zetta	Zb	ZB	$2^{70} = 1,180,591,620,717,411,303,424$
Yotta	Yb	YB	$2^{80} = 1,208,925,819,614,629,174,706,176$

Figure 26-6   Binary measurements for bits and bytes

26.2 Binary

Binary Numbers (26.2.1, 26.2.2)

Computers were originally designed to process numerical data, and today's computers still carry out many tasks involving calculations. Because computers are electronic devices, they manipulate bits: 1s and 0s. The **binary number system** also uses 1s and 0s to represent numbers, so this system is used to represent numbers in most digital devices.

In binary notation, numbers are represented using only the digits 0 and 1. This system is sometimes called **base-2** because it uses two digits.

When counting in binary, begin with 0. The next number is 1. But what comes next? There is no "2" digit. To make the next number, you need to use more than one digit. The number two is represented by 10, pronounced "one zero." The 1 stands for "one quantity of two" and the 0 stands for "no ones." It's the same logic you're familiar with when you use the decimal system for numbers, but with different quantities. The number 23 in decimal ("twenty-three") means "three ones" and "two tens."

Counting in binary goes like this (**Figure 26-7**):

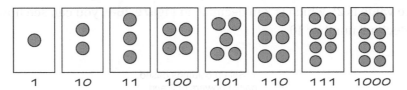

| 1 | 10 | 11 | 100 | 101 | 110 | 111 | 1000 |

Figure 26-7   Counting in binary

Q After 1000, what's the next binary number?

A The next binary number is 1001.

In computer memory, binary numbers are stored in microscopic electronic circuits called **capacitors**. The symbol for a capacitor looks like the letter *T* and its upside-down reflection. A charged capacitor represents a 1 bit. An uncharged capacitor represents a 0 bit. **Figure 26-8** illustrates a series of capacitors that represent the binary number 00000101.

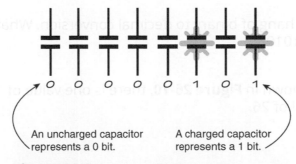

0 0 0 0 0 1 0 1

An uncharged capacitor represents a 0 bit.

A charged capacitor represents a 1 bit.

Figure 26-8   Computer memory uses capacitors to represent binary data

It is usually easy to identify a binary number because it is typically a long string of 1s and 0s. However, a number such as 101 could mean five in binary or one hundred and one in decimal. To differentiate, binary numbers can be written using any of the following notations:

- 101b
- 101_2
- %101
- 0b101
- 101_{binary}

An additional clue that a number is binary are zeros in the left place values. Binary numbers are often written as bytes containing 8 bits. A binary number such as 101 could be written as 00000101. The leftmost zeros do not add any value to the number and may be omitted.

Binary to Decimal (26.2.3)

Programmers are expected to understand how binary can be used to represent prices, miles, wages, quantities, and other numbers that computers manipulate for everyday tasks. Suppose a computer stores 1010 for the number of penguins in a zoo. That number is more understandable when converted into our familiar decimal system.

In the binary number system, each place value is a power of 2. The rightmost place value is 2^0, which is 1 in decimal. The next place value is 2^1, which is 2 in decimal. In **Figure 26-9**, you can see how to convert the binary number 1010 into the decimal number 10.

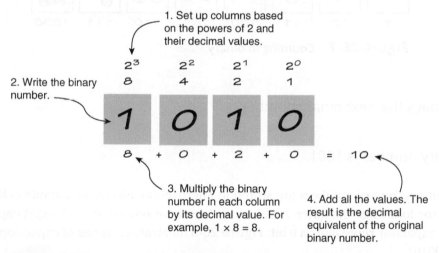

Figure 26-9   Converting binary to decimal

Q Let's see if you have the hang of binary to decimal conversion. What is the decimal equivalent of the binary number 11010?

A Here's the answer. As shown in **Figure 26-10**, there is one value of 16 plus one value of 8 and one value of 2 for a total of 26.

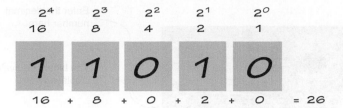

2^4 2^3 2^2 2^1 2^0
16   8   4   2   1

1   1   0   1   0

16 + 8 + 0 + 2 + 0 = 26

Figure 26-10   11010 is the binary representation of 26

Decimal to Binary (26.2.4)

A palindrome is a string (a word or number) that reads the same backward as forward. The word *kayak* is a palindrome. Numbers can also be palindromes. The number 15351 is a palindrome with a secret. To discover that secret, you'll need to know how to convert decimal numbers to binary.

Converting decimal numbers to binary is easy if you use a division trick. The algorithm goes like this:

Write down the decimal number.
Divide the decimal number by 2.
If there is a remainder, write 1 in the remainder column.
If there is no remainder, write 0 in the remainder column.
Continue dividing until you reach 0.
Read up the remainder column for the binary number.

Figure 26-11 shows how this algorithm works to convert 18 into binary.

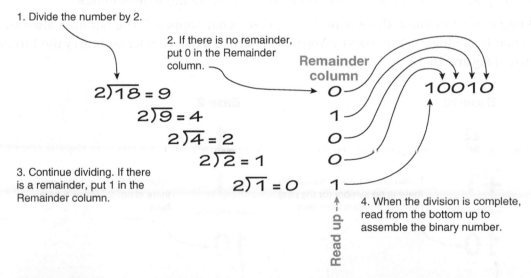

1. Divide the number by 2.

2. If there is no remainder, put 0 in the Remainder column.

3. Continue dividing. If there is a remainder, put 1 in the Remainder column.

Remainder column

$2\overline{)18} = 9$ 0

$2\overline{)9} = 4$ 1

$2\overline{)4} = 2$ 0

$2\overline{)2} = 1$ 0

$2\overline{)1} = 0$ 1

10010

Read up →

4. When the division is complete, read from the bottom up to assemble the binary number.

Figure 26-11   Converting a decimal number to binary requires repeated division by 2

Converting the palindrome 15351 into binary involves lots of division operations. You can use a programmer's calculator like the one in **Figure 26-12** to find the result.

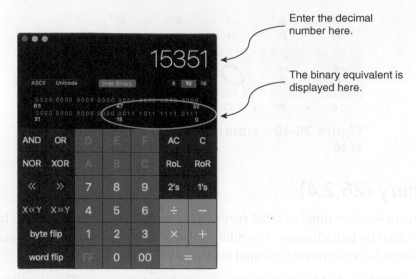

Figure 26-12   Use a scientific or programmer calculator for decimal to binary conversions

The binary for 15351 is 11101111110111. Both the decimal and binary numbers are palindromes! That's the secret of 15351.

Binary Addition (26.2.5)

Computers perform arithmetic operations based on binary numbers. Understanding binary addition can give you insight into digital arithmetic and the way computers represent negative numbers.

When adding 1 + 1 in binary, there is no "2" digit. So, what happens? The addition algorithm for binary numbers is similar to adding 9 + 1 in base-10. You write a zero as a placeholder and carry the 1 to the next place value, as shown in **Figure 26-13**.

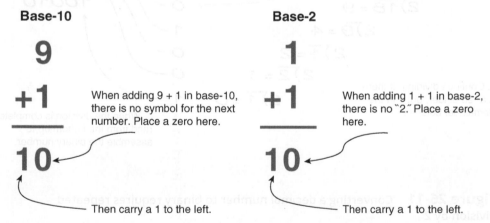

Figure 26-13   The algorithm for binary addition is similar to using a "carry" in base-10

Q **Figure 26-14** shows a few more examples of binary addition. Which are correct and which are not?

A The third sum is not correct. 1011 + 10 = 10101.

$$1 \quad\quad 101 \quad\quad 1011 \quad\quad 1111$$
$$+\ 11 \quad +\ 10 \quad\quad +\ 10 \quad\quad +\ 111$$
$$\overline{100} \quad \overline{111} \quad \overline{1001} \quad \overline{10110}$$

Figure 26-14   Examples of binary addition

Negative Numbers (26.2.6, 26.2.7, 26.2.8)

Computers have to deal with negative numbers, but there is no electronic negative symbol. Computers represent negative numbers in three ways:

- Signed magnitude
- One's complement
- Two's complement

Signed magnitude uses the leftmost bit to indicate whether a number is positive or negative. If that bit is 0, the number is positive. If that bit is 1, the number is negative.

Q Which of these numbers is negative?

00001100
10001100

A The first number begins with a 0, so it is positive: $12_{decimal}$. The second number is negative: $-12_{decimal}$.

The **one's complement** of a binary number is another binary number that, when added to the original number, produces all 1 bits. To produce the one's complement, simply flip the bits as shown in **Figure 26-15**.

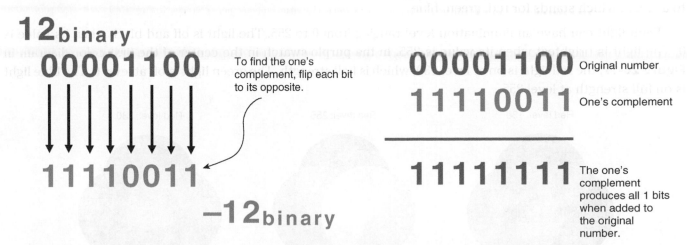

Figure 26-15   The one's complement of a binary number can represent its negative

The **two's complement** of a binary number is another binary number that, when added to the original number, produces all 0 bits. Producing the two's complement is a multistep algorithm as shown in **Figure 26-16**.

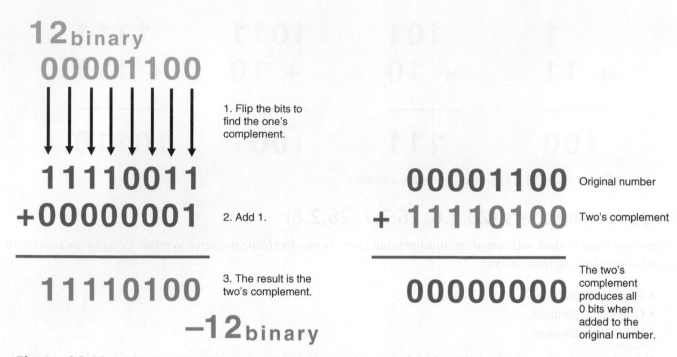

Figure 26-16   The two's complement of a binary number can represent its negative

With three ways of representing negative numbers, you might be thinking that 10001100, 11110011, and 11110100 all could represent –12. You would be correct, but most modern computers use the two's complement for negative numbers.

26.3 Hexadecimal

Colors (26.3.1, 26.3.2)

The color display on a computer or smartphone is divided into thousands of picture elements called **pixels**. Each pixel contains a group of three miniature lights: one red, one green, and one blue. This color system is referred to as **RGB**, which stands for red, green, blue.

Each light can have an illumination level ranging from 0 to 255. The light is off and black when its value is 0. The light is brightest when its value is 255. In the purple swatch in the center of the first color diagram in **Figure 26-17**, the red light is on at level 130, which is half strength. The green light is off at level 0. The blue light is on full strength at level 255.

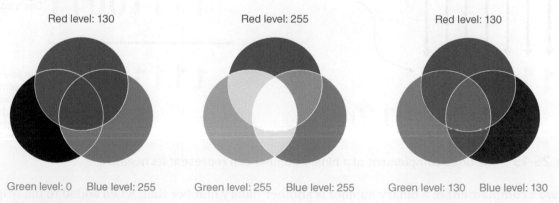

Figure 26-17   RGB color

Q   What color is a pixel when all its light levels are 255?

A   When red, green, and blue levels are 255, the pixel is white.

Computers store colors as binary numbers. In **Figure 26-18**, the decimal values have been converted to binary.

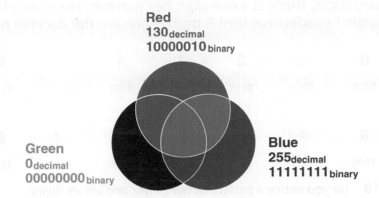

Red
130 decimal
10000010 binary

Green
0 decimal
00000000 binary

Blue
255 decimal
11111111 binary

RGB: 10000010 00000000 11111111

Figure 26-18   Binary values for red, green, and blue combine to display purple

The 24-bit binary number for the color purple is 100000100000000011111111. That's very long. Computers don't have any trouble with such a long number, but humans find it cumbersome. Programmers use hexadecimal notation to deal with colors because it requires only six digits instead of 24.

The hexadecimal notation for the purple swatch is #8200FF. That's much shorter than the 24-bit binary notation. Finding out why hexadecimal notation is so much shorter requires a quick introduction to the hexadecimal number system.

Hexadecimal Numbers (26.3.3, 26.3.4)

The **hexadecimal number system**, or base-16, has 16 digits: 0 1 2 3 4 5 6 7 8 9 A B C D E F. This number system is commonly used to specify the colors of icons, images, and text. Web designers are well versed in hexadecimal for specifying the colors of text and links on webpages.

Programmers usually say "hex" instead of "hexadecimal." Counting in hex goes like this:

0 1 2 3 4 5 6 7 8 9 A B C D E F 10 11 12 13 14 15 16 17 18 19

To distinguish hex numbers from binary and decimal numbers, you might see any of these notations:

- 0x101
- #101
- 101h
- 0h101
- 101_{hex}
- 101_h
- 101_{16}
- &H101
- U+0101

Binary-Hex-Binary Conversions (26.3.5, 26.3.6, 26.3.7)

Q Here's something interesting. Take a look at the binary numbers in **Figure 26-19** and their hex equivalents. Do you notice a pattern?

A For every four binary digits, there is a one-digit hex number. For example, the four binary digits 1011 and the single hexadecimal digit B both represent the decimal number 11.

Hex	0	1	2	3	4	5	6	7
Binary	0000	0001	0010	0011	0100	0101	0110	0111

Hex	8	9	A	B	C	D	E	F
Binary	1000	1001	1010	1011	1100	1101	1110	1111

Figure 26-19   Do you notice a pattern between hex and binary digits?

This correspondence makes it easy to convert from binary to hex. The algorithm for converting binary numbers into hex is shown in **Figure 26-20**.

101011111001001	1. Begin with the original number.
10101111100 1001	2. Working from the right, separate a group of four digits.
101 0111 1100 1001	3. Continue separating into groups of four.
0101 0111 1100 1001	4. If the leftmost group has less than four bits, pad it with zeros.
5 7 C 9	5. For each group of four digits, write the corresponding hex value.
#57C9	6. The result is the hexadecimal value.

Figure 26-20   Convert binary to hex

To convert from hex to binary, just reverse the process. For each hex digit, write out the 4-bit binary number.

Q To be sure you can convert hex to binary, try converting A1 into binary.

A The binary for A is 1010. The binary for 1 is 0001. So A1 is 10100001 in binary.

Hex-Decimal Conversion (26.3.8)

The hexadecimal system has place values that are powers of 16. The algorithm for converting hex to decimal is shown in **Figure 26-21**.

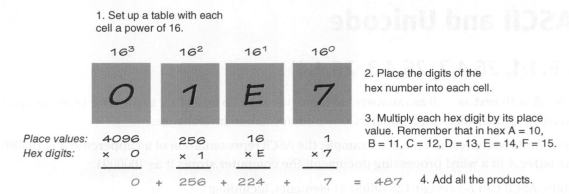

1. Set up a table with each cell a power of 16.

16^3 16^2 16^1 16^0

| O | 1 | E | 7 |

2. Place the digits of the hex number into each cell.

Place values: 4096   256   16   1
Hex digits: × O   × 1   × E   × 7

3. Multiply each hex digit by its place value. Remember that in hex A = 10, B = 11, C = 12, D = 13, E = 14, F = 15.

O + 256 + 224 + 7 = 487   4. Add all the products.

Figure 26-21   Convert hex to decimal

Information Density (26.3.9, 26.3.10, 26.3.11)

Information density is the amount of information that can be represented by a single symbol. You've worked with three number systems: decimal, binary, and hex. Which system do you think has the greatest information density?

Recall that $15_{decimal}$ is 1111_{binary} or F_{hex}. In decimal, the number requires two digits. In binary, four digits. In hex, only one digit. Hexadecimal provides higher information density than binary or decimal, so it is more efficient—at least for humans.

Because hex notation is efficient and relatively easy to read, it is used not only for designating colors, but also for memory readouts, raw file readouts, IPv6 Internet addresses, and storage addresses in computer memory.

Hollywood uses hex, too. You've seen all the garble that appears on hacker screens in movies. That Hollywood illusion is created by displaying the contents of a file with binary bits converted to hex. In **Figure 26-22**, each two-digit pair is a hex value.

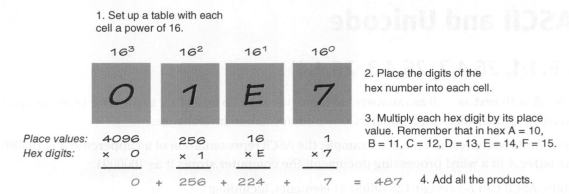

Figure 26-22   A raw file readout displays hex values for the binary data in a document or program

26.4 ASCII and Unicode

ASCII (26.4.1, 26.4.2, 26.4.3, 26.4.4)

Computers work with text as well as numbers, so there has to be an **encoding system** for representing text with 0 and 1 bits. **ASCII** is the American Standard Code for Information Interchange.

ASCII uses 7 bits to represent text. For example, the ASCII representation of an uppercase *A* is 1000001. When you type the letter *A* in a word processing document, the computer stores it as 1000001.

With 7 bits, ASCII can represent 128 different elements, including:

- Lowercase and uppercase letters of the alphabet
- Numerals from 0 to 9
- Punctuation symbols
- Arithmetic operators
- Symbols such as @ # $ % &
- Control characters, which include non-printable data such as a space and a line feed

The characters and their encoded equivalents are called a **character set**. The character set table in **Figure 26-23** illustrates the binary and decimal representations for each character.

Dec	Bin	Char	Dec	Bin	Char	Dec	Bin	Char	Dec	Bin	Char
0	000 0000	[NUL]	32	010 0000	space	64	100 0000	@	96	110 0000	`
1	000 0001	[SOH]	33	010 0001	!	65	100 0001	A	97	110 0001	a
2	000 0010	[STX]	34	010 0010	"	66	100 0010	B	98	110 0010	b
3	000 0011	[ETX]	35	010 0011	#	67	100 0011	C	99	110 0011	c
4	000 0100	[EOT]	36	010 0100	$	68	100 0100	D	100	110 0100	d
5	000 0101	[ENQ]	37	010 0101	%	69	100 0101	E	101	110 0101	e
6	000 0110	[ACK]	38	010 0110	&	70	100 0110	F	102	110 0110	f
7	000 0111	[BEL]	39	010 0111	'	71	100 0111	G	103	110 0111	g
8	000 1000	[BS]	40	010 1000	(	72	100 1000	H	104	110 1000	h
9	000 1001	[TAB]	41	010 1001	)	73	100 1001	I	105	110 1001	i
10	000 1010	[LF]	42	010 1010	*	74	100 1010	J	106	110 1010	j
11	000 1011	[VT]	43	010 1011	+	75	100 1011	K	107	110 1011	k
12	000 1100	[FF]	44	010 1100	,	76	100 1100	L	108	110 1100	l
13	000 1101	[CR]	45	010 1101	–	77	100 1101	M	109	110 1101	m
14	000 1110	[SO]	46	010 1110	.	78	100 1110	N	110	110 1110	n
15	000 1111	[SI]	47	010 1111	/	79	100 1111	O	111	110 1111	o
16	001 0000	[DLE]	48	011 0000	0	80	101 0000	P	112	111 0000	p
17	001 0001	[DC1]	49	011 0001	1	81	101 0001	Q	113	111 0001	q
18	001 0010	[DC2]	50	011 0010	2	82	101 0010	R	114	111 0010	r
19	001 0011	[DC3]	51	011 0011	3	83	101 0011	S	115	111 0011	s
20	001 0100	[DC4]	52	011 0100	4	84	101 0100	T	116	111 0100	t
21	001 0101	[NAK]	53	011 0101	5	85	101 0101	U	117	111 0101	u
22	001 0110	[SYN]	54	011 0110	6	86	101 0110	V	118	111 0110	v
23	001 0111	[ETB]	55	011 0111	7	87	101 0111	W	119	111 0111	w
24	001 1000	[CAN]	56	011 1000	8	88	101 1000	X	120	111 1000	x
25	001 1001	[EM]	57	011 1001	9	89	101 1001	Y	121	111 1001	y
26	001 1010	[SUB]	58	011 1010	:	90	101 1010	Z	122	111 1010	z
27	001 1011	[ESC]	59	011 1011	;	91	101 1011	[	123	111 1011	{
28	001 1100	[FS]	60	011 1100	<	92	101 1100	\	124	111 1100	|
29	001 1101	[GS]	61	011 1101	=	93	101 1101	]	125	111 1101	}
30	001 1110	[RS]	62	011 1110	>	94	101 1110	^	126	111 1110	~
31	001 1111	[US]	63	011 1111	?	95	101 1111	_	127	111 1111	[DEL]

Figure 26-23   The ASCII character set

Q What is the binary representation for an uppercase letter *M* and its decimal equivalent?

A An uppercase *M* is 100 1101 in binary. The decimal equivalent for 100 1101 is 77.

Extended ASCII (26.4.5)

Seven bits provide 128 possible elements for the ASCII character set. Recall that the number of units of information represented by binary digits corresponds to powers of 2.

$$2^1 = 2 \text{ units}$$
$$2^2 = 4 \text{ units}$$
$$2^3 = 8 \text{ units}$$
$$2^4 = 16 \text{ units}$$
$$2^5 = 32 \text{ units}$$
$$2^6 = 64 \text{ units}$$
$$2^7 = 128 \text{ units}$$

Seven-bit ASCII was fine for English text, but it lacked symbols for international monetary units such as the £ (pound) and ¥ (yen). It also lacked letters of the alphabet with diacritic marks, such as ë and à, found in Spanish, French, and other languages.

ASCII was eventually extended to 8 bits, which allows representation of 256 (that's 2^8) different elements. Those elements include diacritic marks, international symbols, and a variety of small lines and shapes. **Figure 26-24** illustrates some symbols added to the Extended ASCII character set.

Figure 26-24   Symbols from the Extended ASCII character set

Unicode (26.4.6, 26.4.7)

As the popularity of computers spread throughout the world, it became important to support languages, such as Russian, Mandarin, Hindi, and Arabic, that use non-European character sets. **Unicode** is a variable-length standard that is at least 16 bits but may extend to 48 bits.

Unicode assigns each symbol a binary number called a codepoint. A codepoint is usually written as a hexadecimal number such as U+006F. The U+ means Unicode. Hexadecimal notation is used instead of binary because it is easier to read.

Q Here's a challenge. You know that 8-bit ASCII can be used to represent 256 characters. The decimal number 256 is 0100 in hex. Which of these symbols would not be in the ASCII character set, but would be in the Unicode character set?

€ U+20AC
@ U+0040
$ U+0024

A The euro symbol € is not in the 8-bit ASCII character set. Its hexadecimal assignment is 20AC, which is 8,364 in decimal—a number far higher than the limit of 256 placed on the ASCII character set. The @ symbol is hex 0040, which is 64 in decimal. The $ symbol is hex 0024, which is 36 in decimal. Because 64 and 36 are within the 256 ASCII limit, the @ and $ symbols are in the ASCII character set.

There are several versions of Unicode. **UTF-8** is a popular standard today. It is the most common character set used on the web.

With encoding methods such as ASCII, Extended ASCII, Unicode, and UTF-8, programmers and web designers may have to specify which one to use. If you have received an email message sprinkled with weird symbols such as HĐ⁻â¾€ or connected to a webpage that contained garbled text, you've seen the result of a mismatched encoding method. Your device might have been expecting UTF-8 but was sent data formatted for plain ASCII text.

Programming languages and web design tools make provisions for specifying encoding systems and character sets. Keep this fact in mind when working on a coding project that involves languages other than English.

26.5 Memory Allocation

Memory and Storage (26.5.1)

The terms "memory" and "storage" are used inconsistently in the computer industry. **Storage** technically refers to devices that hold data permanently, in contrast to **memory** that holds data only temporarily. But devices such as flash drives are popularly called "memory sticks" even though they store data permanently. Disk drives are sometimes called "secondary memory" even though they essentially store data permanently. You can see why there is confusion.

To take a programmer's view, however, memory is different from storage. Memory has a direct line to the processor. Storage is a step removed from the processor. **Figure 26-25** is a useful abstraction showing a programmer's view of memory and storage.

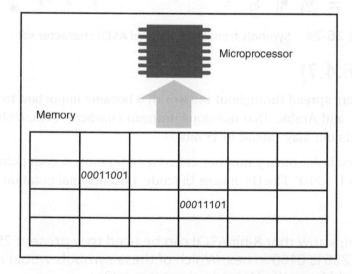

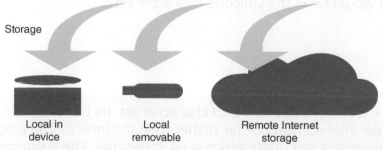

Figure 26-25   A programmer's view of memory and storage

Storage Devices (26.5.2, 26.5.3, 26.5.4, 26.5.5, 26.5.6)

The bits and bytes that represent data and computer programs can be stored in a variety of devices, such as hard drives, flash drives, solid state drives, SD cards, and CD/DVD drives.

Storage devices can be classified in several ways.

Locality. **Online storage** is provided by Internet-based cloud services, such as Amazon Web Services, Microsoft Azure, and Google Cloud Platform. **Offline storage** (local storage) includes devices such as hard drives that are typically connected directly to a digital device and removable devices such as flash drives.

Volatility. **Volatile storage** requires a power source to hold data. **Nonvolatile storage** holds data even when a device is turned off. Nonvolatile storage is sometimes referred to as "permanent storage," whereas volatile storage is sometimes referred to as "temporary storage."

Changeability. Most storage devices save data by a process called "writing," and they retrieve data by a process called "reading." Storage devices such as CD ROMs are **read-only**, which means that the data they contain cannot be changed. Other storage devices, such as hard drives and flash drives, have **read-write** capabilities that allow data to be stored, retrieved, and changed.

Technology. **Magnetic storage technology** arranges microscopic magnetic particles that represent 0s and 1s. **Optical storage technology** recognizes the presence or absence of reflected light. **Solid state storage technology** opens or shuts miniature logic gates to represent "on" or "off" bits (**Figure 26-26**).

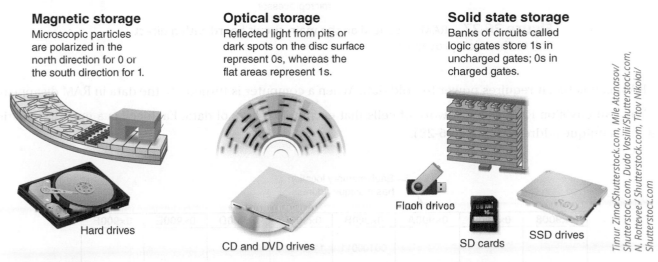

Magnetic storage
Microscopic particles are polarized in the north direction for 0 or the south direction for 1.

Hard drives

Optical storage
Reflected light from pits or dark spots on the disc surface represent 0s, whereas the flat areas represent 1s.

CD and DVD drives

Solid state storage
Banks of circuits called logic gates store 1s in uncharged gates; 0s in charged gates.

Flash drives

SD cards

SSD drives

Timur Zima/Shutterstock.com, Mile Atanasov/Shutterstock.com, Duda Vasilii/Shutterstock.com, N. Rottevee / Shutterstock.com, Titov Nikolai/Shutterstock.com

Figure 26-26 Storage technologies

Computer storage is divided into locations for holding data. Those locations can be designated as blocks, pages, tracks, or sectors, each with a unique address. A byte consisting of 8 bits is usually the minimum amount of space allocated to store a single item of data. Several bytes can be combined to store longer data, such as Unicode characters, integers, or floating-point numbers.

Memory (26.5.7, 26.5.8, 26.5.9)

Programmers are interested in **RAM (random access memory)** because it provides local, temporary storage for data, programs, and the computer's operating system. When programmers use RAM effectively, programs run efficiently. For example, a list stored in successive memory locations can be accessed more quickly than if the list is scattered randomly in memory.

RAM is classified as memory because it is directly linked to the processor. RAM is housed within one or more integrated circuits that reside on the main circuit board of a digital device (**Figure 26-27**).

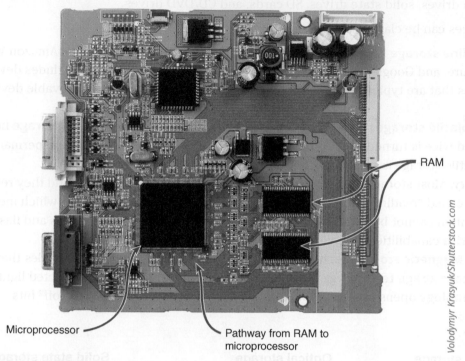

Volodymyr Krasyuk/Shutterstock.com

Figure 26-27   RAM is located on the main circuit board with a direct link to the microprocessor

RAM is volatile. It requires power to hold data. When a computer is turned off, the data in RAM disappears.

You can envision RAM as a gridwork of cells that each hold a byte of data. Each cell is a memory location that has a unique address (**Figure 26-28**).

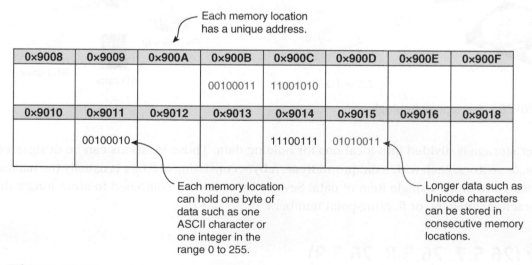

0×9008	0×9009	0×900A	0×900B	0×900C	0×900D	0×900E	0×900F
			00100011	11001010			

0×9010	0×9011	0×9012	0×9013	0×9014	0×9015	0×9016	0×9018
	00100010			11100111	01010011		

Figure 26-28   RAM addresses and data

A **memory address** such as 0x9FFF begins with 0x to indicate it is in hexadecimal. Familiarity with this notation is helpful for two reasons:

Manual memory management. Occasionally when coding, you might want to directly manipulate the contents of a memory location.

Tracking down coding errors. You might want to check the contents of memory variables to fix coding errors.

RAM capacity is typically measured in gigabytes, in contrast to storage options, which may hold terabytes of data. Today's computers and smartphones are usually shipped with somewhere between 1 and 16 GB of RAM.

Summary

- Data representation refers to the way information is abstracted so that it can be manipulated, transmitted, and stored as data by today's computing devices.
- Whether data takes the form of radio signals, electric charges, magnetized particles, or reflected light, it retains two important characteristics: it is digital, and it is binary.
- One binary digit is called a bit. Eight bits are a byte.
- Digital devices use the binary number system to represent positive and negative numbers. Text data is represented using ASCII, Unicode, and UTF-8 encoding.
- Binary representations are typically long strings of 0s and 1s, which are difficult for humans to read. Hexadecimal notation is easier to read than binary and has higher information density, so it is often the preferred notation used by programmers. Hexadecimal is used to refer to memory addresses and for raw file readouts.
- Digital data is held temporarily in memory and more permanently in storage devices, such as hard drives and flash drives.
- Storage devices can be classified in several ways, including by technology. Magnetic storage technology arranges microscopic magnetic particles that represent 0s and 1s. Optical storage technology recognizes the presence or absence of reflected light. Solid state storage technology opens or shuts miniature logic gates to represent "on" or "off" bits.
- RAM is classified as memory because it is directly linked to the processor. RAM provides local, temporary storage for data, programs, and the computer's operating system. Each RAM location has a unique address and holds one byte of data.

Key Terms

analog data	digital data	pixels
ASCII	encoding system	RAM (random access memory)
base-2	hexadecimal number system	read-only
binary	information density	read-write
binary digits	magnetic storage technology	RGB
binary measurements	memory	signed magnitude
binary number system	memory address	solid state storage technology
bit	nonvolatile storage	storage
byte	offline storage	two's complement
capacitors	one's complement	Unicode
character set	online storage	UTF-8
data representation	optical storage technology	volatile storage

Module 27

Programming Paradigms

Learning Objectives:

27.1 Imperative and Declarative Paradigms

27.1.1 Define the term "programming paradigm."

27.1.2 Differentiate between imperative and declarative programming paradigms.

27.2 The Procedural Paradigm

27.2.1 Associate procedural programming with step-by-step algorithms that specify *how* a computer should perform a task.

27.2.2 Associate the procedural paradigm with imperative programming.

27.2.3 List the key characteristics of the procedural paradigm.

27.2.4 List advantages and disadvantages of the procedural paradigm.

27.2.5 Associate procedural programming with early high-level languages such as Fortran, BASIC, Pascal, and C.

27.3 The Object-Oriented Paradigm

27.3.1 Associate the object-oriented paradigm with creating data models of a problem's entities, actions, and relationships.

27.3.2 Explain the significance of classes, objects, attributes, and methods in the object-oriented paradigm.

27.3.3 List the key characteristics of OOP.

27.3.4 List advantages and disadvantages of the object-oriented paradigm.

27.3.5 Identify problems that can best be solved using the object-oriented paradigm.

27.3.6 Identify programming languages that support the object-oriented paradigm.

27.3.7 State that a programming language can support multiple paradigms.

27.4 Declarative Paradigms

27.4.1 Identify the approach of declarative paradigms as expressing the logic of a problem rather than specifying a step-by-step algorithm.

27.4.2 List the key characteristics of declarative paradigms.

27.4.3 Identify problems that can best be solved using the declarative paradigm.

27.4.4 List logic programming, functional programming, and database query as examples of the declarative paradigm.

27.4.5 Associate various programming languages with each type of declarative paradigm.

27.4.6 List advantages and disadvantages of the declarative paradigm.

27.1 Imperative and Declarative Paradigms

Think Outside the Box (27.1.1, 27.1.2)

Q Can you use pen and paper to duplicate the drawing in **Figure 27-1** without lifting the pen from the paper?

Figure 27-1   Can you draw this diagram without lifting your pen from the paper?

A The trick is to fold over a corner of the paper as shown in **Figure 27-2**.

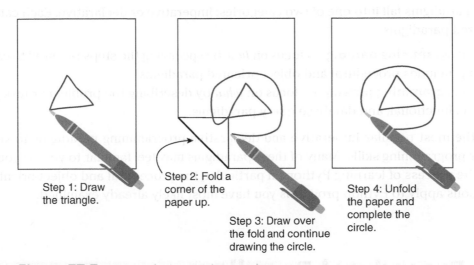

Step 1: Draw the triangle.

Step 2: Fold a corner of the paper up.

Step 3: Draw over the fold and continue drawing the circle.

Step 4: Unfold the paper and complete the circle.

Figure 27-2   One solution to the puzzler

The circle puzzler has another solution. Using a ballpoint pen, you can retract the point after drawing the triangle, move the pen, and then extend the point to draw the circle.

Solving the circle-drawing challenge requires creative thinking and illustrates that there can be more than one approach to a solution.

Programmers have several ways to approach a programming task:

• View the task as a problem that can be solved by specifying a series of steps for the computer to execute.
• Visualize the computer manipulating data for several objects, people, or places.
• Create a solution based on a series of rules.

The various approaches to programming are referred to as **programming paradigms**. To use an analogy, suppose you are planning a trip from New York City to Philadelphia. As in **Figure 27-3**, you have several "paradigms" for transportation: car, plane, train, or scooter!

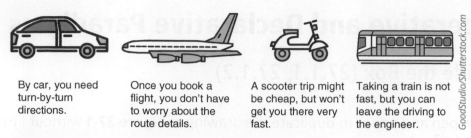

By car, you need turn-by-turn directions.

Once you book a flight, you don't have to worry about the route details.

A scooter trip might be cheap, but won't get you there very fast.

Taking a train is not fast, but you can leave the driving to the engineer.

GoodStudio/Shutterstock.com

Figure 27-3   Transportation paradigms

Each transportation paradigm has advantages and disadvantages. You might even use more than one paradigm by driving to the airport and then taking a plane. Programming paradigms also have advantages and disadvantages. Here are the important takeaways:

- A programming paradigm affects the way you think about a program and the style in which you code it.
- Each programming paradigm has advantages and disadvantages.
- One paradigm might be a more suitable approach to a programming problem than another paradigm.
- Some programs might require you to use more than one paradigm.
- The features for implementing paradigms vary from one programming language to another.

Programming paradigms fall into one of two categories: imperative or declarative. Each category includes a subset of specialized paradigms.

- **Imperative programming paradigms** focus on *how* by specifying the steps required to carry out a task. This category includes procedural and object-oriented paradigms.
- **Declarative programming paradigms** focus on *what* by describing the problem or task. This category includes logic, functional, and database query paradigms.

Let's look at the most popular imperative and declarative programming paradigms to see how they can contribute to your programming skills. Many of these paradigms may feel familiar to you, as you've instinctually adapted them in the process of learning Python. In particular, the procedural and object-oriented paradigms in the following sections apply to Python programs you have most likely already examined.

27.2 The Procedural Paradigm

Procedural Basics (27.2.1, 27.2.2)

The traditional approach to programming uses the **procedural paradigm**, which helps you visualize a program as a step-by-step algorithm. Programs based on the procedural paradigm typically consist of instructions that indicate *how* a computer should perform a task or solve a problem.

Because the procedural paradigm focuses on step-by-step algorithms, it is classified as an imperative programming paradigm.

Let's use a road trip as an example and look at a program that calculates the total cost of gas for two trips. One trip is along the 2,700-mile, once-glamorous Route 66. The other trip is along the scenic but rugged 2,000-mile Alaska Highway. You would like the program to determine which trip would have the lowest total gas cost. A procedural algorithm for this calculation might look like the steps in **Figure 27-4**.

In keeping with the step-by-step focus of the procedural paradigm, the code for this program would closely match the steps of the algorithm; one line of program code for each step in the algorithm.

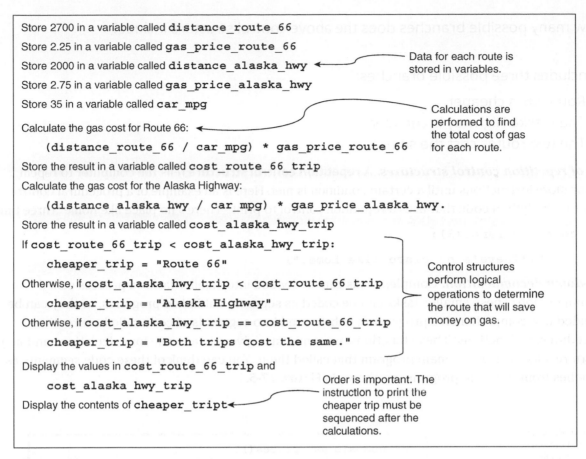

Store 2700 in a variable called `distance_route_66`

Store 2.25 in a variable called `gas_price_route_66`

Store 2000 in a variable called `distance_alaska_hwy` ← ⌐ Data for each route is stored in variables.

Store 2.75 in a variable called `gas_price_alaska_hwy`

Store 35 in a variable called `car_mpg`

Calculate the gas cost for Route 66: ← ⌐ Calculations are performed to find the total cost of gas for each route.

    (distance_route_66 / car_mpg) * gas_price_route_66

Store the result in a variable called `cost_route_66_trip`

Calculate the gas cost for the Alaska Highway:

    (distance_alaska_hwy / car_mpg) * gas_price_alaska_hwy.

Store the result in a variable called `cost_alaska_hwy_trip`

If `cost_route_66_trip` < `cost_alaska_hwy_trip`:

    cheaper_trip = "Route 66"

Otherwise, if `cost_alaska_hwy_trip` < `cost_route_66_trip` ⌐ Control structures perform logical operations to determine the route that will save money on gas.

    cheaper_trip = "Alaska Highway"

Otherwise, if `cost_alaska_hwy_trip` == `cost_route_66_trip`

    cheaper_trip = "Both trips cost the same."

Display the values in `cost_route_66_trip` and

    cost_alaska_hwy_trip

Display the contents of `cheaper_trip`← ⌐ Order is important. The instruction to print the cheaper trip must be sequenced after the calculations.

Figure 27-4   A procedural algorithm specifies how the computer determines the trip with the lowest gas cost

Characteristics of Procedural Programs (27.2.3)

The three sections of the algorithm in Figure 27-4 are typical of programs based on the procedural paradigm. The program has an input section where data is loaded into variables, a processing section where calculations are performed, and an output section where data is displayed, printed, or transmitted. Here are some other characteristics of programs based on the procedural paradigm:

Order is important. A crucial element of procedural programming is specifying the correct order of the steps in an algorithm.

Use of variables. Procedural programs typically store data in variables and use those variables for computations, output, and other operations.

Use of selection control structures. Simple procedural programs execute the steps of an algorithm in sequence. But control structures can change that sequence. A **selection control structure** tells the computer what to do based on whether a condition is true or false. The following Python code for a section of the road trip program tells the computer to put **"Route 66"** in the variable **cheaper_trip** if the cost of gas for traveling Route 66 is cheaper than the cost on the Alaska Highway.

```
if cost_route_66_trip < cost_alaska_hwy_trip:

    cheaper_trip = "Route 66"

elif cost_alaska_hwy_trip < cost_route_66_trip:

    cheaper_trip = "Alaska Highway"

elif cost_alaska_hwy_trip == cost_route_66_trip:

    cheaper_trip = "Both trips cost the same."
```

How many possible branches does the above control structure include?

 It includes three possible branches:

1. Route 66 is cheaper.
2. The Alaska Highway is cheaper.
3. The two routes cost the same.

Use of repetition control structures. A **repetition control structure** tells the computer to repeat one or more instructions until a certain condition is met. Here is an example of a procedural control structure in Python code that uses a repetition control to print "There's no place like home" three times.

```
for count in range(3):

    print("There's no place like home.")
```

Top-down decomposition. Complex tasks can be divided into smaller tasks, a process called decomposition. These smaller tasks can be coded as separate but linked programs, or they can be included in a comprehensive program but abstracted into segments of code called subroutines, procedures, or functions. These functions are sometimes given data to use for calculations and may return results back to the main program that called them. You can think of these code segments as branches from the main program, as shown in **Figure 27-5**.

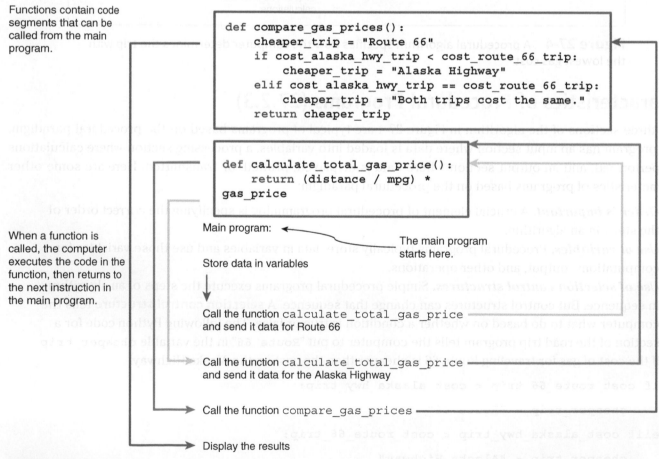

Figure 27-5   Procedural programs have a main execution path, but subroutines, procedures, and functions serve as side trips

Procedural Paradigm Applications (27.2.4, 27.2.5)

As a programmer, you can apply the procedural paradigm to any programming problems that can be approached as a series of steps. It is a particularly effective approach for problems and tasks such as those in **Figure 27-6**.

Repetitive tasks where the same set of steps can be applied to different data sets

Large applications that can be divided into modules

Systems that require optimized performance

Any problem where the solution naturally involves a series of sequential steps or calculations

Processing paychecks requires the same calculations every week, but for varying work hours

Online stores with modules for inventory management, shopping carts, payment processing, and delivery logistics

Launching spacecraft

Processing survey data

davooda/Shutterstock.com

Figure 27-6   The procedural paradigm works well for these types of applications

Advantages of the procedural paradigm include the following:

- Program structure corresponds closely to the linear sequence in which the CPU executes instructions, so programs run quickly and efficiently
- Easy to learn and is a classic approach understood by most programmers
- Most popular programming languages support the procedural approach
- Flexibility for successfully implementing a wide range of problems and coding tasks
- Modularity allows a team of programmers to contribute code segments to a comprehensive application

The disadvantage of the procedural paradigm is that it does not fit gracefully with certain categories of problems. You might want to select a different paradigm when developing a program for the following types of problems:

- Applications that do not have a clear order of events, start point, or end point
- Unstructured problems, such as assessing the quality of a vintage wine, that may require solutions based on subjective, incomplete, or uncertain data
- Activities, such as social media trends, that do not have a clear algorithm
- Language-based problems, such as speech recognition, that manipulate textual data rather than numerical data
- Complex problems, such as blocking hackers and malware, that have unusually complex logic

Early programming languages such as Fortran and COBOL were designed to support procedural programming. BASIC, Pascal, and C are also well-known languages for coding in the procedural style. More recent languages, such as C++, Python, and Java, support the procedural style but also provide features for other programming paradigms.

27.3 The Object-Oriented Paradigm

Objects, Classes, and Methods (27.3.1, 27.3.2)

The **object-oriented paradigm** is based on the idea that programs can be designed by visualizing objects that interact with each other. You might already be familiar with **objects** in an object-oriented program, which are abstractions of real-world entities, such as people, places, and things.

For a road trip, you might be considering whether to drive your Mustang or your friend's Camaro. You can create Mustang and Camaro objects as specific instances of a template called a **class**. **Figure 27-7** explains. The figure uses the Unified Modeling Language (UML) to describe a class in general terms. Even if you are unfamiliar with UML, look at the callouts to guide your understanding of how the classes should be structured.

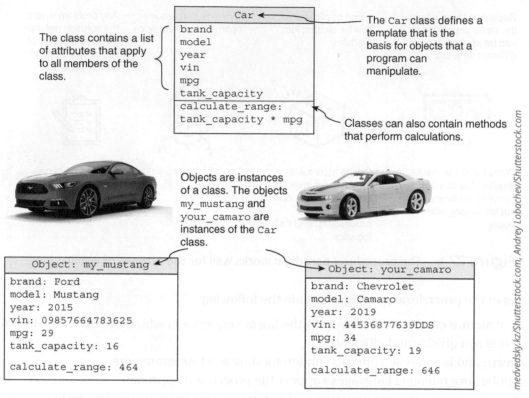

The class contains a list of attributes that apply to all members of the class.

The `Car` class defines a template that is the basis for objects that a program can manipulate.

Classes can also contain methods that perform calculations.

Objects are instances of a class. The objects `my_mustang` and `your_camaro` are instances of the `Car` class.

```
                Car
brand
model
year
vin
mpg
tank_capacity
calculate_range:
tank_capacity * mpg
```

```
Object: my_mustang
brand: Ford
model: Mustang
year: 2015
vin: 09857664783625
mpg: 29
tank_capacity: 16

calculate_range: 464
```

```
Object: your_camaro
brand: Chevrolet
model: Camaro
year: 2019
vin: 44536877639DDS
mpg: 34
tank_capacity: 19

calculate_range: 646
```

medvedsky.kz/Shutterstock.com, Andrey Lobachev/Shutterstock.com

Figure 27-7   The object-oriented paradigm focuses on defining classes and creating objects

A class defines **attributes**, such as `mpg` and `tank_capacity`. Classes also define **methods** that perform tasks, such as collecting input, executing decisions, making calculations, or producing output.

Q In Figure 27-7, what is the method in the `Car` class?

A The `Car` class contains the `calculate_range` method, which computes the range of a car using the formula `tank_capacity * mpg`.

A `Car` class could be part of a program that determines the cost of a road trip. You need another class for the road trip program, one that generates objects for various trip routes such as those in **Figure 27-8**.

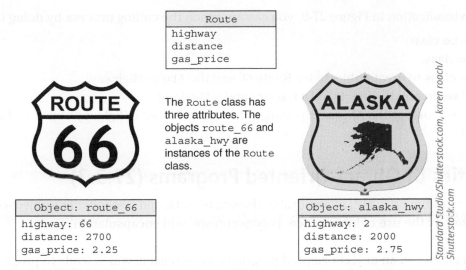

The Route class has three attributes. The objects route_66 and alaska_hwy are instances of the Route class.

```
Route
highway
distance
gas_price
```

```
Object: route_66
highway: 66
distance: 2700
gas_price: 2.25
```

```
Object: alaska_hwy
highway: 2
distance: 2000
gas_price: 2.75
```

Figure 27-8   A class and objects for trip routes

From an object-oriented perspective, you might visualize the road trip program as the interaction between objects shown in **Figure 27-9**.

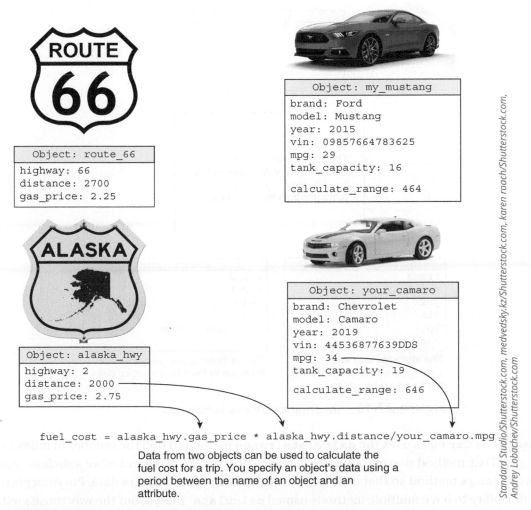

```
Object: route_66
highway: 66
distance: 2700
gas_price: 2.25
```

```
Object: my_mustang
brand: Ford
model: Mustang
year: 2015
vin: 09857664783625
mpg: 29
tank_capacity: 16

calculate_range: 464
```

```
Object: alaska_hwy
highway: 2
distance: 2000
gas_price: 2.75
```

```
Object: your_camaro
brand: Chevrolet
model: Camaro
year: 2019
vin: 44536877639DDS
mpg: 34
tank_capacity: 19

calculate_range: 646
```

fuel_cost = alaska_hwy.gas_price * alaska_hwy.distance/your_camaro.mpg

Data from two objects can be used to calculate the fuel cost for a trip. You specify an object's data using a period between the name of an object and an attribute.

Figure 27-9   In the object-oriented paradigm, objects interact

Based on the visualization in Figure 27-9, you can approach the coding process by doing the following:

Define the `Route` class.

Define the `Car` class.

Use the `Route` class to create objects for Route 66 and the Alaska Highway.

Use the `Car` class to create objects for a Camaro and a Mustang.

Calculate the fuel cost for the Alaska trip using data from the Alaska Highway object and the Camaro object.

Characteristics of Object-Oriented Programs (27.3.3)

Object-oriented programming (OOP) incorporates classes, objects, and methods. The object-oriented paradigm is also characterized by the use of inheritance, polymorphism, and encapsulation.

Inheritance. The classes in an object-oriented program can be reused, which leads to programming efficiencies. Suppose you're thinking of taking an electric car on your road trip. Gas mileage won't apply.

Instead of making a completely different class for electric cars, you can use the `Car` class for attributes that apply to all types of cars but create one subclass for gas guzzlers and another subclass for electric cars.

Inheritance is a feature of OOP that allows subclasses to acquire common attributes from a parent class, as shown in **Figure 27-10**.

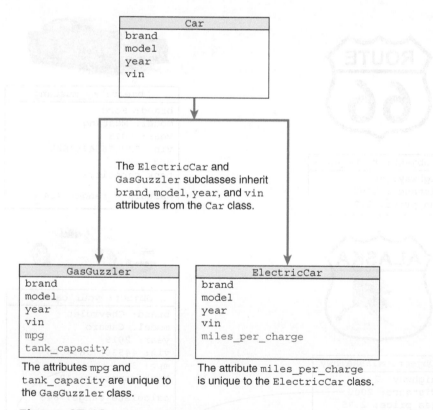

Figure 27-10   Inheritance creates subclasses

Polymorphism. The `Car` class uses the `calculate_range` method to find the number of miles a car can drive on a tank of gas. That method doesn't apply to electric cars. For the `ElectricCar` subclass, you can modify the `calculate_range` method so that it simply uses the `miles_per_charge` data. **Polymorphism** gives your program the flexibility to have multiple methods named `calculate_range`, but the way those methods process objects depends on their class. See **Figure 27-11**.

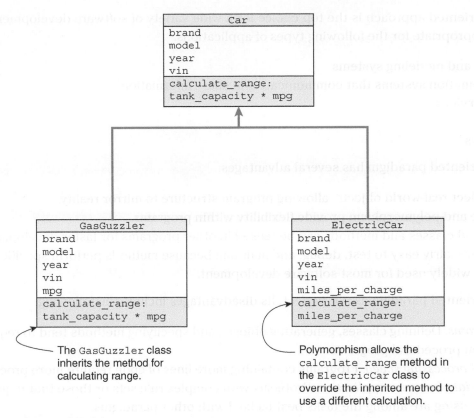

Figure 27-11 Polymorphism provides flexibility for methods

Encapsulation. Classes are abstractions, which can be visualized as black boxes that **encapsulate** data attributes and methods. After a class is defined, its methods can be triggered by sending a message. In the road trip program, a message to "calculate the range of my Mustang" enters the black box, triggers the appropriate method, and produces the specified output as in **Figure 27-12**.

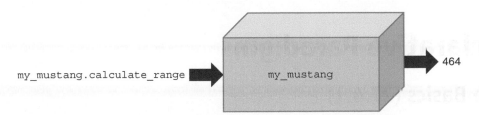

Figure 27-12 Encapsulation treats classes as black boxes

The object-oriented paradigm joins the procedural paradigm under the umbrella of imperative programming. With both paradigms, programmers specify the steps for *how* to accomplish a task or perform a method defined in a class.

Object-Oriented Applications (27.3.4, 27.3.5, 27.3.6, 27.3.7)

If you score a job on a programming team, you'll most likely work on a project that is based on an object-oriented approach. Familiarity with OOP is mandatory for today's IT and computer science careers.

The object-oriented approach is the top choice for a wide variety of software development projects, but it is particularly appropriate for the following types of applications:

- Simulation and modeling systems
- Office automation systems that communicate and share information
- Internet services
- Web apps
- Mobile apps

The object-oriented paradigm has several advantages:

- Classes reflect real-world objects, allowing program structure to mirror reality.
- Inheritance and polymorphism provide flexibility within programs.
- Encapsulated classes and methods can be reused in other programs for faster development.
- Programs are fairly easy to test, debug, and maintain because methods perform specific tasks.
- Today, it is widely used for most software development.

The object-oriented paradigm is not perfect. Its disadvantages include the following:

- *Large programs.* Defining classes, generating objects, and specifying methods tend to require more lines of code than procedural programs.
- *Nonoptimal processing speed.* Programs containing more lines of code require more processing time.
- *Not appropriate for every application.* Problems with complex rule sets or those that require natural language processing are among the tasks best tackled with other paradigms.

Simula, developed in the 1960s, and SmallTalk, developed in the 1970s, were two of the original programming languages for object-oriented programming. The paradigm was not popular, however, until the 1990s when languages such as Java, Python, Ruby, and C++ started to appear.

Many of today's popular programming languages support both procedural and object-oriented programming approaches. Such languages allow programmers to create classes, objects, and methods, but do not require them as the foundation for program code.

27.4 Declarative Paradigms

Declarative Basics (27.4.1)

Although the dominant programming paradigms are procedural and object oriented, other programming paradigms are worth your attention. Declarative paradigms approach programming by describing what a program is supposed to accomplish. This approach is very different from imperative paradigms, which focus on the steps for how to accomplish a task.

Declarative paradigms are like booking a flight: You specify when you want to leave, where you want to go, and the fare class that you can afford. Your specifications tell the booking app what you want, not how to book the flight or pilot the plane to your destination.

To get a handle on the declarative approach, let's delve into the fascinating world of logic programming.

In logic programming, you use three types of statements: facts that form a database, rules that define the logic, and queries that trigger processing. A fact supplies basic information in the form of a **predicate expression** that specifies a relationship. **Figure 27-13** explains.

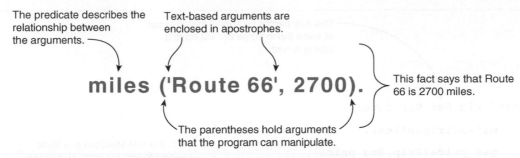

The predicate describes the relationship between the arguments.

Text-based arguments are enclosed in apostrophes.

miles ('Route 66', 2700).

This fact says that Route 66 is 2700 miles.

The parentheses hold arguments that the program can manipulate.

Figure 27-13   Logic programming uses predicate expressions

Using predicate expressions, you can create a program that contains facts about routes, gas prices, and cars. Without viewing the facts it contains, users who understand the way facts are structured can interact with the program to enter queries. **Figure 27-14** shows a set of facts and the results of a query that asks, "What is the price of gas on the Alaska Highway?"

```
miles('Route 66', 2700).

miles('Alaska Hwy', 2000).

gas_price('Route 66', 2.25).

gas_price('Alaska Hwy', 2.75).

mpg('Camaro', 34).

mpg('Mustang', 29).


?- gas_price('Alaska Hwy', What).


What = 2.75
```

Facts specify data about the routes and cars.

This query has two arguments: **'Alaska Hwy'** and **What**. Because **What** is capitalized and not set off by apostrophes, it is a variable. The query looks for a **gas_price** fact with an **'Alaska Hwy'** argument. When it finds one, it replaces **What** with the value of the second argument: 2.75.

The result of the query specifies the value of the variable **What**.

Figure 27-14   A query searches the database for matching facts

Q What do you think will be produced by the query `?- miles('Alaska Hwy', What)`?

A The query produces **What = 2000**, based on the fact `miles('Alaska Hwy', 2000)`.

Adding a rule to the program specifies the logic for calculating the cost of any trip, as **Figure 27-15** explains.

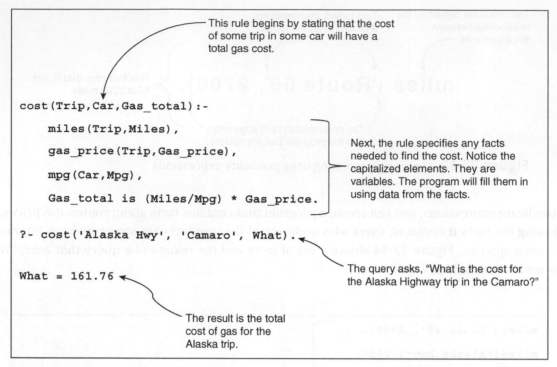

Figure 27-15   Rules provide the logic for processing the data provided by the program's facts

Q   How would you change the query in Figure 27-15 to ask for the cost of a trip on Route 66 in the Mustang?

A   The query would be `cost('Route 66', 'Mustang', What)`.

To automate the query, you can add a `show_costs` rule. Does it matter where you put that rule? No. One of the key characteristics of the declarative paradigm is that the sequence of instructions is not important. That contrasts with the imperative paradigm where instructions must be coded in sequence for the program to produce the correct result. Here is the rule:

```
show_costs:-
cost(Trip, Car, Gas_total),
write(Trip), write(' '),
write(Car), write(' '),
write(Gas_total).
```

With the `show_costs` rule in place, the query `?- show_costs.` produces this output:

```
Route 66 Camaro 178.67
Route 66 Mustang 209.48
Alaska Hwy Camaro 161.76
Alaska Hwy Mustang 189.65
```

Notice that the program repeated this query for both routes and both cars without a repetition control. Programming languages that support the declarative paradigm have internal mechanisms to handle the flow of control.

Characteristics of the Declarative Paradigm (27.4.2)

The main takeaway about the declarative paradigm is that you don't have to specify the steps for producing output. Instead, you need only specify *what* rather than *how*: what are the facts, what are the rules, and what are the queries.

Let's recap two other characteristics that surfaced in the logic programming example:

- Declarative programs are not based on a step-by step algorithm, so the order of statements is much less important than in imperative programs.
- The programming language handles the flow of control, so repetition controls are not needed.

Applications for Declarative Paradigms (27.4.3, 27.4.4, 27.4.5, 27.4.6)

The declarative approach shines for applications that involve complex relationships, interrelated rules, statistical analysis, and database queries. You might encounter several variations of the declarative paradigm, each with its unique focus and corresponding programming languages, as shown in **Figure 27-16**.

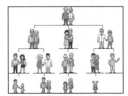
Logic programming paradigm. Genealogy involves complex relationships between mothers, fathers, children, siblings, and spouses. The data is text-based, not numerical. Processing involves relationships, rather than calculations. The **logic programming paradigm** is an effective approach for dealing with complex relationships, decisions, and rule sets that are expressed as text. Programming languages such as Prolog support this declarative approach.

Functional programming paradigm. Social networking services have policies against spam, malware, and other inappropriate activities. Identifying abuses involves statistical analysis and processing policy rules. The **functional programming paradigm** is an effective approach for applications that have interacting text-based or numerical rules. Programming languages such as Haskell, Scheme, OCaml, Scala, and Clojure support a declarative approach to programs that deal with mathematical functions.

Database query programming. Databases may contain hundreds or millions of records. Database query languages such as SQL include built-in declarative commands, such as **SELECT**. The following statement uses the **SELECT** command to find the price of gas along the Alaska Highway:
```
SELECT gas_price FROM TripDatabase WHERE Trip =
"Alaska Highway"
```
This statement is another example of the declarative paradigm's focus on *what*, rather than *how*. It is in contrast to the imperative paradigm, which would require many lines of code specifying how to look at every entry in the database until finding the Alaska Highway trip and its corresponding gas price.

Figure 27-16   Variations of the declarative paradigm

In addition to applications for which they are well suited, declarative paradigms have some general advantages and disadvantages that are important to keep in mind:

Advantage: Because languages that support the declarative paradigm handle program flow, programmers do not have to code background control structures.

Advantage: Relatively simple program code is required for tasks that involve complex and interrelated rules or conditions.

Disadvantage: Program execution speed is not optimal because declarative programming languages handle program flow in the same way for every program.

Disadvantage: Programmers have to think outside of the imperative-paradigm box.

Summary

- Programming paradigms provide various approaches to designing, developing, and implementing computer programs.
- Programming paradigms can be classified as imperative or declarative. Imperative programming paradigms focus on *how* by specifying the steps required to carry out a task. Declarative programming paradigms focus on *what* by describing the problem or task.
- The procedural paradigm is an imperative approach based on step-by-step algorithms. It is characterized by the use of variables, selection control structures, repetition control structures, and top-down decomposition. Programs based on the procedural paradigm typically run efficiently, but the approach is not optimal for all types of applications.
- The object-oriented paradigm is an imperative approach based on the concept of objects interacting with each other. Programmers define templates called classes, generate objects from these classes, and define methods that perform tasks related to the objects. Features such as inheritance, polymorphism, and encapsulation provide flexibility and reusability, but at a possible cost to execution speed.
- Declarative paradigms include logic programming, functional programming, and database query programming. These paradigms shine for applications that involve complex relationships, interrelated rules, statistical analysis, and database queries.

Key Terms

attributes	inheritance	predicate expression
class	methods	procedural paradigm
declarative programming paradigms	object-oriented paradigm	programming paradigms
encapsulate	objects	repetition control structure
imperative programming paradigms	polymorphism	selection control structure

Module 28

User Interfaces

Learning Objectives:

28.1 User Interface Basics

28.1.1 Define the term "user interface."

28.1.2 Explain the difference between a user interface and a user experience.

28.1.3 Describe the focus of the computer science discipline called Human-Computer Interaction.

28.1.4 Distinguish between physical and abstract interface components.

28.1.5 Describe how programmers select appropriate user interfaces.

28.1.6 Explain the purpose of APIs in the context of user interfaces.

28.2 Command-Line User Interfaces

28.2.1 List the characteristics of command-line user interfaces.

28.2.2 Identify use cases for command-line user interfaces.

28.2.3 Delineate the general algorithm for programs with command-line user interfaces.

28.2.4 Identify and apply conventions for formatting command-line input and output.

28.3 Graphical User Interfaces

28.3.1 List the characteristics of graphical user interfaces.

28.3.2 Explain how APIs relate to developing programs with graphical user interfaces.

28.3.3 Explain the relevance of event-driven programs to graphical user interfaces.

28.3.4 Recall the steps for the high-level algorithm on which an event-driven program is based.

28.4 Voice User Interfaces

28.4.1 Identify use cases for voice user interfaces.

28.4.2 Outline the algorithm for speech recognition.

28.4.3 Describe the process of concatenative speech synthesis.

28.4.4 Compare and contrast voice user interfaces to other types of user interfaces.

28.5 Virtual Environment Interfaces

28.5.1 Differentiate between applications of virtual reality, augmented reality, and mixed reality.

28.5.2 List user interface components for virtual environment interfaces.

28.5.3 Explain the significance of vector graphics for virtual reality programs.

28.5.4 List three types of tools for building programs with virtual environments.

28.6 Accessibility and Inclusion

28.6.1 Define "accessibility" as it relates to software design and use.

28.6.2 Match examples of common accessibility problems with best practices solutions.

28.6.3 Define "inclusion" as it relates to software design and use.

28.6.4 Match examples of common inclusion problems with best practices solutions.

28.6.5 Classify usability problems as accessibility or inclusion.

28.1 User Interface Basics

UI and UX (28.1.1, 28.1.2, 28.1.3)

In *Star Trek IV: The Voyage Home*, the crew of the starship *Enterprise* travels back in time to 1986. Scotty, the ship's engineer, walks over to an Apple Macintosh computer like the one in **Figure 28-1**. When he says, "Hello, computer!" nothing happens, so he picks up the mouse and tries to use it as a microphone.

Is it a microphone?

iStock/RyanJLane

Figure 28-1   The way to interact with a digital device might not be obvious to everyone

Scotty is familiar with computers that respond to voice commands. The way he expects to interact with the Macintosh computer is not the way the computer is expecting to interact with him. Scotty has a user interface problem.

In the context of programming, a **user interface (UI)** is a collection of physical, graphical, and logical constructs that facilitate interaction between humans and digital devices. The purpose of a user interface is to simplify a complex system so it is easy to use.

A similar concept, **user experience (UX)** is broader in scope and goes beyond user interaction to include an entire realm of consumer involvement. Apple provides an example of a crafted user experience that includes physical stores, online stores, product packaging, branding, equipment design, product support, and a standard look and feel for devices' home screens and apps.

The takeaway is this: UX design is all about an overall product experience, while UI design is all about the way users interact with a digital device.

In computer science, **Human–Computer Interaction (HCI)**, is an important and in-demand discipline. HCI encompasses UI and UX design. It is a key aspect of all software design, from creating fantastic game worlds to formulating mundane online tax forms.

UI Components (28.1.4)

User interfaces have both physical and abstract components. Physical components, such as those in **Figure 28-2**, include input and output devices.

Figure 28-2 User interfaces have physical components

Elena Blokhina/Shutterstock.com, JenWalters/ Shutterstock. com, wacpan/Shutterstock.com, iceink/Shutterstock.com, Benoit Daoust/Shutterstock.com, gd_project/Shutterstock. com, AG-PHOTOS/Shutterstock.com

Q What are the main physical components of a smartphone user interface?

A The touch screen and microphone are the primary physical UI components, but the phone's speaker is also a UI component. Some phones have a Home button that is a key UI component.

User interfaces also have abstract components. Modern programs contain abstract user interface components, such as the screen-based controls in **Figure 28-3** that represent actions and objects.

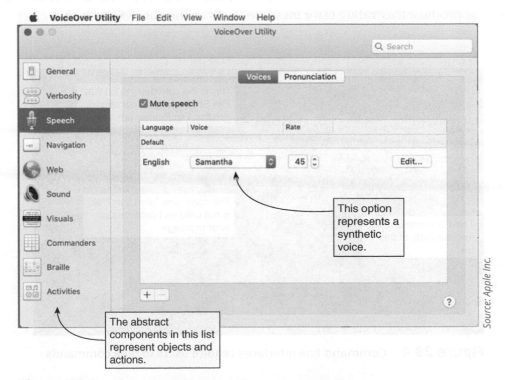

Source: Apple Inc.

Figure 28-3 User interfaces have abstract components

Selecting a UI (28.1.5, 28.1.6)

The user interface for a software product does not emerge from the vacuum of space. It has context defined by the platform conventions of operating systems, programming languages, design standards, and web protocols, including HTTP and HTML. Your selection of user interface elements for a program should reflect this context.

Operating systems, such as Microsoft Windows, Android, macOS, and iOS, each feature a unique user interface defined by the look and feel of menus, icons, and other screen-based controls. When programming, you can access **application programming interfaces (APIs)** that contain platform-specific interface elements, such as the Windows toolbar or a scrollable iPhone menu.

Physical and abstract interface components combine in various ways to produce four main classifications of user interfaces. Let's take a look at each one to discover the applications where they shine.

28.2 Command-Line User Interfaces

Command-Line Basics (28.2.1, 28.2.2)

Early generations of computers featured **command-line user interfaces** that required users to type commands. Some modern digital devices provide access to a command-line interface that you can use to expertly work with the operating system. On computers running the Windows operating system, the command line is accessed using the Windows command prompt. On an Apple computer running macOS, access is provided by the Terminal app.

Although command-line interaction with the operating system is similar to carrying out a conversation with the computer, the conversation is based on a set of command words and punctuation rules that users have to memorize. Mistakes produce frustrating error messages such as the one in **Figure 28-4**.

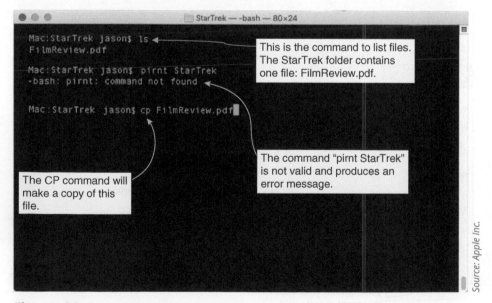

Figure 28-4   Command-line interfaces require users to type commands

Command-Line Program Design (28.2.2, 28.2.3, 28.2.4)

Command-line user interfaces can be incorporated into software applications. Judicious use of prompts and a sprinkling of artificial intelligence (AI) can alleviate the burden of memorizing commands.

A chatbot program called Eliza is an iconic example of a program based on a command-line user interface. **Chatbots** such as Eliza are designed to carry out a conversation. Originally, chatbots used bland generic replies, but more sophisticated chatbots use artificial intelligence algorithms to determine the meaning of user input. **Figure 28-5** shows a typical Eliza conversation.

```
I am the psychotherapist. Please describe your problems.
Each time you are finished talking, type RET twice.

>I seem to have trouble making decisions.
Can you elaborate on that?
>You know, trouble deciding what to do.
Why do you say that?
> I can't make up my mind.
Really?
>You're not being very helpful.
What makes you believe that I'm not being very helpful?
```

Figure 28-5   A conversation with the Eliza chatbot software

The overarching algorithm for a program with a command-line user interface is similar to a conversation in which the computer and user take turns asking questions and making responses.

Repeat until task is complete:
Computer prompts user to enter a query or other input data.
User enters data.
Computer responds to input data.

For simple entry-level practice programs, you may choose to use command-line user interfaces. You can incorporate some basic user interface principles to format input and output, as shown in **Figure 28-6**.

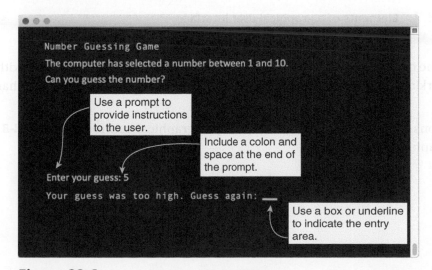

Figure 28-6   Command line best practices

28.3 Graphical User Interfaces

GUI Basics (28.3.1)

Most digital devices today are equipped with a **graphical user interface (GUI)**, which displays screen-based objects and menus that can be manipulated using a mouse, keyboard, or touch gesture. The acronym for "graphical user interface" is GUI, sometimes pronounced "gooey."

A GUI is based on a desktop or home screen populated with graphical representations of objects and actions. GUIs are sometimes called "WIMP" user interfaces because they contain workspaces, icons, menus, and a pointer, as shown in **Figure 28-7**.

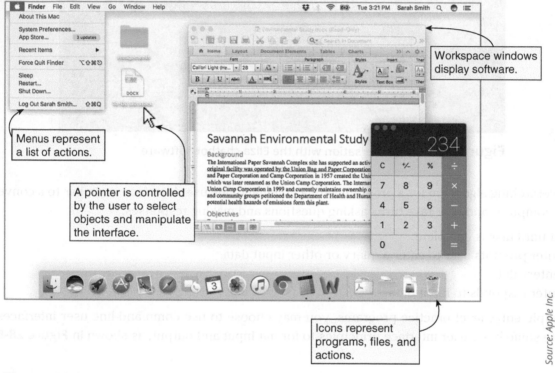

Source: Apple Inc.

Figure 28-7   Elements of a graphical user interface

Menus, such as the one in Figure 28-7, address the memorization problem associated with command-line user interfaces. When working with a GUI, users can select commands from a menu rather than typing memorized commands.

In addition to icons and menus, GUIs offer a variety of graphical controls. **Figure 28-8** illustrates the most common types of graphical controls.

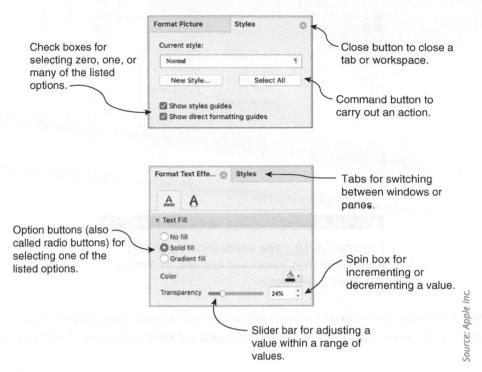

Check boxes for selecting zero, one, or many of the listed options.

Close button to close a tab or workspace.

Command button to carry out an action.

Tabs for switching between windows or panes.

Option buttons (also called radio buttons) for selecting one of the listed options.

Spin box for incrementing or decrementing a value.

Slider bar for adjusting a value within a range of values.

Source: Apple Inc.

Figure 28-8   Graphical controls

Q Can you identify the controls in **Figure 28-9**?

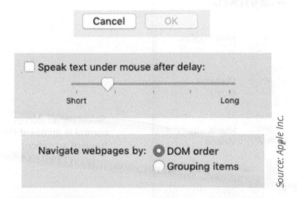

Source: Apple Inc.

Figure 28-9   Can you identify these GUI controls?

A From the top, these controls are command buttons, a slider bar, and option, or "radio," buttons.

GUI Program Design (28.3.2, 28.3.3, 28.3.4)

Graphical user interfaces provide a layer of abstraction that hides the computer operating system's command-line detail. As a programmer, you can include graphical user interface components in your programs by using libraries and APIs. When developing software for the Windows platform, for example, you can use the Windows API to design menus that look and act like those on the Windows desktop and Microsoft Office applications. See **Figure 28-10**.

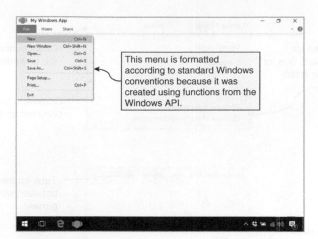

Figure 28-10   The Windows API provides
tools for menus, command buttons, and other
Windows UI elements

Programs with GUI interfaces have an open-ended **event-driven** flow, rather than a linear flow from beginning to end. The flow of the program is determined by user actions called "events," as shown in **Figure 28-11**.

Source: Apple Inc., GreenLandStudio/Shutterstock.com

Figure 28-11   UI events

For example, your smartphone's music app might have a menu with options for accessing albums, randomizing a playlist, and playing a specific song. You can select these options in any order. Your selection is an event that triggers an action such as playing the *Star Trek* soundtrack. Your code for handling an event is referred to as an **event handler**.

The high-level algorithm for developing an event-driven program goes something like this:

Create the icons, menus, and other interface elements that can trigger events.

Organize those interface elements inside a screen window.

Define and code an event-handler function for each interface element.

Initiate the program as an infinite event-loop that waits for users to trigger events.

28.4 Voice User Interfaces

Voice Interface Basics (28.4.1)

Today, Scotty could pick up any smartphone and speak to a digital assistant using a **voice user interface** characterized by spoken communication. Just think of the ways that voice user interfaces shine:

- Hands-free communication while driving
- Text message dictation
- Digital assistants, such as Siri and Alexa
- Telephone interactive voice response systems
- Word processor dictation systems

Voice user interfaces are based on two technologies: speech recognition and speech synthesis. **Speech recognition** uses sophisticated algorithms to identify spoken words and convert them into text that can be processed for meaning. During **speech synthesis**, machines such as computers generate audio output that sounds like human speech.

Speech Recognition (28.4.2)

To get a handle on the complexity of speech recognition algorithms, suppose you use a voice command to call a phone number beginning with "six." A microphone collects samples from the sound wave and attempts to identify a unit of speech, called a **phoneme**, that corresponds to each sample. Those phonemes then have to be interpreted to find the correct meaning. **Figure 28-12** highlights the difficulty of this process.

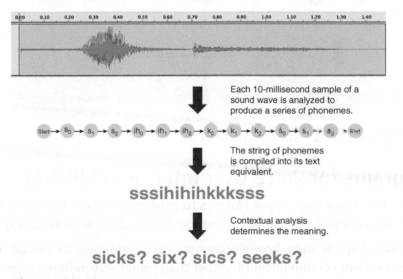

Each 10-millisecond sample of a sound wave is analyzed to produce a series of phonemes.

The string of phonemes is compiled into its text equivalent.

sssihihihkkksss

Contextual analysis determines the meaning.

sicks? six? sics? seeks?

Figure 28-12   Speech recognition

To efficiently convert speech to text, computer scientists apply sophisticated algorithms such as Connectionist Temporal Classification, Fourier transforms, and Hidden Markov Models. The process is computationally intensive, as you can imagine. A typical sentence contains thousands of 10-millisecond speech samples, and each one has to be compared to a huge universe of possible phonemes.

After converting speech to text, further processing is required to determine its context and meaning. Is it a number? Is it part of a phone number? Is it the area code? As speech input becomes more complex, deriving meaning requires algorithms based on a branch of artificial intelligence called natural language processing.

Speech Synthesis (28.4.3)

The first generation of speech synthesizers produced robotic voices that mangled the pronunciation of many words. Modern speech synthesis produces speech that sounds natural. The most common speech synthesis technology, **concatenative synthesis**, is based on a collection of prerecorded phonemes that can be assembled into words and sentences.

To derive the phonemes, live voice actors record words and sentences contained in a series of phoneme-rich scripts. Expert linguists slice the recordings into speech components, such as frequently used words and language-specific phonemes. The experts tag these speech segments and then load them into an extensive database. Speech segments are retrieved from this database during the speech synthesis process outlined in **Figure 28-13**.

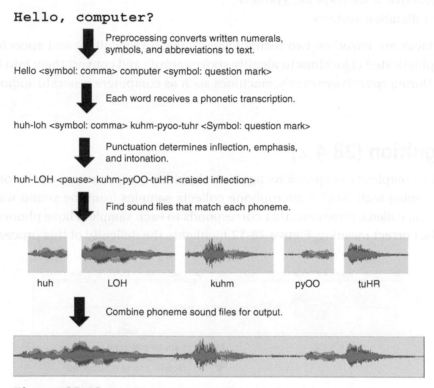

Figure 28-13   Speech synthesis

Designing Programs for Voice User Interfaces (28.4.4)

Programmers can add audio input and output features to existing software. For example, text messaging apps accept either typed or spoken input. Such applications can be classified as GUIs with speech input capabilities.

A purely voice-activated application, however, has no visual interface. Its design requires a programming mindset based on conversational communication rather than visual screen-based interactions.

To design a voice-activated application, your first step is to define the contextual domain. Are you creating a game? A digital assistant? By mapping out typical interactions, you can design a series of audio prompts and responses.

Q Would you say that the logic underlying a program with a voice user interface resembles a program with a command-line interface or a GUI?

A The logic of a program with a voice user interface surprisingly has more similarities to command-line user interfaces than to GUIs. The conversation that takes place is linear rather than event driven.

Implementing voice user interfaces requires speech recognition and speech synthesis APIs. Programs can access comprehensive speech recognition from cloud-based services such as Google Cloud, but access requires an Internet connection. Speech recognition within local devices is more limited, but advancements in speech processing algorithms continue to provide better functionality for programs that operate independently of the Internet.

28.5 Virtual Environment Interfaces

Virtual Environments (28.5.1)

Virtual reality uses computer technology to create a simulated, three-dimensional world that users can manipulate through head, hand, and body movements. Doesn't that sound a lot like the futuristic holodeck on the starship *Enterprise* where the crew could "vacation" in exotic simulated locations?

While waiting for holodecks, you can work with virtual reality games, flight simulators, field trips, and architectural walkthroughs. Technologies similar to virtual reality include **augmented reality** and **mixed reality**. See **Figure 28-14**.

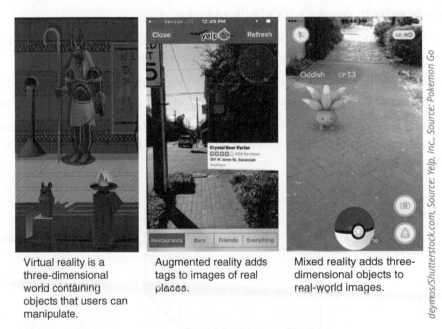

Virtual reality is a three-dimensional world containing objects that users can manipulate.

Augmented reality adds tags to images of real places.

Mixed reality adds three-dimensional objects to real-world images.

deymos/Shutterstock.com, Source: Yelp, Inc., Source: Pokemon Go

Figure 28-14   Virtual environments

Virtual Environment Interface Components (28.5.2, 28.5.3)

The primary input device for virtual reality software is a head-mounted display, which contains two display screens—one for each eye. As shown in **Figure 28-15**, the two images are slightly offset and produce the sense of three dimensions when viewed.

Haptic technologies play an increasingly important role as part of a virtual interface. **Haptic** devices simulate the sense of touch. For example, users wearing haptic gloves in a virtual environment would be able to "feel" the surface of a simulated object.

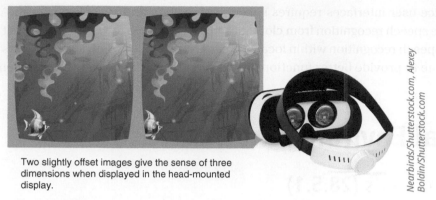

Nearbirds/Shutterstock.com, Alexey Boldin/Shutterstock.com

Two slightly offset images give the sense of three dimensions when displayed in the head-mounted display.

Figure 28-15   Virtual reality head-mounted display

Virtual, augmented, or mixed reality user interfaces may also include one or more of the following devices:

Hand-held controllers, such as joysticks and digital wands, to select objects

Smartphone cameras to capture real-world images

Smartphone displays to provide the screen for a head-mounted display

Haptic gloves for tactile feedback from virtual objects

Microphones for speech recognition

Motion tracking body suits to sense a user's body movements.

Programming virtual applications is all about collecting data from interface devices and using it to control variables that affect the virtual environment and the objects it contains.

Environments can be based on footage from 360-degree motion photography or three-dimensional vector animations. **Vector graphics** define shapes as a set of instructions for drawing lines and curves.

Vector graphic instructions can form three-dimensional objects. The structure for a vector graphic is called a wireframe, and that wireframe can be filled with color, shaded, highlighted, and endowed with various levels of transparency. See **Figure 28-16**.

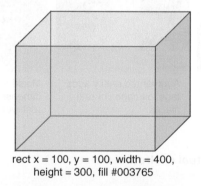

rect x = 100, y = 100, width = 400,
height = 300, fill #003765

Figure 28-16   3D vector graphics
are formed from instructions that
specify shape, size, color, and lighting

Assembling a collection of vector graphics produces a virtual reality environment that users can navigate in three dimensions, viewing objects from all sides. Because each vector object is independent, users can also move them within the virtual world.

Programming the Virtual Interface (28.5.4)

Extending the user interface to a three-dimensional environment requires linkages from the user's equipment. For example, if haptic gloves are used to manipulate objects, each glove gesture is an interface input that you have to deal with in program code.

Development tools provide functions and libraries for assigning actions to the entire spectrum of inputs. Development tools for virtual environments include the following:

- Modeling languages such as VRML
- Application program interfaces such as WebVR
- Game engines such as Unity

28.6 Accessibility and Inclusion

Accessibility Guidelines (28.6.1, 28.6.2)

Imagine using digital devices with your eyes closed. You can't see the screen. You can't look at the labels on your keyboard. Millions of people with disabilities use braille keyboards, screen narrators, and other adaptive technologies such as the eyes-free texting app in **Figure 28-17**.

Figure 28-17   Adaptive devices include this app for eyes-free texting

In the context of software development, **accessibility** means providing user interfaces that can be used by everyone, including people with disabilities. Most software development projects include detailed accessibility requirements based on in-house guidelines and standards developed by advocacy organizations.

Both Microsoft and Apple have detailed guidelines for developing accessible software and apps. The W3C organization promotes its Web Content Accessibility Guidelines (WCAG) and a variation of those guidelines for nonweb information and communications technologies. Many countries, including the United States, have enacted laws and regulations that apply to hardware and software accessibility.

Programming for accessibility may require you to provide alternative modes of interaction for people with visual, audio, motor, or cognitive limitations. Including individuals with special needs in software testing cycles can help you gauge the success of your accessibility efforts. Best practice guidelines for accessibility include the following.

Visual accessibility. Many people have impaired vision. Individuals without sight may use special adaptive equipment to interact with digital devices. Color blindness prevents people from differentiating some colors. People with low vision may have difficulty deciphering text that blends into the background.

To increase accessibility for individuals with impaired vision:

- Provide an audio alternative to visual cues. Alt text, for example, provides an audio description of a graphic, image, or diagram.
- Organize screen elements to make sense when interpreted by a screen reader.
- Avoid using color as the only cue for differentiating significant text and controls.
- Select a color palette that presents high contrast between foreground objects, text, and backgrounds.

Audio accessibility. Because audio interaction with digital devices has become popular, developers should take the following steps to assist individuals with acute hearing loss:

- Avoid using audio as the only cue signaling events and alerts.
- Provide an option to view a transcript of audio exchanges.
- Provide closed captioning for video streams.

Motor and cognitive accessibility. Physical disabilities can make using a keyboard and mouse difficult. Because adaptive devices interact with the operating system, software is generally more accessible when it adheres to standard conventions of the host operating system. Also consider the following guidelines:

- Ensure that your software functions correctly when users have activated accessibility features provided by the operating system.
- Be mindful of response times, allowing for delayed responses from persons with motor disabilities.
- Avoid flashing screen objects that may cause seizures in some people.
- Provide alternatives to mouse operations, such as drag and drop, that may be difficult for individuals with impaired motor skills.
- Consider ways someone might use your software by issuing voice commands.

Inclusive Design (28.6.3, 28.6.4, 28.6.5)

Inclusive design ensures that a software product is usable by people with diverse abilities, backgrounds, and equipment access. It includes accessibility principles but extends to encompass gender identity, ethnicity, nationality, technical skill level, and equipment availability.

Best practices for inclusive design require you as a developer to view projects from the perspective of people who may speak different languages, identify with different genders, have various skill sets, and who may not have access to state-of-the-art equipment.

Inclusive language. You may not be able to speak Hindi or read Devanagari script, but you can probably identify the Search link in **Figure 28-18** because the software developers included a magnifying glass icon.

Figure 28-18   Icons and images can help to overcome language barriers

Tech products get worldwide use, so think globally when you design software.

- Use simple language and intuitive controls to increase usability for people with diverse language preferences.
- Enhance on-screen controls with icons to show their purpose.
- Use standard buttons and menus placed at standard locations, which may help users transfer skills from other similar software.

Inclusive identity. Cultural heritage and personal identity affect the way people use and interpret content. Wording and visual techniques can help to ensure a positive experience for every user. See **Figure 28-19**.

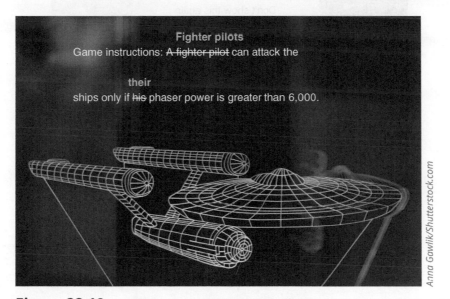

Figure 28-19   Inclusive language is gender neutral

Guidelines for identity inclusion include the following:

- Be mindful of pronouns. Using plurals, such as "their," helps to avoid use of "he," "she," and other gender-specific terms.
- Remain aware of cultural sensitivities, including the meanings attached to colors, symbols, and gestures.
- Avoid sarcasm and inside jokes that may be easily misinterpreted by users with diverse cultural backgrounds.

Inclusive skill sets. Novice users may need help to overcome the initial learning curve for your software, but expert users don't want to wade through multiple help screens before getting right to the task. In **Figure 28-20**, expert users can opt out of the introductory help.

Following are guidelines for including users of varying skill sets:

- Assume your users could have skill levels ranging from novice to expert.
- Supply a full range of cues to help novice users, but do not let them interfere with the streamlined interaction demanded by power users.

Inclusive equipment. Consumers use many devices to access software, and not everyone has a high-speed Internet connection. Designing your software to include as many devices as practical might require different versions for computer and mobile platforms, as shown in **Figure 28-21**.

Figure 28-20   Let users opt out of hints and instructions that they don't want

Figure 28-21   Different platforms may require different versions of a software product

Here are some additional tips for extending your software to a larger user base:

- Test your software on legacy devices that might not have state-of-the-art processing power, cutting-edge graphics capability, or high-speed Internet access.
- Customize versions of your software for various screen sizes, orientations, and resolutions to accommodate users with smartphones, desktop computers, tablets, or laptops.
- Aim for cross-platform compatibility so that your software works on multiple operating systems and your online apps operate with multiple browsers.

Q In the scene from *Star Trek* when Scotty tries to use voice commands to interact with a 1986 Macintosh computer, how would you classify his interface problem? Is it an accessibility problem or an inclusive problem?

A Scotty does not have a hearing, visual, cognitive, or motor disability, so his problem must be with inclusive design. In theory, the Macintosh computer design did not consider the experiences and expectations of a person from another cultural time period. In reality, this fanciful example also points out that developers can only implement available technologies but may have opportunities to add accessible and inclusive features in the future.

Summary

- A user interface (UI) is a collection of physical, graphical, and logical constructs that facilitate interaction between humans and digital devices. A broader concept, user experience (UX) goes beyond user interaction to include an entire realm of consumer involvement.
- User interfaces have both physical and abstract components. Programmers have control over abstract user interface components, such as screen-based controls that represent actions and objects. Programmers can access application program interfaces (APIs) that contain platform-specific interface elements, such as the Windows toolbar or a scrollable iPhone menu.
- Command-line user interfaces requiring typed interaction can be used to manipulate the operating system and for simple entry-level practice programs.
- A graphical user interface (GUI) displays graphical objects and menus that can be manipulated using a mouse, keyboard, or touch gesture. GUIs are sometimes called "WIMP" user interfaces because they contain workspaces, icons, menus, and a pointer.
- Programs with GUI interfaces have an open-ended, event-driven flow, rather than a linear flow from beginning to end. The flow of the program is determined by user actions called "events."
- A voice user interface is characterized by spoken communication, based on underlying speech recognition and speech synthesis technologies. The logic of a program with a voice user interface has similarities to command-line user interfaces.
- Virtual reality uses computer technology to create a simulated, three-dimensional world that users can manipulate through head, hand, and body movements. Augmented reality tags real-world scenes with computer-generated data. Mixed reality layers three-dimensional interactive objects over real-world scenes.
- When developing the user interface for a program, be sure to consider accessibility and use inclusive design so that your work is available to the widest possible audience.

Key Terms

accessibility	event handler	phoneme
application programming interfaces (APIs)	graphical user interface (GUI)	speech recognition speech synthesis
augmented reality	haptic	user experience (UX)
chatbots	Human–Computer	user interface (UI)
command-line user interfaces	Interaction (HCI)	vector graphics
concatenative synthesis	inclusive design	virtual reality
event-driven	mixed reality	voice user interface

Module
29

Software Development Methodologies

Learning Objectives:

29.1 Software Development

29.1.1 List the key tasks that take place during the software development process.

29.1.2 Describe the importance of efficiency, security, and quality throughout the software development process.

29.2 The Waterfall Model

29.2.1 Describe the general methodology of the waterfall development model.

29.2.2 Identify each phase of the waterfall model.

29.2.3 List advantages and disadvantages of the waterfall model.

29.2.4 Select software development projects that can be best approached using the waterfall model.

29.3 The Agile Model

29.3.1 Describe the general approach of incremental, iterative development methods.

29.3.2 Classify Scrum, Extreme Programming, Feature-Driven Development, and Rapid Application Development as agile development methodologies.

29.3.3 List advantages and disadvantages of agile development.

29.3.4 Select software projects that can be best approached using an agile development methodology.

29.4 Coding Principles

29.4.1 Describe the DRY principle.

29.4.2 Describe the single responsibility principle.

29.4.3 Explain the purpose of clean coding.

29.4.4 Explain how statement blocks assist readability and constrain scope in a structured program.

29.4.5 Describe the importance of secure coding.

29.4.6 List principles for secure coding.

29.4.7 List success factors for creating top-notch software.

29.5 Testing

29.5.1 Identify testing levels for software development.

29.5.2 Describe unit testing and the use of test cases.

29.5.3 State the purpose of integration testing.

29.5.4 Explain why system testing is classified as a "black box" methodology.

29.5.5 Explain the use of alpha and beta passes in the acceptance test phase.

29.5.6 Identify the purpose of regression testing.

29.1 Software Development

The Software Development Life Cycle (29.1.1)

Like plants and animals, software has a life cycle. This **software development life cycle** begins with conception and progresses through the phases as shown in **Figure 29-1**.

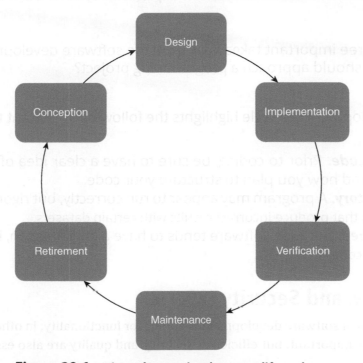

Figure 29-1   The software development life cycle

As an individual or as part of a development team, you'll contribute to one or more phases of the software development life cycle.

Conception and Planning. The initial idea for an information system, software program, or app is based on business necessities, problems that need to be solved, niches that need to be filled, or markets that have profit potential. The software begins as a plan, which contains requirements for *what* the software is expected to do. Those requirements are created by various stakeholders, such as users, business owners, consultants, and programmers.

Design. In the design phase, developers formulate a model of the software using algorithms and data structures that specify *how* the software is supposed to accomplish the list of requirements.

Implementation. The software materializes as programmers generate lines of code and populate data structures to implement the design.

Verification. Testing is an integral phase in which software gains durability and stability as programmers correct errors and optimize performance.

Maintenance. After deployment, software can perform for months, years, or decades. Its lifetime may span generations of hardware and encompass innovations that affect its functionality. Software evolves in the maintenance phase as programmers supply incremental improvements to maintain peak performance.

Retirement. Eventually, the useful lifespan of a software program comes to an end because of factors such as changing user requirements and hardware innovations. As software nears the end of its useful life, maintenance activities wind down and user support is discontinued. If new, updated software is required, then stakeholders restart the software development life cycle for a new state-of-the-art edition.

Q Can you identify three important takeaways from the software development life cycle that affect the way you should approach a programming project?

A The software development life cycle highlights the following important takeaways for you as a programmer:

- *Plan before you code.* Prior to coding, be sure to have a clear idea of what the software is supposed to do and how you plan to structure your code.
- *Testing is mandatory.* A program may appear to run correctly, but rigorous testing can eliminate coding errors that produce incorrect results with certain datasets.
- *Done is not finished.* Because software tends to have a long lifespan, be prepared to revise and improve your code.

Efficiency, Quality, and Security (29.1.2)

It might seem like the focus of software development is coding for functionality; in other words, making software that works. Functionality is important, but efficiency, security, and quality are also essential in all phases of the software life cycle.

Efficiency. Efficient programs have a smaller hardware footprint but better response time.

Security. Secure software protects itself, its users, its underlying hardware, and its communication system from unauthorized activities.

Quality. Software rises to the top of the quality scale when it is correct, reliable, easy to use, flexible, testable, and maintainable.

The checklist in **Figure 29-2** provides examples of best practices that integrate efficiency, security, and quality during every phase of the software life cycle.

Conception

☑ Make sure the list of requirements is targeted to essential tasks.

☑ Include a list of security concerns in the requirements document.

☑ Gather factors that define usage expectations.

Design

☑ Decompose the software scope into modules, functions, and classes that perform specific tasks.

☑ Ensure that the design incudes all of the required tasks.

☑ Include directives for secure coding practice in the software specifications.

Implementation

☑ Follow secure coding practices.

☑ Write code that can be easily understood and modified.

☑ Walk through code to identify potential inefficiencies and security vulnerabilities.

Verification

☑ Follow a testing plan that verifies correct operation for all branches of the program.

☑ Include tests that attempt to gain unauthorized access to the software code or data.

Maintenance

☑ Provide ways to monitor the software's performance throughout its life.

☑ Provide monitoring routines to log attempted security breaches.

Retirement

☑ Have a plan for gracefully decommissioning the software.

Figure 29-2   Best practices for software efficiency, quality, and security in each phase of software development

29.2 The Waterfall Model

Structured Analysis and Design (29.2.1, 29.2.2)

Back in the days when computers were room-sized mainframes, going digital was all about converting manual business processes into computerized information systems. Teams of systems analysts were nearly overwhelmed by all the tasks associated with implementing new information systems. See **Figure 29-3**.

Write detailed specifications

Compile corporate wish list

Create software

Test software

Catalog manual business processes

Schedule tasks

Write documentation

Purchase and install equipment

Generate cost estimates

Train users

Stick to the budget

Daniela Barreto/Shutterstock.com

Figure 29-3   Developing new information systems involves many tasks

Out of the chaos emerged a systematic approach to software development based on a rigidly structured sequence of analysis and design phases. This approach, known as the **waterfall model**, divides software development into a series of cascading tasks that are performed one after the other. As shown in **Figure 29-4**, each phase produces a deliverable that is the input for the next phase.

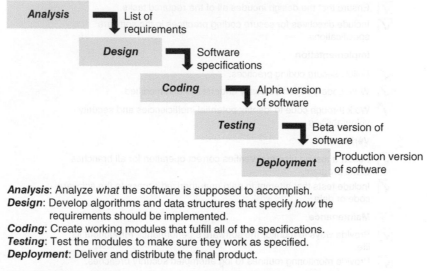

Analysis: Analyze *what* the software is supposed to accomplish.
Design: Develop algorithms and data structures that specify *how* the
     requirements should be implemented.
Coding: Create working modules that fulfill all of the specifications.
Testing: Test the modules to make sure they work as specified.
Deployment: Deliver and distribute the final product.

Figure 29-4   **Phases of the waterfall development model**

Q Suppose you are a member of a development team producing an advanced driver assistance system (ADAS) that monitors blind spots, helps drivers stay in their lane, and autonomously avoids collisions. Your team is using the waterfall development method. What documentation would you be given as you begin coding the collision detection module?

A The software specifications documentation.

Waterfall Advantages and Disadvantages (29.2.3, 29.2.4)

The main advantage of the waterfall model is its emphasis on planning. During the analysis and design phases, developers lock down specifications for the software. These two phases may take up to 40 percent of the total development time, and once coding begins, few changes are made to the specifications. Additional advantages include:

- With specifications locked down, programmers have a clear mandate and don't need to be concerned with last-minute change orders that might have a domino effect throughout the code.
- The documentation created during the analysis and design phases needs only minor edits to become documentation for the final software product.

The major criticism of the waterfall model is its lack of flexibility. During the analysis and design phases, developers rarely can anticipate every way in which users will interact with the software. Business policies and regulations might change while development is ongoing. Because the software specifications are locked down at the beginning, developers have limited leeway to add or improve features during the coding phase.

Based on its advantages and disadvantages, the waterfall model is appropriate for development projects when:

- The scope and size of the project are well defined.
- The requirements are clear at the beginning of the project.
- The underlying system and use cases are stable.
- The project has a defined completion date during which requirements are not likely to change.

Q How suitable is the waterfall model for developing your collision avoidance module of the ADAS system?

A The waterfall method might not be suitable because as you develop the system, you could discover additional requirements based on scenarios that were not anticipated during the design phase.

29.3 The Agile Model

Incremental Development (29.3.1)

In response to the waterfall model's rigid approach to software development, an **incremental development model** emerged in which software is designed, coded, and tested in a succession of cycles. Each cycle produces a module that works and adds value to the project but is not necessarily feature complete. In each cycle, requirements can change as the software gradually takes its final form.

You can visualize the incremental development model as a series of loops like those pictured in **Figure 29-5**.

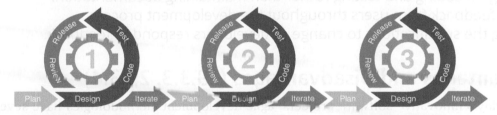

Plan: Determine the scope and focus of the iteration.
Design: Create specifications for coding an instance of a module.
Code: Write the code for the module.
Test: Test the module.
Release: Circulate the module to get user feedback.
Review: Analyze user feedback.
Iterate: Launch the next iteration to improve and extend the feature set and functionality.

Figure 29-5   **The incremental iterative design approach**

Agile Methodologies (29.3.2)

Incremental, iterative development is the basis for today's popular **agile development methodologies**. When you hear team leaders mention Scrum, Extreme Programming, Rapid Application Development, or Feature-Driven Development, they are referring to various agile methodologies.

The general agile approach was devised by a group of programmers who published the Agile Manifesto, shown in **Figure 29-6**.

The Agile Manifesto

We are uncovering better ways of developing software by
doing it and helping others do it. Through this work we have
come to value:

Individuals and interactions over processes and tools

Working software over comprehensive documentation

Customer collaboration over contract negotiation

Responding to change over following a plan

That is, while there is value in the items on the right, we value
the items on the left more.

———

© 2001–2019 **Agile Manifesto** Authors
This declaration may be freely copied in any form, but only
in its entirety through this notice.

Source: Agile Alliance

Figure 29-6   **The Agile Manifesto**

Q From reading the Agile Manifesto, what are the four important principles of the Agile philosophy?

A The four important principles of the Agile philosophy are:

- Interacting with users and team members rather than following a set process.
- Focusing on coding and testing rather than maintaining documentation.
- Getting feedback from users throughout the development process.
- Allowing the specifications to change as developers respond to feedback.

Agile Advantages and Disadvantages (29.3.3, 29.3.4)

For many of today's innovative software projects, agile development methodologies have several advantages over the waterfall model:

- Agile methodologies are more flexible, allowing programmers to alter requirements going into each iteration.
- Functional software is released at the end of each iteration, unlike the waterfall model, which produces a functional product only at the end of the testing phase.
- Each release is thoroughly tested to ensure software quality.
- User interaction during multiple deployment and review phases provides developers with continuous feedback that can be incorporated into the final product.
- Because of feedback during each iteration, the final product tends to satisfy user needs.

Q In agile methodologies, how does user involvement differ from the waterfall method?

A In the waterfall method, users typically provide input once during the analysis phase and then again during the testing phase. With agile methodologies, users participate in each iteration.

The major criticisms of agile methodologies include:

- Measuring progress is difficult.
- The number of iterations that will be required for the final product is unknown.
- Developers can get sidetracked by requests to add features that are not essential to the software functionality.
- The lack of a comprehensive design plan tends to be reflected in haphazard documentation.

Q Which criticism of agile methodologies is most likely to affect the software delivery date?

A Because the number of iterations is unknown, the software delivery date may be difficult to estimate.

Based on advantages and disadvantages, an agile methodology is appropriate for development projects when:

- The requirements are not obvious when the project begins.
- It is acceptable for the design to emerge through prototyping.
- It is important to get users involved in the development process.

29.4 Coding Principles

Efficient Coding (29.4.1)

DRY, WET, DIE, SRP, Clean, STRIDE, KISS. Programmers toss these terms around like baseballs at an MLB game warmup. These terms are acronyms for principles that can help you during the coding phase of the software development cycle.

> **Don't Repeat Yourself (DRY)** is a programming principle that promotes efficient code through efficient use and reuse of functions, classes, and methods. **Duplication is Evil (DIE)** is the same idea.
>
> **Write Every Time (WET)** is the opposite of DRY. WET code contains needless repetition. **Figure 29-7** shows the difference between WET and DRY code.

The takeaway from the DRY principle is to check your code for redundancies. If necessary, restructure your algorithms, classes, or methods to eliminate repetitive code.

```
# WET code
if hazard.moving == "right":
    if speed > 30:
        swerve("left")
    else:
        brake_lights = True
        alarm.sound()
        accelerate = False
        brake(hazard)

if hazard.moving == "left":
    if speed > 30:
        swerve("right")
    else:
        brake_lights = True
        alarm.sound()
        accelerate = False
        brake(hazard)

# DRY code
if hazard.moving == "right":
    if speed > 30:
        swerve("left")
    else:
        stop_car()

if hazard.moving == "left":
    if speed > 30:
        swerve("right")
    else:
        stop_car()

def stop_car():
    brake_lights = True
    alarm.sound()
    accelerate = False
    brake(hazard)
```

The logic for stopping is repeated in this WET code.

This DRY code eliminates the repetition by calling a function.

The function contains code for stopping the car that can be called from multiple locations in the main program.

Figure 29-7 The difference between WET and DRY code

Modularized Code (29.4.2)

The **single responsibility principle (SRP)** suggests each function or class should have only one responsibility and one reason to change. When you have more than one reason to change a function or a class, it might have too much responsibility and is a candidate for restructuring.

Your collision avoidance module for the ADAS software needs to deal with various hazards. You might initially think that hazards should be defined in a class like the one shown in **Figure 29-8**.

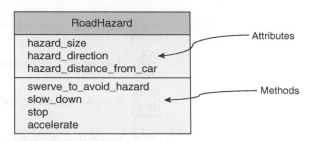

Figure 29-8   **A class that violates SRP**

Q Can you guess why the RoadHazard class violates SRP?

A The RoadHazard class has four methods, so it is handling many possible hazards. The code for the class or its methods might need to change for many reasons. In the future, sensors might be able to detect the speed of a hazard, which could require changes to several methods in the class. Another reason: it might become apparent that collision avoidance with the car ahead should be handled differently than avoiding random hazards that pop up from the side of the road.

To ensure that your code follows SRP, consider the purpose of each function, class, and method. Make sure these elements are fully decomposed and focus on one task. Look at the dependencies and make sure that changes won't have a domino effect that requires altering multiple class structures or methods.

Clean Coding (29.4.3, 29.4.4)

Clean code can be easily understood not just by you but by other programmers who might test your modules or modify them in the future. Clean code should be elegant, readable, simple, and testable. To produce clean code, keep the following best practices in mind:

- Use descriptive names for variables, functions, methods, and classes.
- Use consistent naming conventions for functions and methods. Don't prefix some functions with "get," but use "calculate" with other similar functions.
- Adopt a naming and coding style that is consistent with accepted conventions for the programming language.
- Keep functions and methods short and focused on doing one task. Aim for functions that have 15 lines of code or less.
- Use white space to create statement blocks that delineate functions, classes, and other program segments.
- Use comments sparingly. Your code should be self-explanatory. Be sure to update comments with each release.

Q How can you create a visual delineation for a block of code that represents a decision control structure?

A Insert an extra line to add white space before and after the decision block.

Secure Coding (29.4.5, 29.4.6)

When you find your STRIDE in programming, you're in the habit of taking steps to make sure your code is secure. STRIDE is a mnemonic for the six types of security threats shown in **Figure 29-9** that take advantage of code vulnerabilities.

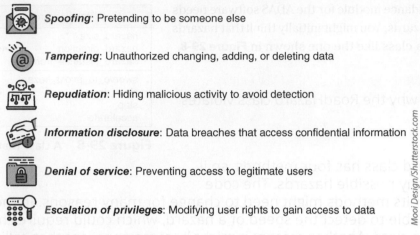

Spoofing: Pretending to be someone else

Tampering: Unauthorized changing, adding, or deleting data

Repudiation: Hiding malicious activity to avoid detection

Information disclosure: Data breaches that access confidential information

Denial of service: Preventing access to legitimate users

Escalation of privileges: Modifying user rights to gain access to data

Figure 29-9   **The STRIDE framework of security vulnerabilities**

You might wonder what these threats have to do with your code. Let's look at an example: buffer overflows. A **buffer overflow** is a condition in which data in memory exceeds its boundaries and flows into memory areas intended for other data or program code. **Figure 29-10** illustrates a simplified example of a buffer overflow exploit.

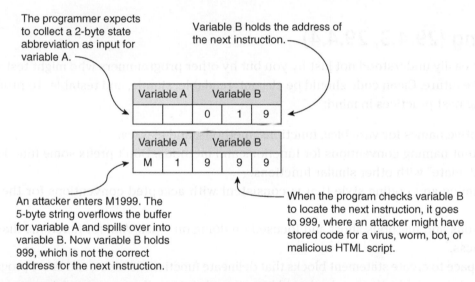

The programmer expects to collect a 2-byte state abbreviation as input for variable A.

Variable B holds the address of the next instruction.

Variable A	Variable B
	0 1 9

Variable A	Variable B
M 1	9 9 9

An attacker enters M1999. The 5-byte string overflows the buffer for variable A and spills over into variable B. Now variable B holds 999, which is not the correct address for the next instruction.

When the program checks variable B to locate the next instruction, it goes to 999, where an attacker might have stored code for a virus, worm, bot, or malicious HTML script.

Figure 29-10   **How a buffer overflow exploit works**

Cybercriminals can trigger buffer overflows with input specifically designed to execute malicious code, such as a computer virus. In the STRIDE model, buffer overflow exploits are an example of tampering that can lead to information disclosure.

You can protect your code from buffer overflows and other security exploits by implementing the following principles of **secure coding**:

Security from the start. Be mindful of ways in which your application might be exploited by cybercriminals.

Separation of privilege. Allow each user to access only those parts of a program that are required to perform their allocated tasks. By doing so, you minimize exposure if an account is compromised.

Economy of mechanism. Follow the KISS (Keep It Simple and Secure) doctrine that simpler code means less can go wrong.

Code defensively. Check user input for suspicious nonprintable control characters, and place strict boundaries on the values that can be stored in variables. Check the validity of input parameters in methods. Use containers that don't allow overruns instead of raw buffers that do.

Fail securely. Anticipate and handle exceptions that might cause your program to fail. Log all failures or suspicious activity. For example, if a user enters an incorrect password many times, it may be a break-in attempt.

Q If you allow open access to the ADAS system, it might be possible for remote users to control the braking system for a car. Which two principles of secure coding does this violate?

A It violates the security-from-the-start principle and the separation-of-privilege principle.

Success Factors (29.4.7)

When creating software, your initial concern might be "I hope it works!" But that is not the only criteria for successful coding. In a production environment, the quality of your code depends on several **success factors**. **Figure 29-11** offers a checklist of success factors that can increase the quality of the software you create.

Success factor	Self-check
☑ Efficiency	I've looked for ways to optimize performance by tightening up the algorithm using techniques to reduce repetition, encapsulate code into functions, and restructure classes.
☑ Usability	I've created a user interface that is intuitive, attractive, and responsive.
☑ Accessibility	I have made every effort to make the software accessible to people with disabilities.
☑ Functionality	I've tested the software to ensure that it performs correctly under all the required use cases and for all data sets.
☑ Security	I've tried to anticipate and block ways in which my software could be compromised by attackers.
☑ Reliability	I am alert to ways in which my software might fail and have incorporated recovery routines.
☑ Flexibility	I've written code that is structured and modularized so that necessary modifications can be implemented in narrowly targeted segments of code.
☑ Maintainability	I've written code that can be understood by other programmers who might be revising it.
☑ Testability	I've written and executed unit tests for my code which can be easily run again for regression testing after any future changes.

Figure 29-11   Coding success factors

29.5 Testing

Levels of Testing (29.5.1)

Developing software to assist drivers is not trivial. Drivers' lives depend on the reliability of the code that you contribute. Testing is crucial.

Software development involves four levels of testing, shown in **Figure 29-12**.

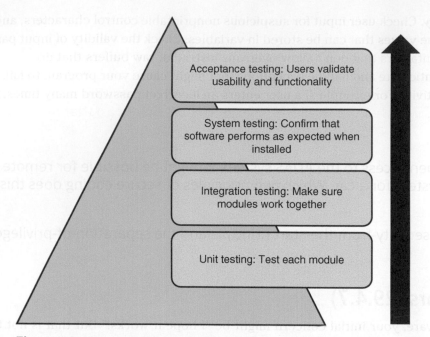

Figure 29-12   Software testing levels

Unit Testing (29.5.2)

Unit testing ensures that each module operates correctly for a comprehensive range of test cases. A **test case** is a set of preconditions, steps, and data that should produce a specific result called a "post condition." When a test case is executed, the actual results should correspond to the expected post condition.

If your module of the ADAS is supposed to stop the vehicle before an imminent collision, you must ensure that it correctly accounts for factors such as vehicle speed, stopping distance, and road conditions.

Unit testing can be carried out by manually entering test data, or testing can be automated using a companion program to feed in test cases. The goal of unit testing is to try all probable combinations of data, statements, decisions, branches, and conditions to ensure that they produce the expected output.

When setting up test cases, you should include boundary cases. A **boundary case** is a data point that is just at or beyond the maximum or minimum limits of expected data. See **Figure 29-13**.

Figure 29-13   Boundary conditions for vehicle speed

Q Based on Figure 29-13, what boundary cases would you check for in the collision avoidance module that relate to vehicle speed?

A One boundary case would be collision avoidance at 160 mph because that is the maximum vehicle speed. But what about 165 mph? Even if cars do not go that fast, you would also want to know what your program does when given that input. Another boundary case would be at 0 mph when the vehicle is stopped.

Savvy programmers always set up test cases for zero or null values. Division by 0 produces errors and exceptions that can terminate a program. Testing the zero-boundary condition ensures that your program handles the result gracefully.

Integration Testing (29.5.3)

Integration testing verifies that all of the units or modules work together. Most software contains a collection of modules that may have been created by several programmers or supplied as libraries and other preprogrammed tools. When combined, these modules might not coordinate as expected.

Integration testing is based on test cases that focus on the flow of data between modules. For example, in the ADAS software, the module that detects objects has to send actionable data to the module that controls the vehicle's speed. When the detection module sends data such as "Large objected detected," the speed module should process that data to stop the vehicle (**Figure 29-14**).

⚠ Large object detected. Stop vehicle.

Figure 29-14   Collision avoidance

System Testing (29.5.4)

System testing validates that the fully integrated software application performs as expected when installed on target hardware platforms. The software is tested under load to make sure it maintains good response time and stability.

System testing is classified as "black box testing" because it focuses on inputs and outputs rather than the underlying code. In contrast, unit testing is classified as "white box testing" because all the details of the code are under scrutiny. See **Figure 29-15**.

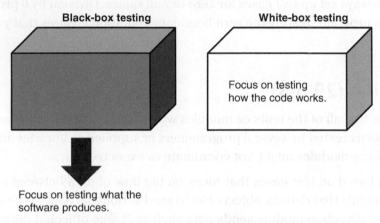

Black-box testing   White-box testing

Focus on testing how the code works.

Focus on testing what the software produces.

Figure 29-15   Black box and white box testing

Acceptance Testing (29.5.5)

Acceptance testing is typically performed with the help of users to ensure that the software meets usability requirements and the objectives for which it was created. Acceptance testing includes alpha and beta test passes.

Alpha testing is performed internally by professional testers. Your ADAS system would likely be tested on a closed course with professional drivers. **Beta testing** is performed by a select group of "real users" who are not members of the development team or professional testers. This phase of testing helps to identify problems that may occur in real-world environments on various hardware platforms and in a wide variety of unexpected scenarios.

Q Software for complex information systems requires a formal test plan prepared by developers. What level of testing is appropriate for casual programming projects and course assignments?

A For casual programming, unit testing can verify that your software functions correctly for a variety of datasets. You can also carry out simple acceptance testing by imagining that you are a typical user.

Regression Testing (29.5.6)

One additional type of testing is important in multiple phases of the software development cycle. **Regression testing** is performed to ensure that recent code modifications do not have adverse effects. This type of testing can be performed during unit, integration, system, or acceptance testing. It may also be required for changes made during the maintenance phase of the system life cycle.

Whenever code is modified, no matter how small the change, appropriate tests should be performed. Usually, you can use existing test cases; if not the entire test suite, then a subset that probes any likely side effects of the modified code.

Summary

- Software has a life cycle that begins with conception and ends when the software is decommissioned.
- During the software development process, members of the development team focus on efficiency, security, and quality, in addition to functionality.
- The waterfall development model divides software development into a series of cascading tasks that are performed one after the other. This development approach is suitable when the application domain is well defined and stable but leaves little room for flexibility and changing requirements.
- Agile methodologies are based on an incremental, iterative approach to software development. Software is designed, coded, and tested in a succession of cycles. Each cycle produces a module that works and adds value to the project but is not necessarily feature complete. In each cycle, requirements can change as the software gradually takes its final form.
- Don't Repeat Yourself (DRY) is a programming principle that promotes efficient code. The opposite is Write Every Time (WET) code that contains repetitions and redundancies.
- The single responsibility principle (SRP) suggests that each function or class should have only one responsibility and one reason to change.
- Clean code can be easily understood not just by you but by other programmers who might test your modules or modify them in the future.
- Secure coding begins with an awareness of exploits that can compromise code and continues throughout the coding process in the form of simplifying code, establishing input checks, and handling exceptions.
- Software quality, security, functionality, and usability are evaluated during four testing phases: unit testing, integration testing, system testing, and acceptance testing.

Key Terms

acceptance testing	Don't Repeat Yourself (DRY)	software development life cycle
agile development methodologies	Duplication is Evil (DIE)	success factors
alpha testing	incremental development model	system testing
beta testing	integration testing	test case
boundary case	regression testing	unit testing
buffer overflow	secure coding	waterfall model
clean code	single responsibility principle (SRP)	Write Every Time (WET)

Module
30

Pseudocode, Flowcharts, and Decision Tables

Learning Objectives:

30.1 Pseudocode

30.1.1 Define the term "pseudocode" as a generalized description of a program.

30.1.2 Explain the purpose of pseudocode.

30.1.3 Contrast pseudocode with code written in a programming language.

30.1.4 Recognize the relationship between algorithm steps and pseudocode statements.

30.1.5 Apply an organized approach to writing pseudocode.

30.2 Flowcharts

30.2.1 Define the term "flowchart" as a diagrammatic representation of an algorithm.

30.2.2 State that flowcharts can be used instead of, or in conjunction with, pseudocode.

30.2.3 Identify the shapes used in flowcharts and the purpose of each.

30.2.4 Trace a path through a flowchart.

30.2.5 List tools that can be used to create flowcharts.

30.3 Decision Tables

30.3.1 Define a decision table as a grid of rows and columns used to distill a set of complex decisions and actions into a set of rules that can become the statements in a computer program.

30.3.2 Identify the four quadrants of a decision table.

30.3.3 Calculate the maximum number of conditions.

30.3.4 Formulate the unique combinations of conditions.

30.3.5 Specify the action for each unique combination.

30.3.6 Interpret the rules produced by a decision table.

30.3.7 Optimize the rule set.

30.3.8 Check the decision table for completeness and accuracy.

30.1 Pseudocode

From Algorithms to Pseudocode (30.1.1, 30.1.2, 30.1.4)

A company has gathered a team of programmers to create a fantastic new multiplayer adventure game. You're on the team and responsible for the module that walks players through creating a wizard or warrior for the game.

The adventure game begins by allowing each player to create a game character. **Figure 30-1** explains the initial parameters for wizards and for warriors.

(a) (b)

Wizard
Energy points: 25
Spells: 3
Location: 0,0

Warrior
Energy points: 25
Weapon: 1
Weapon choice: bow
Location: 0,0

Algol/Shutterstock.com

tsuneomp/Shutterstock.com

Figure 30-1   Adventure game characters

Creating the characters can be complicated to program all at once. Instead of thinking in specific Python syntax, think in general goals. Try to visualize the algorithm necessary to help a game player create a character. Here is one sequence of steps that could accomplish that task.

Ask player to enter a name for the game character.
Give player's character 25 energy points.
Give player the choice of being a wizard or a warrior.
If the character is a warrior, then allow the player to choose one weapon.
If the character is a wizard, then allow the player to choose three spells.
Set the character at the starting location.

Writing down the steps for an algorithm is a good start but refining those steps into pseudocode can reduce the time you spend coding and help you produce a more efficient program.

Pseudocode is a set of human-readable statements for delineating the steps of an algorithm. This development tool is more than a simple list of steps because it should help you focus on the specifics needed for Python without worrying about syntax, scope, object design, and other program elements.

Writing pseudocode can help you develop the detail and precision for expressing an algorithm in terms that can be easily transformed into statements coded in a programming language such as Python.

In **Figure 30-2**, compare the pseudocode to the algorithm. The pseudocode is still not a program you could run, but it provides more detail than the algorithm. Remember, the purpose is not to figure out everything, but to make the transition from idea to programming easier.

Pseudocode	Algorithm Steps
Prompt What is your character's name? Store the input in character_name	Ask player to enter a name for the game character
Store the value 25 in the energy_points variable	Give player's character 25 energy points
Prompt Is your character a wizard or warrior?	Give player the choice of being a wizard or a warrior
Store the input in character_type	

If the value in character_type is warrior then:
        Display the weapons list
        Prompt for a weapon selection
        Store the input in selected_weapon
	If the character is a warrior, then allow the player to choose one weapon

Otherwise, if the value in character_type is wizard then:
        Repeat three times:
            Display the spells list
            Prompt for a spell selection
            Store the input in selected spells list
	If the character is a wizard, then allow the player to choose three spells

Set the location to 0,0	Set the character at the starting location

Figure 30-2   Pseudocode expresses an algorithm in more detail

Pseudocode Guidelines (30.1.5)

There are no hard and fast rules for pseudocode syntax, punctuation, or phrasing, but some keywords and style conventions are derived from programming languages. Use terms that convey the idea of what should happen in code, such as the word **repeat** for loops.

In pseudocode, you work with variables and computations. **Variables** hold values that might change during program execution. Computations, functions, and methods often trigger those changes.

Writing pseudocode is not complex if you follow these steps:

1. Begin by jotting down the algorithm in your own words.
2. Identify variables in the algorithm and assign names to them.
3. Begin your pseudocode in a new column or document by writing statements that declare and initialize the variables.
4. Continue working through each step of the algorithm using more detailed pseudocode steps.
5. Identify computations and write them as mathematical expressions using variables as necessary.
6. Identify decision structures and write them in **if..then** format. Use **otherwise** when dealing with a catch-all case to do if none of the other decisions are true.

7. Identify repetition structures. Write the repetition pseudocode block using `repeat x times` or `repeat until` as appropriate.
8. Use indents for multiline decision and repetition structures.
9. Use blank lines as whitespace to set off decision and repetition structures.

30.2 Flowcharts

Flowchart Basics (30.2.1, 30.2.2)

A **flowchart** is a diagram that represents the sequence and flow of steps in an algorithm. Programmers sometimes use flowcharts instead of pseudocode. Some development projects require the use of both flowcharts and pseudocode.

Flowcharts use a standard set of shapes that are connected by flowline arrows. The most commonly used flowchart shapes are described in **Figure 30-3**.

Shape	Name	Purpose
⬤▬	Terminator	Represents the start or end of the algorithm
▬	Process	Indicates a mathematical or logical operation
◆	Decision	Represents a decision point that branches to different sets of steps
▱	Data	Represents data input or output
●	Connector	Indicates a connection between two separate sections of a flowchart

Figure 30-3   Flowchart shapes

Drawing Flowcharts (30.2.3, 30.2.4)

Flowcharts begin and end with a **terminator shape**. The first shape contains the word Start. Additional shapes are stacked vertically to indicate sequential program flow, as shown in **Figure 30-4**.

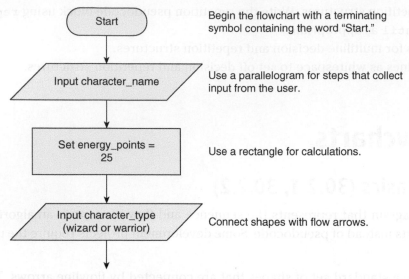

Begin the flowchart with a terminating symbol containing the word "Start."

Use a parallelogram for steps that collect input from the user.

Use a rectangle for calculations.

Connect shapes with flow arrows.

Figure 30-4   **Sequential flow**

Flowchart decision control structures correspond to `if..then` statements in pseudocode. Use a diamond shape and branching arrows for decisions in your flowchart, as shown in **Figure 30-5**.

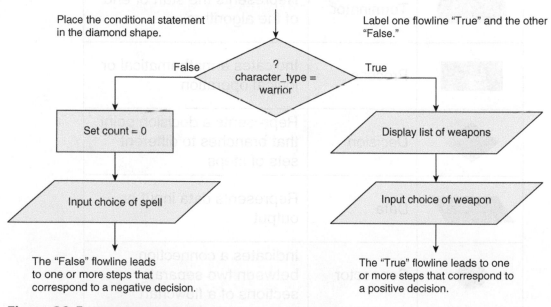

Place the conditional statement in the diamond shape.

Label one flowline "True" and the other "False."

The "False" flowline leads to one or more steps that correspond to a negative decision.

The "True" flowline leads to one or more steps that correspond to a positive decision.

Figure 30-5   **Decision structures**

You can represent repetition control structures in your flowcharts using the shapes and flowlines in **Figure 30-6**.

Flowchart Tools (30.2.5)

To create a flowchart, you can use diagramming software or an online diagramming app. Trace the flow of steps shown in **Figure 30-7** to discover how the shapes fit together to diagram an algorithm that creates a character for an adventure game.

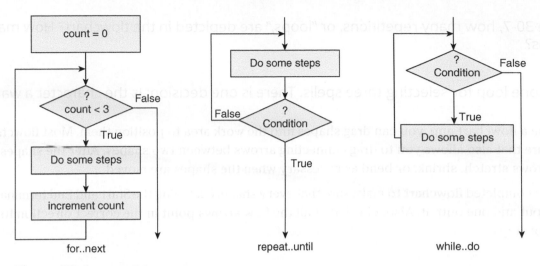

Figure 30-6 Repetition structures

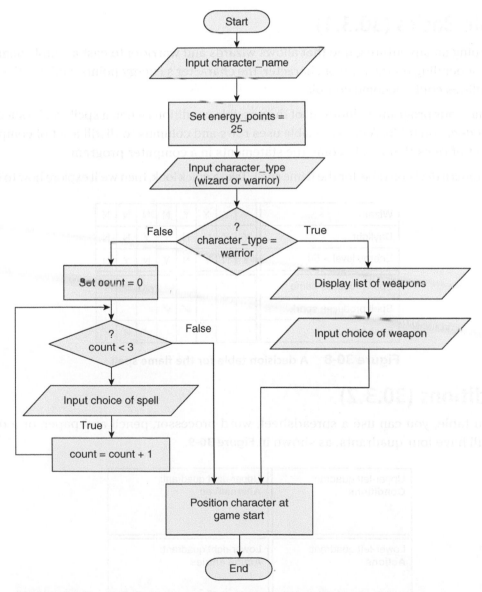

Figure 30-7 Flowchart for creating a new adventure game character

Q In Figure 30-7, how many repetitions, or "loops," are depicted in the flowchart? How many decisions?

A There is one loop for selecting three spells. There is one decision: Is the character a warrior?

When using a flowchart app, you can drag shapes into the work area to position them. Most flowchart apps include a feature that also allows you to drag connecting arrows between two shapes. After the shapes are connected, the arrows stretch, shrink, or bend as necessary when the shapes are moved.

Check your completed flowchart to make sure that every shape, excluding the Start and End terminators, has at least one input and one output. Also, check that all the flow arrows point in the correct direction to indicate the sequence of steps.

30.3 Decision Tables

Decision Table Basics (30.3.1)

Think about developing an adventure game that allows wizards and warriors to cast a simple flame spell under certain conditions, depending on the type of character, the character's energy points, and whether there is daylight. All the possibilities could become complex.

To make sure that your program includes all of the possible conditions when a spell can be successfully cast, you can construct a decision table. A **decision table** uses rows and columns to distill a set of complex decisions and actions into a set of rules that can become the statements in a computer program.

Figure 30-8 illustrates a decision table for the flame spell. Take a quick look, then we'll explore how to construct one.

Wizard	Y	Y	Y	Y	N	N	N	N
Daylight	Y	Y	N	N	Y	Y	N	N
Energy level > 50	Y	N	Y	N	Y	N	Y	N
Spell produces flame	✔	✔	✔					
Spell produces spark				✔	✔			
Spell fails						✔	✔	✔

Figure 30-8 A decision table for the flame spell

List the Conditions (30.3.2)

To create a decision table, you can use a spreadsheet, word processor, pencil and paper, or a decision table wizard. The table will have four quadrants, as shown in **Figure 30-9**.

Upper-left quadrant: **Conditions**	Upper-right quadrant: **Alternatives**
Lower-left quadrant: **Actions**	Lower-right quadrant: **Action entries**

Figure 30-9 Decision table quadrants

Begin by filling in the **Conditions quadrant** with factors that affect the decision. Three conditions affect flame spells. Those conditions go in the upper-left quadrant. See **Figure 30-10**.

Wizard									
Daylight									
Energy level > 50									

Figure 30-10 The Conditions quadrant

Q What do you notice about the way these conditions are formulated?

A They all have yes or no possibilities. For example, the condition Wizard would be "yes" for wizards but "no" for warriors.

List All Possible Alternatives (30.3.3, 30.3.4)

For each condition, there are two alternatives: Y or N. A character can be a wizard (Y) or not (N). It can be daylight (Y) or not (N). The character's energy can be more than 50 (Y) or not (N).

To identify all the options for the **Alternatives quadrant**, first calculate the number of possible combinations. For the spell, there are two alternatives (Y and N) and three conditions (wizard, daylight, and energy level). The calculation is 23, or $2 \times 2 \times 2$, which is 8. You will have eight columns in the Alternatives quadrant. Fill in the alternatives as shown in **Figure 30-11**.

Wizard	Y	Y	Y	Y	N	N	N	N
Daylight	Y	Y	N	N	Y	Y	N	N
Energy level > 50	Y	N	Y	N	Y	N	Y	N

Figure 30-11 The Alternatives quadrant

Notice the pattern in each row. In the first row, one half is filled with Ys and the other half is filled with Ns, so four Ys are followed by four Ns. In the second row, the pattern is two Ys followed by two Ns. The last row alternates between Ys and Ns.

Reading from top to bottom, each column has a unique set of alternatives.

Q What is the first set of alternatives?

A The first set is Y Y Y, indicating that the character is a wizard, it is daylight, and the character's energy level is above 50.

Specify Results and Rules (30.3.5)

Your next step is to specify possible actions in the **Action quadrant**. There are three possible actions: the spell will produce a steady flame, the spell will produce a small spark, or the spell will fail. See **Figure 30-12**.

Wizard	Y	Y	Y	Y	N	N	N	N
Daylight	Y	Y	N	N	Y	Y	N	N
Energy level > 50	Y	N	Y	N	Y	N	Y	N
Spell produces flame								
Spell produces spark								
Spell fails								

Figure 30-12   **The Action quadrant**

The fun part is filling in the **Action Entries quadrant**. For each series of Ys and Ns in a vertical column, place a checkmark in the lower-right quadrant to indicate the correct action. The set of alternatives and the action entries combine to form a rule. See **Figure 30-13**.

Wizard	Y	Y	Y	Y	N	N	N	N
Daylight	Y	Y	N	N	Y	Y	N	N
Energy level > 50	Y	N	Y	N	Y	N	Y	N
Spell produces flame	✔	✔	✔					
Spell produces spark				✔	✔			
Spell fails						✔	✔	✔

Figure 30-13   **Decision table rules**

For the first set of alternatives, Y Y Y, the character is a wizard, it is daylight, and the wizard has an energy level that is greater than 50. This character can cast the flame spell to produce a steady flame.

Q   Take a close look at the other sets of alternatives. What happens when nonwizards cast the flame spell?

A   A warrior can use a flame spell to produce a spark only when it is daylight and the warrior has more than 50 energy points.

Interpret Rules (30.3.6)

The information in a decision table can be converted into pseudocode and eventually into program code. For the first rule, the character is a wizard, it is daylight, and the character's energy level is above 50, so the spell produces a flame. The pseudocode for this rule might be:

```
if wizard is Y and daylight is Y and energy_level is greater than 50 then:

    flame_spell creates flame
```

Can a wizard always cast the flame spell? Rule 4 says that if there is no daylight and the wizard has an energy level less than 50, the spell will only produce a spark. The pseudocode for this rule would be:

```
if wizard is Y and daylight is N and energy_level is less than or equal to 50 then:
    flame_spell creates spark
```

Q Recall that a nonwizard can create a spark if daylight is Y and the energy level is higher than 50. How would you express this rule in pseudocode?

A The rule is the fifth column of alternatives. The pseudocode would be:

```
if wizard is N and daylight is Y and energy_level is greater than 50 then:
    flame_spell creates spark
```

This decision table has eight rules. Are all eight rules required, or can these rules be combined to produce pseudocode and program code that is more efficient? Is the table complete and is it accurate? Before depending on a decision table for the logic that is the basis for program code, three simple steps help to ensure optimization, completeness, and accuracy.

Optimize the Rules (30.3.7)

Some rules can be combined. Notice the pattern of Ys in the first and second rules of **Figure 30-14**. Those rules both produce a flame as long as the character is a wizard and it is daylight. The wizard's energy level doesn't matter.

Wizard	Y	Y	Y	Y	N	N	N	N
Daylight	Y	Y	N	N	Y	Y	N	N
Energy level > 50	Y	N	Y	N	Y	N	Y	N
Spell produces flame	✔	✔	✔					
Spell produces spark					✔	✔		
Spell fails							✔	✔	✔

Figure 30-14   Redundant rules

Rules 1 and 2 can be combined using a dash to eliminate the energy level. The resulting table looks like **Figure 30-15**.

Wizard	Y	Y	Y	N	N	N	N
Daylight	Y	N	N	Y	Y	N	N
Energy level > 50	–	Y	N	Y	N	Y	N
Spell produces flame	✔	✔					
Spell produces spark			✔	✔			
Spell fails					✔	✔	✔

Figure 30-15   A dash indicates combined rules

Q Can you combine the last two rules?

A Yes, the energy level has no effect on nonwizards who are in the dark. The revised decision table will look like **Figure 30-16**.

Wizard	Y	Y	Y	N	N	N
Daylight	Y	N	N	Y	Y	N
Energy level > 50	–	Y	N	Y	N	–
Spell produces flame	✔	✔				
Spell produces spark			✔	✔		
Spell fails					✔	✔

Figure 30-16   The last two rules combined

Check for Completeness and Accuracy (30.3.8)

The final step for creating a decision table is to make sure it is complete and accurate.

Check for completeness. The optimized decision table contains six rules. The table is complete if it contains all of the possible conditions and actions. Suppose that nonwizard users could cast flame spells if they carried a magic candle. That condition is not included in the upper-left quadrant, so the decision table would be incomplete. To complete the table, it would need to be revised for four conditions and sixteen rules.

Check for accuracy. Sometimes decision tables produce redundant rules or impossible situations. **Redundant rules** exist when two rules have the same conditions and produce the same result. **Impossible rules** contain conditions that contradict each other.

Q Here is a slightly different decision table. Can you find any redundant rules or impossible rules in **Figure 30-17**?

	1	2	3	4	5	6	7	8
Wizard	Y	Y	Y	Y	N	N	N	N
Energy level <= 50	Y	Y	N	N	Y	Y	N	N
Energy level > 50	Y	N	Y	N	Y	N	Y	N
Spell produces flame	✔	✔						
Spell produces spark			✔	✔				
Spell fails					✔	✔	✔	✔

Figure 30-17   Can you find any redundant or impossible rules in this decision table?

A Did you find these problems?

- Rules 1 and 5 are impossible. A character cannot have an energy level greater than 50 and less than or equal to 50 at the same time.
- Rules 4 and 8 are impossible. These refer to a character that does not have an energy level above, equal to, or below 50!
- Rules 5, 6, and 7 are redundant. They can be combined.

Decision tables are fun to construct and can help you sort through complex logic. Make sure to keep this tool handy in your program development toolbox.

Summary

- Pseudocode is a set of human-readable statements for delineating the steps of an algorithm, including control structures.
- There are no hard-and-fast rules for pseudocode syntax, punctuation, or phrasing, but some keywords and style conventions are similar to programming languages.
- A flowchart is a diagram that represents the sequence and flow of steps in an algorithm. Flowcharts use a standard set of shapes that are connected by flowline arrows.
- Control structures are easy to visualize when depicted in a flowchart.
- When drawing flowcharts, make sure that every shape, excluding terminators, has at least one input and one output.
- A decision table uses rows and columns to distill a set of complex decisions and actions into a set of rules that can become the statements in a computer program.
- To create a decision table, fill in the four quadrants: Conditions, Alternatives, Actions, and Action Entries. Read down each vertical column of Ys, Ns, and checkmarks to formulate rules.
- Decision tables can be optimized by combining rules to eliminate rules that are redundant and those that are impossible.

Key Terms

Action Entries quadrant	decision table	redundant rules
Action quadrant	flowchart	terminator shape
Alternatives quadrant	impossible rules	variables
Conditions quadrant	pseudocode	

Module 31

Unified Modeling Language

Learning Objectives:

31.1 Purpose of Unified Modeling Language (UML)

31.1.1 Associate "UML" with "unified modeling language."

31.1.2 Define the purpose of UML as helping programmers visualize the design of a software system.

31.2 UML Diagram Parts

31.2.1 Define a class diagram.

31.2.2 Identify the parts of class notation.

31.2.3 Differentiate class notation from object notation.

31.2.4 Define a use case diagram.

31.2.5 Identify the parts of use cases.

31.2.6 Demonstrate a use case with UML.

31.2.7 Define a sequence diagram.

31.2.8 Identify the parts of a sequence diagram.

31.3 Using UML To Structure Programs

31.3.1 Associate UML with the analysis and design of systems that will be implemented with object-oriented programming.

31.3.2 Construct a class diagram for a real-world object.

31.3.3 Contrast real-world examples for relationship diagrams.

31.3.4 Showcase UML associations and their notations for class diagrams.

31.3.5 Demonstrate the translation of UML to code.

31.1 Purpose of Unified Modeling Language (UML)

Communicating Ideas to Other Programmers (31.1.1, 31.1.2)

The way you communicate with others relies on your mutual agreement about what terms mean. When you see or hear the word "teapot," you probably think of an item similar to the one shown in **Figure 31-1**. If "teapot" means something else to a friend or colleague, you might end up arguing about how to use the item. Communication requires agreement on the representation of ideas.

Figure 31-1 Standard teapot

Computer scientists also need to agree on terms when communicating ideas. Instead of reading someone else's code, which can be time-consuming and difficult, you can use the **Unified Modeling Language (UML)**. UML helps programmers visualize the design of complicated programs and coordinate large projects where many people are working on parts of a whole. Each of those parts needs to work with the other parts. Using UML, programmers define the code relationships and behaviors for everyone to reference. UML can also be used for tasks other than programming, such as communicating or creating use cases for programs.

31.2 UML Diagram Parts

Class Diagram Basics (31.2.1, 31.2.2, 31.2.3)

UML is used to define the components of a system, or scenario, including consistent names. UML consists of many types of diagrams, including a **class diagram**, which represents the structure of a system, showing relationships between classes, objects, methods, functions, and member variables.

For example, suppose you need to create a `Teapot` class that contains all of the methods and variables associated with a teapot. Instead of writing the code for the `Teapot` class, you can start by creating a class diagram in UML to describe the structure of the class, as shown in **Figure 31-2**.

Teapot
-color : string
-temperature : double
-water_amount : double
-tea_type : string
+heat_up(temperature : double) : void
+add_water(amount : double) : void
+change_tea(tea : string) : void
+pour(amount : double) : void

Figure 31-2 Class diagram of the `Teapot` class

In a class diagram, a class is represented by a rectangle divided into sections. A class diagram includes the following symbols and notations:

Class name. Write the class name in the top section of the rectangle. Format it as bold, centered, and with the first letter capitalized, as in `Teapot`.

Attributes. List the class attributes in the second section. Attributes are left-aligned, lowercase, and not bold. Each attribute is listed in the format `identifier : variable_type`, as in `color : string`.

Methods. List the methods in the third section. Methods are left-aligned, lowercase, and not bold. Each method is listed in the format `method_name( argument(s) ) : return_type`. Each argument appears in the format `argument_name : type`. For example, a complete method is `heat_up(temperature : double) : void`.

Visibility markers. A **visibility marker** specifies what should be able to access the methods and attributes in a class. The public marker is a **+** sign and the private marker is a **–** sign. For example, `-color : string` indicates that `color` is a private attribute. Therefore, it should be named `self._color` in Python. Markers are optional.

Q Since an object is an instance of a class, can I represent an object in UML using the same notation as in a class diagram?

A For the most part, yes. The only difference in the notation is that you write the object name in the top section instead of the class name. In addition, the object name is underlined, as in `redteapot`, to distinguish an object from a class.

Use Case Diagram Basics (31.2.4, 31.2.5, 31.2.6)

In UML, a **use case diagram** communicates how a user interacts with the system to achieve a goal. In general, a **use case** is a list of actions or steps showing the interactions between a person and a system in order to accomplish a task. The use case depicts who does what with the system and for what purpose.

Specifying use cases helps to organize the **functional requirements** of the system. In software engineering, functional requirements are the behaviors that a system must perform, usually specified by the customer. For example, for a teapot to be useful, it must have the functional requirements of allowing a person to add water, heat the water, change the tea, and pour out the contents.

Q What's the relationship between a functional requirement and a use case?

A You can think of use cases as a way to identify and document the functional requirements of a system.

A **scenario** is a single use case, or a single action path through the system. Generally, a use case diagram communicates a high-level overview of the relationships between system components. A use case diagram of the Making Tea system is displayed in **Figure 31-3**.

A use case diagram consists of the following components:

System. Represent the system being described by a bounding box. Anything outside of the box is considered as outside of the system. In the example, Making Tea is the system.

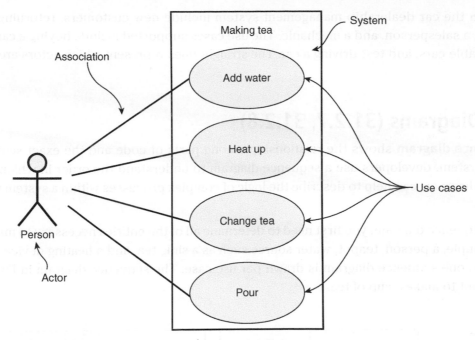

Figure 31-3   Use case diagram for the Making Tea system

Actors. The **actors** are the types of people using the system. An actor is represented by a stick figure. Other systems that interact with this system can also be represented as actors. In the example, a generic Person is the actor.

Use cases. The use cases describe the actions a user can take in the system. The use cases are represented by horizontal ovals. In the example, the use cases are Add water, Heat up, Change tea, and Pour.

Association. An **association** is a line drawn between an actor and a use case. In complex diagrams with many actors and use cases, the associations help to clarify which actors are associated with which use cases.

A more complex example involving a car dealership management system is shown in **Figure 31-4**.

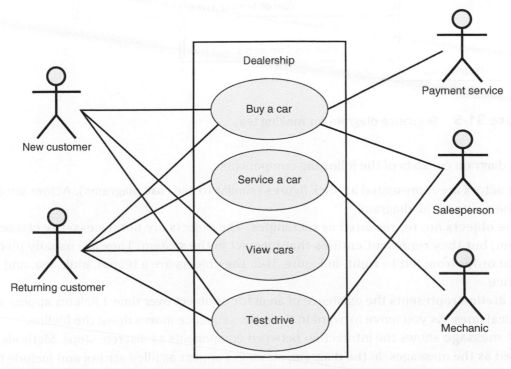

Figure 31-4   Use case diagram for a Dealership management system

The actors in the car dealership management system include new customers, returning customers, the payment service, a salesperson, and a mechanic. The use cases supported include buying a car, servicing a car, viewing the available cars, and test driving a car. The straight lines represent which actors are associated with which use cases.

Sequence Diagrams (31.2.7, 31.2.8)

In UML, a **sequence diagram** shows the relationship among parts of code and the exact sequence of events. When coding a system, developers use a sequence diagram to understand the order in which actions need to occur. Sequence diagrams can help to describe the logic of complex processes within a system without focusing on small details.

To create a sequence diagram, you first need to determine all of the entities necessary to make the code run. In the teapot example, a person, teapot, water source such as a sink, tea, and a heating device are necessary to make tea. Usually, one sequence diagram is drawn per use case. The sequence diagram in **Figure 31-5** shows how to use a teapot to make a cup of tea.

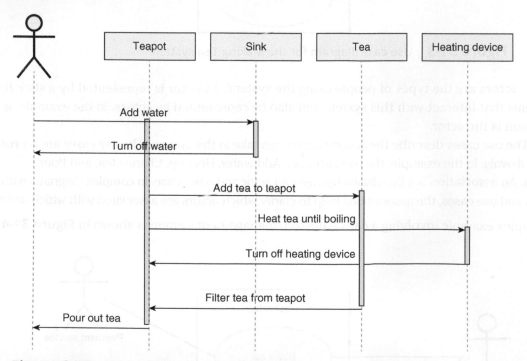

Figure 31-5   Sequence diagram for making tea

A sequence diagram consists of the following components:

Actors. The actors are represented as stick figures (similar to use case diagrams). Actors are always outside of the scope of the diagram.

Objects. The objects are represented as rectangles. The objects are not necessarily classes in the system, but they represent entities that interact in the system. They are usually placed in sequential order from left to right. In Figure 31-5, the objects are a teapot, sink, tea, and heating device.

Lifelines. A **lifeline** represents the existence of an actor or object over time. Lifelines appear as dashed vertical lines. As you move forward in time, the sequence moves down the lifeline.

Messages. A **message** shows the interaction between components as discrete steps. Methods are often used as the messages. In the diagram, messages appear as filled arrows and include text describing the interaction, as in "Add water." Generally, messages point from left to right; however, a **return message** (or reply message) points from right to left, usually indicating the result of an action, similar to a return value. If a message requests information, a return message indicates the result. The return message is denoted with a dashed line. The sequence diagram in Figure 31-5 does not use any return messages.

Activation boxes. An **activation box** shows when and how long an object performs an action or is otherwise active. An activation box is depicted as a long narrow rectangle on the lifeline, extending from the object's first message to its last message.

31.3 Using UML to Structure Programs

UML Associations (31.3.1, 31.3.2, 31.3.3, 31.3.4)

Professional programming teams use UML to design and analyze systems that will be coded using object-oriented programming. The teams use the UML diagrams as a rule book, where everyone agrees on how parts of the program should work. If everyone agrees on the parts and how they fit together, they break the project into smaller tasks for others to work on. In this way, UML provides a cheat sheet for communication in big projects.

Class diagrams can be combined with other classes in a **relationship diagram**. The lines connecting the classes indicate how the classes relate to, and interact with, the other classes, also known as their associations.

Figure 31-6 shows the UML class diagram for a car using **inheritance**. The arrow with a solid line and an unfilled triangle signifies that the class inherits from the class it points to. The `Car` class inherits from `MotorVehicle`, the `ElectricCar` class inherits from `Car`, and the `GasCar` class inherits from `Car`.

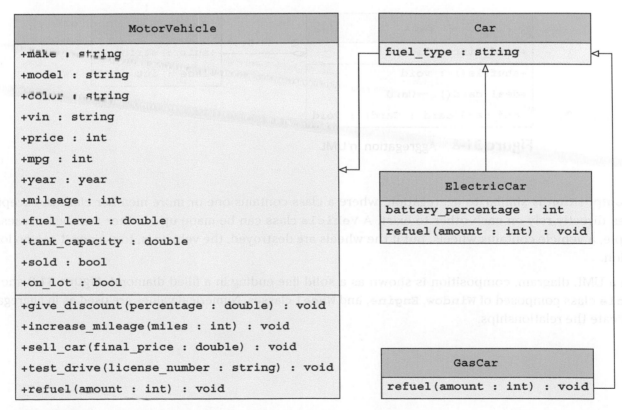

Figure 31-6   Inheritance in UML

Sometimes classes depend on the definition of another class even though they are not literally part of that class. For example, a washing machine can clean clothes, but it does not own them. To represent this dependency in UML, you use a dashed line with an open arrow. **Figure 31-7** shows a `WashingMachine` class that has a **dependence** on the `Clothing` class.

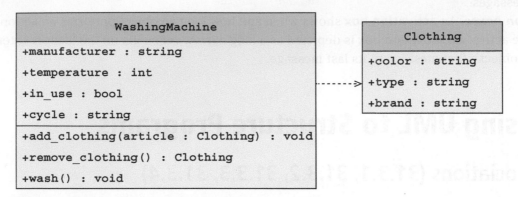

Figure 31-7 Dependency in UML

Aggregation describes a class that contains one or more members of another class, but the lifetimes of those members are not inherently connected to the containing class. For example, a business has multiple stores to manage, but if one store closes, the business still exists. A deck of cards contains many cards, but some cards can be removed without destroying the deck.

In a UML diagram, aggregation is represented by a solid line ending in an unfilled diamond. **Figure 31-8** shows a `Deck` class that aggregates multiple objects of a `Card` class. The numbers on the aggregation line indicate the numerical relationship between the two classes. Here, zero or more cards make up one deck, and each card can exist in only one deck.

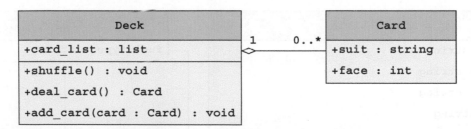

Figure 31-8 Aggregation in UML

Composition is similar to aggregation, where a class contains one or more member classes, except the classes directly rely on each other to exist. A `Vehicle` class can be made up of other member classes. For example, a vehicle contains wheels, but if the wheels are destroyed, the vehicle is, too, since it can no longer function.

In a UML diagram, composition is shown as a solid line ending in a filled diamond. **Figure 31-9** shows a `Vehicle` class composed of `Window`, `Engine`, and `Wheel` classes. Numerical values are used as in aggregation to indicate the relationships.

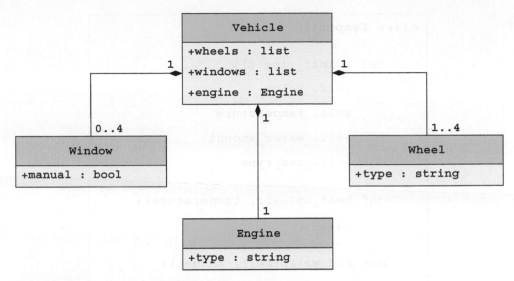

Figure 31-9 Composition in UML

The term **realization** is used in UML when an interface is fulfilled by a class. Realization is shown as a dashed line ending in an unfilled triangle. In **Figure 31-10**, the `VideoPlayer` and `AudioPlayer` realize the `MediaPlayer` interface.

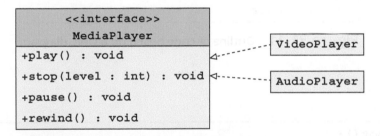

Figure 31-10 Realization in UML

Translating UML to Code (31.3.5)

Suppose you've created a `Teapot` class diagram like the one shown in Figure 31-2, and you want to translate it to code. The best way to start is to outline the code based on the items in the UML diagram, as in **Figure 31-11**.

Depending on how the programming team determined that these methods should behave, you can fill in the rest of the code as shown in **Figure 31-12**.

```
class Teapot():

    def __init__(self):
        self._color
        self._temperature
        self._water_amount
        self._tea_type

    def heat_up(self, temperature):
        pass

    def add_water(self, amount):
        pass

    def change_tea(self, tea):
        pass

    def pour(self, amount):
        pass
```

Figure 31-11   Outline of code based on a UML diagram

```
class Teapot():

    def __init__(self, color):
        self._color = color
        self._temperature = 0
        self._water_amount = 0
        self._tea_type = "Green"

    def heat_up(self, temperature):
        self._temperature = temperature

    def add_water(self, amount):
        self._water_amount += amount
```

Figure 31-12   Implementing the `Teapot` class (*Continued*)

```
        def change_tea(self, tea):

            self._tea_type = tea

        def pour(self, amount):

            self._water_amount -= amount

        def __str__(self):

            string = "Teapot status:\n"
            string += "Color: " + self._color + "\n"
            string += "Temperature: " + str(self._temperature) + "\n"
            string += "Tea Type: " + self._tea_type + "\n"
            string += "Water Amount: " + str(self._water_amount) + "\n"

            return string

if __name__ == '__main__':
    t = Teapot("Blue")
    t.change_tea("Oolong")
    t.add_water(25.5)
    t.heat_up(95)
    t.pour(2.75)
    print(t)
OUTPUT:
Teapot status:
Color: Blue
Temperature: 95
Tea Type: Oolong
Water Amount: 22.75
```

Figure 31-12 Implementing the `Teapot` class

Summary

- The Unified Modeling Language (UML) is a standardized way for computer scientists to communicate ideas to other programmers. Using a common means of communication helps to ensure that everyone on a project team has the same understanding of the program design and solution.
- A class diagram is a visual representation of a class to be used by a program. The diagram uses a rectangle to indicate each class, with sections inside the class rectangle to show the member variables and methods. Access modifiers are also included in the class diagram.
- A use case diagram conveys how a user will interact with the programmed system. The use case diagram is made up of use cases that organize the functional requirements of the system.
- The use case diagram consists of the system, actors, use cases, and associations.
- A scenario represents a single path of action through the system at a high level.
- A sequence diagram shows the relationships of entities within code and the exact sequence of events. This information helps developers understand the logic and process of the system. A sequence diagram also conveys how long each object is active within the system.
- A sequence diagram consists of actors, objects, lifelines, messages, return messages, and activation boxes.
- Classes that rely on other classes but don't own other classes as part of their design are called dependent. UML diagrams show dependency with a dotted line ending with an open arrow.
- A class can contain other classes and use them as part of its whole definition, as in a deck of cards, but the containing class and its member classes are not directly connected. This relationship is called aggregation. UML diagrams show aggregation with a solid line ending in an unfilled diamond.
- When one class is made up of another class and cannot exist without the second class, the relationship is called composition. UML diagrams show composition with a solid line ending with a filled diamond.
- Implementing an interface is called realization. UML diagrams show realization with a dashed line ending in an unfilled triangle.
- Based on UML diagrams, you can create skeleton outlines of a class to fill in with code later. This strategy can help in structuring your code while brainstorming a solution.

Key Terms

activation box	functional requirements	scenario
actors	inheritance	sequence diagram
aggregation	lifeline	Unified Modeling Language (UML)
association	message	use case
class diagram	realization	use case diagram
composition	relationship diagram	visibility marker
dependence	return message	

Glossary

A

absolute file path   A notation that indicates the exact location of a file on the computer, from a point starting at the hard drive.

abstract class   Any class that has one or more pure virtual methods.

abstraction   The process of hiding details or substituting a generalization for something specific.

acceptance testing   A user-focused testing process designed to ensure that the software meets usability requirements and the objectives for which it was created.

access point   A point such as a cursor that keeps track of your current position in a file.

accessibility   The availability of a place, service, or software to people with disabilities.

accessor methods   Methods designed to control how a property of a class is accessed; also known as *getters*.

Action Entries quadrant   The lower-right quadrant of a decision table that contains actions corresponding to each set of alternatives.

Action quadrant   The lower-left quadrant of a decision table that contains a list of possible outcomes.

activation box   In a sequence diagram, a narrow rectangle that shows when and how long an object is performing an action or is active.

actors   The types of people using a system in a UML use case diagram.

adjacency matrix   A way to represent a graph in code with a two-dimensional matrix of edge weights.

aggregation   When a class contains other independent classes as part of its structure.

agile development methodologies   A variety of incremental, iterative approaches based on the Agile Manifesto.

algorithm   A series of steps for solving a problem or task.

alpha testing   A type of acceptance testing performed by internal testers.

Alternatives quadrant   The upper-right quadrant of a decision table that contains Ys and Ns denoting all possible combinations of conditions.

analog data   Data that has continuous values.

ancestors   Any classes that have one or more classes derived from them.

append   A mode to open a file for writing so that you can add data to it, without writing over any existing data.

application programming interfaces (APIs)   A set of routines that can be included in programs to enhance functionality, such as constructing platform-specific user interfaces.

arguments   The term for the values provided to a method or function that are placed inside the parameters.

arithmetic logic unit (ALU)   The component of the CPU that performs arithmetic and logical operations.

arithmetic operators   Mathematical symbols such as +, −, *, /, and %.

ASCII (American Standard Code for Information Interchange)   A method for encoding letters, symbols, and numerals using seven bits or eight bits.

assembly language   A low-level programming language that corresponds closely to the machine language instruction set for a CPU.

assignment statement   A statement that sets or changes the value that is stored in a variable.

association   A line drawn between items in a UML diagram.

asymptotic analysis A method for evaluating the performance of an algorithm in relation to the size of the data set.

asymptotic notation The expression of asymptotic analysis, typically as Big-O, Big-Omega, or Big-Theta.

attributes The characteristics that describe an object.

augmented reality The use of computer technology to add digital tags to real-world images.

auxiliary space The memory required to temporarily hold variables and data as a program runs.

average-case runtime The amount of time an algorithm needs to run to completion on average, given a random order of data.

B

base case A situation in which a recursive function can stop trying to solve a problem.

base-2 Another name for the binary number system.

behavior Describes what an object can do; typically thought of in terms of the methods or actions that an object can perform.

best-case runtime The smallest amount of time possible an algorithm needs to run to completion.

beta testing A type of acceptance testing performed by a select group of users in real-world environments.

Big-O A generalization of a runtime. Only the largest growing factor of the polynomial matters in Big-O.

Big-O notation Asymptotic notation for the worst-case time complexity or space complexity of an algorithm.

Big-Omega notation Asymptotic notation for the best-case time complexity or space complexity.

Big-Theta notation Asymptotic notation that encompasses both the upper and lower bounds of an algorithm, a situation sometimes referred to as a tight bound.

binary A representation of data that can have one of two states.

binary digits A binary digit is a 0 or 1 representing the smallest unit of information in a computer.

binary file A file that stores the contents in binary format (ones and zeros) that is not human readable but takes up less space.

binary measurements Megabytes, gigabytes, and similar measures based on powers of 2.

binary number system A system for counting that uses only numerals 0 and 1.

binary search algorithm An algorithm that divides the search space in half until the target value is located.

binary search tree (BST) A binary tree that enforces a meaning to the left and right children. Stored items are sorted by putting items "less than" the current node to the left, and items "greater than" to the right.

binary trees Trees limited to two children per node.

bit A binary digit; 0 or 1.

Boolean expressions Expressions containing relational operators and operands, such as `choice == 1`, that evaluate to `True` or `False`.

Boolean literal A literal that has a value of `True` or `False`.

boundary case A data point that is just at or beyond the maximum or minimum limits of expected data.

branching recursion A type of recursion that makes more than one recursive function call.

breadth first (BF) traversal A traversal that visits the nodes in a tree by depth level.

breakpoint A location with program code that triggers the debugging utility to halt while a programmer identifies an error.

bubble sort A simple algorithm that sorts items by swapping adjacent pairs if the two items are out of order.

buffer The common piece of memory used to transfer pieces of information into and out of memory during file input and output.

buffer overflow A condition in which data flows into unexpected memory locations.

buffered stream An input or output stream that uses an intermediary buffer when reading from a file or writing to a file.

buffering Moving data, bit by bit, into and out of a common piece of memory (called a *buffer*) that is accessed by your code and an external source (like memory).

build tools Tools, such as a preprocessor, compiler, and linker, that convert source code into a program that a computer can execute.

built-in function A term that has special meaning to the programming language. A built-in function name cannot be used as a variable name.

byte A group of 8 bits; commonly used to store a number, letter, symbol, or punctuation mark.

bytecode Code that is compiled into an intermediate file that a virtual machine compiles and executes.

C

camel case A text format that begins with a lowercase letter but uses an uppercase letter for subsequent words.

capacitors Electronic circuits that store an electrical charge and are commonly used to store signals that represent data in computers.

case sensitivity The differentiation that makes a lowercase letter different from its uppercase version.

central processing unit (CPU) The components of a computer that perform processing tasks.

character Variables that hold one character of data.

character literal A single character or symbol.

character set Alphanumeric characters and their encoded equivalents.

chatbots Interactive programs that respond with seeming intelligence to user interaction.

child In a tree data structure, a node that is below and connected to another node.

child class A class created using methods and data members inherited from the parent class.

circular linked list A linked list in which each node links sequentially to one other node and there is no null pointer to the end.

class diagram A diagram in UML that details the structure of classes.

class name A noun that identifies the class by a specific name.

classes The blueprint containing attributes and methods that describe a collection of objects.

classification patterns The pattern of attributes and methods that apply to a collection of objects.

clean code The principle that code should be easily understood, elegant, simple, and testable.

clone method A method that creates a deep copy of an object.

code block A group of program statements that perform a specific function and that may be visually set off from other statements or blocks using blank lines.

code editor A type of text editor that is specially designed for entering program code.

coercion The process by which a literal is automatically converted into a different data type.

comma-delimited text file A text file in which chunks of data resemble records in a table separated by a comma.

comma-separated values A style of storing data in a text file where each element or value is separated by a comma.

command-line user interfaces A form of interacting with a computer that requires typed commands.

comment An explanatory notation within program code that is not executed by a computer.

compiler Utility software that translates code written in one programming language into another language.

complete graph A graph in which each node has an edge to every other node.

complex data types Data types that store more than one kind of primitive data.

complex instruction set computers (CISC) An instruction set that includes many operations, some of which require multiple CPU cycles.

composite data types Data types that are programmer defined, available as functions, or provided by methods.

composition When a class contains other dependent classes as part of its structure.

compound operators Mathematical operators that offer shortcuts for basic assignment operations.

computational thinking A set of techniques, such as decomposition, pattern identification, and abstraction, designed to formulate problems and their solutions.

computer   A multipurpose device that accepts input, processes that input based on a stored set of instructions, and produces output.

computer program   A collection of statements written in a programming language, such as C++, Java, or Python, that performs a specific task when executed by a digital device.

concatenation   Combining data using the + concatenation operator.

concatenative synthesis   The process of combining a series of prerecorded phonemes to create synthesized speech.

condition-controlled loop   A repetition control structure that is governed by a logical expression either at the beginning or the end of the loop.

conditional logical operator   Operators, such as AND and OR, that combine the outcomes of two or more Boolean expressions.

conditional statement   A statement, such as `if choice == 1`, that initiates a decision control structure.

Conditions quadrant   The upper-left quadrant of a decision table that contains factors affecting a decision.

connected graph   A graph where all nodes are connected by at least one edge to the rest of the group of nodes.

constant   A named memory location that holds data, which is used but not changed by the statements in a program.

constant space complexity   The asymptotic, or Big-O, status for algorithms that do not require additional space as the dataset increases.

constant time   The asymptotic, or Big-O, status for algorithms that are not affected by the size of the data set.

constructor   The dunder method, which is called upon creation of a new object from a class.

contents   The text or information contained in a file.

control statement   A statement that controls the conditions under which a loop continues to execute.

control structure   One or more statements that alter the sequential execution of a computer program.

control unit   The component of the CPU that interprets instructions and manages processing activity.

count-controlled loop   A repetition control structure that repeats a specified number of times.

D

data representation   The way data is presented and abstracted.

data space   The memory required to hold data that is accessed by a program, input to a program, or generated by the program.

data structure   A specific layout of values in memory and a set of operations that can be applied to those values.

data type   A category of data such as integer, floating point, or character.

debugging   The process of finding and correcting errors—bugs—in a computer program.

debugging utilities   Software that can be used to find and correct errors in program code.

decision control structure   One or more statements that alter the sequential flow based on a condition or decision.

decision table   A grid of rows and columns that distill a set of complex decisions and actions into a set of rules that can become the statements in a computer program.

declarative programming paradigms   Any approach to software development and programming that focuses on "what" by describing the problem or task that is the scope of a computer program.

declare a variable   The process of specifying a name that is assigned, or bound, to a memory location.

decomposition   A technique for breaking a task into smaller parts.

deep copy   A copy of an object in which all member variables from the source object are copied into the destination object.

default exceptions   A generic exception handling statement to catch any unhandled exception event.

default parameters   A default value to use for a parameter if no argument is provided (not available in all languages).

default value   A value in the parameter list that is used if no argument is provided for the parameter.

delimiter   A punctuation mark or tab character that denotes the separation of information in a file.

dependence   When a class depends on another independent class's definition.

depth first (DF) traversal   A traversal that tries to go as deep as possible in a tree before backing up to find more nodes to visit.

dequeue   The operation that removes a data element from the front of a queue.

descendant   Any class that has been derived from a parent class.

dictionary   A collection of keys that map to values.

digital data   Data that has discrete, rather than continuous, values.

directed graph   A graph where edges are one-way paths.

directive   In the context of programming, a statement that tells the computer how to handle the program rather than how to perform an algorithm.

directory structure   A hierarchy of folders and files on a computer.

divide-and-conquer technique   An algorithmic technique in which each step divides the problem space and eliminates part of it on the path to a solution.

Don't Repeat Yourself (DRY)   A programming principle that encourages programmers to eliminate redundancies in their code.

double precision   Floating-point numbers stored usually in 8 bytes of memory.

doubly linked list   A linked list in which each element has two pointers: one to the next element and one to the previous element.

dunder methods   Methods that Python uses in default syntactic behaviors; short for "double underscore methods."

Duplication is Evil (DIE)   An acronym for the concept that programmers should eliminate redundancies in their code.

dynamically typed   A programming language feature that allows a variable to take on any type of data during program execution.

E

E notation   A way of expressing floating-point numbers as powers of 10.

edge weights   The cost to take an edge, sometimes used to represent a physical distance, but can be a value that represents other measurements.

edges   The connections between nodes in a nonlinear data structure.

element-based traversal   Traversing a list by viewing each of the elements stored within.

else-if structure   A decision control structure that handles multiple conditions.

encapsulate   A feature of object-oriented programming in which classes become black box abstractions.

encapsulation   An object-oriented concept of constructing objects by bundling relevant data with the actions they can perform.

encoding system   A method for converting data, such as the letters of the alphabet, into a format such as binary.

end of file (EOF)   A special character to represent the last element in a file.

enqueue   The operation that adds a data element to the rear of a queue.

equal operator   The == symbol that compares one value to another and returns `True` if the values are equal.

escape characters   An alternate interpretation of a character that has another meaning.

escape sequence   Embedded characters beginning with a backslash (\ ) to insert special symbols into a string.

event-driven   A paradigm for a program controlled by user events, such as clicking an icon.

event handler   The code for handling a program event.

exception   An event triggered by a situation that cannot be resolved by the program; also a package of information about the situation.

executable file   A file that has been compiled into machine code and that can be directly executed by a computer.

expression   A programming statement that has a value and usually includes arithmetic operators and operands.

F

fall through   Program execution that continues to the next sequential statement.

field   Each piece of data separated by a delimiter (such as a comma) in a table.

FIFO   The acronym for "first in, first out."

file   A digital container that stores data, information, settings, or program commands. In programming, a file can provide input to a program or store the results of a program's execution.

file access point   A special variable that acts like a cursor indicating your position in a file.

file handler   A special, built-in feature that allows you to interact with a file, in abstract terms.

file handling   Reading data into programs and storing data that your program produces.

file input   Using code to read information from a file.

file I/O   The common term for the combined acts of file input and output.

file name   The name of a file, including the extension.

file output   Using code to write information into a file.

filtering   Creating a list containing values that meet a condition, such as only even numbers.

floating-point data types   Numbers that include decimal and fractional parts; expressed in decimal or E notation.

flowchart   A diagram that represents the sequence and flow of steps in an algorithm.

Floyd's Algorithm   A simple algorithm that calculates the value of the shortest paths between all nodes in a graph given an adjacency matrix.

folder   A digital storage space for organizing files and other folders; also called a *directory*.

for-loop   A count-controlled loop that is controlled by the conditions in a statement beginning with the keyword `for`.

formatting parameters   Elements that can alter the appearance of numeric and text output.

function   A named procedure that performs a specific task.

function argument   The data that is passed in parentheses to a function by the function call.

function body   The block of code in a function that defines what the function does.

function call   A statement that transfers program flow to a function.

function declaration   The first line of a function that provides the function name and optionally parameters and return type.

function name   The name of a function, which ends with parentheses ( ).

function parameters   The variables enclosed in parentheses in the function declaration.

function signature   The function name and parameters that uniquely define a function.

functional decomposition   A technique for dividing modules into smaller actions, processes, or steps.

functional requirements   The specific behaviors a system must perform.

G

getters   Methods designed to control how a property of a class is accessed. Also known as accessor methods.

global variable   A variable that is visible throughout the entire program.

graphical user interface (GUI)   A type of user interface that displays graphical objects such as workspaces, icons, menus, and a pointer.

graphs   A nonlinear data structure with no hierarchical structure; has no starting point or ending point.

H

haptic   A term used for devices that simulate the sense of touch.

has-a relationship   A class relationship where a class contains an object of another class as a data member.

head   The first element in a data structure.

heterogeneous   A data structure that can contain different data types.

hexadecimal number system   A system for counting that uses 16 digits: 0 1 2 3 4 5 6 7 8 9 A B C D E F.

high-level programming languages   Systems for issuing instructions to a CPU that abstract away the detail of low-level machine language to provide programmers with natural language commands.

Human-Computer Interaction (HCI)   A computer science discipline that focuses on improving ways that people interact with digital devices.

I

identity   A way to refer to unique objects in order to distinguish them from other objects created from the same class. Oftentimes the identity is synonymous with the variable's name.

if-then structure   A decision control structure with one branch based on a `True` Boolean expression.

if-then-else structure   A decision control structure that has two branches: one for `True` and one for `False`.

immutable   When a class is designed such that no mutator methods exist and all properties are private.

imperative programming paradigms   Any approach to software development and programming that focuses on "how" by specifying the steps required for a computer to carry out a task.

importing   The process of bringing in code from outside files known as modules.

impossible rules   Rules in a decision table that have contradictory actions.

in-place algorithm   An algorithm that does not need additional memory beyond the input.

inclusive design   The concept of developing software and other consumer items so they are available and acceptable to the widest possible audience.

incremental development model   An approach to software development in which software is designed, coded, and tested in a succession of cycles.

index   The position of a character in a string, beginning with position [0].

index-based traversal   Traversing a list by creating an index access for each of the elements stored within.

index error   A coding fault in which the index value is not within the range of index values associated with an array.

infinite loop   A loop that never terminates.

infinite recursion   A recursive function that does not modify its parameters and therefore never stops.

information density   The amount of information that can be represented by a single symbol.

information hiding   The object-oriented programming principle to only allow the object to have

access to the underlying details of the object and hide the data and internal workings from entities outside of it.

inheritance   A feature of object-oriented programming in which subclasses acquire attributes of a parent class.

inheritance hierarchy   Graphical depiction of the inheritance relationship between classes.

initialization method   Another term for constructor, the dunder method named `__init__()`.

initialize a variable   The process of specifying a name and value for a variable.

instance   An object created from a class.

instance field   A variable of an object that is never seen or accessed by anything outside of the object.

instance variables   Another term for "member variables."

instruction cycle   The activity that takes place in the CPU to complete a single instruction: fetch, interpret, execute.

instruction pointer   A component of the CPU's control unit that indicates the location of each instruction to be executed.

instruction register   A component of the CPU's control unit that holds the instruction that is currently being executed.

instruction set   The collection of operations that a computer's CPU can perform.

instruction space   The memory used to store the code for a program.

integer data types   Whole numbers that can be signed or unsigned and expressed in decimal, binary, or hexadecimal notation.

integrated circuit   A thin slice of silicon that contains microscopic electronic circuitry.

integrated development environment (IDE)   Software that includes all of the tools needed to code, compile, link, and debug programs.

integration testing   A testing process for verifying that all of the software units or modules work together.

interfaces   The instructions for how to interact with a piece of code; includes how to call it, what arguments it expects, and what to expect back from the code.

interpreter In the context of computer software, it is utility software that preprocesses and executes program statements one by one.

is-a relationship A class relationship between a parent and a child, in which a child inherits directly from a parent class or one of its descendants.

iteration One repetition of a loop.

iterative sequence A sequence of values that can be visited one after another.

Java Virtual Machine (JVM) The virtual machine software that compiles and executes bytecode produced by the Java programming language.

K

key A reference point (usually a string) used to look up elements in a dictionary.

keywords Words in a programming language that have special meaning, such as a command to perform an action.

L

leaf nodes In a tree data structure, nodes at the bottom, which have no children.

level of abstraction The degree to which the details of an object or concept are hidden.

lifeline In a sequence diagram, represents the existence of an actor or object over time.

LIFO The acronym for "last in, first out."

linear access Reading a file in memory, consecutively, byte by byte, in a sequence.

linear data structure A data structure such as an array, linked list, stack, or queue that arranges data elements in a sequence.

linear recursion A type of recursion that represents a single line of problem solving and therefore makes one recursive function call.

linear search A type of search algorithm that examines each item in a list or array one by one to find a particular value.

linear space complexity The asymptotic, or Big-O, status for algorithms that require additional space for each data element as the size of the data set increases.

linear time The asymptotic, or Big-O, status for algorithms that require one step for each element

in the data set and therefore increase linearly as the data set grows.

linked list A data structure that organizes a collection of data elements in nonconsecutive memory locations.

list An iterative sequence containing values, similar to a bunch of variables put together.

list comprehension A way to create lists using a for-loop within square brackets [].

list index An integer value used to reference a specific element in a list, based on its position; starts at 0 for the first element.

literal An element of data used by a computer program.

local variable A variable that is visible in a function or other defined area of a program.

logarithmic time The asymptotic, or Big-O, status for algorithms with a time or space complexity that tends to level out as the size of the data set increases.

logic errors Another term for semantic error; a flaw in the logic of one or more statements that causes a program to produce incorrect results.

logic gate A circuit that manipulates electrical signals to perform logical and arithmetic operations.

loop A structure in a program that repeats.

loop counter The variable that tracks the number of times a count-controlled loop executes.

low-level programming language A system for issuing instructions using machine language or assembly language that corresponds closely to the CPU instruction set.

M

machine code A series of binary machine language instructions.

machine language The set of binary instructions that a CPU can directly execute.

magnetic storage technology Devices that polarize magnetic particles as a means to store data.

main function A function that is run only if the current module is run directly, not when the current module is imported.

mapping Creating a list containing modified values, such as doubling the numbers.

member variables   Variables that comprise the data that is stored in a class.

memory   A temporary data-holding area that is typically integrated into the main circuit board of a digital device.

memory address   A location in memory with a unique identifier, usually written as a hexadecimal number.

merge sort   An algorithm that guarantees a fast runtime at the expense of additional memory; uses divide-and-conquer.

message   In a sequence diagram, shows the interaction between components as discrete steps; generally a method or function.

metacharacters   Characters that describe the patterns used in regular expressions.

method body   The list of statements that the method executes to perform its operations.

method call   The way in which a method in an object is invoked.

method name   The way in which a method is referred to in code when it is being used; conventionally consists of a verb followed by a noun.

method overriding   Functionality that allows a child class to provide its own implementation of a method that is already inherited by one of its ancestors.

Method Resolution Order (MRO)   The order in which Python searches for a method when used on an object.

methods   The actions that an object can perform.

microprocessor   A complex integrated circuit that contains the components for a computer's CPU.

mixed reality   The use of computer technology to add interactive, three-dimensional objects to a real or simulated experience.

modules   When used in an abstract context, these are cohesive, structural units of algorithm. When used in application with Python code, these are the external files that store code, which can be brought over to other programs by importing.

Moore's Law   The prediction that manufacturers would be able to double the number of components in an integrated circuit every two years.

multiple inheritance   A child class that is derived from more than one parent class.

mutator methods   Methods designed to control how a property of a class is changed; also known as *setters*.

N

nested-if structures   Decision control structures that have a decision within a decision.

nested-loop   A loop within a loop.

nested modules   Modules stored within other modules to help organize code.

newline   A special character (usually \n) indicating the end of a line.

node   A basic unit of a data structure, usually containing a data element and optionally a link to other nodes.

nonlinear data structure   A data structure such as a tree or graph that arranges data elements in a hierarchy, web, or network.

nonvolatile storage   Storage or memory devices that do not require power to hold data.

null variable   A variable that has no value.

numeric literal   A literal composed of one or more digits that represent integers or floating-point numbers.

O

O(C)   The Big-O notation for constant time or space.

O(log _n_)   The Big-O notation for logarithmic time or space complexity.

O(_n_)   The Big-O notation for linear time or space.

O(_n_²)   The Big-O notation for quadratic time.

object code   The binary program code that is produced by a compiler.

object identity   The specific object itself: two variables have the same object identity only if they are the exact same object.

object-oriented decomposition   A technique for dividing a problem or task into logical and physical objects that a computer program will manipulate.

object-oriented paradigm   A type of imperative programming based on the idea that programs can be designed by visualizing objects that interact with each other.

object-oriented programming (OOP)   Programming that relies heavily on the concept of objects.

objects Specific instances of a class; for example, Rover is a specific object of the class Dog.

offline storage Local storage devices that are connected to a computer or can be conveniently removed.

one-dimensional list A list that contains individual value elements, like a queue at a movie theater.

one's complement A binary number that when added to another binary number produces all 1 bits.

online IDE An integrated development environment that runs in a browser and requires no installation; also called a *web IDE*.

online storage Storage provided by Internet-based cloud services.

op code An operation code that is the machine language or assembly language command for a processing instruction.

operands The part of a machine language or assembly language instruction that specifies the data to be processed, its location in memory, or its destination register.

operator overriding Changing the default behavior of Python by overriding the dunder methods for operators such as + or ==.

optical storage technology Devices that use light to store and access data.

order of operations The sequence in which addition, subtraction, and other mathematical operations are performed.

P

parameter list The identifiers representing the input to the function; part of the function signature.

parent In a tree data structure, a node that is above and connected to another node.

parent class The class from which other classes are created during inheritance.

pass by reference A function call that passes a pointer to the actual data.

pass by value A function call that passes a copy of an argument to a function.

pattern identification A technique for finding patterns in procedures and tasks.

peek The operation that accesses the first item in a stack or queue without removing it.

phoneme The smallest sound that is a part of speech.

pip command A command-line Python module used to install established Python modules including all dependencies.

pixels The miniature picture elements of a display screen that emit red, green, and blue light.

pointer A variable that holds the address of another variable.

polymorphism A concept of object-oriented programming in which an object in a child class can be treated uniquely by redefining methods derived from an inherited class.

pop The operation that removes the top element from a stack.

predicate expression The basic format for statements in logic and functional programming.

pre-test loop A condition-controlled loop that begins with a condition and loops only if that condition is true.

primitive data types Data types that are built into a programming language.

procedural paradigm A type of imperative programming paradigm that specifies how a computer is supposed to carry out a task using variables, control structures, and ordered instructions.

procedural programming Code that is written "step-by-step," like a set of instructions or a recipe, for the computer to follow.

program animation A feature of debugging utilities that steps through code one statement at a time.

program code The set of statements written in a programming language.

programming algorithm A set of steps that specify the underlying logic and structure for the statements in a computer program.

programming language A formal language with semantics and syntax for instructing a computer to perform a specific task.

programming paradigms Various approaches to software development and programming. Major paradigms are classified as imperative or declarative.

prompt A message that specifies what a user should enter when a program is running.

properties A way of describing the variables connected to an object as an aspect or feature.

pseudocode A set of structured statements for delineating the steps of an algorithm.

pure virtual method A method that requires the derived classes to override the implementation of its functionality.

push The operation that adds a data element to the top of a stack.

Q

quadratic time The asymptotic, or Big-O, status for algorithms with a time or space complexity that increases more sharply than linear time as the data set grows.

queue A limited-access, linear data structure in which the first data element added is the first element removed.

quicksort An approximation of a fast algorithm that uses probability and divide-and-conquer to achieve a good runtime.

R

raise When a program stops executing code and moves to error-handling in a situation where it cannot continue.

RAM (random access memory) A volatile type of memory that provides a temporary holding area for data.

random access Reading a file in memory by accessing each character directly without first reading the character before it.

range function A function that generates an iterative sequence, typically used with for-loops.

read A mode to open a file to examine its contents.

read-only A device or file that can be accessed but not altered.

read-write A device or file that can be created, accessed, altered, or deleted.

realization When a class implements an interface.

record One line of fields in a table.

recursion A problem-solving approach that divides large problems into smaller, identical problems.

recursive function A function that calls itself at least once.

reduced instruction set computers (RISC) A streamlined instruction set with a roster of simple operations.

redundant rules Two or more rules in a decision table that have the same outcome when differences in alternatives are eliminated.

refactoring The process of revisiting code to reorganize it into a better, more efficient design; frequently used by but not limited to inheritance design.

reference A name, usually in the form of a variable, that refers to a specific location in memory of a value or other data object.

registers Temporary areas for holding data in the CPU.

regression testing Testing to ensure that modifications to code do not have unexpected side effects.

regular expression A string of characters that describe the pattern of the text you are searching for.

relational operator An operator such as ==, >, or < that specifies a comparison between two operands.

relationship diagram A UML diagram showing how classes interact.

relative file path Tells the location of a file from another location in the file system.

relative import When inside nested modules the path to import another module's code is done relative to the current module's location rather than an absolute path.

repetition control structures Blocks of code that are executed repeatedly based on a control condition.

reserved words The words that a programming language reserves for its use to specify commands and other actions.

return message A type of message, similar to a return value.

return statement A statement signaling a value (or not) to return from a method or function.

return value The data that is passed from a function back to the main program.

RGB A color system that uses a mixture of red, green, and blue light to produce the spectrum of colors.

root   In a tree data structure, the topmost node, which has no parents; also considered the "starting point" of a tree.

runtime   How long an algorithm takes to complete in terms of the total number of items, "n."

runtime error   A flaw in a program that causes a program to fail during execution.

S

scenario   A single use case or single action path through a system.

scope   The visibility of program components, such as variables.

script mode   A mode in Python's code editor, IDLE, used for long-term projects; will save code as .py files on your computer.

search algorithms   Special algorithms that find a specific piece of information within a large set of data as efficiently as possible.

search space   The amount of data you are searching.

secure coding   Programming that includes routines to protect code from security exploits.

selection control structure   An executable statement that directs program flow based on a condition or decision.

self-reference keyword   The keyword used in object methods to reference itself.

semantic error   A flaw in the logic of one or more statements that causes a program to produce incorrect results.

semantics   In the context of programming, the meaning and validity of program statements.

sentinel value   A special value in an algorithm that signals the end of a loop or recursion.

sequence diagram   A UML diagram used to show how parts of code are related and the exact sequence of events.

setters   Methods designed to control how a property of a class is changed; also known as *mutator methods*.

shallow copy   Pointing the reference variable for a new object to another, preexisting object.

shell mode   A mode in Python's code editor, IDLE, used for short-term code tests; does not save progress.

shortest path   The path between two nodes that costs the least, as represented by the sum of the edges taken along the path.

signed integer   A whole number that is preceded by a + or – sign.

signed magnitude   The use of the leftmost bit in a binary representation to indicate a negative number.

single precision   Floating-point numbers usually stored in 4 bytes of memory.

single responsibility principle (SRP)   The concept that each function or class should have only one responsibility and one reason to change.

singly linked list   A linked list in which a single pointer links one element to the next element.

snake case   A text format that uses all lowercase letters and separates words with an underscore.

software development kit (SDK)   A set of tools for developing platform-specific software.

software development life cycle   The progression of a software application from conception to retirement.

solid state storage technology   Devices that use nonvolatile circuitry to store data.

sorting   The act of placing items in a deterministic order, typically numerically or alphabetically.

sorting algorithms   Programming approach to sorting items stored in computer memory.

source code   A set of statements usually written in a high-level programming language.

space complexity   The amount of memory required by an algorithm as a function of the size of the data set.

sparse graph   A graph with few edges between the nodes.

speech recognition   The process by which spoken words are transformed into digital text.

speech synthesis   The process by which digital text is transformed into audible speech.

stable algorithm   An algorithm that does not mix up equivalent items' relative orders.

stacks   A limited access, linear data structure in which the last data element added is the first element removed.

state   Represents the data held in an object's member variables at any time.

statement   Each instruction written in a high-level programming language.

static method   A special method that is independent of any particular object of the class and can be called without making an instance of the object; this type of method is called on the class itself.

static variable   A member variable of a class that contains the same value in all instances of the class.

statically typed   A programming language feature that requires a variable to hold only the type of data that was specified when the variable was declared or initialized.

storage   A term used to refer to devices that can hold data on a relatively permanent basis.

stream   A channel that allows you to interact with files stored on your computer or another drive.

streamreader   A programming language device that creates a stream for reading data from a file.

streamwriter   A programming language device that creates a stream for writing data to a file.

string   A sequence of characters.

string data type   The data type assigned to variables that hold a sequence of characters.

string literal   A literal that contains more than one character.

structural decomposition   A process that identifies structural units of a task or problem.

structural equality   The contents of the object; two variables are structurally equivalent if they have the exact same contents but do not have to be the same memory location.

success factors   Best practices that can improve the quality of a programmer's code.

syntax   In the context of programming languages, the grammar rules for word order and punctuation.

syntax error   A flaw in a program statement that results from incorrectly using punctuation or word sequencing.

system testing   A testing process for validating that the fully integrated software application performs as expected when installed on target hardware platforms.

T

table   A collection of records.

tail recursion   A way to structure recursive code so that the program requires no additional memory during function calls.

terminator shape   The rounded rectangle shape at the beginning or end of a flowchart.

test case   A set of preconditions, steps, and data that should produce a specific result called a "post condition."

text editor   Software that can be used to enter plain ASCII text.

text file   A file that stores its contents as ASCII characters.

time complexity   The amount of time, measured in number of operations, required to run an algorithm as its data set grows.

transistor   A key component of integrated circuits because of its ability to amplify signals, act as a switch, and form logic gates.

traversal   A way to visit all nodes in a tree.

traversing a list   The process of visiting each element in a list.

tree   A nonlinear data structure that enforces a hierarchical form and looks like an upside-down tree.

truth table   A table that specifies the outcome of conditional logical operators such as AND and OR.

try   An attempt for code to complete as normal, unless an exception occurs; then the code stops trying and moves to handle the thrown exception.

try-except block   A syntactic block of code where exceptions occur and are handled. The try part indicates code to try, and the except part catches and handles exceptions from the try part.

two-dimensional list   A list that contains lists as each of its elements, like a tic-tac-toe board.

two's complement   A binary number that when added to another binary number produces all 0 bits.

type casting   Converting a variable of one type into another type.

type inference   A programming language feature that deduces the data type based on the presence or absence of a decimal point.

U

unconnected graph   A graph with isolated groups of nodes not connected by edges.

undefined variable   A variable that has not been specified by the programmer.

undirected graph   A graph where edges are two-way paths.

Unicode   A variable-length encoding system that includes representation for the written glyphs used by most of the world's languages.

Unified Modeling Language (UML)   A standardized way of visualizing programs to enable better communication with others.

unit testing   A process that tests each program module to ensure that it operates correctly.

unsigned integer   A positive whole number that has no + or − sign.

use case   A list of actions or steps showing the interactions between a person and a system in order to accomplish a task.

use case diagram   A UML diagram that communicates how a user interacts with a system.

user-controlled loop   A loop that executes or terminates based on input collected from the user at run-time.

user experience (UX)   A concept that encompasses aspects of user activities beyond interacting with the user interface.

user interface (UI)   A collection of physical, graphical, and logical constructs that facilitate interaction between humans and digital devices.

UTF-8   A popular version of Unicode, used extensively on the web.

V

value   The data element stored in a dictionary that can be accessed and modified by its associated key.

variable   A named memory location that temporarily holds text or a numeric value.

vector graphics   A format for specifying digital images as instructions for lines, colors, and basic shapes.

virtual machine   Utility software that operates on a specific hardware platform to execute bytecode.

virtual reality   The use of computer technology to create simulated three-dimensional worlds populated by objects that users can manipulate.

visibility marker   UML symbols that indicate the access modifiers of variables or methods.

voice user interface   A type of user interface characterized by spoken communication between a user and a digital device.

void function   A function that does not return a value to the main program.

volatile storage   Storage or memory that requires power to hold data.

W

waterfall model   An approach to software development in which the project is divided into a series of cascading tasks that are performed one after the other.

while-loop   A pre-test loop that begins with a while statement.

worst-case runtime   The largest amount of time possible an algorithm needs to run to completion.

write   A mode to open a file and insert content, writing over any existing content.

Write Every Time (WET)   The opposite of DRY; code that contains redundancies.

Index